Investments in Conflict Zones

Nijhoff International Investment Law Series

Series Editors

Prof. Eric De Brabandere (*Leiden University*)
Prof. Tarcisio Gazzini (*University of East Anglia*)
Prof. Stephan W. Schill (*University of Amsterdam*)
Prof. Attila Tanzi (*University of Bologna*)

Editorial Board

Andrea K. Bjorklund (*Montreal*) – Juan Pablo Bohoslavsky (*El Bolson, Rio Negro*) – Chester Brown (*Sydney*) – Patrick Dumberry (*Ottawa*) – Michael Ewing-Chow (*Singapore*) – Susan D. Franck (*Lexington*) – Ursula Kriebaum (*Vienna*) – Makane Mbengue (*Geneva*) – Catherine A. Rogers (*Carlisle*) – Christian Tams (*Glasgow*) – Andreas Ziegler (*Lausanne*)

VOLUME 15

The titles published in this series are listed at *brill.com/iils*

Investments in Conflict Zones

The Role of International Investment Law in Armed Conflicts, Disputed Territories, and 'Frozen' Conflicts

Edited by

Tobias Ackermann and Sebastian Wuschka

BRILL

NIJHOFF

LEIDEN | BOSTON

Library of Congress Cataloging-in-Publication Data

Names: Ackermann, Tobias, editor. | Wuschka, Sebastian, editor.
Title: Investments in conflict zones : the role of international investment law in armed conflicts, disputed territories, and 'frozen' conflicts / edited by Tobias Ackermann and Sebastian Wuschka.
Description: Leiden, The Netherlands : Koninklijke Brill NV, [2021] | Series: Nijhoff international investment law series, 2351-9542 ; volume 15 | Includes bibliographical references and index. | Summary: "In Investments in Conflict Zones, a selected group of experts explores how armed conflicts, territorial disputes, and 'frozen' conflicts impact the application and interpretation of international investment law and how investment protection can be reconciled with such politically charged circumstances." – Provided by publisher.
Identifiers: LCCN 2020036616 (print) | LCCN 2020036617 (ebook) | ISBN 9789004442801 (hardback) | ISBN 9789004442832 (ebook)
Subjects: LCSH: Investments, Foreign (International law) | Investments, Foreign–Law and legislation. | War–Economic aspects. | International commercial arbitration.
Classification: LCC K3830 .I6838 2021 (print) | LCC K3830 (ebook) | DDC 346/.092–dc23
LC record available at https://lccn.loc.gov/2020036616
LC ebook record available at https://lccn.loc.gov/2020036617

Typeface for the Latin, Greek, and Cyrillic scripts: "Brill". See and download: brill.com/brill-typeface.

ISSN 2351-9542
ISBN 978-90-04-44280-1 (hardback)
ISBN 978-90-04-44283-2 (e-book)

Copyright 2021 by Koninklijke Brill NV, Leiden, The Netherlands.
Koninklijke Brill NV incorporates the imprints Brill, Brill Hes & De Graaf, Brill Nijhoff, Brill Rodopi, Brill Sense, Hotei Publishing, mentis Verlag, Verlag Ferdinand Schöningh and Wilhelm Fink Verlag.
All rights reserved. No part of this publication may be reproduced, translated, stored in a retrieval system, or transmitted in any form or by any means, electronic, mechanical, photocopying, recording or otherwise, without prior written permission from the publisher. Requests for re-use and/or translations must be addressed to Koninklijke Brill NV via brill.com or copyright.com.

This book is printed on acid-free paper and produced in a sustainable manner.

Contents

Foreword: The Role of International Investment Law in Conflict Scenarios IX
   Marco Sassòli
Acknowledgements XVI
Abbreviations XVII
Notes on Contributors XX
Table of Cases XXVI

Introduction: Investments in Conflict Zones 1
   Tobias Ackermann and Sebastian Wuschka

PART 1
Investment Law and Armed Conflicts

1   International Law in Revolutionary Upheavals: On the Tension between International Investment Law and International Humanitarian Law 19
   Tillmann Rudolf Braun

2   The Genealogy of Extended War Clauses: Requisition and Destruction of Property in Armed Conflicts 54
   Ira Ryk-Lakhman

3   Full Protection and Security from Physical Security to Environmental Security: Its Limitations and Future Possibilities 84
   Emily Sipiorski

4   The Effect of Armed Hostilities on Investment Treaty Obligations: A Case of *Force Majeure*? 112
   Christina Binder and Philipp Janig

PART 2
Investment Law and Disputed Territories

5 The Concept of 'Territory' in BITS of Disputing Sovereigns 139
   Markus P Beham

6 The Protection of Foreign Investments in Disputed Maritime Areas 176
   Marco Benatar and Valentin J Schatz

7 Parallel Proceedings Arising from Uncertain Territorial and Maritime Boundaries 209
   Christine Sim

8 Representation of States in Investment Arbitrations Involving Governments Competing for International Recognition 246
   Réka A Papp

9 The Substantive and Procedural Protection of Investments under Article 1 Protocol 1 to the ECHR and Its Value in Cases of Territorial Conflicts 280
   Isabella Risini

PART 3
Investment Law and Its Application to Annexed Territories and in 'Frozen' Conflicts

10 The Application of Investment Treaties in Occupied or Annexed Territories and 'Frozen' Conflicts: *Tabula Rasa* or *Occupata*? 319
   Kit De Vriese

11 The Duty of Non-Recognition and EU Free Trade Agreements: Lessons for Investment Law from the Case of *Front Polisario* 359
   Stefan Lorenzmeier

12 Assessing the Role and Effects of Domestic Investment Statutes in Frozen Conflict Situations: The Example of Transnistria/Pridnestrovie 387
   Vladlena Lisenco and Karsten Nowrot

13   Investment Law and the Conflict in the Donbas Region: Legal
     Challenges in a Special Case   431
        Stefan Lorenzmeier and Maryna Reznichuk

14   International Investment Law in the Context of State Fragility: Full
     Protection and Security and Fair and Equitable Treatment   458
        Johanna Baumann

     Index   487

Foreword: The Role of International Investment Law in Conflict Scenarios

Marco Sassòli

This book deals mainly, but not only, with investments protected by particular rules of international law in situations of armed conflicts, including occupation. Disputes on maritime or territorial boundaries obviously do not only arise in or follow armed conflicts. It is true that they can equally have an impact on investment disputes, and this book deals with them. Armed conflicts nevertheless raise six particular interrelated questions, which fascinate more generally international lawyers. I will list them hereafter; the reader of this book will encounter them, sometimes explicitly, often implicitly, in nearly all contributions. I will, however, enter into a discussion in both theory and practice only on the first two questions.

1 General Debates in International Law to Which This Book Points

First, several contributions inevitably discuss how different branches of international law interrelate, ie what the editors call conflicts between norms. This refers to *jus in bello* (which comprises mainly but not only international humanitarian law (IHL)) and *jus ad bellum* on the one hand, and international investment protection law on the other.

Second, affected persons understandably try to enforce the rules of one branch of international law that lacks enforcement mechanisms for them to trigger through the mechanisms of other branches, which function and are relatively able to enforce their findings. Accordingly, IHL or *jus ad bellum* can benefit from adjudication in investment arbitration and regional human rights courts.

Third, in this book we also encounter tectonic clashes between two layers of international law. On the one hand, there is the (usually older) layer of international law, which covers interstate relations. This includes *jus ad bellum* and the old-fashioned rules that protect (but, in reality, allow freezing, if not, confiscation of) property in wartime for the mere reason that such property belongs to enemy 'subjects'. On the other hand, the (newer) layer consists of the law of the international community of 7.7 billion human beings; putting them at the centre as addressees of rights and obligations, piercing the corporate veil of the state. In our case, the latter comprises certainly international human rights law (IHRL) and international criminal law (a branch that we should not totally forget in our context). IHL (or at least its branch applicable to international armed conflicts) and the law of neutrality are based upon interstate relations, which designate those who are protected, but also protect individuals. In the case of IHL, an increasing number of rules do not refer to nationality (or, for combatants and prisoners of war, to the power on which they depend). Whether IHL gives individuals rights remains controversial. It certainly gives them only in rare case remedies. International investment protection law too has an ambiguous position between the two layers. On the one hand, it protects individuals and gives them remedies against states. On the other hand, it protects those individuals based upon their nationality – a traditional issue of the first layer – and upon treaties between their home state, and the state on the territory of which they invest.

Fourth, while international law is still largely state-centred, non-state actors play an increasing role in international affairs. Even when international rules apply to non-state actors, often no international forum exists in which individual victims, injured states, third states, intergovernmental organizations, or NGOs could invoke the responsibility of a non-state actor and obtain relief. Investment protected by international law may fall under the control of, or be affected by, armed non-state actors or *de facto* regimes. Contributions in this book show how investments can be protected in such situations; either through a state based upon its own or the *de facto* regime's conduct, or through and by the non-state actor itself, *eg* through 'legislation' adopted by the *de facto* regime – a method equally used to implement IHL applicable in non-recognized *de facto* regimes.

Fifth and sixth, as the editors point out in their introduction, underlying the object of this book are largely philosophical debates on the tension between collective and individual interests; and, between allegedly higher values such as peace, equality, survival of war affected populations, and egoistic individual patrimonial interests. I may only add that those interests are in reality not always so individual and egoistic, because of pension funds and the number of livelihoods depending on investments.

2   How to Deal with Contradictions between International Investment Protection Law and IHL?

The first issue is widely discussed under the titles of fragmentation, *lex specialis*, or systemic integration. Such discussion is sometimes conducted at the

FOREWORD: INTERNATIONAL INVESTMENT LAW IN CONFLICT SCENARIOS   XI

theoretical level, but much more frequently concerning the relationship between IHL and IHRL; and between international trade law, on the one hand, and IHRL or international environmental law on the other. The relationship between other branches, such as between the Second Geneva Convention protecting the shipwrecked[1] and international maritime safety conventions,[2] is nearly totally ignored by scholars. These could be rare playgrounds for doctoral students unwilling to engage into sociological enquiries, but ready to approach unchartered waters of practical relevance, while demonstrating that they are able to discuss basic theoretical problems of international law. When it comes to international investment protection law, I have the impression that a lot has been written about its relation with international environmental law and IHRL. However, very little has been written about the relationship between international investment protection and IHL or *jus ad bellum*. This book fills a genuine gap.

To determine how investment protection law and other branches of international law applicable in conflict scenarios interact in a given case, one first has to make sure that each branch applies in its own terms. Next, one has to clarify whether they contradict each other (which presupposes that we define what constitutes a contradiction). Finally – and this is the issue which fascinates most scholars – one has to solve the contradiction if it exists – in extreme cases, to clarify which rule prevails.

First, one must clarify when two rules actually lead to different outcomes. The most restrictive understanding is that two rules only differ if one rule prescribes certain conduct that the other prohibits. If this were correct, I would expect no contradictions in our case. This is because IHL, *jus ad bellum* or the law of neutrality, never prescribe conduct that would violate obligations under investment protection law. An exception could be the prohibition of adverse distinction in IHL (and the principle of non-discrimination in IHRL). They could be at stake in cases involving a differential treatment of investment by nationals benefitting from an investment protection treaty, in comparison to other investments. However, this can be overcome by considering that the nationality of the investor can neither be a prohibited, nor a suspicious ground of distinction. Further, that in any event, the respect of an applicable international obligation outside of IHL can be a legitimate ground for differentiations.

---

[1] Geneva Convention for the Amelioration of the Condition of Wounded, Sick and Shipwrecked Members of Armed Forces at Sea (adopted 12 August 1949, entered into force 21 October 1950) 75 UNTS 85 (Second Geneva Convention).
[2] See, most importantly, the International Convention for the Safety of Life at Sea (adopted 1 November 1974, entered into force 25 May 1980) 1184 UNTS 278 (SOLAS).

A broader understanding of contradictions, which is preferable in my view, would also cover potential conflicts, where international investment protection law prohibits conduct that IHL does not prohibit or which IHL – according to many – even authorizes. This in turn raises the debate whether, and to what extent, IHL authorizes certain conduct; or, if it only prohibits or prescribes certain conduct, leaving other conduct unregulated – at best, giving a weak permission. Indeed, prohibitions in investment protection treaties may overrule such permissions.

When international investment protection law and other branches of international law lead to divergent results, the nature of the relationship between them is a controversial matter. Such controversy exists in terms of both the terminology used to describe the relationship, and the practical outcomes, namely, the rule that must be respected in such a situation. At the centre of these controversies, is the *lex specialis* principle, which is increasingly contested in scholarly writings, including in this book.

We may ignore here those who claim that the *lex specialis* principle applies only to contradictions between rules in the same treaty, or the same branch of international law. This is because, if that were correct, the principle would not help reconcile conflicting international investment protection law, and other branches. Some insist that the *lex specialis* principle is only an interpretative rule to avoid norm conflicts and, therefore, cannot solve them. However, a strict distinction between norm conflict avoidance and norm conflict resolution is artificial, especially in international law.

Some hold that the principle concerns the overall relationship between two branches of law, concluding that IHL always prevails in armed conflicts. For some of them that one could label as 'absolute IHL supremacists', who are frequent in military circles, any silence in IHL is deliberate and means that no rule of international law regulates the respective conduct or issue. None of the contributors of this book adopts such an approach, neither in favour of IHL, nor investment law. Others, who might be labelled 'moderate IHL supremacists', admit that issues IHL does not regulate remain governed by other branches in an armed conflict. However, they contend that IHL must prevail as *lex specialis* as soon as it regulates a given issue, at least if a suitable interpretation of the rules of both branches cannot avoid a genuine norm conflict. I would label the probably majoritarian view – following the terminology suggested by one of my former LLM students – as 'the common contact surface area' approach. It seeks to determine the *lex specialis* in every case of application, according to logic and the overall systemic purposes of international law. In my view, the principle does not even determine, once and for all, the relationship between two rules. Rather, it determines which rule prevails over another in a particular situation. Each case must be analysed individually. Several factors determine which rule is 'special' in relation to a certain problem. Specialty, in the logical sense, implies that the norm that applies to a certain set of facts, must give way to the norm that applies to that same set of facts, as well as to an additional fact that is present in a given situation. A norm that is either more precise, or that has a narrower material or personal scope of application, constitutes the *lex specialis*. The norm addressing a problem explicitly prevails over the one that treats it implicitly. A norm that provides more details prevails over another's generality; while one that is more restrictive, prevails over one that covers a problem fully, but in a less exacting manner.

Some of the principle's critics argue that IHL and other branches of international law applicable in armed conflicts should apply cumulatively. They may indeed base their views upon the practice of international tribunals, and upon a textual reading of most UN Security Council resolutions, concerning the relationship between IHL and IHRL. This leads, however, to unrealistic results that even proponents of this approach do not suggest, and – more importantly – that clearly do not comport with state practice. Others seek to solve possible contradictions through systemic integration or interpretation that takes into account other applicable rules of international law, as required by article 31(3)(c) of the Vienna Convention on the Law of Treaties.[3] Finally, some seek to abandon the pretence that the legal order provides only one solution (I would add: any solution). They prefer to solve the few real conflicts that exist through the political process. However, in my view, this is a surrender of the law as a distinct science. The essence of the rule of law (and at the same time its grand fiction) is that decision-makers apply norms, including when they contradict other norms, according to legal rules and not (their) policy preferences.

Academic writings discuss these fascinating questions widely. In practice, they have, however, only a limited impact on the actual investment protection in and after armed conflicts. Several contributions in this book show that IHL and investment protection lead nearly always to the same results. Where possible divergences exist, investment treaties contain particular war clauses, full protection and security standards, as well as vague and open terms, which may be interpreted in light of IHL and *jus ad bellum*. The concept of territory refers to *jus ad bellum* and other rules of public international law. Unlike IHL obligations, sometimes some investment treaty obligations may also be suspended during armed conflicts. Indeed, the violation of the latter obligations may be

---

3   Vienna Convention on the Law of Treaties (adopted 22 May 1969, entered into force 27 January 1980) 1155 UNTS 331 (VCLT).

justified by circumstances precluding unlawfulness, such as *force majeure*, extensively and restrictively interpreted in contributions to this book.

The other way around, it seems to be more difficult to use investment protection treaties to interpret the many vague terms appearing in IHL, *eg* in the definition of military objectives, proportionality, precautionary measures, or on the admissibility of destructions, confiscations and requisitions in enemy hands. These rules refer to interests other than those protected by investment treaties. A major exception is article 38 of the Fourth Geneva Convention,[4] which prescribes that the regulations concerning aliens in time of peace – which include investment protection – continue to regulate the treatment of enemy aliens on a belligerent's own territory, by that belligerent in the power of which they are, in case of armed conflict. It may also be that the jurisprudence of investment dispute settlement mechanisms can be used to clarify the concept of property, which is not defined but largely protected in IHL, *eg* of military occupation. For the rest, the specificities of an armed conflict – rather than the fact that an investment protection treaty also covers certain property – will generally point, at least for enemy investment, to IHL as the *lex specialis*. This takes equally into account the consideration that protection by IHL is generally much more detailed than the vague clauses in investment protection law. Finally, for the protection of property in the power of a party, but not in the conduct of hostilities, the nationality of the investor will play a crucial role in determining the *lex specialis*. IHL and the old-fashioned and very permissive customary rules on the treatment of enemy property (the relationship between the two is rarely discussed) will play – to a large extent – the role of the *lex specialis* for enemy property. Investment protection treaties will fill in the more general provisions of the law of neutrality and play a greater role for neutral property.

3   May Investment Arbitrators Apply IHL?

A second general issue underlying debates in this book, transversal to many discussions in international law, is whether mechanisms of one branch should (be used to) adjudicate issues governed by another branch. This issue is particularly relevant in international law, because it lacks a regular ordinary court adjudicating the whole of international law. On the one hand, this raises

---

4   Geneva Convention Relative to the Protection of Civilian Persons in Time of War (adopted 12 August 1949, entered into force 21 October 1950) 75 UNTS 287 (Fourth Geneva Convention).

questions of competence (both in the sense of jurisdiction and of knowledge). Such decisions may also undermine the credibility of a certain mechanism. No one expects that Russia would withdraw from Crimea because an investment arbitration holds on a preliminary question that it belongs to Ukraine. How do we prevent such lack of acceptance and enforcement from spilling over into acceptance that prisoners continue to be detained in violation of European Court of Human Rights decisions, and that investors are expropriated without compensation in violation of arbitral decisions on investment protection? On the other hand, no branch of international law can be seen in clinical isolation. In particular, when it takes binding decisions, a mechanism cannot simply decide that a state violated one treaty, which has instituted the mechanism. It must also be able to add that no other rule of international law could justify the conduct incompatible with that treaty. Otherwise, a state found in violation of the treaty the mechanism adjudicates could argue that it will not comply with the decision, because it is justified – if not obliged – to do so under another rule of international law.

Here too the theoretical debate can be avoided in most cases by a practical approach: the investment arbitration (or human rights) tribunal only decides whether its constituent treaty was violated. However, as mentioned above, it has inevitably to interpret the terms of that treaty such as 'territory', 'investment', 'fair and equitable treatment', 'full protection and security', 'property', or 'necessity of the situation' by taking other rules of international law into account. Nevertheless – and here I differ with the authors of two chapters – the concept of effective control under investment protection treaties, IHRL and IHL must be understood in light of the realities on the ground. This, therefore, cannot imply a violation of the duty of non-recognition.

The lack of understanding by the judges or arbitrators of a mechanism can be overcome by training, including university curricula that avoid very early overspecialization. The contributors to this book have visibly avoided this trap, as investment law specialists visibly know IHL, for example. What remains is that an investment protection arbitrator will inevitably approach problems with an investment protection focus, and a human rights court judge with a human rights approach. This problem can only be fully overcome in a very different international society, with ordinary tribunals of general jurisdiction. In recent years, international reality has moved away, rather than come closer, to such a world. In the meantime, reading this book, members of different epistemic communities, including investment arbitrators and attorneys, can come closer to each other.

Acknowledgements

This volume emanates from an expert workshop that was held at Ruhr-University Bochum, Germany, in early March 2019. A group of international humanitarian law and international investment law experts – many of whom have contributed to this volume – came together to discuss the interplay between international investment law and the legal regimes that apply in armed or 'frozen' conflicts and to disputed territories. Reports about the workshop have been published by Maximilian Bertamini (Kluwer Arbitration Blog, 2 June 2019) and by Valentin J Schatz ((2019) 2 JILPAC 107).

Both the workshop and the work on this publication have been generously supported by Ruhr-University Bochum's Research School PLUS, funded by Germany's Excellence Initiative [DFG GSC 98/3]. We wish to express our sincerest thanks in this respect also to Dr Sarah Gemicioglu, who greatly contributed to the successful organisation of the workshop and beyond in her capacity as coordinator of RUB Research School PLUS. Our gratitude further goes to Maximilian Bertamini, Benedikt Behlert, Theresa Bosl, Van Hoang, Tim Potthast, Robin Ramsahye, and Ella Schönleben, who ensured that the workshop in Bochum was the success that it became, and to Rouven Diekjobst for his editorial assistance during the preparation of this volume. Additionally, we are indebted to Dr Isabella Risini and Tim Rauschning, who contributed their expertise and significant time to help us peer-review the drafts of the contributions in this volume.

Finally, we wish to express our thanks to the editors of the Nijhoff International Investment Law Series for accepting this volume into the series, to Brill Nijhoff generally, and to Kelley Baylis for her support in particular.

Tobias Ackermann and Sebastian Wuschka
Berlin and Hamburg, June 2020

Abbreviations

AJIL	American Journal of International Law
ARIEL	Austrian Review of International and European Law
ASEAN	Association of Southeast Asian Nations
BIICL	British Institute of International and Comparative Law
BIT	Bilateral investment treaty
BLEU	Belgium–Luxembourg Economic Union
CARICOM	Caribbean Community and Common Market
CDDH	Council of Europe Steering Committee for Human Rights
CETA	Comprehensive Economic and Trade Agreement between Canada and the European Union
CJEU	Court of Justice of the European Union
co	company
COMESA	Common Market for Eastern and Southern Africa
corp	corporation
CRCICA	Cairo Regional Centre for International Commercial Arbitration
CUTS	Consumer Unity & Trust Society
CUP	Cambridge University Press
DNR	Peoples' Republics of Donetsk
DRC	Democratic Republic of the Congo
ECJ	European Court of Justice
ECHR	Convention for the Protection of Human Rights and Fundamental Freedoms
ECOWAS	Economic Community of the West African States
ECtHR	European Court of Human Rights
EJIL	European Journal of International Law
EU	European Union
EuGRZ	Europäische Grundrechte-Zeitschrift
EWC	Extended war clause
FET	Fair and equitable treatment
FPS	Full protection and security
FTA	Free trade agreement
GATT	General Agreement on Tariffs and Trade
GDP	Gross domestic product
HKIAC	Hong Kong International Arbitration Centre
IACtHR	Inter-American Court of Human Rights
IASB	International Accounting Standards Board of the IFRS Foundation
ICC	International Chamber of Commerce

ICCPR	International Covenant on Civil and Political Rights
ICESCR	International Covenant on Economic, Social and Cultural Rights
ICJ	International Court of Justice
ICLQ	International and Comparative Law Quarterly
ICSID	International Centre for Settlement of Investment Disputes
ICTY	International Criminal Tribunal for the former Yugoslavia
IFRS	International Financial Reporting Standards
IHL	International humanitarian law
IIA	International investment agreement
ILC	International Law Commission
ILR	International Law Reports
IPC	Immovable Property Commission
IUSCTR	Iran-US Claims Tribunal Reports
JERL	Journal of Energy & Natural Resources Law
JIDS	Journal of International Dispute Settlement
JILPAC	Journal of International Law of Peace and Armed Conflict / Humanitäres Völkerrecht
LCIA	London Court of International Arbitration
LNR	Peoples' Republic of Luhansk
LRTWC	Law Reports of Trials of War Criminals
JWIT	Journal of World Investment & Trade
JWELB	Journal of World Energy Law & Business
LCIA	London Court of International Arbitration
Max Planck UNYB	Max Planck Yearbook of United Nations Law
MFN	Most-favoured nation (treatment)
MLR	Modern Law Review
MSSR	Moldavian Soviet Socialist Republic
MUP	Manchester University Press
NATO	North Atlantic Treaty Organization
OECD	Organization for Economic Co-operation and Development
OHADA	Organisation pour l'Harmonisation en Afrique du Droit des Affaires
OHCHR	Office of the High Commissioner for Human Rights
OUP	Oxford University Press
OSCE	Organization for Security and Co-operation in Europe
PCA	Permant Court of Arbitration
PCIJ	Permanent Court of International Justice
RIAA	Reports of International Arbitral Awards
SCC	Stockholm Chamber of Commerce

SIAC	Singapore International Arbitration Centre
SFRY	Socialist Federal Republic of Yugoslavia
TDM	Transnational Dispute Management
TRNC	Turkish Republic of Northern Cyprus
TWC	Trials of War Criminals Before the Nuernberg Military Tribunals
UCLJLJ	UCL Journal of Law and Jurisprudence
UDHR	Universal Declaration of Human Rights
UN	United Nations
UNCITRAL	United Nations Commission on International Trade Law
UNCTAD	United Nations Conference on Trade and Development
UNESCO	United Nations Educational, Scientific and Cultural Organization
UNGA	United Nations General Assembly
UNSC	United Nations Security Council
UQLJ	University of Queensland Law Journal
US-GAAP	United States Generally Accepted Accounting Principles
USSR	Union of Soviet Sovereign Republics
VCLT	Vienna Convention on the Law of Treaties
VCST	Vienna Convention on the Succession of States in Respect of Treaties
WTO	World Trade Organization
YBILC	Yearbook of the International Law Commission

Notes on Contributors

Tobias Ackermann
is currently completing the bar qualification scheme ('Referendariat') with the Kammergericht in Berlin, Germany, during which he, among others, worked with the German Federal Ministry for Economic Affairs and Energy's unit handling cases before the European Court of Justice. He has completed his doctoral thesis on the effects of armed conflict on investment treaties at Ruhr-University Bochum, Germany. Previously, Tobias was a research assistant at Ruhr-University Bochum's Institute for International Law of Peace and Armed Conflict and with Berlin-based law firm Blomstein, where he specialised in public procurement and foreign trade law.

Johanna Baumann
is a doctoral candidate at the International Investment Law Centre Cologne, Germany. She studied law with a focus on international and European law at the University of Cologne. Her research concentrates on the implications of economic, political, and legal changes on international investment protection. Johanna worked as a research assistant at several international law firms and as a legal trainee in Düsseldorf, Germany, and New York, USA. She is currently a trainee lawyer with the disputes practice group of Herbert Smith Freehills LLP in Düsseldorf.

Markus P Beham
is assistant professor at the Chair of Constitutional and Administrative Law, Public International Law, European and International Economic Law of the University Passau, Germany, and an adjunct lecturer in international law at the University of Vienna, Austria. Prior to that, he was as an associate in the International Arbitration Group at Freshfields Bruckhaus Deringer LLP, resident in the firm's Vienna office, and a fellow at the Department of Legal Philosophy of the University of Vienna. He holds a joint doctoral degree in law from the Université Paris Nanterre and the University of Vienna and a doctoral degree in history from the latter as well as an LLM degree from Columbia Law School in New York, USA.

Marco Benatar
is an Associate Legal Officer at the International Tribunal for the Law of the Sea. Before joining the Tribunal, he was a research fellow at the Max Planck

Institute Luxembourg for Procedural Law. In addition to advising governments on various international legal matters, he has acted as assistant to counsel and advisor in inter-state proceedings. He has taught international humanitarian law and the law of international organisations as visiting lecturer at the Brussels School of International Studies (University of Kent). Marco serves in the editorial boards of the Military Law and the Law of War Review and the Chinese (Taiwan) Yearbook of International Law and Affairs as well as in the scientific board of the Belgian Review of International Law. He is an associate member of the Centres for International Law of the Vrije Universiteit Brussel and the Université libre de Bruxelles.

Christina Binder

holds the Chair for International Law and International Human Rights Law at the Bundeswehr University Munich, Germany, since April 2017. Before, she was University Professor of International Law at the Department of European, International and Comparative Law at the University of Vienna, Austria, and Deputy Director of the interdisciplinary Research Centre 'Human Rights'. She is member of the International Law Association's Committees on the Implementation of the Rights of Indigenous Peoples and on Human Rights in Times of Emergency. Christina is member of the Executive Board and former Vice-President of the European Society of International Law (ESIL), was member of the Executive Board of the European Inter-University Center for Human Rights and Democratization (EIUC) (2016–19) and is member of the Council of the Global Campus for Human Rights and Democratization since 2019.

Tillmann Rudolf Braun

serves in the German Federal Ministry for Economic Affairs and Energy, Directorate-General for External Economic Policy, lectures international investment law and public international law at the Faculty of Law, Humboldt-University Berlin, Germany, and publishes on these subjects. He was a visiting fellow at the Lauterpacht Centre for International Law University of Cambridge, UK, a visiting research scholar at the American University in Cairo, Law Department, Egypt, and a Global Hauser Fellow at New York University School of Law, USA. He holds a doctoral degree (*summa cum laude*) in international investment law and public international law from the University of Cologne, Germany, an MPA from the John F Kennedy School of Government, Harvard University, Cambridge, USA, and is a member of the Advisory Council of the International Investment Law Centre, Cologne, Germany.

Kit De Vriese

LLM (Cambridge), LLM (Leuven), presently works at Lindeborg Counsellors at Law, a public international law boutique in London, UK. In that capacity, his main focus has been on investor-state and other public international law arbitrations, including their human rights aspects. Although he is an international law generalist, he has a particular interest in international organisations law and the intersection of fragmented fields, including investment arbitration and armed conflict.

Philipp Janig

is a researcher and lecturer at the Chair for International Law and International Human Rights Law at the Bundeswehr University Munich, Germany. He studied law at the University of Vienna, where he is currently writing his dissertation, as well as in Turku, Finland. His research focuses on the interaction of domestic and international law, international dispute settlement as well as fundamental and human rights. Moreover, he is the Managing Editor of the Austrian Review of International and European Law (ARIEL), member of the Editorial Team of the University of Vienna Law Review (VLR) and teaches international law at the IMC FH Krems.

Vladlena Lisenco

PhD, is Associate Professor of International and European Law at the Pridnestrovian Shevchenko State University in Tiraspol. She has been a visiting professor at a number of European, Russian as well as American universities and has professional experience as consultant, trainer, and project manager.

Stefan Lorenzmeier

Dr iur, LLM (Lugd), is a senior researcher and lecturer at the Law Faculty of the University of Augsburg, Germany. His research and teaching focuses on European Union law and public international law. He is the author of numerous publications in these areas.

Karsten Nowrot

Dr iur, LLM (Indiana), is Professor of Public Law, European Law and International Economic Law, Director of the Research Institute for Economic Law and Labour Law as well as the current Head of the Department of Law at the School of Socio-Economics of the Faculty of Business, Economics and Social Sciences at Hamburg University, Germany. He also serves as Deputy Director of the Master Programme 'European and European Legal Studies' at the Institute for European Integration of the Europa-Kolleg in Hamburg.

NOTES ON CONTRIBUTORS

Réka A Papp

is a senior associate to Professor Pierre Tercier, acting as tribunal secretary in complex international commercial and investment arbitrations. Previously, she was a lecturer at the Geneva MIDS LLM programme with a focus on international arbitration, private international law, and European competition law. She holds a *summa cum laude* PhD from the University of Nancy, France, and a JD from ELTE University in Budapest, Hungary. She worked as a teaching assistant at the University of Nancy and interned at the Court of Justice of the European Union. For several years, she coached the team of the University of Nancy for the ICC International Commercial Mediation Competition. While living in Vienna, Austria, she worked as a law firm associate in the field of international commercial arbitration and energy law and also coached the team of the University of Vienna for the Vis Moot and the Hong Kong International ADR Moot.

Maryna Reznichuk

is a PhD student at the Institute of International Relations of Taras Shevchenko National University of Kyiv, Institute of International Relations, Ukraine, from which she also received her bachelor's degree (2014) and master's degree with honors (2016). While studying at the Institute of International Relations, she completed an internship at the Ministry of Foreign Affairs of Ukraine (Department of the European Union). In 2018/2019, she stayed at the University of Augsburg, Germany, on a DAAD scholarship. During her postgraduate studies, she worked as Junior Legal Approximation Fellow in the Ministry of Foreign Affairs of Ukraine (Directorate General for International Law).

Isabella Risini

is a senior research associate at Ruhr-University Bochum, where she teaches, *inter alia,* human rights law and international economic law. She studied law at the University of Augsburg, the Chicago-Kent College of Law (LLM in International and Comparative Law), and the Hague Academy of International Law. During her qualification period for the German bar exam at the Higher Regional Court of Munich, she completed a stage at the headquarters of the German Foreign Office in Berlin. Subsequently, she also had the opportunity of a stage at the European Court of Human Rights. Isabella's research interests include international law, in particular human rights law in a universal and European context, the law of the European Union and international economic law. At the national level, her focus is on constitutional law and public economic law. Her PhD thesis entitled *The Inter-State Application under the European Convention on Human Rights – Between Collective Enforcement of Human Rights and International Dispute Settlement* was published by Brill in 2018.

Ira Ryk-Lakhman
is a senior associate at Tadmor Levy & Co, where she leads the FinTech and innovation practice as well as consults both states and corporations on questions of international law. Ira holds a PhD in investment arbitration and war law and an LLM (distinction) from University College London, UK. She lectures on international law, technology, and financial regulation and serves as an expert on international committees and workgroups concerning the resolution of disputes involving technology and the use of blockchain and AI in trade. Ira is the Chairperson of the alumni association of the Hebrew University's law school, Israel, and a mentor at the TradeLab law clinic.

Marco Sassòli
is Professor of International Law at the University of Geneva and Director of the Geneva Academy of International Humanitarian Law and Human Rights, Switzerland. He is also a Commissioner of the International Commission of Jurists (ICJ) and Special Advisor (pro bono) on international humanitarian law to the Prosecutor of the International Criminal Court. From 2001 to 2003, he taught at the Université du Québec à Montreal, Canada, where he remains an associate professor. From 1985 to 1997, he worked for the International Committee of the Red Cross (ICRC), notably as Deputy Head of its Legal Division, Head of the ICRC delegations in Jordan and Syria and as Protection Coordinator for the former Yugoslavia. During a sabbatical in 2011, he rejoined the ICRC as a legal adviser to its delegation in Islamabad. Professor Sassòli has also served as Executive Secretary of the ICJ, a registrar at the Swiss Supreme Court and Chair of the Board of Geneva Call, an NGO that promotes respect for humanitarian norms among armed non-state actors.

Emily Sipiorski
is a visiting lecturer at the University of Hamburg, Germany, and an associated researcher at NOVA University Lisbon, Portugal. She completed her PhD at Martin Luther University in Halle-Wittenberg, Germany, and worked on a post-doctoral project on international investment law in the Department of Law at the University of Hamburg, School of Socio-Economics of the Faculty of Business, Economics and Social Sciences.

Valentin J Schatz
is a research associate and PhD candidate at the Chair of International Law of the Sea and International Environmental Law, Public International Law and Public Law of Professor Alexander Proelß and a member of the Institute for the Law of the Sea and for Maritime Law at the University of Hamburg, Germany.

His research interests include public international law, the international law of the sea, international environmental law, and international dispute settlement. Particular focus areas in which Valentin has published or provided expertise include international fisheries law, international marine environmental law, and international maritime security law. He is a recipient of the Diploma of the Hague Academy of International Law (2020) and of the Prix Daniel Vignes of the Association Internationale du Droit de la Mer (2018).

Christine Sim

is an associate at Herbert Smith Freehills in New York, specializing in international commercial and investment treaty arbitration. Christine has clerked for arbitrators in investment arbitrations, represented commercial clients up to the appellate level in courts and performed counsel work in international arbitrations, multi-jurisdictional enforcement and law of the sea proceedings. She has worked with states and state-related entities, and currently advises and represents financial institutions and multi-national corporations. She holds a Master in International Dispute Settlement (MIDS) from the University of Geneva and the Graduate Institute Geneva and is admitted to the Supreme Court of Singapore as an advocate and solicitor as well as to the New York State bar.

Sebastian Wuschka

LLM (Geneva MIDS), is a member of German law firm Luther's complex disputes practice group in Hamburg, Germany. In that capacity, his focus has been mainly on investment arbitration and public international law matters since 2014. During his bar qualification period with the Higher Regional Court of Hamburg, he *inter alia* also worked on international law and EU law matters at Germany's Federal Maritime and Hydrographic Agency, on human rights law questions relating to mineral supply chains at the German Corporation for International Cooperation (GIZ) in Bonn, Germany, and with the arbitration practice of US law firm Hughes Hubbard & Reed LLP in Washington, DC, USA. He is an associated member of Ruhr-University Bochum's Institute for International Law of Peace and Armed Conflict and a visiting lecturer at Ruhr-University Bochum and Martin Luther University of Halle-Wittenberg, Germany.

Table of Cases

Permanent Court of International Justice

Acquisition of Polish Nationality (Advisory Opinion) [1923] PCIJ Series B no 7   43n112
Brazilian Loans (France v Brazil) [1929] PCIJ Series A no 21   123n62
Certain German Interests in Polish Upper Silesia (Germany v Poland) [1925] PCIJ Series A no 6   231n131
Electricity Company of Sofia and Bulgaria (Belgium v Bulgaria) [1939] PCIJ Ser A/B no 77   237n175
Factory at Chorzów (Germany v Poland) (Merits) [1928] PCIJ Series A no 17   216, 216–217n38
Legal Status of Eastern Greenland (Denmark v Norway) [1933] PCIJ Rep Series A/B No 53   68n72
Mavrommatis Palestine Concessions (Greece v UK) [1924] PCIJ Series A no 2   230, 230n126, 232, 232n141, 234
Phosphates in Morocco (Italy v France) [1938] PCIJ Series A/B no 74   237, 237n174
Serbian Loans (France v Yugoslavia) [1929] PCIJ Series A no 20   122, 122n62
SS 'Wimbledon' (Great Britain et al v German) [1923] PCIJ Series A no 1   37n79
Status of Eastern Carelia (Advisory Opinion) [1923] PCIJ Rep Series B no 5   187n70

International Court of Justice

Accordance with International Law of the Unilateral Declaration of Independence in Respect of Kosovo (Advisory Opinion) [2010] ICJ Rep 403   350n231, 396n22, 432n11
Accordance with International Law of the Unilateral Declaration of Independence in Respect of Kosovo (Advisory Opinion, Separate Opinion of Judge Cançado Trindade) [2010] ICJ Rep 523   226n92
Aegean Sea Continental Shelf Case (Greece v Turkey) [1978] ICJ Rep 3   185n58
Ahmadou Sadio Diallo (Guinea v DRC) (Merits) [2010] ICJ Rep 639   40n93
Applicability of the Obligation to Arbitrate under Section 21 of the United Nations Headquarters Agreement of 26 June 1947 (Advisory Opinion) [1988] ICJ Rep 12   231, 231–232n138, 445n62, 445n66

Application of the Convention on the Prevention and Punishment of the Crime of Genocide (Bosnia and Herzegovina v Serbia and Montenegro) [2007] ICJ Rep 43   443n51, 443n53, 443n55, 446n72

Application of the International Convention for the Suppression of the Financing of Terrorism and of the International Convention on the Elimination of All Forms of Racial Discrimination (Ukraine v Russia) (Preliminary Objections) [2019] <www.icj-cij.org/en/case/166> accessed 12 May 2020   213n18

Application of the International Convention on the Elimination of All Forms of Racial Discrimination (Georgia v Russia) (Separate Opinion of President Owada) [2011] ICJ Rep 170   231n134

Application of the International Convention on the Elimination of All Forms of Racial Discrimination (Georgia v Russia) (Joint Dissenting Opinion of President Owada, Judges Simma, Abraham, and Donoghue and Judge *ad hoc* Gaja) [2011] ICJ Rep 142   232n137

Application of the International Convention on the Elimination of All Forms of Racial Discrimination (Georgia v Russia) [2011] ICJ Rep 70   191n97, 232n138

Armed Activities on the Territory of the Congo (DRC v Uganda) (Provisional Measures, Order of 1 July 2000, Separate Opinion of Judge Oda) [2000] ICJ Rep 131   249n15

Armed Activities on the Territory of the Congo (DRC v Uganda) [2005] ICJ Rep 168,   27n 37, 35, 434, 434n21, 445, 445n64, 449n83

Armed Activities on the Territory of the Congo (DRC v Uganda) (Separate Opinion of Judge Kooijmans [2005] ICJ Rep 306   434n17, 434, 434nn23–26

Armed Activities on the Territory of the Congo (New Application: 2002) (DRC v Rwanda) [2006] ICJ Rep 6   236n168

Avena and Other Mexican Nationals (Mexico v USA) (Judgment) [2004] ICJ Rep 12   31n58

Barcelona Traction, Light and Power Co, Ltd (Belgium v Spain) (2nd Phase) [1970] ICJ Rep 3   40n93

Case Concerning the Northern Cameroons (Cameroon v UK) [1963] ICJ Rep 15   230–232n143, 234n156

Case Concerning the Temple of Preah Vihear (Cambodia v Thailand) [1962] ICJ Rep 6   401n38

Certain Phosphate Lands in Nauru (Nauru v Australia) (Preliminary Objections) [1992] ICJ Rep 240   350n230

Certain Property (Liechtenstein v Germany) [2005] ICJ Rep 6   224n128

Certain Questions of Mutual Assistance in Criminal Matters (Djibouti v France) (Merits) [2008] ICJ Rep 1   70n84

Corfu Channel (UK v Albania) (Merits) [1949] ICJ Rep 18   46–47n122

Corfu Channel (UK v Albania) (Merits, Dissenting Opinion of Judge Azevedo) [1949] ICJ Rep 78   121n52

East Timor (Portugal v Australia) [1995] ICJ Rep 90   187n70, 228, 228n105, 236n168, 366n15, 369n52, 371n63

Elettronica Sicula SpA (ELSI) (USA v Italy) (Oral Arguments) [1987] III ICJ Pleadings 1   78n115

Elettronica Sicula SpA (ELSI) (USA v Italy) (Counter-Memorial of Italy) [1988] II ICJ Pleadings 1   78n115

Elettronica Sicula SpA (ELSI) (USA v Italy) (Rejoinder of Italy) [1988] II ICJ Pleadings 417   78n115

Elettronica Sicula SpA (ELSI) (USA v Italy) (Judgment) [1989] ICJ Rep 15   34n67, 40n93, 94, 94n58, 114n12

Fisheries Jurisdiction (Germany v Iceland) (Jurisdiction) [1973] ICJ Rep 49   55n9, 332n97

Gabčíkovo-Nagymaros Project (Hungary v Slovakia) [1997] ICJ Rep 7   32n63, 129, 129–130n105, 332n97, 398n25

Haya de la Torre (Colombia v Peru) [1951] ICJ Rep 71   366n41

Kasikili/Sedudu Island (Botswana v Namibia) [1999] ICJ Rep 1045   55n9

Land and Maritime Boundary (Cameroon v Nigeria) (Preliminary Objections) [1998] ICJ Rep 275   232–233n153, 236n168

Legal Consequences for States of the Continued Presence of South Africa in Namibia (South West Africa) notwithstanding Security Council Resolution 276 (1970) (Advisory Opinion) [1971] ICJ Rep 16   11n30, 55n9, 257, 257n69, 328–329n73, 340n148, 344n185, 360n9, 363n23, 366–367n45, 376n88

Legal Consequences of the Construction of a Wall in the Occupied Palestinian Territory (Advisory Opinion) [2004] ICJ Rep 136   11n30, 27n37, 165n152, 323n30, 343–344n182, 361n14, 361n16, 361n18, 396n22

Legal Consequences of the Separation of the Chagos Archipelago from Mauritius in 1965 (Advisory Opinion) [2019] <www.icj-cij.org/en/case/169/advisory-opinions> accessed 21 January 2020   361n16, 366–367n38

Legality of the Threat or Use of Nuclear Weapons (Advisory Opinion) [1996] ICJ Rep 226   24n21, 323n30

Maritime Delimitation in the Black Sea (Romania v Ukraine) [2009] ICJ Rep 61   375nn85–86

Maritime Delimitation in the Indian Ocean (Somalia v Kenya) (Preliminary Objections) [2017] ICJ Rep 3   210n5, 212n13

Maritime Delimitations and Territorial Questions between Qatar and Bahrain (Qatar v Bahrain) [2001] ICJ Rep 40   375nn85–86

Military and Paramilitary Activities in and against Nicaragua (Nicaragua v USA) (Merits) [1986] ICJ Rep 14   141n15, 344n182, 444n59, 446n71

TABLE OF CASES   XXIX

Military and Paramilitary Activities in and against Nicaragua (Nicaragua v USA)
    (Memorial of Nicaragua) [1985] IV ICJ Pleadings 1   78n115
Monetary Gold Removed from Rome in 1943 (Italy v France, UK, and USA) (Preliminary Question) [1954] ICJ Rep 19   4, 4n25, 11n104, 193, 228, 228n104, 350n229
Navigational and Related Rights (Costa Rica v Nicaragua) [2009] ICJ Rep 213   325n45
North Sea Continental Shelf (Germany v Denmark, Germany v Netherlands) [1969] ICJ Rep 3   43n112, 182n36, 375n87
North Sea Continental Shelf (Germany v Denmark, Germany v Netherlands) (Separate Opinion of Judge Ammoun) [1969] ICJ Rep 101   119n37
Obligations Concerning Negotiations Relating to Cessation of the Nuclear Arms Race and to Nuclear Disarmament (Marshall Islands v UK) (Preliminary Objections, Dissenting Opinion of Judge Crawford) [2016] ICJ Rep 1093   194n111
Oil Platforms (Iran v USA) (Merits) [2003] ICJ Rep 161   70, 70n82, 325n41
Oil Platforms (Iran v USA) (Merits, Separate Opinion of Judge Higgins) [2003] ICJ Rep 225   38n87
Questions of Interpretation and Application of the 1971 Montreal Convention Arising from the Aerial Incident at Lockerbie (Libya v UK) (Preliminary Objections) [1998] ICJ Rep 9   236n168
Questions of Interpretation and Application of the 1971 Montreal Convention Arising from the Aerial Incident at Lockerbie (Libya v USA) (Preliminary Objections) [1998] ICJ Rep 115   334n102
Right of Passage over Indian Territory (Portugal v India) (Preliminary Objections) [1957] ICJ Rep 125   36n76, 237n175
Rights of Nationals of the United States of America in Morocco (France v USA) [1952] ICJ Rep 176   231n131
South West Africa (Ethiopia v South Africa, Liberia v South Africa) (Preliminary Objections) [1962] ICJ Rep 319   231, 231–232n142,
South West Africa (Ethiopia v South Africa, Liberia v South Africa) (Preliminary Objections, Joined Dissenting Opinion of Judges Spender and Fitzmaurice) [1962] ICJ Rep 465   232n144, 234n157
South West Africa (Ethiopia v South Africa, Liberia v South Africa) (Preliminary Objections, Dissenting Opinion of Judge Morelli) [1962] ICJ Rep 564   232n144, 234n157
Territorial and Maritime Dispute (Nicaragua v Colombia) [2012] ICJ Rep 624   182n36, 375nn85–87
United States Diplomatic and Consular Staff in Tehran (USA v Iran) (Provisional Measures) [1979] ICJ Rep 7   236, 236n167

United States Diplomatic and Consular Staff in Tehran (USA v Iran) (Oral Arguments on the Request for the Indication of Provisional Measures) [1979] ICJ Pleadings 13   78n115

United States Diplomatic and Consular Staff in Tehran (USA v Iran) (Oral Arguments) [1980] ICJ Pleadings 249   78n115

United States Diplomatic and Consular Staff in Tehran (USA v Iran) [1980] ICJ Rep 3   37n79, 232n143, 234n156, 236

Western Sahara (Advisory Opinion) [1975] ICJ Rep 12   359, 359n6, 372, 372nn65–66

International Tribunal for the Law of the Sea

Delimitation of the Maritime Boundary in the Bay of Bengal (Bangladesh/Myanmar) (Judgment) [2012] ITLOS Rep 4   180n27

Delimitation of the Maritime Boundary in the Bay of Bengal (Bangladesh/Myanmar) (Merits) [2012] ITLOS Rep 169   180n26

Dispute Concerning Delimitation of the Maritime Boundary between Ghana and Côte d'Ivoire in the Atlantic Ocean (Ghana/Côte d'Ivoire) (Provisional Measures, Written Statement of Ghana) [2015] <www.itlos.org/cases/list-of-cases/case-no-23/case-no-23-provisional-measures/> accessed 12 May 2020   215n26

Dispute Concerning Delimitation of the Maritime Boundary between Ghana and Côte d'Ivoire in the Atlantic Ocean (Ghana/Côte d'Ivoire) (Provisional Measures, Order of 25 April 2015) [2015] ITLOS Rep 146   177n9, 212n11, 215n26, 215–216n32

Dispute Concerning Delimitation of the Maritime Boundary between Ghana and Côte d'Ivoire in the Atlantic Ocean (Ghana/Côte d'Ivoire) (Counter Memorial of Côte d'Ivoire) [2016] <www.itlos.org/cases/list-of-cases/case-no-23/> accessed 12 May 2020   215n27, 215n30

Dispute Concerning Delimitation of the Maritime Boundary between Ghana and Côte d'Ivoire in the Atlantic Ocean (Ghana/Côte d'Ivoire) (Reply of Ghana) [2016] <www.itlos.org/cases/list-of-cases/case-no-23/> accessed 13 May 2020   215n30

Dispute Concerning Delimitation of the Maritime Boundary between Ghana and Côte d'Ivoire in the Atlantic Ocean (Ghana/Côte d'Ivoire) (Rejoinder of Côte d'Ivoire) [2016] <www.itlos.org/cases/list-of-cases/case-no-23/> accessed 12 May 2020   213n15

Dispute Concerning Delimitation of the Maritime Boundary between Ghana and Côte d'Ivoire in the Atlantic Ocean (Ghana/Côte d'Ivoire) (Merits) [2017] ITLOS Rep 4   177n9, 201n152, 213n15, 216n31

TABLE OF CASES   XXXI

M/V "Norstar" (Panama v Italy) (Preliminary Objections) [2016] <www.itlos.
  org/en/cases/list-of-cases/case-no-25/>   193n106
M/V "Saiga" (No 2) Case (Saint Vincent and the Grenadines v Guinea) [1999] IT-
  LOS Rep 10   334n102
MOX Plant (Ireland v UK) (Provisional Measures) [2001] ITLOS Rep 95   185n60
Southern Blue Fin Tuna Cases (New Zealand v Japan, Australia v Japan) (Provi-
  sional Measures) (Order of 27 August 1999) [1999] ITLOS Rep 280   232n140

Inter-State Arbitrations, Mixed Arbitrations, and Claims Commissions

Administrative Decision No VII (The Vinland Case), US–Germany Mixed Claims
  Commission (25 May 1925) 7 RIAA 203   63n48
American Electric and Manufacturing Co (Concession), US–Venezuela Mixed
  Claims Commission (1903) 9 RIAA 306   63n47
Arbitration under the Timor Sea Treaty (Timor-Leste v Australia), PCA Case no
  2013–16   210n5, 215n24
Barbados/Trinidad and Tobago (2006) 45 ILM 800   248n13
Bembelista Case (Netherlands/Venezuela) (1903) 10 RIAA 717   21n10, 63n46
Bolívar Railway Co Case (UK/Venezuela) (1903) 9 RIAA 445   25n23
Chagos Marine Protected Area Arbitration (Mauritius v UK), PCA Case no 2011-
  03, Award (18 March 2015)   182n37, 195n122, 195n124, 235, 235n161
Company General of the Orinoco Case (France/Venezuela) (1905) 10 RIAA
  184   130n106
Dame Franz (France) v Germany (1922) 1 ILR 169   125n79
Deserters of Casablanca (France v Germany) (1909) 3 AJIL 755   322
Delagoa Bay Railway Arbitration (Great Britain and USA v Portugal) (1898) 2
  Moore Int'l Arb 1865   98nn80–82
*Dispute Concerning Coastal State Rights in the Black Sea, Sea of Azov, and Kerch
  Strait (Ukraine v Russia)*, PCA Case no 2017-06, Award on Preliminary Objec-
  tions (21 February 2020)   182n37, 192n103, 195n122, 195n124, 213n18
*Eastern Extension, Australasia and China Telegraph Co, Ltd (Great Britain) v
  USA*, (1923) 6 RIAA 112   62n43
Ecuador v USA, PCA Case no 2012–5, Expert Opinion on the Construction of
  Article VII of Christian Tomuschat (24 April 2012)   231n135
Ecuador v USA, PCA Case no 2012–5, Expert Opinion with Respect to Jurisdic-
  tion of W Michael Reisman (24 April 2012)   231n135, 350n235
Ecuador v USA, PCA Case no 2012–5, Memorial on Objections to Jurisdiction of
  the USA (25 April 2012)   231–232n138

Ecuador v USA, PCA Case no 2012–5, Expert Opinion of Alain Pellet (23 May 2012)   232n138, 234n158

Georges Pinson (France) v Mexico (1928) 5 RIAA 327   248n12

Island of Palmas (Netherlands v USA) (1928) 11 RIAA 829   141, 141n20, 149n43

Italy v Cuba, Interim Award (15 March 2005)   227

Italy v Cuba, Final Award (15 January 2008)   227

Larsen v Hawaiian Kingdom, PCA Case no 1999-01, Award (5 February 2001)   123, 123n64, 131, 131n112, 193n109

Loss of Property in Ethiopia Owned by Non-Residents – Eritrea's Claim 24 (Ethiopia v Eritrea), Eritrea–Ethiopia Claims Commission, Partial Award (19 December 2005) 26 RIAA 429   59n23

Ottoman Empire Lighthouses Concession (Greece v France) (1956) 12 RIAA 155   120n46

Pious Fund Case (USA v Mexico) (1902) 9 RIAA 1   228n112

Rainbow Warrior (New Zealand v France) (1990) 82 ILR 499   119n39, 122n61, 129n96

Sambiaggio Case (Italy/Venezuela) (1903) 10 RIAA 499   25n26

South China Sea Arbitration (Philippines v China), PCA Case no 2013–19, Award on Jurisdiction and Admissibility (29 October 2015)   181n28, 193n106, 195n124, 199, 199n149, 209n4, 232, 232–233n154, 235, 235n162, 235nn164–165

South China Sea Arbitration (Philippines v China), PCA Case no 2013–19, Award (12 July 2016)   181n29, 181n31, 181n34

Spanish Zone of Morocco (Great Britain v Spain) (1925) 2 RIAA 615, 2 ILR 157   4, 4nn17–18, 21n10, 25n25, 63, 63n52, 95, 95n62, 120, 120–121n53, 476n90

The Dunn Case (Chile/UK) (1895)   21n10

Timor Sea Conciliation (Timor-Leste v Australia), PCA Case no 2016-10, Decision on Competence (19 September 2016)   210n5

Tinoco Arbitration (Great Britain v Costa Rica) (1923) 1 RIAA 369   251n26, 255, 255–256

Trail Smelter (USA v Canada) (1941) 3 RIAA 1905   101n104, 228n112

William Hardman (Great Britain) v US (1913) 6 RIAA 25   61

Wipperman Case (USA/Venezuela) (1887) 3 Moore Int'l Arb 3039   120

Court of Justice of the European Union

C-104/16 P *Front Polisario II* [2016] ECLI:EU:C:2016:973   359, 365, 371–372, 376, 378

C-162/96 *Racke* [1998] ECR I-3655, 3 CMLR 219   112n7, 332nn96–97, 364nn26–27, 372n69

C-181/73 *Haegeman* [1974] ECR 449   364–365n28

TABLE OF CASES   XXXIII

C–266/16 *Western Sahara Campaign* [2018] ECLI:EU:C:2018:118   359n5, 374
C–266/16 *Western Sahara Campaign*, Opinion by Advocate-General Wathelet [2018] ECLI:EU:C:2018:1   374–375
C–284/16 *Achmea* [2018] ECLI:EU:C:2018:158   282, 381n105
C–363/18 *Organisation juive europénne* [2019] ECLI:EU:C:2019:954   364n25
C-386/08 *Firma Brita GmbH v Hauptzollamt Hamburg-Hafen* [2010] ECR-I-01289   166n161, 170n186
C-420/07 *Meletis Apostolides v David Charles Orams and Linda Elizabeth Orams* [2009] ECR-I-03571   160n116
Opinion 1/17 [2019] ECLI:EU:C:2019:341   381n106
T–512/12 *Front Polisario I* [2015] ECLI:EU:T:2015:953   359, 365, 369, 371–372, 376, 378

European Court of Human Rights

Albert and others v Hungary, App no 5294/14 (ECtHR, 7 July 2020)   286n32
Agrotexim and others v Greece, App no 14807/89 (ECtHR, 24 October 1995)   286n34
Ališić and others v Bosnia and Herzegovina, Croatia, Serbia, Slovenia, and the Former Yugoslav Republic of Macedonia, App no 60642/08 (ECtHR, 16 July 2014)   291n64
Assanidze v Georgia, App no 71503/01 (ECtHR, 8 April 2004)   286n31
Bimer SA v Moldova, App no 15084/03 (ECtHR, 10 July 2007)   302n115
Blečić v Croatia, App no 59532/00 (ECtHR, 8 March 2006, Merits)   295n82
Broniowski v Poland, App no 31443/96 (ECtHR, 28 September 2005, Friendly Settlement)   303
Burmych and others v Ukraine, App no 46852/13 (ECtHR, 12 October 2017, Striking Out)   305
Catan and Others v Moldova and Russia, App no 43370/04 (ECtHR, 19 October 2012 [GC])   451n89, 451
Chiragov and others v Armenia, App no 13216/05 (ECtHR, 16 June 2015, Merits)   290n58, 290n60, 296
Cyprus v Turkey, App no 25781/94 (ECtHR, 10 May 2001, Merits)   293n74, 344
Damayev v Russia, App no 36150/04 (ECtHR, 29 May 2012, Merits and Just Satisfaction)   290n58, 296n89
Demopoulos and others v Turkey, App nos 46113/99 and others (ECtHR, 1 March 2010, Decision)   258, 296
Drozd and Janousek v France and Spain, App no 12747/87 (ECtHR, 26 June 1992)   293n75

EG and 175 other Bug River Applications v Poland, App no 50425/99 (ECtHR, 23 September 2008, Decision)   303n129

Folgerø and others v Norway, App no 15472/02 (ECtHR, 14 February 2006, Decision)   297n95

Gasus Dosier- und Fördertechnik GmbH v The Netherlands, App no 15375/89 (ECtHR, 23 February 1995)   309n158

Georgia v Russia (II), App no 38263/08 (ECtHR)   294n79

Hassan v United Kingdom App no 29750/09 (ECtHR, 16 September 2014)   284n23

Hilal Mammadov v Azerbaijan, App no 81553/12 (ECtHR, 4 February 2016)   297n95

Iatridis v Greece, App no 31107/96 (ECtHR, 25 March 1999, Just Satisfaction)   302n119

Icyer v Turkey, App no 18888/02 (ECtHR, 12 January 2006, Decision)   304n131

Ilaşcu and others v Moldova and Russia, App no 48787/99 (ECtHR, 4 July 2001, Decision)   286n31

Ilaşcu and others v Moldova and Russia, App no 48787/99 (ECtHR, 8 July 2004, Merits and Just Satisfaction)   195n122, 286n31, 291, 344, 399n35

Industrial Financial Consortium Investment Metallurgical Union v Ukraine, App no 10640/05 (ECtHR, 26 June 2018, Merits and Just Satisfaction)   299

Isayeva v Russia, App no 57950/00 (ECtHR, 24 February 2005, Merits and Just Satisfaction)   296n87

Issa and others v Turkey, App no 31821/96 (ECtHR, 16 November 2004, Merits)   294n74

James and others v UK, App no 8793/79 (ECtHR, 21 February 1986)   288n45

Kerimova and others v Russia, App no 17170/04 (ECtHR, 3 May 2011, Merits and Just Satisfaction)   290n56, 296nn87–88

Khamidov v Russia, App no 72118/01 (ECtHR, 15 November 2007, Merits and Just Satisfaction)   290n56

Khlebik v Ukraine, App no 2945/16 (ECtHR, 25 July 2017)   453n102

Likvidējamā p/s Selga and Vasiļevska v Latvia, App no 17126/02 (ECtHR, 1 October 2013, Decision)   291n64

Lithgow and others v UK, App no 9006/80 (ECtHR, 8 July 1986, Merits)   280, 288, 302n114

Loizidou v Turkey, App no 15318/89 (ECtHR, 18 December 1996, Merits)   290, 295n83

Loizidou v Turkey, App no 15318/89 (ECtHR, 23 March 1995, Preliminary Objections)   293n74, 343n175

Loizidou v Turkey, App no 15318/89 (ECtHR, 28 July 1998, Just Satisfaction)   290, 299

TABLE OF CASES   XXXV

Marckx v Belgium, App no 6833/74 (ECtHR, 13 June 1979, Merits and Just Satisfaction)   287

Marini v Albania, App no 3738/02 (ECtHR, 18 December 2007)   302n116

Matthews v UK, App no 24833/94 (ECtHR, 18 February 1999, Merits and Just Satisfaction)   44n115

Meleagrou and others v Turkey, App no 14434/09 (ECtHR, 2 April 2013, Decision)   296n92

National Union of Rail, Maritime and Transport Workers v UK, App no 31045/10 (ECtHR, 8 April 2014, Merits and Just Satisfaction)   297n100

Oao Neftyanaya Kompaniya Yukos v Russia, App no 14902/04 (ECtHR, 20 September 2011, Merits)   297, 299

Oao Neftyanaya Kompaniya Yukos v Russia, App no 14902/04 (ECtHR, 31 July 2014, Just Satisfaction)   297, 299, 307

Peraldi v France, App no 2096/05 (ECtHR, 7 April 2009, Decision)   297n100

Preussische Treuhand GmbH & Co KG aA v Poland, App no 47550/06 (ECtHR 7 October 2008, Decision)   295n82

Rosenzweig and Bonded Warehouses Ltd v Poland, App no 51728/99 (ECtHR, 5 June 2012, Just Satisfaction)   294n117

Sandu and others v Moldova and Russia App nos 21034/05 and seven others (ECtHR, 17 July 2018)   399n29, 402n41, 402nn43–44

Sargsyan v Azerbaijan, App no 40167/06 (ECtHR, 16 June 2015, Merits [GC])   290n58, 296n90, 451nn89–93

Selçuk and Asker v Turkey, App nos 23184/94 and 23185/94 (ECtHR, 24 April 1998, Merits and Just Satisfaction)   290n56

Sovtransavto Holding v Ukraine, App no 48553/99 (ECtHR, 25 July 2002)   291n64

Suljagić v Bosnia and Herzegovina, App no 27912/02 (ECtHR, 3 November 2009)   304

Ukraine v Russia (re Crimea) App no 20958/14 (ECtHR, 11 September 2019)   336n120

Wolkenberg v Poland, App no 50003/99 (ECtHR, 4 December 2007, Decision)   303n128

Xenides-Arestis v Turkey, App no 46347/99 (ECtHR, 22 December 2005, Merits)   296, 304

Yuriy Nikolayevich Ivanov v Ukraine, App no 40450/04 (ECtHR, 15 October 2009, Merits and Just Satisfaction)   305

Zadrić v Bosnia and Herzegovina, App no 18804/04 (ECtHR, 16 November 2010, Decision)   304n133

Zslinsat, Spol SRO v Bulgaria, App no 57785/00 (ECtHR, 10 January 2008, Just Satisfaction)   302n116

Iran-US Claims Tribunal

Anaconda-Iran Inc v Government of Iran and the National Iranian Copper Industries Co (1986) 31 IUSCTR 199   119n37, 125n79

Dadras International and Per-Am Construction Corp v Iran and Tehran Redevelopment Co (1995) 31 IUSCTR 127   120n45

Gould Marketing, Inc, as Successor to Hoffman Export Corp v Ministry of Defence of Iran (1983) 3 IUSCTR 147   120n45, 121n52, 122n56

Mobil Oil Iran Inc and Mobil Sales and Supply Corporation v Government of Iran and National Iranian Oil Co (1987) 16 IUSCTR 3   119n37

Sylvania Technical Systems, Inc v Iran (1985) 8 IUSCTR 298   25n25, 122n60, 124n77, 129n98

USA v Iran (1996) 32 IUSCTR 162   25n23

Investor-State Arbitration

Achmea BV (formerly Eureko BV) v Slovakia, PCA Case no 2008–13, Award on Jurisdiction, Arbitrability, and Suspension (26 October 2010)   36n77

ACP Axos Capital GmbH v Republic of Kosovo, ICSID Case no ARB/15/22, Award (3 May 2018)   140n10

ADC v Hungary, ICSID Case no ARB/03/16, Award (2 October 2006)   76n106

ADF Group Inc v USA, ICSID Case no ARB(AF)/00/1, Award (9 January 2003)   41n97, 78n117

Aeroport Belbek LLC and Mr. Igor Valerievich Kolomoisky v Russia, PCA Case 2015-07   196n130, 209n3, 335n112, 348

Aeroport Belbek LLC and Mr. Igor Valerievich Kolomoisky v Russia, PCA Case no 2015-07, Interim Award (24 February 2017) (not public)   334n101

AES Summit Generation Ltd and AES-Tisza Erömü Kft v Hungary, ICSID Case no ARB/07/22, Award (23 September 2010)   468n54

Africa Holding Co v DRC, ICSID Case no ARB/05/21, Sentence sur les déclinatoires de compétence et la recevabilité (29 July 2008)   25n23

Aguas del Tunari v Bolivia, ICSID Case no ARB/02/3, Decision on Jurisdiction (21 October 2005)   66n65, 185n60

Amco Asia Corp and others v Indonesia, ICSID Case no ARB/81/1, Award (20 November 1984)   92n45, 291n61

American Manufacturing & Trading Inc (AMT) v Zaire, ICSID Case no ARB/93/1, Award (21 February 1997)   28n43, 88n21, 92n45, 92–93n50, 116–117n27, 467n50, 475n85

Ampal-American Israel Corp and others v Egypt, ICSID Case no ARB/12/11, Decision on Jurisdiction (1 February 2016)   227n96, 229

TABLE OF CASES XXXVII

Ampal-American Israel Corp and others v Egypt, ICSID Case no ARB/12/11, Decision on Liability and Heads of Loss (21 February 2017)   5n20, 28, 98, 227n96, 478nn95–96, 481n104

Archer Daniels Midland Co and Tate & Lyle Ingredients Americas, Inc v Mexico, ICSID Case no ARB(AF)/04/5, Award (21 November 2007)   188n75

Asian Agricultural Products Ltd (AAPL) v Sri Lanka, ICSID Case no ARB/87/3, Dissenting Opinion of Samuel KB Asante (15 June 1990), (1991) 6 ICSID Rev 574   19n3

Asian Agricultural Products Ltd (AAPL) v Sri Lanka, ICSID Case no ARB/87/3, Award (27 June 1990)   5, 19, 27–29n51, 37–38n88, 40n94, 45–46, 88n21, 92n46, 94nn56–57, 97, 114–115n20, 117n28, 117–118n32, 126, 324–325, 335, 467n49, 467n52, 475, 477n93

Autopista Concesionada de Venezuela CA (Aucoven) v Venezuela, ICSID Case no ARB/00/5, Award (23 September 2003)   119n39, 321n13

AWG Group Ltd v Argentina, UNCITRAL, Decision on Liability (30 July 2010)   90–91

Azurix Corp v Argentina, ICSID Case no ARB/01/12, Decision on Jurisdiction (8 December 2003)   212n10

Azurix Corp v Argentina, ICSID Case no ARB/01/12, Award (14 July 2006)   89–90n35

Bayindir Insaat Turizm Ticaret Ve Sanayi AS v Pakistan, ICSID Case no ARB/03/29, Decision on Jurisdiction (14 November 2005)   212n10

Bayindir Insaat Turizm Ticaret Ve Sanayi AS v Pakistan, ICSID Case no ARB/03/29, Award (27 August 2009)   468n56, 470nn69–70, 472n75

Bayview Irrigation District and others v Mexico, ICSID Case no ARB(AF)/05/1, Award (19 June 2007)   349n220

Bernardus Henricus Funnekotter and others v Zimbabwe, ICSID Case no ARB/05/6, Award (22 April 2009)   127n90

Bernhard von Pezold and others v Zimbabwe, ICSID Case no ARB/10/15, Award (28 July 2015)   89n25

Biwater Gauff (Tanzania) Ltd v Tanzania, ICSID Case no ARB/05/22, Award (24 July 2008)   28n43, 94, 114n12

Burlington Resources Inc v Ecuador, ICSID Case no ARB/08/5, Decision on Ecuador's Counterclaims (7 December 2017)   84n12

Camuzzi International SA v Argentina, ICSID Case no ARB/03/2, Decision on Objection to Jurisdiction (11 May 2005)   211n10

Canadian Cattlemen for Fair Trade v USA, Award on Jurisdiction (28 January 2008)   349n220

Cargill, Inc v Mexico, ICSID Case no ARB(AF)/05/2, Award (28 September 2009)   188n75

Casinos Austria International GmbH and Casinos Austria AG v Argentina, ICSID Case no ARB/14/32, Decision on Jurisdiction, Dissenting Opinion and Declaration of Dissent of Santiago Torres Bernárdez (20 June 2018)   187n71

Cengiz İnşaat Sanayi ve Ticaret AS v Libya, ICC Case no 21537/ZF/AYZ, Award (7 November 2018)   5n21, 112n3, 473n79

Chevron Corp and Texaco Petroleum v Ecuador, PCA Case no 34877, Partial Award on the Merits (30 March 2010)   71n90

Chevron Corp and Texaco Petroleum v Ecuador, PCA Case no 2009–23, Third Interim Award on Jurisdiction and Admissibility (27 February 2012)   193n108, 228

CME Czech Republic BV (The Netherlands) v Czech Republic, Partial Award (13 September 2001)   211n10

CME Czech Republic BV (The Netherlands) v Czech Republic, Legal Opinion Prepared by Christoph Schreuer and August Reinisch (20 June 2002)   228n110

CMS Gas Transmission Co v Argentina, ICSID Case no ARB/01/8, Award (12 May 2005)   129–130n107

CMS Gas Transmission Co v Argentina, ICSID Case no ARB/01/8, Annulment Decision (25 September 2007)   32n63, 112n8, 130n100

Compañiá de Aguas del Aconquija SA and Vivendi Universal SA (formerly Compañía de Aguas del Aconquija, SA and Compagnie Générale des Eaux) v Argentina, ICSID Case no ARB/97/3, Award (21 November 2000)   90n35

Compañiá de Aguas del Aconquija SA and Vivendi Universal SA v Argentina, ICSID Case no ARB/97/3, Award (20 August 2007)   89n24

Compañía del Desarrollo de Santa Elena SA v Costa Rica, ICSID Case no ARB/96/1, Award (17 February 2000)   101n99

Continental Casualty Co v Argentina, ICSID Case no ARB/03/9, Award (5 September 2008)   32n61, 416n93

Copper Mesa Mining Corp v Ecuador, UNCITRAL, PCA Case no 2012-2, Award (15 March 2016)   98–99

Corn Products International, Inc v Mexico, ICSID Case no ARB(AF)/04/1, Decision on Responsibility (15 January 2008)   188n75

Daimler Financial Services AG v Argentina, ICSID Case no ARB/05/1, Award (22 August 2012)   193n108, 389n10

David R Aven and others v Costa Rica, ICSID Case no UNCT/15/3, Award (18 September 2018)   104n118

Deutsche Bank AG v Sri Lanka, ICSID Case no ARB/09/02, Award (31 October 2012)   97n72

Deutsche Telekom v India, PCA Case no 2014-10, Interim Award (13 December 2017)   113n8

Diag Human SE v Czech Republic Ministry of Health, Case no RSP 06/2003, Final Award (4 August 2008)   249–250

DS Construction FZCO v Libya, PCA Case no 2017–21   461n9

Duke Energy Electroquil Partners & Electroquil SA v Ecuador, ICSID Case no ARB/04/19, Award (16 August 2008)   469–470n71

East Mediterranean Gas SAE v Egyptian General Petroleum Corp, Egypitan Natural Gas Holding Co, and Israel Electric Corp Ltd, ICC Case no 18215/GZ/MHM   227

Eastern Sugar v Czech Republic, SCC Case no 088/2004, Partial Award (27 March 2007)   291n61

ECE Projektmanagement v Czech Republic, PCA Case no 2010–5, Award, 13 September 2013   140n10

Egyptian General Petroleum Corp and Egyptian Natural Gas Holding Co v East Mediterranean Gas SAE, CRCICA Case no 829/2012   227

El Paso Energy International Co v Argentina, ICSID Case no ARB/03/15, Award (31 October 2011)   88–89, 476n87

Electrabel SA v Hungary, ICSID Case no ARB/07/19, Decision on Jurisdiction, Applicable Law, and Liability (30 November 2012)   36n76

Emilio Agustín Maffezini v Spain, ICSID Case no ARB/97/7, Decision on Objections to Jurisdiction (25 January 2000)   236–237

Emilio Agustín Maffezini v Spain, ICSID Case no ARB/97/7, Award (13 November 2000)   472n76

Empresas Lucchetti SA and Lucchetti Peru SA v Peru, ICSID Case no ARB/03/4, Award (7 February 2005)   227n102

EnCana Corp v Ecuador, LCIA Case no UN3481, Award (3 February 2006)   469n58

Enron Corp and Ponderosa Assets LP v Argentina, ICSID Case no ARB/01/3, Decision on Jurisdiction (14 January 2004)   37n81

Enron Corp and Ponderosa Assets LP v Argentina, ICSID Case no ARB/01/3, Award (22 May 2007)   119n39, 122n61, 129–130n100, 132n122

Etrak İnşaat Taahut ve Ticaret Anonim Sirketi v Libya (ICC Arbitration)   46n9

European American Investment Bank AG (Austria) v Slovak Republic, Award on Jurisdiction (22 October 2012)   399n28

Everest Estate LLC and others v Russia, PCA Case no 2015–36, Press Release (9 August 2016)   320n9, 331n89

Everest Estate LLC and others v Russia, PCA Case no 2015–36, Decision on Jurisdiction (20 March 2017) (not public)   67n70, 196n130, 209n3, 334n101, 341, 348–349n225, 352

Feldman v Mexico, ICSID Case no ARB(AF)/99/1, Award (16 December 2002)   48n125

Franz Sedelmayer v Russia, Arbitration Award (7 July 1998)   249n17, 270

Frontier Petroleum Services Ltd v Czech Republic, Final Award (12 November 2010)   470n72

Gamesa Eólica SLU v Syria, PCA Case no 2012-11, Award (5 April 2014) (not public)   112n2

Generation Ukraine, Inc v Ukraine, ICSID Case no ARB/00/9, Award (16 September 2003)   469–470n67

Glamis Gold Ltd v USA, Procedural Order no 2 (Revised) (31 May 2005)   335n113

Grand River Enterprises Six Nations Ltd et al v USA, Award (12 January 2011)   36n77

Gujarat State Petroleum Corp Ltd et al v Yemen and the Yemeni Ministry of Oil and Minerals, ICC Case no 19299/MCP, Final Award (10 July 2015)   48n125

Güriş İnşaat ve Mühendislik AŞ v Libya (ICC Arbitration)   46n9

Himpurna California Energy Ltd v PT (Persero) Perusahaan Listruik Negara, ICC, Final Award (4 May 1999), (2000) 25 YB Comm Arb 13   113n9

Hrvatska Elektroprivreda dd v Slovenia, ICSID Case no ARB/05/24, Tribunal's Ruling Regarding the Participation of David Mildon QC in Further Stages of the Proceedings (6 May 2008)   265nn97–98

Hulley Enterprises Ltd (Cyprus) v Russia, UNCITRAL, PCA Case no 226, Final Award (18 July 2014)   297

International Thunderbird Gaming Corp v Mexico, Award, Separate Opinion of Thomas Wälde (1 December 2005)   198n138

Interocean Development Company and Interocean Oil Exploration Co v Nigeria, ICSID Case no ARB/13/20, Procedural Order No. 5 on the Claimants' Requests Regarding (i) the Authority of Volterra Fietta Lawyers to Represent the Respondent and (ii) the Source and Terms of the Funding of the Respondent's Defence (15 October 2016)   265n97

Joseph Houben v Burundi, ICSID Case no ARB/13/7, Award (12 January 2016)   28n46

LESI SpA and ASTALDI SpA v Algeria, ICSID Case no ARB/05/3, Decision on Jurisdiction (12 July 2006)   185n60

LESI SpA and ASTALDI SpA v Algeria, ICSID Case no ARB/05/3, Award (12 November 2008)   126n86, 476n91, 478n96

LG&E Energy Corp, LG&E Capital Corp and LG&E International Inc v Argentina, ICSID Case no ARB/02/1, Decision on Liability (3 October 2006)   129–130n100, 325n42, 470n71

Libyan Arab Foreign Investment Co (LAFICO) v Burundi, Award (4 March 1991) 96 ILR 279   119n39, 124

Limited Liability Co Lugzor and others v Russia, PCA Case no 2015–29   197n130, 209n3

Limited Liability Co Lugzor and others v Russia, PCA Case no 2015–29, Press Release (28 November 2019)   320n9

TABLE OF CASES   XLI

Limited Liability Co Lugzor and others v Russia, PCA Case no 2015–29, Tribunal's
    Letter (29 August 2017) (not public)   334n101, 341n164, 341n166
Mabco Constructions SA v Republic of Kosovo, ICSID Case no ARB/17/
    25   168n177
Metalclad Corp v Mexico, ICSID Case no ARB(AF)/97/1, Award (30 August
    2000)   101n99, 470n67
Methanex Corp v USA, Award (3 August 2005)   41n97, 43n113, 48n125, 344n184
Middle East Cement v Egypt, ICSID Case no ARB/99/6, Award (12 April 2002)
    76n106
MNSS BV and Recupero Credito Acciaio NV v Montenegro, ICSID Case no ARB(AF)/12/8, Award (4 May 2016)   89n25, 220n61
Mondev International Ltd v USA, ICSID Case no ARB(AF)/99/2, Award (11 October 2002)   40n91, 78n117
MTD Equity Sdn. Bhd. and MTD Chile SA v Chile, ICSID Case no ARB/01/7, Award
    (25 May 2004)   470n67
National Grid v Argentina, UNCITRAL, Award (3 November 2008)   89n24
Niko Resources (Bangladesh) Ltd v Bangladesh Petroleum Exploration & Production Co Ltd ('Bapex') and Bangladesh Oil Gas and Mineral Corp ('Petrobangla'), ICSID Case no ARB/10/11, Decision on Jurisdiction (19 August
    2013)   193n108
NJSC Naftogaz of Ukraine (Ukraine) and others v Russia, PCA Case no
    2017-16   197n130, 346n194
Noble Ventures, Inc v Romania, ICSID Case no ARB/01/11, Award (12 October
    2005)   469n61, 483n105
Nykomb Synergetics Technology Holding AB v Latvia, SCC Case no 118/2001, Arbitral Award (16 December 2003)   113n9
Occidental Petroleum Corp and Occidental Exploration and Production Co v Ecuador, ICSID Case no ARB/06/11, Award (5 October 2012)   90n35, 98
Olin Holdings Ltd v Libya, ICC Case no 20355/MCP, Final Award (25 May
    2018)   466n46
Oschadbank v Russia, PCA Case no 2016-14   197n130, 209n3, 346n194
PacRim v El Salvador, ICSID Case no ARB/09/12, Decision on Jurisdiction (1
    June 2012)   348n208
Pantechniki SA Contractors & Engineers (Greece) v Albania, ICSID Case no ARB/
    07/21, Award (30 July 2009)   28n46, 92–93, 100n87, 114–115n18, 476–478n94,
    478nn96–97, 480n101
Parkerings-Compagniet AS v Lithuania, ICSID Case no ARB/05/8, Award (11
    September 2007)   88n21, 92–94, 474
Patrick Mitchell v DRC, ICSID ARB/99/7, Decision on the Application for Annulment of the Award (1 November 2006)   132n117

Peter A Allard v Barbados, PCA Case no 2012-06, Award (27 June 2016)   101n100, 104

Peteris Pildegovics and SIA North Star v Norway, ICSID Case no ARB/20/11   176n6

Philip Morris Asia Ltd (Hong Kong) v Australia, PCA Case no 2012-12, Award on Jurisdiction and Admissibility (17 December 2015)   237

Phoenix Action Ltd v Czech Republic, ICSID Case no ARB/06/5, Award (15 April 2009)   2n4, 38n83, 401n40

Ping An v Belgium, ICSID Case no ARB/12/29, Award (30 April 2015)   193n108, 228

PJSC CB PrivaBbank and Finance Co Finilion LLC v Russia, PCA Case no 2015–21   196n130, 209n3

PJSC CB PrivatBank and Finance Co Finilon LLC v Russia, PCA Case no 2015–21, Interim Award (24 February 2017) (not public)   334n101, 348

PJSC Ukrnafta v Russia, PCA Case no 2015–34, Award on Jurisdiction (26 June 2017) (not public)   11, 196n130, 209n3, 222, 330–332, 340–341, 346–349, 351

Plama v Bulgaria, ICSID Case no ARB/03/24, Decision on Jurisdiction (8 February 2005)   185n60

PSEG Global Inc and others v Turkey, ICSID Case no ARB/02/5, Award (19 January 2005)   90n35

Rompetrol Group NV v Romania, ICSID Case no ARB/06/3, Decision of the Tribunal on the Participation of a Counsel (14 January 2010)   265n97, 265n99

Rompetrol Group NV v Romania, ICSID Case no ARB/06/3, Award (6 May 2013)   44n116

Ronald S Lauder v Czech Republic, Final Award (3 September 2001)   93n50, 96

RosInvest Co UK Ltd v Russia, SCC Case no V079/2005, Award on Jurisdiction (5 October 2007)   42n103

RSM Production Corp v Central African Republic, ICSID Case no ARB/07/2, Decision on Jurisdiction and Liability (7 December 2010)   113n9

RSM Production Corp v Grenada, ICSID Case no ARB/05/14, Final Award (18 March 2009)   194n117

RSM Production Corp v Saint Lucia, ICSID Case no ARB/12/10, Decision on Saint Lucia's Request for Provisional Measures (12 December 2013)   194n119

Rumeli Telekom AS and Telsim Mobil Telekomunikasyon Hizmetleri AS v Kazakhstan, ICSID Case no ARB/05/16, Award (29 July 2008)   48n125, 437n45

Saluka Investments BV v Czech Republic, Jurisdiction over the Counterclaim (7 May 2004)   220

Saluka Investments BV v Czech Republic, Partial Award (17 March 2006)   28n38, 28n41, 40n91, 72n90, 74n98, 92n45, 291n61, 467n51, 469n57, 470n66, 470n71

TABLE OF CASES   XLIII

Sanum Investments Ltd v Laos, PCA Case no 2013-13, Award on Jurisdiction (13 December 2013)   140n9, 183n42, 196n127, 218, 221–222n71, 338, 340, 399n30

Sempra Energy International v Argentina, ICSID Case no ARB/02/16, Award (28 September 2007)   119n39, 122n61, 129n97, 467n54

Sempra Energy International v Argentina, ICSID Case no ARB/02/16, Decision on Annulment (29 June 2010)   41n97

Sempra Energy International v Argentina, ICSID Case no ARB/02/16, Decision on Objections to Jurisdiction (11 May 2005)   211n10

Siemens AG v Argentina, ICSID Case no ARB/02/8, Award (17 January 2007)   89n24, 232n137, 467n54

South American Silver Ltd v Bolivia, PCA Case no 2013–15, Award (30 August 2018)   130n107, 132

Spyridon Roussalis v Romania, ICSID Case no ARB/06/1, Award (1 December 2011)   32n60

Stabil LLC and others v Russia, PCA Case no 2015–35, Award on Jurisdiction (26 June 2017) (not public)   11, 196n130, 198–199n150, 209n3, 222, 330, 332, 334n101, 338, 340–341, 346–348n208, 448n77

Suez, Sociedad General de Aguas de Barcelona, SA and Vivendi Universal SA v Argentina, ICSID Case no ARB/03/19, Decision on Liability (30 July 2010)   468n54

Técnicas Medioambientales Tecmed, SA v Mexico, ICSID Case no ARB(AF)/00/2, Award (29 May 2003)   466–467n51, 469n58

Tidewater Inc and others v Venezuela, ICSID Case no ARB/10/5, Award (15 March 2015)   195n118

Toto Costruzioni Generali SpA v Lebanon, ICSID Case no ARB/07/12, Decision on Jurisdiction (11 September 2009)   126

Toto Costruzioni Generali SpA v Lebanon, ICSID Case no ARB/07/12, Award (7 June 2012)   126, 470n70, 474n81

Trasta Energy v Libya (UNCITRAL)   473n79

Tza Yap Shum v Peru, ICSID Case no ARB/07/6, Decision on Jurisdiction and Competence (19 June 2009)   140n9

Tza Yap Shum v Peru, ICSID Case no ARB/07/6, Award (7 July 2011)   221

Unión Fenosa Gas SA v Egypt, ICSID Case no ARB/14/4, Award (31 August 2018)   127n90, 129n97

Urbaser SA and others v Argentina, ICSID Case no ARB/07/26, Award (8 December 2016)   84n12, 104–105, 401n40

Valores Mundiales SL and Consorcio Andino SL v Venezuela, ICSID Case no ARB13/11 – Annulment Proceedings Procedural Resolution no 2 (29 August 2019)   266, 269–270n111, 274–276

Veteran Petroleum Ltd (Cyprus) v Russia, UNCITRAL, PCA Case no AA228, Final Award (18 July 2014)   297

Waste Management Inc v Mexico, ICSID Case no ARB(AF)/00/2, Final Award (20 April 2004)   37n80

Waste Management, Inc v Mexico ("Number 2"), ICSID Case no ARB(AF)/00/3, Award (30 April 2004)   78n117, 466n40, 469n61

Way2B ACE v Libya, Award (24 May 2018)   5n21, 112n3

Wena Hotels Ltd v Egypt, ICSID Case no ARB/98/4, Award (8 December 2000)   88n21, 90n35, 92–94, 475n85

Wena Hotels Ltd v Egypt, ICSID Case no ARB/98/4, Decision on Annulment (28 January 2002)   211n10

William Nagel v Czech Republic, SCC Case no 049/2002, Award (9 September 2003)   474

Wintershall AG v Argentina, ICSID Case no ARB/04/14, Award (8 December 2008)   195n118

WJ Holding Ltd v Transdniestrian Moldovan Republic, ICC Case no 21717/MHM, Award (6 June 2018) and Addendum (30 August 2018)   12n34

World Wide Minerals v Kazakhstan, Award (22 December 2010) (not public)   220

World Wide Minerals v Kazakhstan (case 2), Decision on Jurisdiction (15 October 2015) (not public)   140n10

Yosef Maiman, Merhav (Mnf) Ltd, Merhav Ampal Group Ltd, and Merhav Ampal Energy Holdings Ltd Partnership v Egypt, PCA Case no 2012-26   227n96, 473n79

Yukos Universal Ltd (Isle of Man) v Russia, UNCITRAL, PCA Case no 2005-04/AA 227, Final Award (18 July 2014)   99n84, 288n18, 297

WTO and GATT

GATT Panel, *United States – Taxes on Petroleum and Certain Imported Substances*, Report of the Panel adopted on 17 June 1987, L/6175 - 34S/136   389n8

European Communities – Measures Affecting the Approval and Marketing of Biotech Products (29 September 2006) WT/DS291/R, WT/DS292/R, and WT/DS293/R   70n78

Peru – Additional Duty Imports of Certain Agricultural Products (20 July 2015) WT/DS457/AB/R   70n80

Russia – Measures Concerning Traffic in Transit – Panel Report (5 April 2019) WT/DS512/R   389n8

United States – Sections 301–310 of the Trade Act of 1974 – Panel Report (11 December 1999) WT/DS152/R   389n9

United States – Anti-Dumping and Countervailing Duties (China) (11 March 2011) WT/DS379/AB/R 38n87

International Criminal Law

Nuremberg Trials
United States v List (Wilhelm) and others (Hostage Case) (1948) 11 TWC 757, 15 ILR 632 61, 117n26
United States v Carl Krauch et al (IG Farben Trial) (1948) 8 TWC 1081 100n95

International Criminal Court
Prosecutor v Katanga (Judgment pursuant to article 74 of the Statute) ICC-01/04-01/07 (7 March 2014) 60nn28–29, 77n112
Prosecutor v Mbarushimana (Decision on the Confirmation of Charges) ICC-01/04-01/10 (16 December 2011) 60n28
Prosecutor v Mudacumura (Decision on the Prosecutor's Application under Article 58) ICC-01/04-01/12 (13 July 2012) 60n28
Prosecutor v Ntaganda (Decision Pursuant to Article 61(7)(a) and (b) of the Rome Statute on the Charges of the Prosecutor Against Bosco Ntaganda), ICC-01/04-02/06 (9 June 2014) 60n28

International Criminal Tribunal for the Former Yugoslavia
Prosecutor v Hadzihasanoviæ and Kubura, IT-01-47-T (15 March 2006) 39n90
Prosecutor v Dusko Tadic, IT-94-1-A (15 July 1999) 444
Prosecutor v Naletilic and Martinovic, IT-98-34-T (31 March 2003) 434n22
Prosecutor v Boškoski, IT-04-82-T (10 July 2008) 26n31
Prosecutor v Kupreškić et al, IT-95-16-T (14 January 2000) 31n57, 42n108
Prosecutor v Kunarac et al, IT-96-23-T, IT-96-23/1-T (22 February 2001) 43

National Courts
Bridge of Varvarin [2013] Case no 2 BvR 2660/06 (German Federal Constitutional Court) 47
Chen Li Hong and others v Ting Lei Miao and others [2000] 3 HKCFAR 9 150
Diaz v USA, 222 US 574 (1912) 62n38
Government of Laos v Sanum Investments Ltd [2015] SGHC 15 140n9, 209n2, 218n66
Herrera v United States, 222 US 558 (1912) 62n38
Hesperides Hotels v Aegean Holidays Ltd [1978] QB 205 267n106

Jenny and Hedwige R v Belgium, Case no 133 (1933) 7 ILR 323 (Court of Appeal of Brussels)   120n44
John Doe I et al v Unocal Corp et al, 963 F Supp 880 (CD Cal 1997)
Juragua Iron Co, Ltd v USA, 212 US 297 (1909)   62n38
Kiobel v Royal Dutch Shell Petroleum Co, 569 US 108 (2013)   100n92
OI European Group v Venezuela, no 16-cv-01533, Memorandum Opinion and Order (DDC, 1 November 2019)   261–262n87
OI European Group v Venezuela, no 16-cv-1533, Memorandum Opinion (DDC, 21 May 2019)   261–262n87
Presbyterian Church of Sudan v Talisman Energy, 374 F Supp 2d 331 (SDNY 2005)   100n93
Public Committee against Torture in Israel et al v Government of Israel et al [2006] HCJ 769/02 (Supreme Court of Israel sitting as the High Court of Justice)   35n75
R v Reeves Taylor [2019] WLR(D) 648, [2019] UKSC 51, [2019] 3 WLR 1073   252n30
Rusoro Mining Ltd v Venezuela, no 18–7044, Order (DC Cir, 1 May 2019)   260n75
Sanum Investments Ltd v Laos [2016] SGCA 57 (Singapore Court of Appeal)   140n9, 151n59, 209n2, 218, 221, 237n171
Seadrill Ghana Operations Ltd v Tullow Ghana Ltd [2018] EWHC 1640 (Comm)   212n12
Russia v A (Russia v Ukrnafta) [2018] Case no 4A_396/2017, BGE 144 III 559 (Swiss Federal Tribunal)   11, 196n134, 213n17, 222, 330–332n91, 338, 340–341, 346–348n222, 380n101, 448
Russia v A and others (Russia v Stabil and others) [2018] Case no 4A_398/2017, (2019) 17(2) German Arb J 93 (Swiss Federal Tribunal)   11, 196n134, 213n17, 222, 330–332n91, 338, 340–341, 346–348n222, 380n101, 448
VEB Carl Zeiss Jena v Firma Carl Zeiss Heidenheim, ATF 91 II 117 (Swiss Federal Tribunal)   262n86
Wiwa v Royal Dutch Shell Petroleum Co, 392 F3d 812 (5th Cir 2004)   100n91

Introduction: Investments in Conflict Zones

Tobias Ackermann and Sebastian Wuschka

This book is about investment law and conflicts. The notion of conflict runs – in different meanings and on different layers – as a common thread through the contributions in this volume. Primarily, the book explores the role of investment law in various *conflict situations*, ranging from armed to 'frozen' conflicts, from geopolitical conflicts over territories and boundaries to conflicting claims over areas controlled by states or – in some instances – by non-state actors. Given the continuously expanding reach of international investment law and arbitration, it is not surprising that such scenarios increasingly play a role in investment disputes. Recent arbitral awards rendered in the context of the annexation of Crimea[1] or the civil war in Libya[2] are emblematic of this development. The same holds true, among other examples, for the increasing awareness that border disputes can impact investors seeking to extract natural resources in disputed zones.[3] The present volume intends to help closing the gap in scholarship on precisely such legal implications.

On another level, this book concerns *normative conflicts* or, in more general terms, the interaction between different legal regimes. As investment law does not operate in a closed system,[4] its relationship to other fields of international law continues to be the subject of much debate.[5] In addressing, for example, the interplay between investment treaties and the law of armed conflict or the impact of the duty of non-recognition when determining the application of

---

1   For reports on these cases, see, *eg*, Mykhaylo Soldatenko, 'Ongoing Territorial Challenges in Crimea Cases: Putting Everest v. Russia in Context' (*Kluwer Arbitration Blog*, 5 November 2018) <http://arbitrationblog.kluwerarbitration.com/2018/11/05/territorial-challenges-expected-in-crimea-cases-putting-everest-v-russia-in-context> accessed 10 May 2020.
2   See Luke Eric Peterson, 'Investigation: As Fight Continues over $1 bil Award, Libya Facing at Least a Dozen Investment Treaty Arbitrations – Possibly More – in Aftermath of Arab Spring' (*IAReporter*, 31 March 2017) <www.iareporter.com/articles/investigation-as-fight-continues-over-1bil-award-libya-facing-at-least-a-dozen-investment-treaty-arbitrations-possibly-more-in-aftermath-of-arab-spring> accessed 10 May 2020.
3   See Christine Sim, 'Investment Disputes Arising out of Areas of Unsettled Boundaries: Ghana/Côte d'Ivoire' (2018) 11 J World Energy L & Bus 1; Peter Tzeng, 'Investment Protection in Disputed Maritime Areas' (2018) 19 JWIT 828.
4   *Cf*, *eg*, *Phoenix Action, Ltd v Czech Republic*, ICSID Case no ARB/06/5, Award (15 April 2009) paras 77 et seq.
5   See, *eg*, Freya Baetens (ed), *Investment Law within International Law: Integrationist Perspectives* (CUP 2013).

investment treaties to annexed territories, the contributions in this volume present a novel angle in the debate on the relationship between investment law and other legal regimes and, more generally, that on specialization and fragmentation of international law.[6] Taking this perspective, the book seeks to foster a better understanding of what role international investment law may assume in the universe of public international law.

Investment law and its operation in conflict situations finally also touches upon fundamental *interests that conflict* with one another. For example, the question of a state's liability for emergency measures taken in conflict situations goes to the core of the commonly perceived conflict between particular interests of foreign investors and public interests of the state. After all, the much-invoked backlash against investment law[7] finds one of its origins in arbitral awards rendered in the aftermath of the Argentinian financial and economic crisis.[8] In conflict situations, the state's interest in the greatest possible leeway for emergency measures or policy changes increases, but so does the investors' interest in protection and stability. This volume, by exploring, *inter alia*, the limits of liability in times of armed conflicts or state fragility, adds to the debate of how a balance can be stricken between the diverse interests at stake and whether the current system is fit for the job or in need of reform.[9]

1   One Step Back: a Sceptic's Perspective

Before opening the floor for the in-depth analyses provided by the contributors to this volume, we believe it is helpful to take a step back and question, in general and from a policy perspective, the role of investment law in conflict situations. After all, at first glance, foreign investments and the international rules relating to their protection seem to play only a marginal role in these circumstances. In light of much greater issues at play – issues of violence and

---

6   See generally, *eg*, ILC, 'Fragmentation of International Law: Difficulties Arising from the Diversification and Expansion of International Law' (2006) UN Doc A/CN.4/L.682; Bruno Simma and Dirk Pulkowski, 'Of Planets and the Universe: Self-contained Regimes in International Law' (2006) 17 EJIL 483.
7   See, *eg*, Michael Waibel and others (eds), *The Backlash against Investment Arbitration* (Kluwer Law International 2010).
8   For an overview, see José E Alvarez and Kathryn Khamsi, 'The Argentine Crisis and Foreign Investors: A Glimpse into the Heart of the Investment Regime' in Karl P Sauvant (ed), *Yearbook on International Investment Law and Policy 2008–2009* (OUP 2009).
9   See, *eg*, Steffen Hindelang and Markus Krajewski (eds), *Shifting Paradigms in International Investment Law: More Balanced, Less Isolated, Increasingly Diversified* (OUP 2016).

security, of boundaries and sovereignty, of control and title – the legal protection of foreigners and their assets may appear almost irrelevant. One could even regard the involvement of investment law as counterproductive, fearing that it could disturb legal balances created by other rules of greater importance and general application.

When, for example, one prominent publication by the International Committee of the Red Cross famously asks 'How Does Law Protect in War?', the answer given by Marco Sassòli – who kindly authored this volume's foreword – and his co-authors does surely not involve investment law.[10] The laws of armed conflict are not concerned with investments; they have more pressing issues to address. International humanitarian law certainly also safeguards property when it protects civilian objects from the effects of military operations and the grasp of warring states, but it does so primarily for humanitarian reasons, not to protect economic values as such.[11] Why should, against this backdrop, foreign investors profit from a special regime, while others are protected only by a seemingly rudimentary set of rules that is already too often ignored?

In case of disputed territories, it seems doubtful, at first blush, whether investment tribunals possess any authority at all to deal even indirectly with highly complex political conflicts between sovereigns.[12] Should investment tribunals, in proceedings between individuals and (only) one state party to the territorial conflict, address these issues at all?[13] Should they not rather abstain from fuelling the dispute with an award that speaks in favour of one of the states involved? After all, history shows that escalations of territorial disputes have all too often led to the outbreak of hostilities.[14] Similarly, in other conflict situations, investment disputes will involve, at least indirectly, the conflict between two or more states over territory. In such cases, the mere application of a treaty may legitimize factual circumstances that arise from illegal acts, endowing such cases with an 'explosive' nature.

In sum, there may be reason to question the role of investment law in all of these highly sensitive contexts of competing claims of sovereignty and use

---

10 Marco Sassòli, Antoine A Bouvier, and Anne Quintin, *How Does Law Protect in War? Cases, Documents and Teaching Materials on Contemporary Practice in International Humanitarian Law* (3rd edn, ICRC 2011).
11 See Lea Brillmayer and Geoffrey Chepiga, 'Ownership or Use? Civilian Property Interests in International Humanitarian Law' (2008) 49 Harvard Int LJ 413.
12 For an alternative suggestion, see Peter Tzeng, 'Sovereignty over Crimea: A Case for State-to-State Investment Arbitration' (2016) 41 Yale Int'l LJ 459.
13 See Peter Tzeng, 'Investments on Disputed Territory: Indispensable Parties and Indispensable Issues' (2017) 14 Braz J Int'l L 122.
14 John A Vasquez, *The War Puzzle Revisited* (CUP 2009) 371 et seq.

of force. And yet, the fact remains that investment treaties continue to apply in conflict situations, sometimes even in explicit anticipation of them.[15] Legal issues that have already arisen or are likely to arise in the near future demand solutions. Judicial restraint by arbitrators can hardly be the answer to these challenges. After all, one of the purposes of the investment law regime is the guarantee of certain standards to the benefit of the individual investor precisely in times when compliance becomes politically unwelcome, legally complicated, or practically difficult. It is, therefore, important to analyse how investment law pursues or should pursue its goals in the context of conflict situations and how conflicting norms and interests can best be taken into account.

2 Investment Law and Armed Conflicts

The first part of the book approaches these objectives by addressing the role of investment law in armed conflicts. The historical roots of the law of investment protection show that investment disputes in this context are not a new phenomenon. As is well-known, modern investment law is highly influenced by the traditional law on the treatment of aliens. These customary rules, in turn, were shaped by the case law of various mixed claims commissions at the end of the nineteenth and the beginning of the twentieth century.[16] Such commissions were often put in place to come to terms precisely with the economic or personal damage caused to foreign individuals during internal insurrections and unrest. For instance, in 1925, sole arbitrator Huber in the infamous *Spanish Zone of Morocco* case had little difficulty to identify as custom that a state was generally not responsible for acts of insurgencies and revolts but that the authorities merely had a duty of vigilance to protect foreigners within their territory.[17] As for military operations conducted by the Spanish authorities themselves, Huber found that a state was, again, generally not responsible for the consequences arising from engaging the enemy, but this only included acts necessary for military purposes.[18]

---

15 Many investment treaties include so-called 'war clauses' or security exceptions which expressly reference armed conflicts and other emergency situations.

16 See, on these, Rudolf Dolzer, 'Mixed Claims Commissions', *Max Planck Encyclopedia of Public International Law* (2011) <http://opil.ouplaw.com/home/MPIL> accessed 10 May 2020.

17 *Spanish Zone of Morocco (Great Britain v Spain)* (1925) 2 RIAA 615, 642.

18 ibid 645.

Huber's award reflects fundamental questions on the state's liability during conflict situations for losses sustained by foreigners, which continue to accrue today. In modern investment arbitration, the very first BIT-based arbitration stands out in that effect: *AAPL v Sri Lanka* concerned an operation of Sri Lankan security forces during an internal conflict that ultimately led to the destruction of the claimant company's investment and the death of some of its employees.[19] Similar to Huber, the tribunal was concerned with the question of liability of the state for the conduct of its own forces as well as for damage presumably caused by the rebel group opposing the regime in power. However, after 1990 – the year that award was rendered – armed conflicts have not featured prominently in investment law and practice. Only more recently, this trend has begun to shift with tribunals delivering awards concerning the protection of investments from terrorist attacks in Egypt[20] or from rioting and looting in conflict-affected Libya,[21] and with more armed conflict-related cases pending.

Considering this development, the chapter authored by Tillmann Rudolf Braun sheds light on the operation of investment treaties during armed conflicts and examines their relationship to international humanitarian law. In particular, the chapter questions the relevance of a *lex specialis* approach to this relationship and the quality of the normative overlap. All too often, international humanitarian law is held to generally supersede other rules – seemingly a relic of the debunked idea of a strict dichotomy between peace and war and an equally strict separation of the rules applicable to each state of affairs. Braun points out, however, that the overlap of humanitarian and investment law is unlikely to create normative conflicts in the strict sense. As it is, certain clauses in investment treaties, often labelled '(extended) war clauses', expressly acknowledge possible tensions between investment protection and the conduct of hostilities. Braun discusses the interpretation of these understudied

---

[19] *Asian Agricultural Products Ltd (AAPL) v Sri Lanka*, ICSID Case no ARB/87/3, Award (27 June 1990).

[20] *Ampal-American Israel Corp and others v Egypt*, ICSID Case no ARB/12/11, Decision on Liability and Heads of Loss (21 February 2017).

[21] *Cengiz İnşaat Sanayi ve Ticaret AS v Libya*, ICC Case no 21537/ZF/AYZ, Award (7 November 2018); *Way2B ACE v Libya*, Award (24 May 2018) (not public), as reported by Luke Eric Peterson, 'Tribunal Finds that BIT's War-Losses Clause Does Not Exclude Operation of Other BIT Protections (Including Full Protection & Security), but Foreign Investor Fails to Meet Evidentiary Burdens' (*IAReporter*, 8 January 2019) <www.iareporter.com/articles/tribunal-finds-that-bits-war-losses-clause-does-not-exclude-operation-of-other-bit-protections-including-full-protection-security-but-foreign-investor-fails-to-meet-evidentiary-burdens> accessed 10 May 2020.

clauses and encourages their autonomous interpretation, that is, on their own terms.

Ira Ryk-Lakhman's contribution ties in with this discussion. Her chapter provides an in-depth analysis of extended war clauses that provide for compensation in case investments are requisitioned or destroyed in the context of hostilities. Ryk-Lakhman traces the origins of these provisions and argues, in contrast to the proposal developed by Braun, that their language reflects terms of art, originating from customary rules on the protection of foreign property during armed conflict. Pointing out how these findings not only inform the meaning of these clauses but also clear up the other relevant issues, the chapter advocates that the rules of armed conflict must critically inform legal assessments under war clauses found in investment treaties.

Apart from clauses explicitly drafted for cases of armed conflict, the guarantee of full protection and security (FPS) commonly found in investment treaties stands out as one of the most important clauses in any conflict scenario. In cases of widespread turmoil and violence, protecting the physical integrity of investments becomes crucial. After giving an overview of the (partly contentious) contents of the FPS standard and its relevance to the context scenario, Emily Sipiorski provides a fresh perspective on this type of treaty clause. She focuses on the possible implications an investor's involvement in a conflict might have on the protection it can expect from the host state. In this context, the chapter analyses the limits of the FPS standard and evaluates whether treaty reforms are necessary to ensure a proper equilibrium between interests of the state and those of investors.

The limits of a host state's responsibility in times of armed conflict are also the subject of Christina Binder's and Philipp Janig's contribution to this volume. Armed conflicts were traditionally often labelled situations of *force majeure*.[22] Non-responsibility was therefore deemed to be the rule in these exceptional circumstances. Binder and Janig revisit this assessment and explore whether states may invoke the *force majeure* defence to escape liability with a view to both investment treaties as well as investor-state contracts. Whereas in the latter context, details depend on the contractual *force majeure* clause in question, for investment treaties, *force majeure* becomes relevant as a customary circumstance precluding wrongfulness.[23] Binder and Janig highlight that states will only rarely be able to invoke the customary defence of *force majeure*,

---

22 See, extensively on this, Federica I Paddeu, 'A Genealogy of *Force Majeure* in International Law' (2012) 82 Brit YB Int'l L 381, 408 et seq.

23 ILC, 'Articles on Responsibility of States for Internationally Wrongful Acts' (2001), annexed to UNGA Res 56/83 (12 December 2001) UN Doc A/56/83, art 23.

due to its strict requirements and procedural safeguards, and evaluate whether this outcome strikes a sensible balance between the competing interests in the context of armed conflicts.

Taken together, the first part of the book discusses investment law never in isolation, but within the broader context of general international law as well as international humanitarian law. The latter is an area of international law that has so far been associated rarely with investment law. One certainly does not go too far in suggesting that investment lawyers and humanitarian lawyers, as members of different epistemic communities, know rather little of each other. Still, war clauses or the guarantee of protection and security in times of violence show that investment treaties are meant to also apply during precisely such situations. This book's first part reflects an effort to bring investment and humanitarian lawyers a step closer.

3   Investment Law and Disputed Territories

Escalating geopolitical tensions between states have long been recognized as a source of armed conflicts, but they are also likely to adversely impact by the economies involved, weakening, for example, tourism, trade, as well as foreign investment flows.[24] Yet, territorial disputes need not even escalate in order to taint investments and investment treaties. The book's second part focuses on the significance of latent territorial disputes for investment law and the impact of investment law and arbitral proceedings on such disputes.

It seems indeed inevitable in a globalized economy that foreign investments become, in one way or another, entangled with some of the numerous unresolved border conflicts. In case of disputed sovereignty over territories, transboundary waters, or maritime areas, investors who are active in these regions will be faced with legal uncertainty on several levels, beginning with the fundamental question which state is to be considered the 'rightful' host state and, accordingly, which treaty applies.

Markus Beham embarks on a survey of the various concepts of 'territory' used in investment treaties, alleviating the persisting uncertainty associated with the term. Investment agreements usually limit their territorial application and hence their protective reach to the respective 'territory' of the contracting states. However, details vary as to how and by what degree of detail

---

24   Michelle V Remo, 'S&P Warns against Impact of Territorial Disputes' (*Philippine Daily Inquirer*, 15 February 2014) <http://business.inquirer.net/164034/sp-warns-against-impact-of-territorial-disputes> accessed 10 May 2020.

these treaties define their spatial scope of application. The chapter illustrates different approaches found in treaty practice and analyses their legal implications, focusing on particularly relevant states involved in territorial disputes, *eg* China and Taiwan as well as North Korea and South Korea. It further addresses the treaty practice of Cyprus, Georgia, Israel with regard to Palestine, and Kosovo in relation to the (former) Autonomous Province of Serbia. Beham shows whether and how these states anticipate and attempt to clarify uncertainty resulting from disputed territories – and whether they truly succeed with these attempts.

The case of disputed maritime zones is the subject of Marco Benatar's and Valentin Schatz's chapter. Given that, for instance, many oil companies exploit or seek to exploit resources in disputed maritime zones, the question which investment treaty applies becomes crucial. The key, again, is the notion of 'territory' and the relevant treaties' spatial scope. Benatar and Schatz discuss the interpretation of territorial clauses and the application of these treaties to disputed areas in light of both the investor's interest in legal protection as well as the danger of jeopardizing the conclusion of delimitation agreements. They close with observations on consequences of territorial disputes for investor-state arbitral proceedings, pointing to the relevance of notions of estoppel or the *Monetary Gold* doctrine.[25]

The subsequent piece by Christine Sim takes up the procedural aspect of territorial disputes. It analyses the special scenario in which investors solve their legal dilemma by invoking various available treaties before different tribunals and by initiating parallel proceedings, in addition to proceedings the disputing sovereigns themselves might initiate. Sim discusses the consequences of such tactics and highlights the relevance to further define procedural rules and principles applicable to such parallel proceedings, discussing in particular the principles of *res judicata* and *lis pendens*[26] as well as the possibility to use a further refined definition of the notion of 'legal dispute'.

The possibility to initiate parallel proceedings for investment claims is indeed not necessarily confined to investment arbitration. Investors may also

---

25   The *Monetary Gold* or 'indispensable party' doctrine may be invoked before international courts and tribunals in opposition to claims the core of which concerns legal interests of an absent third party. See, initially, *Monetary Gold Removed from Rome in 1943* (*Italy v France, UK, and USA*) (Preliminary Question) [1954] ICJ Rep 19, 32.

26   *Res judicata* provides that once a suit is decided, the same issue cannot be contested again (in other fora), while *lis pendens* allows a court or tribunal to refuse the exercise of jurisdiction when a parallel proceeding is already pending.

seek to rely on a different legal regime that similarly offers dispute mechanisms to the individual, namely human rights law. The jurisdictional requirements before human rights bodies or courts might make such a claim more likely to proceed to the merits. Similar to humanitarian law, human rights law does not concern itself with foreign investments. However, it does concern itself with the protection of property. European human rights law, with its explicit protection of the right to property[27] and relatively effective court system, may therefore be an attractive alternative for the protection of foreign investments and for investors seeking compensation for losses sustained in disputed territories. Isabella Risini provides an analysis of the availability and scope of investment protection under the European Convention in such circumstances. Based on a review of existing case law of the European Court of Human Rights (on, for instance, Northern Cyprus) and with a view to the European Convention's history as well as recent developments (in particular with a view to the Ukraine-Russia conflict), she examines investors' access to protection. She assesses the substantive protection and the available remedies under the European Convention and its first Protocol, as well as the enforcement of judgments rendered by the Court. In particular, the chapter addresses the relative merits of the protection available to investors under the European Convention in comparison to investor-state arbitral proceedings in situations of territorial conflicts.

Competing claims for sovereignty can also arise on the state-internal level and can then trigger questions relating to the proper representation in international legal proceedings. In particular, reports of decisions rendered by investment tribunals on the proper representation of states in investment disputes involving Venezuela, Yemen, as well as Libya have continually emerged during the course the last few years.[28] Réka Papp's contribution tackles the questions that arise in the politically charged atmosphere where two entities – that both

---

27   Protocol (No 1) to the Convention for the Protection of Human Rights and Fundamental Freedoms (signed 20 March 1952, entered into force 18 May 1954) 213 UNTS 221 (ECHR Protocol no 1) art 1.

28   See, *eg*, Tom Jones and Sebastian Perry, 'ICSID Committee Rebuffs Guaidó' (*Global Arbitration Review*, 10 May 2019) <http://globalarbitrationreview.com/article/1192627/icsid-committee-rebuffs-guaido> accessed 1 May 2020; Damien Charlotin, 'Revealed: Reasons Why BIT Tribunal Retracted 2016 Consent Award; Confusion Swirling Around Libya's True Government Had Offered Opportunity for Investor to Strike What Tribunal Initially Viewed as a Respondent-Authorized Settlement' (*IAReporter*, 25 July 2019) <www.iareporter.com/articles/revealed-reasons-why-bit-tribunal-retracted-2016-consent-award-confusion-swirling-around-libyas-true-government-had-offered-opportunity-for-investor-to-strike-what-tribunal-initially-viewed-as-a-r> accessed 10 May 2020.

claim to be the legitimate representative of a state and that both enjoy varying degrees of recognition in the international community – compete for the acknowledgment of arbitral tribunals as the state's sole representative. As Papp highlights, it is of particular importance that arbitral tribunals thread with caution in order to avoid undermining the legitimacy of the decision-making process and in particular to refrain from adopting politically motivated or poorly reasoned decisions. Her chapter seeks to elaborate a coherent legal framework for their analysis that takes into account the full legal and factual context of the issue and considers all possible sources for workable solutions.

In sum, the second part of the book illustrates and provides answers to the various questions arising out of disputes over territory – be they international or internal. In the process, it constantly touches upon the conflict between the interests of ensuring the effective protection of individuals and of taking the clashing claims of sovereignty into account. And yet, sovereignty or the question of legal title over territory often remains the elephant in the room. The issue can be avoided more easily – and is in fact often avoided – in the context of human rights law, since the European Convention bases its application on the actual exercise of jurisdiction, not on the question of legal title.[29] For human rights lawyers, it is crucial who holds actual power over a territory, since that actor will be under a duty to respect and protect individual rights and freedoms. For investment law and its reliance on the notion of territory, the legal and practical consequences of territorial disputes are more difficult to handle – an insight that is carried into the final part of this volume.

4 Investment Law and Annexed Territories and 'Frozen' Conflicts

Investment law in the context of annexations and 'frozen' conflicts forms the final theme of the book. These situations usually result from armed conflict, since annexation connotes the forceful incorporation of foreign territory and frozen conflicts describe situations in which hostilities have ended, while the underlying conflict remains unresolved. Annexations or the establishment of non-state entities on a state's territory, in turn, often form part of frozen conflicts, in which either a foreign state or a *de facto* regime establishes stable control over territory. Situations of annexed territories and frozen conflicts pose unique challenges to investment law. At the bottom of these challenges lies a

---

29 On the notion of jurisdiction in human rights treaties, see Marko Milanović, 'From Compromise to Principle: Clarifying the Concept of State Jurisdiction in Human Rights Treaties' (2008) 8 Hm Rts L Rev 411.

fundamental discrepancy between the legal situation and the factual realities. On the one hand, annexation violates the prohibition of the use of force, is legally void, and must not be recognized as having any legal effects.[30] On the other hand, a factual shift of effective control over territory is often undeniable. With the annexation of Crimea, for example, the situation on the ground diverges widely from the legal assertion of continuing Ukrainian sovereignty. From the perspective of investors, what may in practice matter more than continuity of the *status quo ante* is the fact that Russia sees Crimea as fully integrated into the Russian Federation, that Russian and not Ukrainian laws are applied and enforced in the region, and that Russian courts were created and exercise jurisdiction over the peninsula, which is now even physically connected to Russia's (lawful) territory by a newly built bridge across the Kerch strait.

Against this backdrop, the pragmatic solution found by recent arbitral awards in the Crimea cases is certainly understandable. Several tribunals, most recently backed by the Swiss Federal Tribunal, found that they could exercise jurisdiction over claims brought by Ukrainian investors against the Russian Federation in connection with its conduct on Crimea.[31] In his contribution to this book, Kit De Vriese critically reviews the approach taken by these arbitrators and judges. They opted to define the territorial scope of Russia's investment treaties not with a view to sovereignty but to effective control, begging the question how this interpretation of the treaties' reference to 'territory' relates to the law of treaties as well as the duty of non-recognition. After all, applying one state's treaties to the territory of another might imply a prohibited recognition that the territory in question now belongs to the annexing state. De Vriese offers an alternative approach to the one so far taken by arbitral tribunals, which he suggests to apply to current and future situations of occupation and annexation.

The question that connects De Vriese's contribution with the subsequent one by Stefan Lorenzmeier is whether investment tribunals, although

---

30   UNGA, Resolution 2625 (XXV) (1970) UN Doc A/RES/25/2625, annex para 1; *Legal Consequences for States of the Continued Presence of South Africa in Namibia (South West Africa) Notwithstanding Security Council Resolution 276 (1970)* (Advisory Opinion) [1971] ICJ Rep 16, paras 117 et seq; *Legal Consequences of the Construction of a Wall in the Occupied Palestinian Territory* (Advisory Opinion) [2004] ICJ Rep 136, paras 87, 159.

31   The decisions in these cases remain unpublished for now. Yet, the jurisdictional decisions in the arbitrations *PJSC Ukrnafta v Russia*, PCA Case No 2015–34 and *Stabil and others. v Russia*, PCA Case no 201515/35, have been confirmed in annulment proceedings by the Swiss Federal Tribunal. See *Russia v A* [2018] Case no 4A_396/2017, BGE 144 III 559 (Swiss Federal Tribunal); *Russia v A and others* [2018] Case no 4A_398/2017 (Swiss Federal Tribunal).

nominally dealing with specific disputes between an investor and a state, could be regarded as unintentionally legitimizing illegal situations. This is precisely the argument Stefan Lorenzmeier espouses. He continues the discussion of the duty of non-recognition from a different angle, focusing on the consequences of the case of *Front Polisario* before the Court of Justice of the European Union. That case concerned the application of several agreements between the European Union and Morocco to the territory of the Western Sahara.[32] Since Morocco's presence in Western Sahara is illegal and disregards the right of self-determination of the Sahrawi people (represented by Front Polisario), applying these treaties to the territory of Western Sahara and thus treating it as legally belonging to Morocco violated, in the Court's view, international law. Lorenzmeier initially explores the relevance of the duty of non-recognition and its application in international jurisprudence with regard to the case of *Front Polisario*. He subsequently draws critical conclusions from this case study and recommends to refrain from expanding exceptions for the sake of pragmatism in the case of investment treaties and their application to annexed territories.

A structurally similar divergence between law and fact as observed for illegally annexed or occupied territory can also be found in cases of *de facto* regimes. *De facto* regimes are entities, which exercise control over a defined territory and consider themselves to govern independent states, but which lack recognition by most other states.[33] The entity's claim to sovereignty thus clashes with that of the territorial or 'parent' state as in the conflict between the *de jure* sovereign and the annexing power. Similar to the case of annexation, where the *de facto* regime is created through unlawful acts, such as an unlawful use of force assisted by third states, the duty of non-recognition applies. Examples of unrecognized *de facto* regimes include Northern Cyprus, Abkhazia, and South Ossetia, but it is the case of Transnistria, which Vladlena Lisenco and Karsten Nowrot take a closer look at in their chapter. Transnistria claims to be an independent state, but Moldova continues to assert sovereignty over the territory, designating it merely an 'autonomous territorial unit with special legal status'. Yet, Transnistria as well as other stabilized *de facto* regimes possess their own *de facto* authorities and *de facto* legislation. Their relevance as actors in international investment law was recently underscored, when a first arbitral award against Transnistria surfaced in 2019 during enforcement proceedings

---

32 Case C-104/16 P, *Council of the European Union v Front populaire pour la libération de la saguia-el-hamra et du rio de oro (Front Polisario)*, ECLI:EU:C:2016:973.

33 Jochen A Frowein, 'De Facto Regime', *Max Planck Encyclopedia of Public International Law* (2013) para 1 <http://opil.ouplaw.com/home/MPIL> accessed 17 February 2020.

before the US District Court for the Southern District of New York.³⁴ Lisenco and Nowrot first describe and evaluate the investment law context and the relevant regulatory regime adopted by the self-proclaimed Pridnestrovian Moldavian Republic. They discuss, in particular, the legal and practical relevance of the legislation adopted by *de facto* regimes, showing in how far investment protection can be regulated in case of frozen conflict situations.

The dilemma of foreign investors in territory controlled by a non-state actor is further expounded in the subsequent chapter authored by Stefan Lorenzmeier together with Maryna Reznichuk. They scrutinize the relationship between the legal order of the territorial sovereign and that of the unlawful regime in control, using the example of Ukraine's Donbas region as a basis for their analysis. In that region, the so-called Donetsk and Luhansk People's Republics, two non-state regimes internationally perceived as being supported by the Russian Federation, have been proclaimed and continue to be in open hostilities with Ukraine to this date. Lorenzmeier and Reznichuk use this case study to demonstrate how a state's loss of effective control over part of its territory impacts its domestic investment legislation and how non-state actors as territorial entities themselves address the issue of investment protection and regulation. The chapter surveys potential avenues for investors to seek redress and to receive compensation for losses sustained in the affected territory, particularly looking into rules of IHL, investment law and human rights law.

In case a sovereign state loses control over part of its territory, either to a foreign state or to a *de facto* regime, the relevance of its own laws and the practical impact of its authority, in any event, fade into the background. While the previous chapters largely concern the rules applicable to the actor in control, Johanna Baumann takes us back to the investment treaty obligations of the sovereign state. In the final contribution to this volume, she considers the state's responsibility under investment treaties in case of state fragility. Not limited to cases of annexation and *de facto* regimes but also addressing cases of ongoing armed conflicts and complete state failure, Baumann sheds light on the limits of the state's investment treaty obligations, especially with a view to the full protection and security and fair and equitable treatment standards. She analyses in how far a state can still be legally expected to comply with obligations that are generally premised on the proper functioning of the state apparatus when that apparatus is no longer effective.

---

34   See *WJ Holding Ltd v Transdniestrian Moldovan Republic*, ICC Case no 21717/MHM, Award (6 June 2018) and Addendum (30 August 2018).

The final chapter thus forges a bridge to the questions addressed by the first chapters of this book, concentrating on the effects of crisis and conflict on the workings of international investment law. It is at the same time the final piece of the important and necessary debates surrounding the implications of conflict situations on investment law, reaching from issues of treaty application and interpretation to the interaction with relevant other (general or specific) rules of international law as well as to the quest for balance between the various interests at stake.

5 Outlook

Looking at this volume, there is hope to believe that the involvement of investment law in conflict situations can have a positive impact beyond satisfying particular investor interests. Investor-state arbitration may constitute a welcome forum to strengthen compliance with the rule of law in conflict situations, all too often characterized by disregard to legal rules. Expectations must however not overburden investment law either. Investment treaties and their dispute settlement procedures are not meant to solve underlying conflicts; they exist, after all, to solve concrete disputes between states and investors. In politically sensitive contexts, this feature may be helpful, since investment law, with its promise of de-politicization, could strengthen the position of individuals without being burdened by the greater political quarrels.

On the other hand, emphasizing the specialization of investment law must not lead to viewing it in isolation but to embrace its broader international legal environment. This book highlights what it means that international investment law does not and must not operate as a closed system: whether general international law or specialized set of rules, the influence of extraneous rules on investment law remains an important issue, especially in light of an arbitral practice that is often criticized for its reclusive positions. Yet, arbitral tribunals are in a difficult position to find the proper balance: they must take into account the different circumstances of conflicts to live up to the requirements set out by international life, but they must also avoid letting themselves be used for political agendas. To ensure that investment law benefits the investor and the state at fair balance and at the same time works to the improvement of international law, those involved in international investment law should adhere to three elements: consciousness of factual situations and their practical implications, proper legal methodology, and a dialogue with other branches of international law.

As editors of this volume, it is our modest hope that this book contributes to the achievement of that goal. Investment law has a role to play in conflict situations and it is necessary to follow the contributors of this book on the path to constantly improve its inner workings through further research.

Bibliography

Alvarez JE and K Khamsi, 'The Argentine Crisis and Foreign Investors: A Glimpse into the Heart of the Investment Regime' in KP Sauvant (ed), *Yearbook on International Investment Law and Policy 2008–2009* (OUP 2009).

Baetens F (ed), *Investment Law within International Law: Integrationist Perspectives* (CUP 2013).

Brillmayer L and G Chepiga, 'Ownership or Use? Civilian Property Interests in International Humanitarian Law' (2008) 49 Harvard Int L J 413.

Charlotin D, 'Revealed: Reasons Why BIT Tribunal Retracted 2016 Consent Award; Confusion Swirling Around Libya's True Government Had Offered Opportunity for Investor to Strike What Tribunal Initially Viewed as a Respondent-Authorized Settlement' (*IAReporter*, 25 July 2019) <www.iareporter.com/articles/revealed-reasons-why-bit-tribunal-retracted-2016-consent-award-confusion-swirling-around-libyas-true-government-had-offered-opportunity-for-investor-to-strike-what-tribunal-initially-viewed-as-a-r> accessed 10 May 2020.

Dolzer R, 'Mixed Claims Commissions', *Max Planck Encyclopedia of Public International Law Online Edition* (2011) <http://opil.ouplaw.com/home/EPIL> accessed 10 May 2020.

Frowein JA, 'De Facto Regime', *Max Planck Encyclopedia of Public International Law* (2013) para 1 <http://opil.ouplaw.com/home/EPIL> accessed 17 February 2020.

Hindelang S and M Krajewski (eds), *Shifting Paradigms in International Investment Law: More Balanced, Less Isolated, Increasingly Diversified* (OUP 2016).

Jones T and S Perry, 'ICSID Committee Rebuffs Guaidó' (*Global Arbitration Review*, 10 May 2019) <http://globalarbitrationreview.com/article/1192627/icsid-committee-rebuffs-guaido> accessed 1 May 2020.

Milanović M, 'From Compromise to Principle: Clarifying the Concept of State Jurisdiction in Human Rights Treaties' (2008) 8 Hm Rts L Rev 411.

Paddeu FI, 'A Genealogy of *Force Majeure* in International Law' (2012) 82 Brit YB Int'l L 381.

Peterson LE, 'Investigation: As Fight Continues over $1 bil Award, Libya Facing at Least a Dozen Investment Treaty Arbitrations – Possibly More – in Aftermath of Arab Spring' (*IAReporter*, 31 March 2017) <www.iareporter.com/articles/investigation-as-fight-continues-over-1bil-award-libya-facing-at-least-a-dozen-investment-treaty-arbitrations-possibly-more-in-aftermath-of-arab-spring> accessed 10 May 2020.

Peterson LE, 'Tribunal Finds that BIT's War-Losses Clause Does Not Exclude Operation of Other BIT Protections (Including Full Protection & Security), but Foreign Investor Fails to Meet Evidentiary Burdens' (*IAReporter*, 8 January 2019) <www.iareporter.com/articles/tribunal-finds-that-bits-war-losses-clause-does-not-exclude-operation-of-other-bit-protections-including-full-protection-security-but-foreign-investor-fails-to-meet-evidentiary-burdens> accessed 10 May 2020.

Remo MV, 'S&P Warns against Impact of Territorial Disputes' (*Philippine Daily Inquirer*, 15 February 2014) <http://business.inquirer.net/164034/sp-warns-against-impact-of-territorial-disputes> accessed 10 May 2020.

Sassòli M, AA Bouvier, and A Quintin, *How Does Law Protect in War? Cases, Documents and Teaching Materials on Contemporary Practice in International Humanitarian Law* (3rd edn, International Committee of the Red Cross 2011).

Sim C, 'Investment Disputes Arising out of Areas of Unsettled Boundaries: Ghana/Côte d'Ivoire' (2018) 11 J World Energy L & Bus 1.

Simma B and D Pulkowski, 'Of Planets and the Universe: Self-contained Regimes in International Law' (2006) 17 EJIL 483.

Soldatenko M, 'Ongoing Territorial Challenges in Crimea Cases: Putting Everest v. Russia in Context' (*Kluwer Arbitration Blog*, 5 November 2018) <http://arbitrationblog.kluwerarbitration.com/2018/11/05/territorial-challenges-expected-in-crimea-cases-putting-everest-v-russia-in-context> accessed 10 May 2020.

Tzeng P, 'Sovereignty over Crimea: A Case for State-to-State Investment Arbitration' (2016) 41 Yale Int'l LJ 459.

Tzeng P, 'Investments on Disputed Territory: Indispensable Parties and Indispensable Issues' (2017) 14 Braz J Int'l L 122.

Tzeng P, 'Investment Protection in Disputed Maritime Areas' (2018) 19 JWIT 828.

Vasquez JA, *The War Puzzle Revisited* (CUP 2009).

Waibel M and others (eds), *The Backlash against Investment Arbitration* (Kluwer Law International 2010).

PART 1

Investment Law and Armed Conflicts

CHAPTER 1

International Law in Revolutionary Upheavals: On the Tension between International Investment Law and International Humanitarian Law

Tillmann Rudolf Braun

1   Introduction

An investor's production site was overrun by government forces in a counter-insurgency operation against suspected revolutionary powers. The site was destroyed, and managers and staff killed. From the perspective of international investment law, which arose in recent times mainly from bilateral investment treaty (BIT) practice, a state's failure to exercise sufficient due diligence in such cases, 'which requires undertaking all possible measures that could be reasonably expected to prevent the eventual occurrence of killings and property destructions',[1] may lead to a breach of a BIT and therefore trigger the host state's obligation to compensate a foreign investor.

The destruction of the production site occurred, in this instance, in the course of a non-international armed conflict. Would therefore a different interpretation also be conceivable or even compelling? International humanitarian law arose – from the late nineteenth century onwards – essentially from multilateral treaty practice in response to international armed conflicts (the Hague and Geneva Rules, *ie*, the *jus in bello*). So, if it can also be considered to be applicable in a non-international armed conflict on the basis that 'there [was] no doubt that the destruction of the [investment] took place during the hostilities',[2] it would – as formulated in the dissenting opinion to the *AAPL v Sri Lanka* arbitral award – 'take into account the national emergency and extraordinary conditions under which the government mounted a strategic and

---

1 *Asian Agricultural Products Ltd (AAPL) v Sri Lanka*, ICSID Case no ARB/87/3, Final Award (27 June 1990) para 85(d) (in the context of the full protection and security standard of the applicable Sri Lanka–UK BIT (1980)). President of the tribunal was Ahmed S El-Kosheri, arguably the doyen of international law and arbitration in the Arab world, whom the author had the opportunity to interview in Cairo and who passed away on 18 March 2019.
2 ibid para 59.

highly sensitive security operation to regain its sovereign control'.[3] Hence it would allow a state to take 'all necessary security and military measures',[4] and therefore, such a 'legitimate act of a sovereign government to regain control cannot be faulted merely because of incidental destruction of property'.[5] If the destruction was 'demanded by the necessities of war', then the state action could be seen to be authorised by 'military necessity'[6] and therefore lawful.

If, in such a scenario, international investment law possibly establishes a state's liability for an action which, in turn, would be lawful under international humanitarian law of non-international armed conflicts, a normative conflict may possibly arise, in which each subfield, if one follows a broad understanding of norm conflicts, might 'suggest different ways of dealing with a problem'.[7] This leads to the overriding question of the relationship and interplay of international investment law with other subfields of international law, which have emerged essentially independently of each other and have very different institutional features, dispute resolution (if at all) and enforcement mechanisms. How can and should one deal with the particularistic reality of international law, consisting of international law's specialised subfields and competing normative systems responsive to distinct stakeholders,[8] with neither a hierarchy nor stated relationship to each other?[9] How then should the

---

3   *AAPL v Sri Lanka*, ICSID Case no ARB/87/3, Final Award, Dissenting Opinion of Samuel KB Asante (15 June 1990), (1991) 6 ICSID Rev 574, 593 et seq. Interestingly, the dissenting opinion takes up arguments and concepts that could have been broadly borrowed from international humanitarian law applicable to non-international armed conflicts at the time.
4   ibid.
5   ibid.
6   The principle of 'military necessity' is, for instance, built in article 23(g) of the Regulations Respecting the Laws and Customs of War on Land, Annex to Convention (IV) Respecting the Laws and Customs of War on Land (adopted 18 October 1907, entered into force 26 January 1910) 205 CTS 277 (Hague Regulations), which, by virtue of its customary status, also applies to non-international armed conflicts: '[...] it is especially forbidden [...] To destroy or seize the enemy's property, *unless* such destruction or seizure be imperatively demanded by the *necessities of war*' (emphasis added).
7   ILC, 'Fragmentation of International Law: Difficulties Arising from the Diversification and Expansion of International Law, Report of the Study Group of the International Law Commission' (2006) UN Doc A/CN.4/L.682, paras 21 et seq, which arguably follows a broad understanding of norm conflicts, according to which a norm conflict already exists when different (though not incompatible) balancing of interests is found in varying fields of international law.
8   Martti Koskenniemi and Päivi Leino, 'Fragmentation of International Law? Postmodern Anxieties' (2002) 15 LJIL 553, 562.
9   However, the debate triggered by the ILC Fragmentation Report has lost some momentum in recent years. See Christopher Greenwood, 'Unity and Diversity in International Law' in Mads Andenas and Eirik Bjorge (eds), *A Farewell to Fragmentation: Reassertion and*

interplay and tension between international investment law and international humanitarian law be conceptualised, last but not least, by investment arbitration tribunals?

It is, unfortunately, hardly an entirely new phenomenon in the history of international investment that revolutionary upheavals often escalate into non-international armed conflicts, as the period of revolutions and civil wars in many countries during the late nineteenth and early twentieth centuries has shown.[10] Investments are especially vulnerable since they involve long term commitments and cannot thrive under conditions such as riots, revolutions and civil wars.[11] Nevertheless, the related questions of international law, such as the interplay and relationship between international investment law and international humanitarian law of non-international armed conflicts have not yet been sufficiently clarified or even remain controversial. It has been generally identified that '[t]here is relatively little in fact, until recently, astonishingly little judicial or arbitral practice on normative conflicts'.[12] Moreover, it is especially non-international armed conflicts rather than international armed conflicts that account for by far the largest number of all armed conflicts worldwide.[13] Non-international armed conflicts 'have become the most widespread, the most destructive, and the most characteristic form of organised human violence.'[14] It is very likely that

---

Convergence in International Law (CUP 2015) 38; Laurence Boisson de Chazournes, 'Plurality in the Fabric of International Courts and Tribunals: The Threads of a Managerial Approach' (2017) 27 EJIL 13.

10   In those first awards of this time, on the one hand, no compensation was awarded, *eg*, for state actions 'compelled by the imperious necessity of war' (*Bembelista Case (Netherlands/Venezuela)* (1903) 10 RIAA 717) or for a 'legitimate act of war' (*The Dunn Case (Chile/UK)* (1895), quoted after ILC, '"*Force majeure*" and "Fortuitous Event" as Circumstances Precluding Wrongfulness: Survey of State Practice, International Judicial Decisions and Doctrine' (1978) II(1) YBILC 61, para 356). On the other hand, however, as arbitrator Huber held, 'if the state is not responsible for the revolutionary events themselves, it could nevertheless be responsible for what the authorities do or not do to avert, to the extent possible, the consequence', *Spanish Zone of Morocco (Great Britain v Spain)* (1925) 2 RIAA 615, 639, 642.

11   Christoph Schreuer, 'War and Peace in International Investment Law' in Katia Fach Gómez, Catharine Titi, and Anastasios Gourgourinis (eds), *International Investment Law and the Law of Armed Conflict* (Springer 2019) 2.

12   ILC, 'Fragmentation of International Law' (n 7) para 27.

13   Annyssa Bellal, *The War Report: Armed Conflict in 2018* (The Geneva Academy of International Humanitarian Law and Human Rights 2019) 31 ('18 IACs and 51 NIACs [...] took place in 2018') <www.geneva-academy.ch/joomlatools-files/docman-files/The%20War%20Report%202018.pdf> accessed 19 January 2020.

14   David Armitage, *Civil Wars: A History in Ideas* (Knopf 2017) 7.

issues resulting from such conflicts will come before international courts and arbitral tribunals much more frequently in the future.

The latest example of conflicts culminating in many countries in non-international armed conflicts is the revolutionary upheavals which became known – rightly or wrongly – as the 'Arab Spring'. The act of desperation of a 26-year-old fruit vendor, Mohamed Bouazizi, who set himself on fire on 17 December 2010 in protest against his continuous ill-treatment and humiliation by the police in his hometown of Sidi Bouzid, Tunisia, triggered a wave of unprecedented revolutionary upheavals for 'bread, freedom, social justice and human dignity'[15] in the Arab world. This marked the beginning of the end of the Middle East as we knew it.[16] We have since witnessed the toppling of long-standing regimes, protracted civil wars, the political and violent escalation of frequently confessional tensions and the erosion of the state monopoly of the use of force.

These profound revolutionary upheavals have not only made a deep impact on political and social life, but also inevitably on *economic* life, with far-reaching repercussions for the interests of many public and private commercial entities.[17] Civil war, revolution, state of emergency, revolt, insurrection,

---

15 The term used to describe these upheavals, 'Arab Spring', was coined by Marc Lynch, 'Obama's 'Arab Spring'?' (*Foreign Policy*, 6 January 2011) <http://foreignpolicy.com/2011/01/06/obamas-arab-spring/> accessed 19 January 2020. However, *vis-à-vis* this – rather Western – narrative and attribution, the Arab world's main description of choice was 'Arab Revolutions', or '*al-Thawrat al-Arabiya*'. Later, Lynch published his analysis in Marc Lynch, *The New Arab Wars: Uprisings and Anarchy in the Middle East* (Public Affairs 2016); Marc Lynch, 'New Arab World Order' (*Foreign Affairs*, 16 August 2018) <www.foreignaffairs.com/articles/middle-east/2018-08-13/new-arab-order> accessed 19 January 2020. At the time of writing, in early 2020, a 'second wave' of Arab Spring can be observed in Algeria, Iraq, Lebanon, and Sudan. This time the call is 'we are a people', which has already prompted a comparison to the 'Arab Spring'; see Marwan Muasher, 'Is this the Arab Spring 2.0?' (*Carnegie*, 30 October 2019) <https://carnegieendowment.org/2019/10/30/is-this-arab-spring-2.0-pub-80220> accessed 19 January 2020; Sarah J Feuer and Carmit Valensi, 'Arab Spring 2.0? Making Sense of the Protests Sweeping the Region' (1 December 2019) Institute for National Security Studies Insight no 1235 <www.inss.org.il/publication/arab-spring-2-0-making-sense-of-the-protests-sweeping-the-region/> accessed 19 January 2020.

16 For the historic development, see David Fromkin, *A Peace to End All Peace: The Fall of the Ottoman Empire and the Creation of the Modern Middle East* (20th ed, Macmillan 2009); James Barr, *A Line in the Sand: Britain, France and the Struggle That Shaped the Middle East* (Simon & Schuster 2011).

17 From an economic perspective, see Valerie Noury, 'North African Revolution: Counting the Cost', *African Business* (April 2011) 46; Fida Karam and Chahir Zaki, 'How Did Wars Dampen Trade in the MENA Region?' (2016) 48 Applied Economics 5909.

riot[18] and pre-existing armed conflicts during these revolutionary upheavals have also all left their mark on foreign investors' production facilities. Many of these facilities have had to be closed, with many investors forced to withdraw and evacuate, and facilities – whether accidentally or intentionally – have also been completely destroyed. Above all, foreign investors with investments in the construction, energy and hospitality sectors that have been affected by this dynamic have claimed that the damage caused during the revolutionary upheavals amounts to a breach of obligations under BITs, especially those of Egypt[19] and Libya.[20]

In the present constellation, there is an inherent tension between the investor's and the respondent state's interests, which forms a *leitmotif* that runs through almost all questions of international law concerning possible compensation following a revolutionary upheaval. From the *investor's* point of view, having invested personnel, operations and capital in the host state, the destruction of this investment means that the precise political risk which the BIT provides protection for has materialised. From the respondent *host state's* point of view, however, the revolutionary upheaval originated in a political crisis which the state is neither responsible for nor the cause of. When revolutionary upheavals culminate in non-international armed conflicts, the state authority generally sees itself required to use all possible force at its disposal.

---

18   See this enumeration in Pakistan–Philippines BIT (1999) art 5.
19   A large number of arbitral actions were filed at ICSID against Egypt following the Egyptian revolutions in the aftermath of the 25 January 2011 revolution. See World Bank Group, 'International Centre for Settlement of Investment Disputes – Cases' <https://icsid.worldbank.org/en/Pages/cases/AdvancedSearch.aspx> accessed 19 January 2020 (search for Egypt as respondent). Moreover, several non-ICSID investment arbitration proceedings have been commenced against Egypt with a clear upsurge from 2011 onwards. See 'Egypt has faced $14 bn worth of cases from investors since 2011' (*Ahram Online*, 22 April 2014) <http://english.ahram.org.eg/NewsContent/3/12/99606/Business/Economy/Egypt-has-faced--bn-worth-of-cases-from-investors-.aspx> accessed 19 January 2020. Remarkably, although faced with this unprecedented number of investment claims, Egypt did not terminate any of its BITs and stayed in ICSID (which it had joined in 1972), apparently to signal an open and transparent legal framework for investment.
20   Numerous investment treaty claims that relate to disputes following the first Libyan Civil War have been raised by Turkish construction companies under the Turkey–Libya BIT (2009), as Turkey and Libya enjoyed particularly close economic relations. These claims have, however, *inter alia*, to deal with the fact that Turkey failed to ratify the treaty until 22 April 2011, some two months *after* the civic revolt began and long after the security situation had deteriorated precipitously.

This contribution focuses on the particularly interesting section of questions of international law which arise here, *ie* the interaction and tension between international investment law and international humanitarian law applicable in non-international armed conflicts. Are international humanitarian law and international investment law at all applicable to these constellations? When such a normative overlap does indeed lead to a genuine normative conflict, one possible method of conflict resolution could be the principle of *lex specialis*. Are rules of international humanitarian law *lex specialis* as they constitute 'intransgressible'[21] principles of customary international law – or should international investment law be considered as *lex specialis* for the treatment of investments in times of conflict as this provides the individual's property with more specific and more favourable protection (section 2)?

Yet, is there really a normative conflict between international humanitarian law and international investment law? Should there be reservations concerning a *lex specialis* approach and should instead a more *informative approach* be taken, in which international humanitarian law's rules and concepts would inform the interpretation of BIT norms, and vice versa (section 3.1)? Is it useful and advisable, for example, to interpret the term 'necessity of the situation' in so-called extended war clauses in the light of humanitarian law's principle of 'military necessity'? Or, are there compelling arguments for an *autonomous* treaty interpretation on its own terms (sections 3.2 and 3.3)? Finally, should the burden of proof really remain on the investor, not only in cases of extended war clauses (section 4)?[22]

---

21 *Legality of the Threat or Use of Nuclear Weapons* (Advisory Opinion) [1996] ICJ Rep 226, paras 25, 79.

22 This contribution examines in the context of investment treaty claims for damages after revolutionary upheavals *only* the interplay and relationship between international investment law and international humanitarian law. There remains the additional question of the use of other possible interpretative tools, such as (1) disregarding the loss of profit in situations of political crises and armed conflicts, (2) considering the country risk also when determining the level of compensation, (3) finding equitable solutions derived from the applicable law at the level of enforcement, (4) assigning a corresponding quota to the instrument permitting enforcement (such as the non-enforcement order imposed by the UN Security Council on Iraq's creditors by virtue of UNSC Res 1483 (22 May 2003) UN Doc S/RES/1483), (5) a fund solution where an affected state would establish a structured multi-stage process for settling damages of predominantly similar claims of foreign investors, or (6) establishing mass claims commissions when there is an overriding international interest.

2 Relationship between International Investment Law and International Humanitarian Law of Non-International Armed Conflicts

2.1 *Fundamental Applicability of Both Regimes*

2.1.1 International Investment Law

Even after revolutionary upheavals and radical changes of government, the state's international obligations such as those arising from BITs remain valid as 'nations do not die when there is a change of their rulers or in their forms of government. [...] "The king is dead; long live the king!" has typified this thought for ages. [...] and that responsibility continues through all changing forms of government.'[23] That means when the new government is formed by a revolutionary movement, this insurrectional government will be held responsible for acts of the pre-revolutionary government *and* for all of the acts committed during the revolution.[24] The essential justification for this generally recognised *retroactive* attribution is that '[t]he basis for the attribution of conduct of a successful insurrectional or other movement to the state under international law lies in the continuity between the movement and the eventual government'.[25] If the government is – still – the pre-revolutionary government, it will not be held responsible for damages caused by the unsuccessful revolutionary movement as 'governments are responsible, as a general principle, [only] for the acts of those they control'.[26] Therefore, in this constellation, the government merely remains responsible for the actions of its own forces.

This question must be distinguished from that of the applicability of BITs during *international* armed conflicts. This is rightly the conclusion of a variety of arguments: First, there are already standards contained in BITs in the form

---

23 *Bolívar Railway Co Case (UK/Venezuela)* (1903) 9 RIAA 445, 452 et seq. See also *USA v Iran* (1996) 32 IUSCTR 162; *Africa Holding Co v DRC*, ICSID Case no ARB/05/21, Sentence sur les déclinatoires de compétence et la recevabilité (29 July 2008) para 1.

24 *Cf* ILC, 'Articles on Responsibility of States for Internationally Wrongful Acts' (2001), annexed to UNGA Res 56/83 (12 December 2001) UN Doc A/56/83, art 10(1): 'The conduct of an insurrectional movement which becomes the new government of a State shall be considered an act of that State under international law.'

25 *Spanish Zone of Morocco* (n 10) 642; *Sylvania Technical Systems Inc v Iran* (1985) 8 IUSCTR 298, 310.

26 *Sambiaggio Case (Italy/Venezuela)* (1903) 10 RIAA 499, 513. Responsibility arises, however, if it can be shown that the government of that state was negligent in the use of, or in the failure to use, the forces at its disposal for the prevention or suppression of the insurrection. Ian Brownlie, *System of the Law of Nations: State Responsibility, Part I* (OUP 1986) 452 et seq; Danielle Morris, 'Revolutionary Movements and *De Facto* Governments – Implications of the "Arab Spring" for International Investors' (2012) 28 Arb Int'l 721.

of extended war clauses, which explicitly provide protection in times of armed conflict and war. Secondly, article 3 of the International Law Commission's (ILC) 2011 Draft Articles on the Effects of Armed Conflicts on Treaties clearly states that 'the existence of an armed conflict does not *ipso facto* terminate or suspend the operation of the treaty',[27] thus affirming legal stability and continuity. Finally, those treaties mentioned in the annex to article 7 of the 2011 ILC Draft Articles also clearly include reciprocal BITs as they grant private entities third-party beneficiary rights.[28]

2.1.2 International Humanitarian Law of Non-International Armed Conflict

When revolutionary upheavals culminate in non-international armed conflicts such as civil wars, the application of international humanitarian law to such non-international armed conflicts is much more complicated. In principle, the applicability of international humanitarian law is known to depend on whether these revolutionary upheavals go beyond mere 'internal disturbances and tensions' and culminate in armed conflicts. As article 1(2) of Additional Protocol II to the Geneva Conventions makes clear, the law of armed conflicts 'shall not apply to situations of internal disturbances and tensions, such as riots, isolated and sporadic acts of violence and other acts of a similar nature, as not being armed conflicts'.[29] The existence of a non-international armed conflict[30] – as the *de facto* trigger for applicability – in turn requires both, a minimum of

---

27 ILC, 'Draft Articles on the Effects of Armed Conflicts on Treaties' (2011) annexed to UNGA Res 66/99 (9 December 2011) UN Doc A/RES/66/99.

28 See Tobias Ackermann, 'The ILC Draft Articles on the Effects of Armed Conflicts on Treaties: Room for Termination or Suspension of Bilateral Investment Treaties?' (2016) Minerva Center for the Rule of Law under Extreme Conditions Working Paper <http://minervaextremelaw.haifa.ac.il/images/Ackermann_Armed_Conflicts_and_BITs_Minerva_Working_Paper.pdf> accessed 19 January 2020.

29 (Second) Protocol Additional to the Geneva Conventions of 12 August 1949, and Relating to the Protection of Victims of Non-International Armed Conflicts (adopted 8 June 1977, entered into force 7 December 1978) 1125 UNTS 609 (Additional Protocol II) art 1(2).

30 See Geneva Conventions (adopted 12 August 1949, entered into force 21 October 1950) 75 UNTS 31 (Geneva Conventions) common art 3: 'In the case of armed conflict not of an international character occurring in the territory of one of the High Contracting Parties [...].' As is well-known, there are two distinct thresholds for non-international armed conflicts, to which partially different sets of rules apply: On the one hand, there is common article 3 of the Geneva Conventions with a lower threshold of applicability and, on the other, there is the Additional Protocol II with a higher one.

organisation[31] of the non-state armed group (which, however, must not reach the level of a well-organised state army) as well as a minimum of intensity[32] of the armed conflict, which generally requires the use of (military) force on each side.

The precise demarcation required for applicability between the poles of internal disturbances and tensions – which includes riots, spontaneous uprising of populations, looting leading to large-scale arrests, disappearances and emergency legislation, on the one hand, and intense armed conflicts, on the other hand, is not always easy. Very often, 'there is a gradual escalation of internal disturbances and no hard and fast line could be taken lock, stock and barrel.'[33] Yet, a prime example of such a possible applicability of international humanitarian law of non-international armed conflicts originating from revolutionary upheavals would very likely be the circumstances underlying the award presented at the outset of this analysis – *AAPL v Sri Lanka*.[34]

Depending on the circumstances, the following differentiation must be made regarding the applicability of international humanitarian law of non-international armed conflicts (in the following: international humanitarian law): If the internal disturbances and tensions accompanying a revolutionary upheaval do not exceed the required threshold of armed conflict, then international humanitarian law is not applicable to those situations and international investment law is exclusively applicable.[35] When, in fact, the threshold of armed conflict[36] is crossed, then international humanitarian law is applicable

---

31   The factors demonstrating the existence of a sufficient degree of organization are very well summarised in *Prosecutor v Boškoski*, (Judgment) IT-04-82-T (10 July 2008) paras 199 et seq.
32   On the factors required for this, see ibid para 190.
33   Robert Kolb, *International Humanitarian Law* (Cheltenham 2014) 104.
34   *AAPL v Sri Lanka*, Final Award (n 1) para 59.
35   However, even in situations that are still below the threshold of 'armed conflict', for example, due to a lack of sufficient organization of the revolutionary forces or non-state armed groups – as is typical in the case of flowing transitions between internal disturbances and tensions – massive use of force and destruction regularly occurs. The so-called 'Turku Declaration of Minimum Humanitarian Standards' (adopted 2 December 1990), which was developed for this constellation and formulates minimum humanitarian standards, has so far been discussed within the UN without any significant progress having been made towards a binding treaty. See Emily Crawford, 'Road to Nowhere? The Future for a Declaration on Fundamental Standards of Humanity' (2012) 3 J Int'l Human Legal Stud 43; Tilman Rodenhäuser, 'Fundamental Standards of Humanity: How International Law Regulates Internal Strife' (2013) JILPAC 121.
36   Geneva Conventions common art 3.

including the principle of military necessity,[37] which gives states greater leeway to have recourse to the use of force than in times of peace.

2.2 A Normative Conflict?

Investment law's full protection and security standard and humanitarian law's military necessity can both be applicable to the same factual situation. However, international investment law and international humanitarian law seem to balance property interests differently. International investment law protects as 'a necessary element alongside the overall aim of encouraging foreign investment'[38] the investor's *ownership* interest in compensation for its investment damaged by an unlawful act. In contrast, international humanitarian law's property protection is primarily designed to protect the *use* of civilian property to assure the survival of civilians and mitigate human suffering.[39] Moreover, international humanitarian law balances the principle of humanity and the principle of military necessity, while international investment law balances the protection of foreign investors' rights *vis-à-vis* the state's regulatory power. With these very different objectives and values, it is not surprising that they attach different consequences to the same action. One can see that 'to comply with one rule only by thereby failing to comply with another rule'[40] could produce conflicting results.

International investment law's full protection and security standard, which 'applies essentially when the foreign investment has been affected by civil strife and physical violence',[41] requires states 'to protect more specifically the physical integrity of an investment against interference by use of force.'[42] States are obliged to exercise due diligence, that is, to take reasonable measures of vigilance to protect investors from forcible interference of both non-state and

---

37 This is also the case as a matter of customary international law. See Jean-Marie Henckaerts and Louise Doswald-Beck, *Customary International Humanitarian Law*, vol 2 (ICRC and CUP 2005) 1000 et seq; Kolb (n 33) 86 et seq. Generally, the near universal acceptance of the Geneva Conventions has allowed them to be become accepted as customary international law, see *Legal Consequences of the Construction of a Wall in the Occupied Palestinian Territory* (Advisory Opinion) [2004] ICJ Rep 136, para 92; *Armed Activities on the Territory of the Congo (DRC v Uganda)* [2005] ICJ Rep 168, para 218. On analogies, see Marco Sassóli, *International Humanitarian Law* (Edward Elgar 2019) 224.

38 *Saluka Investments BV v Czech Republic*, Partial Award (17 March 2006) para 300.

39 Lea Brilmayer and Geoffrey Chepiga, 'Ownership or Use? Civilian Property Interests in International Humanitarian Law' (2008) Harv Int'l LJ 413, 427, 430.

40 ILC, 'Fragmentation of International Law' (n 7) para 24.

41 *Saluka v Czech Republic* (n 38) paras 483 et seq.

42 ibid. See also, on the standard and its scope, Emily Sipiorski, chapter 3 in this volume.

state actors.⁴³ The due diligence obligation, as already our initial award *AAPL v Sri Lanka* held, 'requires undertaking all possible measures that could be *reasonably* expected'.⁴⁴ Therefore, arbitral tribunals increasingly examine the underlying situation, in particular regarding the impact of what constitutes the standard's due diligence effort of protection, and formulate a 'sliding scale of liability'.⁴⁵ Such an approach also takes the situation of the *host state* into account as 'a failure of protection and security is [...] likely to arise in an unpredictable instance of civic disorder which could have been readily controlled by a powerful state but which overwhelms the limited capacities of one which is poor and fragile'.⁴⁶ Even if one takes such an adapted due diligence standard as a basis, as the tribunal in the first 'Arab Spring' related award in *Ampal v Egypt* did,⁴⁷ there remains the test of whether possible and *reasonable* 'security measures were not taken and implemented.'⁴⁸ Let us return to the facts described in the initial case cited, namely *AAPL v Sri Lanka*. How, in comparison, would international humanitarian law assess such a situation?

Certainly, international humanitarian law's principle of military necessity⁴⁹ requires belligerents to *distinguish* between civilian objects and military

---

43   *Biwater Gauff (Tanzania) Ltd v Tanzania*, ICSID Case no ARB/05/22, Award (24 July 2008) para 730 ('The Arbitral Tribunal also does not consider that the "full security" standard is limited to a State's failure to prevent actions by third parties, but also extends to actions by organs and representatives of the State itself.'). However, the tribunal in *AAPL v Sri Lanka* carefully avoided the question of attribution of state's acts altogether – an approach that was followed by many subsequent tribunals. See, *eg, American Manufacturing & Trading Inc v Zaire*, ICSID Case no ARB/93/1, Award (21 February 1997) para 6.10.

44   *AAPL v Sri Lanka*, Final Award (n 1) para 85(d).

45   ibid para 26.

46   *Pantechniki SA Contractors & Engineers (Greece) v Albania*, ICSID Case no ARB/07/21, Award (30 July 2009) para 77. These impulses were taken up in subsequent cases dealing with the full protection and security standard. See, *eg, Joseph Houben v Burundi*, ICSID Case no ARB/13/7, Award (12 January 2016) paras 160 et seq.

47   *Ampal-American Israel Corp v Egypt*, ICSID Case no ARB/12/11, Decision on Liability and Heads of Loss (21 February 2017) para 284: 'the tribunal acknowledges that the circumstances in the North Sinai Egypt were difficult in the wake of the Arab Spring Revolution. Armed militant groups took advantage of the political instability, security deterioration and general lawlessness [...]'.

48   ibid. The tribunal held, even under consideration of these circumstances, that given the failure to make sufficient efforts to prevent further attacks after the 'warning' of an initial four attacks, Egypt had not sufficiently fulfilled its due diligence and, therefore, breached its full protection and security obligation.

49   In the framework of this contribution, only a woodcut summary can be given of the principles, prohibitions, and obligations under (First) Protocol Additional to the Geneva Conventions of 12 August 1949, and Relating to the Protection of Victims of International

objectives as well as between civilians and combatants (*ie* objects and persons), to take *precautions* against 'collateral damage' to civilian objects, and to respect the principle of *proportionality* relative to the concrete military advantage.[50] Yet civilian protection of property is lost comparatively quickly under international humanitarian law if, and as soon as, a civilian object qualifies as a military objective, when its destruction offers an – even only indirect – effective contribution to the military action (and in the case of mistaken target identification even in good faith).[51] Finally, an attack directed at a specific military objective[52] but expected to incidentally cause damage to civilian objects (for example, those of an investor) is unlawful only in the case that such 'collateral damage' to civilian objects is excessive in relation to the concrete and direct military advantage anticipated.

Furthermore, the principle of military necessity can also be found *directly* expressed in certain norms of international humanitarian law. These prescribe the conditions for a lawful exemption or deviation, for example towards

---

Armed Conflicts (adopted 8 June 1977, entered into force 7 December 1978) 1125 UNTS 3 (Additional Protocol I) arts 48, 52, 51, 57, 58. These rules are widely recognised as customary international law. See Jean-Marie Henckaerts and Louise Doswald-Beck, *Customary International Humanitarian Law*, vol 1 (ICRC and CUP 2005). See also, with regard to the principle of military necessity, Nobuo Hayashi, 'Contextualizing Military Necessity' (2013) 27 Emory Int'l L Rev 190; Nobuo Hayashi, 'Requirements of Military Necessity in International Humanitarian Law and International Criminal Law' (2010) 28 Boston U Int'l LJ 39.

50   The prohibition of indiscriminate attacks includes the prohibition of attacks, which may be expected to cause incidental civilian loss or destruction, which would be excessive in relation to the concrete and direct military advantage anticipated.

51   In our initial case, *AAPL v Sri Lanka*, the tribunal did not, however, classify the respondent state's submission as credible. See *AAPL v Sri Lanka*, Final Award (n 1) para 85(c): 'the Respondent's version of the events has to be considered lacking convincing evidence with regard to the allegation that the farm became a "terrorist facility" which "violently resisted the Special Task Force" through an "Intense combat action" that "occurred at the Farm". Apparently, the officers' version of the events, which are not substantiated with any credible evidence, and which are contradicted by the Affidavits submitted by eye-witnesses, were intended to cover up their liability to prevent the destruction of the farm.'

52   Two-pronged test pursuant to article 52(2) Additional Protocol I assesses (1) whether the object in question makes an effective contribution to military action and (2) whether its destruction offers a definite military advantage. See, in depth, Ira Ryk-Lakhman, 'Foreign Investments as Non-Human Targets' in Björnstjern Baade, Linus Mührel, and Anton O Petrov (eds), *International Humanitarian Law in Areas of Limited Statehood: Adaptable and Legitimate or Rigid and Unreasonable?* (Nomos 2018) 184 ('In sum, the definition of "military objective" is broad and ambiguous enough to allow in practice for the classification of varied economic assets as military objectives, which may be subject to direct attack.'). See also Ira Ryk-Lakhman, chapter 2 in this volume.

property, for reasons of military necessity. For example, article 23(g) of the Hague Regulations forbids to 'destroy or seize the enemy's property, unless such destruction or seizure be imperatively demanded by the *necessities of war*'.[53] That means, in accordance with the respective provisions, as applicable, if and because the destruction of civilian objects is necessary from the military standpoint, such a destruction by state forces may be lawful. As a result, our initial question can be answered as follows: If the breach of international investment law's full protection and security standard (due to lack of due diligence) establishes a state's liability for an action which, in turn, would be lawful under international humanitarian law, then there may be a normative conflict.

2.3 Lex Specialis?

In such a constellation of a normative conflict, one possible method to resolve the conflict could be the application of the (increasingly contested) principle of *lex specialis*, according to which the norm prevails 'which is "special", that is, the rule with a more precisely delimited scope of application.'[54]

So, should international humanitarian law be considered *lex specialis* both in terms of its subject matter, its greater normative attachment to the object of regulation 'armed conflict', and its universal reach addressing all parties affected, state actors, non-state actors, including civilians in (also non-international) armed conflicts? Furthermore, it could be argued that international humanitarian law is 'to be observed by all States whether or not they have ratified the conventions that contain them, because [these fundamental rules] constitute intransgressible principles of international customary law'.[55] As a result, the 'widespread accession of States to the four Geneva Conventions […] suggests that these constitute customary international law norms that can only be derogated from with express, clear, and unequivocal terms',[56]

---

53 Hague Regulations art 23(g). See also Geneva Convention (IV) relative to the Protection of Civilian Persons in Time of War (adopted 12 August 1949, entered into force 21 October 1950) 75 UNTS 287 (Geneva Convention IV) art 53 ('Any destruction by the Occupying Power of real or personal property belonging individually or collectively to private persons […] is prohibited, except where such destruction is rendered absolutely *necessary by military operations*'), art 147 ('Grave breaches to which the preceding Article relates shall be those involving any of the following acts, if committed against persons or property protected by the present Convention: […] extensive destruction and appropriation of property, not justified by *military necessity* […]').
54 ILC, 'Fragmentation of International Law' (n 7) para 57.
55 *Nuclear Weapons* (n 21) para 79.
56 Gleider I Hernández, 'Book Symposium Investment Law: The Interaction between Investment Law and the Law of Armed Conflict in the Interpretation of Full Protection

which is not discernible from BITs. A further consideration could be derived from the structure of international humanitarian law, given that it contains 'absolute', as opposed to reciprocal, obligations under international law.[57] This then also means, however, that the conflict rules of the Vienna Convention on the Law of Treaties (VCLT),[58] which are essentially *lex specialis* and *lex posterior*, cannot be applied. On that basis, it could be concluded that, if humanitarian conventions apply between two states, a BIT that is also applicable between these states cannot be *lex specialis* to the humanitarian conventions.

Alternatively, should international investment law be considered as *lex specialis* for the treatment of investments as it addresses specific groups of subjects, investors and states? It provides, compared to international humanitarian law, unambiguously the more specific and most favourable protection[59] to the investor's property, and thus offers investors an inherently more specific protection.[60] Also, BITs as well as investment arbitration offer numerous parameters in order to also address the challenges that may be associated with

---

and Security Clauses' (*Opinio Juris*, 2 October 2013) <http://opiniojuris.org/2013/10/02/book-symposium-investment-law-interaction-investment-law-law-armed-conflict-interpretation-full-protection-security-clauses/> accessed 19 January 2020. See also Gleider I Hernández, 'The Interaction between Investment Law and the Law of Armed Conflict' in Freya Baetens, *Investment Law within International Law* (CUP 2013) 21. Also, in favour of international humanitarian law as *lex specialis*, Ofilio Mayorga, 'Arbitrating War: Military Necessity as a Defense to the Breach of Investment Treaty Obligations' (2013) Harvard Program on Humanitarian Policy and Conflict Research Policy Brief <http://hpcrresearch.org/sites/default/files/publications/081213%20ARBITRATING%20WAR%20%28final%29.pdf> accessed 19 January 2020; William W Burke-White, 'Inter-Relationships between the Investment Law and Other International Legal Regimes' (2015) E15 Task Force on Investment Policy Think Piece <http://e15initiative.org/wp-content/uploads/2015/09/E15-Investment-Burke-White-FINAL.pdf> accessed 19 January 2020.

57   *Prosecutor v Kupreškić et al* (Judgment) IT-95-16-T (14 January 2000) paras 517 et seq.
58   Vienna Convention on the Law of Treaties (adopted 22 May 1969, entered into force 27 January 1980) 1155 UNTS 331 (VCLT). The interpretive rules in article 31 VCLT are generally accepted as reflecting customary international law. See *Avena and Other Mexican Nationals (Mexico v USA)* (Judgment) [2004] ICJ Rep 12, 37 et seq.
59   According to the principle of most-favoured-nation treatment, preference is given to a better treatment also in international humanitarian law. See, *eg*, Additional Protocol I art 75(8): 'No provision of this Article may be construed as limiting or infringing any other more favourable provision granting greater protection, under any applicable rules of international law [...]'.
60   See, also with respect to human rights, *Spyridon Roussalis v Romania*, ICSID Case no ARB/06/1, Award (1 December 2011) para 322 ('[...] given the higher and more specific level of protection offered by the BIT to the investors compared to the more general protections offered to them by the human rights instruments [...]').

non-international armed conflicts, for example (as we have already seen) by considering the factual situation of revolutionary upheavals and armed conflicts in the interpretation of the full protection and security standard's due diligence requirements. Furthermore, essential security exceptions clauses in BITs exempt the defending state from its treaty obligations if important national interests are at stake,[61] or possibilities of defence under the customary international law of state responsibility such as *force majeure*[62] to excuse the defending state's non-performance exist.[63]

Apart from this, an overarching legal thought could be inferred from the wording of article 38 of Geneva Convention IV, applicable (however exclusively) in international armed conflict, according to which 'the situation of protected persons shall continue to be regulated, in principle, by the provisions concerning aliens in time of peace'.[64] This means that international humanitarian law does not *per se* exclude such regulations. BITs' extended war clauses, which offer compensation for investments demonstrably destroyed by state organs in cases in which the destruction was not required by the necessity

---

61 For example, in these, the notion of 'public order' is 'intended as a broad synonym for "public peace," which can be threatened by actual or potential insurrections, riots and violent disturbances of the peace', *Continental Casualty Co v Argentina*, ICSID Case no ARB/03/9, Award (5 September 2008) para 174; William W Burke-White and Andreas von Staden, 'Investment Protection in Extraordinary Times: The Interpretation and Application of Non-Precluded Measure Provisions in Bilateral Investment Treaties' (2008) 48 Va J Int'l L 307, 360; José E Alvarez and Tegan Brink, 'Revisiting the Necessity Defense: Continental Casualty v. Argentina' in Karl P Sauvant (ed), *Yearbook on International Investment Law & Policy 2010–2011* (OUP 2012).

62 However, they do pose high thresholds for their successful invocation. See Federica Paddeu, *Justification and Excuse in International Law: Concept and Theory of General Defences* (CUP 2018) 285; Jure Zrilič, 'Armed Conflict as Force Majeure in International Investment Law' (2019) 16 Manchester J Int'l Econ L 28. See also Christina Binder and Philipp Janig, chapter 4 in this volume.

63 However, a distinction must be made here: (1) The question of whether there is a conflict to be resolved possibly by means of *lex specialis* concerns the *primary* rules of international humanitarian law and international investment law which define the content and extent of the actual obligations in international law. This needs to be distinguished from (2) the (further) question of whether certain justifications under the system of state responsibility can be put forward for the non-fulfilment of the primary rule which concerns the *secondary* rules that would, here, refer to armed conflicts. See *Gabčíkovo-Nagymaros Project (Hungary v Slovakia)* [1997] ICJ Rep 7, para 47; *CMS Gas Transmission Co v Argentina*, ICSID Case no ARB/01/8, Annulment Decision (25 September 2007) para 134.

64 Geneva Convention IV art 38: 'With the exception of special measures authorized by the present Convention, in particular by Articles 27 and 41 thereof, the situation of protected persons shall continue to be regulated, in principle, by the provisions concerning aliens in time of peace.'

of the situation,[65] show, in accordance with the intention of the contracting states, that BITs should also apply in times of upheavals and armed conflicts. Finally, the *lex specialis* argument could still be enhanced by the *lex posterior* priority rule in article 30 VCLT, as BITs are likely to be the much more recent treaties.[66]

Yet, it seems questionable overall whether the tension between different specialised branches of international law, which frequently have their own features and rules, can indeed be resolved by the *lex specialis* approach. Displacing the entire body of the respective other law is a far-reaching consequence. Such a step can hardly be assumed to be implicitly intended by the states and, in case of doubt, would probably require an *explicit* expression of the intent of the states affected.[67] Moreover, if, for example, international humanitarian law were considered *lex specialis* and, as a result, international investment law were superseded by international humanitarian law in situations in which investments may be most in need of protection, the question arises whether it would be within an investment arbitration tribunal's jurisdiction and competence to interpret such a hierarchical relationship.[68] And, if international humanitarian law were in fact to override international investment law, should it then also take precedence over other subfields of law such as human rights law? Is there any neutral perspective from which it would be possible to identify unambiguously which subfield is now the more relevant?[69] Is and can there be

---

65   *Eg* Austria–Libya BIT (2004) art 5(2): 'An investor of a Contracting Party who [...] suffers loss resulting from: [...] or (b) destruction of its investment or part thereof by the forces or authorities of the other Contracting Party, which was not required by the necessity of the situation, shall in any case be accorded by the latter Contracting Party restitution or compensation [...].'
66   Further arguments may also be derived from the existence, as here, of a *non-international armed conflict*: One may question to what extent international humanitarian rules applicable to such conflicts which are often derived by analogy to those applicable to international armed conflicts (or as customary law) prevail as *lex specialis*. See Sassòli (n 37) 441.
67   *Elettronica Sicula SpA (ELSI) (USA v Italy)* (Judgment) [1989] ICJ Rep 15, para 50.
68   As defined by the contracting treaty parties, the states, and, if available, the applicable law; for arbitral proceedings based on the Convention on the Settlement of Investment Disputes between States and Nationals of Other States (adopted 18 March 1965, entered into force 14 October 1966) 575 UNTS 159 (ICSID Convention), if there is no applicable law clause, article 42 of the Convention applies. According to article 52(1)(a) of the ICSID Convention, a disputing party could demand annulment of the award if the tribunal manifestly exceeded its powers, namely by deciding the dispute by applying a legal rule it was not empowered to apply, or conversely, by not applying a legal rule it was under duty to apply.
69   Joost Pauwelyn and Ralf Michaels, 'Conflict of Norms or Conflict of Laws? Different Techniques in the Fragmentation of Public International Law' (2012) 22 Duke J Int'l & Comp L 349, 367.

for any given situation *only* one expression of state consent or intent as to how that situation is to be regulated?[70]

Finally, the International Court of Justice (ICJ) itself progressively abandoned the *lex specialis* maxim in *Armed Activities on the Territory of the Congo* and concluded, as already stated in its previous *Wall* opinion,[71] 'that both branches of international law, namely international human rights law and international humanitarian law, would have to be taken into consideration.'[72] However, as the ICJ (as is well known) decided once more in this case *not* to describe humanitarian law as *lex specialis* in relation to human rights law, this could also apply *a fortiori* here, so that both international humanitarian law and international investment law would have to be taken into consideration.

3 Informing Extended War Clauses or Autonomous Treaty Interpretation?

3.1 *An Informative Approach*

Let us return to a situation in which revolutionary upheavals lead to a non-international armed conflict, a situation in which international investment law as well as international humanitarian law are, in principle, equally applicable. Does such a normative overlap necessarily lead to a 'genuine'[73] normative conflict in which the norms are incompatible and for whose resolution one would depend on the aforementioned principle of *lex specialis*? Essentially, a conflict of laws exists only if the norm addressee cannot simultaneously comply with two differing standards, because the legal consequences of both standards are mutually exclusive. Observance of one standard would necessarily lead to an infringement of the other standard. This narrow understanding of conflicts of norms was questioned in the course of the 'fragmentation' debate and a broader understanding of conflicts of norms was called for. According to this broader understanding, a conflict of norms already exists when differing (though not irreconcilable) balancing of interests is found in various fields of international law.

Let us take a closer look again at the claims of concrete standards which both BIT's full protection and security standard and humanitarian law's principle

---

70 Joost Pauwelyn, *Conflict of Norms in Public International Law: How WTO Law Relates to Other Rules of International Law* (CUP 2003) 388.
71 *Construction of a Wall* (n 37) para 106.
72 *Armed Activities* (n 37) para 216.
73 Pauwelyn, *Conflict of Norms* (n 70) 240 et seq, 272.

of 'military necessity' impose. International investment law obliges the state to protect investments with sufficient due diligence – while international humanitarian law, in addition to its restrictive nature, substantially enhances the state's authority to employ force and allows greater emphasis on the sovereign prerogative to handle situations of armed conflicts. Put differently, while international investment law limits the use of force to a measure of last resort, under international humanitarian law, military force can be used in the first instance in accordance with its specific rules. However, although humanitarian law authorises[74] the state to use force to destroy property in accordance with its specific rules, it does not necessarily oblige the state to do so.[75] Therefore, there may indeed be a normative overlap here, but not necessarily a normative conflict in a strict legal sense.

So, if there is no normative conflict in a strict legal sense, should there be reservations concerning a *lex specialis* approach and should instead a more *informative approach* be taken? Such an approach would be consistent at least with the presumption that subfields are not necessarily in conflict with each other.[76] This approach would be in line with article 31(3)(c) VCLT, which directs that there 'shall be taken into account, together with the context [...] [a]ny relevant rules of international law applicable in the relations between the parties'. Such an *informative approach* would also be much more appropriate for arbitrators in an investment arbitral tribunal because this approach allows the sufficient taking into account of the possibilities and limits of the relevant jurisdictional scope of the BIT. Since the arbitral tribunal is appointed to interpret and apply the standards of that treaty, depending on the scope of arbitration clause, in principle, only the violation of such a treaty may serve as a normative point of reference when issuing the arbitral award.[77] Normatively,

---

74 On 'authorisations' in humanitarian law, see Sassóli (n 37) 490.

75 Not to mention the use of human rights law in order to complement and possibly restrict the applicable rules of humanitarian law. See, *eg, Public Committee against Torture in Israel et al v Government of Israel et al* [2006] HCJ 769/02, para 40 (Supreme Court of Israel sitting as the High Court of Justice).

76 *Right of Passage over Indian Territory (Portugal v India)* (Preliminary Objections) [1957] ICJ Rep 125, 142. See, however, *Electrabel SA v Hungary*, ICSID Case no ARB/07/19, Decision on Jurisdiction, Applicable Law, and Liability (30 November 2012) para 4.173, holding that 'there is no general principle under international law compelling the harmonious interpretation of all existing legal rules.'

77 *Grand River Enterprises Six Nations Ltd et al v USA*, Award (12 January 2011) para 71; *Achmea BV (formerly Eureko BV) v Slovakia*, PCA Case no 2008–13, Award on Jurisdiction, Arbitrability, and Suspension (26 October 2010) para 290.

an investor's claim for damages against the host state would therefore always be derived from a BIT.

According to the 'principle of systemic integration', this means that 'although a tribunal may only have jurisdiction in regard to a particular instrument, it must always interpret and apply that instrument in its relationship to its normative environment – that is to say "other" international law.'[78] Therefore, investment arbitrators must distinguish between, on the one hand, the possible *consideration* of rules from that 'other' international law that may be 'taken into account' as interpretive guidance for the relevant treaty term – and, on the other hand, a *de facto application* of the rules of this other law, which is hardly likely to be covered by the specific consent of the parties. Equally, tribunals should appreciate the contexts, similarities and differences contained in such subfields because, basically, these differing fields and concepts can, and should, benefit from each other. However, these subfields may be substantially different – in their formation, their actual effects, their specific institutional context, their specialised expertise and methodology and their specific dispute resolution mechanism. These features may also have their reasons and merits. Elements of these, and lessons learnt from one subfield, can inform another subfield after careful adaption while taking into consideration their systemic and structural contexts as well as their differences.

The prerequisite for such an approach is that BITs are open to such informative interpretations. This leads to the fundamental question of whether international investment law should be understood as a *self-contained regime*,[79] in which general international law and its subfields play no additional role in the interpretation of its norms,[80] or whether it is instead to be understood as part of general international law with the result that norms of international investment law can indeed be interpreted in the light of general international law including its subfields.[81] Certainly, the procedural formation of investor-state arbitration, for example within the framework of the ICSID Convention, displays a characteristic of *lex specialis*. However, international investment law *overall* cannot be understood as a self-contained regime but rather as a part

---

78   ILC, 'Fragmentation of International Law' (n 7) para 90.
79   The term was coined by the Permanent Court of International Justice in SS *'Wimbledon'* (*Great Britain et al v German*) PCIJ Series A no 1, 23, 24. See also *United States Diplomatic and Consular Staff in Tehran (USA v Iran)* [1980] ICJ Rep 3, para 86.
80   *Waste Management Inc v Mexico*, ICSID Case no ARB(AF)/00/2, Final Award (20 April 2004) para 85.
81   *Enron Corp and Ponderosa LP v Argentina*, ICSID Case no ARB/01/3, Decision on Jurisdiction (14 January 2004) para 46; Bruno Simma and Dirk Pulkowski, 'Of Planets and the Universe: Self-contained Regimes in International Law' (2006) 17 EJIL 483.

of general international law.[82] Hence, a basic principle applies which was formulated already in the arbitral award that precedes this analysis – in the first award based on a BIT, *AAPL v Sri Lanka*, the tribunal found:

> [...] the Bilateral Investment Treaty is not a self-contained closed legal system limited to provide for substantive material rules of direct applicability, but it has to be envisaged within a wider juridical context in which rules from other sources are integrated through implied incorporation methods, or by direct reference to certain supplementary rules.[83]

3.2   *Informing Extended War Clauses?*

Under such an *informative approach*, specific assessments of humanitarian law could, possibly, be used to *inform* the interpretation of BIT norms and *vice versa*. For example, extensive extended war clauses offer compensation for investments demonstrably destroyed by state organs in cases in which the destruction was not required by the necessity of the situation. For instance, article 5(2) of the Austria–Libya BIT, entitled 'Compensation for Losses', provides:

> An investor of a Contracting Party who [...] suffers loss resulting from: [...] (b) destruction of its investment or part thereof by the forces or authorities of the other Contracting Party, which was not required by the *necessity of the situation*, shall in any case be accorded by the latter Contracting Party restitution or compensation [...].[84]

Is it advisable and necessary to interpret the term 'necessity of the situation' in light of humanitarian law's 'military necessity' and the specific rules of customary international law applicable in non-international armed conflict, such as the principle of differentiation, the prohibition of excesses and the

---

82   ILC, 'Fragmentation of International Law' (n 7) para 414; Campbell McLachlan, 'Investment Treaties and General International Law' (2008) 58 ICLQ 361, 366.

83   *AAPL v Sri Lanka*, Final Award (n 1) para 21. But see also ibid para 42 ('The construction of the Treaty's comprehensive system governing all aspects related to the extent of the special protection conferred upon the investors in question would permit the evaluation of the Treaty's effective contribution in this respect; ie in view of determining with regard to each issue whether the Sri Lanka/U.K. Treaty intended, merely, to consolidate the pre-existing rules of international law, or, on the contrary, it tended to innovate [...].'); *Phoenix Action Ltd v Czech Republic*, ICSID Case no ARB/06/5, Award (15 April 2009) para 78 ('[international investment law] cannot be read and interpreted in isolation from public international law, and its general principles').

84   Austria–Libya BIT (2004) art 5(2).

obligation to take precautionary measures? The meaning of which rule would then come into play under article 31(3)(c) VCLT,[85] when '(a) the treaty rule is unclear or open-textured [and yet] (b) the terms used in the treaty have a recognized meaning in customary international law'.[86] In favour of such an interpretation,[87] it has been argued that the '[necessity of the situation] follows a pattern long established in practice [...] that these destructions were compelled by the imperious necessity of war',[88] so that this interpretation would correspond to the situation under traditional customary international law.[89]

This would mean, for example, that if the investor's property were indeed assessed as a military objective, its destruction would be lawful, if no excessive incidental civilian damage was to be expected and if the necessary precautions in attack have been taken. If an investor's property were a civilian object and were destroyed as a result of an attack on a military objective, then it would depend on whether such 'collateral damage' was excessive in relation to the concrete and direct military advantage anticipated.[90] The result would be that

---

85   Certainly, sometimes it is not easy to distinguish an interpretation in light of general international law according to article 31(3)(c) VCLT from a direct application of customary international law and general principles of law.

86   ILC, 'Conclusions of the Work of the Study Group on the Fragmentation of International Law: Difficulties Arising from the Diversification and Expansion of International Law' (2006) II(2) YBILC 177, conclusion 20.

87   However, in order to be 'relevant' for purposes of interpretation in the sense of article 31(3)(c) VCLT, a similarity is required between the subject matter of the treaty to be interpreted and that of the rules of international law which is to be taken into account. *US – Anti-Dumping and Countervailing Duties (China)* (11 March 2011) WT/DS379/AB/R, para 308. Subject matter of a BIT is the promotion and protection of investments, while subject matter of international humanitarian law is the conduct of war (*jus in bello*). It could appear questionable whether there is sufficient similarity of the subject matter, not least because – as has been stressed in a different context – 'Article 31, paragraph 3 [VCLT] requires "the context" to be taken into account: and "the context" is clearly that of an economic and commercial treaty', *Oil Platforms (Iran v USA)* (Merits, Separate Opinion of Rosalyn Higgins) [2003] ICJ Rep 225, para 46.

88   *AAPL v Sri Lanka*, Final Award (n 1) para 63. However, in the absence of sufficient evidence whether the farm was a terrorist facility and who finally was responsible for the effective destruction of the farm premises, the tribunal in *AAPL v Sri Lanka* did *not* analyse, as such, the notion of 'the necessity of the situation'. See ibid para 64: 'Under these circumstances, it would be extremely difficult to determine whether the destruction and losses were caused as an inevitable result of the "necessity of the situation" [...].'

89   Christoph Schreuer, 'The Protection of Investments in Armed Conflict' in Freya Baetens (ed), *Investment Law within International Law* (CUP 2013) 14.

90   *Prosecutor v Hadzihasanoviæ and Kubura* (Trial Judgment) IT-01-47-T (15 March 2006) para 45: 'The Chamber finds that collateral damage to civilian property may be justified by military necessity and may be an exception to the principles of protection of civilian property.'

a militarily necessary destruction of an investor's property, if lawful under international humanitarian law, would *not* render the state liable for compensation under international investment law.

3.3   *An Autonomous Treaty Interpretation*

Are there, however, compelling arguments that speak for an autonomous treaty interpretation, and against a (mere) reference to customary law? The thesis that such an understanding is essentially an incorporation of custom into treaty[91] can be countered in principle by the fact that, historically, international investment law certainly had its origins in customary international law. However, the procedural unpredictability of state-centred diplomatic protection in customary international law, being mainly tailored for intergovernmental relations, and the uncertainty of the material standards of general international law, led in the late 1950s and 1960s to an increasing desire to develop new specific forms of protection and arbitration. This desire was equally true for non-state economic actors and states themselves. As a consequence, a dynamic system was created based predominantly on bilateral international treaties starting with the Germany–Pakistan BIT in 1959.[92] The treaty's aim was to develop new tailor-made forms of protection for international investment relations. This was achieved, firstly, through the independent 'treatyfied' concretization of standards of treatment promoting the rule of law[93] – as many of these rights, such as the standard of national treatment, compensation for

---

91   This may apply to the full protection and security standard being informed by customary law, or, *eg*, where states have explicitly limited the scope of this standard to the international minimum standard under customary international law. See *Mondev International Ltd v USA*, ICSID Case no ARB(AF)/99/2, Award (11 October 2002) para 120. But see also the disputes about the scope of treaty rules of full protection and security, *Saluka v Czech Republic* (n 38) paras 483 et seq.

92   The Germany–Pakistan BIT (1959) entered into force in 1962. A new BIT was signed in 2009.

93   Martins Paparinskis, 'Investment Arbitration and the Law of Countermeasures' (2008) Brit YB Int'l L 264, 265: 'The results of the more recent efforts of law-making sometimes accept and incorporate the classic rules; sometimes clarify the classic ambiguities or replace the unsatisfactory solutions; sometimes permit different approaches in parallel; and quite often maintain constructive ambiguity regarding the precise relationship between different rules.' This investment treaty-making process was most likely, arguably counterintuitively, also supported by the ICJ jurisprudence in *Barcelona Traction, Light and Power Co, Ltd (Belgium v Spain)* (*2nd Phase*) [1970] ICJ Rep 3; *ELSI* (n 67); *Ahmadou Sadio Diallo (Guinea v DRC)* (Merits) [2010] ICJ Rep 639. See, generally, Christoph Schreuer, 'Shareholder Protection in International Investment Law' in Pierre-Marie Dupuy and others (eds), *Common Values in International Law: Festschrift Christian Tomuschat* (Engel 2006) 606.

expropriation and the guarantee of free transfer were not necessarily part of the customary international law of diplomatic protection or the law relating to the protection of aliens, and, finally, through the provision of a party-driven dispute settlement mechanism in BITs.[94] Certainly, there may be other narratives,[95] but what follows from this, at least basically, is that the thesis of an incorporation or mere replication of (humanitarian) customary law into (investment) treaty law is, in any case, difficult to maintain consistently and must be examined very carefully in each individual case.

In our particular case, it is striking to say the least that the text of extended war clauses – as 'the starting point of interpretation'[96] (and against the background of the paramount importance of its ordinary meaning under article 31(1) VCLT)[97] uses the phrase 'necessity of the situation', which is not congruent with 'military necessity'. Furthermore, the terminology contained in extended war clauses concerning the 'necessity of the *situation*' conceptualises the category of '*conflicts*' in much wider terms – in contrast to, and well below, the threshold for 'non-international armed conflicts' in international humanitarian law. The reason for this is that international investment law's extended war clauses cover not only 'armed conflicts' as understood in international humanitarian law but also lesser instances of civil unrest, such as internal disturbances and tensions. They are invariably formulated in a broader fashion with open-ended formulations such as 'or other similar events' or 'other armed conflicts'.[98] Some BITs employ terms that may fall significantly short of armed conflict, such as 'rebellion',[99] 'revolt',[100] 'mutiny'[101] or 'riot'.[102]

---

94 Starting with the Italy–Chad BIT (1969) art 7, but the 1990 arbitral award in *AAPL v Sri Lanka* was the first investment arbitral award on the basis of an investor-state dispute resolution clause in a BIT.

95 Andreas Kulick, 'Narrating Narratives of International Investment Law: History and Epistemic Forces' in Stephan W Schill, Christian J Tams, and Rainer Hofmann (eds), *Investment Law and History* (Edward Elgar 2018) 41; Taylor St John, *The Rise of Investor-State Arbitration: Politics, Law, and Unintended Consequences* (OUP 2018).

96 ILC, 'Draft Articles on the Law of Treaties with Commentaries' (1966) II YBILC 187, 220.

97 *Wintershall v Argentina*, ICSID Case no ARB/04/14, Award (8 December 2008) para 78; *Methanex Corp v USA*, Final Award (3 August 2005) pt I ch B paras 22, 37; *ADF Group Inc v USA*, ICSID Case no ARB(AF)/00/1, Award (9 January 2003) para 147; *Sempra Energy International v Argentina*, ICSID Case no ARB/02/16, Decision on Annulment (29 June 2010) para 188.

98 Pakistan–Philippines BIT (1999) art 5.

99 Libya–Switzerland BIT (2003) art 6(2).

100 Syria–Azerbaijan BIT (2009) art 7(1); Libya–Korea BIT (2006) art 4(1).

101 Syria–Pakistan BIT (1996) art 3(4).

102 Yemen–Czech Republic BIT (2008) art 4(1); Libya–Belarus BIT (2000) art 5(1).

If it were desirable to apply the understanding of 'military necessity' – also – to such situations, this would possibly undermine the recognised threshold for the applicability of international humanitarian law of non-international armed conflicts. By such an extension of the understanding of 'necessity of the situation' to 'military necessity' also in these situations, protection under international investment law would very probably be significantly reduced. It seems doubtful whether the contracting parties to a BIT would have intended such a consequence.

The question still remains whether an interpretation in accordance with the understanding of international humanitarian law of non-international armed conflicts should apply to situations that clearly cross the threshold of armed conflict. This can possibly be contradicted by the fact that the contracting states have agreed on an autonomous standard of an extended war clause to create an absolute form of protection also for armed conflicts. Thereby, they have expressed their intention that international investment law remains applicable also in such situations. These extended war clauses are part of BITs which are 'regulating a particular area of the relations between one party and the other,'[103] where 'a bargain is a reciprocal bargain',[104] in which 'the parties must be held to what they agreed to, but not more, or less'.[105] Certainly, this is a very pronounced description,[106] but it draws attention to the fact that those BITs can, basically, (still)[107] be characterised by reciprocity and individual enforcement of the obligations – characteristics which distinguish them from multilateral humanitarian law treaties which, on the other hand, are characterised by 'absolute' non-reciprocity and collective enforcement.[108]

---

103   *RosInvest Co UK Ltd v Russia*, SCC Case no V079/2005, Award on Jurisdiction (5 October 2007) para 40, differentiating between human rights treaties *vis-à-vis* investment treaties.
104   ibid.
105   ibid.
106   See, generally, Christoph Schreuer and Ursula Kriebaum, 'From Individual to Community Interest in International Investment Law' in Ulrich Fastenrath and others (eds), *From Bilateralism to Community Interest: Essays in Honour of Bruno Simma* (OUP 2011) 1079.
107   Certainly, there may be tendencies towards a 'multilateralization' of international investment law as impressively demonstrated by Stephan W Schill, *The Multilateralization of International Investment Law* (CUP 2009). However, it is not yet apparent that BITs would be completely exempt from the reciprocity principle.
108   *Prosecutor v Kupreškić et al* (n 57) paras 517 et seq, contrasting the absolute nature of international humanitarian law treaties with reciprocal commercial treaty norms: '[...] the bulk of this body of law lays down absolute obligations, namely obligations that are unconditional or in other words not based on reciprocity. [...] Unlike other international norms, such as those of commercial treaties which can legitimately be based on the protection of reciprocal interests of States, compliance with humanitarian rules could not be

It can then be concluded from these structural distinctions that notions – to paraphrase the International Criminal Tribunal for the former Yugoslavia in *Prosecutor v Kunarac* – developed in the field of humanitarian law can be transposed to international investment law only if they take into consideration the specificities of the latter body of law.[109] However, this essentially reciprocal bargain would be significantly thrown out of balance if the regime-specific assessments of humanitarian law's principle of 'military necessity' were to be adopted for the interpretation of the term 'necessity of the situation' contained in investment treaties' extended war clauses. This is due to the fact, as evidenced by the clear wording, that states have provided through these extended war clauses – at least in the given situation – that 'unnecessary' damages to investments must be compensated for. Thereby, these clauses provide some protection for investments specifically in violent and particularly dangerous exceptional situations. Furthermore, the wording ('which was not required by the *necessity of the situation*') clearly demonstrates as the main source of the parties' intention that destroyed investments are not entirely considered to be a case of 'collateral damages' in armed conflicts for which investors are usually neither responsible nor the cause. A comparable assessment can also be found in the law of state responsibility, namely the ILC's article 27,[110] which deals with the obligation for a possible compensation for acts which, although contrary to international law, are precluded from responsibility. The underlying principle of article 27 is that there is no reason for which the party harmed by an act should be required to suffer loss in the interests of the injuring state if it did not contribute to, let alone cause, the situation.[111]

Finally, the wording of extended war clauses show that investors should not, in principle, bear the full economic consequences of armed conflicts and civil disturbances, and thus it expresses a certain concept of *risk allocation*. This

---

made dependent on a reciprocal or corresponding performance of these obligations by other States.'

109 *Prosecutor v Kunarac et al* (Judgment) IT-96-23-T, IT-96-23/1-T (22 February 2001) para 471: 'The Trial Chamber is therefore wary not to embrace too quickly and too easily concepts and notions developed in a different legal context. [...] notions developed in the field of human rights can be transposed in international humanitarian law only if they take into consideration the specificities of the latter body of law'.

110 ILC, 'Articles on Responsibility of States for Internationally Wrongful Acts' (n 24) art 27: 'The invocation of a circumstance precluding wrongfulness in accordance with this chapter is without prejudice to: [...] (b) the question of compensation for any material loss caused by the act in question.'

111 James Crawford, 'Revising the Draft Articles on State Responsibility' (1999) 10 EJIL 435, 444 et seq.

wording, as the expression of what the contracting states of BITs intended, indicates that such a compensation under certain conditions then goes just beyond and supersedes the assessments of customary international law.[112] Therefore, the clear treaty terms of extended war clauses (and in particular the 'necessity of the situation', such as in revolutionary upheavals and civil wars, as 'the text and the drafters' intention, which this manifests)[113] shows that it should be carefully interpreted[114] *on its own terms* and not just exclusively from a purely military perspective.

Following on from the view represented here of an autonomous treaty interpretation, the fact remains, however, that the mere existence of a 'non-international armed conflict' automatically triggers the application of international humanitarian law, according to which a different decision would possibly be made on the basis of the applicable legal rules. Thus, in this case, both subfields – investment law and humanitarian law – are applicable in parallel. Yet, as has been established, there is not necessarily a norm conflict between international investment law and international humanitarian law in a strict legal sense: international humanitarian law may authorize (but not necessarily oblige) a state to destroy private property in times of war to the extent necessary for military purposes, while the same state would possibly be held liable for this under international investment law. Nevertheless, the state can – in principle – comply with both legal regimes. For example, if it adheres to the narrower regime, *ie* international investment law, this does not force it to violate international humanitarian law.

Regardless of this, the applicability of both legal subfields does not change the obligation to decide on the legality of state actions in those institutions of the respective subfields. The longest-standing regional human rights court,

---

112   That treaty provisions may validly derogate from previously existing rules of international law has been recognised in *Acquisition of Polish Nationality* (Advisory Opinion) [1923] PCIJ Series B no 7, 15 et seq; *North Sea Continental Shelf (Germany v Denmark, Germany v Netherlands)* [1969] ICJ Rep 3, para 72.
113   *Methanex v USA* (n 97) pt IV ch B para 37.
114   Certainly, in practice, a tribunal may have the burden of justification for the intention of the parties departing from customary rules and the harmonizing principles of article 31 VCLT, but this latter rule of treaty interpretation may, in turn, also be read as providing enough flexibility for a tribunal to 'develop the written terms [of the rule] in a different direction than the customary rule'. Mark E Villiger, *Customary International Law and Treaties: A Manual on the Theory and Practice of the Interrelation of Sources* (Springer 1997) 265, 422. See also ILC, 'Conclusions of the Work of the Study Group' (n 86) conclusion 20, whereby, in the case that the treaty term is clear and leads to a different result than the customary rule, one should apply the treaty rule to the exclusion of that rule.

the European Court of Human Rights, has already proceeded in this way.[115] An arbitral investment tribunal must decide the question of compensation submitted to it, while the question of legality under humanitarian law must be addressed by the bodies of humanitarian law, whose 'remedies will continue to be available and will be unaffected by whatever decision the tribunal gives in the present case'.[116]

In this context, finally, it is striking that respondent states have apparently not yet attempted to use humanitarian law's 'military necessity' as a defence in an investment arbitration in a comparable situation. So far, arbitral tribunals have not yet had to address the possible interplay of international investment law and international humanitarian law of non-international armed conflicts. The almost classic reason for this is that states are, apparently, in any case reluctant to admit to the existence of non-international armed conflicts and, not least, wish to avoid the applicability of international humanitarian law of non-international armed conflicts to, from their point of view, internal affairs.[117] In these cases, the respondent states are anyway often accommodated by the fact that it is, frequently, challenging for the plaintiff investor to prove attributability and causality.

4 Burden of Proof

The 'fog of war',[118] the classically occurring *uncertainty* in situational awareness in armed conflicts, also applies equally to investment arbitrations dealing

---

115 With regard to the *parallel* relationship between the European Convention for the Protection of Human Rights and Fundamental Freedoms (adopted 3 September 1953, entered into force 4 November 1950) 213 UNTS 221 (ECHR) and other treaty obligations, see – with respect to *Matthews v UK*, App no 24833/94 (ECtHR, 18 February 1999, Merits and Just Satisfaction) – Marko Milanovic, 'A Norm Conflict Perspective on the Relationship between International Humanitarian Law and Human Rights Law' (2010) 15 J Confl & Sec L 459, 470: 'The Court thus found the UK responsible for violating the ECHR, irrespective of its other treaty obligations. This did not mean, however, that the treaty prohibiting the extension of the franchise to the inhabitants of Gibraltar was invalid, or that the ECHR prevailed over it in some hierarchical sense. Both treaties were formally of equal stature, and no norm conflict resolution was possible – the UK could not fulfil its obligations under either treaty without violating the other, thereby incurring State responsibility. [...] but [...] this simply did not matter for answering the question that was posed to the Court [...].'

116 *Rompetrol Group NV v Romania*, ICSID Case no ARB/06/3, Award (6 May 2013) para 170 regarding the interaction between the investor-state dispute settlement and ECHR regime.

117 Kolb (n 33) 29, 104.

118 The term 'fog' in reference to uncertainty in war was introduced by Carl von Clausewitz, *On War* (first published in German 1832, N Trübner 1873), ch 3: 'War is the realm of

with such situations. In our initial case, *AAPL v Sri Lanka*, with respect to the extended war clause, the investor had essentially to establish as cumulative requirements, first, the causality between the property's destruction and the government forces' action and, secondly, the *'necessity* of the situation'. The tribunal in *AAPL v Sri Lanka* found:

> In the present case, neither Party was able to provide reliable evidence explaining with precision the conditions under which the destructions and other losses [...] took place. Under these circumstances, it would be extremely difficult to decide whether the destruction and losses were caused as an inevitable result of the "necessity of the situation", or, on the contrary, were avoidable if the governmental security forces would have been keen to act with due diligence. [...] Consequently, all three conditions necessary for the applicability of Article 4.(2) are proven to be non-existent [...].[119]

As the claimant who bore the burden of proving these cumulative requirements could not establish the relevant facts, a claim based on the extended war clause had to be dismissed. In this frequently occurring situation, where the investor is usually merely an onlooker, the tribunal in *AAPL v Sri Lanka* soberly noted that 'the foreign investor who invokes the applicability of said Article 4(2) assumes a heavy burden of proof'.[120]

Such a 'heavy burden of proof' for the claimant, not only in cases of extended war clauses, but also based on the full protection and security standard, often has the consequence that investors, but also their states (which receive the claim by way of 'subrogation'),[121] waive the assertion of this treaty claim from the outset in the absence of foreseeable demonstrability of attributability and causality. Thus, the legal instrument of a BIT, which is available in itself, often does not come into effect in these situations. It seems indeed questionable

---

uncertainty; three quarters of the factors on which action in war is based are wrapped in a fog of greater or lesser uncertainty.'

119   *AAPL v Sri Lanka*, Final Award (n 1) para 64.
120   ibid para 58.
121   BITs contain a 'subrogation clause' for the case that the investor has secured its investment with an investment guarantee and, in the event of loss, makes use of this guarantee. In these cases, the claim resulting from the investment treaty against the host state is usually transferred ('subrogated') from the investor, as the previous claimant, to the home state as guarantor. See, *eg*, Germany–Egypt BIT (2007) art 6: '[...] The latter Contracting State shall also recognize the subrogation of the former Contracting State to any such right or claim (assigned claims) which that Contracting State shall be entitled to assert to the same extents as its predecessor in title.'

how such a sole burden of proof is compatible with the principles of fair trial and procedural equality of parties. One could refer to general principles of international law on the burden of proof, as they have found expression, inter alia, in the case law of the ICJ. For such comparable cases, the ICJ in the *Corfu Channel* case has proposed the easing of the burden of proof:

> [...] the fact of this exclusive territorial control exercised by a state within its frontiers has a bearing upon the methods of proof available to establish the knowledge of that state as to such events. By reason of this exclusive control [...], the victim of a breach of international law, is often unable to furnish direct proof of facts giving rise to responsibility. Such a [victim] should be allowed a more liberal recourse to inferences of fact and circumstantial evidence.[122]

Also, domestic courts, such as the German Federal Constitutional Court in a constitutional complaint relating to civilian casualties of a NATO air raid on a bridge in the Serbian town of Varvarin during the Kosovo War, are in favour of easing the burden of proof:

> [...] that the party who is not charged with the burden of proof may impose a so-called *secondary burden* of proof if the party required to provide proof is outside the course of events which it is obliged to present and has no further knowledge of the relevant facts, whereas the respondent has those facts and can reasonably be expected to provide further details.[123]

Prerequisite for such *prima facie* evidence to be sufficient is, therefore, that, on the one hand, the information in question must be inaccessible to the claimant and, on the other hand, under the exclusive control of the respondent state. Indeed, the constellations presented here are characterised precisely by the fact that it is often almost impossible to reconstruct the exact facts of revolutionary upheavals and armed conflicts which brings to mind the 'fog of war.' The essentially decision-relevant circumstances lie almost exclusively within the state's sphere of power. The respondent state has sovereignty over the sensitive, often confidential information of the state forces' actions, which, in case of doubt, are not accessible to the public. Moreover, the respondent state would, in any

---

122 *Corfu Channel (UK v Albania)* (Merits) [1949] ICJ Rep 18.
123 *Bridge of Varvarin* [2013] Case no 2 BvR 2660/06, para 64 (German Federal Constitutional Court) (translation by the author).

event, have no incentive to make this information available to the claimant, *ie* the investor. Finally, extended war clauses usually contain a wording that the 'destruction of its investment [...] was *not* required by the necessity of the situation [...].' This forces the claimant to prove a *negative* which raises the question of how this is compatible with the basic procedural principle that 'the burden of proof lies upon him who affirms, not him who denies'.[124]

For reasons of procedural equality of parties, therefore, it follows that in such a constellation that *prima facie* evidence for the plaintiff investor must suffice. The respondent state can then, in turn, counter with its own (secondary) evidence as to why the destruction of the investor's property was necessary for reasons of the 'necessity of the situation.' If the respondent state does not present sufficient evidence, the tribunal, if necessary, 'may be prepared to draw appropriate inferences from the respondent's apparent non-production of documents' under these circumstances.[125]

5   Conclusion

In a decentralised system such as public international law with its many specialised subfields, the question of how to conceptualize the relationship and interplay of its distinct subfields becomes especially salient. Moreover, this question becomes even more acute when these subfields simultaneously claim authority and possibly arrive at quite different, if not conflicting, results. When revolutionary upheavals culminate in civil war, and in the course of a non-international armed conflict, a foreign investor's production site is destroyed by government forces, this may be the very question which needs to be answered. Under international investment law, on the one hand, such a situation may lead to a breach of a BIT – under international humanitarian law of non-international armed conflicts, however, if the destruction was authorised by 'military necessity', on the other hand, this state action must be regarded as lawful.

Though, in principle, both legal regimes are applicable in a such a situation, the assumption of a normative conflict, as this contribution shows, seems premature: While humanitarian law authorizes the state to use force to destroy

---

124 Or '*ei incumbit probatio qui dicit non qui negat.*'
125 *Feldman v Mexico*, ICSID Case no ARB(AF)/99/1, Award (16 December 2002) para 178; *Methanex v USA* (n 97) pt II ch C para 24, ch G para 25; *Rumeli Telekom AS and Telsim Mobil Telekomunikasyon Hizmetleri AS v Kazakhstan*, ICSID Case no ARB/05/16, Award (29 July 2008) paras 709 et seq; *Gujarat State Petroleum Corp Ltd et al v Yemen and the Yemeni Ministry of Oil and Minerals*, ICC Case no 19299/MCP, Final Award (10 July 2015) para 102.

property in accordance with its specific rules, it does not necessarily oblige the state to do so. Therefore, there may indeed be a normative overlap here, but not necessarily a normative conflict in a strict legal sense. Moreover, it also seems questionable for convincing reasons whether the principle of *lex specialis* is at all suitable for resolving potential normative conflicts between international law's different specialised subfields. As a consequence, an informative approach whereby specific assessments of humanitarian law could, possibly, be used to *inform* the interpretation of BIT norms and vice versa seems preferable overall.

The extended war clauses of investment treaties offer compensation for investments demonstrably destroyed by state organs in cases in which the destruction was not required by the 'necessity of the situation'. If this term is understood in light of humanitarian law's 'military necessity' and the specific rules of customary international law applicable in non-international armed conflicts, a militarily necessary destruction of an investor's property, which is lawful under international humanitarian law, would not render the state liable for compensation under international investment law. The better arguments, as this contribution shows, however, speak in favour of an *autonomous* treaty interpretation of the 'necessity of the situation' on its own terms and not exclusively from a purely military perspective. The wording shows, inter alia, that destroyed investments are not entirely considered to be a case of 'collateral damages' in armed conflicts, for which investors are usually neither responsible nor the cause, and, therefore, indicates that a possible compensation under certain conditions then goes just beyond and supersedes the assessments of customary international law.

Yet, the fact remains, that both subfields – international investment law and international humanitarian law – are applicable in parallel. This does, however, not change the obligation to decide on the legality of state actions in those institutions of the respective subfield. An arbitral investment tribunal must decide the question of compensation submitted to it, while the question of legality under humanitarian law must be addressed by the bodies of humanitarian law.

Finally, for reasons of fair trial and procedural equality of parties, *prima facie* evidence of attributability and causality for the claimant, *ie* the investor, is to be considered sufficient, if and because the essentially decision-relevant circumstances in question lie almost exclusively within the respondent state's sphere of power and are, in addition, under its exclusive control. The respondent state can then, in turn, counter with its own secondary evidence as to why the destruction of the investor's property was necessary for reasons of 'necessity of the situation.'

Note on the Text

The author would like to thank the American University in Cairo, Egypt, for inviting him as a visiting research scholar, and is grateful to the Fritz Thyssen Stiftung, Cologne, Germany, for its support of his research. The author's views are strictly his own.

Bibliography

'Egypt has faced $14 bn worth of cases from investors since 2011' (*Ahram Online*, 22 April 2014) <http://english.ahram.org.eg/NewsContent/3/12/99606/Business/Economy/Egypt-has-faced--bn-worth-of-cases-from-investors-.aspx> accessed 19 January 2020.

Ackermann, T 'The ILC Draft Articles on the Effects of Armed Conflicts on Treaties: Room for Termination or Suspension of Bilateral Investment Treaties?' (2016) Minerva Center for the Rule of Law under Extreme Conditions Working Paper <http://minervaextremelaw.haifa.ac.il/images/Ackermann_Armed_Conflicts_and_BITs_Minerva_Working_Paper.pdf> accessed 19 January 2020.

Alvarez JE and T Brink, 'Revisiting the Necessity Defense: Continental Casualty v. Argentina' in KP Sauvant (ed), *Yearbook on International Investment Law & Policy 2010–2011* (OUP 2012).

Armitage D, *Civil Wars: A History in Ideas* (Knopf 2017).

Barr J, *A Line in the Sand: Britain, France and the Struggle That Shaped the Middle East* (Simon & Schuster 2011).

Bellal A, *The War Report: Armed Conflict in 2018* (The Geneva Academy of International Humanitarian Law and Human Rights 2019) <www.geneva-academy.ch/joomlatools-files/docman-files/The%20War%20Report%202018.pdf> accessed 19 January 2020.

Boisson de Chazournes L, 'Plurality in the Fabric of International Courts and Tribunals: The Threads of a Managerial Approach' (2017) 27 EJIL 13.

Brilmayer L and G Chepiga, 'Ownership or Use? Civilian Property Interests in International Humanitarian Law' (2008) Harv Int'l LJ 413.

Brownlie I, *System of the Law of Nations: State Responsibility, Part I* (OUP 1986).

Burke-White WW and von Staden A, 'Investment Protection in Extraordinary Times: The Interpretation and Application of Non-Precluded Measure Provisions in Bilateral Investment Treaties' (2008) 48 Va J Int'l L 307.

Burke-White WW, 'Inter-Relationships between the Investment Law and Other International Legal Regimes' (2015) E15 Task Force on Investment Policy Think Piece

<http://e15initiative.org/wp-content/uploads/2015/09/E15-Investment-Burke-White-FINAL.pdf> accessed 19 January 2020.

von Clausewitz C, *On War* (first published in German 1832, N Trübner 1873).

Crawford E, 'Road to Nowhere? The Future for a Declaration on Fundamental Standards of Humanity' (2012) 3 J Int'l Human Legal Stud 43.

Crawford J, 'Revising the Draft Articles on State Responsibility' (1999) 10 EJIL 435.

Feuer SJ and Valensi C, 'Arab Spring 2.0? Making Sense of the Protests Sweeping the Region' (1 December 2019) Institute for National Security Studies Insight no 1235 <www.inss.org.il/publication/arab-spring-2-0-making-sense-of-the-protests-sweeping-the-region/> accessed 19 January 2020.

Fromkin D, *A Peace to End All Peace: The Fall of the Ottoman Empire and the Creation of the Modern Middle East* (20th ed, Macmillan 2009).

Greenwood C, 'Unity and Diversity in International Law' in M Andenas and E Bjorge (eds), *A Farewell to Fragmentation: Reassertion and Convergence in International Law* (CUP 2015).

Hayashi N, 'Contextualizing Military Necessity' (2013) 27 Emory Int'l L Rev 190.

Hayashi N, 'Requirements of Military Necessity in International Humanitarian Law and International Criminal Law' (2010) 28 Boston U Int'l LJ 39.

Henckaerts J-M and L Doswald-Beck, *Customary International Humanitarian Law*, vol 1 (ICRC and CUP 2005).

Henckaerts J-M and L Doswald-Beck, *Customary International Humanitarian Law*, vol 2 (ICRC and CUP 2005).

Hernández GI, 'Book Symposium Investment Law: The Interaction between Investment Law and the Law of Armed Conflict in the Interpretation of Full Protection and Security Clauses' (*Opinio Juris*, 2 October 2013) <http://opiniojuris.org/2013/10/02/book-symposium-investment-law-interaction-investment-law-law-armed-conflict-interpretation-full-protection-security-clauses/> accessed 19 January 2020.

Hernández GI, 'The Interaction between Investment Law and the Law of Armed Conflict' in Freya Baetens, *Investment Law within International Law* (CUP 2013).

Karam F and C Zaki, 'How Did Wars Dampen Trade in the MENA Region?' (2016) 48 Applied Economics 5909.

Kolb R, *International Humanitarian Law* (Cheltenham 2014).

Koskenniemi M and P Leino, 'Fragmentation of International Law? Postmodern Anxieties' (2002) 15 LJIL 553.

Kulick A, 'Narrating Narratives of International Investment Law: History and Epistemic Forces' in SW Schill, CJ Tams, and R Hofmann (eds), *Investment Law and History* (Edward Elgar 2018).

Lynch M, 'New Arab World Order' (*Foreign Affairs*, 16 August 2018) <www.foreignaffairs.com/articles/middle-east/2018-08-13/new-arab-order> accessed 19 January 2020.

Lynch M, 'Obama's 'Arab Spring'?' (*Foreign Policy*, 6 January 2011) <http://foreignpolicy.com/2011/01/06/obamas-arab-spring/> accessed 19 January 2020.

Lynch M, *The New Arab Wars: Uprisings and Anarchy in the Middle East* (Public Affairs 2016).

Mayorga O, 'Arbitrating War: Military Necessity as a Defense to the Breach of Investment Treaty Obligations' (2013) Harvard Program on Humanitarian Policy and Conflict Research Policy Brief <http://hpcrresearch.org/sites/default/files/publications/081213%20ARBITRATING%20WAR%20%28final%29.pdf> accessed 19 January 2020.

McLachlan C, 'Investment Treaties and General International Law' (2008) 58 ICLQ 361.

Milanovic M, 'A Norm Conflict Perspective on the Relationship between International Humanitarian Law and Human Rights Law' (2010) 15 J Confl & Sec L 459.

Morris D, 'Revolutionary Movements and *De Facto* Governments – Implications of the "Arab Spring" for International Investors' (2012) 28 Arb Int'l 721.

Muasher M, 'Is this the Arab Spring 2.0?' (*Carnegie*, 30 October 2019) <https://carnegieendowment.org/2019/10/30/is-this-arab-spring-2.0-pub-80220> accessed 19 January 2020.

Noury V, 'North African Revolution: Counting the Cost', *African Business* (April 2011) 46.

Paddeu F, *Justification and Excuse in International Law: Concept and Theory of General Defences* (CUP 2018).

Paparinskis M, 'Investment Arbitration and the Law of Countermeasures' (2008) Brit YB Int'l L 264.

Pauwelyn J and R Michaels, 'Conflict of Norms or Conflict of Laws? Different Techniques in the Fragmentation of Public International Law' (2012) 22 Duke J Int'l & Comp L 349.

Pauwelyn J, *Conflict of Norms in Public International Law: How WTO Law Relates to Other Rules of International Law* (CUP 2003).

Rodenhäuser T, 'Fundamental Standards of Humanity: How International Law Regulates Internal Strife' (2013) JILPAC 121.

Ryk-Lakhman I, 'Foreign Investments as Non-Human Targets' in B Baade, L Mührel and AO Petrov (eds), *International Humanitarian Law in Areas of Limited Statehood: Adaptable and Legitimate or Rigid and Unreasonable?* (Nomos 2018).

Sassóli M, *International Humanitarian Law* (Edward Elgar 2019).

Schill SW, *The Multilateralization of International Investment Law* (CUP 2009).

Schreuer C and U Kriebaum, 'From Individual to Community Interest in International Investment Law' in U Fastenrath and others (eds), *From Bilateralism to Community Interest: Essays in Honour of Bruno Simma* (OUP 2011).

Schreuer C, 'Shareholder Protection in International Investment Law' in PM Dupuy and others (eds), *Common Values in International Law: Festschrift Christian Tomuschat* (Engel 2006).

Schreuer C, 'The Protection of Investments in Armed Conflict' in F Baetens (ed), *Investment Law within International Law* (CUP 2013).

Schreuer C, 'War and Peace in International Investment Law' in K Fach Gómez, C Titi, and A Gourgourinis (eds), *International Investment Law and the Law of Armed Conflict* (Springer 2019).

Simma B and D Pulkowski, 'Of Planets and the Universe: Self-contained Regimes in International Law' (2006) 17 EJIL 483.

St John T, *The Rise of Investor-State Arbitration: Politics, Law, and Unintended Consequences* (OUP 2018).

Villiger ME, *Customary International Law and Treaties: A Manual on the Theory and Practice of the Interrelation of Sources* (Springer 1997).

Zrilič J, 'Armed Conflict as Force Majeure in International Investment Law' (2019) 16 Manchester J Int'l Econ L 28.

CHAPTER 2

The Genealogy of Extended War Clauses: Requisition and Destruction of Property in Armed Conflicts

Ira Ryk-Lakhman

1   Introduction

This chapter focuses on the treatment of foreign investors in case their investments suffer losses owing to armed conflict.[1] Specifically, the chapter looks into the treaty obligation to compensate investors for the requisition or destruction of their property during hostilities.

Many investment instruments, including the instruments of conflict-ridden states contain explicit stipulations that prescribe a right to compensation under circumstances of 'war'.[2] One type of these 'war clauses' merely requires non-discrimination in the treatment of losses incurred as a result of the armed conflict and similar situations.[3] The other type of provisions – which is the focus of this chapter – goes further and mandates the payment of compensation to investors for losses resulting from hostilities provided that certain conditions are met.

Typically, these clauses enumerate a list of situations using ascertainable expressions, such as war, armed conflict, revolution, revolt, insurrection, or riot. Alongside this list, some provisions use more open-ended terms, such as 'a state of national emergency' or 'like situations'.[4] Such language indicates that the list of events covered by the clause is not exhaustive, thereby covering not only inter-state conflicts or other modern forms of hostilities, such

---

1   Aware of the conceptual, practical, and terminological differences between these concepts, for the purposes of convenience alone the terms 'armed conflict', 'hostilities', and 'war' are mostly used interchangeably in this chapter.
2   As of March 2020, according to publicly available information approximately 1,000 instruments contain such clauses.
3   This chapter is not concerned with the non-discrimination obligation of the war clause. For an analysis of scholarship and arbitral practice of this provision and its origins, see Facundo Perez-Aznar, 'Investment Protection in Exceptional Situations: Compensation-for-Losses Clauses in IIAs' (2017) 32 ICSID Review 696.
4   *Eg* Brazil–Ethiopia BIT (2018) art 8(1); Kazakhstan–UAE BIT (2018) art 5(1); Singapore–Kazakhstan BIT (2018) art 7.

as non-international armed conflicts.[5] These treaty mechanisms are known as 'extended war clauses' (EWC). For instance, article 9 of the Morocco–Nigeria BIT (2016) reads:

> 1) Investors of one Party whose investments in the territory of the other Party *suffer losses due to war, armed conflict*, revolution, state of national emergency, insurrection, civil disturbances or other similar events, shall be accorded by the latter Party treatment, as regards restitution, indemnification, compensation or other settlement, no less favorable treatment than that which the latter Party accords to its own investors or to investors of a third State.
> 2) Without prejudice to paragraph 1 of this Article, investors of one Party who, in any of the situations referred to in that paragraph suffer losses in the territory of the other Contracting Party resulting from:
>   a) requisitioning of their property by its forces or authorities; or
>   b) destruction of their property by its forces or authorities, which was not caused in combat action or was not required by the necessity of the situation; shall be accorded restitution or adequate compensation.[6]

While such treaty mechanisms are relatively common, they have gained little attention in scholarly and arbitral jurisprudence. And so, many questions concerning the origins, meaning, and scope of this treaty instrument remain. Accordingly, this chapter is concerned with the meaning and scope of the circumstances under which the EWC seems to require the state to compensate the investor for losses owing to armed conflict: 'requisition' of property and destruction 'not required by the necessity of the armed conflict' (and like formulations).[7]

To this end, this chapter adopts a doctrinal approach that seeks to ascertain the meaning and content of this international norm by way of using the methodology of sources[8] and interpretation. Hence, the meaning of treaty rules is

---

5   This chapter is concerned with the treatment of investments during armed conflicts, and therefore it does not address the question of whether, absent an explicit stipulation to that effect, the war clause extends to economic crises.
6   Morocco–Nigeria BIT (signed 3 December 2016, not yet in force) art 9 (emphasis added).
7   This chapter does not deal with the meaning of the standard 'adequate compensation' under the EWC, which far exceeds the scope of this discussion. See, *eg*, Diane Desierto, 'The Outer Limits of Adequate Reparations for Breaches of Non-Expropriation Investment Treaty Provisions: Choice and Proportionality in *Chorzów*' (2017) 55 Colum J Transnat'l L 395.
8   The sources of international law are generally considered to be listed in article 38 of the Statute of the International Court of Justice (1945) 1 UNTS xvi.

determined by way of applying rules on treaty interpretation, which are codified in the Vienna Convention on the Law of Treaties (VCLT).[9] The content of customary norms is ascertained by way of examining state practice and *opinio juris*.[10] The reasoning and conclusions that follow from the analysis of treaties and customs are then checked and verified against the decisions of international courts and tribunals, domestic instances, and contemporaneous authorities.

Within the boundaries of the traditional rules of sources and interpretation, the discussion is also assisted by historical analysis. The premise here is that law is imbued with a meaning and a function only when placed in its context, and only by looking at the temporal context can it be determined what the relevant actors understood the law to mean at various times in the past.[11] Historical context also offers a better understanding of the political, socio-cultural, and economic conditions under which particular ideas, such as the protection of 'aliens' and their property during 'war' from 'destruction' and 'requisition', became conceivable as legal concepts that yield certain rights and obligations. Importantly, a careful assessment of the development of international law allows us to identify continuities and discontinuities in the perception and application of the law and thus, to identify the emergence of binding norms on the treatment of investments in armed conflict.[12]

The chapter proceeds as follows. Section 2 briefly outlines the rules of international humanitarian law (IHL), the field of international law that

---

9 Vienna Convention on the Law of Treaties (1969) 1155 UNTS 33 (VCLT). For authorities that recognized and applied the VCLT as a reflection of customary law, see *Legal Consequences for States of the Continued Presence of South Africa in Namibia (South West Africa) notwithstanding Security Council Resolution 276 (1970)* (Advisory Opinion) [1971] ICJ Rep 16, para 94; *Fisheries Jurisdiction (Germany v Iceland)* (Jurisdiction) [1973] ICJ Rep 49, paras 24 et seq; *Kasikili/Sedudu Island (Botswana v Namibia)* [1999] ICJ Rep 1045, para 18.

10 On this point, the chapter takes note and makes use of the works of the International Law Association (ILA) and the International Law Commission (ILC), *ie* Committee on the Formation of Customary (General) International Law, 'Final Report of the Committee: Statement of Principles Applicable to the Formation of General Customary International Law' (200) 69 ILA Rep Conf 712; ILC, 'Draft Conclusions on Identification of Customary International Law with Commentaries' (2018) UN Doc A/73/10 at 122.

11 Marcus M Payk, 'The History of International Law – or International Law in History? A Reply to Alexandra Kemmerer and Jochen von Bernstorff' (*EJIL:Talk!* 8 January 2015) <www.ejiltalk.org/the-history-of-international-law-or-international-law-in-history-a-reply-to-alexandra-kemmerer-and-jochen-von-bernstorff/> accessed 13 April 2020; Kate Miles, 'History and International Law: Method and Mechanism – Empire and "Usual" Rupture' in Stephan W Schill, Christian J Tams, and Rainer Hofmann (eds) *International Investment Law and History* (Edward Elgar 2018) 139 et seq.

12 Heather L Bray, 'Understanding Change: Evolution from International Claims Commissions to Investment Treaty Arbitration' in ibid 105 et seq.

regulates the conduct of hostilities, on the treatment of private property during situations of armed conflict. The section establishes that during the twentieth century several rules on the treatment of private property during war attained customary status. Namely, that appropriation of private property is lawful only if it is required by military necessity and against compensation and destruction of private property is prohibited unless when exceptionally allowed due to military necessity. Section 3 then demonstrates how these customary rules on the conduct of hostilities infiltrated the law on state responsibility for losses to alien property during war, and shaped and informed the content of the customary standard of treatment of aliens and their property in war.

Using the inferences from the analyses in sections 2 and 3, section 4 hones in on the language of the EWC. The starting point of this analysis, pursuant to the provisions of the VCLT, is the ordinary meaning of the provision. It is suggested that under article 31(1) VCLT, the ordinary meaning of the language of the EWC ('destruction not required by the necessity of the situation' and 'requisition by the armed forces') makes a reference to customary law on the treatment of alien property in wartime (section 4.1). Then, a different interpretive route to an arguably similar outcome is considered. Here, the analysis considers the implications of introducing customary war law rules on the appropriation and destruction of property as 'relevant rules of international law' that contextualize the ordinary meaning of the EWC pursuant to article 31(3)(c) VCLT (section 4.2). Next, the analysis examines whether it may be said that the treaty language 'destruction not required by the necessity of war' and 'requisition by the armed forces' has a special meaning (pursuant to article 31(4) VCLT) that departs from the IHL meaning of these terms (section 4.3). The interpretive analysis concludes with a discussion of the implications of the suggested IHL-informed interpretation of the EWC (section 4.4).

Overall, this chapter demonstrates that the codification of war law and its rules on the treatment of private property in the early twentieth century facilitated a progressive development in international law that resulted in the emergence of a set of specific rules on state responsibility for damage to private foreign property during war. It is also argued that these rules are effectively incorporated into the modern treaty language of EWC, since pursuant to the VCLT, the language 'requisition by forces and authorities' and 'destruction not required by the necessity of the situation' are terms of art that make a reference to customary law. Therefore, the meaning of the treaty rule in the EWC is ascertained through the content of the customary norms on requisition and destruction of foreign private property in wartime. This chapter also suggests that such an IHL-informed meaning of the EWC brings further clarity to practical, contested aspects of the provision, namely the burden of proof and the threshold of invocation of the EWC.

2   The Hague Law Rules on Appropriation and Destruction of Property in War

This section deals with customary war law standards on the treatment of property, focusing namely on the qualifications on lawful appropriation of property and the prohibition on destruction of property.

Traditionally, under war law the belligerents were entitled to exercise any measures, including dispossession and destruction, against enemy property.[13] Over time, however, the ability to arbitrarily appropriate spoils of war made way for the obligation of belligerents to protect enemy property in their territory.[14] The change in the perceptions of private property may be attributed to the codification of war law during the peace conferences at The Hague in 1899 and 1907, where state delegates sought to ascertain and codify the rules of warfare. The Hague conferences resulted in the adoption of a body of laws that deal with the conduct of hostilities and which establish restrictions on the means and methods of warfare, collectively known as the Hague Conventions and Regulations[15] or the 'Hague Law'.

The Hague Law codified the notion that the destruction or appropriation of enemy property is subject to qualifications and that such measures must not be adopted as means of injuring the enemy, unless military necessity so requires. Illustratively, requisition under the Hague Regulations is a formal authoritative demand in belligerent occupation for the temporary or permanent use of movable or immovable property or services, in return to compensation.[16] The right to requisition is secondary to the primary duty of the occupying power, which is ensuring the survival, safety, health, or wellbeing of the occupied

---

13   Edwin M Borchard, 'Private Pecuniary Claims Arising Out of War' (1915) 9 AJIL 113, 120; Edwin M Borchard, *The Diplomatic Protection of Citizens Abroad: or the Law of International Claims* (Banks Law Publishing 1916) 253.

14   See, generally, Edwin M Borchard, 'Are We Entitled to Confiscate Enemy Private Property?' (1923) 23 Colum L Rev 383; Philip C Jessup, 'Enemy Property' (1955) 49 AJIL 57.

15   Hague Convention (IV) Respecting the Laws and Customs of War on Land and Its Annex: Regulations Concerning the Laws and Customs of War on Land (adopted 18 October 1907, entered into force 26 January 1910) 205 CTS 277 (HC IV and Hague Regulations, respectively).

16   Hague Regulations arts 52 et seq.

population.[17] Accordingly, customary law, as reflected in the 1907 Hague Regulations,[18] mandates immediate cash payments against requisition or the issuance of receipts that will guarantee a payment as soon as possible.[19] As with other forms of property dispossession, the requirement to pay compensation is a condition of the lawfulness of requisition.[20] Hence, 'requisition, though lawful when originally made, becomes unlawful, when after a reasonable time no adequate compensation was paid.'[21]

Aside from requisition (which concerns situations of occupation), IHL recognizes other forms of deprivation of property during hostilities, such as confiscation (the permanent appropriation of certain types of movable property belonging to the enemy, which can be used for military operations, without compensation)[22] and seizure (the temporary taking of state or private immovable or movable property).[23] Customary war law also recognized

---

17 Geneva Convention (IV) Relative to the Protection of Civilian Persons in Time of War (adopted 12 August 1949, entered into force 21 October 1950) (1950) 75 UNTS 287 (GC IV) art 55. For further discussion of occupation and its interaction with the protection of investments, see Kit De Vriese, chapter 10 in this volume.

18 For earlier authorities, see John Bassett Moore, *History and Digest of the International Arbitrations to Which the United States Has Been a Party International Arbitrations*, vol 4 (US Government Printing Office 1898) 3720 et seq; Clyde Eagleton, 'Responsibility for Damages to Persons and Property of Aliens in Undeclared War' (1938) 32 Am Soc'y Int'l L Proc 127, 130.

19 Hague Regulations art 52. See Borchard, 'Private Pecuniary Claims' (n 13) 133 et seq; Michael Bothe, 'Expert Opinion: Limits of the Right of Expropriation (Requisition) and of Movement Restrictions in Occupied Territory' (2 August 2012), <www.diakonia.se/globalassets/blocks-ihl-site/ihl-file-list/ihl--expert-opionions/limits-of-the-right-of-expropriation-requisition-and-of-movement-restrictions-in-occupied-territory.-dr.-iur.-prof-michael-bothe.pdf> accessed 13 April 2020; Jean-Marie Henckaerts and Louise Doswald-Beck, Customary International Humanitarian Law, vol 1 (CUP 2005), rule 51. See also Australia, *Law of Armed Conflict: Commander's Guide* (Australian Defence Force Publication 1994), § 610, cited by Jean-Marie Henckaerts and Louise Doswald-Beck, Customary International Humanitarian Law, vol 2 (CUP 2005) 1047. The most updated version of the International Committee of the Red Cross's study on the rules and practice of customary IHL is available at <https://ihl-databases.icrc.org/customary-ihl/eng/docs/home> (accessed 20 January 2020).

20 Arnold McNair, 'The Seizure of Property and Enterprises in Indonesia' (1959) 6 Netherlands J Int'l L 218, 250.

21 ibid.

22 Henckaerts and Doswald-Beck (n 19) rule 51.

23 *Loss of Property in Ethiopia Owned by Non-Residents – Eritrea's Claim 24 (Ethiopia v Eritrea)*, Eritrea–Ethiopia Claims Commission, Partial Award (19 December 2005) 26 RIAA 429, paras 21 et seq.

sequestration[24] and angary,[25] but these forms of appropriation are no longer mentioned in contemporary military manuals or in post-1977 sub-sets of IHL.[26]

Further, subject to certain conditions, property may be lawfully and deliberately destroyed during hostilities. Article 23(g) of the Hague Regulations, which reflects customary law,[27] prohibits the destruction of the enemy's property, 'unless such destruction be imperatively demanded by the necessities of war.' 'Destruction' denotes certain *conduct*, such as burning houses or 'setting ablaze, demolishing, or otherwise damaging property',[28] but it does not require a particular *result*, such as the complete shattering of property. It is accepted that 'badly damaged property may be akin to partial destruction', which qualifies as 'destruction'.[29] The phrase 'imperatively demanded by the necessities of war', in turn, is an exceptional language that modifies the content of the humanitarian rule on the protection of property to which it is attached.[30] In other words, article 23(g) of the Hague Regulations is a rule on the protection

---

24 'Sequestration' is the temporary use or taking of private *enemy* property in order to prevent it from being used against the sequestering state during hostilities. See Thomas Kleinlein, 'Sequestration', *Max Planck Encyclopedia of Public International Law* (2010) paras 1 et seq <https://opil.ouplaw.com/home/MPIL> accessed 10 June 2018.

25 'Angary' is the right of the belligerent to requisition certain *neutral* property for his own usage, subject to 'exceptional' military necessities, and in return for compensation. See Borchard, 'Private Pecuniary Claims' (n 13) 119, 122, 133.

26 The authority of the belligerent to take such measures still exists, it is however flanked by more modern conducts. See Jean-Marie Henckaerts and Louise Doswald-Beck, Customary International Humanitarian Law, vol 2 (n 19) 1029 et seq (practice relating to rule 51). See also International and Operational Law Department, The Judge Advocate General's Legal Center & School, *Operational Law Handbook* (17th edn, US Army 2017), ch 2, appendix B and the references to other modern manuals therein.

27 See Henckaerts and Doswald-Beck (n 19) rule 50.

28 *Prosecutor v Mbarushimana* (Decision on the Confirmation of Charges) ICC-01/04-01/10 (16 December 2011) para 174. See also *Prosecutor v Mudacumura* (Decision on the Prosecutor's Application under Article 58) ICC-01/04-01/12 (13 July 2012) paras 51 et seq; *Prosecutor v Katanga* (Judgment pursuant to article 74 of the Statute) ICC-01/04-01/07 (7 March 2014), paras 917 et seq and 924; *Prosecutor v Ntaganda* (Decision Pursuant to Article 61(7)(a) and (b) of the Rome Statute on the Charges of the Prosecutor Against Bosco Ntaganda), ICC-01/04-02/06 (9 June 2014) paras 72 et seq.

29 *Prosecutor v Katanga* (n 28) para 891.

30 See, for other examples using the language 'imperative necessities', 'urgent military necessity', and 'not justified by military necessity', respectively, Geneva Convention (I) for the Amelioration of the Condition of the Wounded and Sick in Armed Forces in the Field (adopted 12 August 1949, entered into force 21 October 1950) 75 UNTS 31 (GC I) arts 8, 33 et seq, and 50; Geneva Convention (II) for the Amelioration of the Condition of the Wounded, Sick and Shipwrecked Members of the Armed Forces at Sea (adopted 12 August 1949, entered into force 21 October 1950) 75 UNTS 85 (GC II) arts 8, 28, and 51; Geneva Convention (III) Relative to the Treatment of Prisoners of War (adopted 12 August 1949,

of property that also prescribes the conditions for its exemption.[31] It is neither a permission to destruct property nor is it a justification or an excuse for an unlawful destruction of property.[32]

As regards the conduct that may be construed as required by 'the necessity of war', it is not limited to measures that are required to secure the submission of the enemy;[33] the notion is rather broad. For instance, in the *William Hardman* case, the Anglo-American Tribunal held that the measures taken by the American force for the maintenance of its sanitary conditions constituted military necessity. Thus, the destruction of private foreign property was allowed and no compensation was due.[34] In *Hostage*, as another example, the Military Tribunal held that, 'the destruction of public and private property by retreating military forces which would give aid and comfort to the enemy may constitute a situation coming within the exceptions contained in Article 23(g) [of the Hague Regulations].'[35]

It follows that during the early twentieth century, the customary rules and qualifications to appropriation and destruction of property crystalized in the framework of the codification of the Hague Law. These instruments anchored in treaty language the customary rules whereby appropriation of property is lawful only when it is required by military necessity and against compensation (in the case of requisition) and destruction of property is prohibited; exceptionally destruction, may be permitted for reasons of military necessity.

3 The Customary Standard of Treatment: Appropriation and Destruction of Alien Property in War

This section suggests that during the twentieth century, the Hague Law rules on the treatment of property infiltrated the law on state responsibility for

---

entered into force 21 October 1950) 75 UNTS 135 (GC III) art 126; GC IV arts 49, 53, 143, and 147.

31 Nils Melzer, *Targeted Killing in International Law* (OUP 2008) 287; Nobuo Hayashi 'Requirements of Military Necessity in International Humanitarian Law and International Criminal Law' (2010) 28 BU Int'l LJ 39, 50 et seq; Michael N Schmitt, 'Military Necessity and Humanity in International Humanitarian Law: Preserving the Delicate Balance' (2010) 50 Va J Int'l L 795, 801 et seq.

32 No amount of necessity can justify or excuse what is otherwise unlawful under IHL. See *In re Rauter* [1949] 16 ILR 526, 543 (Special Court of Cassation, The Hague); Melzer (n 31) 279 et seq; Hayashi (n 31) 52; Yoram Dinstein, *The Conduct of Hostilities under the Law of International Armed Conflict* (2nd edn, CUP 2010) 18; Schmitt (n 31) 798.

33 APV Rogers, *Law on the Battlefield* (3rd edn, MUP 2012) 4–6; Hayashi (n 31) 60.

34 *William Hardman (Great Britain) v US* (1913) 6 RIAA 25, 26.

35 *Hostage Case, United States v List (Wilhelm) and others* (1948) 11 TWC 757.

losses to alien property during war.³⁶ This development occurred in the framework of claims for injuries to, or wrongful seizures of, private foreign property by revolutionists during civil unrest and by armed forces during the World Wars. In turn, this progressive development resulted in the emergence of a set of specific customary rules on state responsibility for damage to private foreign property in war. And so, only eight years after the adoption of 1907 Hague Conventions and Regulations, Borchard observed that 'a long course of practice and The Hague Regulations have given some authority to certain rules for the treatment of alien property in the country of the territorial sovereign'.³⁷

American practice is illustrative. Following the Spanish–American War, the US Court of Claims and US Supreme Court repeatedly addressed the legal status of American property in Cuba, holding that the 'property of citizens of the United States in Cuba was during the war with Spain to be regarded as enemy property subject to the laws of war, and to be destroyed whenever military necessity so demanded.'³⁸ During the 1920s and 1930s, the policy of the State Department with respect to international claims on behalf of its nationals was that 'war damages which are caused in due course in the conduct of hostilities do not ordinarily form the basis for international reclamation.'³⁹ What was considered as 'due course in the conduct of hostilities' was 'determinable by reference chiefly' to war law.⁴⁰ Similarly, Borchard explained in 1915 that 'no compensation is due to private individuals, on account of injuries to their persons or property, resulting from legitimate acts of war.'⁴¹ As for 'what is a legitimate act of war', it is answered by reference to 'The Hague Regulations, and the instructions issued by national to their own armies.'⁴²

In 1923, as another example, the US contended before a British–US Arbitral Tribunal that it was entitled to treat a British-owned property 'as having the character of enemy property', and insofar as its destruction 'was a necessity of war [it gave] rise to no obligation to make compensation'.⁴³ The Tribunal

---

36 Borchard, *Diplomatic Protection* (n 13) 246.
37 Borchard, 'Private Pecuniary Claims' (n 13) 117, 128.
38 The same was held with respect to the treatment of Spanish property in the US. Eg *Juragua Iron Co, Ltd v USA*, 212 US 297, 306, 308 et seq (1909); *Diaz v USA*, 222 US 574 (1912); *Herrera v United States*, 222 US 558 (1912).
39 Letter from the Legal Adviser of the Department of State (Green Haywood Hackworth) to Albion W Johnson (7 June 1937), cited in Green Haywood Hackworth, *Digest of International Law*, vol 5 (US Government Printing Office 1943) 684.
40 ibid.
41 Borchard, 'Private Pecuniary Claims' (n 13) 123.
42 ibid.
43 *Eastern Extension, Australasia and China Telegraph Co, Ltd (Great Britain) v USA* (1923) 6 RIAA 112, 114.

agreed and maintained that British property was 'subject to destruction without compensation in case of necessity of war.'[44] The Tribunal also explained that requisition of foreign property in wartime for certain purposes is a right of the belligerent; this right is 'not absolute but limited, and is in reality only itself acquired in consideration of the payment of compensation.'[45]

Along a similar line, international fora that were established during the twentieth century to hear claims for the interferences with private foreign property during hostilities, such as the Netherlands–Venezuela,[46] the US–Venezuela,[47] and the US–Germany Mixed Claims Commissions,[48] as well as the Spanish Treaty Claims Commission,[49] the Nicaraguan Mixed Claims Commission,[50] the American–Turkish Claims Settlement,[51] and Max Huber in the *Spanish Zone of Morocco* case,[52] all assumed that the destruction and appropriation of private foreign property were lawful only subject to the qualifications of military necessity and the limitations of customary war law.[53]

Codification attempts that were made by the League of Nations also evince the relationship between the Hague Law and the protection of foreign property abroad.[54] Illustratively,[55] Basis 21 of the 1930 Hague Codification Conference was formulated based on the positions of the participating states regarding

---

44 ibid 116.
45 ibid 115.
46 *Eg Bembelista Case (Netherlands/Venezuela)* (1903) 10 RIAA 717.
47 *Eg American Electric and Manufacturing Co (Concession)*, US–Venezuela Mixed Claims Commission (1903) 9 RIAA 306.
48 *Eg Administrative Decision No VII (The Vinland Case)*, US–Germany Mixed Claims Commission (25 May 1925) 7 RIAA 203, 248.
49 See US Government, *Final Report of the Spanish Treaty Claims Commission* (US Government Printing Office 1910) 10 et seq.
50 See Otto Schoenrich, 'The Nicaraguan Mixed Claims Commission' (1915) 9 AJIL 859.
51 Fred K Nielsen, *American-Turkish Claims Settlement: Opinions and Report* (US Government Printing Office 1937) 154 et seq, 174 et seq.
52 *Spanish Zone of Morocco (Great Britain v Spain)* (1925) 2 RIAA 615, 645.
53 Borchard, *Diplomatic Protection* (n 13) 255.
54 League of Nations Committee of Experts for the Progressive Codification of International law, 'Questionnaire No. 4 adopted by the Committee at its Second Session, held in January 1926: Responsibility of States for Damage Done in Their Territories to the Person or Property of Foreigners', reported in (1926) 20 AJIL Spec Sup 176. While the works and conclusions of this Subcommittee were widely criticized, this part was welcomed. See Edwin M Borchard, 'Responsibility of States for Damage Done in their Territories to the Person or Property of Foreigners' (1926) 20 AJIL 738, 744 et seq.
55 See, likewise, Institut de Droit International, 'Responsabilité internationale des Etats à raison des dommages causés sur leur territoire à la personne et aux biens des étrangers' (Lausanne 1927) art 7 <www.idi-iil.org/app/uploads/2017/06/1927_lau_05_fr.pdf> accessed 13 April 2020.

the instances when the state is under an obligation to compensate aliens for losses to their property owing to various forms of hostilities. From these responses, the Codification Commission distilled a consensus over the standard of treatment of private foreign property in war and the consequences of its violations.[56] Basis 21 reads:

> A State is not responsible for damage caused to the person or property of a foreigner by its armed forces or authorities [...]. The State must, however:
> (1) Make good damage to foreigners by the requisitioning [...] their property by its armed forces or authorities;
> (2) Make good damage caused to foreigners by destruction of property by its armed forces or authorities, or by their orders, unless such destruction is the direct consequence of combat acts;
> (3) Make good damage caused to foreigners by acts of its armed forces or authorities where such acts manifestly went beyond the requirement of the situation or where its armed forces or authorities behaved in a manner manifestly incompatible with the rules generally observed by civilized States [...].[57]

It should be clarified that the term 'requisition' in the above-cited Basis 21 is used as a shorthand for a taking of private property for military purposes against compensation, and *not* in its strict sense as a formal demand of the occupying force for the use of property or services. A review of the materials from which the language of Basis 21 derives confirms this view[58]

Overall, it is suggested that the cited Basis 21 reflects the governing legal position on the standard of treatment of private foreign property during war and the state's responsibility to compensate for losses to such property. The contemporaneous works of scholars, such as Brochard and Hyde, support this proposition.[59] Also of note here is Eagleton, who handily summarized the customary standard of treatment of alien property during war:

---

56 Shabtai Rosenne (ed) *League of Nations Conference for the Codification of International Law (1930)*, vol 2 (Oceana Publications 1975) 538.

57 ibid 529. See also ibid 526 et seq, especially the positions of Finland, Germany, GB, Hungary, Norway, New Zealand, and Poland.

58 ibid 526 (point IX). Additionally, see the response of GB, which also bound India and New Zealand (ibid 527 et seq), Finland (ibid 527) and Czechoslovakia (ibid 529). See also the Conclusions, Annexed to the Report of M Guerro, Rapporteur of the Committee of Experts for the Progressive Codification of International Law (ibid 252 et seq).

59 Borchard, *Diplomatic Protection* (n 13) 246; Charles Cheney Hyde, *International Law: Chiefly as Interpreted and Applied by the United States*, vol 2 (Little, Brown, and Co 1922) 306 et

The belligerent may requisition, but he must pay for what he takes; he may destroy or damage, but only [...] 'that property which, unless seized or destroyed, presents an obstacle to a military operation or jeopardizes the safety of his troops.' If the belligerent does not observe these principles, he may be held responsible in international law, and may be called upon to make reparation [...].[60]

4 Modern Investment Treaties: 'Destruction Not Required by the Necessity of War' and 'Requisition'

This section focuses on the meaning of the EWC. At this point, it is convenient to refer again to the typical language and structure of the EWC using the above example of article 9 of the Morocco–Nigeria BIT (2016):

1) Investors of one Party whose investments in the territory of the other Party suffer losses due to war, armed conflict, revolution, state of national emergency, insurrection, civil disturbances or other similar events [...]
2) [...] resulting from:
    a) requisitioning of their property by its forces or authorities; or
    b) destruction of their property by its forces or authorities, which was not caused in combat action or was not required by the necessity of the situation;
   shall be accorded restitution or adequate compensation.[61]

The cited language ordinarily indicates that such clauses encompass instances when, say, a Moroccan investment in Nigeria suffers losses owing to its destruction by Nigerian forces in the framework of a military operation against the so-called 'Niger Delta Avengers', a militant group that has repeatedly attacked oil-producing facilities in the Niger Delta.[62] This clause also covers the 'requisition' or 'destruction' of, say, a Nigerian investment in Morocco by Moroccan forces during a massive protest in Rabat. A separate question is what do these

---

seq; Edwin M Borchard, 'The Law of Responsibility of States for Damage Done in Their Territory to the Person or Property of Foreigners' (1929) 23 AJIL Spec Supp 131, 167.
60   Eagleton (n 18) 129, citing Hyde (n 59) 306.
61   The following discussion focuses on paragraph 2, while paragraph 1 and the standard of compensation under the EWC are left outside the scope of this chapter.
62   Bello Muhammad, 'Hostilities in Nigeria's Niger Delta Blamed on Government Neglect' (*DW*, 11 July 2017) <www.dw.com/en/hostilities-in-nigerias-niger-delta-blamed-on-government-neglect/a-41270034> accessed 13 April 2020.

concepts of 'destruction' and 'requisition' mean in the context of investment treaties? As this is an interpretive issue, it is resolved by way of applying the customary rules of treaty interpretation, as codified in the VCLT.

Accordingly, this section proceeds in four main steps. The first steps looks at the ordinary meaning of the treaty language 'requisition by the armed forces' and 'destruction not required by military necessity' (and like formulations) in EWCs and suggests that these are technical terms of art with a recognized meaning under IHL, which informs their treaty meaning (section 4.1). Second, the analysis considers war law rules on the appropriation (including destruction) of property as 'relevant rules of international law' that form part of the context against which EWC are interpreted. The analysis suggests that customary rules on the treatment of alien property in war should be taken into account together with the context in the interpretation of the EWC (section 4.2). Then, the analysis asks whether the a 'special meaning shall be given to a terms' of the EWC pursuant to article 31(4) VCLT. It is suggested that there is no evidence to indicate that states award the terms of the EWC a special meaning that depart from IHL (section 4.3). Finally, the conceptual and practical implications of the proposition that the EWC effectively incorporates customary war law rules are addressed (section 4.4).

4.1   A Recognized Meaning of Treaty Terms under Customary War Law: Article 31(1) and (4) VCLT

The first element of the general rule of interpretation under article 31 VCLT requires giving the terms of the treaty an ordinary meaning, *ie*, identifying the 'regular, normal, or customary' use of the term.[63] The idea is that words are interpreted in the technical and professional meaning they have in the particularly relevant community of word-users.[64] Therefore, to ascertain the ordinary meaning of 'requisition' and 'destruction not required by the necessity of armed conflict', under article 31(1) VCLT, the interpreter is required to look not to dictionaries but to the manner in which these phrases were used in 'the

---

[63] Richard K Gardiner, *Treaty Interpretation* (2nd edn, OUP 2015) 183. See also Georg Schwarzenberger, 'Myths and Realities of Treaty Interpretation: Articles 27–29 of the Vienna Draft Convention on the Law of Treaties' (1968) 9 Va J Int'l L 1; Oliver Dörr, 'Article 31' in Oliver Dörr and Kirsten Schmalenbach (eds), *Vienna Convention on the Law of Treaties: A Commentary* (2nd edn, Springer 2018) 581 (para 40).

[64] ILC, 'Draft Articles on the Law of Treaties with Commentaries' (1966) UN Doc A/CN.4/SER.A/1966/Add.1, II YB ILC at 187, 221 (para 12); Thomas W Wälde, 'Interpreting Investment Treaties: Experiences and Examples' in Christina Binder and others (eds), *International Investment Law for the 21st Century: Essays in Honour of Christoph Schreuer* (OUP 2009) 771.

parlance of lawyers'[65] in the particular context of investment treaties, *ie* to the technical meaning of these expressions.

The analysis of state practice, jurisprudence, and doctrine from the previous section, demonstrates that in the first half of the twentieth century, the language 'requisition by the armed forces' and 'destruction not required by the necessity of war' (and like formulations) was used in the context of state responsibility for losses to alien property during war as a reference to customary war law. Post-World War II authorities followed the same practice. The words of the Abs–Shawcross Draft Convention on Investments Abroad may be taken as representative of the prevailing legal position in 1960, whereby 'the generally accepted laws of war delineated the treatment of aliens':[66] First, 'the destruction of or damage to the property of an alien is wrongful, unless it is required by the circumstances of urgent necessity'.[67] Second, 'requisition by the authorities' of foreign property is considered a 'valid exercise of belligerent rights' in return for compensation.[68]

Importantly, as with the language of Basis 21 of the Hague Codification Conference, the term 'requisition' is used in modern investment instruments as a shorthand for appropriation of private property by the state's armed forces during armed conflict for military needs and against compensation. By using the term 'requisition' in investment treaties states do *not* intend to prescribe rules for the taking of investments in occupation specifically.[69] In fact, 'occupation' is not enumerated under a single war clause as one of the 'situations' covered by the provision (eg: 'war, armed conflict, revolution, state of national emergency'). That being so, there is no reason to assume that 'requisition' under the EWC pertains to a situation that is *not* stipulated in the provision, namely occupation, but does *not* pertain to any of the situations that are expressly covered by the provision.

Moreover, a strict IHL-reading of 'requisition', whereby the scope of takings covered by the EWC would be *limited* to situations of occupation

---

65 Gidon Gottlieb, 'The Interpretation of Treaties by Tribunals' (1969) Am Soc'y Int'l Proc 122, 131. See also *Aguas del Tunari v Bolivia*, ICSID Case no ARB/02/3, Decision on Jurisdiction (21 October 2005) para 230; Ulf Linderfalk, *On the Interpretation of Treaties: The Modern International Law as Expressed in the 1969 Vienna Convention on the Law of Treaties* (Springer 2007) 65 et seq.
66 Hermann Abs and Hartley Shawcross, 'Draft Convention on Investments Abroad' (1960) 9 J Pub L 115, 116 et seq (art V).
67 Louis B Sohn and RR Baxter, 'Responsibility of States for Injuries to the Economic Interests of Aliens' (1961) 55 AJIL 545, 551 et seq (art 9).
68 ibid 553 et seq.
69 Hague Regulations arts 46 et seq, 52 et seq, 56; GC IV art 57.

alone, leaves out all other prevalent forms of armed conflict and leads to an absurd outcome that cannot be reconciled with practice. Why would states address the protection of investments in belligerent occupation but not, say, in non-international armed conflicts, the more prevalent type of hostilities? Arguably, some states, such as Israel, might be interested in arranging the regulation of foreign investments in occupied territories, which may explain why a provision on requisition (*sensu stricto*) will appear in their investment treaties. However, this does not explain over 1,000 other treaty mechanisms of states that have no involvement in occupation and no reason to arrange the regulation of dispossession of investments in occupation specifically.[70]

Accordingly, it is argued that the term 'requisition' in the EWC is a technical term with a 'special' meaning in the sense of article 31(4) VCLT,[71] which does not correspond with the ordinary meaning of the term under the *jus in bello*. Although the VCLT does not explain how or where to find the special meaning of a term,[72] it is suggested that article 31(4) VCLT is likely to assume relevance where the 'special meaning' can be derived from materials and circumstances that are extrinsic to the treaty subject matter of interpretation.[73] The above review of the materials of the 1930 Hague Codification Conference and contemporary treaty language reveals the intention of states to give the term 'requisition', in the context of investment protection, a broad meaning that encompasses appropriation of property during armed conflict by the state forces for military needs against compensation.

---

[70] On the applicability of the investment instrument (and EWC) to occupied territories, see Daniel Costelloe, 'Treaty Succession in Annexed Territory' (2016) 65 ICLQ 343; Ofilio J Mayorga, 'Occupants, Beware of BITs: Applicability of Investment Treaties to Occupied Territories' (2017) 19 Palestine Ybk Int'l L 136. See also: *Everest Estate LLC and others v Russia*, PCA Case no 2015-36, Decision on Jurisdiction (20 March 2017) (not public).

[71] See also György Haraszti, *Some Fundamental Problems of the Law of Treaties* (Akadémiai Kiadó 1973) 86; Linderfalk (n 65) 64 et seq; Mark E Villiger, *Commentary on the 1969 Vienna Convention on the Law of Treaties* (Martinus Nijhoff 2009) 434; Wälde (n 64) 771. In investment arbitration, article 31(4) VCLT was referred to in barely one percent of investment cases. See J Romesh Weeramantry, *Treaty Interpretation in Investment Arbitration* (OUP 2012) 95 and appendix III.

[72] Article 31(4) VCLT is rather focused on the burden of proving the 'special meaning'. See ILC, 'Draft Articles on the Law of Treaties with Commentaries' (n 64) 222 et seq; ILC, 'Third Report of the Special Rapporteur, Sir Humphrey Waldock, Special Rapporteur' (1964) II YB ILC 5, 57; *Legal Status of Eastern Greenland (Denmark v Norway)* PCIJ Rep Series A/B no 53, 49 Isabelle Van Damme, *Treaty Interpretation by the WTO Appellate Body* (OUP 2009) 350.

[73] Weeramantry (n 71) 96; Dörr (n 63) 610 (para 102).

Overall, it is proposed that the meaning of the phrases 'requisition by armed forces' and 'destruction of property not required by the necessity of the situation' has a recognized meaning under international law, which references customary law. If the technical, be it ordinary or be it special, meaning of 'requisition by armed forces' and 'destruction of property not required by the necessity of the situation' references the customary standard of treatment of foreign property, then under the VCLT, the meaning of the EWC is ascertained by way of examining the content of the customary rules on the treatment of alien property.

This proposition finds support in supplementary means of interpretation.[74] For instance, during the negotiations of the Euro–Arab Draft Convention on the Reciprocal Promotion and Protection of Investments in the early 1980s, when addressing the language of article 5, the EWC in the draft, the parties agreed that 'the formulation of Article 5 as a whole was based on our understanding of customary international law on the question of compensation for damage inflicted during armed conflict' and that 'the formulation of Article 5 derives the formulation prepared by the preparatory committee for the Hague Codification Conference of 1930'.[75] To illustrate this point, Eileen Denza, the Legal Adviser for the UK delegation, went on to cite verbatim the above-mentioned Basis 21 for discussion from the works of the Hague Conference.[76]

4.2 *War Law Rules on Appropriation and Destruction of Property as Part of the Context in the Interpretation of the EWC: Article 31(3)(c) VCLT*

It was proposed above that the customary rules on the treatment of alien property, which derive from war law, inform the ordinary meaning of the EWC. A different interpretive route to an arguably similar outcome may be found in article 31(3)(c) VCLT, whereby the IHL norms on the appropriation and destruction of property are brought into the interpretive exercise by way of 'taking it into account' as a 'relevant rule of international law'. Indeed, the ILC proposed that, custom is 'of particular relevance to the interpretation of a treaty under article 31(3)(c)' where the 'terms used in the treaty have a recognized meaning in customary international law'[77] and the EWC is arguably one such case.

74　VCLT art 32.
75　Office of the UK Permanent Representative to the EU, 'Memo of Eileen Denza to Dr Labib Shokaire, Economic and Legal Adviser to the Arab Monetary Fund' (3 August 1981) (on record with the author).
76　ibid.
77　ILC, 'Fragmentation of International Law: Difficulties Arising from the Diversification and Expansion International Law', UN Doc A/CN.4/L.702 (2006) para 14, conclusion (20).

For the purpose of the present analysis suffice it to say that, for a certain legal instrument to be 'taken into account' under article 31(3)(c), it must meet several cumulative admissibility conditions. It must be a rule of international law; which is relevant; and applicable; between the parties and their relations. Briefly put, the concept of 'rules' encompasses treaties, custom, and general principles.[78] The notion of 'parties' denotes an overlap between the parties to the treaty subject matter of interpretation and the other 'rules of International law'.[79] Finally, there seems to be a spectrum of 'relevant rules'. On one end of the scale is the view that, 'in order to be "relevant" for purposes of interpretation, rules of international law [...] must concern the same subject matter as the treaty terms being interpreted',[80] while on the opposite end is the notion that almost all rules of international law are 'relevant' if treated with a certain amount of abstraction.[81]

If a rule passes these admissibility hurdles it will be taken into account 'together with the context'. It is suggested that both, the rule that appropriation of property in war is lawful only if it is military necessary and against compensation as well as the prohibition on destruction of property other than in exceptional situations of military necessity, pass these admissibility hurdles. As explained, these are rules of customary international law that apply to all types of armed conflicts and bind all states. They are also relevant. In the *Oil Platforms* case, the International Court of Justice stated that customary *jus ad bellum* principles were 'relevant' to the interpretation of treaties of Friendship Commerce and Navigation, the predecessors of modern investment treaties.[82]

---

[78] WTO, *European Communities – Measures Affecting the Approval and Marketing of Biotech Products* (29 September 2006) WT/DS291/R, WT/DS292/R, and WT/DS293/R, para 7.67.

[79] Joost Pauwelyn, *Conflict of Norms in Public International Law: How WTO Law Relates to other Rules of International Law* (CUP 2003) 261 et seq; Linderfalk (n 65) 343 et seq; Gardiner (n 63) 302 et seq.

[80] WTO, *Peru – Additional Duty Imports of Certain Agricultural Products* (20 July 2015) WT/DS457/AB/R, para 5.101.

[81] Bruno Simma and Theodore Kill, 'Harmonizing Investment Protection and International Human Rights: First Steps Towards a Methodology' in Binder and others (n 64) 696. For scholarship that followed this approach, see Melaku Geboye Desta, 'GATT/WTO Law and International Standards: An Example of Soft Law Instruments Hardening Up?' in Andrea K Bjorklund and August Reinisch (eds) *International Investment Law and Soft Law* (Edward Elgar 2012) 185 et seq; Nicolas Klein, 'Human Rights and International Investment Law: Investment Protection as Human Right?' (2012) 4 GoJIL 199; Gleider I Hernández, 'The Interaction Between Investment Law and the Law of Armed Conflict in the Interpretation of Full Protection and Security Clauses' in Freya Baetens (ed) *Investment Law within International Law: Integrationist Perspectives* (CUP 2013) 29 et seq.

[82] *Oil Platforms (Iran v USA)* (Merits) [2003] ICJ Rep 161, para 41.

It is almost certain that the same would apply to the relevance of *jus in bello* customary norms to the interpretation of modern investment treaties.[83] Therefore, these customary norms should be taken into account in the interpretation of the EWC. But what does that mean? Taking a rule 'into account' does not mean that it supplants the treaty language under examination.[84] This rather entails something on the continuum between 'drawing inspiration',[85] 'consideration',[86] and direct 'application' of this relevant rule.[87]

What follows from the above is that compared to the suggested interpretation technique of the language 'destruction not required by the necessity of war' and 'requisition by the armed forces' (and like formulations) through article 31(1) or (4) VCLT, the relative weight of the interpretive technique of article 31(3)(c) VCLT is rather limited. Under article 31(3)(c) VCLT, the customary rules on appropriation (including destruction) of foreign property do not inform the meaning of the EWC, they are but 'proper reference points'[88] from which to draw meaning for international investment agreements. Put a different way, the two ways of bringing customary law into the process of interpretation entail different assessments and different effects.

The next question is then, which interpretive path correctly captures the instructions of the VCLT? It is suggested that if the language 'destruction not required by the necessity of war' and 'requisition by the armed forces' (and like expressions) has an identifiable (ordinary or special) meaning in international law – and it is argued that it does – then this should be accounted for through the language itself, not its context.[89] As one commentator explained:

---

83 Bruno Simma, 'Foreign Investment Arbitration: A Place for Human Rights?' (2011) 63 ICLQ 573, 585.
84 *Certain Questions of Mutual Assistance in Criminal Matters (Djibouti v France)* (Merits) [2008] ICJ Rep 1, para 114.
85 African Charter on Human Rights and Peoples' Rights (adopted 27 June 1981, entered into force 21 October 1986) (1982) 21 ILM 58, art 60.
86 Valentina Vadi, *Cultural Heritage in International Investment Law and Arbitration* (CUP 2014) 266.
87 Philippe Sands, 'Treaty, Custom and Cross-Fertilization of International Law' (1998) 1 Yale Hum Rts & Dev LJ 85, 102.
88 Simma (n 83) 584. The language 'reference point' was used by Simma to describe the function of human right norms that pass the qualifications of article 31(3)(c) VCLT and thus form part of the broader normative context that informs the meaning of investment treaty standards.
89 Martins Paparinskis, 'Investment Treaty Interpretation and Customary Investment Law: Preliminary Remarks' in Chester Brown and Kate Miles (eds) *Evolution in Investment Treaty Law and Arbitration* (CUP 2011) 77 et seq; Anne-Marie Carstens, 'Interpreting Transplanted Treaty Rules' in Andrea Bianchi, Daniel Peat and Matthew Windsor (eds)

In the argument by Article 31(1) or Article 31(4) the benchmark is the content of (the reference in) the treaty rule and the interpretative weight directly affects ordinary or special meaning. In the argument by Article 31(3)(c), the benchmark of admissibility is the subject matter of the treaty rule and the interpretative weight is limited to that of context.[90]

4.3 A Special Meaning to the Language of the EWC that Breaks from War Law Has Not Developed

It was above proposed that a VCLT-consistent interpretation leads to an IHL-informed meaning of the EWC. Nevertheless, it may be argued that even if in the mid-twentieth century, states introduced the EWC to investment treaties with the intention to award them a recognized meaning under customary war law, modern instruments reflect no such intention. Arguably, over time, a special meaning, which is detached from the Hague Law and IHL, has developed for the terms 'requisition by the armed forces' and 'destruction not required by necessity' in the context of foreign investments.

Yet, it is submitted that if the treaty language itself makes a reference to customary law pursuant to article 31 VCLT (as suggested in section 4.1 above), then to preclude this reference and to award phrases, such as 'destruction not required by the necessity of the situation', a meaning *other than* their technical recognized meaning in customary law is only possible if it is 'established that the parties so intended', that is, to award it any such different meaning.[91] Such is the case with the use of the term 'requisition', for instance, which entails

---

Interpretation in International Law (OUP 2015) 238 et seq; Eirik Bjorge, 'The Vienna Rules, Evolutionary Interpretation, and the Intentions of the Parties' in ibid 197 et seq.

90   Martins Paparinskis, *The International Minimum Standard and Fair and Equitable Treatment* (OUP 2013) 159. See an example for this distinction in *Chevron v Ecuador*, Partial Award on Merits (30 March 2010), para 242, where the Tribunal addressed the impact of the customary law of denial of justice on the treaty obligation which required the state to 'provide effective means of asserting claims and enforcing rights'. On the point of the interaction of treaty and custom, the Tribunal first concluded that the treaty rule did not make a reference to custom and only then proceeded to asses context. By contrast, see *Saluka v Czech Republic*, Partial Award (17 March 2006), paras 305 et seq, where the Tribunal did not distinguish between the methods of reliance on customary law. There, the Tribunal assumed that a treaty norm concerning 'deprivation' made a reference to customary rule on expropriation and incorporated the customary qualifications to the treaty rule through its context under article 31(3)(c) VCLT, not the meaning under article 31(1) and (4) VCLT. See also Paparinskis, 'Investment Treaty Interpretation' (n 89) 74 et seq and 90 et seq.

91   VCLT art 31(4).

'appropriation of private foreign property for military needs during armed conflict' and not the accepted meaning of 'requisition' under the law of occupation. As explained above, it is possible to demonstrate the intention of states to award the term 'requisition', in the context of the discussion of compensation for losses to alien property during war, a meaning that is broader than the occupation-centric meaning of the term under IHL.

This is not the case, however, for the phrase 'destruction of property not required by the necessity of the situation' (and like formulations). As explained, there is nothing in the express treaty language, negotiations history, or the use of this treaty language over time to evince a clear intention of the parties to break from the customary IHL meaning of this phrase. On the contrary, this seems to be precisely the meaning that states awarded to this phrase over time and the reason for which this language was introduced into investment treaties.[92]

4.4 The Implications of the Suggested Interpretation of War Clauses

The proposition that the language of the EWC makes a reference to customary law, pursuant to article 31 VCLT, has several conceptual and practical implications.

Conceptually, what follows from the suggested interpretation is that the EWC deals with the obligation of states to pay compensation for lawful conduct and for unlawful conduct in the same breath. While compensation is prescribed as part of the primary rule for *any* requisition of investments, insofar as it is carried out by the host state's forces or authorities, the EWC also mandates compensation for destruction that *fails* to comply with certain conditions ('not caused in' and 'not required by'), *ie*, compensation as part of the secondary obligation.[93]

---

92   See Office of the UK Permanent Representative to the EU (n 75).

93   As noted, this chapter does not deal with the question of what compensation are considered 'adequate' for losses resulting from requisition or destruction. Suffice it to note in this respect that the common construction of the EWC suggests that the obligation to accord 'adequate' compensation modifies *both* the rule on lawful requisition and the consequences for unlawful destruction of foreign property. In almost every instance, the EWC comprises two sub-paragraphs that deal with requisition and destruction of property, respectively, which are followed by a separate, and final, sentence that requires the states to accord 'adequate compensation'. The placement of the language 'shall be accorded adequate compensation' (and like formulations) in a separate sentence below both sub-paragraphs demonstrates that it modifies both conducts. This is the logical consequence of the two-fold use of the phrase, which acts as part of the primary or secondary rule depending on the sub-paragraph to which it relates.

Although it may not appear elegant, it is only logical that the EWC includes elements of both primary and of secondary rules of international law. International law, in particular the law on the protection of foreign property, did not develop under the strict separation between rules that address the scope and content of international obligation on one hand, and the rules that deal with the legal consequences of the breach of any such obligation, on the other. Rather, the treatment of foreign property and the international responsibility thereof were construed in an 'integrated' manner.[94] Traditional attitudes, such as those reflected in the materials of the 1930 Hague Conference, considered the subject of state responsibility as a matter concerned with injuries caused to foreigners.[95] Illustratively, Basis 21, as cited above, dealt with state responsibility for lawful requisition *and* for unlawful destruction under the umbrella of a single rule.[96] The EWC – as UK negotiators explained in 1981[97] – essentially reiterates this 1930 'integrated' norm structure.

In practical terms, the reference to IHL means that the customary qualifications on dispossession are incorporated into the unqualified investment treaty provision.[98] Therefore, irrespective of treaty language, which does not mention IHL's core principles, proportionality or humanity,[99] destruction of foreign investments is in principle subject to an IHL proportionality assessment, which prohibits excessive destruction.[100] Likewise, notwithstanding the treaty

---

94 Martins Paparinskis, 'Investment Arbitration and the Law of Countermeasures' (2009) 37 British Ybk Int'l L 264, 307.

95 Federica Paddeu, 'A Genealogy of *Force Majeure* in International Law' (2012) 82 British Ybk Int'l L 381, 433.

96 Rosenne (n 56) Basis 21.

97 See Office of the UK Permanent Representative to the EU (n 75).

98 For a discussion along these lines in the context of the customary rules on appropriation and treaty rules, see *Saluka v Czech Republic* (n 90) paras 254 and 265.

99 Humanity is a broad open-ended term that is commonly associated with the 'Martens Clause'. The Martens Clause instructs that even in situations that are *not* expressly covered by IHL instruments, both combatants and civilians enjoy a minimum level of protection, namely that all armed conflicts should be regulated by the principles of international law 'as they result from the usages established between [states] from the laws of humanity and the requirements of the public conscience', Declaration Renouncing the Use, in Time of War, of Explosive Projectiles Under 400 Grammes Weight (signed 29 November / 11 December 1868) 138 CTS 297, preamble. See Karl Josef Partsch, 'Article 1: General Principles and Scope of Application' in Michael Bothe, Karl Josef Partsch, and Waldemar A Solf (eds), *New Rules for Victims of Armed Conflicts: Commentary on the Two 1977 Protocols Additional to the Geneva Conventions of 1949* (2nd edn, Martinus Nijhoff 2013) 43; Waldemar A Solf, 'Article 35: Basic Rules' in ibid 224.

100 IHL proportionality essentially mandates that even attacks that comply with the principles of distinction and military necessity are prohibited if they 'may be expected to cause incidental loss of civilian life, injury to civilians, damage to civilian objects, or a

language, which does not mention 'military necessity', a *lawful* dispossession of foreign investments in armed conflict is only one that is justified by military necessity and against compensation. This also means that, as with compensation for lawful expropriation, the stipulation on the obligation to compensate in the EWC ('adequate compensation') is part of the primary obligation.[101]

In turn, this potential resemblance between the EWC and expropriation raises the question of the interaction between both forms of property dispossession and the question whether the expropriation provision deems the EWC redundant. This concern over the possible redundancy of the EWC arises from the fact that while provisions that deal with the transfer of title and/or outright physical seizure of property are commonly known as 'expropriation clauses', they encompass other takings.[102] Different concepts, such as 'expropriation', 'taking', 'nationalization', 'deprivation', 'dispossession', or a combination thereof,[103] can be encountered in investment instruments. These terms are often used interchangeably with no clear elucidation as to their differences;[104] their

---

combination thereof, which would be excessive in relation to the concrete and direct military advantage anticipated', see Henckaerts and Doswald-Beck (n 19) rule 14.

101 It is argued that with expropriation as well as with the EWC, the obligation to compensate is a qualification of the primary rule, not a secondary rule on compensation. The obligation to provide reparations for a breach of a primary obligation arises once a breach of the primary rule is ascertained. In this case, the primary rule requires conduct that comprises several different acts and omissions, including the act, or refusal, of offering compensation. If the state refuses to compensate where the provision mandates it to do so, one aspect of the multifaceted conduct is breached, and the conduct is therefore tainted with illegality. This wrongful act gives rise to the obligation to compensate as a modality of reparation. For a review of the obligation to pay compensation for expropriation and its application by investment tribunals, see Steven R Ratner, 'Compensation for Expropriations in a World of Investment Treaties: Beyond the Lawful/Unlawful Distinction' (2017) 111 AJIL 7.

102 Notably, foreign assets may be subjected to trade and establishment restrictions involving licensing or quotas, anti-trust limitations, consumer protection laws, environmental standards, and even land planning. Although these measures affect the ability to own or enjoy assets and are essential to the efficient functioning of the state, they are not necessarily expropriatory. See M Sornarajah, *The International Law of Foreign Investments* (4th edn, CUP 2018) 472; James Crawford, *Brownlies' Principles of Public International Law* (9th edn, OUP 2019) 604.

103 North American Free Trade Agreement (adopted 17 December 1992, entered into force 1 January 1994) 32 ILM 289 (NAFTA) art 1110.

104 UNCTAD proposed that, 'while "nationalizations" are undertaken for political purposes and may often affect entire sectors of the economy, "expropriations" are takings that are often limited to one specific firm and do not have a political background', UNCTAD, *Bilateral Investment Treaties 1995–2006: Trends in Investment Rulemaking* (2007) 134 at fn 69. A similar view is espoused by Sornarajah (n 102) 472 set seq.

use typically depends on legal tradition and translation. Potentially, the dispossession of private property in armed conflict may be said to be covered by the wide concept of 'expropriation'.

However, the regulation of expropriation does not negate the need for rules on appropriation of investments in armed conflict. While 'requisition' is a form *sui generis* of expropriation for reasons of public utility that requires compensation, it substantively differs from expropriation. First, whereas expropriation may be grounded in various national priorities including health and safety, environmental consideration, and political agenda, the only national need that is capable of justifying appropriation of property (whether requisition, seizure, angary, etc.) in hostilities is military necessity.[105]

Second, expropriation must also comply with due process.[106] Dispossession of property under IHL is not conditioned upon these qualifications. In the case of requisition, in contrast to expropriation, the investor is not entitled to, say, an independent right of review or prior notification. In practical terms this means that a taking for a legitimate purpose against compensation that is lacking in due process may constitute lawful requisition but unlawful expropriation. Hence, the expropriation provision and the EWC do not fully overlap.

An additional consequence that arises from the proposition that the EWC references customary law concerns the stringency of the treaty standard. Any legal norm may be made more or less stringent through the formulation of different burdens of proof, evidentiary standards, and thresholds of invocation.[107] Placing the EWC in the broader normative framework of IHL assists to elucidate the burden of proof under the EWC. It clarifies how to construe the language 'destruction of property [...] that was not required by the necessity of the situation' with respect to the burden of proof.

This language may be taken to establish a presumption of illegality, whereby the state must show that the destructing measure was necessary to accomplish

---

105 Hague Regulations arts 46 et seq, 52 et seq, 56; Borchard, 'Private Pecuniary Claims' (n 13) 122.
106 'Due process' is a wide term which mostly requires that the measure (expropriation) complies with procedures established in domestic legislation and that the affected investors will be allowed to have the case reviewed before an independent and impartial instance (right to an independent review). For examples in treaties, see Montenegro–Switzerland BIT (adopted 7 December 2005, entered into force 11 July 2007) art XX; Austria–Mexico BIT (adopted 29 June 1998, entered into force 26 March 2001) art 4(3). For arbitral practice that focused on the requirement of due process and its breach, see, *eg*, *Middle East Cement v Egypt*, ICSID Case no ARB/99/6, Award (12 April 2002) para 143; *ADC v Hungary*, ICSID Case no ARB/03/16, Award (2 October 2006) para 435.
107 Ryan Goodman, 'The Power to Kill or Capture Enemy Combatants' (2013) 24 EJIL 819, 828.

a military purpose. Alternatively, this language may be construed as a presumption of legality under which the destructing measure is assumed to be lawful unless it is established that the measure was unnecessary to accomplish a military purpose. The former assumption disfavours the state, while the latter presumption favours the state. In this respect Eagleton proposed that, 'the wording of the Hague Convention', which is referenced by the treaty language of the EWC, 'makes it reasonable to say that the burden of proof is upon the belligerent to show that his seizure or destruction of private property was imperiously demanded by the necessities of war.'[108]

Further, placing the EWC in the broader normative framework of IHL assists to ascertain the threshold of the provision's invocation, as it brings further clarity to the meaning and role of the qualifiers of 'necessity', which may allow, in exceptional cases, to destroy property. In IHL instruments, the threshold of invocation of military necessity varies from 'necessity' (unqualified) through 'imperative necessity' under article 23(g) of the Hague Regulations[109] to 'absolute necessity' and like formulations.[110] In contrast to IHL instruments, the EWC usually instructs that destruction that is 'necessary' (unqualified) will not invoke the responsibility of the state. Does the use of qualifiers imply that IHL sets a different, potentially higher threshold of invocation relative to the unqualified EWC, thereby also raising the question of the interaction between the unqualified treaty rule and the customary standard?

On this point, it is suggested that both, the unqualified 'necessity' under the EWC and the 'imperative' threshold under the Hague Law, represent the same standard, since under IHL the qualifier 'imperative' is conceived as a cosmetic, not a substantive adjective. In fact, the same question arose with respect to the Statute of the International Criminal Court, which instructs that destruction of property is not punishable under article 8(2)(b)(xiii) and (e)(xii) if it is 'imperatively demanded by the necessities of war'.[111] Schabas explained that the language 'imperatively demanded by the necessities of war' is 'an archaic expression borrowed from the 1907 Hague Convention.'[112] Dinstein went even further and asserted on this point that, 'the modern tendency is to regard all

---

108 Eagleton (n 18) 135.
109 Hague Regulations art 23(g) ('destruction or seizure be imperatively demanded by the necessities of war').
110 GC IV art 42.
111 Rome Statute of the International Criminal Court (adopted 17 July 1998, entered into force 1 July 2002) (2004) 2187 UNTS 3, art 8(2)(b)(xii) and (e)(xiii).
112 William Schabas, *The International Criminal Court: A Commentary on the Rome Statute* (2nd edn, OUP 2016) 294. See also *Prosecutor v Katanga* (n 28) para 894 and fn 2116.

such adverbs [*ie absolute* and *imperative* necessity] as synonymous and self-evident, and, therefore, redundant.'[113] The same is true for the 'necessity' of the EWC and its reference to customary law on the treatment of aliens.

However, propositions as those expressed above have led some commentators to opine that EWCs 'are arguably superfluous in light of the protection afforded private property under the laws of war.'[114] But this is not accurate. First, the incorporation of custom into treaties removes any ambiguity over the acceptance of the customary rule, and its scope of application to investments.[115] Additionally, incorporation of custom ensures that the (customary) standard as applied to covered investment 'is enforceable through the investor-state and state-state disputes provisions'.[116]

Further, that the EWC references customary law, by way of using technical terms of art with a recognized meaning under the Hague Law, does not mean that modern investment instruments should be interpreted in accordance with 1907 war law. Of course, states are free to agree that a treaty norm is to be interpreted in accordance with customary law as it stood at a certain point in time.[117] But the EWC does not explicitly reflect any such agreement. In fact, seeing as war law, and its exclusive focus on military necessity, has evolved considerably since the Hague Law into modern humanitarian law, it is absurd

---

113 Yoram Dinstein, 'Military Necessity', *Max Planck Encyclopedia of Public International Law* (2015) paras 12 et seq <https://opil.ouplaw.com/home/MPIL> accessed 15 February 2019.

114 Scott K Gudgeon, 'United States Bilateral Investment Treaties: Comments on Their Origin, Purpose, and General Treatment Standards' (1986) 4 Int'l Tax & Bus Law 105, 128. In fn 83, the author refers specifically to the Hague instruments and their subsequent codification in Geneva Law. See also Sohn and Baxter (n 67) 551.

115 *Elettronica Sicula SpA (ELSI) (USA v Italy)* (Counter-Memorial of Italy) [1988] II ICJ Pleadings 1, 30 et seq and 39 et seq; *Elettronica Sicula SpA (ELSI) (USA v Italy)* (Rejoinder of Italy) [1988] II ICJ Pleadings 417, 457; *Elettronica Sicula SpA (ELSI) (USA v Italy)* (Oral Arguments) [1987] III ICJ Pleadings 1, 92 et seq, 111 et seq (arguments for the USA); *United States Diplomatic and Consular Staff in Tehran (USA v Iran)* (Oral Arguments on the Request for the Indication of Provisional Measures) [1979] ICJ Pleadings 13, 25 et seq (arguments for the US); *United States Diplomatic and Consular Staff in Tehran (USA v Iran)* (Oral Arguments) [1980] ICJ Pleadings 249, 273, 284, and 296 (arguments for the US); *Military and Paramilitary Activities in and against Nicaragua (Nicaragua v USA)* (Memorial of Nicaragua) [1985] IV ICJ Pleadings 1, paras 398 et seq. See also Wälde (n 64) 742.

116 Kenneth J Vandevelde, *Bilateral Investment Treaties: History, Policy, and Interpretation* (OUP 2010) 232 et seq.

117 *Mondev International Ltd v USA*, ICSID Case no ARB(AF)/99/2, Award (11 October 2002) para 111; *ADF Group Inc v USA*, ICSID Case no ARB(AF)/00/1, Award (9 January 2003) para 179; *Waste Management v Mexico ("Number 2")*, ICSID Case no ARB(AF)/00/3, Award (30 April 2004) paras 93 et seq.

to propose that twenty-first century EWCs intend to apply war law norms, which modern war law itself no longer recognizes. Therefore, it is suggested that the interpretation of the language of the EWC as a reference to customary law, pursuant to article 31(1) and (4) VCLT, accommodates flexibility and allows for development. Thus, if the customary rules on requisition and destruction of property evolve – and indeed the Hague Law has evolved in the Geneva Law – then the treaty reference will reflect any such change.

5   Conclusion

Many international investment agreements contain an EWC. This provision regulates the treatment to be granted to foreign investors in case their investments suffer losses owing to the lawful requisition or unlawful destruction of their property during armed. While common, these treaty mechanisms have received little attention by arbitral tribunals and scholarship. Accordingly, this chapter attempted to trace their origins and to elucidate their meaning and content.

To that end, it was established that under customary war law, as codified in the Hague Law, appropriation of private foreign property is lawful if it is required by military necessity and against compensation. Destruction of property is, conversely, prohibited. Exceptionally, property may be destroyed only when required by military necessity and subject to a proportionality assessment. Because destruction of property is prohibited as a rule, in contrast to requisition, when the destruction is lawful for military needs it does not denote compensation. It was then established that these IHL rules infiltrated the law on the protection of foreign property abroad during the twentieth century and shaped the customary standard of treatment of foreign property during war.

It was next suggested that the practical implication of this historical development is that today IHL is effectively incorporated in the language of the EWC. This is because the language of the EWC provision uses terms of art with a recognized meaning under IHL ('requisition by the armed forces' and 'destruction not required by military necessity' (and similar wording)). Thus, under the VCLT, the ordinary (or special) meaning of the treaty standard makes a reference to customary IHL. Therefore, the content of the IHL rule informs the meaning of the investment standard. Overall, this chapter traced the roots of the treaty rules on the treatment of the property of foreign investors to the codification of war law in the Hague Regulations and used this historical context to gain a better understanding of the language of the EWC.

Bibliography

Abs H and Shawcross H, 'Draft Convention on Investments Abroad' (1960) 9 J Pub L 115.

Bjorge E, 'The Vienna Rules, Evolutionary Interpretation, and the Intentions of the Parties' in Andrea Bianchi, Daniel Peat and Matthew Windsor (eds) *Interpretation in International Law* (OUP 2015).

Borchard EM, 'Private Pecuniary Claims Arising Out of War' (1915) 9 AJIL 113.

Borchard EM, 'Are We Entitled to Confiscate Enemy Private Property?' (1923) 23 Colum L Rev 383.

Borchard EM, 'Responsibility of States for Damage Done in their Territories to the Person or Property of Foreigners' (1926) 20 AJIL 738.

Borchard EM, 'The Law of Responsibility of States for Damage Done in Their Territory to the Person or Property of Foreigners' (1929) 23 AJIL Spec Supp 131.

Borchard EM, *The Diplomatic Protection of Citizens Abroad: or the Law of International Claims* (Banks Law Publishing 1916).

Bothe M, 'Expert Opinion: Limits of the Right of Expropriation (Requisition) and of Movement Restrictions in Occupied Territory' (2 August 2012), <www.diakonia.se/globalassets/blocks-ihl-site/ihl-file-list/ihl--expert-opionions/limits-of-the-right-of-expropriation-requisition-and-of-movement-restrictions-in-occupied-territory.-dr.-iur.-prof-michael-bothe.pdf> accessed 13 April 2020.

Bray HL, 'Understanding Change: Evolution from International Claims Commissions to Investment Treaty Arbitration' in Stephan W Schill, Christian J Tams, and Rainer Hofmann (eds) *International Investment Law and History* (Edward Elgar 2018).

Carstens A-M, 'Interpreting Transplanted Treaty Rules' in Andrea Bianchi, Daniel Peat and Matthew Windsor (eds) *Interpretation in International Law* (OUP 2015).

Committee on the Formation of Customary (General) International Law, 'Final Report of the Committee: Statement of Principles Applicable to the Formation of General Customary International Law' (200) 69 ILA Rep Conf 712.

Costelloe D, 'Treaty Succession in Annexed Territory' (2016) 65 ICLQ 343.

Crawford J, *Brownlies' Principles of Public International Law* (9th edn, OUP 2019).

Desierto D, 'The Outer Limits of Adequate Reparations for Breaches of Non-Expropriation Investment Treaty Provisions: Choice and Proportionality in Chorzów' (2017) 55 Colum J Transnat'l L 395.

Desta MG, 'GATT/WTO Law and International Standards: An Example of Soft Law Instruments Hardening Up?' in Andrea K Bjorklund and August Reinisch (eds) *International Investment Law and Soft Law* (Edward Elgar 2012).

Dinstein Y, *The Conduct of Hostilities under the Law of International Armed Conflict* (2nd edn, CUP 2010).

Dinstein Y, 'Military Necessity' *Max Planck Encyclopedia of Public International Law* (2015) <https://opil.ouplaw.com/home/MPIL> accessed 15 February 2019.

Dörr O, 'Article 31' in Oliver Dörr and Kirsten Schmalenbach (eds), *Vienna Convention on the Law of Treaties: A Commentary* (2nd edn, Springer 2018).

Eagleton C, 'Responsibility for Damages to Persons and Property of Aliens in Undeclared War (1938)' 32 Am Soc'y Int'l L Proc 127.

Gardiner RK, *Treaty Interpretation* (2nd edn, OUP 2015).

Gottlieb G, 'The Interpretation of Treaties by Tribunals' (1969) Am Soc'y Int'l Proc 122.

Gudgeon SK, 'United States Bilateral Investment Treaties: Comments on Their Origin, Purpose, and General Treatment Standards' (1986) 4 Int'l Tax & Bus Law 105.

Hackworth GH, *Digest of International Law*, vol 5 (US Government Printing Office 1943).

Haraszti G, *Some Fundamental Problems of the Law of Treaties* (Akadémiai Kiadó 1973).

Hayashi N 'Requirements of Military Necessity in International Humanitarian Law and International Criminal Law' (2010) 28 BU Int'l LJ 39.

Henckaerts J-M and Doswald-Beck L, Customary International Humanitarian Law, vol 1 (CUP 2005).

Henckaerts J-M and Doswald-Beck L, Customary International Humanitarian Law, vol 2 (CUP 2005).

Hernández GI, 'The Interaction Between Investment Law and the Law of Armed Conflict in the Interpretation of Full Protection and Security Clauses' in Freya Baetens (ed) *Investment Law within International Law: Integrationist Perspectives* (CUP 2013).

Hyde CC, *International Law: Chiefly as Interpreted and Applied by the United States*, vol 2 (Little, Brown, and Company 1922).

Institut de Droit International, 'Responsabilité internationale des Etats à raison des dommages causés sur leur territoire à la personne et aux biens des étrangers' (Lausanne 1927) <www.idi-iil.org/app/uploads/2017/06/1927_lau_05_fr.pdf> accessed 13 April 2020.

International and Operational Law Department, The Judge Advocate General's Legal Center & School, *Operational Law Handbook* (17th edn, US Army 2017).

Jessup PC, 'Enemy Property' (1955) 49 AJIL 57.

Klein N, 'Human Rights and International Investment Law: Investment Protection as Human Right?' (2012) 4 GoJIL 199.

Kleinlein T, 'Sequestration' *Max Planck Encyclopedia of Public International Law* (2010) <https://opil.ouplaw.com/home/MPIL> accessed 10 June 2018.

League of Nations Committee of Experts for the Progressive Codification of International law, 'Questionnaire No. 4 adopted by the Committee at its Second Session, held in January 1926: Responsibility of States for Damage Done in Their Territories to the Person or Property of Foreigners', reported in (1926) 20 AJIL Spec Sup 176.

Linderfalk U, *On the Interpretation of Treaties: The Modern International Law as Expressed in the 1969 Vienna Convention on the Law of Treaties* (Springer 2007).

Mayorga OJ, 'Occupants, Beware of BITs: Applicability of Investment Treaties to Occupied Territories' (2017) 19 Palestine Ybk Int'l L 136.

McNair A, 'The Seizure of Property and Enterprises in Indonesia' (1959) 6 Netherlands J Int'l L 218.

Melzer N, *Targeted Killing in International Law* (OUP 2008).

Miles K, 'History and International Law: Method and Mechanism – Empire and "Usual" Rupture' in Stephan W Schill, Christian J Tams, and Rainer Hofmann (eds) *International Investment Law and History* (Edward Elgar 2018).

Moore JB, *History and Digest of the International Arbitrations to Which the United States Has Been a Party International Arbitrations*, vol 4 (US Government Printing Office 1898).

Muhammad B, 'Hostilities in Nigeria's Niger Delta Blamed on Government Neglect' (*dw*, 11 July 2017) <www.dw.com/en/hostilities-in-nigerias-niger-delta-blamed-on-government-neglect/a-41270034> accessed 13 April 2020.

Nielsen FK, *American-Turkish Claims Settlement: Opinions and Report* (US Government Printing Office 1937).

Office of the UK Permanent Representative to the EU, 'Memo of E Danza to Dr Labib Shokaire, Economic and Legal Adviser to the Arab Monetary Fund' (3 August 1981) (on record with the author).

Paddeu F, 'A Genealogy of *Force Majeure* in International Law' (2012) 82 British Ybk Int'l L 381.

Paparinskis M, 'Investment Arbitration and the Law of Countermeasures' (2009) 37 British Ybk Int'l L 264.

Paparinskis M, 'Investment Treaty Interpretation and Customary Investment Law: Preliminary Remarks' in Chester Brown and Kate Miles (eds) *Evolution in Investment Treaty Law and Arbitration* (CUP 2011).

Paparinskis M, *The International Minimum Standard and Fair and Equitable Treatment* (OUP 2013).

Partsch KJ, 'Article 1: General Principles and Scope of Application' in Michael Bothe, Karl Josef Partsch, and Waldemar A Solf (eds), *New Rules for Victims of Armed Conflicts: Commentary on the Two 1977 Protocols Additional to the Geneva Conventions of 1949* (2nd edn, Martinus Nijhoff 2013).

Pauwelyn J, *Conflict of Norms in Public International Law: How WTO Law Relates to other Rules of International Law* (CUP 2003).

Payk MM, 'The History of International Law – or International Law in History? A Reply to Alexandra Kemmerer and Jochen von Bernstorff' (*EJIL:Talk!* 8 January 2015) <www.ejiltalk.org/the-history-of-international-law-or-international-law-in-history-a-reply-to-alexandra-kemmerer-and-jochen-von-bernstorff/> accessed 13 April 2020.

Perez-Aznar F, 'Investment Protection in Exceptional Situations: Compensation-for-Losses Clauses in IIAs' (2017) 32 ICSID Review 696.

Ratner SR, 'Compensation for Expropriations in a World of Investment Treaties: Beyond the Lawful/Unlawful Distinction' (2017) 111 AJIL 7.

Rogers APV, *Law on the Battlefield* (3rd edn, MUP 2012).

Rosenne S (ed) *League of Nations Conference for the Codification of International Law (1930)*, vol 2 (Oceana Publications 1975).

Ryan Goodman, 'The Power to Kill or Capture Enemy Combatants' (2013) 24 EJIL 819.

Sands P, 'Treaty, Custom and Cross-Fertilization of International Law' (1998) 1 Yale Hum Rts & Dev LJ 85.

Schabas W, *The International Criminal Court: A Commentary on the Rome Statute* (2nd edn, OUP 2016).

Schmitt MN, 'Military Necessity and Humanity in International Humanitarian Law: Preserving the Delicate Balance' (2010) 50 Va J Int'l L 295.

Schoenrich O, 'The Nicaraguan Mixed Claims Commission' (1915) 9 AJIL 859.

Schwarzenberger G, 'Myths and Realities of Treaty Interpretation: Articles 27–29 of the Vienna Draft Convention on the Law of Treaties' (1968) 9 Va J Int'l L 1.

Simma B and Kill T, 'Harmonizing Investment Protection and International Human Rights: First Steps Towards a Methodology' in Christina Binder and others (eds), *International Investment Law for the 21st Century: Essays in Honour of Christoph Schreuer* (OUP 2009).

Simma B, 'Foreign Investment Arbitration: A Place for Human Rights?' (2011) 63 ICLQ 573.

Sohn LB and Baxter RR, 'Responsibility of States for Injuries to the Economic Interests of Aliens' (1961) 55 AJIL 545.

Solf WA, 'Article 35: Basic Rules' in Michael Bothe, Karl Josef Partsch, and Waldemar A Solf (eds), *New Rules for Victims of Armed Conflicts: Commentary on the Two 1977 Protocols Additional to the Geneva Conventions of 1949* (2nd edn, Martinus Nijhoff 2013).

Sornarajah M, *The International Law of Foreign Investments* (4th edn, CUP 2018).

UNCTAD, *Bilateral Investment Treaties 1995–2006: Trends in Investment Rulemaking* (2007).

US Government, *Final Report of the Spanish Treaty Claims Commission* (US Government Printing Office 1910).

Vadi V, *Cultural Heritage in International Investment Law and Arbitration* (CUP 2014).

Van Damme I, *Treaty Interpretation by the WTO Appellate Body* (OUP 2009).

Vandevelde KJ, *Bilateral Investment Treaties: History, Policy, and Interpretation* (OUP 2010).

Villiger ME, *Commentary on the 1969 Vienna Convention on the Law of Treaties* (Martinus Nijhoff 2009).

Wälde TW, 'Interpreting Investment Treaties: Experiences and Examples' in Christina Binder and others (eds), *International Investment Law for the 21st Century: Essays in Honour of Christoph Schreuer* (OUP 2009).

Weeramantry JR, *Treaty Interpretation in Investment Arbitration* (OUP 2012).

CHAPTER 3

Full Protection and Security from Physical Security to Environmental Security: Its Limitations and Future Possibilities

Emily Sipiorski

1 **Introduction**

The full protection and security (FPS) standard reigns in its usefulness and applicability when armed conflict impacts foreign investment.[1] Christoph Schreuer has already highlighted its value in the relationship between investment protection and situations of armed conflict or other violence as the most important clause.[2] There has been a growing reliance on FPS, where the protections are available, in states touched by internal unrest, particularly arising out of the Arab Spring.[3] While dependent on whether the language is limited in its application by the no less favourable treatment provisions,[4] it remains central to providing protection in situations where investors would be otherwise exposed.

This usefulness is also ideally formed and limited in its application by the interaction with other fields of international law, building on the increased recognition of beneficial systemic integration in all fields and systems of international law.[5] Freya Baetens has indicated a potential movement of investment

---

1 Ana Maria Daza-Clark and Daniel Behn, 'Between War and Peace: Intermittent Armed Conflict and Investment Arbitration' in Katia Fach Gómez, Anastasios Gourgourinis, and Catharine Titi (eds), *International Investment Law and the Law of Armed Conflict* (Springer 2019) 58 et seq.

2 Christoph Schreuer, 'War and Peace in International Investment Law' in Katia Fach Gómez, Anastasios Gourgourinis, and Catharine Titi (eds), *International Investment Law and the Law of Armed Conflict* (Springer 2019) 10.

3 Heather L Bray, 'SOI – Save Our Investments: International Investment Law and International Humanitarian Law' (2013) 14 JWIT 578, 583, 593 et seq (discussing the case of Libya).

4 See, *eg*, Zimbabwe–Germany BIT (2000) art 4(3).

5 Martti Koskenniemi and Päivi Leino, 'Fragmentation of International Law? Postmodern Anxieties' (2002) 15 LJIL 553; Joost Pauwelyn, 'Bridging Fragmentation and Unity: International Law as a Universe of Inter-Connected Islands' (2004) 25 Mich J Int'l L 903, 916; ILC, 'Fragmentation of International Law: Difficulties arising from the Diversification and Expansion of International Law' (2006) UN Doc A/CN.4/L.702; Anthea Roberts, 'Clash of Paradigms: Actors and Analogies Shaping the Investment Treaty System' (2013) 107 AJIL

law towards closer interactions with international humanitarian law (IHL): 'It is true that international investment law transcends its origins as a primarily self-contained regime; and indeed, there are areas in which investment law has borrowed extensively by analogy from international humanitarian law, such as the protection of aliens.'[6] The law on state responsibility similarly provides an opportunity for bettering the broader system of international investment treaty law.[7] Furthermore, drawing from the basic purposes of the standard of protection, there remains substantial basis for a further interaction with other fields of international law,[8] including international environmental standards.[9] Respect for these necessary interactions have already been provided for in soft law mechanisms. The United Nations (UN) Guiding Principles on Business and Human Rights have promoted corporate accountability and indicated that 'enterprises should respect the standards of international humanitarian law.'[10] In addition, The OECD Guidelines for Multinational Corporations recommends that enterprises 'take due account of the need to protect the environment, public health and safety, and generally to conduct their activities in a manner contributing

---

45; Ulf Linderfalk, 'Cross-Fertilization in International Law' (2015) 84 Nord J Int'l L 428; Steffen Hindelang and Markus Krajewski, 'Shifting Paradigms in International Investment Law – More Balanced, Less Isolated, Increasingly Diversified' (2016) 27 EJIL 545, 551.

[6] Freya Baetens, 'When International Rules Interact: International Investment Law and the Law of Armed Conflict' (*IISD Investment Treaty News*, 7 April 2011) <www.iisd.org/itn/2011/04/07/when-international-rules-interact-international-investment-law-and-the-law-of-armed-conflict/> accessed 11 March 2020. See also Teerawat Wongkaew, 'The Cross-Fertilisation of International Investment Law and International Humanitarian Law: Prospects and Pitfalls' in Katia Fach Gómez, Anastasios Gourgourinis, and Catharine Titi (eds), *International Investment Law and the Law of Armed Conflict* (Springer 2019) 386 et seq; Jure Zrilič, *The Protection of Foreign Investment in Times of Armed Conflict* (OUP 2019).

[7] ILC, 'Articles on Responsibility of States for Internationally Wrongful Acts' (2001), annexed to UNGA Res 56/83 (12 December 2001) UN Doc A/56/83 (ILC Articles on State Responsibility).

[8] See critically, José E Alvarez, 'Beware: Boundary Crossings – A Critical Appraisal of Public Law Approaches to International Investment Law' (2016) 17 JWIT 171.

[9] Shyami F Puvimanasinghe, *Foreign Investment, Human Rights, and the Environment: A Perspective from South Asia on the Role of Public International Law for Development* (Martinus Nijhoff 2007); Kate Miles, 'International Investment Law: Origins, Imperialism and Conceptualizing the Environment' (2010) 21 Colo J Int'l Envtl L & Pol'y 1; Jorge E Viñuales, *Foreign Investment and the Environment in International Law* (CUP 2012); Saverio Di Benedetto, *International Investment Law and the Environment* (Edward Elgar 2013); Kate Miles, *The Origins of International Investment Law: Empire, Environment and the Safeguarding of Capital* (CUP 2013).

[10] UN Office of the High Commissioner for Human Rights, 'Guiding Principles on Business and Human Rights' (2011) UN Doc HR/Pub/11/04, Principle 12. See also ILC, 'Second Report on Protection of the Environment in Relation to Armed Conflicts by Marja Lehto, Special Rapporteur' (2019) UN Doc A/CN.4/728, 32 et seq.

to the wider goal of sustainable development.'[11] The increased recognition of a state's right to counterclaim – now somewhat limited in scope to treaties providing broad language in the provisions[12] – holds potential for expansion and incorporation of norms arising out of other systems of international law.

This contribution is formed, has evolved, and draws from the rapidly changing notions and transforming landscape of investment protection.[13] Underlying these criticisms and discussions is a basic question of how the rule of law is being upheld, particularly in light of international investment protection within the general umbrella of public international law.[14] Undoubtedly one of the reasons for the need to re-examine the investment protection system is the increased awareness of this overlap in responsibilities from other branches of international law – in particular, human rights law and environmental law[15] – and the complexity in equitably binding private actors, despite their position in public international law, to responsibilities attributable only to sovereign states operating within the international system.[16] FPS, unique in its limited

---

11 Organisation for Economic Co-operation and Development (OECD), *Guidelines for Multinational Enterprises* (OECD Publishing 2011) 42.

12 *Urbaser SA and Consorcio de Aguas Bilbao Bizkaia, Bilbao Biskaia Ur Partzuergoa v Argentina*, ICSID Case no ARB/07/26, Award (8 December 2016) paras 1143 et seq; *Burlington Resources Inc v Ecuador*, ICSID Case no ARB/08/5, Decision on Ecuador's Counterclaims (7 December 2017) para 60.

13 Regarding the use of arbitral tribunals, see Charles N Brower and Stephan W Schill, 'Is Arbitration a Threat or a Boon to the Legitimacy of Investment Arbitration?' (2009) 9 Chicago J Int'l L 471; Daniel Behn, 'Legitimacy, Evolution, and Growth in Investment Treaty Arbitration: Empirically Evaluating the State-of-the-Art' (2015) 46 Geo J Int'l L 363, 367. Regarding consistency, see for example, Susan D Franck, 'The Legitimacy Crisis in Investment Treaty Arbitration: Privatizing Public International Law through Inconsistent Decisions' (2005) 73 Fordham L Rev 1521, 1625.

14 Thomas Schultz and Cédric Dupont, 'Investment Arbitration: Promoting the Rule of Law or Over-Empowering Investors? A Quantitative Empirical Study' (2014) 25 EJIL 1147; Julian Donaubauer, Eric Neumayer, and Peter Nunnenkamp, 'Winning or Losing in Investor-to-State Dispute Resolution: The Role of Arbitrator Bias and Experience' (2018) 26 Rev Int'l Econ 892.

15 Pierre-Marie Dupuy, Francesco Francioni and Ernst-Ulrich Petersmann (eds), *Human Rights in International Investment Law and Arbitration* (OUP 2009); Viñuales, *Foreign Investment and the Environment* (n 9).

16 Barnali Choudhury, 'Recapturing Public Power: Is Investment Arbitration's Engagement of the Public Interest Contributing to the Democratic Deficit?' (2008) 41 Vand J Transnat'l L 775; William W Burke-White and Andreas von Staden, 'Private Litigation in a Public Law Sphere: The Standard of Review in Investor-State Arbitrations' (2010) 35 Yale J Int'l L 283; Stephan W Schill, 'Enhancing the Legitimacy of International Investment Law: Conceptual and Methodological Foundations of a New Public Law Approach' (2011) 52 Va J Int'l L 57; Julie Maupin, 'Public and Private in International Investment Law: An

application and (arguable) potential for a closer relationship with other fields of international law demonstrates the valuable interaction of regimes[17] that could push international investment law into a more balanced and agreeable future. This future envisions an acceptance of the value of IHL and environmental standards as well as the evolving (albeit still undefined) role of private actors within this complicated web of regimes.

On the most basic level, this chapter attempts to find the limits to the FPS standard and how these limitations in fact speak to a more broadly-framed issue within the ongoing reforms of the international investment regime – namely, whether the system is ready for an integration with other fields of international law to maintain its longevity. But more specifically, the chapter drives at the role that the provision could or should take in future disputes – as the very foundation of ideas of physical security and conflict push past war between two distinct regimes or between sovereign states and move towards conflict resulting from nature itself through climatic changes; this interaction plays with the developing role of private individuals in impacting that security. Although the FPS standard has been broadly discussed in the literature, there is limited discussion on its future and the profound relevance of these relationships on its full potential for application in the new era of investment protection, particularly as it continues to be included in the most recent investment agreements and chapters on investment protection.[18]

This contribution pushes ideas of conflict and their impact on an investment past these basic assumptions and towards a reading of physical protection in light of environmental impacts. However, this extension of the provision to environmental impacts lives in two directions: impacting the role and responsibilities for both states and investors. Drawing on its typical applicability to conflict, the discussion examines the relevance of investor contributions, towards the idea of 'militarized commerce', in limiting the applicability of the

---

Integrated Systems Approach' (2014) 54 Va J Int'l L 367; Kevin Crow, 'Corporations and Crimes Against Humanity: Financial Liability Through ISDS?' in Katia Fach Gómez, Anastasios Gourgourinis, and Catharine Titi (eds), *International Investment Law and the Law of Armed Conflict* (Springer 2019) 466.

17   Roberts (n 5) 45; Hindelang and Krajewski (n 5) 551.
18   See, *eg*, Comprehensive Economic and Trade Agreement between Canada and the European Union (signed 30 October 2016, not in force) [2017] OJ L 11/23 (CETA) art 8.10; EU–Viet Nam Investment Protection Agreement (signed 30 June 2019, not in force), Annex to the Proposal for a Council Decision on the Conclusion of the Investment Protection Agreement between the European Union and its Member States, of the One Part, and the Socialist Republic of Viet Nam of the Other Part, COM(2018) 693 final (17 October 2018) art 2.5; Argentina–Japan BIT (2018) art 4.

FPS standard to investors, and then uses this as a framework for understanding the nature of similar limitations of the standard under emerging environmental standards, both domestically and on an international level. The question remains whether this provision could lead to a more balanced interaction between other relevant fields of international law by way of its scope and interpretation in customary international law.

Section 1 examines the accepted application of the principle as a means for setting the groundwork for its use in the current landscape of international investment law as well as understanding its deeper relationship with international law. Section 2 discusses the limitations in the application of FPS protection based on the behaviour of the investor, which then leads to a theoretical critique on the use of the standard of protection for a regime-integrated future of international investment protection. Section 3 turns to the possibility and practice of extending FPS to situations where physical security of an investment has been compromised by an environmental impact, highlighting recent case law. Namely, this section considers the implications that environmental damage has on the application of the protection – analysing this from both the perspective of the state's behaviour (the traditional application of standards of protection in international investment law) and the investor's behaviour (a growing possibility of impact with the opening of counterclaims and the re-development of language of investment protection). The final section considers the results of such applications of FPS to the general integrity of international investment protection in individual cases as well as the more broadly conceived impacts on the debated legitimacy of the system (section 4). The chapter intends to challenge the typical applications of investment protection and provide an integrated analysis of one of the broad standards of protection consistently included in investment agreements.

2   Positioning and Defining Full Protection and Security

FPS, its definition formed in customary law[19] but its application part of the evolving system of international investment law,[20] can be generally understood

---

19   Ira Ryk-Lakhman, 'Protection of Foreign Investments Against the Effects of Hostilities: A Framework for Assessing Compliance with Full Protection and Security' in Katia Fach Gómez, Anastasios Gourgourinis, and Catharine Titi (eds), *International Investment Law and the Law of Armed Conflict* (Springer 2019) 269.

20   See, generally, Stephan W Schill, *The Multilateralization of International Investment Law* (CUP 2009).

as a due diligence standard by states to ensure the physical security of investments.[21] As early as the first bilateral investment treaty (BIT), the value of 'protection and security' of investments was identified as the basis and central purpose of the treaty; the preamble indicated '[i]nvestments by nationals or companies of either Party shall enjoy protection and security in the territory of the other Party.'[22] The tribunal in *El Paso Energy v Argentina* clarified the mechanism of the protection with respect to due diligence:

> [...] the obligation to show 'due diligence' does not mean that the State has to prevent each and every injury. Rather, the obligation is generally understood as requiring that the State take reasonable actions within its power to avoid injury when it is, or should be, aware that there is a risk of injury. The precise degree of care, of what is 'reasonable' or 'due', depends in part on the circumstances.[23]

This provision is rarely further defined or limited in the treaty provisions, which has controversially pushed its application beyond physical security and towards other protections, namely legal security.[24] As this provision has been applied and understood historically, such physical protection relates to times of internal strife or civil unrest as well as other conflicts with another state.[25]

FPS – like many of the other standards of protection in investment protection agreements – is full of ambiguity and lacks clearly defined modes for application.[26] A typical FPS clause in a BIT or investment chapter of a trade

---

21   See, *eg, Asian Agricultural Products Ltd (AAPL) v Sri Lanka*, ICSID Case no ARB/87/3, Final Award (27 June 1990) paras 67 et seq; *American Manufacturing & Trading Inc (AMT) v Zaire*, ICSID Case no ARB/93/1, Award (21 February 1997) para 6.05; *Wena Hotels Ltd v Egypt*, ICSID Case no ARB/98/4, Award (8 December 2000) para 84; *Parkerings-Compagniet AS v Lithuania*, ICSID Case no ARB/05/8, Award (11 September 2007) para 351.
22   Pakistan–Germany BIT (1959) art 3.
23   *El Paso Energy International Co v Argentina*, ICSID Case no ARB/03/15, Award (31 October 2011) para 523.
24   See, *eg, Azurix Corp v Argentina*, ICSID Case no ARB/01/12, Award (14 July 2006) para 406; *Siemens AG v Argentina*, ICSID Case no ARB/02/8, Award (17 January 2007) paras 286, 308; *Compañiá de Aguas del Aconquija SA and Vivendi Universal SA v Argentina*, ICSID Case no ARB/97/3, Award (20 August 2007) para 7.4.12; *National Grid v Argentina*, Award (3 November 2008) para 187. See also Rudolf Dolzer and Christoph Schreuer, *Principles of International Investment Law* (2nd edn, OUP 2012) 149 et seq.
25   See, *eg, Bernhard von Pezold and others v Zimbabwe*, ICSID Case no ARB/10/15, Award (28 July 2015) paras 597 et seq; *MNSS BV and Recupero Credito Acciaio NV v Montenegro*, ICSID Case no ARB(AF)/12/8, Award (4 May 2016) paras 352 et seq.
26   See, generally, Brian Bix, *Law Language and Legal Determinacy* (Clarendon 1993); Neil MacCormick, *Rhetoric and the Rule of Law: A Theory of Legal Reasoning* (OUP 2005); Ralf

agreement provides for 'protection and constant security' – sometimes qualified with 'full' – or 'most constant protection and security'.[27] With these variations often disregarded in significance,[28] considered by some as a 'starting point for the tribunal's reasoning, but [...] not seem[ing] to play a decisive role in the result.'[29] Instead, the standard appears as a particular ideal of treatment.

Guidance beyond these terms is not included in the language or definitions of the treaties, save for the indication found in several instances that the standard is no less than that provided in international law.[30] Indeed, the protection of foreigners is typically defined by customary law.[31] In its form in the North American Free Trade Agreement (NAFTA), the standard is expressly linked to international minimum standard under customary international law.[32] This calibrating of the standard within the international context does not sufficiently clarify the scope of protection or the limits to it. Reverting to the Vienna Convention on the Law of Treaties (VCLT),[33] article 31 and the consequential consideration of the ordinary meaning frames the tribunal's approach to this standard, as with other treaty provisions; it also enables a more integrated interpretation of the standard that may release it from the black letter, 'contractual' reading of the protections.[34]

FPS can be both closely (at times included in the same provision or paragraph) as well loosely (in terms of language) connected to fair and equitable treatment (FET).[35] In fact, the provision is frequently argued by investors in

---

Poscher, 'Ambiguity and Vagueness in Legal Interpretation' in Lawrence M Solan and Peter M Tiersam (eds), *Oxford Handbook of Language and Law* (OUP 2012); Andreas Kulick, 'From Problem to Opportunity? An Analytical Framework for Vagueness and Ambiguity in International Law' (2016) 59 German YB Int'l L 258. See also Maupin (n 16) 384 et seq.

27 Christoph Schreuer, 'The Protection of Investments in Armed Conflict' in Freya Baetens (ed), *Investment Law within International Law* (CUP 2013).
28 ibid.
29 Giuditta Cordero Moss, 'Full Protection and Security' in August Reinisch (ed), *Standards of Investment Protection* (OUP 2008) 134.
30 ibid.
31 Ryk-Lakhman (n 19) 269.
32 North American Free Trade Agreement (adopted 17 December 1992, entered into force 1 January 1994) 32 ILM 289 (NAFTA) art 1105.
33 Vienna Convention on the Law of Treaties (adopted 23 May 1969, entered into force 27 January 1980) 1155 UNTS 331 (VCLT).
34 Campbell McLachlan, 'The Principle of Systemic Integration and Article 31(3)(c) of the Vienna Convention' (2005) 54 ICLQ 279.
35 Alejandro M Garro, 'Trade and Investment Treaties, the Rule of Law, and Standards of the Administration of Justice' (2011) 42 U Miami Inter-Am L Rev 267, 268 et seq; Nigel Blackaby and others, *Redfern and Hunter on International Arbitration* (6th edn, OUP 2014) para 8.113; Kendra Leite, 'The Fair and Equitable Treatment Standard: A Search for

relation to FET.³⁶ Questions regarding its fluctuating requirements depending on the development status of the host state have been approached in several cases.³⁷ It has also been at times considered part of the linkage among the three concepts: FPS, FET, and the international minimum standard.³⁸ Notably, the creation of the standard in the same provision can create an obstacle to an independent exploration of the exact contents of the provision. In some respects, FPS tends to be the shadow of its much brighter and more readily applied partner, the FET standard. The two provisions, if they are drafted into one article, allow for a disregard to FPS – as something that fails to stand on its own. When clearly separated from FET, the applicability of the FPS standard, as formed under customary international law, is more limited in breadth.³⁹ This limitation was expressly stated by the tribunal in *AWG Group Ltd v Argentina*:

> The present Tribunal, however, takes the view that under Article 3, quoted above, the concept of full protection and security is included within the concept of fair and equitable treatment, but that the scope of full protection and security is narrower than the fair and equitable treatment. Thus, State action that violates the full protection and security clause would of necessity constitute a violation of fair and equitable treatment under the French BIT. On the other hand, all violations of fair and equitable treatment are not automatically also violations of full protection and security.⁴⁰

---

a Better Balance in International Investment Agreements' (2016) 32 Am U Int'l L Rev 363. For cases combining the FPS and FET standards, see, *eg*, *Wena Hotels v Egypt* (n 21) para 77; *Compañiá de Aguas del Aconquija SA and Vivendi Universal SA (formerly Compañía de Aguas del Aconquija, SA and Compagnie Générale des Eaux) v Argentina*, ICSID Case no ARB/97/3, Award (21 November 2000); *PSEG Global Inc and others v Turkey*, ICSID Case no ARB/02/5, Award (19 January 2005) para 258; *Azurix v Argentina* (n 24) para 408; *Occidental Petroleum Corp and Occidental Exploration and Production Co v Ecuador*, ICSID Case no ARB/06/11, Award (5 October 2012) para 404.

36 Cordero Moss (n 29) 131; Stanimir A Alexandrov, 'The Evolution of the Full Protection and Security Standard' in Meg Kinnear and others (eds), *Building International Investment Law: The First 50 Years of ICSID* (Wolters Kluwer 2015) 329.

37 Ursula Kriebaum, 'The Relevance of Economic and Political Conditions for Protection under Investment Treaties' (2011) 10 L & Prac Int'l Cts & Tribunals 383, 384.

38 Eric De Brabandere, 'Fair and Equitable Treatment and (Full) Protection and Security in African Investment Treaties between Generality and Contextual Specificity' (2017) 18 JWIT 530.

39 Schreuer (n 2) 11.

40 *AWG Group Ltd v Argentina*, Decision on Liability (30 July 2010) para 171.

Nonetheless, there has been some caution in including the standard in BITs by less economically developed states.[41] The provision has at times been omitted from treaties, reflecting a concern over the application. Both, Annex 1 of the Southern African Development Community (SADC) Protocol on Finance and Investment (2006) and the Investment Agreement for the Common Market for Eastern and Southern Africa (COMESA) Common Investment Area (2007) omit the provision.[42] Mahnaz Malik has indicated that this omission 'reflects the growing concern among developing countries about this standard.'[43] He also posits that it 'remains to be seen, however, if countries will follow this regional approach in their BITs, particularly when negotiating with a partner that insists otherwise.'[44]

Ultimately, FPS can be condensed down to two essential prongs: a due diligence obligation on the part of the state (section 2.1) to protect the physical security of an investment (section 2.2).

2.1 *Due Diligence*

The clause, in its typical manifestation, puts a level of burden on the host state to actively protect the 'physical integrity' of an investment against the occurrence of adverse effects.[45] These adverse effects could be the result of the host state's own action – whether military in nature or a more basic failure to provide police protection where necessary.[46] In that sense, FPS is considered a 'standard of due diligence.'[47] The flexibility of due diligence in its application

---

41 Mahnaz Malik, 'The Full Protection and Security Standard Comes of Age: Yet Another Challenge for States in Investment Treaty Arbitration?' (2011) IISD Best Practice Series <www.iisd.org/pdf/2011/full_protection.pdf> accessed 16 March 2020.
42 See also ibid.
43 ibid.
44 ibid.
45 See *Amco Asia Corp and others v Indonesia*, ICSID Case no ARB/81/1, Award (20 November 1984) (breach of treaty obligations because of the state's failure to protect the investment from take-over); *AMT v Zaire* (n 21); *Saluka Investments BV v Czech Republic*, Partial Award (17 March 2006) para 483; *Eastern Sugar v Czech Republic*, SCC Case no 088/2004, Partial Award (27 March 2007); *Rumeli Telekom AS and Telsim Mobil Telekomunikasyon Hizmetleri AS v Kazakhstan*, ICSID Case no ARB/05/16, Award (29 July 2008) paras 669 et seq; Schreuer (n 2) 1.
46 *AAPL v Sri Lanka* (n 21).
47 Eric De Brabandere, 'Host States' Due Diligence Obligations in International Investment Law' (2015) 42 Syracuse J Int'l L & Com 319. See *AMT v Zaire* (n 21); *Wena Hotels v Egypt* (n 21); *Parkerings v Lithuania* (n 21) para 351. See also Nartnirun Junngam, 'The Full Protection and Security Standard in International Investment Law: What and Who is Investment Fully (?) Protected and Secured From?' (2018) 7(1) Am U Bus L Rev 1.

was dramatized by the *Pantechniki v Albania* decision. In considering the application of the standard, the arbitrator noted that the Respondent's witness

> testified that the police said they were *unable* to intervene. That is crucially different from a *refusal* to intervene given the scale of the looting. [The arbitrator] conclude[d] that the Albanian authorities were powerless in the face of social unrest of this magnitude. [...] The Claimant ha[d] not shown that Albania failed to comply with its duty to extend full protection and security in the circumstances that gave rise to this case.[48]

Ursula Kriebaum indicates that

> the due diligence obligation means that host States have to take measures which are reasonable under the circumstances to protect the investment. What is reasonable will be influenced by the circumstances prevailing in the host State, including the resources at its disposal. This would suggest that there is enough flexibility in the legal standards in investment law to take account of the different stages of development across nations.[49]

While some tribunals have limited the protection to acts of third parties rather than actions by the state, in general the state owes investors due diligence to protect the investment from destructive aspects of a disturbance or conflict.[50] This approach was explicitly applied by the *Eastern Sugar* tribunal, disregarding the applicability of FPS as the actions were committed by the Czech Republic's Ministry of Agriculture:

> As the Tribunal understands it, the criterion in Art. 3(2) of the BIT concerns the obligation of the host state to protect the investor from third parties, in the cases cited by the Parties, mobs, insurgents, rented thugs and other engaged in physical violence against the investor in violation of the state monopoly of physical force. Thus, where a host state fails to grant full protection and security, it fails to act to prevent actions by third parties that it is required to prevent.[51]

---

48 *Pantechniki SA Contractors & Engineers (Greece) v Albania*, ICSID Case no ARB/07/21, Award (30 July 2009) paras 82, 84.
49 Kriebaum (n 37) 384.
50 *Eastern Sugar v Czech Republic* (n 45) para 203. See also *AMT v Zaire* (n 21); *Wena Hotels v Egypt* (n 21); *Ronald S Lauder v Czech Republic*, Final Award (3 September 2001) para 308; *Parkerings v Lithuania* (n 21) para 351.
51 *Eastern Sugar v Czech Republic* (n 45) para 203.

In fact, the language of the provisions varies between requiring due diligence with respect to government actions or non-state actors.[52] These limitations, however, are not widely accepted and state actions are frequently included in the breadth of protections. The *Parkerings* tribunal indicated that a

> violation of the standard of full protection and security could arise in case of failure of the State to prevent the damage, to restore the previous situation or to punish the author of the injury. The injury could be committed either by the host State, or by its agencies or by an individual.[53]

The extension of the standard of treatment was similarly followed by the *Biwater Gauff* tribunal, which did 'not consider that the "full security" standard is limited to a State's failure to prevent actions by third parties, but also extends to actions by organs and representatives of the State itself.'[54]

As stated by the tribunal in *Wena Hotels v Egypt* in connection with fair and equitable treatment, the provision requires protection of the investment and in particular, even when there is no ability to prevent the action, some level of action by the authorities after an illegal seizure would be required.[55] Yet, this standard is not an 'absolute obligation which guarantees that no damages will be suffered, in the sense that any violation thereof creates automatically a "strict liability" on behalf of the host State.'[56] The host state does not 'accept an absolute responsibility for all injuries to foreigners',[57] supported by the tribunal's consideration of several older bilateral treaties that used similar and more forceful expressions of the standard. The International Court of Justice (ICJ) in the *ELSI* decision poignantly provided that '[t]he reference in Article v to the provision of "constant protection and security" cannot be construed as the giving of a warranty that property shall never in any circumstances be occupied or disturbed.'[58]

This due diligence aspect of the standard is central to its re-imagining in other interactions with other aspects of international law. Namely, a state only

---

52 Nasser Alreshaid, 'Revisiting the Notion of Full Protection and Security of Foreign Direct Investments in Post-Gadhafi Libya: Two Governments, Tribunal Violence, Militias, and Plenty More' (2016) 28 Fla J Int'l L 63, 76 et seq.
53 *Parkerings v Lithuania* (n 21) para 355.
54 *Biwater Gauff (Tanzania) Ltd v Tanzania*, ICSID Case no ARB/05/22, Award (24 July 2008) para 730.
55 *Wena Hotels v Egypt* (n 21) paras 84, 88.
56 *AAPL v Sri Lanka* (n 21) 545.
57 ibid paras 545 et seq.
58 *Elettronica Sicula SpA (ELSI) (USA v Italy)* (Judgment) [1989] ICJ Rep 15, para 108.

possesses a certain level of ability to prevent certain consequences, but the levels are malleable over time, inherently transforming by both internal and external factors. This may significantly lessen its impact to an environmental claim while leaving the question of how such a reversion could be used to bind the investor. While the standard could not be applied without this limiting effect for the state, its relevance more broadly in international law defines its characteristics.

The due diligence aspects of FPS can be refined by interpreting it based on IHL.[59] While not directly applicable in an investment claim, the already well-developed law on the responsibility of states for violations of humanitarian law provides an existing framework for the application of the due diligence standard as it is applied in a similar respect in international investment law. In particular, there is an obvious overlap in the protection of civilians and property during armed conflict that enables a closer interaction between the two systems of law. Teerawat Wongkaew has referred to this interaction and its potential for 'cross-fertilization', referring in particular to the interpretation of the due diligence standard of FPS based on common article 1 of the Geneva Conventions[60] and article 58(c) of the Additional Protocol I.[61]

The liability of a state and their due diligence obligations to prevent or punish unlawful actions of armed groups was considered by sole arbitrator Huber as early as 1925 in the *British Claims in the Spanish Zone of Morocco* case, in which he distinguished between a state's culpability for actions directly committed by it and by actions by others that it failed to prevent.[62]

Rule 149 of the International Committee of the Red Cross's study on customary IHL from 2005, explaining the responsibility of a state for violations of the IHL, provides a practical explanation for the extension of state responsibility.[63] This rule, reflecting article 51 of the 1949 Geneva Convention I,[64] article 52 of

---

59   Wongkaew (n 6) 397 et seq.
60   Geneva Conventions (adopted 12 August 1949, entered into force 21 October 1950) 75 UNTS 287 (Geneva Conventions).
61   (First) Protocol Additional to the Geneva Conventions of 12 August 1949, and Relating to the Protection of Victims of International Armed Conflicts (adopted 8 June 1977, entered into force 7 December 1978) 1125 UNTS 3 (Additional Protocol I). See Wongkaew (n 6) 397 et seq.
62   *Spanish Zone of Morocco (Great Britain v Spain)* (1925) 2 RIAA 615, 639, 642 et seq.
63   Jean-Marie Henckaerts and Louise Doswald-Beck, *Customary International Humanitarian Law*, vol 1 (ICRC and CUP 2005) rule 149.
64   Geneva Convention (I) for the Amelioration of the Condition of the Wounded and Sick in Armed Forces in the Field (adopted 8 June 1977, entered into force 21 October 1950) 75 UNTS 31 (Geneva Convention I).

the 1949 Geneva Convention II,[65] article 131 of the 1949 Geneva Convention III,[66] and article 148 of the 1949 Geneva Convention IV,[67] provides for the liability of a state for breaches of the Geneva Conventions. This realization of this responsibility and its subsequent application connects with the requirements for liability and a grounded interpretation of those requirements, respecting customary international law on responsibility.

While FPS provides a due diligence obligation on the part of the state to protect the physical security of an investment as it has been applied, what does that mean in the current landscape of investment protection existing within the broader framework of public international law?

2.2 *Physical Security*

The FPS standard has been at times interpreted broadly to include both physical as well as legal security.[68] The relevant language allowing for such a breadth of inclusion has been debated in particular in the more recent European Union trade agreements[69] with the legal security aspect allowing the power of judicial interpretation to determine its breadth. The provisions provide little definition, as stated by the *Lauder* tribunal:

> Article II(2)(a) of the Treaty provides that "[i]nvestment [...] shall enjoy full protection and security". There is no further definition of this obligation in the Treaty. The Arbitral Tribunal is of the opinion that the Treaty obliges the Parties to exercise such due diligence in the protection of foreign investment as reasonable under the circumstances. However, the Treaty does not oblige the Parties to protect foreign investment against any loss of value caused by persons whose acts could not be attributed to the State. Such protection would indeed amount to

---

65   Geneva Convention (II) for the Amelioration of the Condition of Wounded, Sick and Shipwrecked Members of Armed Forces at Sea (adopted 8 June 1977, entered into force 21 October 1950) 75 UNTS 85 (Geneva Convention II).

66   Geneva Convention (III) Relative to the Treatment of Prisoners of War (adopted 8 June 1977, entered into force 21 October 1950) 75 UNTS 135 (Geneva Convention III).

67   Geneva Convention (IV) Relative to the Protection of Civilian Persons in Time of War (adopted 8 June 1977, entered into force 21 October 1950) 75 UNTS 287 (Geneva Convention IV).

68   Helge E Zeitler, 'The Guarantee of "Full Protection and Security" in Investment Treaties Regarding Harm Caused by Private Actors' (2005) 3 Stockholm Int'l Arb Rev 1; Cordero Moss (n 29) 131.

69   Catharine Titi, 'Full Protection and Security, Arbitrary or Discriminatory Treatment and the Invisible EU Model BIT' (2014) 15 JWIT 534, 542 et seq.

strict liability, which cannot be imposed to a State absent any specific provision in the Treaty.[70]

Furthermore, there are few standards for interpretation attributed to FPS,[71] resulting in diverse applications of the standard and divergent persuasive authority.[72] However, there is a general consensus that has formed that distinguishes the FPS provision because of its applicability to physical protection.[73]

The story of FPS – as well as investor-state dispute resolution, more generally – begins with *AAPL v Sri Lanka*.[74] The claim was brought in part based on the FPS standard in the UK–Sri Lanka BIT (1980) as well as the most favoured nation clause, referencing directly the possibility of armed conflict. Article 2(2) of the UK–Sri Lanka BIT (1980) provides that investors 'shall enjoy full protection and security in the territory.' In addition, article 4(1) of the UK–Sri Lanka BIT (1980) provides:

> Nations or companies of one Contracting Party whose investments in the territory of the other Contracting Party suffer losses owing to war or to armed conflict, revolution, a state of national emergency, revolt, insurrection or riot in the territory of the latter Contracting Party shall be accorded by the latter Contracting Party treatment, as regards restitution, indemnification, compensation or other settlement, no less favourable than that which the latter Contracting Party accords to its own nationals or companies or to nationals or companies of any third State.

In *AAPL v Sri Lanka*, a shrimp farm was destroyed:

> According to the Claimant, the Company's farm, which was its main producing center, was destroyed on January 28, 1987, during a military operation conducted by the security forces of Sri Lanka against installations reported to be used by local rebels. As a direct consequence of said action, AAPL alleged having suffered a total loss of its investment, and claimed from the Government of Sri Lanka compensation for the damages incurred as a result thereof.[75]

---

70 *Lauder v Czech Republic* (n 50) para 308.
71 Malik (n 41) 2.
72 *Deutsche Bank AG v Sri Lanka*, ICSID Case no ARB/09/02, Award (31 October 2012) para 535.
73 Schreuer (n 2) 11.
74 *AAPL v Sri Lanka* (n 21).
75 *AAPL v Sri Lanka* (n 21) para 3.

The relevance of FPS in times of conflict has again emerged in some of the claims coming out of disputes in Libya as well as Egypt.[76] In the *Ampal v Egypt* dispute, for example, the standard of protection was brought because the investor suffered loss as a result of internal insurgencies.[77] In short, the aggressive force resulted in the loss of the investment.

2.3 Limitations on the Application of the FPS Standard: Contribution and Complicity in International Law

The FPS provision is considered limited to a small number of activities by the state. The scope and current understanding of the breadth of the FPS standard under customary international law can be identified as the reason for the limited application of the provision by investment tribunals. However, in the case of conflict, the limitations on the application can also be attributed to the actions of the investors. In terms of general international law, the contribution of others, including the victim, to a violation of international law can impact the outcome of a dispute, in particular, with respect to the issue of reparations between two states.[78]

It could be argued that an FPS claim would similarly be limited by the investors' own behaviour – both from the standpoint of contribution, or contributory fault, as well as complicity. This aspect of contribution has relevance in a conflict situation, but these applications will be discussed more dynamically below with respect to environmental impacts. These general ideas of contribution and complicity of the investor in domestic issues are beginning to draw more attention within the legitimacy debate.[79]

2.3.1 Damages and Contribution

Damages calculations have frequently referred to the behaviour of claimants in the injury caused – and the consequential impact on reparations.[80] Article 39 of the ILC Articles on State Responsibility provides for 'Contribution to

---

76   See Bray (n 3); Alreshaid (n 52).
77   *Ampal-American Israel Corp and others v Egypt*, ICSID Case no ARB/12/11, Decision on Liability and Heads of Loss (21 February 2017) paras 235 et seq.
78   See ILC Articles on State Responsibility art 47; James Crawford, *Brownlie's Principles of Public International Law* (9th edn, OUP 2019) 537.
79   Jorge E Viñuales, 'International Investment Law and Natural Resource Governance' in Kati Kulovesi and Elisa Morgera (eds), *Research Handbook on International Law and Natural Resources* (Edward Elgar 2016).
80   *Delagoa Bay Railway Arbitration (Great Britain and USA v Portugal)* (1898) 2 Moore Int'l Arb 1865; Marjorie Whiteman, *Damages in International Law* (US Government Printing Office 1937) 1694.

Injury': 'In the determination of reparation, account shall be taken to the contribution to the injury by wilful or negligent action or omission of the injured State or any person or entity in relation to whom reparation is sought.' In investment decisions, for example, in *Occidental Petroleum v Ecuador*, the tribunal considered the contribution of the claimant through a proportionality analysis.[81] Further reasoning with respect to reparations was followed in *Copper Mesa Mining v Ecuador*.[82] Caroline Henckels has advanced this approach, indicating that

> [a]n argument can be made that governments should bear primary responsibility for balancing the interests of stakeholders in the course of governance, particularly where a measure has been adopted following wide public participation or in response to public concerns. Balancing, or determining whether a measure is reasonable, risks highly subjective decision-making that is influenced by adjudicators' own political, ideological and economic beliefs and assumptions.[83]

This concept of contribution and its impact on damages is also applicable with respect to the 'unclean hands' doctrine.[84]

2.3.2 Investor Complicity

While foreign investments suffering losses from conflict situations have protections available under FPS, those protections may be complicated by the

---

[81] *Occidental v Ecuador* (n 35) para 675. The award relies in part on a monograph, *ie*, Brigitte Stern, *Acte de la victim justifiant partiellement l'acte de l'État* (Pedone 1973), and on the award in *Delagoa Bay Railway* (n 80). See also Borzu Sabahi and Kabir Duggal, 'Occidental Petroleum v Ecuador (2012): Observations on Proportionality, Assessment of Damages and Contributory Fault' (2013) 28 ICSID Rev 279. *Cf* Benedict Kingsbury and Stephan W Schill, 'Investor-State Arbitration as Governance: Fair and Equitable Treatment, Proportionality and the Emerging Global Administrative Law' in Albert Jan van den Berg (ed), *50 Years of the New York Convention: ICCA International Arbitration Conference* (Wolters Kluwer 2009).

[82] *Copper Mesa Mining Corp v Ecuador*, PCA Case no 2012-2, Award (15 March 2016) para 6.92, also referring to *Delagoa Bay Railway* (n 80) and the ILC's reliance on it in ILC, 'Articles on Responsibility of States for Internationally Wrongful Acts with Commentaries' (2001) II(2) YBILC 31, art 39 cmt 4 (with respect to the contribution of an injured state and its relevance to reparation).

[83] Caroline Henckels, 'Balancing Investment Protection and the Public Interest: The Role of the Standard of Review and the Importance of Deference in Investor-State Arbitration' (2013) 4 JIDS 197, 207.

[84] See, *eg*, *Yukos Universal Ltd (Isle of Man) v Russia*, PCA Case no 2005-04/AA 227, Final Award (18 July 2014) paras 1634 et seq.

actions of the investors – more specifically, these private actors may participate in a way to ensure the profitability of their investment. The following section examines aspects of investor or corporate complicity[85] – referred to by other scholars as 'militarized commerce'[86] – first considering some examples outside of investment law and then assessing how such involvement impacts the FPS protection.

Complicity by a foreign investor leading to limitations in the application of FPS can be difficult to causally attribute to that investor.[87] Yet, the very nature of commercial gain often translates into associations and relationships made in the interest of preserving the investment or enhancing the profitability. There are significant examples in international law of companies complying with the demands of a repressive regime in the interests of continuing their business operations.[88] For example, Lafarge Cement Syria paid money to the so-called 'Islamic State' and other militant groups to maintain the production at one of its plants.[89] In a similar scenario, brought under the US Alien Tort Claims Act,[90] Shell was brought to US court by twelve Nigerians alleging torture and human rights abuses.[91] In *Doe v Unocal*, Unocal was brought to US court over alleged use of forced labour in the construction of a gas pipeline

---

85   See, *eg*, International Commission of Jurists, 'Corporate Complicity and Legal Accountability' (2008) 58 <www.icj.org/wp-content/uploads/2012/06/Vol.1-Corporate-legal-accountability-thematic-report-2008.pdf> accessed 10 May 2020; Danielle Olson, 'Corporate Complicity in Human Rights Violations under International Criminal Law' (2015) 1(1) Int'l Hm Rts LJ Art 5 <https://via.library.depaul.edu/ihrlj/vol1/iss1/5/> accessed 10 May 2020.

86   Craig Forcese, 'Deterring "Militarized Commerce": The Prospect of Liability for "Privatized" Human Rights Abuses' (2000) 31 Ottawa L Rev 171, 173.

87   From the perspective of complicity of the state in looting activities, see *Pantechniki v Albania* (n 48) para 83.

88   António M Abrantes, *Entre Neutralidade e Cumplicidade o Envolvimento de Agentes Económicos na Comissão de Crimes Internacionais* (Instituto Jurídico da Faculdade de Direito da Universidade de Coimbra 2017) 17 et seq (highlighting the role of commercial entities in military conflicts).

89   Liz Alderman, Elian Peltier, and Hwaida Saad, ' "ISIS Is Coming!" How a French Company Pushed the Limits in War-Torn Syria' *The New York Times* (New York, 10 March 2018) <www.nytimes.com/2018/03/10/business/isis-is-coming-how-a-french-company-pushed-the-limits-in-war-torn-syria.html> accessed 10 May 2020.

90   Alien Tort Statute, 28 US Code § 1350 (providing that '[t]he district courts shall have original jurisdiction of any civil action by an alien for a tort only, committed in violation of the law of nations or a treaty of the United States.'); now limited in extraterritorial application following the decision of the US Supreme Court in *Kiobel v Royal Dutch Shell Petroleum Co* 569 US 108 (2013).

91   *Wiwa v Royal Dutch Shell Petroleum Co*, 392 F3d 812 (5th Cir 2004).

between Burma and Thailand.[92] A claim was brought for a Canadian company's complicity in the Sudanese genocide.[93] Similar matters of complicity have been linked to companies' involvement in the Second World War,[94] including involvement of rail operators as well as the notorious IG Farben involvement in production of chemicals.[95]

Integration of international investment law into the wider body of international law may require an acceptance of this type of role for the investor. The role played by illegal behaviour in international investments complicates decision-making and decisions may draw from other sources of international and domestic law to enhance interpretation and undefined elements.[96] The notion of complicity, arising out of criminal law, however, is difficult to apply in an investment dispute. Namely, it would be a significant risk for an investor to seek compensation in an international forum for losses suffered as a result of a dispute that it fuelled. But, the grey areas of such involvement may allow for such a dispute to reach an arbitral tribunal.

3   Extending the Practice and Application of FPS to Environmental Impacts

A debate has entered the investment reform dialogue regarding environmental law and its implications in investment protection.[97] Some scholars have recommended the inclusion of environmental obligations through 'international civil liability' principles into investment agreements.[98] Environmental

---

92   *John Doe I et al v Unocal Corp et al*, 963 F Supp 880 (CD Cal 1997). See Rachel Chambers, 'The *Unocal* Settlement: Implications for the Developing Law on Corporate Complicity in Human Rights Abuses' (2005) 13(1) Hm Rts Brief 14.
93   *Presbyterian Church of Sudan v Talisman Energy*, 374 F Supp 2d 331 (SDNY 2005).
94   Abrantes (n 88) 31.
95   *Trial of Carl Krauch and Twenty-Two others (IG Farben Trial)* (1948) 10 LRTWC 1.
96   Zachary Douglas, 'The Plea of Illegality in Investment Treaty Arbitration' (2014) 29 ICSID Rev 155.
97   See, generally, Puvimanasinghe (n 9); Miles, 'International Investment Law' (n 9); Viñuales, *Foreign Investment and the Environment* (n 9); Di Benedetto (n 9); Miles, *The Origins of International Investment Law* (n 9).
98   Alessandra Mistura, 'Enhancing Environmental Protection in International Investment Law through the Integration of International Civil Liability Principles' (*IISD Investment Treaty News*, 23 April 2019) <www.iisd.org/itn/2019/04/23/enhancing-environmental-protection-in-international-investment-law-through-the-integration-of-international-civil-liability-principles-alessandra-mistura/> accessed 16 March 2020.

considerations have long been an aspect of tribunals' decisions.[99] And now, the possible intersection between environmental aspects of physical security and the application of the FPS has begun to enter the body of international investment decisions.[100] Despite the growing international regime of climate treaties, including the UN Framework Convention on Climate Change,[101] the Kyoto Protocol,[102] and the Paris Agreement,[103] these mechanisms lack effective enforcement, which makes the integration of these principles into the framework of international investment law both complicated and fascinating. International investment law provides a potential vehicle for a broader realization of environmental goals[104] while continuing to operate for the protection of foreign investments.

FPS could be used to fill the gaps that have been regarding environmental protection with respect to the investor's behaviour. In that sense, it is possible to find a link in the language of the treaties as they already exist to approach the issue of environmental responsibility. This requires looking at the ideas of physical security and conflict more broadly. The physical integrity of foreign investments typically protected in the relevant provisions has essential and necessary implications in times of conflict. However, this becomes more interesting as we read conflict more broadly. Although previous case law guides the current application of the FPS standard, this does not limit re-imagination of the protections in certain new light based on new circumstances surrounding international investment law generally and any specific situations of domestic conflict that result in potential violation of the standard. It is essential to start with an expansion of the idea of conflict – and its close connection to claims arising out of physical security under FPS – before bridging the applicability to environmental impacts. This application of FPS is most relevant if considered with respect to the emerging and developing standards in environmental law. Under a treaty calling for 'most constant protection and security', however, this

---

99   *Compañía del Desarrollo de Santa Elena SA v Costa Rica*, ICSID Case no ARB/96/1, Award (17 February 2000) paras 54 et seq; *Metalclad Corp v Mexico*, ICSID Case no ARB(AF)/97/1, Award (30 August 2000) paras 48 et seq.
100 *Peter A Allard v Barbados*, PCA Case no 2012-06, Award (27 June 2016).
101 UN Framework Convention on Climate Change (adopted 9 May 1992, entered into force 21 March 1994) 1771 UNTS 107.
102 Kyoto Protocol to the UN Framework Convention on Climate Change (adopted 11 December 1997, entered into force 16 February 2005) 2303 UNTS 162.
103 Paris Agreement (adopted 12 December 2015, entered into force 4 November 2016), Annex to UN Doc FCCC/CP/2015/L.9/Rev.1 (2015).
104 With respect to the responsibility in customary international law for damage to private property, see *Trail Smelter Case (USA v Canada)* (1941) 3 RIAA 1938, 1966.

analysis may fail as the standard and plain reading indicates that the security has not changed since the investment was first made.

Conflict has long been understood in its sense of a physical aggression – some type of warfare – between two sovereign states. Other contributions in this volume approach the internal aspects of conflict.[105] While these traditional notions of conflict provide guidance for the manner in which conflict will manifest in the future, the next level takes conflict out of the paradigm of sovereign states and moves it into a more abstract realm. Conflict can be more complex than simply two sovereign states battling for territory. Conflict can manifest itself between people and forces of nature as well. To wit, environmental changes due to climate change have caused conflict and will cause conflict in the future – in the traditional sense – over resources. Conflict, however, may also be used to understand the complexity of resulting impacts on individuals as result of climate change. This conflict may not necessarily result in conflict between individuals but rather towards individuals. This follows the recognition of climate change as directly impacting human rights.[106]

These evolving frameworks for how war and peace are conceptualized are highly relevant in the field of international investment protection. The ambiguous standards, guided in their interpretation by article 31 VCLT, are based on their generally-accepted definitions as well as the interplay, at least in ICSID-administered disputes, with international law through ICSID Convention article 42(1).[107] In this respect, treaty interpretation under customary law as provided for in the VCLT, including in particular article 31(3)(c), allows consideration and application of international law in investment decisions.[108] This is particularly the case where there is either a gap in the treaty provision or lack of clarity that leads to consideration of customary law.[109]

---

105 See Tillmann Rudolf Braun, chapter 1 in this volume, 26–28; Ira Ryk-Lakhman, chapter 2 in this volume; Christina Binder & Philipp Janig, chapter 4 in this volume, 114–118.

106 UNHRC, 'Report of the Special Rapporteur on the Issue of Human Rights Obligations Relating to the Enjoyment of a Safe, Clean, Healthy and Sustainable Environment: Climate Change' (2016) UN Doc A/HRC/31/52. See also the overview at UN Office of the High Commissioner for Human Rights, 'Human Rights and Climate Change' (2020) <www.ohchr.org/EN/Issues/HRAndClimateChange/Pages/HRClimateChangeIndex.aspx> accessed 16 March 2020.

107 Convention on the Settlement of Investment Disputes between States and Nationals of Other States (adopted 18 March 1965, entered into force 14 October 1966) 575 UNTS 159 (ICSID Convention). See also Christoph Schreuer and others, *The ICSID Convention: A Commentary* (2nd edn, CUP 2009) 545 et seq.

108 McLachlan (n 34) 279.

109 Alvarez (n 8); ILC, 'Fragmentation of International Law' (n5) 11.

3.1 FPS Claim Based on Environmental Damage

An FPS claim based on a domestic environmental designation has already been brought forward by an investor. In *Allard v Barbados*, the claimant sought protection under the FPS provision based on the government's failure to maintain the protected status of land surrounding the investment property. In the mid-1990s, a Canadian invested in land in Barbados for the purpose of developing an eco-tourism attraction. The claimant owned part of a larger piece of 240 acres of designated wetland.[110] The designation of the land for recreation and open space required that Allard receive planning permission and conduct an environmental impact assessment.[111] Permission for the development was granted conditionally[112] and construction was begun on the tourism project.[113] But by 2008, changes by the government of Barbados affected the zone – meaning that it was no longer protected territory but had been re-allocated for residential uses and as an urban corridor.[114] The claimant brought a claim under FET, FPS, and non-discrimination based on the state's failure 'to mitigate a significant degradation of the environment and the 'tourist experience' at the Sanctuary, and thereby depriving him of the entire benefit of his investment in Barbados.'[115] Article 11(2) of the Canada–Barbados BIT (1996) provides that 'Each Contracting Party shall accord investments or returns of investors of the other Contracting Party: [...] (b) full protection and security [...].' Focusing on the FPS claim, the tribunal considered the responsibilities of the state based on the due diligence standard, finding that '[i]ts governance of the entire area does not fall short of what was appropriate and sufficient for purposes of the duty of due diligence as required' under the BIT.[116] While this case represents a first step towards an increased breadth of application for FPS towards environmental considerations, the tribunal denied protection under FPS.[117]

3.2 Counterclaims

The arguments presented and the basis of the claim in *Allard v Barbados* presents an antithesis to *Aven v Costa Rica*, in which the projects by the investor were contributing to the environmental degradation of the protected area.[118]

---

110   *Allard v Barbados* (n 100) para 33.
111   ibid para 35.
112   ibid para 37.
113   ibid para 41.
114   ibid para 45.
115   ibid para 50.
116   ibid paras 248 et seq.
117   ibid para 251.
118   *David R Aven and others v Costa Rica*, ICSID Case no UNCT/15/3, Award (18 September 2018).

The Respondent submitted a counterclaim based on environmental damage caused by the project, which was rejected on grounds of timeliness rather than subject matter.[119] In consistency with the counterclaim brought by Costa Rica in *Aven*, most counterclaims approach the issue of human rights violations or environmental harm caused by a project, as in *Urbaser v Argentina*[120] and *Burlington v Ecuador*.[121]

Moreover, Corporate Social Responsibility, along the same lines, could also be contemplated as a soft law mechanism for limiting the application of the FPS protections.[122]

3.3 Contribution to Environmental Impacts

There is already a certain basis for recognizing the contribution of investors in their relationships with the host state. Language that regulates investors' behaviour with respect to human rights and labour standards is increasingly included in new investment chapters and agreements. For example, article 14 of the Economic Community of West African States (ECOWAS) Supplementary Act on Investments (2008)[123] provides that investors

> shall uphold human rights in the workplace and the community in which they are located. Investors shall not undertake or cause to be undertaken, acts that breach such human rights. Investors shall not manage or operate the investments in a manner that circumvents human rights obligations, labour standards as well as regional environmental or social obligations, to which the host State and/or home State are Parties.

Article 14(3) expressly prohibits 'complicity' with public authorities in violating these standards, namely 'by complicity with, or in assistance with others, including public authorities, violate human rights in times of peace or during socio-political upheavals'.

While none of these relate directly to the applicability and enforcement of claims regarding the environment, the close connection with human rights could demonstrate a direction in the language of agreements. Article 28(9) of

---

119 ibid para 745.
120 *Urbaser v Argentina* (n 12) para 1151.
121 *Burlington v Ecuador* (n 12) para 60.
122 *Urbaser v Argentina* (n 12) paras 1195 et seq.
123 Supplementary Act A/Sa.3/12/08 Adopting Community Rules on Investment and the Modalities for Their Implementation with ECOWAS (2008).

the COMESA Investment Agreement (2007) refers to contributions in aspects of enforcement:

> A Member State against whom a claim is brought by a COMESA investor under this Article may assert as a defence, counterclaim, right of set off or other similar claim, that the COMESA investor bringing the claim has not fulfilled its obligations under this Agreement, including the obligations to comply with all applicable domestic measures or that it has not taken all reasonable steps to mitigate possible damages.

This interaction between FPS and environmental law, in particular with respect to the integration of investor behaviour, leaves substantial lingering problems, including first, with acceptance and second, enforcement, but provides a pathway for a more complete consideration of investment protection.

4   Conclusions

While undoubtedly FPS has long been tightly and tenaciously associated with conflict in the traditional sense, the movement forward with respect to the urgency towards sustainability and environmental realities allows and necessitates a push forward for this provision towards more diverse applications. The solution to recognising a more systemically integrated system of investment protection may already be contained within the provisions. The FPS provision is a possible key to a more complete application of international law – allowing a push and pull with respect to rights and obligations resulting in a more complete legal mechanism for protection and actualization of international law.

To recap the argument: 1) FPS protects an investor's physical security with particular relevance in different forms of conflict; 2) such protection of physical security allows an opening in the application to environmental arguments; 3) yet, there are limitations in application of FPS in general, possibly manifesting in situations of complicity as well as contribution, as understood under international criminal law, during times of conflict; 4) such application of limitations will no doubt see future relevance with respect to environmental complicity and the possibility of counterclaims as conflict becomes more broadly defined.

This evolution of the protections demonstrates how the language of investment agreements, in their elaborate ambiguity, leave sufficient manoeuvrability for boundary crossing, regime interaction, and the new generation of investment protection. The standards of protection, in particular FPS with its close relationship with customary law, proves the perfect test case for exploring the possibility of a richer boundary crossing beyond investment law – both towards the more obvious IHL but also towards the emerging standards of international environmental agreements. While lacking enforceability mechanisms, as such environmental standards become more accepted norms of international law,[124] there is an even more profound basis for applying those norms in both the protection – as well as the limitation – of investment under FPS.

The possibility of a multilateral investment instrument and the practicality of renegotiating the 3,000 existing agreements exceeds what could happen during the next decade of reforms. Yet, if the space created during the negotiation of the treaties is considered through a new light, such agreements may prove to be sufficient to take into account the expanding needs and tendencies of the global economic realm. This supports a broader argument that the language of investment agreements – rather than requiring a complete renovation of the treaties and agreements – already holds the keys for taking investment law into a more systemically harmonised future.

Bibliography

Abrantes AM, *Entre Neutralidade e Cumplicidade o Envolvimento de Agentes Econômicos na Comissão de Crimes Internacionais* (Instituto Jurídico da Faculdade de Direito da Universidade de Coimbra 2017).

Alderman L, E Peltier, and H Saad, ' "ISIS Is Coming!" How a French Company Pushed the Limits in War-Torn Syria' *The New York Times* (New York, 10 March 2018) <www.nytimes.com/2018/03/10/business/isis-is-coming-how-a-french-company-pushed-the-limits-in-war-torn-syria.html> accessed 10 May 2020.

Alexandrov SA, 'The Evolution of the Full Protection and Security Standard' in M Kinnear and others (eds), *Building International Investment Law: The First 50 Years of ICSID* (Wolters Kluwer 2015).

Alreshaid N, 'Revisiting the Notion of Full Protection and Security of Foreign Direct Investments in Post-Gadhafi Libya: Two Governments, Tribunal Violence, Militias, and Plenty More' (2016) 28 Fla J Int'l L 63.

Alvarez JE, 'Beware: Boundary Crossings – A Critical Appraisal of Public Law Approaches to International Investment Law' (2016) 17 JWIT 171.

---

124 Louis J Kotzé, 'Constitutional Conversations in the Anthropocene: In Search of Environmental *Jus Cogens* Norms' (2015) 46 Netherlands YB Int'l L 241.

Baetens F, 'When International Rules Interact: International Investment Law and the Law of Armed Conflict' (*IISD Investment Treaty News*, 7 April 2011) <www.iisd.org/itn/2011/04/07/when-international-rules-interact-international-investment-law-and-the-law-of-armed-conflict/> accessed 11 March 2020.

Behn D, 'Legitimacy, Evolution, and Growth in Investment Treaty Arbitration: Empirically Evaluating the State-of-the-Art' (2015) 46 Geo J Int'l L 363.

Bix B, *Law Language and Legal Determinacy* (Clarendon 1993).

Blackaby N and others, *Redfern and Hunter on International Arbitration* (6th edn, OUP 2014).

Bray HL, 'SOI – Save Our Investments: International Investment Law and International Humanitarian Law' (2013) 14 JWIT 578.

Brower CN and SW Schill, 'Is Arbitration a Threat or a Boon to the Legitimacy of Investment Arbitration?' (2009) 9 Chicago J Int'l L 471.

Burke-White WW and von Staden A, 'Private Litigation in a Public Law Sphere: The Standard of Review in Investor-State Arbitrations' (2010) 35 Yale J Int'l L 283.

Chambers R, 'The *Unocal* Settlement: Implications for the Developing Law on Corporate Complicity in Human Rights Abuses' (2005) 13(1) Hm Rts Brief 14.

Choudhury B, 'Recapturing Public Power: Is Investment Arbitration's Engagement of the Public Interest Contributing to the Democratic Deficit?' (2008) 41 Vand J Transnat'l L 775.

Cordero Moss G, 'Full Protection and Security' in A Reinisch (ed), *Standards of Investment Protection* (OUP 2008).

Crawford J, *Brownlie's Principles of Public International Law* (9th edn, OUP 2019).

Crow K, 'Corporations and Crimes Against Humanity: Financial Liability Through ISDS?' in K Fach Gómez, A Gourgourinis, and C Titi (eds), *International Investment Law and the Law of Armed Conflict* (Springer 2019).

Daza-Clark AM and D Behn, 'Between War and Peace: Intermittent Armed Conflict and Investment Arbitration' in K Fach Gómez, A Gourgourinis, and C Titi (eds), *International Investment Law and the Law of Armed Conflict* (Springer 2019).

De Brabandere E, 'Host States' Due Diligence Obligations in International Investment Law' (2015) 42 Syracuse J Int'l L & Com 319.

De Brabandere E, 'Fair and Equitable Treatment and (Full) Protection and Security in African Investment Treaties between Generality and Contextual Specificity' (2017) 18 JWIT 530.

Di Benedetto S, *International Investment Law and the Environment* (Edward Elgar 2013).

Dolzer R and C Schreuer, *Principles of International Investment Law* (2nd edn, OUP 2012).

Donaubauer J, E Neumayer, and P Nunnenkamp, 'Winning or Losing in Investor-to-State Dispute Resolution: The Role of Arbitrator Bias and Experience' (2018) 26 Rev Int'l Econ 892.

Douglas Z, 'The Plea of Illegality in Investment Treaty Arbitration' (2014) 29 ICSID Rev 155.

Dupuy P-M, F Francioni and E-U Petersmann (eds), *Human Rights in International Investment Law and Arbitration* (OUP 2009).

Forcese C, 'Deterring "Militarized Commerce": The Prospect of Liability for "Privatized" Human Rights Abuses' (2000) 31 Ottawa L Rev 171.

Franck SD, 'The Legitimacy Crisis in Investment Treaty Arbitration: Privatizing Public International Law through Inconsistent Decisions' (2005) 73 Fordham L Rev 1521.

Garro AM, 'Trade and Investment Treaties, the Rule of Law, and Standards of the Administration of Justice' (2011) 42 U Miami Inter-Am L Rev 267.

Henckaerts J-M and L Doswald-Beck, *Customary International Humanitarian Law*, vol 1 (ICRC and CUP 2005).

Henckels C, 'Balancing Investment Protection and the Public Interest: The Role of the Standard of Review and the Importance of Deference in Investor-State Arbitration' (2013) 4 JIDS 197.

Hindelang S and M Krajewski, 'Shifting Paradigms in International Investment Law – More Balanced, Less Isolated, Increasingly Diversified' (2016) 27 EJIL 545, 551.

International Commission of Jurists, 'Corporate Complicity and Legal Accountability' (2008) <www.icj.org/wp-content/uploads/2012/06/Vol.1-Corporate-legal-accountability-thematic-report-2008.pdf> accessed 10 May 2020.

Junngam N, 'The Full Protection and Security Standard in International Investment Law: What and Who is Investment Fully (?) Protected and Secured From?' (2018) 7(1) Am U Bus L Rev 1.

Kingsbury B and SW Schill, 'Investor-State Arbitration as Governance: Fair and Equitable Treatment, Proportionality and the Emerging Global Administrative Law' in AJ van den Berg (ed), *50 Years of the New York Convention: ICCA International Arbitration Conference* (Wolters Kluwer 2009).

Koskenniemi M and P Leino, 'Fragmentation of International Law? Postmodern Anxieties' (2002) 15 LJIL 553.

Kotzé LJ, 'Constitutional Conversations in the Anthropocene: In Search of Environmental *Jus Cogens* Norms' (2015) 46 Netherlands YB Int'l L 241.

Kriebaum U, 'The Relevance of Economic and Political Conditions for Protection under Investment Treaties' (2011) 10 L & Prac Int'l Cts & Tribunals 383.

Kulick A, 'From Problem to Opportunity? An Analytical Framework for Vagueness and Ambiguity in International Law' (2016) 59 German YB Int'l L 258.

Leite K, 'The Fair and Equitable Treatment Standard: A Search for a Better Balance in International Investment Agreements' (2016) 32 Am U Int'l L Rev 363.

Linderfalk U, 'Cross-Fertilization in International Law' (2015) 84 Nord J Int'l L 428.

MacCormick N, *Rhetoric and the Rule of Law: A Theory of Legal Reasoning* (OUP 2005).

Malik M, 'The Full Protection and Security Standard Comes of Age: Yet Another Challenge for States in Investment Treaty Arbitration?' (2011) IISD Best Practice Series <www.iisd.org/pdf/2011/full_protection.pdf> accessed 16 March 2020.

Maupin J, 'Public and Private in International Investment Law: An Integrated Systems Approach' (2014) 54 Va J Int'l L 367.

McLachlan C, 'The Principle of Systemic Integration and Article 31(3)(c) of the Vienna Convention' (2005) 54 ICLQ 279.

Miles K, 'International Investment Law: Origins, Imperialism and Conceptualizing the Environment' (2010) 21 Colo J Int'l Envtl L & Pol'y 1.

Miles K, *The Origins of International Investment Law: Empire, Environment and the Safeguarding of Capital* (CUP 2013).

Mistura A, 'Enhancing Environmental Protection in International Investment Law through the Integration of International Civil Liability Principles' (*IISD Investment Treaty News*, 23 April 2019) <www.iisd.org/itn/2019/04/23/enhancing-environmental-protection-in-international-investment-law-through-the-integration-of-international-civil-liability-principles-alessandra-mistura/> accessed 16 March 2020.

Olson D, 'Corporate Complicity in Human Rights Violations under International Criminal Law' (2015) 1(1) Int'l Hm Rts LJ Art 5 <https://via.library.depaul.edu/ihrlj/vol1/iss1/5/> accessed 10 May 2020.

Organisation for Economic Co-operation and Development (OECD), *Guidelines for Multinational Enterprises* (OECD Publishing 2011).

Pauwelyn J, 'Bridging Fragmentation and Unity: International Law as a Universe of Inter-Connected Islands' (2004) 25 Mich J Int'l L 903.

Poscher R, 'Ambiguity and Vagueness in Legal Interpretation' in LM Solan and PM Tiersam (eds), *Oxford Handbook of Language and Law* (OUP 2012).

Puvimanasinghe SF, *Foreign Investment, Human Rights, and the Environment: A Perspective from South Asia on the Role of Public International Law for Development* (Martinus Nijhoff 2007).

Roberts A, 'Clash of Paradigms: Actors and Analogies Shaping the Investment Treaty System' (2013) 107 AJIL 45.

Ryk-Lakhman I, 'Protection of Foreign Investments Against the Effects of Hostilities: A Framework for Assessing Compliance with Full Protection and Security' in Katia Fach Gómez, Anastasios Gourgourinis and Catharine Titi (eds), *International Investment Law and the Law of Armed Conflict* (Springer 2019).

Sabahi B and K Duggal, 'Occidental Petroleum v Ecuador (2012): Observations on Proportionality, Assessment of Damages and Contributory Fault' (2013) 28 ICSID Rev 279.

Schill SW, *The Multilateralization of International Investment Law* (CUP 2009).

Schill SW, 'Enhancing the Legitimacy of International Investment Law: Conceptual and Methodological Foundations of a New Public Law Approach' (2011) 52 Va J Int'l L 57.

Schreuer C and others, *The ICSID Convention: A Commentary* (2nd edn, CUP 2009).

Schreuer C, 'The Protection of Investments in Armed Conflict' in Freya Baetens (ed), *Investment Law within International Law* (CUP 2013).

Schreuer C, 'War and Peace in International Investment Law' in K Fach Gómez, A Gourgourinis, and C Titi (eds), *International Investment Law and the Law of Armed Conflict* (Springer 2019).

Schultz T and C Dupont, 'Investment Arbitration: Promoting the Rule of Law or Over-Empowering Investors? A Quantitative Empirical Study' (2014) 25 EJIL 1147.

Stern B, *Acte de la victim justifiant partiellement l'acte de l'État* (Pedone 1973).

Titi C, 'Full Protection and Security, Arbitrary or Discriminatory Treatment and the Invisible EU Model BIT' (2014) 15 JWIT 534.

UN Office of the High Commissioner for Human Rights, 'Human Rights and Climate Change' (2020) <www.ohchr.org/EN/Issues/HRAndClimateChange/Pages/HRClimateChangeIndex.aspx> accessed 16 March 2020.

Viñuales JE, *Foreign Investment and the Environment in International Law* (CUP 2012).

Viñuales JE, 'International Investment Law and Natural Resource Governance' in Kati Kulovesi and Elisa Morgera (eds), *Research Handbook on International Law and Natural Resources* (Edward Elgar 2016).

Whiteman M, *Damages in International Law* (US Government Printing Office 1937).

Wongkaew T, 'The Cross-Fertilisation of International Investment Law and International Humanitarian Law: Prospects and Pitfalls' in K Fach Gómez, A Gourgourinis, and C Titi (eds), *International Investment Law and the Law of Armed Conflict* (Springer 2019).

Zeitler HE, 'The Guarantee of "Full Protection and Security" in Investment Treaties Regarding Harm Caused by Private Actors' (2005) 3 Stockholm Int'l Arb Rev 1.

Zrilič J, *The Protection of Foreign Investment in Times of Armed Conflict* (OUP 2019).

CHAPTER 4

The Effect of Armed Hostilities on Investment Treaty Obligations: A Case of *Force Majeure*?

Christina Binder and Philipp Janig

1   Introduction

The rules governing the use of military power by sovereign actors belong to the oldest fields of public international law. In comparison, international investment law is a novelty. While inter-state conflicts have become a rare occurrence, the recent decade has seen a number of intra-state conflicts with implications for foreign investors. In particular, the civil unrest in a number of countries resulting from the 'Arab Spring' has given rise to several investment claims,[1] including against Syria[2] and Libya.[3]

The present chapter focuses on the effects of armed hostilities on the obligations of host states in light of *force majeure*. While international law presumes the continuity of treaties in situations of armed hostilities, armed hostilities may give raise to the derogation from treaty obligations by a treaty party under the general law of treaties, either temporarily on the basis of suspension or generally due to the termination of the treaty.[4] Thus, they may allow to invoke a material breach (article 60 VCLT),[5] supervening impossibility of performance

---

1   Eric De Brabandere, '*Jus Post Bellum* and Foreign Direct Investment: Mapping the Debate' (2015) 16 JWIT 590, 596.
2   See, *eg*, *Gamesa Eólica SLU v Syria*, PCA Case no 2012-11, Award (5 April 2014) (not public).
3   See, *eg*, *Way2B ACE v Libya*, Award (24 May 2018) (not public); *Cengiz İnşaat Sanayi ve Ticaret AS v Libya*, ICC Case no 21537/ZF/AYZ, Award (7 November 2018); several other cases are still pending at the time of writing, see United Nations Conference on Trade and Development (UNCTAD), 'Investment Dispute Settlement Navigator' (*Investment Policy Hub*, 2020) <https://investmentpolicy.unctad.org/investment-dispute-settlement> accessed 23 March 2020.
4   See, generally, ILC, 'Draft Articles on the Effects of Armed Conflicts on Treaties with Commentaries' (2011) II(2) YBILC 108; Christoph Schreuer, 'War and Peace in International Investment Law' in Katia Fach Gómez, Anastasios Gourgourinis, and Catharine Titi (eds), *International Investment Law and Law of Armed Conflict* (Springer 2019) 4 et seq.
5   This might potentially be the case in international armed conflicts between the treaty parties.

(article 61 VCLT)[6] or a fundamental change of circumstances (article 62 VCLT).[7] Moreover, treaty provisions enshrined in international investment agreements (IIAS) might provide for carve-outs applicable to situations of armed hostilities. Thus, so-called non-precluded measures (NPM) clauses may give host states the possibility to argue a derogation from their obligations insofar as this concerns measures necessary for the protection of their 'essential security interests'.[8] However, when no party invokes any of these grounds for suspension or termination under the law of treaties and no NPM clause finds application, the IIAS will remain in place and operable.

Thus, the question arises whether host states might rely on the defence of *force majeure* under the law of state responsibility in the context of armed hostilities. This chapter explores to what extent *force majeure* provides host states with relief in investment disputes when faced with the exceptional situation of armed hostilities on their territory. While the concept of *force majeure* may also be enshrined in contractual clauses or domestic law, both of which may find application in investment disputes,[9] the present chapter will be limited to the examination of *force majeure* under general international law. As such, the defence is available in principle to all host states and its applicability does not dependent on the pertinent IIA.

To address this question, this chapter first discusses the most pertinent treatment standards of IIAs in the context of armed hostilities, as these might influence the application of secondary norms (section 2). Thereafter, it addresses *force majeure* under general international law (section 3), including its constituent elements (section 3.1), its practical relevance with regard to

---

6 See Gabriele Gagliani, 'Supervening Impossibility of Performance and the Effect of Armed Conflict on Investment Treaties: Any Room for Manoeuvre?' in Katia Fach Gómez, Anastasios Gourgourinis, and Catharine Titi (eds), *International Investment Law and Law of Armed Conflict* (Springer 2019).

7 See Case C-162/96 *Racke GmbH and Co v Hauptzollamt Mainz* [1998] ECR I-3655 (concerning the civil war in and break-up of Yugoslavia).

8 See William J Moon, 'Essential Security Interests in International Investment Agreements' (2012) 15 J Int'l Econ L 481. See also, *eg, CMS Gas Transmission Co v Argentina*, ICSID Case no ARB/01/8, Annulment Decision (25 September 2007) para 146. Earlier jurisprudence has incorrectly equated these provisions as *lex specialis* to the defence of necessity under customary international law, see also *Deutsche Telekom v India*, PCA Case no 2014-10, Interim Award (13 December 2017) paras 225 et seq.

9 See, *eg*, ICC, *Himpurna California Energy Ltd v PT (Persero) Perusahaan Listruik Negara*, Final Award (4 May 1999), (2000) 25 YB Comm Arb 13; *RSM Production Corp v Central African Republic*, ICSID Case no ARB/07/2, Decision on Jurisdiction and Liability (7 December 2010) paras 145 et seq, 176 et seq. See also *Nykomb Synergetics Technology Holding AB v Latvia*, SCC Case no 118/2001, Arbitral Award (16 December 2003) paras 101 et seq.

armed hostilities (section 3.2), potential procedural requirements (section 3.3) and the legal consequences of a successful invocation (section 3.4). Section 4 concludes.

2 Pertinent Treatment Standards: Full Protection and Security and (Extended) War Clauses

International investment agreements generally enshrine a variety of different treatment standards, including fair and equitable treatment (FET), full protection and security (FPS) and various non-discrimination standards. While all of these might apply in situations of armed hostilities, this section will discuss two standards that are arguably of particular importance. The standard most likely violated as a result of armed hostilities is FPS, which is moreover enshrined in most IIAS. In addition, a (limited) number of IIAS include so-called (extended) war clauses that specifically deal with armed hostilities and similar situations.

The FPS standard primarily serves to safeguard the physical security of the investor and their investment, both from actions of state authorities (such as military or police) as well as private actors (such as insurgents or rioters).[10] As a result, FPS provisions have been applied in a number of cases relating to armed hostilities, most famously in *AAPL v Sri Lanka* in the context of a counter-insurgency operation by governmental forces.[11] The standard requires states to exercise due diligence to prevent physical harm, which is not fulfilled in case of 'a substantive failure to take reasonable, precautionary and preventive action'.[12] However, tribunals partly differ in the specific diligence standard to be applied. While some tribunals assess the conduct of host states against that of a 'well-administered government' (*AAPL v Sri Lanka*), others take account of the specific circumstances of the respective host state (*Pantechniki v Albania*).[13] In particular, in a protracted (civil) war, which may deplete a host

---

10 Merryl Lawry-White, 'International Investment Law in a *Jus Post Bellum* Framework' (2015) 16 JWIT 633, 647 et seq; Schreuer, 'War and Peace' (n 4) 10 et seq.

11 *Asian Agricultural Products Ltd (AAPL) v Sri Lanka*, ICSID Case no ARB/87/3, Award (27 June 1990) paras 45 et seq. See further cases cited in Schreuer, 'War and Peace' (n 4) 13.

12 *Biwater Gauff (Tanzania) Ltd v Tanzania*, ICSID Case no ARB/05/22, Award (24 July 2008) para 725. See also *Elettronica Sicula SpA (ELSI) (USA v Italy)* (Judgment) [1989] ICJ Rep 15, para 108.

13 See *Pantechniki SA Contractors & Engineers (Greece) v Albania*, ICSID Case no ARB/07/21, Award (30 July 2009) paras 76 et seq. See also Lawry-White (n 10) 647 et seq; Ira Ryk-Lakhman, 'Protection of Foreign Investments against the Effects of Hostilities: A Framework for Assessing Compliance with Full Protection and Security' in Katia Fach

state's resources, these different approaches may lead to significantly different results.

Moreover, IIAs may also include war clauses, which come in different variations. 'Simple' war clauses are enshrined in a significant number of IIAs and establish a non-discrimination standard in relation to compensation in cases of losses through armed conflict and similar events,[14] as exemplified by article 12(1) of the Energy Charter Treaty (ECT):[15]

> Except where Article 13 [on expropriation] applies, an Investor of any Contracting Party which suffers a loss with respect to any Investment in the Area of another Contracting Party owing to war or other armed conflict, state of national emergency, civil disturbance, or other similar event in that Area, shall be accorded by the latter Contracting Party, as regards restitution, indemnification, compensation or other settlement, treatment which is the most favourable of that which that Contracting Party accords to any other Investor, whether its own Investor, the Investor of any other Contracting Party, or the Investor of any third state.[16]

Such provisions enshrine non-discrimination obligations based on national treatment (NT) and/or most favoured nation (MFN) treatment regarding compensation paid by the host state in connection with certain types of

---

Gómez, Anastasios Gourgourinis, and Catharine Titi (eds), *International Investment Law and Law of Armed Conflict* (Springer 2019) 262 et seq.

14   For an overview of such provisions, see UNCTAD, 'Bilateral Investment Treaties 1995–2006: Trends in Investment Rulemaking' (2007) <https://unctad.org/en/Docs/iteiia20065_en.pdf> accessed 12 December 2019. For an overview of such clauses in BITs by Libya, Syria, and Yemen, see Suzanne Spears and Maria Fogdestam Agius, 'Protection of Investments in War-Torn States: A Practitioner's Perspective on War Clauses in Bilateral Investment Treaties' in Katia Fach Gómez, Anastasios Gourgourinis, and Catharine Titi (eds), *International Investment Law and Law of Armed Conflict* (Springer 2019). On the treaty practice of China with African countries, see Uche Ewelukwa Ofodile, 'Africa-China Bilateral Investment Treaties: A Critique' (2013) 35 Mich J Int'l L 131, 171 et seq. See also, on the treaty practice of Cuba, Rafael Cox Alomar, 'Investment Treaty Arbitration in Cuba' (2017) 48 U Miami Inter-Am L Rev 1, 42 et seq (terming them *'force majeure'* clauses).

15   Energy Charter Treaty (adopted 17 December 1994, entered into force 16 April 1998) 2080 UNTS 95 (ECT).

16   See also Michail Risvas, 'Non-discrimination and the Protection of Foreign Investments in the Context of an Armed Conflict' in Katia Fach Gómez, Anastasios Gourgourinis, and Catharine Titi (eds), *International Investment Law and Law of Armed Conflict* (Springer 2019) 202 et seq.

occurrences.[17] These obligations are relative, as non-discrimination provisions in general, and will thus only grant relief to the investor if there is a compensation scheme introduced by the host state.[18] Moreover, while their application is limited to circumstances in which the losses suffered by the investors result from a specific type of crisis situation,[19] it is irrelevant who (or what) caused them, contrasting them with so-called extended war clauses.[20]

These extended war clauses are considerably rarer and provide for stand-alone obligations.[21] They are enshrined in a number of pertinent provisions as a second paragraph, such as article 12(2) ECT:

> Without prejudice to paragraph (1), an Investor of a Contracting Party which, in any of the situations referred to in that paragraph, suffers a loss in the Area of another Contracting Party resulting from
> (a) requisitioning of its Investment or part thereof by the latter's forces or authorities; or
> (b) destruction of its Investment or part thereof by the latter's forces or authorities, which was not required by the necessity of the situation, shall be accorded restitution or compensation which in either case shall be prompt, adequate and effective.[22]

These extended war clauses deal with two different situations: firstly, the requisition (of parts) of the investment and, secondly, the destruction (of parts) of the investment that was not required by military necessity. Similar to FPS, they thus protect the physical integrity of the investment. In contrast, their application is limited to certain conflict situations and they generally foresee responsibility of the host state only for damages resulting from its own forces.[23]

---

17 For provisions only entailing MFN obligations, see Australia–Uruguay BIT (2019) art 8; Cyprus–Hungary BIT (1989) art 4(5).

18 Schreuer, 'War and Peace' (n 4) 13 et seq. See also *Pantechniki v Albania* (n 13) para 89 (finding that the invocation of a such a clause was irrelevant as 'the Claimant conceded that it could not prove that other victims of the civil disturbances had been favoured by the Government').

19 But see also UK–Argentina BIT (1990) art 4 (applying further to 'losses […] resulting from arbitrary actions by the authorities in the territory of the [host state]').

20 *AAPL v Sri Lanka* (n 11) para 65.

21 See generally Ira Ryk-Lakhman, chapter 2 in this volume.

22 For similar provisions, see Brazil–Ethiopia BIT (2018) art 8; Kuwait–Pakistan BIT (2011) art 4; Armenia–Latvia BIT (2005) art 6; Austria–Libya BIT (2002) art 5.

23 Schreuer, 'War and Peace' (n 4) 14 et seq. See also *American Manufacturing & Trading, Inc (AMT) v Zaire*, ICSID Case no ARB/93/1, Award (21 February 1997) paras 7.07 et seq.

The specific formulation of these provisions varies. Most treaties foresee an absolute obligation to restitute or compensate losses resulting from requisitioning, such as article 12(2)(a) ECT. However, some limit the responsibility of host states to instances in which the forces or authorities act within their 'competences, duties and command structures' under domestic law,[24] thus abrogating the general rule under article 7 of the ILC Articles on State Responsibility.[25]

In the context of the destruction of property, as covered by article 12(2)(b) ECT, extended war clauses generally limit the obligation to restitute or compensate to circumstances in which that 'was not required by the necessity of the situation'. The reference to (military) necessity requires investors, in particular, to show that damages caused to the investment were disproportional to any (purported) military advantage of the host state.[26] However, other treaties refer to 'combat actions', either instead of (military) necessity[27] or as an alternative element.[28] Still other treaties additionally refer to losses caused by state authorities that were 'not required by the [...] observance of legal requirement'.[29] Given the formulation of extended war clauses, the additional insertion of these elements in effect broadens the responsibility of the host state. This follows from them being phrased as alternative negative requirements for such responsibility ('not [...] or not'). Thus, should a provision enshrine these different elements, it would be sufficient for an investor to, *eg*, show that the

---

24 See Investment Agreement for the Common Market for Eastern and Southern Africa (COMESA) Common Investment Area (2007) art 21(2)(a); Mauritius–India BIT (1998) art 5(2)(a).

25 The article provides that states are responsible for actions of an organ which 'exceeds its authority or contravenes instructions'.

26 This is generally read as a reference to the law of armed conflict, see Lawry-White (n 10) 650. See also (First) Protocol Additional to the Geneva Conventions of 12 August 1949, and Relating to the Protection of Victims of International Armed Conflicts (adopted 8 June 1977, entered into force 7 December 1978) 1125 UNTS 3 (Additional Protocol I) art 51(5)(b); *In re List and others (Hostages Trial)* (1948) 15 ILR 632, 646 et seq. See, however, Ryk-Lakhman (n 13) 263 (noting that '[n]ot a single investment tribunal that adjudicated disputes that arise out of or in relation to armed conflicts considered the laws of armed conflict').

27 See DRC–US BIT (1984) art IV(2)(b) (applied in *AMT v Zaire* (n 23)).

28 Sri Lanka–UK BIT (1980) art IV(2)(b). See, for an interpretation of that provision, *AAPL v Sri Lanka* (n 11) paras 57 et seq. See also Mauritius–India BIT (1998) art 5(2)(b).

29 See Investment Agreement for the COMESA Common Investment Area (2007) art 21(2)(b); Mauritius–India BIT (1998) art 5(2)(b) (terminated on 22 March 2017 through unilateral denunciation).

destruction property was *either* not required by the necessity of the situation *or* not caused in combat action.[30]

Although extended war clauses, depending on their specific formulation, provide for considerable protection of an investor's property during armed hostilities, their relevance in practice might be limited due to the evidentiary problems involved. This follows from the burden of proof lying with the investor,[31] and the difficulty of gathering clear evidence around the conduct of combat operations.[32]

Instead of (extended) war clauses, a few treaties concluded by Italy enshrine so-called 'strict war clauses'.[33] These provide for strict liability of the host state with regard to losses and damages incurred 'due to war, other forms of armed conflict, a state of emergency, civil strife or other similar events' and '[i]rrespective of whether [they] have been caused by governmental forces or other subjects'.[34] While these provisions do not foresee restitution as a remedy, they provide for the farthest-reaching protection of investors by enshrining an absolute obligation to provide adequate compensation in these situations.[35] Nevertheless, most of the evidentiary difficulties mentioned above will persist.

Should a tribunal find a host state responsible for the breach of FPS or some type of a war clause during armed hostilities (or any other standard of treatment for that matter), the question arises whether the respondent state might successfully invoke *force majeure* due to the exceptional situation. Despite the general distinction between primary and secondary norms of international law, the examination of *force majeure* might also be influenced by whether one of the obligations discussed above is in question. As will be discussed below, the due diligence test involved in a FPS breach might overlap with elements of *force majeure* and its invocation might be altogether excluded in cases of breach of a strict or extended war clause.

---

30 See, however, *AAPL v Sri Lanka* (n 11) para 57 (treating the elements as cumulative).
31 ibid para 58. See, critical of this, Christoph Schreuer, 'The Protection of Investments in Armed Conflict' in Freya Baetens (ed), *Investment Law within International Law: Integrationist Perspectives* (CUP 2013) 16.
32 See *AAPL v Sri Lanka* (n 11) paras 63 et seq (with regard to necessity); Lawry-White (n 10) 650 (regarding attribution).
33 See Federico Ortino, 'Italy' in Chester Brown (ed), *Commentaries on Selected Model Investment Treaties* (2013) 335. See also Pakistan–Tajikistan BIT (2004) art IV (providing that adequate compensation shall be paid 'in accordance with customary international law').
34 Italy–Syria BIT (2002) art 4. See also Ecuador–Italy BIT (2001) art 4; Italy–Qatar BIT (2000) art 4; Italy–Pakistan BIT (1997) art 4.
35 Spears and Fogdestam Agius (n 14) 298.

3 *Force Majeure* and International Investment Law

3.1 Force Majeure *under General International Law*

The defence of *force majeure* is firmly accepted as a circumstance precluding wrongfulness under general international law.[36] While most authorities consider it a general principle of law,[37] some see it anchored in customary international law.[38] At any rate, the *force majeure* defence under international law is codified in article 23 of the ILC Articles on State Responsibility:[39]

1. The wrongfulness of an act of a State not in conformity with an international obligation of that State is precluded if the act is due to *force majeure*, that is the occurrence of an irresistible force or of an unforeseen event, beyond the control of the State, making it materially impossible in the circumstances to perform the obligation.
2. Paragraph 1 does not apply if:
   (a) the situation of *force majeure* is due, either alone or in combination with other factors, to the conduct of the State invoking it; or
   (b) the State has assumed the risk of that situation occurring.

---

36 See generally also Christina Binder, 'Circumstances Precluding Wrongfulness' in Marc Bungenberg and others (eds), *International Investment Law: A Handbook* (CH Beck, Hart, and Nomos 2015) 456 et seq.

37 See, *eg, North Sea Continental Shelf (Germany v Denmark, Germany v Netherlands)* (Separate Opinion of Fouad Ammoun) [1969] ICJ Rep 101, para 35; James Crawford, *The International Law Commission's Articles on State Responsibility: Introduction, Text and Commentaries* (CUP 2002) 172 et seq. See, in particular, the jurisprudence of the Iran–US Claims Tribunal, *eg, Anaconda-Iran Inc v Government of Iran and the National Iranian Copper Industries Co* (1986) 31 IUSCTR 199, para 43; *Mobil Oil Iran Inc and Mobil Sales and Supply Corp v Government of Iran and National Iranian Oil Co* (1987) 16 IUSCTR 3, para 117.

38 For an extensive discussion on the matter, see Federica I Paddeu, 'A Genealogy of *Force Majeure* in International Law' (2012) 82 Brit YB Int'l L 381, 476 et seq. See also James Crawford, *State Responsibility: The General Part* (CUP 2013) 295. For a customary rule, see Ana Maria Daza-Clark and Daniel Behn, 'Between War and Peace: Intermittent Armed Conflict and Investment Arbitration' in Katia Fach Gómez, Anastasios Gourgourinis, and Catharine Titi (eds), *International Investment Law and Law of Armed Conflict* (Springer 2019) 63.

39 Crawford, *Articles on State Responsibility* (n 37) 172. For case law applying *force majeure* as codified in that provision (or its predecessor), see *Rainbow Warrior (New Zealand v France)* (1990) 82 ILR 499, para 77; *Libyan Arab Foreign Investment Co (LAFICO) v Burundi*, Award (4 March 1991) 96 ILR 279. See also, similarly, *Autopista Concesionada de Venezuela CA (Aucoven) v Venezuela*, ICSID Case no ARB/00/5, Award (23 September 2003) para 108. See, although with the omission of 'unforeseen events', *Enron Corp and Ponderosa Assets LP v Argentina*, ICSID Case no ARB/01/3, Award (22 May 2007) para 217; *Sempra Energy International v Argentina*, ICSID Case no ARB/02/16, Award (28 September 2007) para 246.

Given that most IIAs do not explicitly refer to *force majeure* as a legal concept, these elements will generally find application should a host states invoke the defence.[40] The requirements outlined in article 23 of the ILC Articles on State Responsibility are strict, so that the defence will only apply in exceptional situations.[41] In the words of the ILC Commentary, *force majeure* 'involves a situation where the State in question is in effect compelled to act in a manner not in conformity with the requirements of an international obligation incumbent upon it'.[42] In particular older cases have – partly by way of *obiter dicta* – considered armed hostilities or civil unrest as prototypical *force majeure* situations.[43] In the *Spanish Zone of Morocco* case, the single arbitrator Max Huber held that 'the State is not responsible for the fact that there is a rising, a revolt, or a civil or international war', as these are regarded as *force majeure*.[44] Similarly, the Iran–US Claims Tribunal found that 'strikes, riots and other civil strife in the course of the Islamic Revolution had created classic *force majeure* conditions at least in Iran's major cities'.[45] However, *force majeure* has rarely been invoked in more recent jurisprudence, and hardly at all in cases involving armed hostilities. The following discussion thus addresses its different elements in general and attempts to draw therefrom for such situations.

Regarding its first element, the state has to be faced with either an 'irresistible force' (a constraint which the state was unable to avoid or oppose by its own means)[46] *or* an 'unforeseen event'.[47] A situation will constitute an

---

40   For an early draft including such a reference, see OECD, 'Draft Convention on the Protection of Foreign Property' (1967) art 6 <www.oecd.org/daf/inv/internationalinvestmentagreements/39286571.pdf> accessed 17 December 2019. See also the discussion below on the inter-relation of extended war clauses with *force majeure*.
41   See Simon Olleson, 'The Impact of the ILC's Articles on Responsibility of States for Internationally Wrongful Acts' (2007) British Institute of International and Comparative Law 154 <www.biicl.org/files/3107_impactofthearticlesonstate_responsibilitypreliminarydraftfinal.pdf> accessed 10 February 2020.
42   Crawford, *Articles on State Responsibility* (n 37) 170.
43   See the cases cited in ibid 172 et seq (fn 376); Sebastián Mantilla Blanco, *Full Protection and Security in International Investment Law* (Springer 2019) 187 et seq.
44   *Spanish Zone of Morocco* (*Great Britain v Spain*) (1925) 2 ILR 157, 159. See also – apparently under Belgian law – *Jenny and Hedwige R v Belgium*, Case no 133 (1933) 7 ILR 323, 323 et seq (Belgium, Court of Appeal of Brussels) ('Before 1914 war damage was deemed to be the result of *force majeure*, and gave no right to a remedy against the State'.).
45   See, with further references, *Gould Marketing, Inc, as Successor to Hoffman Export Corp v Ministry of Defence of Iran* (1983) 3 IUSCTR 147, para 19; *Dadras International and Per-Am Construction Corp v Iran and Tehran Redevelopment Co* (1995) 31 IUSCTR 127, para 275.
46   Crawford, *Articles on State Responsibility* (n 37) 170. A pertinent example might include the *Ottoman Empire Lighthouses Concession* (*Greece v France*) (1956) 12 RIAA 155 discussed in more detail below.
47   Christina Binder, *Die Grenzen der Vertragstreue im Völkerrecht* (Springer 2013) 395 et seq.

'unforeseen event' if it was 'neither foreseen nor [of] an easily foreseeable kind'.[48] For instance, in the *Wipperman* Case in the late nineteenth century, Venezuela was not responsible for the looting of property of the US consul by native tribes, as 'the raid was one of those occasional and unexpected outbreaks against which ordinary and reasonable foresight could not provide'.[49] While isolated incidents might well be considered unforeseeable, it is doubtful whether that would likewise be true for occurrences in a protracted situation, such as rebel attacks in a civil war. In the much more recent *Aucoven* arbitration, the tribunal was concerned with the failure of Venezuela to increase toll rates applicable to the motorway operated by the claimant, as foreseen by a concession agreement. Venezuela argued that it was prevented to do so due to strong public resistance, which would constitute *force majeure*. The tribunal rejected the argument as it considered that the events were foreseeable, given that similar protests had already occurred in 1989, likewise after an increase in the price of transportation.[50]

Moreover, there is a requirement of *externality* to the situation, *ie* it must be 'beyond the control of the State'. This requires that the 'acts or omissions cannot be attributed [to the state] a result of his own wilful behaviour'.[51] Thus, the state may neither have directly created the situation, nor may the state have been able to avert it by the exercise of due diligence.[52] This clearly excludes reliance on *force majeure* by an aggressor state in inter-state conflicts. With regard to civil wars or civil unrest, the required diligence is more difficult to ascertain.[53] According to the Secretariat Study on *force majeure* of 1978 '[t]he Government is liable, however, where it fails to show due diligence

---

48 Crawford, *Articles on State Responsibility* (n 37) 170.
49 *Wipperman Case (USA/Venezuela)* (1887) 3 Moore Int'l Arb 3039, 3043.
50 See *Aucoven v Venezuela* (n 39) paras 111 et seq.
51 ILC, '"Force majeure" and "Fortuitous Event" as Circumstances Precluding Wrongfulness: Survey of State Practice, International Judicial Decisions and Doctrine – Study Prepared by the Secretariat' (1978) II(2) YBILC 61, para 15. See also Andrea Bjorklund, 'Emergency Exceptions: State of Necessity and Force Majeure', in Peter T Muchlinski, Federico Ortino, and Christoph Schreuer (eds), *Oxford Handbook of International Investment Law* (OUP 2008) 500 et seq.
52 Binder, *Die Grenzen der Vertragstreue* (n 47) 394 et seq. See also *Gould Marketing v Iran* (n 45) para 19 (defining *force majeure* as 'social and economic forces beyond the power of the state to control through the exercise of due diligence'); *Corfu Channel (UK v Albania)* (Merits, Dissenting Opinion of Philadelpho Azevedo) [1949] ICJ Rep 78, 94 (arguing that the laying of mines by a another actor might be unforeseeable for a coastal state, however would not have been 'inevitable' for Albania, as it could have used its coastal artillery to drive off the perpetrators).
53 See also *Spanish Zone of Morocco* (n 44) 159 et seq.

in preventing or suppressing the riot, or where the circumstances indicate an insufficiency of protective measures or a complicity of government officers or agents in the disorder'.[54]

Nevertheless, the standard might be 'more flexible when it concerns a general situation',[55] such as protracted civil unrest or civil war. In that regard, the Iran–US Claims Tribunal operated with a general presumption that the core period of the revolution (December 1978 – February 1979) constituted a *force majeure* situation, at least in the larger cities.[56] The more recent *Aucoven* case,[57] discussed below, suggests the same. At any rate, the inextricable connection between *force majeure* and due diligence raises the question whether the defence may find application in the context of investment disputes arising from armed hostilities, as will be discussed below.

This *force majeure* situation must make it 'materially impossible [...] to perform the obligation' in question.[58] This requires a clear causal link between the 'irresistible force' or 'unforeseen event' and the impossibility of performance,[59] which is determined based on the circumstances of each case.[60] While performance must not have become absolutely impossible, it is insufficient that it merely becomes more difficult or burdensome.[61] In that context, purely economic difficulties in discharging the obligations generally do not reach the level of 'material impossibility', as confirmed by the Permanent Court of International Justice (PCIJ) in the context of the payment of loans in *Serbian Loans*:

> It cannot be maintained that the [First World] war itself, despite its grave economic consequences, affected the legal obligations of the contracts between the Serbian Government and the French bondholders.

---

[54] ILC, '"*Force majeure*" and "Fortuitous Event"' (n 51) para 545, quoting Edwin M Borchard, *The Diplomatic Protection of Citizens Abroad or the Law of International Claims* (Banks Law Publishing 1928) 22.

[55] Sandra Szurek, 'Circumstances Precluding Wrongfulness in the ILC Articles on State Responsibility: *Force Majeure*' in James Crawford, Alain Pellet, and Simon Olleson (eds), *The Law of International Responsibility* (OUP 2010) 478.

[56] See, *eg*, *Gould Marketing v Iran* (n 45) para 19.

[57] *Aucoven v Venezuela* (n 39).

[58] This requires a causal link, see Crawford, *Articles on State Responsibility* (n 37) 170 et seq.

[59] ibid 170.

[60] See *Sylvania Technical Systems, Inc v Iran* (1985) 8 IUSCTR 298, para 53.

[61] See Crawford, *State Responsibility* (n 38) 298 et seq. See also *Rainbow Warrior* (n 39) para 77 (holding that 'the test [...] is of absolute and material impossibility and [...] a circumstance rendering performance merely more difficult or burdensome does not constitute a case of *force majeure*'); *Enron v Argentina* (n 39) para 217; *Sempra v Argentina* (n 39) para 246.

The economic dislocations caused by the war did not release the debtor State [...].[62]

However, armed hostilities themselves may well lead to the impossibility of performance, with the ILC Commentary explicitly mentioning the 'loss of control over a portion of the State's territory as a result of an insurrection or devastation of an area by military operations carried out by a third State'.[63]

Similarly, in the *Ottoman Empire Lighthouses Concession* arbitration, the tribunal was concerned with Greece's obligation to restitute a lighthouse to France. Although the lighthouse had suffered significant damages caused by shelling by Turkish batteries, this constituted *force majeure*, therefore excusing Greece from restoring the lighthouse to its original condition.[64] Thus, in case of an overwhelming attack (*ie* an irresistible force), a host state may invoke *force majeure* regardless whether it was reasonably foreseeable or not.

In *Aucoven*, the tribunal addressed what it called the 'requirement of impossibility', although its examination included aspects of the *irresistibility* and *externality* of the situation, as well as the *impossibility* to perform the obligation.[65] This arguably follows from the tribunal's decision to apply the 'impossibility standard under Venezuelan administrative law',[66] although it found that international law did not provide for a different standard.[67] Nevertheless, the applicable standard was arguably lower than the one foreseen in the ILC Articles on State Responsibility, as 'it is not necessary that the *force majeure* event be irresistible; it suffices that by all reasonable judgment the event impedes the normal performance of the [obligation]'.[68] Moreover, in what arguably appears as question of *externality*, the tribunal noted that Venezuela admitted 'that the civil protest was not irresistible in the sense that it could not have been mastered by the use of force'.[69] While that issue was not finally resolved, the tribunal was 'rather inclined to find that, in consideration of the events of 1989 and of the risk of repetition, the impossibility requirement appears met'.[70]

---

62   *Serbian Loans (France v Yugoslavia)* [1929] PCIJ Series A no 20, 39 et seq. See, likewise, *Brazilian Loans (France v Brazil)* [1929] PCIJ Series A no 21, 120.
63   Crawford, *Articles on State Responsibility* (n 37) 170 et seq.
64   See *Ottoman Empire Lighthouses Concession* (n 46) 219 et seq. See also Crawford, *State Responsibility* (n 38) 296.
65   *Aucoven v Venezuela* (n 39) paras 120 et seq.
66   ibid para 121.
67   ibid para 123.
68   ibid para 121.
69   ibid para 124.
70   ibid.

Although *Aucoven* was thus concerned with issues also relevant for situations of armed hostilities, it is unclear how far its approach reflects the applicable standards under general international law.

Moreover, article 23(2) of the ILC Articles on State Responsibility foresees two circumstances in which reliance on *force majeure* is excluded, essentially further determining the required 'externality' of the situation. While the first relates to factual contributions by the state, the second concerns specific commitments undertaken by it. Following article 23(2)(a) of the ILC Articles on State Responsibility, the situation may not be 'due [...] to the state invoking it'. This arguably sets a higher bar than the comparable criterion for exclusion in article 25(2)(b) of the ILC Articles on State Responsibility, which only requires a 'contribution' of the state to the situation of necessity.[71] In particular, it should not include situations in which a state 'contributes unwittingly' to a certain occurrence; rather, its role must be substantial.[72] In *LAFICO v Burundi*, Burundi argued that the participation of LAFICO in the management of a joint venture was 'objectively impossible' as the company and its representatives were absent.[73] However, the tribunal rejected reliance on *force majeure* in that context, as 'the impossibility [was] the result of a unilateral decision' of Burundi, namely the decision to expel all Libyan nationals and prohibit them from entering the country.[74] While the contribution of Burundi thus clearly created the pertinent situation, most cases will generally not be as clear-cut. Especially in the context of civil wars, states will arguably have contributed to the underlying political or social situation and/or to the exacerbation of the conflict.[75] However, jurisprudence suggests that this will generally not suffice. The Iran–US Claims Tribunal found that 'strikes, riots and other civil strife in the course of the Islamic Revolution had created classic *force majeure* conditions', and that those were generally not attributable to Iran.[76] As a result, Iran was excused from certain (contractual) payment obligations.[77] Also the *Aucoven* tribunal found that even though the protest in question had the 'full support of

---

71 Crawford, *Articles on State Responsibility* (n 37) 173. The question of 'contribution' in the context of necessity has been addressed in a number of cases relating to the Argentine financial crisis, see Christina Binder and Philipp Janig, 'Investment Agreements and Financial Crises' in Markus Krajewski and Rhea Tamara Hoffmann (eds), *Research Handbook on Foreign Direct Investment* (Edward Elgar 2019).
72 Crawford, *State Responsibility* (n 38) 300 et seq.
73 *LAFICO v Burundi* (n 39) para 53.
74 ibid para 55.
75 See, with regard to Libya, Daza-Clark and Behn (n 38) 64.
76 *Gould Marketing v Iran* (n 45) paras 19 et seq.
77 *Sylvania v Iran* (n 60) paras 38 et seq.

the local government', it was unclear whether that 'support was causal for the protests or their seriousness'.⁷⁸ Thus, the threshold for excluding reliance of a host state due to its contribution to a situation appears rather high.

Moreover, article 23(2)(b) of the ILC Articles on State Responsibility excludes reliance on *force majeure*, if 'the State has assumed the risk of that situation occurring'.⁷⁹ This includes situations in which a state, through an agreement, 'has undertaken to prevent the particular situation or has otherwise assumed that risk'.⁸⁰ The *extended* war clauses discussed above arguably contain such undertakings. These provisions generally enshrine commitments by the state to compensate investors for certain typical risks that result from 'war or armed conflict [...] or similar event', namely the destruction and requisitioning of private property.⁸¹ While it is reasonable to assume that this applies to extended war clauses in general, this becomes most clear with regard to provisions that explicitly apply to 'acts of God or *force majeure*'.⁸² The same would likewise apply to strict war clauses. As a result, a host state could not excuse the breach of these obligations by invoking *force majeure*.

3.2 *The Practical Relevance of* Force Majeure *in Investment Disputes Involving Armed Hostilities*

While armed hostilities might well meet the requirements for the *force majeure* defence to apply, its potential impact in the context of investment disputes is more limited. So far, host states – at least in public proceedings – have rarely invoked *force majeure* as a defence in situations of armed hostilities. As discussed above, in such situations, tribunals will most likely deal with (purported) violations of FPS provisions and extended war clauses. While the latter might themselves exclude reliance on *force majeure*, it is unlikely that a violation of the former could be excused by *force majeure* in practice. This follows

---

78 *Aucoven v Venezuela* (n 39) para 128. However, as discussed above, the plea failed on other grounds.

79 For an early case, see *Dame Franz (France) v Germany* (1922) 1 ILR 169 (holding that Germany could not invoke *force majeure* for the loss of private property due to World War I, as it had *post facto* accepted responsibility in the Treaty of Versailles). See also *Anaconda v Iran* (n 37) para 43.

80 Crawford, Articles on State Responsibility (n 37) 173 et seq. See also Crawford, *State Responsibility* (n 38) 301.

81 Spears and Fogdestam Agius (n 14) 283, 309.

82 This is particular the case with a number of BITs concluded by Austria, see, *eg*, Austria–Kyrgyzstan BIT (2016) art 8; Austria–Libya BIT (2002) art 5. See also Bulgaria–Morocco BIT (1996) art 5 (including a 'simple' war clause titled 'compensation in case of *force majeure*'/'pepommagement en cas de *force majeure*').

from FPS provisions containing obligations of conduct, paired with the connection of *force majeure* with due diligence. Thus, the factual circumstances giving rise to a *force majeure* situation might already be decisive on the level of primary rules, leading tribunals to find no breach in the first place. Should, reversely, a tribunal find a violation due to a lack of due diligence by the host state, the situation would lack the required externality.[83]

For instance, while the dissenting arbitrator in *AAPL v Sri Lanka* considered that Sri Lanka was 'essentially [confronted] with a *force majeure* situation', he found this to be relevant for the application of the primary rules:

> [t]he Tribunal's enunciation and application of due diligence rule fails to take into account the national emergency and extraordinary conditions under which the Government mounted a strategic and highly sensitive security operation to regain its sovereign control of the area of insurgency.[84]

Similarly, in *Toto Costruzioni v Lebanon*, the tribunal took account of the consequences of the internal armed conflict inside Lebanon and the war between Lebanon and Israel when applying primary rules. It found it had no jurisdiction regarding a denial of justice claim based on the FET standard,[85] and that Lebanon did not breach its obligation with regard to its purported failure to remove Syrian troops.[86]

Thus, tribunals have certain discretion in taking into account the specific (alleviating) circumstances resulting from armed hostilities already when examining whether host states have violated their obligations under IIAs. When faced with primary norms involving due diligence obligations, the *force majeure* defence only appears available to host states should tribunals apply different diligence standards in the context of primary rules and *force majeure*: otherwise, any failure to exercise diligence will both lead to a breach and

---

83　See, generally on this issue, Jure Zrilič, 'Armed Conflict as Force Majeure in International Investment Law' (2019) 16 Manchester J Int'l Econ L 28.

84　*AAPL v Sri Lanka*, ICSID Case no ARB/87/3, Final Award, Dissenting Opinion of Samuel KB Asante (15 June 1990), (1991) 6 ICSID Rev 574, 593.

85　*Toto Costruzioni Generali SpA v Lebanon*, ICSID Case no ARB/07/12, Decision on Jurisdiction (11 September 2009) paras 165 et seq (however finding it decisive that the claimant showed a lack of diligence in pursuing the litigation).

86　*Toto Costruzioni Generali SpA v Lebanon*, ICSID Case no ARB/07/12, Award (7 June 2012) paras 195 et seq (finding that Toto Costruzioni 'was – or should have been aware – of that the Syrian troops occupied areas' relevant for the project). See also Schreuer, 'The Protection of Investments in Armed Conflict' (n 31) 18 et seq; *LESI SpA and ASTALDI SpA v Algeria*, ICSID Case no ARB/05/3, Award (12 November 2008) paras 173 et seq.

prevent reliance on the defence. In most circumstances, it appears unlikely that tribunals would apply different standards. However, should a tribunal be faced with a broader, protracted *force majeure* situation – which might be the case in the context of armed hostilities – it might consider that while a host state has failed to act in due diligence in a specific situation (thus breaching, *eg*, FPS), it nevertheless has *in general* acted diligently in reaction to insurgent groups (thus still allowing for an invocation of *force majeure*).

Moreover, *force majeure* might still find application insofar as the primary rules breached contain obligations of result, such as non-discrimination obligations. This, for example in situations where the host state, faced with a situation of armed hostilities, disproportionately interferes with the rights of foreign investors to address the situation; *eg*, when certain branches of industry are predominantly in the hands of foreign investors. At any rate, the reliance on *force majeure* due to armed hostilities appears all the more exceptional in the context of investment disputes and will only be open to host states under rather specific circumstances.

3.3 *Procedural Requirements of Invoking* Force Majeure

Should a state seek to rely on *force majeure*, the ILC Articles on State Responsibility do not explicitly foresee any procedural obligations. During their drafting, the Special Rapporteur envisioned such obligations as article 34*bis*(1):

> A State invoking a circumstance precluding wrongfulness under this chapter should, as soon as possible after it has notice of the circumstance, inform the other State or States concerned in writing of it and of its consequences for the performance of the obligation.[87]

The Commission considered the provision a progressive development of international law and withdrew it eventually.[88] While it appears clear that there are currently no procedural obligations under customary international law, and jurisprudence generally regards the circumstances precluding wrongfulness as defences that may be invoked *ex post facto*,[89] procedural

---

[87] ILC, 'Report of the Work of the ILC on the Work of Its Fifty-First Session' (1999) II(2) YBILC 1, 83 et seq (fn 239). See also Binder, *Die Grenzen der Vertragstreue* (n 47) 419.

[88] ILC, 'Report of the Work of the ILC on the Work of Its Fifty-First Session' (n 85) 83 et seq (paras 392, 395, 398).

[89] See in more detail, Binder, *Die Grenzen der Vertragstreue* (n 47) 415 et seq. See also Bjorklund (n 51) 508 (considering that prompt notifications are 'unlikely to occur' in practice).

obligations are sometimes foreseen in treaty provisions.⁹⁰ Moreover, it is argued that such requirements might arise from the general principle of good faith.⁹¹ Depending on the circumstances, this might in particular include the earliest possible notification of the other treaty party or parties of the circumstance precluding wrongfulness.⁹² While prior notification will often be impossible in situations of *force majeure*, due to them potentially constituting an 'unforeseen event',⁹³ notification might still be possible and expedient if those situations are protracted, such as in case of armed hostilities. However, this duty to act in good faith should also extend to the non-treaty parties protected by the treaty's provisions, *ie* the pertinent foreign investors. Given that a host state might not be aware of all investors operating in its territory, this should not be understood as a requirement of direct notification. Instead, notifications should arguably reach a certain level of publicity, similarly to the required public proclamation of a state of emergency under human rights treaties.⁹⁴ This would allow investors to take notice and mitigate the consequences of the host state's reliance on *force majeure*. Despite the cautiousness of both the ILC and jurisprudence in this context, a failure to act in good faith might well be taken into account in the context of international law as currently applicable. Thus, procedural requirements would

---

90 See, on the basis of a contract, *Unión Fenosa Gas SA v Egypt*, ICSID Case no ARB/14/4, Award (31 August 2018) para 9.78 ('give prompt notice with relevant information'). *Cf* also *Bernardus Henricus Funnekotter and others v Zimbabwe*, ICSID Case no ARB/05/6, Award (22 April 2009) para 103 (considering, in the context of necessity, that 'Zimbabwe domestic law may [...] provide the Tribunal useful information' and that 'no state of emergency [had been] declared in that country', although 'ultimately international law, not the domestic law of Zimbabwe, must determine the effect any state of emergency would have on the dispute').

91 Binder, *Die Grenzen der Vertragstreue* (n 47) 419 et seq.

92 ILC, 'Second Report on State Responsibility by Mr. James Crawford, Special Rapporteur' (1999) UN Doc A/CN.4/498/Add.2, para 352 ('If a State seeks to rely on a circumstance precluding wrongfulness, *ie* in order to excuse what would otherwise be a breach of international law, it should, as a minimum, promptly inform the other State or States of that fact, and of the consequences for its performance of the obligation.').

93 See also ILC, 'Report of the Work of the ILC on the Work of Its Fifty-First Session' (n 85) 83 et seq (para 392).

94 See, *eg*, International Covenant on Civil and Political Rights (adopted 16 December 1966, entered into force 23 March 1976) 999 UNTS 171 (ICCPR) art 4(1) ('In time of public emergency which threatens the life of the nation *and the existence of which is officially proclaimed* [...]', emphasis added); Human Rights Committee, 'General Comment No 29: State of Emergency (Article 4)' (2001) UN Doc CCPR/C/21/Rev.1/Add.11, para 2 (noting that such a public proclamation 'is essential for the maintenance of the principles of legality and rule of law at times when they are most needed').

not be understood as a separate obligation under international law, but as an element relevant for calculating compensation for 'material losses' suffered by the other party. As will be discussed in the next section, whether the successful invocation of *force majeure* absolves the host state from any responsibility to pay compensation is an unsettled question. Should such an obligation to pay compensation exist, the (lack of a) notification by the host state contrary to good faith which increased the investor's losses may, for instance, be taken into account when determining the amount of compensation to be paid.

3.4 Consequences of a Successful Invocation of Force Majeure

The high threshold to rely on *force majeure* shows that the defence will only apply in exceptional circumstances. However, should a host state be able to successfully invoke *force majeure* in an investment dispute, the question arises as to the legal consequences thereof. These consequences are addressed in part by article 27 of the ILC Articles on State Responsibility:

> The invocation of a circumstance precluding wrongfulness in accordance with this chapter is without prejudice to:
> (a) compliance with the obligation in question, if and to the extent that the circumstance precluding wrongfulness no longer exists;
> (b) the question of compensation for any material loss caused by the act in question.

The first element, encapsulated in article 27(a) of the ILC Articles on State Responsibility, follows from the essentially temporal character of circumstances precluding wrongfulness. It appears largely uncontroversial and was confirmed – in the context of necessity – by the International Court of Justice (ICJ) in the *Gabčíkovo-Nagymaros* case,[95] as well as in inter-state[96] and investor-state arbitrations.[97] This likewise applies in *force majeure* situations.[98] Thus, reliance on *force majeure* does not affect the existence of the underlying

---

95 *Gabčíkovo-Nagymaros Project (Hungary v Slovakia)* [1997] ICJ Rep 7, para 101 ('[a]s soon as the state of necessity ceases to exist, the duty to comply with treaty obligations revives'.).
96 See *Rainbow Warrior* (n 39) para 75.
97 *CMS Gas Transmission Co v Argentina*, ICSID Case no ARB/01/8, Award (12 May 2005) para 382; *Enron v Argentina* (n 39) para 343; *Sempra v Argentina* (n 39) para 392; *Unión Fenosa Gas v Egypt* (n 90) para 8.47.
98 See, in particular, the jurisprudence of the Iran-US Claims Tribunal in this regard, *eg*, *Sylvania v Iran* (n 60) paras 38 et seq.

obligations as such. Safe for any other rule of international law, the obligations in question will apply in their entirety as soon as the situation has passed.[99]

However, much more controversial is whether – and to what extent – the state relying on *force majeure* has to compensate the party to which the obligation was owed to. That question is purposefully left open by article 27(b) of the ILC Articles on State Responsibility, mainly because the provision provides for one common approach for all circumstances precluding wrongfulness.[100] In doctrine, attempts have been made to draw from the classification of defences into justifications and excuses.[101] While a justification (*eg*, self-defence) would result in the *lawfulness* of the conduct in question, excuses (*eg*, necessity) would only protect the state from the consequences of wrongful acts.[102] Thus, with regard to the latter, states would generally remain responsible to compensate for any 'material loss' caused.[103] This is also reflected in jurisprudence in the context of necessity, which generally favours compensation.[104] In *Gabčíkovo-Nagymaros*, for example, the ICJ noted that 'Hungary expressly acknowledged that [...] a state of necessity would not exempt it from its duty to compensate its partner'.[105] While the ICJ itself has not ruled on the matter, older arbitral cases[106] as well as investment tribunals[107] support that contention.

---

99   Crawford, *Articles on State Responsibility* (n 37) 189 et seq; Sandra Szurek, 'The Notion of Circumstances Precluding Wrongfulness' in James Crawford, Alain Pellet, and Simon Olleson (eds), *The Law of International Responsibility* (OUP 2010) 434; Crawford, *State Responsibility* (n 38) 281 et seq. See also *LG&E Energy Corp, LG&E Capital Corp, and LG&E International Inc v Argentina*, ICSID Case no ARB/02/1, Decision on Liability (3 October 2006) para 263.

100   *LG&E v Argentina* (n 99) paras 260, 264; *Enron v Argentina* (n 39) para 345; Bjorklund (n 51) 510 et seq. Insofar, the dictum of the *CMS* tribunal that the provision 'establishes the appropriate rule on the issue' is somewhat misleading, see *CMS v Argentina*, Award (n 97) para 390. See, likewise critical, *CMS v Argentina*, Decision on Annulment (n 8) para 147.

101   See, in particular, Federica Paddeu, *Justification and Excuse in International Law: Concept and Theory of General Defences* (CUP 2018) 77 et seq.

102   ibid.

103   ibid 80.

104   Bjorklund (n 51) 511 et seq. See also Crawford, *Articles on State Responsibility* (n 37) 190.

105   *Gabčíkovo-Nagymaros Project* (n 95) para 48.

106   See *Company General of the Orinoco Case (France/Venezuela)* (1905) 10 RIAA 184 (although labelled '*force majeure*' the constitutive elements of the defence are rather those of necessity).

107   *South American Silver Ltd v Bolivia*, PCA Case no 2013-15, Award (30 August 2018) para 620 ('the invocation of this defense does not preclude the payment of compensation by the State for the damages effectively resulting from acts attributable to it'). See also *CMS v Argentina*, Award (n 97) para 388 ('[t]he plea of state of necessity may preclude the

However, in particular in the context of *force majeure*, which is generally classified as an excuse, that distinction arguably is not determinative.[108] When grappling with the issue, scholars and international judicial bodies sometimes came to widely diverging conclusions. In a recent study, Federica Paddeu considers that 'whether a duty of compensation exists is a matter not currently resolved by positive international law'.[109] While that appears particularly unsatisfactory for investment arbitral tribunals required to decide on specific claims for compensation, it reflects the legal and factual complexities involved in the matter.

Some authors have argued that – in contrast to necessity – the conduct of states in *force majeure* situations lacks an element of free will.[110] As a result, states under *force majeure* should be under no obligation to pay compensation.[111] This contention is reflected in the *Ottoman Empire Lighthouses Concession* arbitration, in which a tribunal held that Greece was not responsible to compensate damages caused by shelling by Turkish batteries, as it constituted a case of *force majeure* 'which would have hit [the lighthouse] even if it remained in the Company's hands'.[112]

Nevertheless, should an obligation to compensate exist also in case of a successful invocation of *force majeure*,[113] its content diverges significantly from the general framework foreseen by the ILC Articles on State Responsibility in the case of an internationally wrongful act. Firstly, article 27 of the ILC Articles

---

wrongfulness of an act, but it does not exclude the duty to compensate the owner of the right which had to be sacrificed'), and see also ibid para 390.
108   Crawford, *State Responsibility* (n 38) 319.
109   Paddeu, *Justification and Excuse* (n 101) 98 et seq.
110   Bjorklund (n 51) 511. See also ILC, 'Second Report on State Responsibility' (n 92) para 356 (draft art 35).
111   See Crawford, *State Responsibility* (n 38) 319 (considering it 'doubtful' whether *force majeure* 'can give rise to an obligation to compensate'); Binder, *Die Grenzen der Vertragstreue* (n 47) 441 (with further references). See also Giovanni DiStefano, *Fundamentals of Public International Law: A Sketch of the International Legal Order* (Brill 2019) 760 et seq, who argues that ILC Articles on State Responsibility art 27(b) is generally only concerned with the payment of *ex gratia* compensation.
112   See *Ottoman Empire Lighthouses Concession* (n 46) 219 et seq (translation by the authors).
113   The matter is further confounded by the question what the source of such an obligation would be. See, in this regard, Bjorklund (n 51) 515; Mathias Forteau, 'Reparation in the Event of a Circumstance Precluding Wrongfulness' in James Crawford, Alain Pellet, and Simon Olleson (eds), *The Law of International Responsibility* (OUP 2010) 891 et seq; Paddeu, *Justification and Excuse* (n 101) 78 et seq. See also Rutsel Silvestre J Martha, *The Financial Obligation in International Law* (OUP 2015) 411 (arguing that the answer should be sought 'in the principles concerning liability for injurious consequences of conduct not prohibited by international law').

on State Responsibility and doctrine suggest that it is limited to the payment of compensation and thus does not encompass restitution (*restitutio in integrum*).[114] Secondly, the *force majeure* situation excludes any duty to perform as long as it persists. Likewise, compensation will be due only after the situation has ended and interest will only accrue thereafter.[115]

Thirdly, the Commission itself distinguishes between compensation as reparation (article 34 and article 36 of the ILC Articles on State Responsibility) and compensation for 'material losses' unaffected by a circumstance precluding wrongfulness (article 27(b) of the ILC Articles on State Responsibility).[116] In particular, the 'reference to 'material loss' is narrower than the concept of damage elsewhere in the articles'.[117] According to the tribunal in *South American Silver v Bolivia*, it encompasses 'damages effectively resulting from acts attributable to' the responsible state.[118] This suggests the requirement of a clear causal link between the acts (or the failure to act) of the host state and the damages incurred by the investor, which in particular excludes lost profits and (for the continuation of the *force majeure* situation) interest.[119] As already indicated above, in that context investment tribunals might take into account whether a host state has failed to notify the investor that it considers to be faced with an ongoing *force majeure* situation, contrary to good faith. To what extent these differences might become relevant in the context of armed hostilities will largely depend on the specific circumstances of the case.

Also, in the absence of an obligation, states may nevertheless pay compensation based on considerations of equity and justice. Although not in the context of investment protection, states have in the past made *ex gratia* payments following *force majeure* situations.[120] Similarly, authors have also suggested a burden sharing between the actors involved.[121] In light of these considerations, as well as the aforementioned legal and practical difficulties, these matters

---

114 See ILC Articles on State Responsibility art 35. Nevertheless, restitution is generally of little relevance within international investment law.
115 See ILC Articles on State Responsibility art 38(2) ('Interest runs from the date when the principal sum should have been paid until the date the obligation to pay is fulfilled'.).
116 Crawford, *Articles on State Responsibility* (n 37) 190.
117 ibid. *Cf* also *Patrick Mitchell v DRC*, ICSID Case no ARB/99/7, Decision on the Application for Annulment of the Award (1 November 2006) para 57.
118 *South American Silver v Bolivia* (n 107) para 620 (in the context of necessity).
119 Note that this would only pertain to interest on the compensation of material losses themselves, and not necessarily interest on prior financial obligations.
120 Paddeu, *Justification and Excuse* (n 101) 78. See also the instances cited in Binder, *Die Grenzen der Vertragstreue* (n 47) 443 et seq.
121 Forteau (n 113) 893. See also Sergey Ripinski and Kevin Williams, *Damages in International Investment Law* (BIICL 2015) 353.

should indeed preferably be settled in negotiations between the host state and the investor.[122] However, in that context and insofar (simple) war clauses are applicable, the host state has to ensure that these payments are made in a non-discriminatory manner. Otherwise, it might trigger the requirement to expand these compensatory schemes to other investors, as the operation of (simple) war clauses is unaffected by the *ex gratia* nature of initial payments.

Based on the observations above, it appears likely that host states successfully invoking *force majeure* are under no obligation to pay compensation. However, even if tribunals do not follow that approach, reliance might still have notable value for host states. Especially, if they are faced with an ongoing and protracted civil war, states might be able to postpone and limit their financial liabilities.

4   Conclusions

Armed hostilities in both inter-state as well as intra-state conflicts are often considered as prototypical examples of a *force majeure* situation. Nevertheless, the *force majeure* defence under general international law will only be available to host states in exceptional circumstances. On the one hand, this follows from the high threshold required in the different elements of *force majeure*, as reflected in article 23 of the ILC Articles on State Responsibility. More importantly, however, it results from the interaction between these elements and the specific primary obligations most likely in question in such disputes. Thus, the failure to act in due diligence by a host state will most likely both result in a violation of FPS, as well as exclude reliance on *force majeure*. In addition, host states will arguably not be able to invoke *force majeure* with regard to a violation of an extended or strict war clause, as they have explicitly undertaken responsibility for these types of risks. Despite these caveats, a number of new cases involving civil unrest or a civil war, lodged against Middle Eastern countries, might well give raise to an increased engagement of tribunals with the principle of *force majeure*.

Bibliography

Binder C, *Die Grenzen der Vertragstreue im Völkerrecht* (Springer 2013).
Binder C, 'Circumstances Precluding Wrongfulness' in M Bungenberg and others (eds), *International Investment Law: A Handbook* (Nomos and Hart 2015).

---

122   Crawford, *Articles on State Responsibility* (n 37) 190. See also *Enron v Argentina* (n 39) para 345.

Binder C and P Janig, 'Investment Agreements and Financial Crises' in M Krajewski and RT Hoffmann (eds), *Research Handbook on Foreign Direct Investment* (Edward Elgar 2019).

Bjorklund A, 'Emergency Exceptions: State of Necessity and *Force Majeure*', in PT Muchlinski, F Ortino, and C Schreuer (eds), *Oxford Handbook of International Investment Law* (OUP 2008).

Borchard EM, *The Diplomatic Protection of Citizens Abroad or the Law of International Claims* (Banks Law Publishing 1928).

Cox Alomar R, 'Investment Treaty Arbitration in Cuba' (2017) 48 U Miami Inter-Am L Rev 1.

Crawford J, *The International Law Commission's Articles on State Responsibility: Introduction, Text and Commentaries* (CUP 2002).

Crawford J, *State Responsibility: The General Part* (CUP 2013).

Daza-Clark AM and D Behn, 'Between War and Peace: Intermittent Armed Conflict and Investment Arbitration' in K Fach Gómez, A Gourgourinis, and C Titi (eds), *International Investment Law and Law of Armed Conflict* (Springer 2019).

De Brabandere E, 'Jus Post Bellum and Foreign Direct Investment: Mapping the Debate' (2015) 16 JWIT 590.

DiStefano G, *Fundamentals of Public International Law: A Sketch of the International Legal Order* (Brill 2019).

Ewelukwa O fodile U, 'Africa-China Bilateral Investment Treaties: A Critique' (2013) 35 Mich J Int'l L 131.

Forteau M, 'Reparation in the Event of a Circumstance Precluding Wrongfulness' in J Crawford, A Pellet, and S Olleson (eds), *The Law of International Responsibility* (OUP 2010).

Gagliani G, 'Supervening Impossibility of Performance and the Effect of Armed Conflict on Investment Treaties: Any Room for Manoeuvre?' in K Fach Gómez, A Gourgourinis, and C Titi (eds), *International Investment Law and Law of Armed Conflict* (Springer 2019).

Lawry-White M, 'International Investment Law in a *Jus Post Bellum* Framework' (2015) 16 JWIT 633.

Mantilla Blanco S, *Full Protection and Security in International Investment Law* (Springer 2019).

Martha RSJ, *The Financial Obligation in International Law* (OUP 2015).

Moon WJ, 'Essential Security Interests in International Investment Agreements' (2012) 15 J Int'l Econ L 481.

OECD, 'Draft Convention on the Protection of Foreign Property' (1967) <www.oecd.org/daf/inv/internationalinvestmentagreements/39286571.pdf> accessed 17 December 2019.

Olleson S, 'The Impact of the ILC's Articles on Responsibility of States for Internationally Wrongful Acts' (2007) British Institute of International and Comparative Law

<www.biicl.org/files/3107_impactofthearticlesonstate_responsibilitypreliminary-draftfinal.pdf> accessed 10 February 2020.

Ortino F, 'Italy' in C Brown (ed), *Commentaries on Selected Model Investment Treaties* (2013).

Paddeu F, *Justification and Excuse in International Law: Concept and Theory of General Defences* (CUP 2018).

Paddeu FI, 'A Genealogy of *Force Majeure* in International Law' (2012) 82 Brit YB Int'l L 381.

Ripinski S and K Williams, *Damages in International Investment Law* (BIICL 2015).

Risvas M, 'Non-discrimination and the Protection of Foreign Investments in the Context of an Armed Conflict' in K Fach Gómez, A Gourgourinis, and C Titi (eds), *International Investment Law and Law of Armed Conflict* (Springer 2019).

Ryk-Lakhman I, 'Protection of Foreign Investments against the Effects of Hostilities: A Framework for Assessing Compliance with Full Protection and Security' in K Fach Gómez, A Gourgourinis, and C Titi (eds), *International Investment Law and Law of Armed Conflict* (Springer 2019).

Schreuer C, 'The Protection of Investments in Armed Conflict' in F Baetens (ed), *Investment Law within International Law: Integrationist Perspectives* (CUP 2013).

Schreuer C, 'War and Peace in International Investment Law' in K Fach Gómez, A Gourgourinis, and C Titi (eds), *International Investment Law and Law of Armed Conflict* (Springer 2019).

Spears S and M Fogdestam Agius, 'Protection of Investments in War-Torn States: A Practitioner's Perspective on War Clauses in Bilateral Investment Treaties' in K Fach Gómez, A Gourgourinis, and C Titi (eds), *International Investment Law and Law of Armed Conflict* (Springer 2019).

Szurek S, 'Circumstances Precluding Wrongfulness in the ILC Articles on State Responsibility: *Force Majeure*' in J Crawford, A Pellet, and S Olleson (eds), *The Law of International Responsibility* (OUP 2010).

Szurek S, 'The Notion of Circumstances Precluding Wrongfulness' in J Crawford, A Pellet, and S Olleson (eds), *The Law of International Responsibility* (OUP 2010).

UNCTAD, 'Bilateral Investment Treaties 1995–2006: Trends in Investment Rulemaking' (2007) <https://unctad.org/en/Docs/iteiia20065_en.pdf> accessed 12 December 2019.

UNCTAD, 'Investment Dispute Settlement Navigator' (*Investment Policy Hub*, 2020) <https://investmentpolicy.unctad.org/investment-dispute-settlement> accessed 23 March 2020.

Zrilič J, 'Armed Conflict as Force Majeure in International Investment Law' (2019) 16 Manchester J Int'l Econ L 28.

PART 2

Investment Law and Disputed Territories

CHAPTER 5

The Concept of 'Territory' in BITs of Disputing Sovereigns

Markus P Beham

1   Introduction

The concept of 'territory' or 'area', as it is often found in bilateral investment treaties (BITs) or multilateral agreements with investment provisions, is usually included as a jurisdictional condition to limit the application to investments with at least some form of territorial nexus.[1] According to Zachary Douglas, this requirement is already implicit in 'the whole architecture of an investment treaty'.[2] 'Territory' is also sometimes used to restrict certain treaty standards such as expropriation and full protection and security or the most-favoured nation or national treatment standard to limit the review of applicable norms.[3] When Russia took control over Crimea in 2014, the question popped up in practice what happens to investment treaties in cases of annexation or occupation of territory.[4] Does the law of

---

1   See on this Christina Knahr, 'Investments "in the Territory" of the Host State' in Christina Binder and others (eds), *International Investment Law for the 21st Century: Essays in Honour of Christoph Schreuer* (OUP 2009); Rudolf Dolzer and Christoph Schreuer, *Principles of International Investment Law* (2nd edn, OUP 2012) 76 et seq; Christina Knahr, 'The Territorial Nexus Between an Investment and the Host State' in Marc Bungenberg and others (eds), *International Investment Law: A Handbook* (CH Beck, Hart, and Nomos 2015); Christopher R Zheng, 'The Territoriality Requirement in Investment Treaties: A Constraint on Jurisdictional Expansionism' (2016) 34 Singapore L Rev 139; Caroline Kleiner and Francesco Costamagna, 'Territoriality in Investment Arbitration: The Case of Financial Instruments' (2018) 9 JIDS 315; Margaret Clare Ryan, 'Is There a "Nationality" of Investment? Origin of Funds and Territorial Link to the Host State' in Emmanuel Gaillard and Yas Banifatemi (eds), *Jurisdiction in Investment Treaty Arbitration* (Juris 2018).
2   Zachary Douglas, 'Property, Investment, and the Scope of Investment Protection Obligations' in Zachary Douglas, Joost Pauwelyn, and Jorge E Viñuales (eds), *The Foundations of International Investment Law: Bringing Theory into Practice* (OUP 2014) 373.
3   See, *eg*, German Model BIT (2008) art 3(5).
4   See Richard Happ and Sebastian Wuschka, '*Horror Vacui*: Or Why Investment Treaties Should Apply to Illegally Annexed Territories' (2016) 33 J Int'l Arb 245; Odysseas G Repousis, 'Why Russian Investment Treaties Could Apply to Crimea and What Would This Mean for the Ongoing Russo–Ukrainian Territorial Conflict' (2016) 32 Arb Int'l 459; Peter Tzeng, 'Investments on Disputed Territory: Indispensable Parties and Indispensable Issues' (2017) 14

treaties[5] or of state succession[6] provide solutions? These issues have been dealt with elsewhere, including in chapters of this book.[7] This is not what this chapter is about. Rather, it embarks on the hermeneutical exercise of looking at the various definitions of territory included in BITs of 'disputing sovereigns', seeking to explore whether there is any connection between political positions and the scope assigned to such treaties.[8]

Arbitral practice regarding the definition and scope of 'territory' is scarce but the question does not bar practical relevance. Tribunals have dealt with the issue of application of BITs to special administrative or overseas areas[9] and decisions have been rendered on the basis of state succession to treaties.[10] The

---

Braz J Int'l L 122; G Matteo Vaccaro-Incisa, 'Crimea Investment Disputes: Are Jurisdictional Hurdles Being Overcome Too Easily?' (*EJIL: Talk!*, 9 May 2018) <www.ejiltalk.org/crimea-investment-disputes-are-jurisdictional-hurdles-being-overcome-too-easily/> accessed 8 May 2020. For an early discussion, see Thomas D Grant, *Aggression against Ukraine: Territory, Responsibility, and International Law* (Palgrave Macmillan 2015) 87 et seq.

5   See Vienna Convention on the Law of Treaties (adopted 23 May 1969, entered into force 23 January 1980) 1155 UNTS 331 (VCLT) art 29. See also ILC, 'Draft Articles on the Effect of Armed Conflicts on Treaties, with Commentaries' (2011) II(2) YBILC 108.

6   See Vienna Convention on Succession of States in Respect of Treaties (adopted 22 August 1978, entered into force 6 November 1996) 1946 UNTS 3 (VCST) art 15. See also Daniel Costelloe, 'Treaty Succession in Annexed Territory' (2016) 65 ICLQ 343. On the general issue of state succession to investment agreements, see Christian J Tams, 'State Succession to Investment Treaties: Mapping the Issues' (2016) 31 ICSID Rev 314.

7   See also Kit De Vriese, chapter 10 in this volume, as well as Stefan Lorenzmeier and Maryna Reznichuk, chapter 13 in this volume.

8   For similar efforts with regards to international trade, see Moshe Hirsch, 'Rules of Origin as Trade or Foreign Policy Instruments? The European Union Policy on Products Manufactured in the Settlements in the West Bank and the Gaza Strip' (2003) 26 Fordham Int'l LJ 572.

9   See, for China, *Mr Tza Yap Shum v Peru*, ICSID Case no ARB/07/6, Decision on Jurisdiction and Competence (19 June 2009); *Sanum Investments Ltd v Laos*, PCA Case no 2013-13, Award on Jurisdiction (13 December 2013). The latter decision was set aside by the Singapore High Court in *Government of Laos v Sanum Investments Ltd* [2015] SGHC 15 – only to be confirmed on appeal by the Singapore Court of Appeals in *Sanum Investments Ltd v Government of Laos* [2016] SGCA 57. See, on both cases, also Odysseas G Repousis, 'On Territoriality and International Investment Law: Applying China's Investment Treaties To Hong Kong And Macao' (2015) 37 Mich J Int'l L 113; Tams (n 6) 339 et seq; John Shijian Mo, 'The Dilemma of Applying Bilateral Investment Treaties of China to Hong Kong and Macao: Challenge Raised by Sanum Investments to China' (2018) 33 ICSID Rev 125. On the *Sanum* case, see Christina Binder, '*Sanum Investments Ltd v The Government of the Lao People's Democratic Republic*' (2016) 17 J World Investment & Trade 280. See further Odysseas G Repousis, 'The Application of Investment Treaties to Overseas Territories and the Uncertain Provisional Application of the Energy Charter Treaty to Gibraltar' (2017) 32 ICSID Rev 170.

10   See *ACP Axos Capital GmbH v Kosovo*, ICSID Case no ARB/15/22, Award (3 May 2018). Serbia could have protested against the application of the treaty which – at least according to

European Court of Justice (ECJ) has held with regard to Western Sahara that the European Union (EU) could not assign an Association Agreement territorial scope that might be contrary to the right to self-determination.[11]

This chapter will first briefly outline the generic definition of 'territory' under international law (section 2) and its use in BITs more generally (section 3). It then looks at how specific treaty provisions in BITs of disputing sovereigns – the analysis does not cover multilateral agreements with investment provisions – have been modelled (section 4). The chapter ends with a brief assessment of what might be learnt from this (section 5).

2 Territory in International Law

Territory is surely one of the framing elements of international relations.[12] As every student of international law will know, it is among the three constitutive elements of a state.[13] According to the seminal article by Malcolm Shaw, territory 'clearly includes land areas, subterranean areas, waters, rivers, lakes, the airspace above the land etc. and the territorial sea'.[14] This is echoed by the International Court of Justice (ICJ) in *Nicaragua*, finding that it 'extends to the internal waters and territorial sea of every State and to the air space above its territory' under both customary international law and common treaty standards.[15]

Hans Kelsen defined territory as 'that space within which a State is authorized by general international law to perform all acts provided for by its national law or [...] the space within which according to general international law the organs determined by a national legal order are authorised to execute

---

the public record – it seems to have not. See also *World Wide Minerals v Kazakhstan* (case 2), Decision on Jurisdiction (15 October 2015) (not public); *ECE Projektmanagement v Czech Republic*, PCA Case no 2010-5, Award (13 September 2013) para 3.139.

11 ECJ, Case C-104/16 P *Council of the European Union v Front Polisario* EU:C:2016:973, para 123; see Stefan Lorenzmeier, chapter 11 in this volume, 371–373.

12 For critical introductions to the concept, see Daniel-Erasmus Khan, 'Territory and Boundaries' in Bardo Fassbender and Anne Peters (eds), *The Oxford Handbook of the History of International Law* (OUP 2012); Daniel-Erasmus Khan, 'Territory Taking Centre Stage in International Law: Some Preliminary Thoughts on the Rise of Territoriality to the Bedrock of Modern Statehood' in Société Française pour le Droit International (ed), *Droit des Frontieères Internationales – The Law of International Borders* (Éditions Pedone 2016).

13 See, exemplary, Georg Jellinek, *Allgemeine Staatslehre* (3rd edn, O Häring 1914) 71.

14 Malcolm N Shaw, 'Territory in International Law' (1982) 13 Netherlands YB Int'l L 61, 66.

15 *Military and Paramilitary Activities in and against Nicaragua (Nicaragua v USA)* (Merits) [1986] ICJ Rep 14, para 212.

this order'.[16] 'Sovereignty' thus entails *de jure* control over territory.[17] Supposedly, it was the Peace of Westphalia that brought about the notion that these two concepts are connected,[18] that through the exercise of sovereignty 'land' becomes 'territory'.[19] As Max Huber found in the *Island of Palmas* case, 'the continuous and peaceful display of territorial sovereignty [...] is as good as title'.[20]

When dealing with disputing sovereigns, the borders between *de jure* and *de facto* control may become blurred. Sovereignty and territory are suddenly contentious.

3   Territory in BITS

Is this customary definition of territory echoed in investment treaties? Since more than one ministry may be tasked with the negotiation of BITs (usually that of economy together with that of foreign affairs, sometimes also that of justice or the attorney general's office) and the *travaux préparatoires* are rarely made public,[21] the answer requires a larger interpretative exercise.

As Michael Waibel argues, investment treaties are 'designed to counterbalance the host state's regulatory authority over investments in its territory'.[22] This teleological view would relate territory to investments falling 'under the control of the host State's legislative, executive and judicial power'.[23] The issue is about exposure to 'sovereign risk'.[24]

---

16   Hans Kelsen, *Principles of International Law* (first published 1952, Lawbook Exchange 2003) 209.
17   Samantha Besson uses the term 'supreme authority', see Samantha Besson, 'Sovereignty', *Max Planck Encyclopedia of Public International Law* (2011) para 1 <https://opil.ouplaw.com/home/MPIL> accessed 8 May 2020.
18   See, on this, Shaw (n 14) 62. See also Besson (n 17) paras 12 et seq.
19   See Anthony Aust, 'Treaties, Territorial Application', *Max Planck Encyclopedia of Public International Law* (2006) para 2 <https://opil.ouplaw.com/home/MPIL> accessed 8 May 2020.
20   *Island of Palmas (Netherlands v USA)* (1928) 2 RIAA 829, 839.
21   See Dolzer and Schreuer (n 1) 31.
22   Michael Waibel, *Sovereign Defaults before International Courts and Tribunals* (CUP 2011) 238.
23   Michael Waibel, 'Investment Arbitration: Jurisdiction and Admissibility' in Marc Bungenberg and others (eds), *International Investment Law: A Handbook* (CH Beck, Hart, and Nomos 2015) 1248 et seq. See also Zheng (n 1) 147.
24   Douglas, 'Property, Investment, and the Scope of Investment Protection Obligations' (n 2) 386.

According to a United Nations Conference on Trade and Development (UNCTAD) publication on the 'Scope and Definition' of investment treaties, 'the purpose of the definition of "territory" generally is not to describe the land territory of the parties, but to indicate that "territory" includes maritime zones over which the host country exercises jurisdiction'.[25] The following analysis will concentrate on the territorial aspect, focusing on this extension to maritime zones only where it goes beyond the usual scope.

Is there such a thing as standard wording for the definition of 'territory' in BITs? According to UNCTAD, '[t]he most common definition is typified' in the 2006 Lebanon–South Korea BIT:[26]

> For the purposes of this Agreement: [...] 'territory' means the territory of the Contracting Parties, including the territorial sea as well as the maritime areas including the exclusive economic zone, its seabed and subsoil adjacent to the outer limit of the territorial sea over which the State concerned exercises, in accordance with national and international law, jurisdiction and sovereign rights.[27]

This relies on a tautological definition (territory equals territory) with a specification that this includes the territorial sea as well as other maritime zones, subject to jurisdiction. Such a generic definition of territory may have to do with the fact that the concept does not appear problematic *a prima vista*. The commentary included in the Consumer Unity & Trust Society's (CUTS) 1998 Model for an International Agreement on Investment finds that '[t]he definition' of territory as 'the land territory, internal waters, and the territorial sea of a Contracting Party, and, in the case of a Contracting Party which is an archipelagic state, its archipelagic waters' contained within the draft 'is self-explanatory'.[28]

Some BITs, however, contain very specific definitions of territory. For example, in the 2012 USA Model BIT, 'territory' means 'the customs territory of the United States, which includes the 50 states, the District of Columbia, and Puerto Rico' and 'the foreign trade zones located in the United States and Puerto Rico'.[29] This Model BIT is, at the same time, an example for a choice

---

25 UNCTAD, *Scope and Definition: A Sequel* (UN 2011) 100.
26 ibid 99.
27 Lebanon–South Korea BIT (2006) art 1(4).
28 CUTS International Agreement on Investment (1998) Definitions.
29 USA Model BIT (2012) art 1. See also Lee M Caplan and Jeremy K Sharpe, 'United States' in Chester Brown (ed), *Commentaries on Selected Model Investment Treaties* (OUP 2013) 772.

TABLE 5.1 Review of 62 model BITs listed by UNCTAD by year indicating the frequency of (1) no definition,[a] (2) a definition in the determination of the scope of application,[b] (3) a generic definition,[c] (4) a specific definition,[d] and (5) a state-specific definition[e] with any of these including references to (a) domestic[f] and/or (b) international law.[g]

	(1) No definition	(2) Scope of application	(3) Generic definition	(4) Specific definition	(5) State-specific definition	(a) Domestic law reference	(b) International law reference
absolute	10	5	41	6	23	2	2
relative	16.13%	8.07%	66.13%	9.68%	37.10%	3.23%	3.23%

[a] USA Model BIT (2004); Burundi Model BIT (2002), Mongolia Model BIT (1998); Germany Model BIT (1998); Switzerland Model BIT (1995); USA Model BIT (1994); Germany Model BIT (1991); Asian-African Legal Consultative Committee Model Agreements (1985); CARICOM Negotiation Guidelines for BITs (1984).

[b] Russia Model BIT (2016) art 11(4); Norway Model BIT (2015) art 1(3) and (4); Norway Model BIT (2007) arts 1(3) and (4); France Model BIT (2006) art 1(4); France Model BIT (1999) art 1(5).

[c] BLEU Model BIT (2019) art 7; Morocco Model BIT (2019) art 3(18); Netherlands Model BIT (2019) art 1(e); Slovakia Model BIT (2019) art 1(4); Azerbaijan Model BIT (2016) art 1(4); Czech Republic Model BIT (2016) art 1(5); Brazil Model BIT (2015) art 1(8); India Model BIT (2015) art 1(3); Serbia Model BIT (2014) art 1(4); Burkina Faso Model BIT (2012) art 1(4); Southern African Development Community (SADC) Model BIT (2012) art 2; Guatemala Model BIT (2010) art 1(5); Macedonia Model BIT (2009) art 1(4); Turkey Model BIT (2009) art 1(4); Austria Model BIT (2008) art 1(6); Colombia Model BIT (2008) art 1(4); Germany Model BIT (2008) art 1(4); Ghana Model BIT (2008) art 1(e); Canada Model BIT (2004) art 1; Netherlands Model BIT (2004) art 1(c); Guatemala Model BIT (2003) art 1(d); Kenya Model BIT (2003) art 1(d); India Model BIT (2003) art 1(f); Israel Model BIT (2003) art 1(e); Italy Model BIT (2003) art 1(7); Uganda Model BIT (2003) art 1(5); Benin Model BIT (2002) art 1(4); Sweden Model BIT (2002) art 1(4); Thailand Model BIT (2002) art 1(4); Finland Model BIT (2001) art 1(4); Greece Model BIT (2001) art 1(4); OPEC Fund for International Development (OPEC Fund) Model Agreement (2001) art 1(e); Denmark Model BIT (2000) art 1(6); Peru Model BIT (2000) art 1(3); Turkey Model BIT (2000) art 1(4); Croatia Model BIT (1998) art 1(6); CUTS International Agreement on Investment (1998) Definitions; Malaysia Model BIT (1998) art 1(1)(c); South Africa Model BIT (1998) art 1; Netherlands Model BIT (1997) art 1(c); Chile Model BIT (1994) art 1(3).

d USA Model BIT (2012) art 1; Colombia Model BIT (2011) art 1(4); Mexico Model BIT (2008) art 1(10); UK Model BIT (2008), arts 1(e), 13; Mauritius Model BIT (2002) art 1(D); UK Model BIT (1991), arts 1(e), 12.

e BLEU Model BIT (2019) art 2(7); Morocco Model BIT (2019) art 3(18); Azerbaijan Model BIT (2016) art 1(4); Czech Republic Model BIT (2016) art 1(5); India Model BIT (2015) art 1(13); Serbia Model BIT (2014) art 1(4); Burkina Faso Model BIT (2012) art 1(4); USA Model BIT (2012) art 1; Colombia Model BIT (2011) art 1(4); Ghana Model BIT (2008) art 1(e); Mexico Model BIT (2008) art 1(10); UK Model BIT (2008) arts 1(e), 13; Canada Model BIT (2004) art 1; USA Model BIT (2004) art 1; Guatemala Model BIT (2003) art 1(d); India Model BIT (2003) art 1(f); Israel Model BIT (2003) art 1(e); Uganda Model BIT (2003) art 1(5); Mauritius Model BIT (2002) art 1(D); Malaysia Model BIT (1998) art 1(1)(c); Croatia Model BIT (1998) art 1(6); UK Model BIT (1991) arts 1(e) 12; Asian–African Legal Consultative Committee Model Agreements (1985) art 1(g).

f India Model BIT (2015) art 1(13); Mauritius Model BIT (2002) art 1(D).

g BLEU Model BIT (2019) art 2(7); Mexico Model BIT (2008) art 1(10).

of state-specific definitions, providing an individual definition for each contracting state.

A number of agreements specify that territory be understood in accordance with either domestic or international law. For example, while the 2015 India Model defines territory as 'the territory of the Republic of India in accordance with the Constitution of India',[30] the 2019 Belgium–Luxembourg Economic Union (BLEU) Model BIT defines it as 'the territory of the Kingdom of Belgium and the territory of the Grand Duchy of Luxembourg, in accordance with international law'.[31]

A review of 62 Model BITs and draft agreements from 1984 to 2019[32] reveals that the broad majority indeed includes generic, tautological definitions as in the 2006 Lebanon–South Korea BIT. Some reference territory not in a separate definition but in connection with the application of a treaty.[33] Only a margin of these BITs specifies an understanding of territory in accordance with either domestic or international law.

Within these draft agreements, generic, tautological definitions may include references to specific aspects of territory such as airspace, internal waters, or the territorial sea which all fall within the definition of territory under international law. The 2008 Austria Model BIT – currently being updated – uses the wording 'with respect to each Contracting Party the land territory, internal waters, maritime and airspace under its sovereignty, including the exclusive economic zone and the continental shelf where the Contracting Party exercises jurisdiction, in conformity with international law.'[34]

A review of 32 Model BITs and draft agreements from 1991 to 2019 referring to individual parts of state territory[35] reveals that the largest portion refers to the territorial sea in its definition of territory, followed by an equal number of treaties referring to both internal waters and territorial sea or all three elements.

The 2008 Austria Model BIT also includes the jurisdictional requirement that 'the land territory, internal waters, maritime and airspace' be 'under its sovereignty'. Roughly a fifth of BITs reviewed include such a jurisdictional

---

30　India Model BIT (2015) art 1(13).
31　BLEU Model BIT (2019) art 2(7).
32　As listed by UNCTAD, 'International Investment Agreement Navigator' (*Investment Policy Hub*, 2020) <https://investmentpolicy.unctad.org/international-investment-agreements> accessed 7 May 2020.
33　Since these are not definitions *stricto sensu*, they were not considered with regard to the existence of further elements in the further tables below.
34　Austria Model BIT (2008) art 1(6).
35　As listed by UNCTAD, 'International Investment Agreement Navigator' (n 32).

THE CONCEPT OF 'TERRITORY' IN BITS OF DISPUTING SOVEREIGNS 147

TABLE 5.2 Review of 32 model BITs listed by UNCTAD by year including references to either (1) airspace, internal waters, and territorial sea,ª (2) airspace and internal waters,ᵇ (3) airspace and territorial sea,ᶜ (4) internal waters and territorial sea,ᵈ (5) airspace,ᵉ and (6) territorial sea.ᶠ

	(1) Airspace, internal waters, and territorial sea	(2) Airspace and internal waters	(3) Airspace and territorial sea	(4) Internal waters and territorial sea	(5) Airspace	(6) Territorial sea
absolute	7	2	5	1	2	15
relative	21.88%	6.25%	15.63%	3.13%	6.25%	46.88%

ª Brazil Model BIT (2015) art 1(8); Macedonia Model BIT (2009) art 1(4); Austria Model BIT (2008) art 1(6); Mexico Model BIT (2008) art 1(10); Canada Model BIT (2004) art 1; Guatemala Model BIT (2003) art 1(d); Finland Model BIT (2001) art 1(4).
ᵇ Slovakia Model BIT (2019) art 1(4); Guatemala Model BIT (2010) art 1(5).
ᶜ India Model BIT (2015) art 1(13); Colombia Model BIT (2008) art 1(4); Ghana Model BIT (2008) art 1(e); India Model BIT (2003) art 1(f); Malaysia Model BIT (1998) art 1(1)(c).
ᵈ CUTS International Agreement on Investment (1998) Definitions.
ᵉ Colombia Model BIT (2011) art 1(4); Peru Model BIT (2000) art 1(3).
ᶠ Netherlands Model BIT (2019) art 1(e); Czech Republic Model BIT (2016) art 1(5); Burkina Faso Model BIT (2012) art 1(4); SADC Model BIT (2012) art 2; USA Model BIT (2012) art 1; Turkey Model BIT (2009) art 1(4); Israel Model BIT (2003) art 1(e); Kenya Model BIT (2003) art 1(d); Mauritius Model BIT (2002) art 1(D); Thailand Model BIT (2002) art 1(4); Greece Model BIT (2001) art 1(4); OPEC Fund Model Agreement (2001) art 1(e); Turkey Model BIT (2000) art 1(4); South Africa Model BIT (1998) art 1; UK Model BIT (1991) arts 1(e).

requirement, with roughly two thirds of that sample divided equally between a nexus to either international or both international and domestic law.[36]

Overall, it has been commented in the literature that definitions of territory in BITs have become more elaborate over time.[37] A review of the Model BITs analysed above shows that the choice of state-specific definitions has

---

36 In doubt, the provisions were interpreted restrictively *in dubio mitius*. For example, in the case of sentences with unclear relative clauses, the jurisdictional requirement would be understood to apply to the entire territory, not just airspace and territorial waters or other maritime zones.
37 See, with regard to the UK, Brown, Chester and Audley Sheppard, 'United Kingdom' in Chester Brown (ed), *Commentaries on Selected Model Investment Treaties* (OUP 2013) 718.

TABLE 5.3 Review of 62 model BITs listed by UNCTAD by year indicating a jurisdictional requirement[a] with possible references to (a) domestic law, (b) international law,[b] or (c) both.[c]

	Jurisdictional requirement	(a) Domestic law	(b) International law	(c) Domestic and international law
absolute	13	0	4	4
relative	20.97%	–	6.45% / 30.77% to sample	6.45% / 30.77% to sample

[a] Slovakia Model BIT (2019) art 1(4); Czech Republic Model BIT (2016) art 1(5); Brazil Model BIT (2015) art 1(8); Serbia Model BIT (2014) art 1(4); Burkina Faso Model BIT (2012) art 1(4); Guatemala Model BIT (2010) art 1(5); Macedonia Model BIT (2009) art 1(4); Austria Model BIT (2008) art 1(6); Guatemala Model BIT (2003) art 1(d); Kenya Model BIT (2003) art 1(d); Greece Model BIT (2001) art 1(4); Denmark Model BIT (2000) art 1(6); Chile Model BIT (1994) art 1(3).
[b] Slovakia Model BIT (2019) art 1(4); Czech Republic Model BIT (2016) art 1(5); Macedonia Model BIT (2009) art 1(4); Kenya Model BIT (2003) art 1(d).
[c] Brazil Model BIT (2015) art 1(8); Serbia Model BIT (2014) art 1(4); Guatemala Model BIT (2010) art 1(5); Guatemala Model BIT (2003) art 1(d).

risen within each sample from just about 7 percent between 1990 and 1999[38] to roughly a third of BITs between 2000 and 2009[39] to almost half of BITs between 2010 and 2019.[40] At the same time, jurisdictional requirements with references to international law or international and domestic law have increased within each sample from zero between 1990 and 1999 to roughly 10 percent between 2000 and 2009[41] to a quarter between 2010 and 2019.[42]

---

38 Croatia Model BIT (1998) art 1(6); Malaysia Model BIT (1998) art 1(1)(c); UK Model BIT (1991) arts 1(e), 12.
39 Ghana Model BIT (2008) art 1(e); Mexico Model BIT (2008) art 1(10); UK Model BIT (2008) arts 1(e), 13; Canada Model BIT (2004) art 1; USA Model BIT (2004) art 1; Guatemala Model BIT (2003) art 1(d); India Model BIT (2003) art 1(f); Israel Model BIT (2003) art 1(e); Uganda Model BIT (2003) art 1(5); Mauritius Model BIT (2002) art 1(D).
40 BLEU Model BIT (2019) art 2(7); Morocco Model BIT (2019) art 3(18); Azerbaijan Model BIT (2016) art 1(4); Czech Republic Model BIT (2016) art 1(5); India Model BIT (2015) art 1(13); Serbia Model BIT (2014) art 1(4); Burkina Faso Model BIT (2012) art 1(4); USA Model BIT (2012) art 1; Colombia Model BIT (2011) art 1(4).
41 Slovakia Model BIT (2019) art 1(4); Czech Republic Model BIT (2016) art 1(5); Brazil Model BIT (2015) art 1(8); Serbia Model BIT (2014) art 1(4); Guatemala Model BIT (2010) art 1(5).
42 Macedonia Model BIT (2009) art 1(4); Guatemala Model BIT (2003) art 1(d); Kenya Model BIT (2003) art 1(d).

But will the concept of 'territory' as construed by disputing sovereigns in their investment treaties differ from these boilerplate definitions? The following sections take an empirical approach, reviewing the text of BITs of a number of disputing sovereigns to see whether there are any patterns or even specific references to their respective state of sovereign or territorial limbo.

4 Territory in BITs of Disputing Sovereigns

How is 'territory' construed by 'disputing sovereigns' in their investment treaties? Since most such situations involve or have involved at some point in time a breach of the peace, Max Huber's dictum[43] cannot hold. Matteo Vaccaro-Incisa proposes that '[i]nvestment arbitration is not the best setting to face complex questions of public international law'.[44] Is that equally the case for the underlying investment treaties themselves? Would states seek to address contentious territorial issues in such an instrument? Or is the premise a pragmatic jurisdiction-based understanding of territory?

When thinking of sovereigns disputing over territory, a typology of three different scenarios comes to mind (sometimes a question of perspective): First, there may be more than one sovereign laying claim to territory over which none of them actually fully exercises control. This is the case between China and Taiwan or North and South Korea (section 4.1). Second, a sovereign may have lost control over parts of its territory to which it still aspires as in the case of Cyprus over the northern parts of the island or Georgia over the provinces of Abkhazia and South Ossetia (section 4.2). Third, a sovereign might factually exercise control over territory claimed by another, aspiring sovereign. This is the case regarding Israel over the Palestinian territories or Kosovo over the (formerly) Serbian province (section 4.3). Each of these scenarios suggests certain likely attitudes towards the definition of territory.

There are, of course, multiple further examples to be thought of, from Kashmir and Nagorno-Karabakh to Moldova and Transnistria,[45] Morocco and Western Sahara,[46] Somalia and Somaliland, to Russia's control over Crimea[47] as well as the peculiar situation of the Donbas region.[48] And this is

---

43 *Island of Palmas* (n 20) 839.
44 Vaccaro-Incisa (n 4).
45 See also Vladlena Lisenco and Karsten Nowrot, chapter 12 in this volume.
46 See, with respect to the EU's treaty relations with Morocco, Stefan Lorenzmeier, chapter 11 in this volume.
47 See also Kit De Vriese, chapter 10 in this volume.
48 See also Stefan Lorenzmeier and Maryna Reznichuk, chapter 13 in this volume.

not taking into account minor territorial or borderline disputes.[49] For the purpose of this book chapter, two examples for each scenario will need to suffice.

As of February 2020, none of the states or entities analysed here had submitted notifications relating to any of these issues in accordance with either article 25(4) or article 70 of the ICSID Convention.[50]

4.1 Competing Sovereigns

Competing sovereigns would be the proudest of them all. They boldly assert territorial sovereignty over the very same piece of territory as another, irrespective of jurisdiction or control. But they might also be pragmatic in their day-to-day affairs. This puts them in front of a dilemma when considering the territorial scope of a treaty. Would the exclusion of certain areas or an omission of the issue altogether be seen as a cementation of the *status quo*? Specifically extending the territorial scope risks accountability for events outside of sovereign control.

4.1.1 China and Taiwan

Following the implications of the One China Policy,[51] the case of China (the People's Republic of China) and Taiwan (the Republic of China or Chinese Taipei as it is known in most international fora) is particular. Asserting title over the entirety of China (from Taiwanese perspective at least until the 1990s),[52] the two disputing governments have settled upon a territorial *status quo* since

---

49 For a wide range of examples, see Markku Suksi, 'Divided States', *Max Planck Encyclopedia of Public International Law* (2013) <https://opil.ouplaw.com/home/MPIL> accessed 8 May 2020.

50 Convention on the Settlement of Investment Disputes between States and Nationals of Other States (adopted 18 March 1965, entered into force 14 October 1966) 575 UNTS 159 (ICSID Convention). See International Centre for Settlement of Investment Disputes (ICSID), 'Contracting States and Measures Taken by Them for the Purpose of the Convention' (February 2019) <https://icsid.worldbank.org/en/Documents/icsiddocs/ICSID%208-Contracting%20States%20and%20Measures%20Taken%20by%20Them%20for%20the%20Purpose%20of%20the%20Convention.pdf> accessed 7 May 2020.

51 See Ministry of Foreign Affairs of the People's Republic of China, 'A Policy of "One Country, Two Systems" on Taiwan' (2014) <www.fmprc.gov.cn/mfa_eng/ziliao_665539/3602_665543/3604_665547/t18027.shtml> accessed 7 May 2020.

52 See Björn Ahl, 'Taiwan', *Max Planck Encyclopedia of Public International Law* (2008) paras 5, 19 et seq <https://opil.ouplaw.com/home/MPIL> accessed 8 May 2020; Suksi (n 49) para 18. It does, however, still formally compete with China for parts of the Spratley Islands. See Michael Strupp, 'Spratly Islands', *Max Planck Encyclopedia of Public International Law* (2008) <https://opil.ouplaw.com/home/MPIL> accessed 8 May 2020.

at least the 1950s.[53] While Taiwan had managed to represent the state of China at the United Nations (UN) until 1971, the subsequent change in representation resulted in a process of 'de-recognition' of Taiwan by the end of the 1970s,[54] resulting in its consideration as a *de facto* regime.[55] Although now largely unrecognised, Taiwan boasts a thriving 'treaty' practice of its own.[56] Its appearance at the international level has been institutionalised through its participation in the World Trade Organization since 2002.[57]

Depending on the wording, an investor affected by measures taken by a Taiwanese agency in Taipei might decide to initiate proceedings against China under a BIT between her home state and China (as opposed to Taiwan). Following the logic of the 2000 judgment of the Hong Kong Court of Final Appeal in *Chen Li Hung v Ting Lei Miao*[58] – albeit arguably made in a more limited context and relevant for that special administrative region alone – the scenario and its chances of success might seem less theoretical. Here, the court accepted the enforceability of a Taiwanese insolvency order in Hong Kong with the simple argument that it might promote reunification. At the same time, China has continuously held that its international agreements only apply to the special administrative regions of Hong Kong and Macao upon the express decision of the Chinese government.[59]

Of the 145 Chinese BITs listed by UNCTAD on its Investment Policy Hub, 116 are available in English, French, German, or Spanish. It was possible, with

---

53 See James Crawford, *The Creation of States in International Law* (2nd edn, OUP 2007) 200.
54 ibid 200 et seq.
55 Jochen A Frowein, 'De Facto Regime', *Max Planck Encyclopedia of Public International Law* (2013) para 1 <https://opil.ouplaw.com/home/MPIL> accessed 8 May 2020.
56 One might argue over the categorisation of agreements with such entities as Taiwan as 'treaties'. For sake of simplicity, this chapter equally describes them as BITs (as does UNCTAD). On the general practice of Taiwan regarding conclusion of agreements, see Crawford (n 53) 219 et seq.
57 See on this, most recently, Pasha L. Hsieh, 'Rethinking Non-Recognition: The EU's Investment Agreement with Taiwan under the One-China Policy' (forthcoming 2021) LJIL, manuscript available at <https://ssrn.com/abstract=3555574> accessed 8 May 2020.
58 *Chen Li Hung and others v Ting Lei Miao and others* [2000] 3 HKCFAR 9. See, on this aspect of the decision, also Pasha L Hsieh, 'An Unrecognized State in Foreign and International Courts: The Case of the Republic of China on Taiwan' (2007) 28 Mich J Int'l L 765, 784 et seq.
59 See, *eg*, the statement by the spokesperson for the Chinese Foreign Ministry regarding the judgment of the Singapore Court of Appeals in *Sanum Investments Ltd v Laos* (n 9), Chinese Foreign Ministry, 'Foreign Ministry Spokesperson Hua Chunying's Regular Press Conference on October 21, 2016' (21 October 2016) <www.fmprc.gov.cn/mfa_eng/xwfw_665399/s2510_665401/t1407743.shtml> accessed 8 May 2020.

assistance, to review two further BITs in Russian, allowing for a review of roughly 80 percent of these treaties.

Neither of the Chinese Model BITs (none listed by UNCTAD) contain a definition of territory.[60] Just over half of China's BITs leave territory simply undefined, most of these belonging to the early generation of BITs concluded by China from the 1980s to the 1990s[61] but also a number of BITs of the millennial years.[62] Some of these only define maritime zones or application thereto.[63] The 1985 China–Kuwait BIT does not contain a definition of territory but specifies the 'host government' to mean the 'government of the Contracting State in whose territory and maritime zones the relevant investment is made or is to be made'.[64]

Other Chinese BITs include generic definitions such as 'national territory',[65] 'areas lying within the land boundaries',[66] 'zones contained within the land

---

60 See Norah Gallagher and Wenhua Shan, 'China' in Chester Brown (ed), *Commentaries on Selected Model Investment Treaties* (OUP 2013) 178.

61 Bahrain–China BIT (1999); Barbados–China BIT (1998); Cape Verde–China BIT (1998); China–Ethiopia BIT (1998); China–Saudi Arabia BIT (1996); China–Syria BIT (1996); China–Zimbabwe BIT (1996); China–Serbia BIT (1995); China–Ecuador BIT (1994, terminated 2018); China–Egypt BIT (1994); China–Peru BIT (1994); Albania–China BIT (1993); China–Croatia BIT (1993); China–Laos BIT (1993); China–Lithuania BIT (1993); China–Uruguay BIT (1993); Bolivia–China BIT (1992); China–Greece BIT (1992); China–Philippines BIT (1992); China–Portugal BIT (1992, terminated 2008); China–South Korea BIT (1992, terminated 2007); China–Vietnam BIT (1992); China–Hungary BIT (1991); China–Mongolia BIT (1991); China–Papua New Guinea BIT (1991); China–Ghana BIT (1989); China–Pakistan BIT (1989); China–Turkey BIT (1990); China–Japan BIT (1988); China–Malaysia BIT (1988); China–New Zealand BIT (1988); China–Poland BIT (1988); China–Sri Lanka BIT (1986); China–Switzerland BIT (1986, terminated 2010); Austria–China BIT (1985); China–Italy BIT (1985); China–Netherlands BIT (1985, terminated 2004); China–Singapore BIT (1985); China–Thailand BIT (1985); BLEU–China Investment Treaty (1984, terminated 2009); China–Finland BIT (1984, terminated 2006); China–Norway BIT (1984); China–Germany BIT (1983, terminated 2005); China–Sweden BIT (1982).

62 China–South Korea BIT (2007); China–Latvia BIT (2004); China–Germany BIT (2003); China–Djibouti BIT (2003, not in force); China–Côte d'Ivoire BIT (2002, not in force); China–Myanmar BIT (2001); Botswana–China BIT (2000, not in force); Brunei–China BIT (2000, not in force); China–Congo BIT (2000); China–Iran BIT (2000).

63 China–France BIT (2007) art 1(4); China–Israel BIT (1995) art 1(5); China–Estonia BIT (1993) art 1(5); Australia–China BIT (1988) art 1(1)(g); China–UK BIT (1986) art 1(2); China–Denmark BIT (1985) art 1(5); China–France BIT (1984, terminated 2010) art 1(4).

64 China–Kuwait BIT (1985) art 1(6).

65 Argentina–China BIT (1992) art 1(5).

66 China–Kenya BIT (2001, not in force) art 1(4); China–Jamaica BIT (1994) art 1(4).

boundaries',[67] 'terrestrial zones',[68] 'land area',[69] 'territorial land',[70] 'land territory',[71] 'territory [...], including the land area, inland area, territorial sea'[72] or simply 'territory'.[73] A number of BITs include a reference to domestic law.[74] Some place territory under a jurisdictional requirement,[75] the 2005 China–Portugal BIT (2005) adding the qualifier 'in accordance with international law and their national laws'.[76] Norah Gallagher and Wenhua Shan, in their commentary on the Chinese Model BIT (not listed by UNCTAD), argue for a significance of these distinctions in the case of disputed territory.[77] In comparison to the analysis of Model BITs above, China is below average when it comes to the number of definitions with a jurisdictional requirement but

---

67 China–United Arab Emirates (1993) art 1(6).
68 Algeria–China BIT (1996) art 1(4).
69 China–Tanzania BIT (2013) art 1(4); China–Uzbekistan BIT (2011) art 1(4); China–Finland BIT (2004) art 1(4); China–Nigeria BIT (2001) art 1(4); China–South Africa BIT (1997) art 1(4).
70 China–North Korea BIT (2005) art 1(4).
71 Canada–China BIT (2012) art 1(22); China–Switzerland BIT (2009) art 1(4); China–Portugal BIT (2005) art 1(4); China–Spain BIT (2005) art 1(4). See also China–Spain BIT (1992, terminated 2008) art 1(4).
72 China–South Africa BIT (1997) art 1(4).
73 China–Malta BIT (2009) art 1(4); China–Mali BIT (2009) art 1(4); China–Colombia BIT (2008) art 1(4); China–Mexico BIT (2008) art 1; China–India BIT (2006, terminated 2018) art 1(d); China–Seychelles BIT (2007, not in force) art 1(5); BLEU–China Investment Treaty (2005) art 1(4); China–Czech Republic BIT (2005) art 1(4); China–Madagascar BIT (2005) art 1(4); China–Namibia BIT (2005, not in force) art 1(4); Benin–China BIT (2004, not in force) art 1(4); China–Tunisia BIT (2004) art 1(4); China–Uganda BIT (2004, not in force) art 1(4); China–Guyana BIT (2003) art 1(5); Bosnia and Herzegovina–China BIT (2002) art 1(4); China–Trinidad and Tobago BIT (2002) art 1(5); China–Cyprus BIT (2001) art 1(4); China–Jordan BIT (2001, not in force) art 1(6); China–Netherlands BIT (2001) art 1(4); China–Qatar BIT (1999) art 1(4); China–Lebanon BIT (1996) art 1(4); China–Indonesia BIT (1994, terminated 2015) art 1(6); China–Kazakhstan BIT (1992) art 1(5); China–Kyrgyzstan BIT (1992) art 1(4); China–Czechoslovakia BIT (1991, still applicable to Slovakia but terminated for the Czech Republic 2006) art 1(4), counted twice for both the Czech Republic and Slovakia; Bulgaria–China BIT (1989) art 1(4).
74 China–North Macedonia BIT (1997) art 1(5); Cambodia–China BIT (1996) art 1(4); China–Mauritius BIT (1996) art 1; China–Cuba BIT (1995) art 1(4); China–Morocco BIT (1995) art 1(4); China–Oman BIT (1995) art 1(6); Azerbaijan–China BIT (1994) art 1(4); Chile–China BIT (1994, terminated 2014) art 1(4); China–Iceland BIT (1994) art 1(4); China–Romania BIT (1994) art 1(4); China–Georgia BIT (1993) art 1(4); China–Slovenia BIT (1993) art 1(4).
75 China–Tunisia BIT (2004) art 1(4); China–South Africa BIT (1997) art 1(4); China–Czechoslovakia BIT (1991, still applicable to Slovakia but terminated for the Czech Republic 2006) art 1(4), counted twice for both the Czech Republic and Slovakia.
76 China–Portugal BIT (2005) art 1(4).
77 Gallagher and Shan (n 60) 178.

TABLE 5.4 Definition of 'territory' in 118 of the 145 Chinese BITs listed by UNCTAD, showing either (1) no definition,[a] (2) a generic definition,[b] possibly including (a) a reference to domestic law[c] or (b) a jurisdictional requirement,[d] or (3) a specific definition.[e]

	BITS reviewed	(1) Without definition	(2) Generic definition	(2)(a) Domestic law reference	(2)(b) Jurisdictional requirement	(3) Specific definition
absolute	118	62	54	12	5	2
relative	81.38%	52.54%	45.76% / 96.43% to sample of BITs with definitions	10.17% / 21.43% to sample of BITs with definitions	4.24% / 8.93% to sample of BITs with definitions	1.70% / 3.57% to sample of bits with definitions

[a] See above n 61–64.
[b] See above n 65–76.
[c] See above n 74.
[d] See above n 75–76.
[e] See above n 77 and below n 78.

sports an extraordinarily high relative portion of provisions with a nexus to its own domestic law.

Only two Chinese agreements address the situation of special administrative regions. The Protocol to the 2006 China–Russia BIT excludes application to Hong Kong and Macao.[78] The 2008 China–Mexico BIT includes the footnote 'authorized by the Central Government of the People's Republic of China, the Governments of Hong Kong and Macao Special Administrative Regions can separately negotiate and sign the Agreement on the Promotion and Reciprocal Protection of Investments with the Government of United Mexican States by themselves'.[79] This might also raise questions as to the scope of the agreement until the date of such a separate agreement.

Beyond the usual extension to maritime zones with or without jurisdictional requirements found in many Chinese BITs, the earlier version of the China–Spain BIT seems to imply application to maritime zones over which

78 Protocol to the Russia–China BIT (2006).
79 China–Mexico BIT (2008) art 1.

the parties might exercise sovereignty at some point in the future.[80] A particularly expansive example is the 1993 China–Slovenia BIT including 'all possible other areas having the status of sovereignty, sovereign rights or jurisdiction in accordance with international law'.[81]

Of the 25 Taiwanese BITs listed by UNCTAD under the category 'Taiwan, Province of China', 13 were available in either English, French, or Spanish, allowing a review of only about 50 percent of BITs. The Taiwanese Ministry of Economic Affairs, which gave the total number of BITs and free trade agreements including investment chapters at 32, provided two additional agreements, one with India[82] and one with the Philippines,[83] which were included in the analysis. The agreements are often concluded by sub-entities such as the Taiwan Industrial Development and Investment Center or the Taipei Economic and Cultural Centers based in various states, as opposed to Taiwan itself.

Both the 1992 Paraguay–Taiwan BIT, as one of the earliest available agreements, and the more recent 2017 Philippines–Taiwan BIT leave territory undefined.[84] Others reference 'territory',[85] 'terrestrial space',[86] or 'land territory'.[87] The 2009 Saint Vincent and the Grenadines–Taiwan BIT defines it as 'the territory of Republic of China (Taiwan)'.[88] One might argue whether this is indeed generic. For sure, the 1990 Singapore–Taiwan BIT, which speaks of 'relevant places', meaning those 'places of operation designated by the [Taiwan Industrial Development and Investment Center] and [Singapore Economic Development Board]',[89] and the similarly worded 1996 Taiwan–Thailand BIT can be labelled specific definitions.[90]

Not a single BIT of China or Taiwan references the respective other 'entity'.

---

80 China–Spain BIT (1992, terminated 2008) art 1(4).
81 China–Slovenia BIT (1993) art 1(4).
82 India–Taiwan BIT (2018).
83 Philippines–Taiwan BIT (2017).
84 Philippines–Taiwan BIT (2017); Paraguay–Taiwan BIT (1992).
85 India–Taiwan BIT (2018) art 1(9); India–Taiwan BIT (2002, terminated 2018) art 1(4); Belize–Taiwan BIT (1999, not in force) art 1(d); Costa Rica–Taiwan BIT (1999) art 1(3); Guatemala–Taiwan BIT (1999) art 1(4); North Macedonia–Taiwan BIT (1999) art 1(d); Burkina Faso–Taiwan BIT (1998) art 1(4); Swaziland–Taiwan BIT (1998, not in force) art 1(d).
86 Dominican Republic–Taiwan BIT (1999) art 1(4).
87 Gambia–Taiwan BIT (2005) art 1(4).
88 Saint Vincent and the Grenadines–Taiwan BIT (2009) art 1(10).
89 Singapore–Taiwan BIT (1990) art 1.
90 Taiwan–Thailand BIT (1996) art 1.

TABLE 5.5 Definition of 'territory' in 13 of the 25 Taiwanese BITs listed by UNCTAD plus additional two agreements provided by the Taiwanese Ministry of Economic Affairs, showing either (1) no definition,[a] (2) a generic definition,[b] or (3) a specific definition.[c]

	BITs reviewed	(1) Without definition	(2) Generic definition	(3) Specific definition
absolute	15	2	11	2
relative	55.56%	13.33%	73.34%	13.33%

[a] See above n 84.
[b] See above n 85–88.
[c] See above n 89–90.

4.1.2 North and South Korea

At the end of the Korean War stood the division of the Korean peninsula into a 'Western'-aligned south and a Communist north.[91] While the goal of reunification has remained a constant in relations between the two, tensions and incidents persist with both governments laying claim to the entire territory.[92] Under those circumstances, could an investor into North Korea argue with a straight face that 'territory' includes South Korea or vice versa?

South Korea was among the earliest states to engage in the active conclusion of investment treaties. Of the 105 South Korean BITs listed by UNCTAD on its Investment Policy Hub, 102 are available in either English, French, or Portuguese, allowing for an almost complete review of BITs.

The earliest South Korean BITs of the 1960s to 1970s together with a few exceptions of later generations contain no definition.[93] The 2002

---

91 See Deok-Young Park, 'Korea', *Max Planck Encyclopedia of Public International Law* (2013) <https://opil.ouplaw.com/home/MPIL> accessed 8 May 2020; Dana Constantin, 'Korean War (1950–53)', *Max Planck Encyclopedia of Public International Law* (2015) <https://opil.ouplaw.com/home/MPIL> accessed 8 May 2020.

92 Jochen A Frowein even lists North Korea among the examples of *de facto* regimes. Frowein (n 55) para 1.

93 China–South Korea BIT (2007); China–South Korea BIT (1992, terminated 2007); South Korea–Uzbekistan BIT (1992); Austria–South Korea BIT (1991); Hungary–South Korea BIT (1988); France–South Korea BIT (1977); South Korea–UK BIT (1976); South Korea–Tunisia BIT (1975); BLEU–South Korea Investment Treaty (1974, terminated 2011); Netherlands–South Korea BIT (1974, terminated 2005); South Korea–Switzerland BIT (1971); Germany–South Korea BIT (1964).

Saudi Arabia–South Korea BIT only clarifies the application to maritime zones.[94]

While the generic, tautological definition as 'the territory of the Republic of Korea' is often seen in 1980s and early 1990s BITs,[95] later ones use 'terrestrial space',[96] 'land territory',[97] 'land',[98] 'territory, including the land area',[99] 'territory, as well as islands',[100] or simply 'territory'.[101] In other instances, they refer to the territory

---

94　Saudi Arabia–South Korea BIT (2002) art 1(4).
95　Azerbaijan–South Korea BIT (2007) art 1(4); Peru–South Korea BIT (1993, terminated 2011) art 1(6); Poland–South Korea BIT (1989) art 1(6).
96　El Salvador–South Korea BIT (1998) art 1(4).
97　Kenya–South Korea BIT (2014) art 1(4); Colombia–South Korea BIT (2010, not in force) art 1(4).
98　Guatemala–South Korea BIT (2000) art 1(4).
99　South Korea–Uzbekistan BIT (2019, not in force) art 1(c).
100　Mauritius–South Korea BIT (2007) art 1(4).
101　Armenia–South Korea BIT (2018) art 1(c); Myanmar–South Korea BIT (2014) art 1(4); Cameroon–South Korea BIT (2013) art 1(4); Rwanda–South Korea BIT (2009) art 1(4); South Korea–Uruguay BIT (2009) art 1(4); Gabon–South Korea BIT (2007) art 1(4); Kyrgyzstan–South Korea BIT (2007) art 1(4); BLEU–South Korea Investment Treaty (2006) art 1(4); Bulgaria–South Korea BIT (2006) art 1(4); Congo–South Korea BIT (2006) art 1(4); Dominican Republic–South Korea BIT (2006) art 1(4); Guyana–South Korea BIT (2006) art 1(4); Lebanon–South Korea BIT (2006) art 1(4); Libya–South Korea BIT (2006) art 1(d); Croatia–South Korea BIT (2005) art 1(d); Democratic Republic of the Congo–South Korea BIT (2005, not in force) art 1(d); Slovakia–South Korea BIT (2005) art 1(4); Burkina Faso–South Korea BIT (2004) art 1(4); Jordan–South Korea BIT (2004) art 1(4); Kuwait–South Korea BIT (2004) art 1(5); Mauritania–South Korea BIT (2004) art 1(4); Albania–South Korea BIT (2003) art 1(4); Netherlands–South Korea BIT (2003) art 1(4); Oman–South Korea BIT (2003) art 1(4); Jamaica–South Korea BIT (2003) art 1(4); South Korea–Trinidad and Tobago BIT (2002) art 1(4); South Korea–United Arab Emirates BIT (2002) art 1(4); Panama–South Korea BIT (2001) art 1(4); Brunei–South Korea BIT (2000) art 1(4); Honduras–South Korea BIT (2000) art 1(4); Costa Rica–South Korea (2000) art 1(4); Algeria–South Korea BIT (1999) art 1(4); Qatar–South Korea BIT (1999) art 1(4); Israel–South Korea BIT (1999) art 1(5); Morocco–South Korea BIT (1999) art 1(4); Iran–South Korea BIT (1998) art 1(4); Nigeria–South Korea BIT (1998) art 1(5); South Korea–Tanzania BIT (1998, not in force) art 1(4); Belarus–South Korea BIT (1997) art 1(4); Cambodia–South Korea BIT (1997) art 1(4); Chile–South Korea BIT (1996, terminated 2004) art 1(4); Egypt–South Korea BIT (1996) art 1(4); India–South Korea BIT (1996, terminated 2017) art 1(4); Kazakhstan–South Korea BIT (1996) art 1(4); Laos–South Korea BIT (1996) art 1(4); Latvia–South Korea BIT (1996) art 1(4); Greece–South Korea BIT (1995) art 1(4); South Korea–Ukraine BIT (1996) art 1(4); Brazil–South Korea BIT (1995, not in force) art 1(1)(d); South Africa–South Korea BIT (1995) art 1(4); South Korea–Sweden BIT (1995) art 1(4); South Korea–Tajikistan BIT (1995) art 1(4); Argentina–South Korea BIT (1994) art 1(4); Philippines–South Korea BIT (1994) art 2(e); Finland–South Korea BIT (1993) art 1(4); Lithuania–South Korea BIT (1993) art 1(4); Czech Republic–South Korea (1992) art 1(4); Russia–South Korea BIT (1990) art 1(4).

over which sovereignty or jurisdiction is exercised[102] with some requiring this be done in accordance with domestic law,[103] international law,[104] or both.[105]

The 1996 Latvia–South Korea BIT includes 'those maritime areas [...] over which a Contracting Party exercises or will exercise sovereign rights and jurisdiction in accordance with international law',[106] as do the 1996 India–South Korea BIT and Kazakhstan–South Korea BIT while making explicit that the reference to international law includes the 1982 UN Convention on the Law of the Sea.[107]

Whereas it may come as a surprise to some that the 'Hermit Kingdom' would allow foreign direct investments in the first place, it has entered into a number of investment agreements. Of the 24 listed North Korean BITs, 14 are available in English or French. It was possible, with assistance, to review two further BITs in Russian and one in Serbian, allowing for a review of around 70 percent of these treaties.

While the 1998 North Korea–Switzerland BIT merely extends application to maritime zones,[108] most treaties use a generic definition such as 'territory',[109] followed by 'territorial land'[110] and 'land'.[111] Only two restrict the definition to 'territory under its sovereignty'.[112]

Not a single BIT of either North or South Korea references the respective other.

---

102 Japan–South Korea BIT (2002) art 1(6); Hong Kong–South Korea BIT (1997) art 1(1) (defining 'area'); Bolivia–South Korea BIT (1996) art 1(5); Paraguay–South Korea BIT (1992) art 1(5); Mongolia–South Korea BIT (1991) art 1(4); South Korea–Turkey BIT (1991) art 1(5); Romania–South Korea BIT (1990, terminated 2008) art 2(4); South Korea–Thailand BIT (1989) art 1(5); Denmark–South Korea BIT (1988) art 1(5); Malaysia–South Korea BIT (1988) art 1(e); Pakistan–South Korea BIT (1988) art 1(5); Bangladesh–South Korea (1986) art 1(5); Senegal–South Korea BIT (1984) art 1(d); South Korea–Sri Lanka BIT (1980) art 1(5).
103 Portugal–South Korea BIT (1995) art 1(4); Indonesia–South Korea BIT (1991) art 1(6).
104 South Korea–Vietnam BIT (2003) art 1(4); South Korea–Vietnam BIT (1993, terminated 2004) art 1(4).
105 Mexico–South Korea BIT (2000) art 1(4); Nicaragua–South Korea BIT (2000) art 1(4); South Korea–Spain BIT (1994) art 1(4); Italy–South Korea BIT (1989) art 2(4).
106 Latvia–South Korea BIT (1996) art 1(4).
107 India–South Korea BIT (1996, terminated 2017) art 1(4); Kazakhstan–South Korea BIT (1996) art 1(4). Both reference the UN Convention on the Law of the Sea (adopted 10 December 1982, entered into force 16 November 1994) 1833 UNTS 3.
108 North Korea–Switzerland BIT (1998) art 1(4).
109 Belarus–North Korea BIT (2006, not in force) art 1(4); North Korea–Thailand BIT (2002) art 1(4); Mali–North Korea BIT (1999, not in force) art 1(d); Czech Republic–North Korea BIT (1998) art 1(4); Egypt–North Korea BIT (1997) art 1(4); North Korea–North Macedonia BIT (1997) art 1(4)(b); North Korea–Russia BIT (1996) art 1(d).
110 North Korea–Singapore BIT (2008) art 1(4); North Korea–Syria BIT (2006, not in force) art 1(4); China–North Korea BIT (2005) art 1(4); Mongolia–North Korea BIT (2003, not in force) art 1(4)(2); Malaysia–North Korea BIT (1998) art 1(1)(d); North Korea–Slovakia BIT (1998) art 1(4).
111 North Korea–Serbia BIT (1998) art 1(4).
112 Bangladesh–North Korea BIT (1999, not in force) art 1(4); Denmark–North Korea BIT (1996) art 1(6).

TABLE 5.6 Definition of 'territory' in 102 of the 105 South Korean BITS listed by UNCTAD, showing either (1) no definition[a] or (2) a generic definition,[b] some adding (a) a jurisdictional requirement[c] with a nexus to either (i) domestic law,[d] (ii) international law,[e] or (iii) both.[f]

	BITs reviewed	(1) Without definition	(2) Generic definition	(a) Jurisdictional requirement	(a)(i) Follows domestic law	(a)(ii) Follows international law	(a)(iii) Follows domestic and international law
absolute	102	13	89	22	2	2	4
relative	97.14%	12.75%	87.26% /	21.57% / 24.72% to sample of BITS with definitions	0.98% / 2.25% to sample of BITS with definitions / 9.09% to sample of BITS with jurisdictional requirement	0.98% / 2.25% to sample of BITS with definitions / 9.09% to sample of BITS with jurisdictional requirement	3.92% / 4.49% to sample of BITS with definitions / 18.18% to sample of BITS with jurisdictional requirement

[a] See above n 93–94.
[b] See above n 95–105.
[c] See above n 102–105.
[d] See above n 103.
[e] See above n 104.
[f] See above n 105.

4.2 *Hopeful Sovereigns*

In situations in which states have lost control over parts of their territory, they face a similar dilemma as do competing sovereigns: either to extend application of a treaty and risk being held accountable for actions outside of their control or to recognise the situation by carving out such areas and, thereby, implicitly cementing the *status quo*. While they may not wish to guarantee treaty standards in areas in which they lack control, they might be tempted by the opportunity of a BIT to assert their positions.

4.2.1 Cyprus

Following its struggle for independence from British rule, the two main ethnicities, Greek and Turkish, were caught up in violence throughout the larger part of the 1960s. Triggered by an unsuccessful *coup d'état* aimed at unification of Cyprus with Greece in 1974, Turkish troops invaded and occupied the northern parts of the island, a situation that has since cemented into a *status quo*.[113] The only recognised government remains that of the Republic of Cyprus, whereas the occupied parts of the island are controlled by a *de facto* regime under the name of Turkish Republic of Northern Cyprus (TRNC),[114] recognised only by Turkey.[115] Since the ECJ confirmed that property rights of displaced persons continued to apply,[116] any investment stands under the threat of claims for compensation. But could a gas exploration company active along the northern coast sue Cyprus for a violation of the full protection and security standard following an incident with a policing organ of the TRNC?[117]

Of the 27 Cypriot BITs listed by UNCTAD on its Investment Policy Hub, 23 were available in English or Greek. It was possible, with assistance, to review

---

113 For concise overviews of the situation, see Ioannis Zelepos, 'The Historical Background of the Cyprus Problem – Just a Conflict of Ethnic Nationalism?' (2014) 19 ARIEL 13; Aristoteles Constantinides, 'The Cyprus Problem in the United Nations Security Council' (2014) 19 ARIEL 29; Frank Hoffmeister, 'Cyprus', *Max Planck Encyclopedia of Public International Law* (2019) <https://opil.ouplaw.com/home/MPIL> accessed 8 May 2020.

114 See, on the legal status of the TRNC, Stefan Talmon, *Kollektive Nichtanerkennung illegaler Staaten: Grundlagen und Rechtsfolgen einer international koordinierten Sanktion, dargestellt am Beispiel der Türkischen Republik Nord-Zypern* (Mohr Siebeck 2006).

115 See UNSC Res 541(18 November 1983) UN Doc S/RES/541.

116 See ECJ, Case C-420/07 *Meletis Apostolides v David Charles Orams and Linda Elizabeth Orams* [2009] ECR I–03571.

117 See, in relation to such disputed maritime zones, also Marco Benatar and Valentin J Schatz, chapter 6 in this volume.

an additional BIT in Russian, allowing for a review of roughly 90 percent of available investments treaties.

Many BITs concluded by Cyprus during the late 1980s and stretching into the early 1990s omit any definition of 'territory'.[118] The first to define the term is the 1992 Cyprus–Greece BIT which does so generically with a jurisdictional requirement.[119] Later BITs simply use 'land territory',[120] 'areas encompassed by land boundaries',[121] 'national territory',[122] or simply 'territory'.[123]

The idea of a future exercise of sovereignty is expressed in the 2008 Cyprus–Qatar BIT stating that territory '[i]n respect of the Republic of Cyprus and, when used in geographical sense, includes the national territory, the territorial sea thereof as well as any area outside the territorial sea, including the contiguous zone, the exclusive economic zone and the continental shelf, which has been or may hereafter be designated, under the laws of Cyprus in accordance with international law, as an area within which Cyprus may exercise sovereign rights or jurisdiction'[124] with similar wording to be found in the 2010 Albania–Cyprus BIT.[125]

4.2.2 Georgia

The turbulent dissolution process of the Soviet Union saw the Georgian Soviet Socialist Republic slide into a civil war throughout which both the provinces of Abkhazia and South Ossetia declared their independence. Until today, the international community assumes that both still belong to Georgia,[126] even

---

118   Cyprus–Egypt BIT (1998); Cyprus–Poland BIT (1992, terminated 2019); BLEU–Cyprus Investment Treaty (1991); Cyprus–Romania BIT (1991); Cyprus–Hungary BIT (1989); Bulgaria–Cyprus BIT (1987).
119   Cyprus–Greece BIT (1992) art 1(4). See also the Armenia–Cyprus BIT (1995) art 1(5); Belarus–Cyprus BIT (1998) art 1(4).
120   Cyprus–Iran BIT (2009) art 1(4); Cyprus–Moldova BIT (2007) art 1(4); Cyprus–Syria BIT (2007) art 1(5); Cyprus–Libya BIT (2004) art 1(3); Cyprus–Lebanon BIT (2001) art 1(4).
121   Cyprus–Serbia and Montenegro BIT (2005, later also applied to Montenegro) art 1(4), counted twice for Serbia and Montenegro respectively.
122   Albania–Cyprus BIT (2010) art 1(4); Cyprus–Qatar BIT (2008) art 1(4).
123   Cyprus–San Marino (2006) art 1(4); Cyprus–India BIT (2002, terminated 2017) art 1(f); Cyprus–Czech Republic BIT (2001) art 1(4); China–Cyprus BIT (2001) art 1(4); Cyprus–Israel BIT (1998) art 1(5); Cyprus–Russia BIT (1997, not in force) art 1(4).
124   Cyprus–Qatar BIT (2008) art 1(4).
125   Albania–Cyprus BIT (2010) art 1(4).
126   See, generally, Angelika Nußberger, 'Abkhazia', *Max Planck Encyclopedia of Public International Law* (2013) <https://opil.ouplaw.com/home/MPIL> accessed 8 May 2020; Angelika Nußberger, 'South Ossetia', *Max Planck Encyclopedia of Public International Law* (2013) <https://opil.ouplaw.com/home/MPIL> accessed 8 May 2020.

TABLE 5.7 Definition of 'territory' in 21 of the 27 Cypriot BITs listed by UNCTAD, showing either (1) no definition[a] or (2) a generic definition,[b] possibly including (a) a jurisdictional requirement.[c]

	BITs reviewed	(1) Without definition	(2) Generic definition	(a) Jurisdictional requirement
absolute	24	6	18	3
relative	88.89%	25%	75%	9.38% / 16.67% to sample of BITs with definitions

[a] See above n 118.
[b] See above n 119–123.
[c] See above n 119.

though the latter has been unable to exert any form of sovereignty despite various attempts at regaining control over these parts of its territory, including the 2008 Russo–Georgian War.[127] Could Georgia still end up facing an investment claim for violation of treaty standard violations in Abkhazia or South Ossetia?

Of the 36 Georgian BITs listed by UNCTAD on its Investment Policy Hub, 23 are available in English, French, or German. It was possible, with assistance, to review two further BITs, one in Russian and one in Swedish, allowing for a review of roughly 70 percent of available investments treaties.

Some BITs of the early 1990s still leave territory undefined[128] (some of them only extend application to the maritime zones).[129] A number of treaties since the mid-1990s begin to use generic wording that includes tautological definitions as 'territory',[130] 'zones contained within the land boundaries',[131] or 'land

---

127 See on this conflict Otto Luchterhandt, 'Völkerrechtliche Aspekte des Georgien-Krieges' (2008) 46 Archiv des Völkerrechts 435; Hannes Hofmeister, ' "Don't Mess with Moscow" – Legal Aspects of the 2008 Caucasus Conflict' (2010) 12 San Diego Int'l LJ 147.
128 Georgia–US BIT (1994); Georgia–Germany BIT (1993); BLEU–Georgia Investment Agreement (1993).
129 Georgia–Netherlands BIT (1998) art 1(c); France–Georgia BIT (1997) art 1(5).
130 Czech Republic–Georgia BIT (2009) art 1(4); Georgia–Romania BIT (1997) art 1(4); Georgia–Kazakhstan BIT (1996) art 1(4); Georgia–Iran BIT (1995) art 1(4); Georgia Israel BIT (1995) art 1(5).
131 Georgia–Italy BIT (1997, terminated 2014) art 1(7).

territory'.¹³² The 1994 Georgia–UK BIT equates it with 'the Republic of Georgia'.¹³³ Some add the requirement that the territory must be under Georgia's sovereignty.¹³⁴ The 1993 China–Georgia BIT – the first treaty to include a definition – makes it 'the territory of each Contracting Party as defined in its laws and the adjacent areas over which each Contracting party has sovereign rights or jurisdiction in accordance with international law'.¹³⁵ Similar wording appears in the 2017 Belarus–Georgia BIT.¹³⁶

A possible acknowledgment of territorial troubles in Georgia appears in the 1999 Egypt–Georgia BIT (not in force), which defines it as

> the territory of Georgia recognized by the international community within the state borders of [...] Georgia, including the internal waters, territorial sea, the air space above them, the exclusive economic zone and continental shelf adjacent to its sea coast, with respect of which [...] Georgia, in accordance with the [*sic*] international law, may exercise sovereign rights.¹³⁷

Similar wording can be found in the 2005 Georgia–Latvia BIT¹³⁸ – on which Martins Paparinskis has commented that it was included 'in light of the non-recognized entities in Georgian territory'¹³⁹ –, the 2005 Georgia–Lithuania BIT,¹⁴⁰ the 2006 Finland–Georgia BIT (which uses 'international law' as opposed to 'international community'),¹⁴¹ the 2008 Georgia–Sweden BIT,¹⁴² the 2009 Georgia–Kuwait BIT,¹⁴³ the Estonia–Georgia BIT,¹⁴⁴ and the 2014 Georgia–Switzerland BIT.¹⁴⁵ This makes up the majority of post-2000 BITs (seven out of nine), making Georgia a statistical outlier by a factor of three when it comes to specific definitions of territory.

---

132 Austria–Georgia BIT (2001) art 1(6).
133 Georgia–UK BIT (1995) art 1(e).
134 Georgia–Greece BIT (1994) art 1(4). See, similarly, also Georgia–Kyrgyzstan BIT (1997) art 1(4).
135 China–Georgia BIT (1993) art 1(4).
136 Belarus–Georgia BIT (2017) art 1(4).
137 Egypt–Georgia BIT (1999, not in force) art 1(3).
138 Georgia–Latvia BIT (2005) art 1(4).
139 Martins Paparinskis, 'Latvia' in Chester Brown (ed), *Commentaries on Selected Model Investment Treaties* (OUP 2013) 441.
140 Georgia–Lithuania BIT (2005) art 1(4).
141 Finland–Georgia BIT (2006) art 1(4).
142 Georgia–Sweden BIT (2008) art 1(4).
143 Georgia–Kuwait BIT (2009) art 1(6).
144 Estonia–Georgia BIT (2009) art 1(5).
145 Georgia–Switzerland (2014) art 1(4).

TABLE 5.8   Definition of 'territory' in 25 of the 36 Georgian BITs listed by UNCTAD, showing either (1) no definition,[a] (2) a generic definition,[b] possibly including (a) reference to domestic law[c] or (b) a jurisdictional requirement,[d] or (3) a specific definition.[e]

	BITs reviewed	(1) Without definition	(2) Generic definition	(2)(a) Domestic law reference	(2)(b) Jurisdictional requirement	(3) Specific definition
absolute	25	5	12	2	2	8
relative	69.44%	20%	48% / 60% to sample of BITs with definitions	8% / 10% to sample of BITs with definitions	8% / 10% to sample of BITs with definitions	32% / 40% to sample of BITs with definitions

[a] See above n 128–129.
[b] See above n 129–136.
[c] See above n 135–136.
[d] See above n 134.
[e] See above n 137–145.

The 1994 Georgia–UK BIT contains an expansive definition of maritime zones, specifying Georgian territory as that of 'the Republic of Georgia, including the territorial sea and any maritime area situated beyond the territorial sea of the Republic of Georgia which has been or might in the future be designated under the national law of the Republic of Georgia in accordance with international law as an area within which the Republic of Georgia may exercise rights with regard to the sea-bed and subsoil and the natural resources'.[146] While this refers to any domestic legislative steps of Georgia, these must be made 'in accordance with international law'.

In any case, a good faith argument that Georgia should face an investment claim for violation of treaty standard violations in Abkhazia or South Ossetia could appear difficult against the background of a piece of domestic legislation called the Law of Georgia on Occupied Territories.[147] It defines the occupied territories as 'the territories of the Autonomous Republic of Abkhazia', the 'Tskhinvali region (the territories of the former South Ossetian Autonomous

146   Georgia–UK BIT (1995) art 1(e).
147   Georgia, Law of Georgia on Occupied Territories, no 431-IIS (23 October 2008) LHG 28.

Region)', and 'on the Black Sea: the inland waters and the territorial sea of Georgia, their bed and subsoil falling within the water area along the state border with the Russian Federation, to the South of the Psou River up to the administrative border at the influx of the Enguri River into the Black Sea, over which Georgia exercises its sovereignty, as well as the following maritime zones: the adjacent zone, the special economic zone, and the continental shelf, where, according to the norms of the legislation of Georgia and the [sic] international law, in particular the UN Convention on the Law of the Sea of 1982, Georgia exercises fiscal, sanitary, immigration and taxation rights in the adjacent zone, and sovereign rights and jurisdiction within the special economic zone and on the continental shelf', as well as the air space above all of these areas.[148] According to the Law, in these occupied territories, any real estate transaction contrary to Georgian law is void[149] and a majority of economic activities there are subject to Georgian governmental approval.[150]

4.3   Factual Sovereigns

This final scenario sees two possible constellations: mere factual control or factual control paired with claims to sovereignty. On the other side might stand an unrecognised entity, a hopeful sovereign or – in the case of conflicting aspirations – competing ones. The category might overlap with other scenarios, depending on perspective.

4.3.1   Israel over the Palestinian Territories

At the end of the Six Day War of 1967, Israel had occupied territory of Egypt, Jordan, and Syria.[151] Two of these areas, the West Bank of the river Jordan and the Gaza Strip are subject to a plight for self-determination on behalf of the Palestinian people.[152] The issue is further complicated by Israel's ambiguous rejection of its status as an occupying power, its settlement policy, particularly in Judea and Samara,[153] and its claims to the Golan Heights and East Jerusalem.[154]

---

148   ibid art 2.
149   ibid art 5(1).
150   ibid art 6.
151   See Benjamin Rubin, 'Israel, Occupied Territories', *Max Planck Encyclopedia of Public International Law* (2009) para 2.
152   See ibid para 5. See also *Legal Consequences of the Construction of a Wall in the Occupied Palestinian Territory* (Advisory Opinion) [2004] ICJ Reports 136, para 118.
153   See, on this, the Israel, Law for the Regularization of Settlement in Judea and Samaria, no 5777-2017 (6 February 2017).
154   See, generally, Rubin (n 151) paras 11, 45 et seq. See also Ralph RA Janik, 'Israel and International Law' (2016) <www.ssrn.com/abstract=2889965> accessed 7 May 2020.

At the same time, Israel is confronted with what is becoming an increasingly recognised entity. In 2011, Palestine became a member of UNESCO, a status only reserved for states.[155] A year later, its observer status at the UN was upgraded to 'non-member observer state'.[156] The relevant resolution speaks of the 'State of Palestine'.[157] In 2015, Palestine joined the Rome Statute of the International Criminal Court, again only open to states.[158] But as the current discussion within the Assembly of States Parties of the International Criminal Court suggests, the scope of Palestine's claims might appear equally unclear.[159]

Today, both Israel and Palestine have BITs in force.[160] The question is whether an investor in whatever tourism industry in East Jerusalem subject to a violation of fair and equitable treatment might bring a claim under an Israeli BIT with its home state. Would the issue be any different in case of an investment into Bethlehem or Judea? If Israel continues to argue for the application of trade agreements to settlements,[161] is it thereby estopped from denying the relevant treaty standards under one of its BITs there?

All 41 Israeli BITs listed by UNCTAD on its Investment Policy Hub are available in either English or French, allowing for a full review. While Israel may have largely based its treaty texts on UK models, among the largest divergences are the definitions.[162] The first BITs of Israel negotiated in the mid-1970s and early 1980s[163] as well as some of the late 1990s[164] do not include a definition of territory. Some BITs include a generic definition of territory as 'territory'[165] or

---

155 Constitution of the United Nations Educational, Scientific and Cultural Organization (adopted 16 November 1945, entered into force 4 November 1956) 4 UNTS 275 (UNESCO Constitution) art II(1)–(2).
156 See UNGA Res 67/19 (29 November 2012) UN Doc A/RES/67/19.
157 ibid.
158 See Rome Statute of the International Criminal Court (adopted 17 July 1998, entered into force 1 July 2002) 2187 UNTS 3 (Rome Statute) art 125(3).
159 See, on this issue recently, *Situation in the State of Palestine* (Prosecution Request Pursuant to Article 19(3) for a Ruling on the Court's Territorial Jurisdiction in Palestine) ICC-01/18-131 (22 January 2020).
160 See Israeli–Palestinian Interim Agreement on the West Bank and the Gaza Strip (signed 28 September 1995) 36 ILM 551, art XVII and annex III, which transfers a wide range of 'powers and responsibilities' over 'civil affairs' with 'territorial jurisdiction' covering 'land, subsoil and territorial waters, in accordance with the provisions of this Agreement'.
161 See ECJ, Case C-386/08 *Firma Brita GmbH v Hauptzollamt Hamburg-Hafen* [2010] ECR I-01289.
162 See Wolfgang Alschner and Dmitriy Skougarevskiy, 'Mapping the Universe of International Investment Agreements' (2016) 19 J Int'l Econ L 561, 582 et seq.
163 France–Israel BIT (1983, terminated 1995); Germany–Israel BIT (1976, not in force).
164 Israel–Romania BIT (1998); Israel–Turkey BIT (1996); China-Israel BIT (1995) art 1(5).
165 Armenia–Israel BIT (2000) art 1(5); Belarus–Israel BIT (2000) art 1(4); El Salvador–Israel BIT (2000) art 1(5); Israel–Thailand BIT (2000) art 1(5); Israel–Slovakia BIT (1999) art

THE CONCEPT OF 'TERRITORY' IN BITS OF DISPUTING SOVEREIGNS   167

TABLE 5.9 Definition of 'territory' in 41 Israeli BITs listed by UNCTAD, showing either (1) no definition[a] or (2) a generic definition.[b]

	BITs reviewed	(1) Without definition	(2) Generic definition
absolute	41	5	36
relative	100.00%	12.20%	87.81%

[a] See above n 163–164.
[b] See above n 165 and below n 166–167.

'national territory'[166] with a larger number as of the mid-1990s choosing 'the territory of the State of Israel'.[167] One might argue whether the latter is indeed generic.

To contrast the sample, of the five BITs listed for Palestine, only one is available in English. It was possible, with assistance, to review a second BIT in Russian. The Germany–Palestine BIT defines territory 'in respect of the Palestinian Authority' as 'the territory under the self-administration of the Palestinian Authority'.[168] The Palestine–Russia BIT considers territory as that of the State of Palestine.[169] In these cases, one could assume that the Germany–Israel BIT would not extend to these areas.[170]

1(5); Cyprus–Israel BIT (1998) art 1(5); Israel–Slovenia BIT (1998) art 1(4); Israel–Uruguay BIT (1998) art 1(5); Israel–Moldova BIT (1997) art 1(4); Albania–Israel BIT (1996) art 1(5); Georgia–Israel BIT (1995) art 1(5); Israel–Kazakhstan BIT (1995) art 1(5); Israel–Turkmenistan BIT (1995) art 1(5); Estonia–Israel BIT (1994) art 1(5); Israel–Latvia BIT (1994) art 1(5); Israel–Uzbekistan BIT (1994) art 1(5); Bulgaria–Israel BIT (1993) art 1(3); Hungary–Israel BIT (1991, terminated 2007) art 1(5); Israel–Poland BIT (1991) art 1(5).

166 Argentina–Israel BIT (1995) art 1(5).
167 Israel–Japan BIT (2017) art 1(g); Israel–Myanmar BIT (2014) art 1(e); Israel–Ukraine BIT (2010) art 1(1)(f); Azerbaijan–Israel BIT (2007) art 1(1)(e); Guatemala–Israel BIT (2006) art 1(1)(e); Israel–Serbia and Montenegro BIT (2004, later also applied to Montenegro) art 1(6), counted twice for Serbia and Montenegro respectively; Israel–South Africa BIT (2004, not in force) art 1(1)(e); Ethiopia–Israel BIT (2003) art 1(6); Israel–Mongolia BIT (2003) art 1(6); Croatia–Israel BIT (2000) art 1(5); Israel–South Korea BIT (1999) art 1(5); Czech Republic–Israel BIT (1997) art 1(5); India–Israel BIT (1996, terminated 2017) art 1(f); Israel–Lithuania BIT (1994) art 1(5); Israel–Ukraine BIT (1994, terminated 2012) art 1(1)(f).
168 Germany–Palestine BIT (2000) art 1(4).
169 Palestine–Russia BIT (2016) art 1.
170 Germany–Israel BIT (1976, not in force).

4.3.2 Kosovo over the (Former) Autonomous Province of Serbia

Kosovo declared independence from Serbia on 17 February 2008, proclaiming that it will 'undertake the international obligations of Kosovo, including those concluded on our behalf by the United Nations Interim Administration Mission in Kosovo (UNMIK) and treaty and other obligations of the former Socialist Federal Republic of Yugoslavia to which we are bound as a former constituent part'.[171] Yet the Serbian Constitution still recognises Kosovo as 'an integral part of the territory of Serbia' and it is established therein as an autonomous province.[172]

Kosovo exercises control over the territory of another sovereign. Could it expect Serbia to fight a claim by an infrastructure investor in Pristina? Should a simple reference to 'territory' be seen as reference to its constitutional understanding or take into account the realities of international relations?

Considering Kosovo as an unrecognised state for the purposes of the United Nations, UNCTAD does not list treaties with Kosovo on its Investment Policy Hub,[173] but it is a member state of the ICSID Convention and has since prevailed in the first case brought against it.[174] According to the Kosovar Ministry of Trade and Industry, investment agreements exist with Albania, Austria,[175] Belgium and Luxemburg,[176] Macedonia, Switzerland,[177] Turkey, the United Arab Emirates, and the US financial development institution DFC (International Development Finance Corporation), formerly named OPIC (Overseas Private Investment Corporation).[178] It was possible to unearth a number of treaties through the legal databases of respective states that have concluded BITs with Kosovo.

---

[171] Kosovo Declaration of Independence (17 February 2008) 47 ILM 467.

[172] Constitution of Serbia (30 September 2006) preamble, art 182. See, in this regard also, above n 10.

[173] Although other such entities seem to be included.

[174] *Axos v Kosovo* (n 10). See Sebastian Perry, 'Victory for Kosovo in First ICSID Case' (*Global Arbitration Review*, 4 May 2018) <https://globalarbitrationreview.com/article/1169154/victory-for-kosovo-in-first-icsid-case> accessed 7 May 2020.

[175] Austria–Kosovo BIT (2010).

[176] BLEU–Kosovo Investment Treaty (2010).

[177] Kosovo–Switzerland BIT (2011). See also *Mabco Constructions SA v Kosovo*, ICSID Case no ARB/17/25 (pending).

[178] See the information provided at Kosovan Ministry of Trade and Industry, 'Investment Environment: Legislation and Agreements' (not dated) <https://kiesa.rks-gov.net/page.aspx?id=2,162> accessed 7 May 2020. See, on Kosovo's positioning generally, Christian W Konrad, 'Kosovo and Arbitration – The Birth of a New State' (*Kluwer Arbitration Blog*, 17 November 2010) <http://arbitrationblog.kluwerarbitration.com/2010/11/17/kosovo-and-arbitration-the-birth-of-a-new-state/> accessed 7 May 2020.

The first such treaties concluded by Kosovo following its declaration of independence was with Austria in 2010[179] and it defines territory as sovereign territory.[180] The 2010 BLEU–Kosovo Investment Agreement contains a somewhat unusual definition as

> the land territory of the Republic of Kosovo comprising the airspace above it over which it exercises, in accordance with international law, its jurisdiction or sovereign rights for the purposes of exploration and conservation of natural resources.[181]

The 2011 Kosovo–Switzerland BIT defines it as the area over which either party exercised jurisdiction and sovereignty in accordance with international law.[182] All three BITs include a jurisdictional requirement, two of them with a nexus to international law.

A number of Serbian BITs immediately preceding and following the unilateral declaration of independence by Kosovo were reviewed for contrast. All post-2008 treaties define territory as 'the area over which the Republic of Serbia exercises, in accordance with its national laws and regulations and international law, sovereign rights or jurisdiction'.[183] The 2013 Serbia–United Arab Emirates BIT adds 'and when used in a geographical sense it means the territory of the Republic of Serbia'.[184] Looking at a sample of the most recent pre-2008 BITs, the requirement of jurisdiction is absent.[185]

---

179 *Cf* Kathleen Claussen, 'Functional States Recognition and International Economic Law' in Chiara Giorgetti and Natalie Klein (eds), *Resolving Conflicts in the Law: Essays in Honour of Lea Brilmayer* (Brill Nijhoff) 166.
180 Austria–Kosovo BIT (2010) art 1(6).
181 BLEU–Kosovo Investment Treaty (2010) art 1(4): 'le territoire terrestre de la République du Kosovo comprenant l'espace aérien situé au dessus sur lequel celle-ci exerce, conformément au droit international, sa juridiction ou ses droits souverains aux fins d'exploration et de conservation des ressources naturelles.'
182 Kosovo–Switzerland BIT (2011) art 1(4).
183 Serbia–Turkey BIT (2018, not in force) art 1(3); Canada–Serbia BIT (2014) art 1; Morocco–Serbia BIT (2013, not in force) art 1(4); Azerbaijan–Serbia BIT (2011) art 1(4); Indonesia–Serbia BIT (2011, not in force) art 1(5); Kazakhstan–Serbia BIT (2010) art 1(4); Montenegro–Serbia BIT (2009) art 1(4). Similarly, Algeria–Serbia BIT (2012) art 1(4); Malta–Serbia BIT (2010) art 1(e); Denmark–Serbia BIT (2009) art 1(5); Portugal–Serbia BIT (2009) art 1(7).
184 See, *eg*, Serbia–United Arab Emirates BIT (2013) art 1(5).
185 Cyprus–Serbia BIT (2005) art 1(4); Egypt–Serbia BIT (2005) art 1(4); Finland–Serbia BIT (2005) art 1(4); Lithuania–Serbia BIT (2005) art 1(4); Serbia–Switzerland BIT (2005) art 1(4).

5 Assessment

The empirical evidence collected for this chapter seems somewhat equivocal (if not, at times, random). Neither a quantitative nor a geographical review produces an overall pattern. Since expansive or open definitions of territory in BITs bring with them wider application and, thus, potentially even more obligations, an interpretation of this fact might mean many things: an assumption of pressure from the other contracting party, an opportunity taken for the assertion of claims, or complete ignorance. Where definitions remain boilerplate, do more restrictive definitions in other BITs suggest an expansive understanding? Should state practice in international relations or domestic legislation inform the interpretative context?

What it boils down to: Can you have your cake and eat it too? Would disputing sovereigns assert territorial claims at the political level and then pragmatically argue that the very same area is not covered by a legal definition of 'territory'? The answer might depend on the overall treaty practice of the other contracting party (the home state of the investor). It could be hard to make a good faith argument that in the case of a state having entered into an agreement both with China and Taiwan (to take but one of the above examples), the Chinese BIT should also apply to Taiwanese territory.[186] Where domestic law extends the scope of a BIT to a particular territory, a tribunal might still follow the considerations of the ECJ in the *Front Polisario* case.[187]

Should it seem remarkable that Cyprus concludes BITs open to more expansive maritime zones and, in some cases, including the idea of sovereign rights to be exercised at a future point in time in treaty relations with its Mediterranean neighbours such as Lebanon and Libya or other member states of the Organisation of Islamic Cooperation[188] such as Iran or Qatar, the latter a close ally of Turkey? But then again, there is no coherent geographical pattern. Many Chinese BITs include jurisdictional clauses with a nexus to domestic law. But only in the BITs of Georgia is the issue of recognition openly addressed.

---

186 *Cf* the logic of the ECJ in *Firma Brita v Hauptzollamt Hamburg-Hafen* (n 161) paras 46 et seq. See Moshe Hirsch, 'The Politics of Rules of Origin' in Tomer Broude, Marc L Busch, and Amelia Porges (eds), *The Politics of International Economic Law* (CUP 2011) 323.

187 See *Council v Front Polisario* (n 11) para 123; see also Stefan Lorenzmeier, chapter 11 in this volume, 371–373.

188 With regard to the role of the Organisation of Islamic Cooperation relating to the TRNC, see Markus P Beham, 'Cyprus Through the Lens of the Organisation of Islamic Cooperation: "The Victim of an Outcome in Which They Have No Fault"' (2017) 19 ARIEL 115.

Are there limits to interpretation? Matteo Vaccaro-Incisa has argued that according to the wording 'in accordance with international law' in the Russia–Ukraine BIT, it would be 'implausible that the BIT coverage may go beyond *de jure* territory'.[189] Judging from the logic of the ICJ's *Wall* advisory opinion,[190] it might be doubtful whether states would have the competence to enter into agreements to that extent.[191]

Even where the Orphean interpretative effort of luring the concept of territory out of the dark succeeds, a claim might dissipate when the view turns back to the questions of jurisdiction or attribution. Could an investment in Taiwan fall under the definition of 'investment' under a Chinese BIT? Douglas offers the rule that '[t]he economic materialization of an investment requires the commitment of resources to the economy of the host state by the claimant entailing the assumption of risk in expectation of a commercial return'.[192] As far as attribution goes, there are, of course, treaty standards such as fair and equitable treatment or full protection and security that could bypass the dilemma. But these standards might, arguably, only apply to investments prior to the events during which the territory became disputed.

The unsatisfactory answer to all these questions must remain cliché: it depends. It will require a case-by-case determination and involve an exercise in treaty interpretation. For sure, were one to look for a solution to the underlying territorial issues at the international level, the picture regarding the notion of 'territory' in investment treaties does not appear overly helpful. But the examples drawn upon for this chapter indicate that the enquiry is relevant: BITs of disputing sovereigns address questions of public international law that go beyond the core issues of international investment law, even if most examples fall short of addressing the question outright.

Note on the Text

BITs relied upon are, unless otherwise indicated, available at the UNCTAD Investment Policy Hub (as of January–March 2020). Nicola Antretter, University

---

189   Vaccaro-Incisa (n 4).
190   See *Construction of a Wall* (n 152).
191   See also, in the context of the EU, *Council v Front Polisario* (n 11); see further Stefan Lorenzmeier, chapter 11 in this volume, 371–373.
192   Zachary Douglas, *The International Law of Investment Claims* (CUP 2009) 189. See also Douglas, 'Property, Investment, and the Scope of Investment Protection Obligations' (n 2) 372 et seq.

of Passau, patiently cross-checked these many references. Alongside the editors, an anonymous peer-reviewer made sure that any loose threads in the preliminary draft of this chapter could be pulled together. The author is further indebted to Tomer Broude and Moshe Hirsch, both Hebrew University of Jerusalem, for context on Israel, to Ketevan Platchiashvili and Giorgi Ustiashvili, both Sulkhan-Saba Orbeliani Teaching University, for context on Georgia, to Christina Letnikova, University of Passau, for help with texts in Russian, to Nikola Hajdin, University of Stockholm, for help with texts in Serbian as well as Swedish, and to E-Nuo Gu and Yi Zhang, both Xi'an Jiaotong University School of Law, for context on China. Matteo Vaccaro-Incisa was kind enough to provide comments on the final draft. Attempts were made to contact the relevant Ministries or agencies of each case study (with the exception of North Korea). Some were helpful, some were not.

Bibliography

Alschner W and D Skougarevskiy, 'Mapping the Universe of International Investment Agreements' (2016) 19 J Int'l Econ L 561.

Ahl B, 'Taiwan', *Max Planck Encyclopedia of Public International Law* (2008) <https://opil.ouplaw.com/home/MPIL> accessed 8 May 2020.

Aust A, 'Treaties, Territorial Application', *Max Planck Encyclopedia of Public International Law* (2006) <https://opil.ouplaw.com/home/MPIL> accessed 8 May 2020.

Beham MP, 'Cyprus Through the Lens of the Organisation of Islamic Cooperation: "The Victim of an Outcome in Which They Have No Fault"' (2017) 19 ARIEL 115.

Besson S, 'Sovereignty', *Max Planck Encyclopedia of Public International Law* (2011) <https://opil.ouplaw.com/home/MPIL> accessed 8 May 2020.

Binder C, '*Sanum Investments Limited v The Government of the Lao People's Democratic Republic*' (2016) 17 J World Investment & Trade 280.

Brown C and A Sheppard, 'United Kingdom' in Chester Brown (ed), *Commentaries on Selected Model Investment Treaties* (OUP 2013).

Caplan LM and JK Sharpe, 'United States' in Chester Brown (ed), *Commentaries on Selected Model Investment Treaties* (OUP 2013).

Chinese Foreign Ministry, 'Foreign Ministry Spokesperson Hua Chunying's Regular Press Conference on October 21, 2016' (21 October 2016) <www.fmprc.gov.cn/mfa_eng/xwfw_665399/s2510_665401/t1407743.shtml> accessed 8 May 2020.

Claussen K, 'Functional States Recognition and International Economic Law' in Chiara Giorgetti and Natalie Klein (eds), *Resolving Conflicts in the Law: Essays in Honour of Lea Brilmayer* (Brill Nijhoff).

Constantin D, 'Korean War (1950–53)', *Max Planck Encyclopedia of Public International Law* (2015) <https://opil.ouplaw.com/home/MPIL> accessed 8 May 2020.

Constantinides A, 'The Cyprus Problem in the United Nations Security Council' (2014) 19 ARIEL 29.

Costelloe D, 'Treaty Succession in Annexed Territory' (2016) 65 ICLQ 343.

Crawford J, *The Creation of States in International Law* (2nd edn, OUP 2007).

Dolzer R and C Schreuer, *Principles of International Investment Law* (2nd edn, OUP 2012).

Douglas Z, *The International Law of Investment Claims* (CUP 2009).

Douglas Z, 'Property, Investment, and the Scope of Investment Protection Obligations' in Z Douglas, J Pauwelyn, and JE Viñuales (eds), *The Foundations of International Investment Law: Bringing Theory into Practice* (OUP 2014).

Frowein JA, 'De Facto Regime', *Max Planck Encyclopedia of Public International Law* (2013) <https://opil.ouplaw.com/home/MPIL> accessed 8 May 2020.

Gallagher N and W Shan, 'China' in Chester Brown (ed), *Commentaries on Selected Model Investment Treaties* (OUP 2013).

Grant TD, *Aggression against Ukraine: Territory, Responsibility, and International Law* (Palgrave Macmillan 2015).

Happ R and S Wuschka, '*Horror Vacui*: Or Why Investment Treaties Should Apply to Illegally Annexed Territories' (2016) 33 J Int'l Arb 245.

Hirsch M, 'Rules of Origin as Trade or Foreign Policy Instruments? The European Union Policy on Products Manufactured in the Settlements in the West Bank and the Gaza Strip' (2003) 26 Fordham Int'l LJ 572.

Hirsch M, 'The Politics of Rules of Origin' in Broude T, Busch ML, and Porges A (eds), *The Politics of International Economic Law* (CUP 2011).

Hoffmeister F, 'Cyprus', *Max Planck Encyclopedia of Public International Law* (2019) <https://opil.ouplaw.com/home/MPIL> accessed 8 May 2020.

Hofmeister H, ' "Don't Mess with Moscow" – Legal Aspects of the 2008 Caucasus Conflict' (2010) 12 San Diego Int'l LJ 147.

Hsieh PL, 'An Unrecognized State in Foreign and International Courts: The Case of the Republic of China on Taiwan' (2007) 28 Mich J Int'l L 765.

Hsieh PL, 'Rethinking Non-Recognition: The EU's Investment Agreement with Taiwan under the One-China Policy' (forthcoming 2021) LJIL, manuscript available at <https://ssrn.com/abstract=3555574> accessed 8 May 2020.

Janik RRA, 'Israel and International Law' (2016) <www.ssrn.com/abstract=2889965> accessed 7 May 2020.

Jellinek G, *Allgemeine Staatslehre* (3rd edn, O Häring 1914).

Kelsen H, *Principles of International Law* (first published 1952, Lawbook Exchange 2003).

Khan D-E, 'Territory and Boundaries' in B Fassbender and A Peters (eds), *The Oxford Handbook of the History of International Law* (OUP 2012).

Khan D-E, 'Territory Taking Centre Stage in International Law: Some Preliminary Thoughts on the Rise of Territoriality to the Bedrock of Modern Statehood' in Société Française pour le Droit International (ed), *Droit des Frontieères Internationales – The Law of International Borders* (Éditions Pedone 2016).

Kleiner C and F Costamagna, 'Territoriality in Investment Arbitration: The Case of Financial Instruments' (2018) 9 JIDS 315.

Knahr C, 'Investments "in the Territory" of the Host State' in C Binder and others (eds), *International Investment Law for the 21st Century: Essays in Honour of Christoph Schreuer* (OUP 2009).

Knahr C, 'The Territorial Nexus Between an Investment and the Host State' in M Bungenberg and others (eds), *International Investment Law: A Handbook* (CH Beck, Hart, and Nomos 2015).

Konrad CW, 'Kosovo and Arbitration – The Birth of a New State' (*Kluwer Arbitration Blog*, 17 November 2010) <http://arbitrationblog.kluwerarbitration.com/2010/11/17/kosovo-and-arbitration-the-birth-of-a-new-state/> accessed 7 May 2020.

Kosovan Ministry of Trade and Industry, 'Investment Environment: Legislation and Agreements' (not dated) <https://kiesa.rks-gov.net/page.aspx?id=2,16> accessed 7 May 2020.

Luchterhandt O, 'Völkerrechtliche Aspekte des Georgien-Krieges' (2008) 46 Archiv des Völkerrechts 435.

Ministry of Foreign Affairs of the People's Republic of China, 'A Policy of "One Country, Two Systems" on Taiwan' (2014) <www.fmprc.gov.cn/mfa_eng/ziliao_665539/3602_665543/3604_665547/t18027.shtml> accessed 7 May 2020.

Mo JS, 'The Dilemma of Applying Bilateral Investment Treaties of China to Hong Kong and Macao: Challenge Raised by Sanum Investments to China' (2018) 33 ICSID Rev 125.

Nußberger A, 'Abkhazia' *Max Planck Encyclopedia of Public International Law* (2013) <https://opil.ouplaw.com/home/MPIL> accessed 8 May 2020.

Nußberger A, 'South Ossetia' *Max Planck Encyclopedia of Public International Law* (2013) <https://opil.ouplaw.com/home/MPIL> accessed 8 May 2020.

Paparinskis M, 'Latvia' in C Brown (ed), *Commentaries on Selected Model Investment Treaties* (OUP 2013).

Park D-Y, 'Korea', *Max Planck Encyclopedia of Public International Law* (2013) <https://opil.ouplaw.com/home/MPIL> accessed 8 May 2020.

Perry S, 'Victory for Kosovo in First ICSID Case' (*Global Arbitration Review*, 4 May 2018) <https://globalarbitrationreview.com/article/1169154/victory-for-kosovo-in-first-icsid-case> accessed 7 May 2020.

Repousis OG, 'On Territoriality and International Investment Law: Applying China's Investment Treaties to Hong Kong and Macao' (2015) 37 Mich J Int'l L 113.

Repousis OG, 'Why Russian Investment Treaties Could Apply to Crimea and What Would This Mean for the Ongoing Russo–Ukrainian Territorial Conflict' (2016) 32 Arb Int'l 459.

Repousis OG, 'The Application of Investment Treaties to Overseas Territories and the Uncertain Provisional Application of the Energy Charter Treaty to Gibraltar' (2017) 32 ICSID Rev 170.

Rubin B, 'Israel, Occupied Territories', *Max Planck Encyclopedia of Public International Law* (2009) <https://opil.ouplaw.com/home/MPIL> accessed 8 May 2020.

Ryan MC, 'Is There a "Nationality" of Investment? Origin of Funds and Territorial Link to the Host State' in E Gaillard and Y Banifatemi (eds), *Jurisdiction in Investment Treaty Arbitration* (Juris 2018).

Shaw MN, 'Territory in International Law' (1982) 13 Netherlands YB Int'l L 61.

Strupp M, 'Spratly Islands', *Max Planck Encyclopedia of Public International Law* (2008) <https://opil.ouplaw.com/home/MPIL> accessed 8 May 2020.

Suksi M, 'Divided States', *Max Planck Encyclopedia of Public International Law* (2013) <https://opil.ouplaw.com/home/MPIL> accessed 8 May 2020.

Talmon S, *Kollektive Nichtanerkennung illegaler Staaten: Grundlagen und Rechtsfolgen einer international koordinierten Sanktion, dargestellt am Beispiel der Türkischen Republik Nord-Zypern* (Mohr Siebeck 2006).

Tams CJ, 'State Succession to Investment Treaties: Mapping the Issues' (2016) 31 ICSID Rev 314.

Tzeng P, 'Investments on Disputed Territory: Indispensable Parties and Indispensable Issues' (2017) 14 Braz J Int'l L 122.

UNCTAD, *Scope and Definition: A Sequel* (UN 2011).

UNCTAD, 'International Investment Agreement Navigator' (*Investment Policy Hub*, 2020) <https://investmentpolicy.unctad.org/international-investment-agreements> accessed 7 May 2020.

Vaccaro-Incisa GM, 'Crimea Investment Disputes: Are Jurisdictional Hurdles Being Overcome Too Easily?' (*EJIL: Talk!*, 9 May 2018) <www.ejiltalk.org/crimea-investment-disputes-are-jurisdictional-hurdles-being-overcome-too-easily/> accessed 8 May 2020.

Waibel M, *Sovereign Defaults before International Courts and Tribunals* (CUP 2011).

Waibel M, 'Investment Arbitration: Jurisdiction and Admissibility' in M Bungenberg and others (eds), *International Investment Law: A Handbook* (CH Beck, Hart, and Nomos 2015).

Zelepos I, 'The Historical Background of the Cyprus Problem – Just a Conflict of Ethnic Nationalism?' (2014) 19 ARIEL 13.

Zheng CR, 'The Territoriality Requirement in Investment Treaties: A Constraint on Jurisdictional Expansionism' (2016) 34 Singapore L Rev 139.

CHAPTER 6

The Protection of Foreign Investments in Disputed Maritime Areas

Marco Benatar and Valentin J Schatz

1   **Introduction**

The oceans with their vast living and non-living marine resources are widely considered a new frontier in international investment protection.[1] Marine resources and other uses of the ocean that are of commercial interest to foreign investors range from oil and gas to other minerals such as gems or precious metals, offshore wind energy, aquaculture and fisheries. In the past, most attention had been paid to the protection of investments in maritime areas adjacent to occupied territories under international humanitarian law rather than international investment law.[2] Currently, particularly investments in offshore energy production are considered an area in which international investment law can play an important role with respect to activities that are otherwise mainly regulated by the law of the sea.[3] Investments in submarine cables and

---

1   Christopher Greenwood, 'Oceans and Space: Some New Frontiers for International Investment Law' (2018) 19 JWIT 775; Stephan W Schill, Christian J Tams, and Rainer Hofmann, 'Oceans and Space: New Frontiers in Investment Protection?' (2018) 19 JWIT 765.

2   On the legal framework applicable to 'occupied maritime areas', see Tassilo Singer, 'Occupation of Sea Territory: Requirements for Military Authority and Comparison to Art. 43 of the Hague Convention IV' in Jörg Schildknecht and others (eds), *Operational Law in International Straits and Current Maritime Security Challenges* (Springer 2018); Marco Longobardo, 'The Occupation of Maritime Territory under International Humanitarian Law' (2019) 95 Int'l L Stud 322. For discussion of the protection of foreign investments in maritime areas in situations of occupation, see, *eg*, Allan Gerson, 'Off-Shore Oil Exploitation by a Belligerent Occupant: The Gulf of Suez Dispute' (1977) 71 AJIL 725; Brice M Clagett and O Thomas Johnson, 'May Israel as a Belligerent Occupant Lawfully Exploit Previously Unexploited Oil Resources of the Gulf of Suez?' (1978) 72 AJIL 558; Susan Power, 'Occupying the Continental Shelf?: A Note Considering the Status of the Continental Shelf Delimitation Agreement Concluded between Turkey and the TRNC during the Belligerent Occupation of Northern Cyprus' (2014) 9 Irish YB Int'l L 91.

3   See, *cg*, Seline Trevisanut, 'Foreign Investments in the Offshore Energy Industry' in Tullio Treves, Francesco Seatzu, and Seline Trevisanut (eds), *Foreign Investment, International Law and Common Concerns* (Routledge 2014); Seline Trevisanut and Nikolaos

pipelines[4] and deep seabed mining beyond national jurisdiction[5] have also attracted academic attention. And most recently, the first ever publicly known investor-State arbitration concerning foreign fishing operations within national jurisdiction has surfaced.[6]

However, it is not uncommon for neighbouring coastal states to disagree over entitlements to maritime areas and/or over the delimitation of their maritime boundaries, particularly where (potentially) abundant offshore resources are at issue. Such situations can create considerable legal uncertainty, which in turn can directly translate into economic risks for foreign investors.[7] The exploitation of resources in disputed maritime areas remains governed by the law of the sea, which continues to develop through international jurisprudence.[8] Noteworthy in this regard are the decisions of the Special Chamber of the International Tribunal for the Law of the Sea (ITLOS) in *Ghana/Côte d'Ivoire*.[9]

Giannopoulos, 'Investment Protection of Offshore Energy Production: Bright Sides of Regime Interaction' (2018) 19 JWIT 789. See also Stuart Bruce, 'International Energy Law', *Max Planck Encyclopedia of Public International Law* (2014) paras 39 et seq, 52, 55 <https://opil.ouplaw.com/home/MPIL> accessed 30 April 2020.

4   Markos Karavias, 'Submarine Cables and Pipelines: The Protection of Investors under International Law' (2018) 19 JWIT 860.

5   Joanna Dingwall, 'International Investment Protection in Deep Seabed Mining beyond National Jurisdiction' (2018) 19 JWIT 890.

6   See *Peteris Pildegovics and SIA North Star v Norway*, ICSID Case no ARB/20/11 (pending); Lisa Bohmer, 'Snow Crab Dispute Prompts First ICSID Arbitration against Norway' (*IAReporter*, 1 April 2020) <www.iareporter.com/articles/snow-crab-dispute-prompts-first-icsid-arbitration-against-norway/> accessed 30 April 2020.

7   See, eg, Nigel Blackaby and Ben Juratowitch, 'Hydrocarbons in Disputed Areas' (2015) 44(4) Int'l L News 1; Saadia Bhatty and Nefeli Lamprou, 'Pitfalls of Investing in Sub-Saharan African Regions with Unsettled Boundaries: How Foreign Investors May Minimize and Manage Investment Risk' (2016) 13(4) TDM 1; Will Thomas, Alexandra van der Meulen, and Shirin Chua, 'Common Offshore Hydrocarbon Deposits: Rights, Risks and Remedies under International Law' (2019) 17 Oil, Gas & Energy L 1.

8   See, eg, Enrico Milano and Irini Papanicolopulu, 'State Responsibility in Disputed Areas on Land and at Sea' (2011) 71 Heidelberg J Int'l L 587; Paul Michael Blyschak, 'Offshore Oil and Gas Projects Amid Maritime Border Disputes: Applicable Law' (2013) 6 J World Energy L & Bus 210; Dominic Roughton, 'Rights (and Wrongs) of Capture: International Law and the Implications of the Guyana/Suriname Arbitration' (2015) 26 JERL 374; BIICL, *Report on the Obligations of States under Articles 74(3) and 83(3) of UNCLOS in Respect of Undelimited Maritime Areas* (BIICL 2016); Constantinos Yiallourides, 'Oil and Gas Development in Disputed Waters under UNCLOS' (2016) 5 UCLJLJ 59.

9   *Dispute Concerning Delimitation of the Maritime Boundary between Ghana and Côte d'Ivoire in the Atlantic Ocean (Ghana/Côte d'Ivoire)* (Provisional Measures) [2015] ITLOS Rep 146; *Dispute Concerning Delimitation of the Maritime Boundary between Ghana and*

Where the rights of foreign investors are harmed in disputed maritime areas, the question arises whether these investors can invoke international investment agreements (IIAS) to seek redress.[10] IIAS cover both bilateral investment treaties (BITS) and multilateral investment agreements (MIAS). BITS can be described as 'reciprocal legal agreement[s] concluded between two sovereign States for the promotion and protection of investments by investors of the one State ("home State") in the territory of the other State ("host State")'.[11] Reciprocal rules and protections of investments may also increasingly be found in multilateral agreements, which can be seen – at least from this perspective – as MIAS.[12] IIAS are the primary instruments for the protection of foreign

---

Côte d'Ivoire in the Atlantic Ocean (Ghana/Côte d'Ivoire) (Merits) [2017] ITLOS Rep 4. For commentary, see Yoshifumi Tanaka, 'Unilateral Exploration and Exploitation of Natural Resources in Disputed Areas: A Note on the Ghana/Côte d'Ivoire Order of 25 April 2015 before the Special Chamber of ITLOS' (2015) 46 Ocean Dev & Int'l L 315; Constantinos Yiallourides, 'Calming the Waters in the West African Region: The Case of Ghana and Côte d'Ivoire' (2018) 26 Afr J Int'l & Comp L 507; Joseph Onele, 'Revisiting Unilateral Exploitation of Mineral Resources in Disputed Water under United Nations Convention on the Law of the Sea: Any New Matter Arising?' (2019) 10 JIDS 160; Millicent McCreath and Zoe Scanlon, 'The Dispute Concerning the Delimitation of the Maritime Boundary Between Ghana and Côte d'Ivoire: Implications for the Law of the Sea' (2019) 50 Ocean Dev & Int'l L 1; Youri van Logchem, 'The Rights and Obligations of States in Disputed Maritime Areas: What Lessons Can Be Learned from the Maritime Boundary Dispute between Ghana and Côte d'Ivoire?' (2019) 52 Vand J Transnat'l L 121; Bin Zhao, 'The Curious Case of Ghana/Côte d'Ivoire: A Consistent Approach to Hydrocarbon Activities in the Disputed Area?' (2020) 10 Asian J Int'l L 94.

10 Marco Benatar, 'Applying International Investment Law to Disputed Maritime Zones: A Case Study of the Falklands (Malvinas)' (2015) 28 Hague YB Int'l L 65; Christine Sim, 'Investment Disputes Arising Out of Areas of Unsettled Boundaries: Ghana/Côte d'Ivoire' (2018) 11 World Energy L & Bus 1; Peter Tzeng, 'Investment Protection in Disputed Maritime Areas' (2018) 19 JWIT 828; Kathryn Khamsi, 'Investments in Unsettled Maritime Boundary Contexts: The Role of Bilateral Investment Treaties in Delivering Certainty' (2020) 34 ICSID Rev 666.

11 Marc Jacob, 'Investments, Bilateral Treaties' *Max Planck Encyclopedia of Public International Law* (2014) para 1 <https://opil.ouplaw.com/home/MPIL> accessed 30 April 2020.

12 Christoph Schreuer, 'Investment Disputes', *Max Planck Encyclopedia of Public International Law* (2013) paras 11 et seq <https://opil.ouplaw.com/home/MPIL> accessed 30 April 2020. See, eg, Energy Charter Treaty (adopted 17 December 1994, entered into force 16 April 1998) 2080 UNTS 95 (ECT); Agreement between the United States of America, the United Mexican States, and Canada (adopted 30 November 2018, not in force) <https://ustr.gov/trade-agreements/free-trade-agreements/united-states-mexico-canada-agreement/agreement-between> accessed 30 April 2020; Trans-Pacific Partnership (text released 26 January 2016, not signed) <https://ustr.gov/trade-agreements/free-trade-agreements/trans-pacific-partnership/tpp-full-text> accessed 30 April 2020.

investments in international investment law.¹³ Typical provisions contained in IIAs include definitions of the notions of investment and investor, substantive protections of foreign investors (*eg*, concerning expropriation, fair and equitable treatment, full protection and security),¹⁴ and dispute settlement clauses (usually providing for both investor-state and state-to-state arbitration).¹⁵

But do they apply to investments in disputed maritime areas? And if this is the case, can an arbitral tribunal established under an IIA's dispute settlement clause make all findings of fact and law required to apply the IIA without exceeding the scope of its jurisdictional mandate?¹⁶

This chapter seeks to answer these questions. In so doing, it will define the concept of 'disputed maritime areas' for present purposes (section 2). Next, it will address the spatial scope of IIAs as a matter of *substantive law* in relation to maritime areas generally and disputed maritime areas specifically (section 3). Thereafter, this chapter will turn to specific challenges of *procedural law* raised by investor-state dispute settlement in relation to investments in disputed maritime areas (section 4). An ensuing section will assess the different approaches investment tribunals could follow in dealing with the aforementioned challenges (section 5), followed by concluding remarks (section 6).

2   Disputed Maritime Areas: a Taxonomy

In simplified terms, the international law of the sea knows three maritime areas¹⁷ of sovereignty (internal waters, territorial sea, and archipelagic waters)¹⁸ and three maritime zones of functional rights and jurisdiction (contiguous zone,¹⁹ exclusive economic zone (EEZ), and continental

---

13   This chapter does not address the protection of investments under investment contracts or political risk insurance. See Tzeng, 'Investment Protection in Disputed Maritime Areas' (n 10) 850 et seq.

14   Schreuer, 'Investment Disputes' (n 12) paras 49 et seq.

15   Arnaud de Nanteuil, *Droit international de l'investissement* (2nd edn, Pedone 2017) 47.

16   The scope *ratione loci* of IIAs and the scope of jurisdiction *ratione loci* of investment tribunals are closely related but separate issues. See Michael Waibel, 'Investment Arbitration: Jurisdiction and Admissibility' in Marc Bungenberg and others (eds), *International Investment Law: A Handbook* (CH Beck, Hart, and Nomos 2015) 1248 et seq.

17   As neither internal waters nor archipelagic waters are strictly speaking maritime *zones* measured from the baselines, it is more accurate to refer to maritime *areas*.

18   *Cf* Wolfgang Graf Vitzthum, 'Maritimes Aquitorium und Anschlusszone' in Wolfgang Graf Vitzthum (ed), *Handbuch des Seerechts* (Beck 2006) 69 et seq.

19   The contiguous zone does not involve rights to marine resources or jurisdiction with respect to economic activities. See Yoshifumi Tanaka, *The International Law of the Sea*

shelf).[20] Disagreement among states in respect of such maritime areas can arise in a multitude of ways and it is beyond the scope of this chapter to identify all imaginable scenarios.[21] For the purposes of this chapter, the term 'disputed maritime area' refers to any maritime area where at least two states claim inconsistent maritime rights as coastal states based on the international law of the sea.[22] Three overarching categories of disputed maritime areas may be identified on the basis of this definition.[23]

2.1 Delimitation of Overlapping Entitlements

The first category is that of delimitation disputes in which two or more coastal states have *overlapping entitlements* (territorial seas, EEZs, or continental shelves)[24] and disagree about how exactly these entitlements should be delimited by a maritime boundary. These are the archetype of maritime boundary delimitation disputes.[25] It is worth mentioning that such disputes may also arise from overlapping maritime entitlements to different maritime zones (*eg*, territorial sea v EEZ).[26] Another example is the situation where a coastal state

---

(3rd edn, CUP 2019) 146 et seq. For this reason, it is not addressed in the remainder of this chapter.

20   See, generally, Maria Gavouneli, *Functional Jurisdiction in the Law of the Sea* (Brill 2007).

21   This chapter does not address 'delineation' disputes as opposed to 'delimitation' disputes. The former concerns maritime areas to which only one coastal state has laid claim, but where one or more other states do not recognise that maritime claim and consider that the relevant maritime area either forms part of the high seas and/or Area or of another maritime zone of the coastal state which involves more limited rights (*eg*, the EEZ rather than the territorial sea).

22   Modified from Tzeng, 'Investment Protection in Disputed Maritime Areas' (n 10) 830.

23   The definition adopted for the purposes of this chapter excludes investment protection in relation to joint development areas or provisionally delimited maritime areas. On these issues, see Tzeng, 'Investment Protection in Disputed Maritime Areas' (n 10) 855 et seq; Khamsi (n 10) 672 et seq.

24   As internal waters and archipelagic waters are not maritime zones measured from the baselines, it is impossible for them to overlap with the maritime zones of other states. In order for such a situation to arise, the validity of the baseline would have to be disputed, rendering the dispute one concerning the existence of maritime entitlements. See section 2.2 below.

25   See, generally, Stephen Fietta and Robin Cleverly, *A Practitioner's Guide to Maritime Boundary Delimitation* (OUP 2016); Alex G Oude Elferink, Tore Henriksen, and Signe Veierud Busch (eds), *Maritime Boundary Delimitation: The Case Law Is It Consistent and Predictable?* (CUP 2018); Yoshifumi Tanaka, *Predictability and Flexibility in the Law of Maritime Delimitation* (2nd edn, Hart 2019).

26   *Delimitation of the Maritime Boundary in the Bay of Bengal (Bangladesh/Myanmar)* (Merits) [2012] ITLOS Rep 4, para 169; Erik Franckx and Marco Benatar, 'Navigating Between Consolidation and Innovation: Bangladesh/Myanmar (International Tribunal for the Law of the Sea, Judgment of 14 March 2012)' (2013) 27 Ocean YB 435, 442.

claims a continental shelf beyond 200 nm that overlaps with an EEZ and continental shelf entitlement within 200 nm of another coastal state.[27]

2.2 Existence of Overlapping Entitlements

The second and most diverse category is that of disputes that concern the *existence of entitlements* claimed by a coastal state in an area claimed also by another coastal state. In many cases, these disputes will coexist with disputes concerning the delimitation of overlapping entitlements.[28] First, there may be disputes about whether a particular feature on which a coastal state bases a claim to an entitlement can indeed be classified as 'high-tide' territory giving rise to such entitlements rather than, for example, a low-tide elevation that does not have such effect except as a base point for baselines.[29] Second, even where the territorial nature of an island is uncontested, there can be disputes about whether the island constitutes a 'rock' within the meaning of article 121(3) of the United Nations Convention on the Law of the Sea (UNCLOS)[30] rather than an 'island proper' under article 121(1) UNCLOS, which would mean that it does not create maritime entitlements beyond a territorial sea.[31] Third, a coastal state may allege that a neighbouring coastal state has drawn baselines that are not in accordance with the applicable rules,[32] resulting in the non-opposability of maritime entitlements claimed from these baselines that reflect the excess of entitlement.[33] Fourth, disputes about the existence or extent of maritime entitlements are common in situations where one or more coastal states claim historic waters and this claim is opposed by another

---

27 See, albeit for a situation of adjacent rather than opposite coasts, *Bangladesh/Myanmar* (n 26) paras 463 et seq; Franckx and Benatar (n 26) 450.
28 However, where overlapping entitlements can be ruled out if the alleged entitlement does not exist, it has been held that such disputes do not concern 'delimitation' in the strict sense. See *South China Sea Arbitration (Philippines v China)*, PCA Case no 2013-19, Award on Jurisdiction and Admissibility (29 October 2015) para 405.
29 *Cf South China Sea Arbitration (Philippines v China)*, PCA Case no 2013-19, Award (12 July 2016) paras 281 et seq.
30 United Nations Convention on the Law of the Sea (adopted 10 December 1982, entered into force 16 November 1994) 1833 UNTS 3 (UNCLOS).
31 *Cf South China Sea Arbitration*, Award (n 29) paras 385 et seq.
32 For an overview, see Tullio Scovazzi, 'Baselines', *Max Planck Encyclopedia of Public International Law* (2007) <https://opil.ouplaw.com/home/MPIL> accessed 30 April 2020.
33 *Cf* ILA, 'Baselines under the International Law of the Sea, Final Report' (2018) 33 <www.ila-hq.org/images/ILA/DraftReports/DraftReport_Baselines.pdf> accessed 30 April 2020. Importantly, climate change-induced rise of sea-levels and uncertainty under the current legal regime carry significant potential to exacerbate existing disputes or cause new ones. See, *eg*, Eike Blitza, *Auswirkungen des Meeresspiegelanstiegs auf maritime Grenzen* (Springer 2019).

coastal state. Claims to historic waters are essentially claims to maritime areas of sovereignty (usually internal waters) that are 'exceptional' in the sense that they are exercised in derogation of the general regime with the acquiescence of the states concerned.[34] Of course, such exceptional claims may clash with claims of other states to maritime entitlements based on the general rules.[35]

2.3 Ownership of Entitlements

The third category of disputed maritime areas for the purposes of this chapter covers disputes concerning *ownership of entitlements* that themselves derive from disputes relating to territorial sovereignty over the land generating the entitlement. Following the principle that 'the land dominates the sea', maritime entitlements are attributed to the state that has sovereignty over the land giving rise to these entitlements.[36] Therefore, if two states claim sovereignty over coastal or island territory, they are also in dispute over the entitlements generated by the relevant land area.[37]

3 Spatial Scope of IIAs and Maritime Areas

In order to explore to what extent investments situated in contested maritime areas are protected by IIAs, it is necessary to analyse their spatial scope (or scope *ratione loci*). As IIAs are treaties within the meaning of article 1(1)(a) of the Vienna Convention on the Law of Treaties (VCLT),[38] their scope must be

---

34 *South China Sea Arbitration*, Award (n 29) para 268. See, generally, Clive R Symmons, *Historic Waters and Historic Rights in the Law of the Sea: A Modern Reappraisal* (2nd edn, Brill 2019).

35 An example would be the dispute between Ukraine and Russia concerning the status of the Sea of Azov, in which Ukraine claims that the general rules on maritime entitlements apply, whereas Russia maintains that the Sea of Azov constitutes shared internal waters of both states (*ie* a 'condominium'). See Valentin J Schatz and Dmytro Koval, 'Russia's Annexation of Crimea and the Passage of Ships Through Kerch Strait: A Law of the Sea Perspective' (2019) 50 Ocean Dev & Int'l L 275.

36 *North Sea Continental Shelf (Germany/Denmark; Germany/Netherlands)* [1969] ICJ Rep 3, para 96. See also *Territorial and Maritime Dispute (Nicaragua v Colombia)* [2012] ICJ Rep 624, para 140.

37 See, *eg*, *Chagos Marine Protected Area Arbitration (Mauritius v UK)*, PCA Case no 2011-03, Award (18 March 2015) paras 163 et seq; *Dispute Concerning Coastal State Rights in the Black Sea, Sea of Azov, and Kerch Strait (Ukraine v Russia)*, PCA Case no 2017-06, Award on Preliminary Objections (21 February 2020) paras 43 et seq.

38 Vienna Convention on the Law of Treaties (adopted 23 May 1969, entered into force 23 January 1980) 1155 UNTS 331 (VCLT).

determined by reference to the law of treaties.[39] While each IIA is to be interpreted on its own terms, some common practices and trends can usefully be identified regarding the scope *ratione loci* of IIAs.[40]

Article 29 VCLT regulates the 'default' territorial scope of treaties by providing that '[u]nless a different intention appears from the treaty or is otherwise established, a treaty is binding upon each party in respect of its entire territory'.[41] It is widely accepted that this provision reflects customary international law.[42] In international law, territory is understood as 'that defined portion of the globe which is subjected to the sovereignty of a state [...] The importance of state territory is that it is the space within which the state exercises its supreme, and normally exclusive, authority'.[43] It comprises the land, subsoil, and inland waters (*eg*, lakes and rivers), as well as the airspace above the land. In addition, as recognised by article 2(1) UNCLOS, a state's sovereignty extends to internal waters, territorial sea, and – in the case of archipelagic states[44] – archipelagic waters,[45] including the seabed, subsoil and the airspace above these areas.[46] As opposed to these maritime areas of sovereignty, coastal states only enjoy functionally limited sovereign rights and/or jurisdiction in the remaining maritime zones, namely the EEZ, continental shelf, and contiguous zone.[47]

---

39   J Romesh Weeramantry, *Treaty Interpretation in Investment Arbitration* (OUP 2012) 157 et seq. Where a party to an IIA is not a party to the VCLT, the customary international law of treaties must be applied, which to a considerable extent mirrors the rules of the VCLT. See, *eg*, Anthony Aust, 'Vienna Convention on the Law of Treaties (1969)', *Max Planck Encyclopedia of Public International Law* (2006) paras 14 et seq <https://opil.ouplaw.com/home/MPIL> accessed 30 April 2020; Malgosia Fitzmaurice, 'Treaties', *Max Planck Encyclopedia of Public International Law* (2010) para 12 <https://opil.ouplaw.com/home/MPIL> accessed 30 April 2020.

40   For in-depth analysis, see Benatar (n 10) 73 et seq. See also Tzeng, 'Investment Protection in Disputed Maritime Areas' (n 10) 834 et seq. Generally, on the definition of territory in BITs of disputing sovereigns over certain territories, see also Markus P Beham, chapter 5 in this volume, 142–149.

41   On VCLT art 29, see, generally, Syméon Karagiannis, 'Art. 29 1969 Vienna Convention' in Oliver Corten and Pierre Klein (eds), *The Vienna Conventions on the Law of Treaties*, vol 1 (OUP 2011) 731 et seq.

42   See, *eg*, *Sanum Investments Ltd v Laos*, PCA Case no 2013-13, Award on Jurisdiction (13 December 2013) para 220.

43   Robert Jennings and Arthur Watts (eds), *Oppenheim's International Law*, vol 1 (9th edn, OUP 2008) 563 et seq.

44   *Cf* UNCLOS art 46.

45   For archipelagic state sovereignty in archipelagic waters, see also UNCLOS art 49.

46   *Cf* Richard Barnes, 'Article 2' in Alexander Proelss (ed), *The United Nations Convention on the Law of the Sea: A Commentary* (Beck, Hart, and Nomos 2017) 33.

47   The 'sovereign rights' notion associated with the EEZ and the continental shelf could nonetheless be viewed as an 'extract of the broader concept of sovereignty'. Alexander

Against this background, a textual reading of article 29 VCLT suggests that – absent an intention of the parties to define the scope *ratione loci* of a treaty differently – it will extend to the internal waters and territorial sea, but not to the EEZ, contiguous zone, or continental shelf of a coastal state.[48] Archipelagic waters are also included where applicable as they are a maritime area of sovereignty located *landward* of the territorial sea and *seaward* of the internal waters.[49] That said, article 29 VCLT is merely the 'default' rule and allows for considerable flexibility in defining the territorial scope of treaties.[50] It also declares itself subsidiary to the 'intention' of the treaty in question.[51]

Turning to the scope *ratione loci* of IIAs, it is notable that as IIAs, and particularly BITs, are usually negotiated on the basis of similar models, they frequently cover the same or very similar content.[52] Rules on the scope *ratione loci* of an IIA are usually found in the provision that defines the notion of investment within the meaning of the IIA. Often, protections under IIAs are restricted to investments made 'in the territory' of one of the parties to the agreement.[53] In this respect, two categories of IIAs may be identified for the present

---

Proelss, 'Article 56' in Alexander Proelss (ed), *The United Nations Convention on the Law of the Sea: A Commentary* (Beck, Hart, and Nomos 2017) 424. See also Amber Rose Maggio, 'Article 77' in Alexander Proelss (ed), *The United Nations Convention on the Law of the Sea: A Commentary* (Beck, Hart, and Nomos, 2017) 605 et seq.

48 Anthony Aust, *Modern Treaty Law and Practice* (3rd edn, CUP 2013) 178. For a more equivocal stance, see Syméon Karagiannis, 'The Territorial Application of Treaties' in Duncan B Hollis (ed), *The Oxford Guide to Treaties* (OUP 2012) 317 et seq. As for the *travaux préparatoires*, the International Law Commission's (ILC) commentary to its final Draft Articles (which were later considered by the Vienna Conference on the Law of Treaties) explains that the notion of 'entire territory' embraces 'all the land and appurtenant territorial waters and air space which constitute the territory of the state', ILC, 'Draft Articles on the Law of Treaties with Commentaries' (1966) II YBILC 187, 213 (draft art 25 cmt 3). The concept of 'appurtenant territorial waters' is not known to contemporary international law. Scholars have construed this passage as referring to internal waters and the territorial sea. See Kerstin von der Decken, 'Article 29' in Oliver Dörr and Kirsten Schmalenbach (eds), *Vienna Convention on the Law of Treaties: A Commentary* (2nd edn, Springer 2018) 530.

49 *Cf* UNCLOS arts 48–50. For an inclusion of archipelagic waters also, see von der Decken (n 48) 530.

50 One particular type of limitation of scope used by metropolitan states is that of territorial limitations. On the role of such territorial limitations in IIAs, see Benatar (n 10) 74 et seq.

51 For discussion, see von der Decken (n 48) 523 et seq.

52 Chester Brown, 'The Evolution of the Regime of International Investment Agreements: History, Economics and Politics' in Marc Bungenberg and others (eds), *International Investment Law: A Handbook* (CH Beck, Hart, and Nomos 2015) 182.

53 Christina Knahr, 'Investments "in the Territory" of the Host State' in Christina Binder and others (eds), *International Investment Law for the 21st Century: Essays in Honour of Christoph Schreuer* (OUP 2009) 42. See also August Reinisch, 'Investment Disputes and

purposes, namely agreements that do not further define the term 'territory' to include maritime zones of sovereign rights and functional jurisdiction and those that do.⁵⁴

As far as the first category is concerned, territory is understood as including land, the internal waters, and the territorial sea.⁵⁵ This is made explicit, for example, in article 1(10)(a) ECT, which refers to 'territory under [a contracting party's] sovereignty, it being understood that territory includes land, internal waters and the territorial sea' – although the ECT does not belong in this category of IIAs. Arguably, archipelagic waters would also be included for archipelagic states. Against this background, it may be asked whether or not the scope of IIAs that simply refer to 'territory' should be interpreted as including the EEZ and continental shelf, which are not maritime zones of sovereignty but merely of 'sovereign rights'.⁵⁶ At first sight, the most intuitive reading may be that most, particularly older, IIAs apply only to territory in the strict sense.⁵⁷

However, there could be agreements containing provisions that implicitly presuppose applicability to the EEZ or continental shelf, prompting a broader interpretation of the IIA's scope *ratione loci*. Depending on the object and purpose of an IIA, its scope might also be open to evolutionary interpretation taking into account the maritime areas of functional rights and jurisdiction that emerged after its conclusion.⁵⁸ Of course, the fact that some IIAs expressly incorporate these maritime areas into the definition of 'territory' may lend support to the contrary view that an omission reflects an intention to adopt a narrow scope.⁵⁹ In any case, any transfer of an interpretation of the scope of one IIA to another should be approached with great caution given that, based on the rules of treaty interpretation in articles 31 and 32 VCLT, each IIA is, arguably, to be interpreted independently.⁶⁰ Finally, there is a teleological

---

Their Boundaries' in Société française pour le droit international (ed), *Droit des frontières internationales/The Law of International Borders* (Pedone 2016) 208 et seq.

54   There are also BITs that do not define the term 'territory' at all, see, *eg*, Austria–Egypt (2001). See also Markus P Beham, chapter 5 in this volume, 142–149.
55   Benatar (n 10) 73 et seq. For an inclusion of the territorial sea, see also Greenwood (n 1) 783; Tzeng, 'Investment Protection in Disputed Maritime Areas' (n 10) 835 et seq.
56   Tzeng, 'Investment Protection in Disputed Maritime Areas' (n 10) 836 et seq.
57   *Cf* Tzeng, 'Investment Protection in Disputed Maritime Areas' (n 10) 836.
58   Greenwood (n 1) 784, with reference to *Aegean Sea Continental Shelf Case (Greece v Turkey)* [1978] ICJ Rep 3, paras 77, 86. *Cf* also Tzeng, 'Investment Protection in Disputed Maritime Areas' (n 10) 837.
59   Greenwood (n 1) 784.
60   As Tzeng, 'Investment Protection in Disputed Maritime Areas' (n 10) 837, points out, this issue is a controversial subject. For the view taken here, he refers to Stephan W Schill, *The Multilateralization of International Investment Law* (CUP 2010) 305 et seq; Andrew D

argument for an application of IIAs to all areas under the jurisdiction and/ or effective control of the parties since the object and purpose of such agreements is to *effectively* protect foreign investments.[61] While none of these arguments conclusively point in one direction, an arbitral tribunal will likely face a selection of them in determining the scope *ratione loci* of the IIA which it has been called upon to apply.

Beyond the (mostly older) IIAs that simply refer to 'territory', there is a clear trend towards the inclusion of maritime areas of functional rights and jurisdiction, *ie* the EEZ and/or continental shelf, into the definition of 'territory' or 'area' – and thus the spatial scope of IIAs.[62] This serves to ensure that the protections afforded by the IIA cover investments in marine industries such as oil and gas extraction facilities, mineral exploration or offshore energy infrastructure located within the host state's maritime jurisdiction.[63] Where maritime areas beyond the territorial sea are included in the scope of IIAs, there is no uniformity but rather a variety of formulas employed.[64] The first group of IIAs expressly lists maritime areas in which the parties exercise sovereign rights or jurisdiction.[65] Within this group, some IIAs contain a particularly

---

Mitchell and James Munro, 'Someone Else's Deal: Interpreting International Investment Agreements in the Light of Third-Party Agreements' (2017) 28 EJIL 669. For the contrary practice of many arbitral tribunals, see Tzeng, 'Investment Protection in Disputed Maritime Areas' (n 10) 837 (fn 44) with reference to *Aguas del Tunari v Bolivia*, ICSID Case no ARB/02/3, Decision on Jurisdiction (21 October 2005) paras 289 et seq; *LESI SpA and ASTALDI SpA v Algeria*, ICSID Case no ARB/05/3, Decision on Jurisdiction (12 July 2006) para 84; *Plama v Bulgaria*, ICSID Case no ARB/03/24, Decision on Jurisdiction (8 February 2005) para 204. It is worth recalling that 'the application of international law rules on interpretation of treaties to identical or similar provisions of different treaties may not yield the same results, having regard to, *inter alia*, differences in the respective contexts, objects and purposes, subsequent practice of parties and *travaux préparatoires*'. *MOX Plant (Ireland v UK)* (Provisional Measures) [2001] ITLOS Rep 95, para 51.

61 Tzeng, 'Investment Protection in Disputed Maritime Areas' (n 10) 836 et seq. For detailed discussion of this approach, see section 5 below.

62 Benatar (n 10) 77 with reference to UNCTAD, *Bilateral Investment Treaties 1995–2006: Trends in Investment Rulemaking* (2006) 17 et seq. See also Tzeng, 'Investment Protection in Disputed Maritime Areas' (n 10) 837 et seq.

63 *Cf* UNCTAD, *Scope and Definition* (1999) 44; UNCTAD, *Scope and Definition: A Sequel* (2011) 100. There also exist IIAs concluded between coastal states and landlocked states which define 'territory' to include maritime areas. See Rudolf Dolzer and Margrete Stevens, *Bilateral Investment Treaties* (Martinus Nijhoff 1995) 44.

64 Benatar (n 10) 78 with reference to UNCTAD (n 62) 18 et seq. See also Tzeng, 'Investment Protection in Disputed Maritime Areas' (n 10) 837 et seq.

65 Benatar (n 10) 78. See, *eg*, Comprehensive Economic and Trade Agreement between Canada and the European Union [2017] OJ L 11/23 (not in force) (CETA) art 8.2(1) in conjunction with art 1.3; Australia–India BIT (1999) art 1(f)(i), (ii). See also Greenwood

comprehensive definition of 'territory' that encompasses even artificial islands, installations and structures in the EEZ or on the continental shelf of the host state.⁶⁶ A second group of IIAs does not expressly make reference to these maritime areas but refers to rights enjoyed under international law for the purposes of exploration and exploitation of natural resources, which implicitly includes sovereign rights in the EEZ and on the continental shelf.⁶⁷ There are also IIAs that combine the approaches of the first and second group because they define their scope differently – at least in wording if not in content – for each party.⁶⁸ A third group of BITs that may be identified opts for even more general and ambiguous wording by merely making reference to areas in which the parties exercise 'jurisdiction' without specifying the nature or spatial extent of such jurisdiction.⁶⁹

4 Limits of Jurisdiction in Investor-State Dispute Settlement

From the perspective of investor-state dispute settlement, investments in disputed maritime areas can pose a variety of intricate procedural conundrums. This chapter focuses on challenges that investment tribunals might face with respect to establishing their jurisdiction over investment disputes in such areas. On the one hand, these challenges concern the applicability of IIAs to disputed maritime areas as a matter of substantive law. On the other hand, there is a cardinal difference between a legal assessment of such a situation and the question of an arbitral tribunal's competence to make such an assessment on the basis of the limited scope of jurisdiction that it has been granted on the basis of the relevant IIA. The principle of consent to jurisdiction, which lies at the core of international dispute settlement, mandates that 'no State can,

---

(n 1) 783 et seq (fn 27) with reference to the USA Model BIT (2012) art 1(c); UK Model BIT (2008) art 1(e). See also the examples given by Tzeng, 'Investment Protection in Disputed Maritime Areas' (n 10) 838 (fn 46), ie Hong Kong–Chile BIT (2016, not in force) art 1; Russia–Morocco BIT (2016, not in force) art 1(4)(a).

66   See, eg, Canada Model BIT (2004) art 1. For coastal state jurisdiction concerning artificial islands, installations, and structures in the EEZ and on the continental shelf, see UNCLOS arts 60, 80.

67   See, eg, Korea–Tajikistan BIT (1995) art 1.4; Energy Charter Treaty art 1(10).

68   See, eg, Trans-Pacific Partnership (n 12) art 1.3 in conjunction with annex 1-A. See also Tzeng, 'Investment Protection in Disputed Maritime Areas' (n 10) 837 (fn 35) with reference to Canada–Hong Kong BIT (2016) art 1; Nigeria–Singapore BIT (2016, not in force) art 1.

69   See, eg, Thailand–Egypt BIT (2000) art 1.4.

without its consent, be compelled to submit its disputes with other States either to mediation or to arbitration, or to any other kind of pacific settlement'.[70] This principle also applies in investor-state dispute settlement.[71] Therefore, the extent of jurisdiction of investment tribunals must be established by reference to the compromissory clauses of the IIAs that form the basis for litigation.[72] In the present context, problems arise with respect to jurisdiction *ratione materiae* and jurisdiction *ratione personae*.

4.1 Limits of Jurisdiction ratione materiae: *Implicated Issues*

Compromissory clauses in IIAs usually confine jurisdiction *ratione materiae* of investor-state tribunals to 'investment disputes', which may be described in simplified terms as disputes between an investor and the host state concerning losses or damages that the investor has incurred through alleged breaches of the IIA by the host state.[73] Therefore, investment tribunals generally have jurisdiction to determine – upon the investor's request – whether its protections under the IIA have been breached by the host state. However, absent a suitable *renvoi*-provision in the IIA,[74] investment tribunals do not ordinarily have jurisdiction to make findings on whether a provision of another treaty or a primary rule of customary international law has been breached.[75] As only investments

---

70 *Status of Eastern Carelia* (Advisory Opinion) [1923] PCIJ Rep Series B no 5, 7, 27; *East Timor (Portugal v Australia)* [1995] ICJ Rep 90, para 26. See also Shabtai Rosenne, 'International Courts and Tribunals, Jurisdiction and Admissibility of Inter-State Applications', Max Planck Encyclopedia of Public International Law (2006) para 2 <https://opil.ouplaw.com/home/MPIL> accessed 30 April 2020.

71 See, *eg, Casinos Austria International GmbH and Casinos Austria AG v Argentina*, ICSID Case no ARB/14/32, Decision on Jurisdiction, Dissenting Opinion and Declaration of Dissent of Santiago Torres Bernárdez (20 June 2018) para 36.

72 Frédéric G Sourgens, 'By Equal Contest of Arms: Jurisdictional Proof in Investor-State Arbitrations' (2012) 38 NCJ Int'l L & Com Reg 876 et seq.

73 See, generally, Schreuer, 'Investment Disputes' (n 12) paras 21 et seq, who also addresses consent to investor-state arbitration via investment contracts and national legislation, which are not addressed in this chapter.

74 For example, many IIAs contain an obligation of host states to accord investments or returns of investors of the other contracting party fair and equitable treatment *in accordance with principles of international law*. These are references to a customary international law standard. See Ioana Tudor, *The Fair and Equitable Treatment Standard in the International Law of Foreign Investment* (OUP 2008) 25 et seq.

75 *Cf* Peter Tzeng, 'The Implicated Issue Problem: Indispensable Issues and Incidental Jurisdiction' (2018) 50 NYU J Int'l Law & Pol 485 et seq. *Cf* also *Archer Daniels Midland Co and Tate & Lyle Ingredients Americas, Inc v Mexico*, ICSID Case no ARB(AF)/04/5, Award (21 November 2007) para 133; *Corn Products International, Inc v Mexico*, ICSID Case no ARB(AF)/04/1, Decision on Responsibility (15 January 2008) paras 181 et seq, 189. The

that fall within the scope *ratione loci* of the IIA are protected, investment tribunals do have jurisdiction to determine whether the investment in question has been made in the 'territory' or 'area' of the host state as defined by the IIA.[76] For this purpose, investment tribunals may interpret the provisions of the IIA to determine its spatial scope, and – in a second step – apply those provisions to the facts of the case in order to establish the nexus between the investment and the 'territory' or 'area' of the host state for the purposes of the IIA.[77]

As shown in the previous section, at least contemporary IIAs tend to cover investments located both in maritime areas of sovereignty (internal waters, territorial sea, and archipelagic waters) and maritime zones of functional rights and jurisdiction (EEZ and continental shelf). This determination is in itself a first step in establishing jurisdiction *ratione materiae*.[78] Assuming, *arguendo*, that the IIA on the basis of which an investor has initiated arbitration does extend to the relevant maritime areas, the question arises whether or not the fact that the relevant maritime area is disputed affects the applicability of the IIA. In such situations, the maritime area is contested among two or more *states* either because there is an outstanding dispute about the delimitation of overlapping entitlements[79] and/or a dispute concerning the existence of overlapping entitlements[80] and/or a dispute in relation to ownership over an entitlement.[81] These inter-state disputes are 'implicated' by the investment dispute because a decision concerning the latter might require, as a preliminary issue or 'prior determination', a decision concerning these inter-state disputes.[82]

---

        issue was not explicitly addressed in the parallel case *Cargill, Inc v Mexico*, ICSID Case no ARB(AF)/05/2, Award (28 September 2009) 379 et seq.

76   Benatar (n 10) 85 et seq; Tzeng, 'Investment Protection in Disputed Maritime Areas' (n 10) 839. As the territorial nexus requirement is often part of the definition of 'investment', which concerns the IIA's scope *ratione materiae*, there is arguably no need to refer to jurisdiction *ratione loci* rather than simply jurisdiction *ratione materiae* in this respect. This is also the approach of article 25 of the ICSID Convention, which only requires an 'investment'. See Christoph Schreuer and others, *The ICSID Convention: A Commentary* (2nd ed, CUP 2009) 137 et seq.

77   This chapter is not concerned with the requirements for the establishment of the nexus between the investment and the spatial scope. On the latter issue, see Lucy Reed, Zoe Scanlon, and Dafina Atanasova, 'Protected Investment', *Max Planck Encyclopedia of Public International Law* (2018) paras 61 et seq <https://opil.ouplaw.com/home/MPIL> accessed 30 April 2020.

78   Tzeng, 'Investment Protection in Disputed Maritime Areas' (n 10) 839 et seq.

79   See section 2.1 above.

80   See section 2.2 above.

81   See section 2.3 above.

82   On the problem of implicated issues generally, see Tzeng, 'The Implicated Issue Problem' (n 75) 447 et seq.

However, deciding a territorial sovereignty dispute or a maritime delimitation dispute is quite different from interpreting and applying the provisions of an IIA, including the provisions concerning the agreement's spatial scope. Therefore, such implicated issues raise intricate questions of jurisdiction *ratione materiae*, which are addressed in the final section of this chapter.[83]

In assessing under which circumstances investment tribunals may have to make determinations on implicated issues, it is helpful to distinguish two categories of IIAs, namely those that do not take account of existing territorial or maritime disputes and those that contain language to this effect.[84]

The first category of IIAs are applicable to maritime areas as established in the previous section but do not contain wording that further circumscribes their spatial scope of application in light of an existing territorial or maritime dispute. Examples cited in the literature include Morocco's BITs[85] (in light of Western Sahara) and Israel's BITs[86] (in light of the question of Palestine).[87] Other IIAs contain an additional requirement that the maritime areas of the host state be established 'in accordance with international law'.[88] One example is the UK Model BIT.[89] There are also IIAs that define the relevant rules of international law in a more detailed fashion. For example, the Argentina–USA BIT (1991) refers to maritime areas 'established in accordance with international law as reflected in the 1982 United Nations Convention on the Law of the Sea'.[90] The Model BIT (2012) of the USA, which is not a party to UNCLOS, refers to customary international law.[91] While the purpose of these clauses is said to reign in exorbitant assertions of maritime rights and jurisdiction,[92] it may be doubted whether they also cover contested maritime entitlements, which themselves are derived from territorial sovereignty disputes.[93] Arguably, the

---

83   See section 5 below.
84   Benatar (n 10) 80 et seq. See also Tzeng, 'Investment Protection in Disputed Maritime Areas' (n 10) 839 et seq.
85   Rwanda–Morocco BIT (2016, not in force) art 1(4)(ii); Morocco–Guinea-Bissau BIT (2015, not in force) art 1(4)(a).
86   Israel–Azerbaijan BIT (2007) art 1(1)(e)(1); Israel–Guatemala BIT (2006).
87   Tzeng, 'Investment Protection in Disputed Maritime Areas' (n 10) 839. On Israel's BITs in light of the question of Palestine, see also Markus P Beham, chapter 5 in this volume, 165–167.
88   Tzeng, 'Investment Protection in Disputed Maritime Areas' (n 10) 838 et seq.
89   UK Model BIT (2008) art 1(e)(i).
90   USA–Argentina BIT (1991) art 1(1)(f).
91   USA Model BIT (2012) art 1.
92   José A Rivas, 'Colombia' in Chester Brown (ed), *Commentaries on Selected Model Investment Treaties* (OUP 2013) 207; Nico Schrijver and Vid Prislan, 'The Netherlands' in Chester Brown (ed), *Commentaries on Selected Model Investment Treaties* (OUP 2013) 558.
93   Benatar (n 10) 82.

same may be said about maritime disputes that either do not concern entitlements as such but the delimitation of overlapping entitlements or that concern technical questions such as the legality of baselines. Either way, in applying these provisions, investment tribunals might have to make determinations regarding territorial and maritime inter-state disputes.[94]

The second category includes IIAs that appear to have been drafted with unsettled territorial or maritime disputes in mind, which is reflected in the definition of their scope.[95] Examples include the BITs to which Georgia is a party, which define Georgian territory as 'recognized by the international community'.[96] It is likely that the choice of wording is influenced by the secessionist conflict over South Ossetia and Abkhazia.[97] The Japan–Peru BIT (2008) offers another illuminating illustration in the context of a maritime disagreement. The definition of Japan's 'Area' mentions the EEZ and the continental shelf, yet the description of Peru's 'Area' is generic, simply referring to 'the maritime zones'.[98] This differentiation, which is out of step with other investment agreements negotiated by Japan in the same period, is due to Peru's claim to a 200 nm territorial sea.[99] Against the background of China's contested territorial and maritime claims in, *inter alia*, the South China Sea, it has been argued that the UK–China BIT's (1986) spatial scope could equally be interpreted very broadly as it merely refers to areas in which sovereignty, sovereign rights, or jurisdiction are *exercised*, without also including a reference to international law.[100] A further example is the BIT between Argentina and Qatar, which refers, for Argentina's 'territory', to 'the territory subjected to the sovereignty

---

94   Benatar (n 10) 82 et seq; Tzeng, 'Investment Protection in Disputed Maritime Areas' (n 10) 841.

95   Benatar (n 10) 81 et seq; Thomas D Grant, 'International Dispute Settlement in Response to an Unlawful Seizure of Territory: Three Mechanisms' (2015) 16 Chicago J Int'l L 1, 28 et seq, 32 et seq; Tzeng, 'Investment Protection in Disputed Maritime Areas' (n 10) 840 et seq.

96   Georgia–Latvia BIT (2005) art 1.4(b); Georgia–Kuwait BIT (2009) art 1.6(b). See Martins Paparinskis, 'Latvia' in Chester Brown (ed), *Commentaries on Selected Model Investment Treaties* (OUP 2013) 441.

97   For an account of some of the relevant facts of the dispute, see *Application of the International Convention on the Elimination of All Forms of Racial Discrimination (Georgia v Russia)* [2011] ICJ Rep 70.

98   Japan–Peru BIT (2008) art 1.7(a), (b). The definition of the term 'Area' is followed by a note declaring that '[n]othing under this paragraph shall affect the rights and obligations of the Contracting Parties under international law'.

99   Luke Nottage and Shotaro Hamamoto, 'Japan' in Chester Brown (ed), *Commentaries on Selected Model Investment Treaties* (OUP 2013) 358. For objections to the Peruvian claim, see J Ashley Roach and Robert W Smith, *Excessive Maritime Claims* (3rd ed, Martinus Nijhoff 2012) 146 et seq.

100   *Cf* Khamsi (n 10) 677 with reference to UK–China BIT (1986) art 1(2).

of the Argentine Republic in accordance with its constitutional and legal provisions'.[101] As these examples show, when confronted with IIAs of this category, investment tribunals might in some cases not have to pass judgment on matters concerning the inter-state disputes concerning the maritime areas in question because they may simply make the relevant determinations by reference to the definitions and sources indicated in the IIA.[102]

Finally, even when faced with an (allegedly) implicated issue, it would be prudent for arbitral tribunals to give due consideration to the nature of the issue and its circumstances. In some situations, it might be necessary to have a test allowing a tribunal to weed out claims by a respondent that, if taken at face value, would constitute implicated issues beyond the tribunal's jurisdiction but – in the circumstances – would also threaten the effective exercise of the tribunal's mandate. While the terminology used in this context is not uniform ('plausibility', 'abuse of rights', 'good faith legal dispute' etc.), it would appear that there exists a (yet to be clearly determined) threshold for a dispute to be considered an obstacle to jurisdiction *ratione materiae*.[103] Where an arbitral tribunal determines that an allegedly implicated issue does not meet this threshold, it is arguably not prevented from accepting jurisdiction. Considerable scope for research remains in this respect.

4.2 Limits of Jurisdiction ratione personae: *Indispensable Parties*

In the context of litigation concerning investments in disputed maritime areas, there will frequently exist a second jurisdictional problem that is distinct from the challenge posed by implicated issues outside the jurisdiction *ratione materiae* of investment tribunals. Assuming that the maritime area is disputed because of contested sovereignty over the territory generating the entitlement, of the contested existence of a maritime entitlement, or an unresolved maritime delimitation dispute, it is inherent in the nature of investor-state dispute settlement that one of the two disputing states will not be a party to the proceedings. This raises a problem of jurisdiction *ratione personae* that will – in these types of cases – almost always exist in addition to the problem of jurisdiction *ratione materiae* discussed above.

---

101   Argentina–Qatar BIT (2016, not in force) art 1(5)(a).
102   Tzeng, 'Investment Protection in Disputed Maritime Areas' (n 10) 841.
103   See, *eg, Dispute Concerning Coastal State Rights in the Black Sea, Sea of Azov, and Kerch Strait* (n 37) 490 et seq, 504; Valentin Schatz, 'The Award Concerning Preliminary Objections in *Ukraine v Russia*: Observations Regarding the Implicated Status of Crimea and the Sea of Azov' (*EJIL:Talk!*, 20 March 2020) <www.ejiltalk.org/the-award concerning-preliminary-objections-in-ukraine-v-russia-observations-regarding-the-implicated-status-of-crimea-and-the-sea-of-azov/> accessed 30 April 2020.

Indeed, according to the 'indispensable party' or '*Monetary Gold*' principle, an international court or tribunal must refrain 'from deciding a case between two parties amenable to its jurisdiction on the merits if the legal interests of a third state would not only be affected by a merits judgment, but would form "the very subject-matter" of the case'.[104] While this principle is best known from the jurisprudence of the International Court of Justice (ICJ),[105] it has been recognised by other international courts and tribunals[106] and is sometimes considered applicable in international dispute settlement more generally.[107] Investment tribunals confronted with objections to jurisdiction based on the *Monetary Gold* principle have, to the knowledge of the present authors, not directly taken a position as to whether the principle applies to them.[108] Notably, however, an arbitral tribunal under UNCITRAL Rules invoked the *Monetary Gold* principle *proprio motu* in support of its decision to decline jurisdiction.[109] Assuming, *arguendo*, that the *Monetary Gold* principle is applicable to investor-state arbitration, the question arises whether or to what extent it

---

104   Tobias Thienel, 'Third States and the Jurisdiction of the International Court of Justice: The *Monetary Gold* Principle' (2014) 54 German YB Int'l L 322, quoting the core phrase in this respect from *Monetary Gold Removed from Rome in 1943 (Italy v France, UK, and USA)* (Preliminary Question) [1954] ICJ Rep 19, 32.

105   Hugh Thirlway, *The Law and Procedure of the International Court of Justice: Fifty Years of Jurisprudence* (OUP 2013) 715 et seq; 1658 et seq.

106   Eg, *M/V "Norstar" (Panama v Italy)* (Preliminary Objections) [2016] para 172 <www.itlos.org/en/cases/list-of-cases/case-no-25/>; *South China Sea Arbitration*, Jurisdiction (n 28) paras 179 et seq. See also Filippo Fontanelli, 'Reflections on the Indispensable Party Principle in the Wake of the Judgment on Preliminary Objections in the *Norstar Case*' (2017) Rivista di Diritto Internazionale 112 et seq.

107   Pro: Ori Pomson, 'Does the Monetary Gold Principle Apply to International Courts and Tribunals Generally?' (2019) 10 JIDS 125. Contra: Noam Zamir, 'The Applicability of the *Monetary Gold* Principle in International Arbitration' (2017) 33 Arb Int'l 531 et seq.

108   *Chevron Corp and Texaco Petroleum Corp v Ecuador*, PCA Case no 2009–23, Third Interim Award on Jurisdiction and Admissibility (27 February 2012) paras 4.59 et seq; *Niko Resources (Bangladesh) Ltd v Bangladesh Petroleum Exploration & Production Co Ltd ('Bapex') and Bangladesh Oil Gas and Mineral Corp ('Petrobangla')*, ICSID Case no ARB/10/11, Decision on Jurisdiction (19 August 2013) paras 516 et seq; *Ping An v Belgium*, ICSID Case no ARB/12/29, Award (30 April 2015) paras 127 et seq, 238. See also Alain Pellet, 'The Case Law of the ICJ in Investment Arbitration' (2013) 28 ICSID Rev 231 (fn 55). Other tribunals have referenced the principle in the context of the requirement of consent to jurisdiction more generally. See *Wintershall AG v Argentina*, ICSID Case no ARB/04/14, Award (8 December 2008) para 160 (fn 135); *Daimler Financial Services AG v Argentina*, ICSID Case no ARB/05/1, Award (22 August 2012) para 175.

109   *Larsen v Hawaiian Kingdom*, PCA Case no 1999-01, Award (5 February 2001) paras 11.8 et seq, 12.1 et seq. See also Patrick Jacob and Franck Latty, 'Arbitrage Transnational et Droit International Général' (2012) 58 Annuaire français de droit international 625 et seq.

could present an obstacle to jurisdiction in disputes concerning investments in disputed maritime areas.[110]

One way in which this could happen is in the context of establishing the territorial link between the investment and the host state. According to the jurisprudence of the ICJ, the *Monetary Gold* principle is restricted to 'prerequisite determination[s]',[111] which means that it applies in situations that would require the Court to make a finding on the legality of a third state's conduct or its legal position.[112] On this basis, an arbitral tribunal might decline jurisdiction over an investment claim because an assessment of whether an investment was made in the 'territory' or 'area' of the host state might require it to make a determination of another state's legal position with regard to territorial sovereignty over the land generating a maritime entitlement or in respect of a maritime delimitation.[113]

5   Potential Approaches to Jurisdictional Limitations in the Context of Implicated Issues and Indispensable Parties

Investment tribunals faced with problems of implicated issues[114] and/or indispensable parties[115] will have to make a decision on how to approach the question of their jurisdiction in a way that ensures the effective exercise of their mandate while respecting the limits of this mandate. Here, it should be noted that the problem of lack of jurisdiction *ratione materiae* over certain categories of implicated issues (territorial sovereignty, maritime entitlements, and maritime boundary delimitation) and the parallel problem of jurisdiction *ratione personae* in relation to the other state's interest

---

110   Also noted by Tzeng, 'Investment Protection in Disputed Maritime Areas' (n 10) 846.
111   Peter Tzeng, 'Investments on Disputed Territory: Indispensable Parties and Indispensable Issues' (2017) 14 Braz J Int'l L 124 et seq. See also *Obligations Concerning Negotiations Relating to Cessation of the Nuclear Arms Race and to Nuclear Disarmament (Marshall Islands v UK)* (Preliminary Objections, Dissenting Opinion of James Crawford) [2016] ICJ Rep 1093, para 32: 'The case law has however set firm limits to the *Monetary Gold* principle. It applies only where a determination of the legal position of a third State is a necessary prerequisite to the determination of the case before the Court'.
112   Malcom N Shaw, *Rosenne's Law and Practice of the International Court: 1920–2015*, vol 1 (5th edn, Brill Nijhoff 2015) 568.
113   For discussion of the *Monetary Gold* principle in the context of investment arbitration proceedings that implicate sovereignty disputes concerning land territory, see Tzeng, 'Investments on Disputed Territory' (n 111) 125 et seq.
114   See section 4.1 above.
115   See section 4.2 above.

in these issues based on the *Monetary Gold* principle will usually be inextricably linked in investor-state dispute settlement. Hence, a potential solution should arguably take into account both problems. *Prima facie*, it may be doubted that jurisdiction *ratione materiae* under IIAs generally extends to the types of inter-state disputes implicated in litigation concerning investments in contested maritime areas, particularly where it would be required to make determinations of breaches of rules of international law not included in the compromissory clause of the IIA or potential *renvoi*-provisions in the IIA.[116] It would also be unexpected for an investment tribunal to involve itself with maritime delimitation, which requires very specific legal and technical expertise.[117]

Case law is not instructive on this particular issue. Although some cases have dealt with investments that happened to be situated in maritime zones[118] – at times even disputed ones[119] – there appears to be no public ruling offering insights as to whether IIAs cover contested maritime areas.[120] Investment tribunals could look to the paths followed by other international courts and tribunals to inform their own methodology. A variety of approaches may be discerned depending on the jurisdictional titles invoked.[121] The three main approaches are (1) to accept ancillary jurisdiction over the implicated issue,[122]

---

116   But see Richard Happ and Sebastian Wuschka, '*Horror Vacui*: Or Why Investment Treaties Should Apply to Illegally Annexed Territories' (2016) 33 J Int'l Arb 255, who consider that investment tribunals may make determinations of territorial sovereignty in situations where such sovereignty is disputed.

117   *RSM Production Corp v Grenada*, ICSID Case no ARB/05/14, Final Award (18 March 2009) para 333: 'ICSID Tribunals are not empowered to delimit maritime boundaries'.

118   *Wintershall v Argentina* (n 108); *Tidewater Inc and others v Venezuela*, ICSID Case no ARB/10/5, Award (15 March 2015); Reinisch (n 53) 210 (fn 13).

119   *RSM Production Corp v Saint Lucia*, ICSID Case no ARB/12/10, Decision on Saint Lucia's Request for Provisional Measures (12 December 2013) paras 14–21; *RSM v Grenada* (n 117). For a discussion of the latter case, see Blyschak (n 8) 230 et seq.

120   *Cf* Roughton (n 8) 400. Arbitral awards deciding whether an investment has been made 'in the territory' of a host state tend to concern entirely disparate topics *eg* financial transactions. See Knahr (n 52) 590 et seq; Jeswald W Salacuse, *The Law of Investment Treaties* (2nd ed, OUP 2015) 188 et seq.

121   See, *eg*, Lawrence Hill-Cawthorne, 'International Litigation and the Disaggregation of Disputes: Ukraine/Russia as a Case Study' (2019) 68 ICLQ 793 et seq.

122   See, *eg, Ilaşcu and others v Moldova and Russia* ECHR 2004–VII 1, paras 333 et seq. Limited ancillary jurisdiction over sovereignty disputes was also accepted by two arbitral tribunals under Annex VII of UNCLOS, but only in *obiter dicta* and not for the categories of sovereignty disputes before them. See *Chagos Marine Protected Area Arbitration* (n 37) para 221; *Dispute Concerning Coastal State Rights in the Black Sea, Sea of Azov, and Kerch Strait* (n 37) paras 191 et seq.

(2) to develop an approach that circumvents the implicated issue and thus the obstacle to jurisdiction,[123] and (3) to decline jurisdiction over claims that implicate issues beyond jurisdiction.[124] In practice, a separate solution may be to find another, unrelated reason to decline jurisdiction and thus have no need to answer the question altogether.[125] Due to a dearth of precedents, it is a matter of some speculation how a tribunal would handle investments in disputed maritime areas. The ensuing paragraphs will explore arguments both for and against potential approaches.[126]

One way of circumventing implicated issues in the present context is to interpret the provisions of IIAs defining their scope *ratione loci* in a functional manner in light of the – arguable – object and purpose of IIAs[127] to protect investments under the 'effective control' of the contracting states.[128] However, given that 'effective control' is a concept that is more easily applied to land territory, artificial islands or installations, or ships than to maritime areas as such, an investment tribunal might choose a test more akin to an exercise of a degree of 'jurisdiction and control' in such a context. Such an approach would focus on the host state's factual exercise of jurisdiction and control over a maritime area (or, where the territory generating the dispute is concerned, 'effective control') – and perhaps the territory generating the relevant maritime entitlement – rather than the legality of the claim as such.[129] It appears that such an

---

123 For example, human rights courts and bodies may consider human rights instruments applicable extraterritorially regardless of the status of the relevant territory. See, *eg*, Marko Milanović and Tatjana Papić, 'The Applicability of the ECHR in Contested Territories' (2018) 67 ICLQ 779; Lea Raible, 'Title to Territory and Jurisdiction in International Human Rights Law: Three Models for a Fraught Relationship' (2018) 31 LJIL 315.

124 Two arbitral tribunals under Annex VII of UNCLOS have declined jurisdiction due to an implicated sovereignty dispute. See *Chagos Marine Protected Area* (n 37) para 220; *Dispute Concerning Coastal State Rights in the Black Sea, Sea of Azov, and Kerch Strait* (n 37) paras 197 et seq. Another tribunal indicated that it would have done the same if the sovereignty dispute at hand was in fact implicated. See *South China Sea Arbitration*, Jurisdiction (n 28) paras 152 et seq.

125 *Cf* Tzeng, 'The Implicated Issue Problem' (n 75) 491.

126 The states parties to the IIA could also consider taking the question of the scope *ratione loci* of the IIA to inter-state arbitration or adjudication – for example based on a compromissory clause in the agreement. See Peter Tzeng, 'Sovereignty over Crimea: A Case for State-to-State Investment Arbitration' (2016) Yale J Int'l L 459 et seq.

127 *Cf Sanum v Laos* (n 42) para 240.

128 Benatar (n 10) 86; Happ and Wuschka (n 116) 260 et seq; Tzeng, 'Investments on Disputed Territory' (n 111) 133; Tzeng, 'Investment Protection in Disputed Maritime Areas' (n 10) 836 et seq, 846 et seq; Khamsi (n 10) 680.

129 Benatar (n 10) 86; Tzeng, 'Investment Protection in Disputed Maritime Areas' (n 10) 836 et seq, 846 et seq. Conversely, while not an investment dispute, the judgment of the European Court of Justice (Grand Chamber) in *Western Sahara Campaign UK* serves as

approach was taken by a number of arbitral tribunals hearing cases brought by Ukrainian private investors and state-owned enterprises with investments in Crimea against Russia pursuant to the Russia–Ukraine BIT (1998),[130] which reportedly upheld their jurisdiction – although these decisions are not publicly available.[131] Afterwards, some of these arbitral tribunals also held Russia liable for breaches of the BIT.[132] Insofar as the reasoning of these awards has come to light, it appears that the arbitral tribunals interpreted the term 'territory' as employed by the Russia–Ukraine BIT (1998)[133] as also including territory over which a contracting state exercises *de facto* control.[134] Interestingly, in

a useful illustration of an approach based on the legality of the claim. The Court held that 'taking account of the fact that the territory of Western Sahara does not form part of the territory of the Kingdom of Morocco [...], the waters adjacent to the territory of Western Sahara are not part of the Moroccan fishing zone referred to in [...] the Fisheries Partnership Agreement' and that 'it must be held that the expression "Moroccan fishing zone", for the purposes of [the Protocol setting out the fishing opportunities provided for by the Agreement], does not include the waters adjacent to the territory of Western Sahara'. Case C–266/16 *Western Sahara Campaign UK* EU:C:2018:118, paras 69, 79.

130 *Aeroport Belbek LLC and Mr. Kolomoisky v Russia*, PCA Case 2015-07; *PJSC CB PrivatBank and Finance Co Finilon LLC v Russia*, PCA Case no 2015–21; *Limited Liability Co Lugzor and others v Russia*, PCA Case no 2015–29; *PJSC Ukrnafta v Russia*, PCA Case no 2015–34; *Stabil LLC and others v Russia*, PCA Case no 2015–35; *Everest Estate LLC and others v Russia*, PCA Case no 2015–36; *Oschadbank v Russia*, PCA Case no 2016-14; *NJSC Naftogaz of Ukraine (Ukraine) and others v Russia*, PCA Case no 2017-16.

131 Alison Ross, 'Crimea Cases against Russia to Proceed' (*Global Arbitration Review*, 9 March 2017) <https://globalarbitrationreview.com/article/1137587/crimea-cases-against-russia-to-proceed> accessed 30 April 2020; Jarrod Hepburn and Ridhi Kabra, 'Investigation: Further Russia Investment Treaty Decisions Uncovered, Offering Broader Window into Arbitrators' Approaches to Crimea Controversy' (*IAReporter*, 17 November 2017) <www.iareporter.com/articles/investigation-further-russia-investment-treaty-decisions-uncovered-offering-broader-window-into-arbitrators-approaches-to-crimea-controversy/> accessed 30 April 2020.

132 See, *eg*, 'Russian Federation Is Hit with $1.3 Billion Dollar UNCITRAL Bilateral Investment Treaty Award' (*IAReporter*, 26 November 2018) <www.iareporter.com/articles/russia-hit-with-1-3-billion-dollar-in-a-new-uncitral-bilateral-investment-treaty-award/> accessed 30 April 2020.

133 Russia–Ukraine BIT (1998) art 1(1).

134 Jarrod Hepburn, 'Investigation: Full Jurisdictional Reasoning Comes to Light in Crimea-related BIT Arbitration vs. Russia' (*IAReporter*, 9 November 2017) <www.iareporter.com/articles/full-jurisdictional-reasoning-comes-to-light-in-crimea-related-arbitration-everest-estate-v-russia/> accessed 30 April 2020; Lisa Bohmer, 'In Now-Public Decisions, Swiss Federal Tribunal Clarifies Reasons for Dismissing Challenges to Two Crimea-Related Investment Treaty Awards against Russia' (*IAReporter*, 16 November 2018) <www.iareporter.com/articles/in-now-public-decisions-swiss-federal-tribunal-clarifies-reasons-for-dismissing-challenges-to-two-crimea-related-investment-treaty-awards-against-russia/> accessed 30 April 2020; Lisa Bohmer, 'Swiss Federal Tribunal Provides Reasons for

subsequent set-aside proceedings before Swiss courts in one of the arbitrations, it appears that Russia did not deny the applicability of the BIT to territories in which *de facto* control is exercised.[135]

Reasoning on the basis of 'effective control' in the context of international investment law can be justified on several grounds. First, and most importantly, such an approach is arguably supported by the abovementioned object and purpose of IIAs to effectively protect investments.[136] Notably, 'effective control' tests for the purpose of establishing extraterritorial application are also employed in international human rights law,[137] which some see as sharing key objectives with international investment law (effective protection of human rights vs. effective protection of foreign investments).[138] Such approaches may also be available to human rights courts and bodies in situations of contested territorial sovereignty and/or occupation.[139]

Second, the territorial nexus requirement could be framed with more flexibility by accentuating the limited specific framework within which it operates.[140] The provisions that define the scope *ratione loci* of IIAs frequently include a chapeau that employs language such as 'for the purposes of this treaty'. Investment tribunals could rely on this wording to qualify any findings on the applicability of the IIA to the maritime area in question

Refusing to Set Aside Two Crimea-Related Awards' (*IAReporter*, 21 January 2020) <www.iareporter.com/articles/swiss-federal-tribunal-provides-reasons-for-refusing-to-set-aside-two-crimea-related-awards/> accessed 30 April 2020; *Russia v A* [2018] Case no 4A_396/2017, BGE 144 III 559, 563 et seq (Swiss Federal Tribunal).

135   See, *eg*, ibid 565 et seq in relation to *Stabil and others v Russia* (n 130).
136   Benatar (n 10) 86; Happ and Wuschka (n 116) 260 et seq; Tzeng, 'Investments on Disputed Territory' (n 111) 133; Tzeng, 'Investment Protection in Disputed Maritime Areas' (n 10) 836 et seq, 846 et seq; Khamsi (n 10) 680. Such reasoning appears to have been used by at least one of the Crimea tribunals. See Hepburn, 'Investigation' (n 134).
137   See, *eg*, Marko Milanovic, *Extraterritorial Application of Human Rights Treaties: Law, Principles and Policy* (OUP 2011); Karen Da Costa, *The Extraterritorial Application of Selected Human Rights Treaties* (Martinus Nijhoff 2012). On the frontiers of this doctrine in the maritime domain, see, *eg*, Efthymios Papastavridis, 'The European Convention of Human Rights and Migration at Sea: Reading the "Jurisdictional Threshold" of the Convention Under the Law of the Sea Paradigm' (2020) 21 German LJ 417; Violeta Moreno-Lax, 'The Architecture of Functional Jurisdiction: Unpacking Contactless Control – On Public Powers, *S.S. and Others v. Italy*, and the "Operational Model"' (2020) 21 German LJ 385.
138   Happ and Wuschka (n 116) 267 with reference to *International Thunderbird Gaming Corp v Mexico*, Award, Separate Opinion of Thomas Wälde (1 December 2005) para 13. See also Khamsi (n 10) 680.
139   See, generally, Milanović and Papić (n 123); Raible (n 123).
140   Benatar (n 10) 91.

as being strictly concerned with the interpretation and application of the IIA – without prejudice to issues of sovereignty and maritime rights and jurisdiction under international law more generally.[141] Third, such an outcome would be supported by an interpretation of ambiguous terms in provisions of IIAs to the advantage of the investor (*in dubio pro investore*), which, according to its proponents, is based on the object and purpose of such agreements to 'create favourable conditions for investment'.[142] Fourth, the tribunal might defer to the definition that the host state gives to its own territory and maritime areas.[143] In situations where a coastal state is exercising control over a maritime area and consistently claims it falls within its sovereignty or sovereign rights and jurisdiction, it is unlikely that it will object to an investment tribunal's jurisdiction on the basis that the relevant waters are not in its 'territory' or 'area'.[144] In addition, an investment tribunal might find support in the doctrine of estoppel and hold that this state is estopped from objecting to jurisdiction *ratione loci*.[145] However, the duty of investment tribunals to examine *proprio motu* their own jurisdiction arguably limits the persuasive power of arguments based on the conduct of the respondent state.[146]

Finally, the attitude of states not party to the dispute that are potentially indispensable based on the *Monetary Gold* principle might exert influence on how arbitral tribunals approach the issue.[147] Within certain limits, a non-disputing state that is party to an IIA may make unilateral submissions to

---

141   ibid.
142   Benatar (n 10) 85 et seq with reference to Michael Waibel, 'International Investment Law and Treaty Interpretation' in Rainer Hofmann and Christian J Tams (eds), *International Investment Law and General International Law* (Nomos 2011) 50 et seq.
143   Waibel, 'Investment Arbitration: Jurisdiction and Admissibility' (n 16) 1249 et seq.
144   Michael Waibel, 'Oil Exploration Around the Falklands (Malvinas)' (*EJIL:Talk!*, 13 August 2012) <www.ejiltalk.org/oil-exploration-around-the-falklands-malvinas/> accessed 30 April 2020. In the context of territorial sovereignty disputes, see also Happ and Wuschka (n 116) 254. Compare also Russia's position in *Stabil and others v Russia* (n 130) as described in *Russia v A* (n 134) 563.
145   Benatar (n 10) 85 et seq (fn 76); Roughton (n 8) 400 (fn 100); Happ and Wuschka (n 116) 261; Tzeng, 'The Implicated Issue Problem' (n 75) 491. *Cf* also *Russia v A* (n 134) 563, which mentions that the arbitral tribunal in *Stabil and others v Russia* (n 130) noted Ukraine's submissions in support of its findings that the BIT applied.
146   Happ and Wuschka (n 116) 254; Tzeng, 'Investment Protection in Disputed Maritime Areas' (n 10) 847. For general discussion, see Jack Wass, 'Jurisdiction by Estoppel and Acquiescence in International Courts and Tribunals' (2016) 86 Brit YB Int'l L 155.
147   Benatar (n 10) 91 et seq.

arbitral tribunals or participate as *amicus curiae*.[148] In at least two sets of cases such a strategy has been applied in a potential *Monetary Gold* situation. First, the arbitral tribunal in the *South China Sea Arbitration* between the Philippines and China ruled that Vietnam was not an indispensable party, stressing that its finding was shared by the government of Vietnam, which had sent a statement to the arbitral tribunal.[149] Second, a similar development may be noted with respect to the previously discussed Crimean investment cases against Russia, in which many of the arbitral tribunals granted Ukraine permission to submit its views as a non-disputing party to the Ukraine–Russia BIT (1998). Seemingly, Kiev aimed to convince the arbitral tribunals that they could accept jurisdiction without having to determine the status of Crimea. It appears that this strategy may have been successful given that Ukraine's submissions were reportedly taken into account by some arbitral tribunals as support for their decision to accept jurisdiction based on their *de facto* control test.[150]

6 Conclusion

This chapter has sought to demonstrate the various substantive and procedural challenges that investment tribunals are likely to face when confronted with claims of investors concerning investments in disputed maritime areas. Particular attention was paid to the potential for cases to touch upon implicated issues concerning an underlying inter-state dispute and the risk of passing judgment on the legal position of a state not party to the proceedings. An overview has been provided of a variety of legal rationales on which arbitrators could rely to either accept or decline jurisdiction, including the possible application of an 'effective control'-type test for the purpose of applying an IIA *ratione loci*. As the applicability of IIAs in disputed maritime areas remains to be adjudicated, it would be difficult to predict the outcome of any future case. Nonetheless, should an investment tribunal accept jurisdiction over claims concerning investments in a disputed maritime area based on an IIA, a host of additional legal questions arise with respect to the *merits* of such claims – particularly in light of the special legal regime that applies in such areas.[151] For

---

148 Loretta Malintoppi and Hussein Haeri, 'The Non-Disputing State Party in Investment Arbitration' in David D Caron and others (eds), *Practising Virtue: Inside International Arbitration* (OUP 2015) 575 et seq.
149 *South China Sea Arbitration*, Jurisdiction (n 28) paras 179 et seq.
150 See, *eg*, *Russia v A* (n 134) 564 regarding *Stabil and others v Russia* (n 130).
151 Sim (n 10) 9 et seq; Tzeng, 'Investment Protection in Disputed Maritime Areas' (n 10) 847 et seq; Khamsi (n 10) 680 et seq.

example, international law does not appear to prohibit states from granting hydrocarbon licenses to foreign investors merely because a maritime area is disputed due to overlapping EEZ and/or continental shelf entitlements. As the Special Chamber in *Ghana/Côte d'Ivoire* observed:

> maritime activities undertaken by a State in an area of the continental shelf which has been attributed to another State by an international judgment cannot be considered to be in violation of the sovereign rights of the latter if those activities were carried out before the judgment was delivered and if the area concerned was the subject of claims made in good faith by both States.[152]

Other questions concern attribution, the correct application of various standards of protection and liability in light of the possibility of coastal states taking measures adversely affecting investments in disputed maritime areas – a situation far more likely to arise at sea than on land. Under what circumstances could an investor rely on legitimate expectations in situations of well-known maritime disputes?[153] In any event, foreign companies would do well to factor the legal risks highlighted in this chapter into their decision-making on whether to invest in contested waters.[154] Part of this process could be to consider investment contracts in addition to existing (but legally uncertain) protections under IIAs as part of an investment protection strategy,[155] although host states might be reluctant to accept commitments regarding risks stemming from actions of other claimants.[156]

Note on the Text

This chapter is based on – and develops further – ideas presented by Marco Benatar at the Expert Workshop *The Role of International Investment Law in Armed Conflicts, Disputed Territories, and 'Frozen' Conflicts* at the Ruhr-University Bochum in March 2019 and in his previous journal article 'Applying

---

152 *Dispute Concerning Delimitation of the Maritime Boundary between Ghana and Côte d'Ivoire in the Atlantic Ocean* (Merits) (n 9) para 592.
153 Khamsi (n 10) 680 et seq.
154 Tim Martin, 'Energy and International Boundaries' in Kim Talus (ed), *Research Handbook on International Energy Law* (Edward Elgar 2014) 193 et seq.
155 *Cf* Tzeng, 'Investment Protection in Disputed Maritime Areas' (n 10) 859.
156 *Cf* Khamsi (n 10) 672 et seq.

International Investment Law to Disputed Maritime Zones: A Case Study of the Falklands (Malvinas)' (2015) 28 Hague YB Int'l L 65. The views expressed in this chapter are personal views and do not represent the opinion of the International Tribunal for the Law of the Sea.

Bibliography

'Russian Federation Is Hit with $1.3 Billion Dollar UNCITRAL Bilateral Investment Treaty Award' (*IAReporter*, 26 November 2018) <www.iareporter.com/articles/russia-hit-with-1-3-billion-dollar-in-a-new-uncitral-bilateral-investment-treaty-award/> accessed 30 April 2020.

Aust A, 'Vienna Convention on the Law of Treaties (1969)', *Max Planck Encyclopedia of Public International Law* (2006) <https://opil.ouplaw.com/home/MPIL> accessed 30 April 2020.

Aust A, *Modern Treaty Law and Practice* (3rd edn, CUP 2013).

Barnes R, 'Article 2' in A Proelss (ed), *The United Nations Convention on the Law of the Sea: A Commentary* (Beck, Hart, and Nomos 2017).

Benatar M, 'Applying International Investment Law to Disputed Maritime Zones: A Case Study of the Falklands (Malvinas)' (2015) 28 Hague YB Int'l L 65.

Bhatty S and N Lamprou, 'Pitfalls of Investing in Sub-Saharan African Regions with Unsettled Boundaries: How Foreign Investors May Minimize and Manage Investment Risk' (2016) 13(4) TDM 1.

BIICL, *Report on the Obligations of States under Articles 74(3) and 83(3) of UNCLOS in Respect of Undelimited Maritime Areas* (BIICL 2016).

Blackaby N and B Juratowitch, 'Hydrocarbons in Disputed Areas' (2015) 44(4) Int'l L News 1.

Blitza E, *Auswirkungen des Meeresspiegelanstiegs auf maritime Grenzen* (Springer 2019).

Blyschak PM, 'Offshore Oil and Gas Projects Amid Maritime Border Disputes: Applicable Law' (2013) 6 J World Energy L & Bus 210.

Bohmer B, 'Snow Crab Dispute Prompts First ICSID Arbitration against Norway' (*IAReporter*, 1 April 2020) <www.iareporter.com/articles/snow-crab-dispute-prompts-first-icsid-arbitration-against-norway/> accessed 30 April 2020.

Bohmer L, 'In Now-Public Decisions, Swiss Federal Tribunal Clarifies Reasons for Dismissing Challenges to Two Crimea-Related Investment Treaty Awards against Russia' (*IAReporter*, 16 November 2018) <www.iareporter.com/articles/in-now-public-decisions-swiss-federal-tribunal-clarifies-reasons-for-dismissing-challenges-to-two-crimea-related-investment-treaty-awards-against-russia/> accessed 30 April 2020.

Bohmer L, 'Swiss Federal Tribunal Provides Reasons for Refusing to Set Aside Two Crimea-Related Awards' (*IAReporter*, 21 January 2020) <www.iareporter.com/articles/swiss-federal-tribunal-provides-reasons-for-refusing-to-set-aside-two-crimea-related-awards/> accessed 30 April 2020.

Brown C, 'The Evolution of the Regime of International Investment Agreements: History, Economics and Politics' in M Bungenberg and others (eds), *International Investment Law: A Handbook* (Beck, Hart, and Nomos 2015).

Bruce S, 'International Energy Law', *Max Planck Encyclopedia of Public International Law* (2014) <https://opil.ouplaw.com/home/MPIL> accessed 30 April 2020.

Clagett BM and OT Johnson, 'May Israel as a Belligerent Occupant Lawfully Exploit Previously Unexploited Oil Resources of the Gulf of Suez?' (1978) 72 AJIL 558.

Da Costa K, *The Extraterritorial Application of Selected Human Rights Treaties* (Martinus Nijhoff 2012).

de Nanteuil A, *Droit international de l'investissement* (2nd edn, Pedone 2017).

Dingwall J, 'International Investment Protection in Deep Seabed Mining beyond National Jurisdiction' (2018) 19 JWIT 890.

Dolzer R and M Stevens, *Bilateral Investment Treaties* (Martinus Nijhoff 1995).

Fietta S and R Cleverly, *A Practitioner's Guide to Maritime Boundary Delimitation* (OUP 2016).

Fitzmaurice M, 'Treaties', *Max Planck Encyclopedia of Public International Law* (2010) <https://opil.ouplaw.com/home/MPIL> accessed 30 April 2020.

Fontanelli F, 'Reflections on the Indispensable Party Principle in the Wake of the Judgment on Preliminary Objections in the *Norstar Case*' (2017) Rivista di Diritto Internazionale 112.

Franckx E and M Benatar, 'Navigating Between Consolidation and Innovation: Bangladesh/Myanmar (International Tribunal for the Law of the Sea, Judgment of 14 March 2012)' (2013) 27 Ocean YB 435.

Gavouneli M, *Functional Jurisdiction in the Law of the Sea* (Brill 2007).

Gerson A, 'Off-Shore Oil Exploitation by a Belligerent Occupant: The Gulf of Suez Dispute' (1977) 71 AJIL 725.

Graf Vitzthum W, 'Maritimes Aquitorium und Anschlusszone' in W Graf Vitzthum (ed), *Handbuch des Seerechts* (Beck 2006).

Grant TD, 'International Dispute Settlement in Response to an Unlawful Seizure of Territory: Three Mechanisms' (2015) 16 Chicago J Int'l L 1.

Greenwood C, 'Oceans and Space: Some New Frontiers for International Investment Law' (2018) 19 JWIT 775.

Happ R and S Wuschka, '*Horror Vacui*: Or Why Investment Treaties Should Apply to Illegally Annexed Territories' (2016) 33 J Int'l Arb 255.

Hepburn J, 'Investigation: Full Jurisdictional Reasoning Comes to Light in Crimea-related BIT Arbitration vs. Russia' (*IAReporter*, 9 November 2017) <www.iareporter.com/articles/full-jurisdictional-reasoning-comes-to-light-in-crimea-related-arbitration-everest-estate-v-russia/> accessed 30 April 2020.

Hepburn J and R Kabra, 'Investigation: Further Russia Investment Treaty Decisions Uncovered, Offering Broader Window into Arbitrators' Approaches to Crimea Controversy' (*IAReporter*, 17 November 2017) <www.iareporter.com/articles/investigation-further-russia-investment-treaty-decisions-uncovered-offering-broader-window-into-arbitrators-approaches-to-crimea-controversy/> accessed 30 April 2020.

Hill-Cawthorne L, 'International Litigation and the Disaggregation of Disputes: Ukraine/Russia as a Case Study' (2019) 68 ICLQ 793.

ILA, 'Baselines under the International Law of the Sea, Final Report' (2018) <www.ila-hq.org/images/ILA/DraftReports/DraftReport_Baselines.pdf> accessed 30 April 2020.

Jacob M, 'Investments, Bilateral Treaties' *Max Planck Encyclopedia of Public International Law* (2014) <https://opil.ouplaw.com/home/MPIL> accessed 30 April 2020.

Jacob P and F Latty, 'Arbitrage Transnational et Droit International Général' (2012) 58 Annuaire français de droit international 625.

Jennings R and A Watts (eds), *Oppenheim's International Law*, vol 1 (9th edn, OUP 2008).

Karagiannis S, 'Art. 29 1969 Vienna Convention' in O Corten and P Klein (eds), *The Vienna Conventions on the Law of Treaties*, vol 1 (OUP 2011).

Karagiannis S, 'The Territorial Application of Treaties' in DB Hollis (ed), *The Oxford Guide to Treaties* (OUP 2012).

Karavias M, 'Submarine Cables and Pipelines: The Protection of Investors under International Law' (2018) 19 JWIT 860.

Khamsi K, 'Investments in Unsettled Maritime Boundary Contexts: The Role of Bilateral Investment Treaties in Delivering Certainty' (2020) 34 ICSID Rev 666.

Knahr C, 'Investments "in the Territory" of the Host State' in C Binder and others (eds), *International Investment Law for the 21st Century: Essays in Honour of Christoph Schreuer* (OUP 2009).

Longobardo M, 'The Occupation of Maritime Territory under International Humanitarian Law' (2019) 95 Int'l L Stud 322.

Maggio AR, 'Article 77' in A Proelss (ed), *The United Nations Convention on the Law of the Sea: A Commentary* (Beck, Hart, and Nomos, 2017).

Malintoppi L and H Haeri, 'The Non-Disputing State Party in Investment Arbitration' in DD Caron and others (eds), *Practising Virtue: Inside International Arbitration* (OUP 2015).

Martin T, 'Energy and International Boundaries' in K Talus (ed), *Research Handbook on International Energy Law* (Edward Elgar 2014).

McCreath M and Z Scanlon, 'The Dispute Concerning the Delimitation of the Maritime Boundary Between Ghana and Côte d'Ivoire: Implications for the Law of the Sea' (2019) 50 Ocean Dev & Int'l L 1.

Milano E and I Papanicolopulu, 'State Responsibility in Disputed Areas on Land and at Sea' (2011) 71 Heidelberg J Int'l L 587.

Milanovic M, *Extraterritorial Application of Human Rights Treaties: Law, Principles and Policy* (OUP 2011).

Milanović M and T Papić, 'The Applicability of the ECHR in Contested Territories' (2018) 67 ICLQ 779.

Mitchell AD and J Munro, 'Someone Else's Deal: Interpreting International Investment Agreements in the Light of Third-Party Agreements' (2017) 28 EJIL 669.

Moreno-Lax V, 'The Architecture of Functional Jurisdiction: Unpacking Contactless Control – On Public Powers, *S.S. and Others v. Italy*, and the "Operational Model"' (2020) 21 German LJ 385.

Nottage L and S Hamamoto, 'Japan' in C Brown (ed), *Commentaries on Selected Model Investment Treaties* (OUP 2013).

Onele J, 'Revisiting Unilateral Exploitation of Mineral Resources in Disputed Water under United Nations Convention on the Law of the Sea: Any New Matter Arising?' (2019) 10 JIDS 160.

Oude Elferink AG, T Henriksen, and SV Busch (eds), *Maritime Boundary Delimitation: The Case Law Is It Consistent and Predictable?* (CUP 2018).

Paparinskis M, 'Latvia' in C Brown (ed), *Commentaries on Selected Model Investment Treaties* (OUP 2013).

Papastavridis E, 'The European Convention of Human Rights and Migration at Sea: Reading the "Jurisdictional Threshold" of the Convention Under the Law of the Sea Paradigm' (2020) 21 German LJ 417.

Pellet A, 'The Case Law of the ICJ in Investment Arbitration' (2013) 28 ICSID Rev 231.

Pomson O, 'Does the Monetary Gold Principle Apply to International Courts and Tribunals Generally?' (2019) 10 JIDS 125.

Power S, 'Occupying the Continental Shelf?: A Note Considering the Status of the Continental Shelf Delimitation Agreement Concluded between Turkey and the TRNC during the Belligerent Occupation of Northern Cyprus' (2014) 9 Irish YB Int'l L 91.

Proelss A, 'Article 56' in A Proelss (ed), *The United Nations Convention on the Law of the Sea: A Commentary* (Beck, Hart, and Nomos 2017).

Raible L, 'Title to Territory and Jurisdiction in International Human Rights Law: Three Models for a Fraught Relationship' (2018) 31 LJIL 315.

Reed L, Z Scanlon, and D Atanasova, 'Protected Investment', *Max Planck Encyclopedia of Public International Law* (2018) <https://opil.ouplaw.com/home/MPIL> accessed 30 April 2020.

Reinisch A, 'Investment Disputes and Their Boundaries' in Société française pour le droit international (ed), *Droit des frontières internationales/The Law of International Borders* (Pedone 2016).

Rivas JA, 'Colombia' in C Brown (ed), *Commentaries on Selected Model Investment Treaties* (OUP 2013).

Roach JA and RW Smith, *Excessive Maritime Claims* (3rd ed, Martinus Nijhoff 2012).

Rosenne S, 'International Courts and Tribunals, Jurisdiction and Admissibility of Inter-State Applications', *Max Planck Encyclopedia of Public International Law* (2006) <https://opil.ouplaw.com/home/MPIL> accessed 30 April 2020.

Ross A, 'Crimea Cases against Russia to Proceed' (*Global Arbitration Review*, 9 March 2017) <https://globalarbitrationreview.com/article/1137587/crimea-cases-against-russia-to-proceed> accessed 30 April 2020.

Roughton D, 'Rights (and Wrongs) of Capture: International Law and the Implications of the Guyana/Suriname Arbitration' (2015) 26 JERL 374.

Salacuse JW, *The Law of Investment Treaties* (2nd ed, OUP 2015).

Schatz VJ and D Koval, 'Russia's Annexation of Crimea and the Passage of Ships Through Kerch Strait: A Law of the Sea Perspective' (2019) 50 Ocean Dev & Int'l L 275.

Schatz VJ, 'The Award Concerning Preliminary Objections in *Ukraine v Russia*: Observations Regarding the Implicated Status of Crimea and the Sea of Azov' (*EJIL:Talk!*, 20 March 2020) <www.ejiltalk.org/the-award-concerning-preliminary-objections-in-ukraine-v-russia-observations-regarding-the-implicated-status-of-crimea-and-the-sea-of-azov/> accessed 30 April 2020.

Schill SW, *The Multilateralization of International Investment Law* (CUP 2010).

Schill SW, CJ Tams, and R Hofmann, 'Oceans and Space: New Frontiers in Investment Protection?' (2018) 19 JWIT 765.

Schreuer C and others, *The ICSID Convention: A Commentary* (2nd ed, CUP 2009).

Schreuer C, 'Investment Disputes', *Max Planck Encyclopedia of Public International Law* (2013) <https://opil.ouplaw.com/home/MPIL> accessed 30 April 2020.

Schrijver N and V Prislan, 'The Netherlands' in C Brown (ed), *Commentaries on Selected Model Investment Treaties* (OUP 2013).

Scovazzi T, 'Baselines', *Max Planck Encyclopedia of Public International Law* (2007) <https://opil.ouplaw.com/home/MPIL> accessed 30 April 2020.

Shaw M, *Rosenne's Law and Practice of the International Court: 1920–2015*, vol 1 (5th edn, Brill Nijhoff 2015).

Sim C, 'Investment Disputes Arising Out of Areas of Unsettled Boundaries: Ghana/Côte d'Ivoire' (2018) 11 World Energy L & Bus 1.

Singer T, 'Occupation of Sea Territory: Requirements for Military Authority and Comparison to Art. 43 of the Hague Convention IV' in J Schildknecht and others (eds), *Operational Law in International Straits and Current Maritime Security Challenges* (Springer 2018);.

Sourgens FG, 'By Equal Contest of Arms: Jurisdictional Proof in Investor-State Arbitrations' (2012) 38 NC J Int'l L & Com Reg 876.

Symmons CR, *Historic Waters and Historic Rights in the Law of the Sea: A Modern Reappraisal* (2nd edn, Brill 2019).

Tanaka Y, 'Unilateral Exploration and Exploitation of Natural Resources in Disputed Areas: A Note on the Ghana/Côte d'Ivoire Order of 25 April 2015 before the Special Chamber of ITLOS' (2015) 46 Ocean Dev & Int'l L 315.

Tanaka Y, *Predictability and Flexibility in the Law of Maritime Delimitation* (2nd edn, Hart 2019).

Tanaka Y, *The International Law of the Sea* (3rd edn, CUP 2019).

Thienel T, 'Third States and the Jurisdiction of the International Court of Justice: The *Monetary Gold* Principle' (2014) 54 German YB Int'l L 322.

Thirlway H, *The Law and Procedure of the International Court of Justice: Fifty Years of Jurisprudence* (OUP 2013).

Thomas W, A van der Meulen, and S Chua, 'Common Offshore Hydrocarbon Deposits: Rights, Risks and Remedies under International Law' (2019) 17 Oil, Gas & Energy L 1.

Trevisanut S, 'Foreign Investments in the Offshore Energy Industry' in T Treves, F Seatzu, and S Trevisanut (eds), *Foreign Investment, International Law and Common Concerns* (Routledge 2014).

Trevisanut S and N Giannopoulos, 'Investment Protection of Offshore Energy Production: Bright Sides of Regime Interaction' (2018) 19 JWIT 789.

Tudor I, *The Fair and Equitable Treatment Standard in the International Law of Foreign Investment* (OUP 2008).

Tzeng P, 'Sovereignty over Crimea: A Case for State-to-State Investment Arbitration' (2016) Yale J Int'l L 459.

Tzeng P, 'Investments on Disputed Territory: Indispensable Parties and Indispensable Issues' (2017) 14 Braz J Int'l L 124.

Tzeng P, 'Investment Protection in Disputed Maritime Areas' (2018) 19 JWIT 828.

Tzeng P, 'The Implicated Issue Problem: Indispensable Issues and Incidental Jurisdiction' (2018) 50 NYU J Int'l Law & Pol 485.

UNCTAD, *Scope and Definition* (1999).

UNCTAD, *Bilateral Investment Treaties 1995–2006: Trends in Investment Rulemaking* (2006).

UNCTAD, *Scope and Definition: A Sequel* (2011).

van Logchem Y, 'The Rights and Obligations of States in Disputed Maritime Areas: What Lessons Can Be Learned from the Maritime Boundary Dispute between Ghana and Côte d'Ivoire?' (2019) 52 Vand J Transnat'l L 121.

von der Decken K, 'Article 29' in O Dörr and K Schmalenbach (eds), *Vienna Convention on the Law of Treaties: A Commentary* (2nd edn, Springer 2018).

Waibel M, 'International Investment Law and Treaty Interpretation' in R Hofmann and CJ Tams (eds), *International Investment Law and General International Law* (Nomos 2011).

Waibel M, 'Oil Exploration Around the Falklands (Malvinas)' (*EJIL:Talk!*, 13 August 2012) <www.ejiltalk.org/oil-exploration-around-the-falklands-malvinas/> accessed 30 April 2020.

Waibel M, 'Investment Arbitration: Jurisdiction and Admissibility' in M Bungenberg and others (eds), *International Investment Law: A Handbook* (Beck, Hart, and Nomos 2015).

Wass J, 'Jurisdiction by Estoppel and Acquiescence in International Courts and Tribunals' (2016) 86 Brit YB Int'l L 155.

Weeramantry JR, *Treaty Interpretation in Investment Arbitration* (OUP 2012).

Yiallourides C, 'Oil and Gas Development in Disputed Waters under UNCLOS' (2016) 5 UCLJLJ 59.

Yiallourides C, 'Calming the Waters in the West African Region: The Case of Ghana and Côte d'Ivoire' (2018) 26 Afr J Int'l & Comp L 507.

Zamir N, 'The Applicability of the *Monetary Gold* Principle in International Arbitration' (2017) 33 Arb Int'l 531.

Zhao B, 'The Curious Case of Ghana/Côte d'Ivoire: A Consistent Approach to Hydrocarbon Activities in the Disputed Area?' (2020) 10 Asian J Int'l L 94.

CHAPTER 7

Parallel Proceedings Arising from Uncertain Territorial and Maritime Boundaries

Christine Sim

A state's existence – and the basis upon which it conducts its international affairs – is intimately dependent on sovereignty over its territory. Through an investment protection treaty, a state generally asserts its sovereignty and accords protection to those investments within its territory. As defined in many investment treaties, such 'territory' includes land and territorial seas, as well as exclusive economic zones and continental shelves.

Yet, the scope of such territorial and maritime boundaries is not always perfectly defined. There are currently more than 150 uncertain territorial and maritime boundary disputes in the world,[1] many of which could trigger investment disputes.

What happens when investments have been made in an area, over which one state asserts its sovereignty, but an international court or tribunal later determines that this area belongs to another state? In that case, whose investment treaty applies? Similar questions may arise based on recent factual events: for instance, the applicability of China's investment treaties to Macau and Hong Kong,[2] the applicability of Russia's investment treaties to annexed Crimean territory,[3] and the possibility of bringing an investment claim against China in the Spratlys for issuing a concession for hydrocarbons exploration which has been affected by a binding arbitral award.[4]

---

1   Max Galka, 'Mapping Every Disputed Territory in the World' (*Metrocosm*, 20 November 2015) <https://metrocosm.com/mapping-every-disputed-territory-in-the-world> accessed 12 May 2020.
2   *Government of Laos v Sanum Investments Ltd* [2015] SGHC 15 (Singapore High Court); *Sanum Investments Ltd v Government of Laos* [2016] SGCA 57 (Singapore Court of Appeal).
3   *Aeroport Belbek LLC and Mr Kolomoisky v Russia*, PCA Case no 2015-07; *Privatbank and Finance Co Finilion LLC v Russia*, PCA Case no 2015–21; *LLC Lugzor and others v Russia*, PCA Case no 2015–29; *PJSC Ukrnafta v Russia*, PCA Case no 2015–34; *Stabil LLC and others v Russia*, PCA Case no 2015–35; *Everest Estate LLC and others v Russia*, PCA Case no 2015–36; *Oschadbank v Russia*, PCA Case no 2016-14.
4   *South China Sea Arbitration (Philippines v China)*, PCA Case no 2013–19, Award on Jurisdiction and Admissibility (29 October 2015); Anders Corr, 'China May Owe the Philippines

Specific situations, for example, of state succession to treaties or illegal annexation of territories require the application of different legal regimes. This chapter sets out the potential scenarios in which parallel proceedings could arise from areas of uncertain territorial and maritime boundaries (sections 1 and 2), analyses the substantive principles that may apply to investments in areas of unsettled or contested boundaries (section 3), and examines the procedural mechanisms available to regulate parallel proceedings, pending the resolution of these substantive questions by international tribunals (section 4). Broadly, parallel proceedings are disputes that arise from the same set of factual circumstances and/or legal issues, but these related disputes are submitted to different dispute settlement fora. Although they would usually not involve exactly the same parties, the parties could be related, such as for instance, in the case of an indirect shareholder and its subsidiary company, or either of several littoral states involved in the dispute. As described in this chapter, parallel proceedings that arise in the context of uncertain territorial and maritime boundaries may involve related factual and legal issues. Is it ideal for various tribunals to resolve related aspects of a larger dispute, or should rules be developed to harmonize parallel proceedings?

Parallel proceedings are not inherently undesirable – they are the choice of states. Instead, this chapter looks at procedural mechanisms available to best manage parallel proceedings when they arise. In reality, uncertainty pervading many land and maritime disputes raises the price of trade and investment globally, and hinders development for some of the world's most economically vulnerable states.[5] Foreign investors face the risk that a petroleum license previously granted will later become contested.[6] Business owners in annexed

$177 Billion in South China Sea Rent & Damages' (*Forbes*, 15 July 2016) <www.forbes.com/sites/anderscorr/2016/07/15/the-philippines-should-sue-china-for-177-billion-in-south-china-sea-rent-and-damages/#d405fda60358> accessed 12 May 2020.

5   To date, fewer than 200 of the approximately 430 potential maritime boundaries worldwide have been delimited (and some only partially), leaving well over 200 latent or active maritime boundary disputes still to be resolved. See Enrico Milano and Irini Papanicolopulu, 'State Responsibility in Disputed Areas on Land and at Sea' (2011) Heidelberg J Int'l L 71; Coalter G Lathrop, 'Why Litigate a Maritime Boundary? Some Contributing Factors' in Natalie Klein (ed) *Litigation International Law Disputes* (CUP 2014) 230. For an example of such disputes, see, *eg*, *Maritime Delimitation in the Indian Ocean (Somalia v Kenya)* (Preliminary Objections) [2017] ICJ Rep 3. With respect to the dispute between Australia and Timor-Leste, see Agreement between Australia and Timor-Leste relating to the Unitisation of the Sunrise and Troubadour Fields (signed 6 March 2003, entered into force 23 February 2007) 2483 UNTS 317; *Timor Sea Conciliation (Timor-Leste v Australia)*, PCA Case no 2016-10, Decision on Competence (19 September 2016) paras 5–12; *Arbitration under the Timor Sea Treaty (Timor-Leste v Australia)*, PCA Case no 2013–16 (pending).

6   See, *eg*, Marie-Christine Aquarone, 'The 1985 Guinea/Guinea-Bissau Maritime Boundary Case and Its Implications' (1995) 26 Ocean Dev & Int'l L 413; Nigel Blackaby and Ben

territories may have the option of commencing an investment treaty arbitration against either state.[7] Tourism resorts on contested islands could be volleyed from one jurisdiction to another.[8] It is therefore important that parallel proceedings arising from uncertain territorial and maritime boundaries are managed by international tribunals through clear procedural rules as a matter of international law.

1 Introduction: Why Is There a Risk of Parallel Proceedings?

First, as a result of treaties providing private parties direct rights to investor-state arbitration and the protection of indirect shareholdings as investments, investors are frequently in a position to directly assert multiple parallel claims arising under various legal instruments such as investor-state contracts, the law of the host state, international treaties, and general international law in relation to the same set of facts.[9] Such parallel proceedings risk (i) double recovery, (ii) conflicting outcomes and legal uncertainty, (iii) investors' abuse of process to increase their chances of success and (iv) increased costs.[10]

   Juratowitch, 'Hydrocarbons in Disputed Areas' (2015) 44(4) Int'l L News 1; Saadia Bhatty and Nefeli Lamprou, 'Pitfalls of Investing in Sub-Saharan African Regions with Unsettled Boundaries: How Foreign Investors May Minimize and Manage Investment Risk' (2016) 4 TDM 3; Pierre-Emmanuel Dupont, 'The Not-So-Curious Case of the Western Sahara Sea' (*The Westphalian*, 13 April 2016) <https://thewestphalian.com/analysis/2016/04/13> accessed on 12 May 2020; Pierre-Emmanuel Dupont, 'Conflicting Maritime Claims in the Gulf of Aden' (15 May 2017) (1) *Int'l L Gazette* 8; Liang Xu, 'China Succeeds in Mining Combustible Ice in South China Sea' (*Xinhua*, 18 May 2017) <www.xinhuanet.com//english/2017-05/18/c_136295598.htm> accessed 12 May 2020.
7 Richard Happ and Sebastian Wuschka, '*Horror Vacui*: Or Why Investment Treaties Should Apply to Illegally Annexed Territories' (2016) 33 J Int'l Arb 245.
8 Raul Dancel, 'Manila Wants South China Sea Outpost to Be Tourism Draw' (*Straits Times*, 17 May 2017) <www.straitstimes.com/asia/se-asia/manila-wants-s-china-sea-outpost-to-be-tourism-draw> accessed 12 May 2020.
9 Mark Feldman, 'Setting Limits on Corporate Nationality Planning in Investment Treaty Arbitration' (2012) 27 ICSID Rev 281; Hanno Wehland, *The Coordination of Multiple Proceedings in Investment Treaty Arbitration* (OUP 2013) paras 2.65, 2.70, 3.75 et seq.
10 Vaughan Lowe, '*Res Judicata* and the Rule of Law in International Arbitration' (1996) 8 Afr J Int'l & Comp L 38, 48; Gilles Cuniberti, 'Parallel Litigation and Foreign Investment Dispute Settlement' (2006) 21 ICSID Rev 381, 395; Robin Hansen, 'Parallel Proceedings in Investor-State Treaty Arbitration: Responses for Treaty Drafters, Arbitrators and Parties' (2010) 73 MLR 523, 529; August Reinisch, 'The Issues Raised by Parallel Proceedings and Possible Solutions' in Michael Waibel and others (eds), *The Backlash against Investment Arbitration* (Kluwer Law International 2010) 113, 115; Jamie Shookman, 'Too Many Forums for Investment Disputes? ICSID Illustrations of Parallel Proceedings and Analysis' (2010)

Second, commercial disputes are likely to arise in relation to contracts entered into in furtherance of the investment project. Following the International Tribunal for the Law of the Sea's granting of provisional measures ordering Ghana to ensure that concession holders stop drilling in disputed maritime areas between Ghana and Côte d'Ivoire,[11] two separate proceedings were commenced under commercial contracts for the lease of drilling rigs in the disputed maritime area. These related disputes were submitted to commercial arbitral tribunals constituted under International Chamber of Commerce (ICC) Rules and to the English Courts.[12]

Third, there is additional potential for state-to-state proceedings in parallel to commercial or investment disputes.[13] The potential commencement of state-to-state proceedings multiplies the number of forums to which a dispute could be brought, and increases the potential of inconsistent decisions. In 2018, Qatar filed multiple international claims arising from the same set of actions by Saudi Arabia, the UAE, Bahrain and Egypt including the closure of their land, naval and aerial borders for travel from Qatar, and expulsion of Qatari diplomats. Qatar claimed that these actions were in violation of their international obligations before international tribunals, including the International Court of Justice (ICJ), the United Nations (UN) Officer of the High Commissioner for Human Rights, the International Civil Aviation Organization,

---

27 J Int'l Arb 361, 362; Jan Ole Voss, *The Impact of Investment Treaties on Contracts between Host States and Foreign Investors* (Brill 2011) 281; Hanno Wehland, 'The Regulation of Parallel Proceedings in Investor-State Disputes' (2016) 31 ICSID Rev 576, 577 et seq. For examples from arbitral practice, see, eg, *CME Czech Republic BV (The Netherlands) v Czech Republic*, Partial Award (13 September 2001) paras 419, 525; *Wena Hotels Ltd v Egypt*, ICSID Case no ARB/98/4, Decision on Annulment (28 January 2002) para 49; *Azurix Corp v Argentina*, ICSID Case no ARB/01/12, Decision on Jurisdiction (8 December 2003) para 101; *Camuzzi International SA v Argentina*, ICSID Case no ARB/03/2, Decision on Objection to Jurisdiction (11 May 2005) para 91; *Sempra Energy International v Argentina*, ICSID Case no ARB/02/16, Decision on Objections to Jurisdiction (11 May 2005) para 102; *Bayindir Insaat Turizm Ticaret Ve Sanayi AS v Pakistan*, ICSID Case no ARB/03/29, Decision on Jurisdiction (14 November 2005) para 270.

11 *Dispute Concerning Delimitation of the Maritime Boundary between Ghana and Côte d'Ivoire in the Atlantic Ocean (Ghana/Côte d'Ivoire)* (Provisional Measures, Order of 25 April 2015) [2015] ITLOS Rep 146.

12 The termination of the relevant drilling rig contract was named 'Project Voldemort'. See Alison Ross, 'Win Declared in West African Offshore Drilling Case' (*Global Arbitration Review*, 18 July 2018) <https://globalarbitrationreview.com/article/1172083/win-declared-in-west-african-offshore-drilling-case> accessed 12 May 2020; *Seadrill Ghana Operations Ltd v Tullow Ghana Ltd* [2018] EWHC 1640 (Comm).

13 See, eg, *Maritime Delimitation in the Indian Ocean (Somalia v Kenya)* (Preliminary Objections) [2017] ICJ Rep 3.

and the World Trade Organization's (WTO) Dispute Settlement Body.¹⁴ The possibility that various international tribunals arrive at different conclusions on the facts and conflicting legal outcomes may lead to non-compliance by the parties and undermine confidence in international dispute settlement.

The potential for contradictory decisions is clear also in the context of investment treaties. Investment arbitral tribunals are not bound by the findings of other international courts and tribunals,¹⁵ especially on issues of compensation for harm to investments. The transfer of control over Crimean territory from Ukraine to Russia led to at least eight known investor-state arbitrations initiated by Ukrainian investors against Russia regarding their investments in Crimea.¹⁶ Several tribunals have since found that investments in Crimea are protected under Russia's investment treaty protection obligations. Russia's argument that the territorial scope of the treaty only encompassed the territory at the specific time when the relevant treaty was concluded (in 1998) was rejected.¹⁷ As a question of interpretation of the investment treaty, the investment was deemed to be within Russia's territory. Parallel proceedings regarding different aspects of the dispute and legal rights were submitted to the ICJ and arbitration under the UN Convention on the Law of the Sea (UNCLOS).¹⁸

---

14   Alexandra Hofer, 'Sanctioning Qatar Continued: The United Arab Emirates Is Brought before the ICJ' (EJIL:Talk!, 22 June 2018) <www.ejiltalk.org/sanctioning-qatar-continued-the-united-arab-emirates-is-brought-before-the-icj/> accessed 12 May 2020.

15   See, *eg*, the respective requests for compensation by Ghana and by Cote d'Ivoire, *Dispute Concerning Delimitation of the Maritime Boundary between Ghana and Côte d'Ivoire in the Atlantic Ocean (Ghana/Côte d'Ivoire)* (Rejoinder of Côte d'Ivoire) [2016] paras 6.70 et seq <www.itlos.org/cases/list-of-cases/case-no-23/> accessed 12 May 2020; *Dispute Concerning Delimitation of the Maritime Boundary between Ghana and Côte d'Ivoire in the Atlantic Ocean (Ghana/Côte d'Ivoire)* (Merits) [2017] ITLOS Rep 4, paras 570 et seq.

16   See above n 3.

17   See also *Russia v A* [2018] Case no 4A_396/2017, BGE 144 III 559 (Swiss Federal Tribunal); *Russia v A and others* [2018] Case no 4A_398/2017, (2019) 17(2) German Arb J 93 (Swiss Federal Tribunal). On these cases, see Lisa Bohmer, 'In Now-Public Decisions, Swiss Federal Tribunal Clarifies Reasons for Dismissing Challenges to Two Crimea-Related Investment Treaty Awards against Russia' (*IAReporter*, 16 November 2018) <www.iareporter.com/articles/in-now-public-decisions-swiss-federal-tribunal-clarifies-reasons-for-dismissing-challenges-to-two-crimea-related-investment-treaty-awards-against-russia/> 12 May 2020.

18   *Application of the International Convention for the Suppression of the Financing of Terrorism and of the International Convention on the Elimination of All Forms of Racial Discrimination (Ukraine v Russia)* (Preliminary Objections) [2019] <www.icj-cij.org/en/case/166> accessed 12 May 2020; *Dispute Concerning Coastal State Rights in the Black Sea, Sea of Azov, and Kerch Strait (Ukraine v Russia)*, PCA Case no 2017-06, Award on Preliminary Objections (21 February 2020) under the United Nations Convention on the

In theory, it is the 'fragmented' nature of international law that could be blamed for multiple proceedings in various international dispute resolution forums, even though they all surround the same set of interrelated disputes. Depending on ripeness and admissibility, investment claims could be commenced in relation to the effects of orders by another tribunal that restrict the rights of an investor or the operation of an investment, such as provisional measures.

2 How do Uncertain Boundaries Affect Investments?

Investment treaty disputes are typically brought within the host state and investor's home state's definitions of boundaries.[19] However, the Westphalian premise of 'bounded territories' has never been absolute.[20] The particular issue of investment arbitration in the context of uncertain boundaries brings the problems of bounded territories in international law and parallel proceedings into even starker relief.

Every scenario which could give rise to investment treaty arbitrations is impossible to describe comprehensively. Instead, this section illustrates two broad categories of historical and recent potential disputes: maritime investments, which often relate to hydrocarbon deposits and territorial investments, which often arise due to changes in jurisdiction.

2.1 *Maritime Investments*

Historically, competition over maritime hydrocarbon deposits have led to examples such as: the 1996 Greece-Turkey disputes in the Aegean over the Imia/Kardak Rocks, ongoing issues regarding oil exploration disputes in the Red Sea between Egypt, Sudan, Saudi Arabia and Yemen, the 1995 confrontation between Eritrea and Yemen over the Hanish islands, the 1936 and 1985 issues between Qatar and Bahrain over the Hawar islands, the 1955 and ongoing dispute over Rockall Plateau between the Faroe Islands, Iceland and the UK, the 1994 disputes between West Africa, Nigeria, Cameroon and Equatorial

---

Law of the Sea (adopted 10 December 1982, entered into force 16 November 1994) 1833 UNTS 3 (UNCLOS).

19 In relation to the definition of territory employed in investment treaties, see, in greater detail, Markus P Beham, chapter 5 in this volume, 141–149.

20 Daniel Bethlehem, 'The End of Geography: The Changing Nature of the International System and the Challenge to International Law' (2014) 25 EJIL 9; Cedric Ryngaert, *Jurisdiction in International Law* (2nd edn OUP 2015).

Guinea in the Gulf of Guinea, and the 1987 and ongoing Colombia–Venezuela dispute.[21]

Uncertain maritime boundaries also have a great impact on international energy security, communications, and financial markets. In the event of a dispute regarding the right to lay and repair submarine cables, submarine cable companies are often dependent on a state willing to invoke compulsory dispute settlement under UNCLOS.[22]

In more recent times, potential investment treaty claims could arise from hydrocarbons concessions granted by China and the Philippines near Reed Bank in South China Sea.[23] In other parts of Asia, boundary tensions in the Gulf of Thailand have implications on the exploitation of hydrocarbon resources. Potential investment treaty claims could have arisen from hydrocarbon concessions in the area of the uncertain maritime boundary between Australia and Timor Leste if the states had not reached an agreement on sharing of the resources around the Greater Sunrise block.[24] The maritime dispute surrounding Gibraltar has become the main flashpoint in the broader Anglo-Spanish dispute over Gibraltar's sovereignty. In direct response to what Britain perceives as unlawful maritime incursions into what it calls 'British Gibraltar Territorial Waters', the Spanish Ambassador to the UK was publicly summoned to Whitehall on five occasions between September 2010 and May 2014.[25]

Similarly, in Africa, for many years, Ghana had conducted oil exploration and production in the area of the Gulf of Guinea which is disputed between Ghana and Côte d'Ivoire.[26] Since 2008, Ghana claimed that the western limit

---

21 Gerald Henry Blake and Richard E Swarbrick, 'Hydrocarbons and International Boundaries: A Global Overview' in Gerald Henry Blake and others (eds), *Boundaries and Energy: Problems and Prospects* (Kluwer Law International 1999) 12 et seq.

22 Tara Davenport, 'Submarine Communications Cables and Law of the Sea: Problems in Law and Practice' (2012) 43 Ocean Dev & Int'l L 201, 202 et seq; Youri Van Logchem, 'Submarine Telecommunication Cables in Disputed Maritime Areas' (2014) 45 Ocean Dev & Int'l L 107, 108.

23 Corr (n 4).

24 *Arbitration under the Timor Sea Treaty* (n 5).

25 Jamie Trinidad, 'The Disputed Waters around Gibraltar' (2016) 86 Brit YB Int'l L 101.

26 *Dispute Concerning Delimitation of the Maritime Boundary between Ghana and Côte d'Ivoire* (Provisional Measures, Order of 25 April 2015) (n 11) para 52, 84. See also *Dispute Concerning Delimitation of the Maritime Boundary between Ghana and Côte d'Ivoire in the Atlantic Ocean (Ghana/Côte d'Ivoire)* (Provisional Measures, Written Statement of Ghana) [2015] <www.itlos.org/cases/list-of-cases/case-no-23/case-no-23-provisional-measures/> accessed 12 May 2020.

of its oil blocks created under these conditions should be adopted as the maritime boundary.[27] On the other hand, Côte d'Ivoire argued that Ghana failed to pay heed to Côte d'Ivoire's repeated calls to cease all activity in the disputed area.[28] It argued claimed 'the right to select the oil companies to conduct exploration and exploitation operations and freely to determine the terms and conditions in its own best interest and in accordance with its own requirements with respect to oil and the environment'.[29] Côte d'Ivoire also claimed compensation for any violations of such rights.[30]

Pending the decision of the International Tribunal for the Law of the Sea (ITLOS) between the Order on Provisional Measures of 25 April 2015 and the judgment on the maritime delimitation,[31] investors that had commenced oil exploration in the area of uncertain maritime zones were indirectly ordered not to conduct any further drilling as Ghana had been ordered not to take all necessary steps to ensure that drilling ceased.[32] The damages caused through business interruption have not been publicly quantified.[33]

2.2 Territorial Investments

In modern history, one important example of an investment dispute arising out of moving frontiers may be traced to the *Chorzów Factory* case of the Permanent Court of International Justice (PCIJ), where the factories expropriated were previously on German land, but the land was taken over by Poland after the war.[34]

---

27 *Dispute Concerning Delimitation of the Maritime Boundary between Ghana and Côte d'Ivoire in the Atlantic Ocean (Ghana/Côte d'Ivoire)* (Counter Memorial of Côte d'Ivoire) [2016] para 12 <www.itlos.org/cases/list-of-cases/case-no-23/> accessed 12 May 2020.
28 ibid para 24.
29 *Dispute Concerning Delimitation of the Maritime Boundary between Ghana and Côte d'Ivoire* (Provisional Measures, Order of 25 April 2015) (n 11) para 48.
30 *Dispute Concerning Delimitation of the Maritime Boundary between Ghana and Côte d'Ivoire* (Counter Memorial of Côte d'Ivoire) (n 27) paras 9.33 et seq; *Dispute Concerning Delimitation of the Maritime Boundary between Ghana and Côte d'Ivoire in the Atlantic Ocean (Ghana/Côte d'Ivoire)* (Reply of Ghana) [2016] paras 5.28 et seq <www.itlos.org/cases/list-of-cases/case-no-23/> accessed 13 May 2020; *Delimitation of the Maritime Boundary* (Rejoinder of Côte d'Ivoire) (n 15) paras 6.66 et seq.
31 Oral proceedings began on 6 February 2017; the judgment was delivered on 23 September 2017, see *Dispute Concerning Delimitation of the Maritime Boundary between Ghana and Côte d'Ivoire* (Merits) (n 15).
32 *Dispute Concerning Delimitation of the Maritime Boundary between Ghana and Côte d'Ivoire* (Provisional Measures, Order of 25 April 2015) (n 11) para 108.
33 See Ross (n 12).
34 *Factory at Chorzów, (Germany v Poland)* (Merits) [1928] PCIJ Series A no 17.

In 1915, a contract had been concluded between the Chancellor of the German Empire, on behalf of the Reich, and the investor, according to which that Company undertook 'to establish for the Reich and forthwith to begin the construction of', amongst other things, a nitrate factory at Chorzów in Upper Silesia.[35] The necessary lands were to be acquired on behalf of the Reich and entered in its name in the land register. The machinery and equipment were to be in accordance with the patents and licences of the Company and the experience gained by it, and the Company undertook to manage the factory until 31 March 1941, making use of all patents, licences, experience gained, innovations and improvements, as also of all supply and delivery contracts of which it had the benefit.[36]

On 15 May 1922, the Convention was signed at Geneva between Germany and Poland concerning Upper Silesia, which would result in the cession of Polish Upper Silesia to Poland.[37] As a result, the investors on 15 November 1922 brought an action before the German–Polish Mixed Arbitral Tribunal at Paris, instituted a parallel action in regard to the movable property existing at Chorzów at the time of the taking over of the factory, against the Polish Treasury before the Civil Court of Katovice, and brought an action on 25 March 1925 before the German-Polish Mixed Arbitral Tribunal against the Polish Treasury with a view to obtaining an annual indemnity until the restitution of the factory.[38] At the same time, the Government of the German Reich submitted a suit to the PCIJ concerning reparation due by the Polish government for the damage suffered by their investors as a result of the Polish government taking possession of the nitrate factory.[39]

As covered in greater detail also in another chapter of this volume,[40] another more recent example of a territorial dispute arises from Crimea. In 2014, Russia established effective control over Crimea by physically occupying Crimea in February 2014, by formally incorporating Crimea into Russia under a March 2014 decree and by adopting a constitution for Crimea.[41] Ukraine acknowledged that Crimea was under Russia's occupation and effective control

---

35 ibid 18 et seq.
36 ibid 19 et seq.
37 Convention between Germany and Poland Relating to Upper Silesia (signed 15 May 1922, entered into force 3 June 1922) 9 LNTS 465.
38 *Factory at Chorzów* (Merits) (n 34) 22 et seq.
39 ibid.
40 See Kit De Vriese, chapter 10 in this volume, 330–335.
41 Bohmer (n 17).

but has protested the act. As described in the introduction, the transfer of control over Crimean territory from Ukraine to Russia led to at least eight known investor-State arbitrations[42] and proceedings before the ICJ as well as arbitration under UNCLOS.[43]

The controversial claims to secession of Catalonia and Kurdistan in more recent times raises issues relating to state succession to treaties that echo similar debates that took place regarding Kosovo and Quebec.[44] Although these are not currently subject to international legal proceedings, they raise similar issues of succession to and application of investment treaties that are worth considering. More recent uncertainty in the application of treaties arose in the *Sanum v Laos* arbitration.[45] After the arbitration under the 1993 China–Laos bilateral investment treaty (BIT) and a subsequent judgment by the Singapore Court of Appeals in 2016,[46] the Chinese Foreign Ministry explained during a press conference that 'as a principle, the investment agreements between the central government and foreign countries do not apply' to Hong Kong and Macao.[47] Without a definitive act under international law, the status of all other investments in, and investors from, Macau or Hong Kong, may need to be further clarified.[48]

---

42   See above n 3.
43   See above n 18.
44   Marc Weller, 'Secession and Self-determination in Western Europe: The Case of Catalonia' (*EJIL:Talk!*, 18 October 2017) <www.ejiltalk.org/secession-and-self-determination-in-western-europe-the-case-of-catalonia/> accessed 12 May 2020; Daniel Grütters, 'Catalonia: The Right to Secede and the Right to Self-Determination' (*Oxford Human Rights Hub*, 23 October 2017) <https://ohrh.law.ox.ac.uk/catalonia-the-right-to-secede-and-the-right-to-self-determination/> accessed 12 May 2020; Marko Milanovic, 'A Footnote on Secession', (*EJIL:Talk!*, 26 October 2017) <www.ejiltalk.org/a-footnote-on-secession/> accessed 12 May 2020; Milena Sterio, 'Self-Determination and Secession under International Law: The Cases of Kurdistan and Catalonia' (2018) 22(1) ASIL Insights <www.asil.org/insights/volume/22/issue/1/self-determination-and-secession-under-international-law-cases-kurdistan> accessed 12 May 2020.
45   *Sanum Investments Ltd v Laos*, PCA Case no 2013-13, Award on Jurisdiction (13 December 2013).
46   *Sanum v Laos* [2016] SGCA 57 (n 2).
47   Chinese Foreign Ministry, 'Foreign Ministry Spokesperson Hua Chunying's Regular Press Conference on October 21, 2016' (21 October 2016) <www.fmprc.gov.cn/mfa_eng/xwfw_665399/s2510_665401/t1407743.shtml> accessed 12 May 2020.
48   Norah Gallagher and Wenhua Shan, *Chinese Investment Treaties: Policies and Practice* (OUP 2009) ch 2.

3 Which Normative Regimes Are Relevant?

The normative regimes of international law are set in a Westphalian background of bounded territories, although as noted above, this concept is not absolute.[49] As part of this background, there is growing tension between those heralding globalization as representing the breaking down of state boundaries,[50] against others who argue that these transboundary challenges have always existed and the organised state will persist.[51]

Those pushing for recognition of globalisation point to a multiplicity of actors – including (regional) international organisations and non-state actors such as individuals, corporations, and non-governmental organisations – becoming involved in international law. This is especially so in some areas of international law, such as environmental law,[52] trade and investment,[53] and the protection of cultural heritage.[54] Mindful of this underlying tension, this section examines the applicability of several legal regimes to investments in areas of uncertain boundaries.

---

49 Bethlehem (n 20); Ryngaert (n 20).
50 Nathaniel Berman, '"But the Alternative Is Despair": European Nationalism and the Modernist Renewal of International Law' (1993) Harv L Rev 1792, 1878; David Kennedy, 'International Law and the Nineteenth Century: History of an Illusion' (1997) 17 Quinnipiac L Rev 99, 110; Karen Knop, *Diversity and Self-Determination in International Law* (CUP 2002) 381; Thomas Friedman, *The World is Flat* (Farrar, Straus and Giroux 2005); Francisco Pereira Coutinho and Francisco Briosa e Gala, 'David and Goliath Revisited' (2014) 10 Tex J Oil Gas & Energy L 429; Carl Landauer, 'The Ever-Ending Geography of International Law: The Changing Nature of the International System and the Challenge to International Law: A Reply to Daniel Bethlehem' (2014) 25 EJIL 31.
51 See Landauer (n 50) 31 et seq.
52 See, *eg*, on the participation of NGOs in the 2015 UN Climate Change Conference, the overview at UN Framework Convention on Climate Change, 'COP21 Observer Participation Page' (*United Nations Climate Change*, 2020) <https://unfccc.int/process/conferences/pastconferences/paris-climate-change-conference-november-2015/Observer-participation-in-COP-21-CMP-11> accessed 13 May 2020.
53 In particular, international organisations, such as the European Union, have played a more active role in the development of international law and institutions, as evidenced by the involvement of the EU in the WTO and the Energy Charter Treaty (adopted 17 December 1994, entered into force 16 April 1998) 2080 UNTS 95 as well as its conclusion of free trade agreements (FTAs), including with Canada, Singapore, and Vietnam. See Comprehensive Economic and Trade Agreement between Canada and the European Union [2017] OJ L 11/23 (signed 30 October 2016, not in force); EU–Singapore FTA (signed 9 October 2018, not in force) [2019] OJ L294/3; EU–Vietnam FTA (signed 30 June 2019, not in force) <https://trade.ec.europa.eu/doclib/press/index.cfm?id=1437> accessed 12 May 2020.
54 See Alessandro Chechi, *The Settlement of International Cultural Heritage Disputes* (OUP 2014) 34 et seq.

Three substantive regimes of public international law have been considered: state succession,[55] customary international law applicable to war and the use of force, illegality and international public policy.[56] These depend on the factual context of the dispute.

3.1 State Succession

Where there are multiple investment treaties or international proceedings that have been invoked in relation to a single event or dispute, the question of which treaties apply arises. This question commonly arises due to the succession of states to treaties. state succession to treaties can arise from several factual scenarios. These must be carefully separated into two categories – (i) formation of new states and (ii) expansion of existing states[57] – because they imply very different concerns.

New states often result from independence of former colonies or break up of unions. After secession or dissolution of a union, it is debated whether the new state should be bound by previous treaty commitments entered into by their predecessors, or be entitled to enjoy a clean slate.[58] Ratification of the

---

[55]   Matthew Craven, 'The Problem of State Succession and the Identity of States under International Law' (1998) 9 EJIL 142; Roda Mushkat, 'Hong Kong and Succession of Treaties' (1997) 46 ICLQ 181; Jan Klabbers, 'Cat on a Hot Tin Roof: The World Court, State Succession, and the *Gabčíkovo-Nagymaros* Case' (1998) 11 LJIL 345; Patrick Dumberry, 'State Succession to Bilateral Treaties: A Few Observations on the Incoherent and Unjustifiable Solution Adopted for Secession and Dissolution of States under the 1978 Vienna Convention' (2014) 28 Leiden J Intl' L 3; Alexandre Genest, 'Sudan Bilateral Investment Treaties and South Sudan: Musings on State Succession to Bilateral Treaties in the Wake of Yugoslavia's Breakup' (2014) 3 TDM; Qerim Qerimi and Suzana Krasniqi, 'Theories and Practice of State Succession to Bilateral Treaties: The Recent Experience of Kosovo' (2013) 14 German LJ 1359; Naomi Hart and Sriram Srikumar, 'Investor-State Arbitration before the High Court of Singapore: Territoriality, Nationality and Arbitrability' (2015) 4 Cambridge J Int'l & Comp L 191; Michael Hwang and Aloysius Chang, '*Government of Laos v Sanum Investments Ltd*: A Tale of Two Letters' (2015) 30 ICSID Rev 506; Christian J Tams, 'State Succession to Investment Treaties: Mapping the Issues' (2016) 31 ICSID Rev 314.

[56]   Milano and Papanicolopulu (n 5); Andreas Zimmermann and James G Devaney, 'Succession to Treaties and the Inherent Limits of International Law', in Christian J Tams, Antonios Tzanakopoulos, and Andreas Zimmermann (eds), *Research Handbook on the Law of Treaties* (Edward Elgar 2014); Sergejs Dilevka, 'Arbitration Claims by Ukrainian Investors under the Russia-Ukraine BIT: Between Crimea and a Hard Place?' (*CIS Arbitration Forum*, 17 February 2016) <www.cisarbitration.com/2016/02/17/arbitration-claims-by-ukrainian-investors-under-the-russia-ukraine-bit-between-crimea-and-a-hard-place/> accessed 13 May 2020; Happ and Wuschka (n 7).

[57]   Tams (n 55) 317. *Cf* Vienna Convention on the Succession of States in Respect of Treaties (adopted 23 August 1978, entered into force 6 November 1996) 1946 UNTS 3 (VCST).

[58]   Zimmermann and Devaney (n 56) 516 et seq; Tams (n 55) 317.

1978 Vienna Convention on Succession of States in Respect of Treaties (VCST) is not universal.[59] In *World Wide Minerals v Kazakhstan,* the tribunal decided that Kazakhstan was bound by an investment treaty concluded by the now-dissolved Soviet Union.[60] Several investment treaties concluded by the Federal Republic of Yugoslavia still exist and may bind states such as Serbia and Montenegro.[61] New states may unilaterally declare that they continue to apply investment treaties previously applicable in that territory.[62] For example, in *Saluka Investments BV v Czech Republic,* the 'Czech Republic confirmed to the Kingdom of The Netherlands that, upon the separation of the Czech and Slovak Federal Republic into two separate republics, the Treaty remained in force between the Czech Republic and the Kingdom of The Netherlands'.[63]

Existing states can expand by combination, incorporation, transfer, or annexation of territories. Macau and Hong Kong were transferred to China in 1997 and 1999 by the UK. In *Tza Yap Shum v Peru,* the tribunal decided that China's investment treaty applied to Hong Kong resident Tza Yap Shun, who had made investments in Peru.[64] In *Sanum v Laos,* the arbitral tribunal and the Singapore Court of Appeal decided that the 'moving treaty-frontiers' rule[65] applied automatically, extending China's investment treaty to cover the dispute between a Macanese investor and Laos.[66] The Singapore Court of Appeal

---

59 The VCST has only 23 state parties. See also Tams (n 55) 318.
60 *World Wide Minerals v Kazakhstan,* Award (22 December 2010) (not public).
61 Tams (n 55) 321, noting that *MNSS BV and Recupero Credito Acciaio NV v Montenegro,* ICSID Case no ARB(AF)/12/8, Award (4 May 2016), 'illustrates that these questions are not of a purely academic character. At the time of the request for arbitration, Montenegro had not ratified the ICSID Convention in its own right, but the Socialist Federal Republic of Yugoslavia [...] (from which Serbia and Montenegro emerged) had'. See also Jarrod Hepburn, 'Montenegro to Face Second Known Investment Treaty Claim, This Time over Bankrupt Steelworks' (*IAReporter,* 10 December 2012) <www.iareporter.com/articles/montenegro-to-face-second-known-investment-treaty-claim-this-time-overbankrupt-steelworks> accessed 13 May 2020.
62 Tams (n 55) fn 123.
63 *Saluka Investments BV v Czech Republic,* Jurisdiction over the Counterclaim (7 May 2004) para 2.
64 *Tza Yap Shum v Peru,* ICSID Case no ARB/07/6, Award (7 July 2011).
65 As reflected in VCST art 15.
66 *Sanum v Laos,* Award on Jurisdiction (n 45) paras 219 et seq; *Sanum v Laos* [2016] SGCA 57 (n 2) para 76. The lower court, the Singapore High Court, disagreed with the application of the 'moving treaty-frontiers' rule to this dispute, thus raising issues of temporality, namely, whether the 'moving treaty-frontiers' rule applied and whether this presumption can be later rebutted by an exchange of diplomatic notes subsequent to the dispute crystallising and being brought to arbitration. See *Government of Laos v Sanum* [2015] SGHC 15 (n 2).

decided the 'moving treaty-frontiers' doctrine was part of customary international law, and as a general rule binds all states.[67] Since Laos and China did not take specific steps to preclude the application of the 'moving treaty-frontiers' doctrine to their BIT, it would extend to Macau upon China resuming sovereignty of that territory.[68]

Tribunals have also referred to principles of interpretation in determining whether an existing investment treaty's territorial scope expands according to subsequent expansions in territory. Article 29 of the Vienna Convention on the Law of Treaties[69] provides that 'Unless a different intention appears from the treaty or is otherwise established, a treaty is binding upon each party in respect of its entire territory'. In *PJSC Ukrnafta v Russia* and *Stabil LLC v Russia*, the tribunal had decided that Article 29 meant that Russia's investment treaty applied to territory acquired by Russia after the treaty was concluded, and the Swiss Federal Tribunal agreed.[70]

State succession principles however do not provide a complete regime for uncertainty and the regulation of parallel proceedings. Although the transfer of the territory of Macau to China occurred in 1999, however for the purposes of the arbitration, the 'critical date' on which the dispute crystallised was when the arbitration proceedings were initiated on 14 August 2012.[71] Therefore, although China's investment treaty, by operation of the 'moving treaty-frontiers' doctrine, automatically extended to Macau as of the 1999 handover, between 1999 to 2012 when the arbitration was initiated, it remained open to China and Laos to record their agreement otherwise. If so, do Macanese investors have the right to invoke investment treaties entered into by China and treaties entered by Macau?[72]

The regime of state succession to treaties is not a complete answer as these rules were not designed with investment arbitration in mind. In many cases, these rules may be of limited relevance to investment treaties considering that:

---

67   *Sanum v Laos* [2016] SGCA 57 (n 2) para 75.
68   ibid paras 76 et seq.
69   Vienna Convention on the Law of Treaties (adopted 23 May 1969, entered into force 27 January 1980) 1155 UNTS 331.
70   *PJSC Ukrnafta v Russia*, PCA Case no 2015–34, Award on Jurisdiction (26 June 2017) (not public); *Stabil LLC and others v Russia*, PCA Case no 2015–35, Award on Jurisdiction (26 June 2017) (not public). See Bohmer (n 17). See further *Russia v A* [2018] Case no 4A_396/2017 (n 17); *Russia v A and others* [2018] Case no 4A_398/2017 (n 17).
71   *Sanum v Laos* [2016] SGCA 57 (n 2) paras 67, 92.
72   Patrick Dumberry, 'State Succession to BITs in the Context of the Transfer of Territory of Macao to China: Lessons Learned from the *Sanum* Saga' (2018) 35 J Int'l Arb 329.

The contemporary incarnation of the investment protection regime, based on bilateral investment treaties and regular access to international arbitration, is of fairly recent origin after all. It was established simply too late to be affected by the main waves of State succession that swept the international system before the 1970s.[73]

Thus specific treaty provisions such as article 12 of the Ghana–UK investment treaty are designed to allow the investment treaty definition of 'territory' to expand according to the expansion of the UK, by an Exchange of Notes.[74]

Finally, and importantly, article 6 of the VCSST clarifies that the convention 'applies only to the effects of a succession of states occurring in conformity with international law and, in particular, the principles of international law embodied in the Charter of the United Nations'.[75] Therefore, in the case of combination, incorporation or transfer of territories into an existing state, the applicable rule may depend on whether the conduct of the expanding state was illegal under international law.

3.2 Illegally Annexed Territories

State succession rules do not apply immediately to situations of illegal occupation of territory.[76] These involve 'ruptures of a particular kind', to which international law responds with particular sets of rules, notably aimed at denying legal validation of the factual situation.[77] Most prominently, in the case of

---

73   Tams (n 55) 315.
74   UK–Ghana BIT (1989) art 12.
75   VCST art 6.
76   VCST art 6. VCST art 39 states that the Convention 'shall not prejudge any question that may arise in regard to the effects of a succession of States in respect of a treaty from the international responsibility of a State or from the outbreak of hostilities between States'. VCST art 40 states that the Convention 'shall not prejudge any question that may arise in regard to a treaty from the military occupation of a territory'.
77   Friendly Relations Declaration, UNGA Res 2625 (XXV) (24 October 1970) principle 1 ('No territorial acquisition resulting from the threat or use of force shall be recognized as legal'); Definition of Aggression, UNGA Res 3314 (XXIX) (14 December 1974) art 5(3) ('No territorial acquisition or special advantage resulting from aggression is or shall be recognized as lawful'); ILC, 'Articles on Responsibility of States for Internationally Wrongful Acts' (2001), Annex to UNGA Res 56/83 (12 December 2001) UN Doc A/56/83, arts 40, 41; Thomas D Grant, *Aggression against Ukraine: Territory, Responsibility, and International Law* (Palgrave 2015) 94; Tams (n 55) 320; Rainer Hofmann, 'Annexation', *Max Planck Encyclopedia of Public International Law* (2020) <https://opil.ouplaw.com/home/MPIL> accessed 13 May 2020; Lauri Mälksoo, *Illegal Annexation and State Continuity* (Brill 2003).

illegally annexed territories by use of force,[78] international public policy prefers that the offending state should not benefit from its illegal act.[79]

As a substantive question, it could be disingenuous for the occupying state to assert that its investment treaties are not automatically extended to its newly annexed territory. After all, sovereignty entails both power and responsibility. In addition, it has been argued that the main purpose why international law should recognise such extension – should be to oblige occupying powers to restore and maintain public order and civil life in the occupied territory.[80] The rationale why investment tribunals should find that they have jurisdiction over an investment damaged in the annexation are largely policy-based. They include that the occupying state should not benefit from its illegal conduct, estoppel, and the 'interest of the international community to sanction illegal acquisition of territory by means of annexation'.[81] It has also been argued that an interpretation otherwise would 'leave investors in a legal vacuum'.[82]

3.3   *Limitations of Substantive Legal Rules*

While the annexing power is unlikely to dispute that the area where the investment was made is part of its territory,[83] it is likely to have other objections to jurisdiction, in particular objections relating to the time that the investment was made and to the time that the dispute arose.

Customary international law mandates that in the case of illegal use of force, the occupying state's treaties should not be recognized as extending to the occupied territory. Would an investment tribunal's assumption of jurisdiction be perceived as recognizing the unlawful acquisition of territory?[84]

The applicable legal regime depends on the context of the contested boundary and the facts relevant in making and maintaining the investment. Under general international law, the obligation of non-recognition of illegally annexed territory is well accepted.[85] Third parties may be under an obligation to respect the territorial integrity and sovereignty of the injured state by various

---

78   Charter of the United Nations (adopted 26 June 1945, entered into force 24 October 1945) 1 UNTS xvi (UN Charter) art 2(4).
79   James Crawford, *Brownlie's Principles of Public International Law* (8th ed, OUP 2012) 220; Malcolm N Shaw, *International Law* (7th ed., CUP 2014) 358.
80   Happ and Wuschka (n 7) fns 24 et seq.
81   ibid 254.
82   ibid 254.
83   ibid 253, 261 et seq.
84   ibid 254.
85   ILC, 'Articles on Responsibility of States for Internationally Wrongful Acts with Commentaries' (2001) II(2) YBILC 31, art 41 cmts 5 et seq.

acts such as (i) refusing to recognise the situation as lawful, (ii) by refraining from entering into formal arrangements with the occupier regarding the unlawful exploitation of natural resources in the occupied territories, and (iii) by not applying existing bilateral economic and commercial treaties to trade from that region.

Note that legal developments regarding the effect of armed conflict on treaties is nascent. To this day, no comprehensive customary regime governs the effect of hostilities on treaties.[86] An occupation in violation of the right to self-determination may require third states not to enter into arrangements with the occupier for exploitation of natural resources in that territory. On the other hand, in cases of secessionist attempts by a people or a minority to undermine the territorial integrity of a state that are not justified under international law, third states should refrain from recognising the secessionist entity and from entering into formal arrangements with that entity.[87]

As illegal annexation results from unlawful belligerent occupation of the relevant piece of land, the customary international rules of belligerent occupation, as recognised in the 1907 Hague Regulations[88] and the Fourth Geneva Convention of 1949,[89] continue to apply throughout the annexation. Third states may be obliged to recognise the states' existing treaties, instead of the occupying power's treaties.[90]

At the same time, the conduct of the occupying state would be governed by the regime of belligerent occupation and international humanitarian law, as

---

86 UN Secretariat, 'The Effect of Armed Conflict on Treaties: An Examination of Practice and Doctrine' (2005) UN Doc A/CN.4/550, para 1; Anthony Aust, *Modern Treaty Law and Practice* (2nd ed, CUP 2007) 308; Benny Tan Zhi Peng, 'The International Law Commission's Draft Articles on the Effects of Armed Conflicts on Treaties: Evaluating the Applicability of Impossibility of Performance and Fundamental Change' (2013) 3 Asian J Int'l L 51, 54.

87 Milano and Papanicolopulu (n 5) 633 et seq.

88 Regulations Respecting the Laws and Customs of War on Land, Annex to Convention (IV) Respecting the Laws and Customs of War on Land (adopted 18 October 1907, entered into force 26 January 1910) 205 CTS 277 (Hague Regulations) art 43.

89 Geneva Convention (IV) Relative to the Protection of Civilian Persons in Time of War (adopted 12 August 1949, entered into force 21 October 1950) (1950) 75 UNTS 287 (GC IV) art 47 et seq.

90 See, *eg*, Valentina Azarova, 'Israel's unlawfully prolonged occupation: consequences under an integrated legal framework' (2017) European Council on Foreign Relations Policy Brief, 12 <www.ecfr.eu/publications/summary/israels_unlawfully_prolonged_occupation_7294> accessed 13 May 2020: 'third states and international organisations cannot enter into agreements with Israel in relation to Palestinian territory that have not received the consent of the Palestinian representatives or that affect existing agreements with them'.

well as by human rights law to the extent that the relevant rules apply extraterritorially. Investment protection treaties would still continue to apply after the outbreak of armed hostilities, particularly where these treaties address the consequences of armed conflicts.[91]

It is not clear why investment treaties should be specially carved out of the whole corpus of other treaties that states enter into. States have treaties which govern almost all aspects of international relations including diplomatic immunity, trade, tax, extradition, international criminal statutes, human rights, environmental protection, and recognition of court judgments.

Policy arguments, although compelling and necessary, suffer the defect of changing from situation to situation, as a 'response or reaction'[92] to new facts as and when they arise. Substantive legal rules are incapable of providing an overarching, stable legal principle. Instead, they only highlight the 'fragmented' nature of the international legal order,[93] the absence of a clear hierarchy of norms, and invite continued jostling between various legal regimes for norm supremacy.

4 Which Procedural Rules Apply?

Substantive legal regimes provide the primary obligations that bind states. States are also bound by secondary obligations such as the regime of state responsibility. At a third level, the rules of international legal proceedings are no less fundamental. Consent to the jurisdiction of an international tribunal,

---

91 Kit De Vriese chapter 10 in this volume, 325–326; Christoph Schreuer, 'The Protection of Investments in Armed Conflicts' in Freya Baetens (ed) *Investment Law within International Law: Integrationist Perspectives* (CUP 2012) 3 et seq; Gleider I Hernández, 'The Interaction between Investment Law and the Law of Armed Conflict in the Interpretation of Full Protection and Security Clause' in Freya Baetens (ed) *Investment Law within International Law: Integrationist Perspectives* (CUP 2012); Ofilio Mayorga, 'Arbitrating War: Military Necessity as a Defense to the Breach of Investment Treaty Obligations' (2013) Harvard Program on Humanitarian Policy and Conflict Research Policy Brief <http://hpcrresearch.org/sites/default/files/publications/081213%20ARBITRATING%20WAR%20%28final%29.pdf> accessed 13 May 2020; Josef Ostřanský, 'The Termination and Suspension of Bilateral Investment Treaties Due to an Armed Conflict' (2015) 6 JIDS 136.

92 *Accordance with International Law of the Unilateral Declaration of Independence in Respect of Kosovo* (Advisory Opinion, Separate Opinion of Antonio A Cançado Trindade) [2010] ICJ Rep 523, paras 136 et seq.

93 Stephan W Schill, 'W(h)ither Fragmentation? On the Literature and Sociology of International Investment Law' (2011) 22 EJIL 875; José E Alvarez, 'Beware: Boundary Crossings' (2016) 17 JWIT 171.

the existence of a dispute and *res judicata* are examples of the procedural legal order.

4.1 Indispensable Third Parties, Res Judicata, Abuse of Process, and Comity

In practice, it only takes a creative counsel to commence parallel international proceedings.[94] For instance, in 2015, many of the Crimea-related arbitrations were commenced by claimants relating to associated with Ukrainian oligarch Igor Kolomoisky.[95] In another instance, four parallel arbitrations were commenced surrounding the same facts, against Egypt and two state-owned companies.[96] Shareholders at different levels of a chain of companies initiated two 'duplicative' investment treaty arbitrations against Egypt under separate investment treaties.[97]

State-to-state proceedings could also arise despite the efforts of investor-state arbitration to depoliticize transnational investment disputes.[98] In *Italy v Cuba*, Italy attempted to exercise diplomatic protection under the Italy–Cuba BIT (1993)[99] even though the treaty provided both state-state and investor-state dispute settlement provisions.[100] The *Peru v Chile* arbitration was brought by Peru as an attempt 'to block or hinder an ongoing investor-state arbitration'.[101] Peru requested suspension of the investor-state proceedings on account of the state-to-state proceedings, however, the investor-state tribunal refused to stay proceedings. State-to-state arbitration was later discontinued.[102]

---

94 Emmanuel Gaillard, 'Abuse of Process in International Arbitration' (2017) 32 ICSID Rev 17, 17.

95 Zoe Williams, 'An Update on Disputes under the Russia-Ukraine BIT' (*IAReporter*, 6 July 2017) <www.iareporter.com/articles/an-update-on-disputes-under-the-russia-ukraine-bit/> accessed 13 May 2020.

96 *Ampal-American Israel Corp and others v Egypt*, ICSID Case no ARB/12/11; *Yosef Maiman, Merhav (MNF) Ltd, Merhav Ampal Group Ltd, and Merhav Ampal Energy Holdings Ltd Partnership v Egypt*, PCA Case no 2012–26; *East Mediterranean Gas SAE v Egyptian General Petroleum Corp, Egyptian Natural Gas Holding Co, and Israel Electric Corp Ltd*, ICC Case no 18215/GZ/MHM; *Egyptian General Petroleum Corp and Egyptian Natural Gas Holding Co v East Mediterranean Gas SAE*, CRCICA Case no 829/2012.

97 Gaillard (n 94) 17.

98 Ibrahim FI Shihata, 'Towards a Greater Depoliticization of Investment Disputes: The Roles of ICSID and MIGA' (1986) 1 ICSID Rev 1.

99 *Italy v Cuba*, Interim Award (15 March 2005); *Italy v Cuba*, Final Award (15 January 2008). See Michele Potestà, 'Republic of Italy v. Republic of Cuba' (2012) 106 AJIL 341, 344.

100 Italy–Cuba BIT (1993) arts 9, 10.

101 Potestà (n 99) 344 (fn 8).

102 *Empresas Lucchetti SA and Lucchetti Peru SA v Peru*, ICSID Case no ARB/03/4, Award (7 February 2005) paras 7, 9.

Two key principles are particularly relevant when facing disputes arising out of investments in areas of uncertain boundaries – the *Monetary Gold* indispensable third party principle and *res judicata*.[103]

In *Monetary Gold*, the ICJ declined to proceed due to the absence of an indispensable third party, because the rights of the absent third party would 'form the very subject-matter of the decision'.[104] This was followed in *East Timor*.[105] The ICJ decided not to proceed because it would be required to decide upon the lawfulness of activities by the absent third states.

The Monetary Gold principle has been raised in the investment arbitrations *Ping An v Belgium*[106] and *Chevron v Ecuador*.[107] In the context of investments in areas of uncertain maritime boundaries between Ghana and Côte d'Ivoire, if an investment tribunal is required to decide on the lawfulness of the actions of the absent third state, it may exercise its adjudicative discretion not to proceed.[108] For example, in an arbitration by an investor against Ghana, a tribunal may have to determine if a part of damage incurred was caused by the actions of Côte d'Ivoire. Third states may have compelling reasons for seeking participation in an investor-state arbitration.[109]

Res judicata protects defendants from having to defend themselves twice in the same manner.[110] *Lis pendens*, an offshoot of the principle of *res judicata*, gives a tribunal discretion to stay its proceedings.[111] It is widely accepted as

---

103 Bin Cheng, *General Principles of Law as Applied by International Courts and Tribunals* (Stevens 1953) 336; Shabtai Rosenne, *The Law and Practice of International Court 1920–1996*, vol 3 (Nijhoff 1997) 1655 et seq; Voss (n 10) 288.
104 *Monetary Gold Removed from Rome in 1943 (Italy v France, UK, and USA)* (Preliminary Question) [1954] ICJ Rep 19, 32.
105 *East Timor (Portugal v Australia)* [1995] ICJ Rep 90.
106 *Ping An Life Insurance Co of China, Ltd and Ping An Insurance (Group) Co of China, Lt v Belgium*, ICSID Case no ARB/12/29, Award (30 April 2015) paras 127 et seq.
107 *Chevron Corp and Texaco Petroleum Corp v Ecuador*, PCA Case no 2009–23, Third Interim Award on Jurisdiction and Admissibility (27 February 2012), paras 3.83 et seq, 3.126 et seq, 3.178 et seq, 4.59 et seq.
108 Odysseas G Repousis, 'Why Russian Investment Treaties Could Apply to Crimea and What Would This Mean for the Ongoing Russo–Ukrainian Territorial Conflict' (2016) 32 Arb Int'l 459, 478.
109 Velimir Živković, 'Rethinking Interested Parties in ISDS: The Sase of 3rd States' (Kluwer Arbitration Blog, 3 December 2015) <https://arbitrationblog.kluwerarbitration.com/2015/12/03/rethinking-interested-parties-in-isds-the-case-of-3rd-states/> accessed 14 May 2020.
110 *CME Czech Republic BV (The Netherlands) v Czech Republic*, Legal Opinion Prepared by Christoph Schreuer and August Reinisch (20 June 2002) para 1. See also IC MacGibbon, 'Estoppel in International Law' (1958) 7 ICLQ 468.
111 Karin Oellers-Frahm, 'Multiplication of International Courts and Tribunals and Conflicting Jurisdiction: Problems and Possible Solutions' (2001) 5 Max Planck UNYB 67,

customary and general international law,[112] but it generally requires a triple identity of (i) the parties, (ii) the object of the proceedings and (iii) the legal ground.[113] The applicability of *res judicata* or *lis pendens* to investment disputes has been doubted since international tribunals do not have any hierarchical authority over one another.[114] In investment arbitrations, it will only be relevant if one and the same entity pursues treaty claims against the same host state.[115] Therefore, it is unlikely to be helpful to either disputing state if an investor brings claims against both states in relation to its investment in a disputed area.

Increasing attention has been paid to the notion of 'abuse of process' in international arbitration.[116] However, the notion of abuse of process may not yet be recognised as a general principle of law, is flexible beyond the literal application of the black letter law,[117] and has given rise to a haphazard approach to parallel proceedings. For instance, in *Ampal*, the tribunal found that the parallel arbitrations did not amount to an abuse of process, but because the tribunal in the parallel arbitration had signalled that it had jurisdiction, the abuse of process had 'crystallised'.[118] However, the tribunal allowed the claimants to elect which proceedings it would pursue,[119] and the claimants divided up their claims between the two arbitrations to hedge their bets.[120] Abuse of process also requires the court or tribunal to identify the 'spirit of the law',[121] or the

---

78; August Reinisch, 'The Use and Limits of *Res Judicata* and *Lis Pendens* as Procedural Tools to Avoid Conflicting Dispute Settlement Outcomes' (2004) 3 L & Prac Int'l Cts & Tribunals 37; Campbell McLachlan, *Lis Pendens in International Litigation* (Brill 2009); Gaillard (n 94) 27 et seq.

112 *The Pious Fund Case (USA v Mexico)* (1902) 9 RIAA 1, 7 et seq; *Trail Smelter (USA v Canada)* (1941) 3 RIAA 1905, 1950; Cheng (n 103) 336.

113 Audley Sheppard, 'Res Judicata and Estoppel' in Bernardo M Cremades and Julian DM Lew (eds), *Parallel State and Arbitral Procedures in International Arbitration* (Kluwer Law International 2005) 233.

114 Voss (n 10) 289 et seq.

115 Wehland, 'The Regulation of Parallel Proceedings' (n 10) 585 et seq.

116 John P Gaffney, '"Abuse of Process" in Investment Treaty Arbitration' (2010) 11 JWIT 515; Eric De Brabandere, '"Good Faith", "Abuse of Process" and the Initiation of Investment Treaty Claims' (2012) 3 JIDS 609; Hervé Ascensio, 'Abuse of Process in International Investment Arbitration' (2014) 13 Chinese J Int'l L 763; Gaillard (n 94) 24 et seq.

117 Gaillard (n 94) 34.

118 *Ampal-American Israel Corp and others v Egypt*, ICSID Case no ARB/12/11, Decision on Jurisdiction (1 February 2016) para 331. See also Gaillard (n 93) 45.

119 *Ampal v Egypt*, Decision on Jurisdiction (n 118) para 334.

120 Gaillard (n 94) 25 et seq.

121 Gaillard (n 94) 36.

'ulterior'[122] motive of the claimant – endeavours that can only be tailored to specific factual situations, and are prone to legal uncertainty.

A measure of awareness and respect between international courts and tribunals would be appropriate.[123] The function of the court or tribunal is closely tied to the way a 'dispute' would be defined. In the *Case Concerning Northern Cameroons*, the ICJ stated that the 'function of the Court is to state the law, but it may pronounce judgment only in connection with concrete cases where there exists at the time of the adjudication an actual controversy involving a conflict of legal interests between the parties'.[124]

4.2 Definition of a 'Dispute'

When tribunals are faced with multiple parallel proceedings, attempting to identify an applicable procedural rule that would govern the tribunal's exercise of jurisdiction could be difficult. Should a tribunal issue a stay in deference to another tribunal, or continue the proceedings in exercise of its duty to address a dispute efficiently?

Instead of choosing between a variety of substantive or procedural rules, it could make the most sense for the tribunal to focus on the definition of a dispute under international law, and determine the scope of the dispute put before it in the context of parallel proceedings arising in areas of uncertain maritime or territorial boundaries.[125] This would enable a tribunal to distinguish between the disputes within its mandate and whether such disputes overlap with those of another tribunal's.

The universally recognized definition of a dispute is stated in the *Mavrommatis* case: 'A dispute is a disagreement on a point of law or fact, a conflict of legal views or of interests between two persons'.[126] Although the PCIJ's *Mavrommatis* definition has been adopted as 'standard phrase and commonplace', it is notably broad, can be fulfilled fairly easily, and not exactly the same as a 'legal dispute'.[127]

---

122 Gaillard (n 94) 26 et seq, 36.
123 Crawford (n 79) 24. See also Ronald A Brand, 'Forum Non Conveniens', *Max Planck Encyclopedia of Public International Law* (2019) <https://opil.ouplaw.com/home/MPIL> accessed 14 May 2020.
124 *Case Concerning the Northern Cameroons (Cameroon v UK)* [1963] ICJ Rep 15, 33 et seq.
125 Hugh Thirlway, 'Territorial Disputes and Their Resolution in the Recent Jurisprudence of the International Court of Justice' (2017) 31 LJIL 1, 4.
126 *Mavrommatis Palestine Concessions (Greece v UK)* [1924] PCIJ Series A no 2, 11.
127 Christian J Tams, 'The Contentious Jurisdiction of the Permanent Court' in Malgosia Fitzmaurice and Christian J Tams (eds), *Legacies of the Permanent Court of International Justice* (Nijhoff 2013) 43.

4.2.1 Opposition

The ICJ in the *South West Africa* case noted that, for a dispute to exist, 'it must be shown that the claim of one party is positively opposed by the other'.[128] The point of crystallisation of the dispute has been identified as 'un accord sur un désaccord' or 'an agreement to disagree'.[129] It is 'when the parties, however they communicate, put forward contradictory contentions and claims they reciprocally reject over the same subject matter'.[130] The jurisdiction over interpretation of the treaty was found in *Certain German Interests in Polish Upper Silesia* and *Rights of Nationals of the United States of America in Morocco*.[131]

Each case brings new facts and unique procedural scenarios which further polish the definition of a dispute in international law. One such instance is the absence of a party. When one party fails to participate, it brings unique challenges to ascertaining the existence of a dispute. In the *Applicability of the Obligation to Arbitrate*, the USA declined to expressly affirm or contradict the UN's view that its legislation constituted a violation of the UN Headquarters Agreement.[132] The court noted that:

> [W]here one party to a treaty protests against the behaviour or a decision of another party, and claims that such behaviour or decision constitutes a breach of the treaty, the mere fact that the party accused does not advance any argument to justify its conduct under international law does not prevent the opposing attitudes of the parties from giving rise to a dispute concerning the interpretation or application of the treaty.[133]

In the context of a requirement of prior negotiation as a pre-condition to jurisdiction, it has been suggested that for a dispute to crystallise, there must be a

---

128 *South West Africa (Ethiopia v South Africa, Liberia v South Africa)* (Preliminary Objections) [1962] ICJ Rep 319, 328. See also *Certain Property (Liechtenstein v Germany)* [2005] ICJ Rep 6, para 23.
129 Georges Abi-Saab, 'Negotiation and Adjudication' in Laurence Boisson de Chazournes, Marcelo Kohen, and Jorge E Viñuales (eds), *Diplomatic and Judicial Means of Dispute Settlement* (Nijhoff 2012) 329.
130 ibid 329.
131 *Certain German Interests in Polish Upper Silesia (Germany v Poland)* [1925] PCIJ Series A no 6; *Rights of Nationals of the United States of America in Morocco (France v USA)* [1952] ICJ Rep 176.
132 Agreement Regarding the Headquarters of the United Nations (signed 26 June 1947, entered into force 21 November 1947) 11 UNTS 11.
133 *Applicability of the Obligation to Arbitrate under Section 21 of the United Nations Headquarters Agreement of 26 June 1947* (Advisory Opinion) [1988] ICJ Rep 12, para 38.

'positive act of manifestation of opposition'.[134] Other scholars have taken the view that a legal dispute exists 'only if the parties are opposed to one another in respect of a specific claim raised by one party against the other which is rejected in whatever form'.[135] The USA argued in *Ecuador v USA* that a dispute requires 'an assertion of a right, claim, or demand on one side, met by contrary claims or allegations on the other'.[136]

A dispute may exist even in the absence of active opposition,[137] as long as 'a party's *actions* make it obvious that its views are positively opposed to another party's views'.[138] In the *South China Sea* case, because of China's non-participation in the proceeding, the tribunal was required to determine whether there was a dispute between the Parties concerning the matters raised by the Philippines and, whether such a dispute concerned the interpretation or application of the Convention.[139] In *Southern Bluefin Tuna*,[140] ITLOS referred to the definition of dispute in *Mavrommatis*[141] and to *South West Africa* in which it was held that 'it must be shown that the claim of one party is positively opposed by the other'.[142] A mere existence of conflicting interests between the parties, a mere institution of proceedings, a mere assertion or denial that a

---

134 *Application of the International Convention on the Elimination of All Forms of Racial Discrimination (Georgia v Russia)* (Separate Opinion of President Owada) [2011] ICJ Rep 170, paras 11 et seq. See also Karel Wellens, *Negotiations in the Case Law of the International Court of Justice: A Functional Analysis* (Routledge 2016) 90.

135 *Ecuador v USA*, PCA Case no 2012-5, Expert Opinion with Respect to Jurisdiction of W Michael Reisman (24 April 2012) para 30; *Ecuador v USA*, PCA Case no 2012-5, Expert Opinion on the Construction of Article VII of Christian Tomuschat (24 April 2012), para 7. See also *South West Africa* (n 128); *Northern Cameroons* (n 124) 33 et seq.

136 *Ecuador v USA*, PCA Case no 2012-5, Memorial on Objections to Jurisdiction of the USA (25 April 2012) 17.

137 *Asian Agricultural Products Ltd. v Sri Lanka*, ICSID Case no ARB/87/3, Award (27 June 1990) para 3; *Siemens AG v Argentina*, ICSID Case no ARB/02/8, Award (17 January 2007) para 159; *Application of the International Convention on the Elimination of All Forms of Racial Discrimination (Georgia v Russia)* (Joint Dissenting Opinion by Judges Owada, Simma Abraham, Donoghue and Judge ad hoc Gaja) [2011] ICJ Rep 142, para 3; Wellens (n 134) 89 et seq.

138 *Ecuador v USA*, Memorial of the USA (n 136) 29. See also *Ecuador v USA*, PCA Case no 2012-5, Expert Opinion of Alain Pellet (23 May 2012) 20; *Applicability of the Obligation to Arbitrate* (n 133) para 38; *Land and Maritime Boundary (Cameroon v Nigeria)* (Preliminary Objections) [1998] ICJ Rep 275; *Application of the International Convention on the Elimination of All Forms of Racial Discrimination (Georgia v Russia)* [2011] ICJ Rep 70.

139 *South China Sea* (n 4) para 131.

140 *Southern Blue Fin Tuna Cases (New Zealand v Japan, Australia v Japan)* (Provisional Measures) (Order of 27 August 1999) [1999] ITLOS Rep 280, para 44.

141 *Mavrommatis Palestine Concessions* (n 126) 11.

142 *South West Africa* (n 128) 328.

dispute exists,[143] or a purely theoretical disagreement on a point of law or fact are alone not conclusive of the existence of a dispute.[144]

The *South China Sea* tribunal's determination of whether there is a dispute between the Philippines and China was complicated because of China's non-participation in the proceeding.[145] China had neither clarified the nature or scope of its claimed historic rights nor its understanding of the meaning of the 'nine-dash line' set out on the map accompanying its notes verbales of 7 May 2009. China had also not expressed a view on the status of contested maritime features.[146] The tribunal pieced together two instances of opposing views in a statement in opposition to a published map and another statement in opposition to a note verbale. First the tribunal found that a dispute was readily apparent in the text and context of China's 'map depicting a seemingly expansive claim to maritime entitlements', opposed to the Philippines' argument that maritime entitlements are to be derived from 'geological features' and based solely on the Convention. Second, the tribunal found a dispute in China's invocation of 'abundant historical and legal evidence' and rejection of the contents of the Philippines' note as 'totally unacceptable'.[147]

Since '[i]nternational law does not require a state to expound its legal arguments before a dispute can arise', the tribunal's task was to 'distinguish between the dispute itself and arguments used by the parties to sustain their respective submissions on the dispute'.[148] It also opined that 'a dispute is not negated by the absence of granular exchanges with respect to each and every individual feature'.[149] The tribunal identified a dispute concerning 'the maritime entitlements generated in the South China Sea'.[150]

The *South China Sea* tribunal developed a holistic definition of a dispute in international law – it should be 'viewed objectively'.[151] In particular, it was

---

143   *Northern Cameroons* (n 124); *United States Diplomatic and Consular Staff in Tehran (USA v Iran)* [1980] ICJ Rep 3.
144   *South West Africa (Ethiopia v South Africa, Liberia v South Africa)* (Preliminary Objections, Joined Dissenting Opinion of Judges Spender and Fitzmaurice) [1962] ICJ Rep 465, 547; *South West Africa (Ethiopia v South Africa, Liberia v South Africa)* (Preliminary Objections, Dissenting Opinion of Judge Morelli) [1962] ICJ Rep 564, 566.
145   *South China Sea* (n 4) para 131.
146   *South China Sea* (n 4) para 160.
147   ibid para 167. See also Keyuan Zou and Qiang Ye, 'Interpretation and Application of Article 298 of the Law of the Sea Convention in Recent Annex VII Arbitrations: An Appraisal' (2017) 48 Ocean Dev & Int'l L 331, 334.
148   *South China Sea* (n 4) para 170.
149   ibid para 170.
150   ibid para 170.
151   ibid para 170.

'conscious that it may emerge, in the course of the Tribunal's examination or in light of further communications from China, that the Parties are not, in fact, in dispute on the status of, or entitlements generated by, a particular maritime feature'.[152] The Tribunal adopted the approach of the ICJ in *Land and Maritime Boundary*[153] that even if 'the exact scope of this dispute cannot be determined at present, a dispute nevertheless exists between the two Parties'.[154]

4.2.2 Subject Matter

Although *Mavrommatis* defines a dispute as a disagreement on a point of law *or* fact, some take the view that a mere theoretical disagreement is not enough:

> A dispute *must* relate to clearly identified issues and must have *specific consequences* in order to serve as a basis for jurisdiction. A disagreement on a theoretical question is not sufficient. This does not mean that actual damage must have occurred, but merely that *the issue must have some practical relevance*.[155]

A mere existence of conflicting interests between the parties, a mere institution of proceedings, a mere assertion or denial that a dispute exists,[156] or a purely theoretical disagreement on a point of law or fact are alone not conclusive of the existence of a dispute.[157] There must be some 'concreteness'.[158] A legal dispute is one where the parties have formulated their claims on the 'basis of rights and/or obligations derived from a legal norm'.[159] Some international disputes are arguably by their very nature beyond the competence of international tribunals or 'non-justiciable'.[160]

---

152 ibid para 171.
153 *Land and Maritime Boundary* (n 138) para 93.
154 *South China Sea* (n 4) paras 170 et seq.
155 Christoph Schreuer, 'What is a Legal Dispute?' in Isabelle Buffard and others (eds), *International Law between Universalism and Fragmentation: Festschrift in Honour of Gerhard Hafner* (Brill 2008) 978 (emphasis added). See also Henry G Schermers and Niels M Blokker, *International Institutional Law: Unity within Diversity* (5th edn, Brill 2011) 841.
156 *Northern Cameroons* (n 124); *United States Diplomatic and Consular Staff in Tehran* (n 143).
157 *South West Africa* (Preliminary Objections, Joined Dissenting Opinion of Judges Spender and Fitzmaurice) (n 144) 547; *South West Africa* (Preliminary Objections, Dissenting Opinion of Judge Morelli) (n 144) 566.
158 *Ecuador v USA*, Expert Opinion of Alain Pellet (n 138) 20.
159 Robert Kolb, *The International Court of Justice* (Hart 2014) 322. See also Hans Kelsen, *The Law of the United Nations: A Critical Analysis of Its Fundamental Problems* (first published 1951, The Lawbook Exchange 2000) 477 et seq.
160 Hersch Lauterpacht, 'The Doctrine of Non-Justiciable Disputes in International Law' [1928] (24) Economica 277.

As claims are crafted by the claimant which commences the proceedings, the definition of a dispute is often dependent on the claimant's submissions. In *South China Sea*, the claimant carefully separated the submission on the status and entitlements of maritime features from the issue of sovereignty over those features. In contrast, in *Chagos*, the tribunal took the view that the issue of sovereignty could not be easily separated from the other issues in dispute.[161]

The *South China Sea* tribunal, which had jurisdiction only over the UNCLOS dispute, was careful to distinguish between territorial sovereignty and maritime disputes. The tribunal set out two scenarios where the submissions could overlap with territorial sovereignty: 'either (a) the resolution of the Philippines' claims would require the Tribunal to first render a decision on sovereignty, either expressly or implicitly; or (b) the actual objective of the Philippines' claims was to advance its position in the Parties' dispute over sovereignty'.[162] Therefore, Schreuer has astutely concluded that:

> The existence of a legal dispute is determined by the type of claim put forward and by the nature of the arguments supporting it. A dispute will be legal if the claim is based on treaties, legislation and other sources of law and if remedies such as restitution or damages are sought. *It is in the hands of the claimant to present its claim in legal terms.* Attempts by respondents to characterize disputes as political rather than legal have not succeeded. What matters are not the political circumstances but the assertion of legal rights.[163]

The *South China Sea* tribunal stated '[s]imply put, the Tribunal is not empowered to act except in respect of one or more actual disputes between the Parties'.[164] The tribunal is required to 'isolate the real issue in the case and to identify the object of the claim'.[165] It observed that it is entirely ordinary and expected that two states with a relationship as extensive and multifaceted as that existing between the Philippines and China would have disputes in respect of several distinct matters. Indeed, even within a geographic area such as the South China Sea, the Parties can readily be in dispute regarding multiple

---

161 *Chagos Marine Protected Area Arbitration (Mauritius v UK)*, PCA case no 2011-03, Award (18 March 2015) para 212.
162 *South China Sea* (n 4) para 153.
163 Schreuer, 'What is a Legal Dispute?' (n 155) 978 et seq (emphasis added).
164 *South China Sea* (n 4) para 148.
165 ibid para 150.

aspects of the prevailing factual circumstances or the legal consequences that follow from them.

The definition of a dispute should be refined to take into account the specificities of an uncertain boundary. Based on a broad definition of 'dispute', the argument that the investor's dispute is really with one state, is unlikely to succeed as an objection to jurisdiction, because legal claims clearly exist against the respondent. Schreuer has hinted at this tautology.[166] The *South China Sea* tribunal agreed with the ICJ in *United States Diplomatic and Consular Staff in Tehran* that there are no grounds to 'decline to take cognizance of one aspect of a dispute merely because that dispute has other aspects, however important'.[167]

The finding of a dispute is objective.[168] The determination of the date of a dispute involves chronological interpretation of facts, ascertaining the nature of views expressed by the parties, and establishing the causal link between the facts and the legal issue.[169] The *Maffezini v Spain* tribunal's description of the genesis of a dispute is helpful:

> [T]here tends to be a natural sequence of events that leads to a dispute. It begins with the expression of a disagreement and the statement of a difference of views. In time these events acquire a precise legal meaning through the formulation of legal claims, their discussion and eventual rejection or lack of response by the other party. The conflict of legal views and interests will only be present in the latter stage, even though the underlying facts predate them. It has also been rightly commented that the existence of the dispute presupposes a minimum of communications between the parties, one party taking up the matter with the other, with the latter opposing the Claimant's position directly or indirectly. This sequence of events has to be taken into account in establishing the critical date for determining when under the BIT a dispute

---

166   Schreuer, 'What is a Legal Dispute?' (n 155) 978.
167   *United States Diplomatic and Consular Staff in Tehran (USA v Iran)* (Provisional Measures) [1979] ICJ Rep 7, para 22.
168   *East Timor* (n 105) 99 et seq; *Land and Maritime Boundary* (n 138) para 87; *Questions of Interpretation and Application of the 1971 Montreal Convention Arising from the Aerial Incident at Lockerbie (Libya v UK)* [1998] ICJ Rep 9, para 22; *Armed Activities on the Territory of the Congo (New Application: 2002) (DRC v Rwanda)* [2006] ICJ Rep 6, para 90.
169   Ibrahim Shihata, *The Power of the International Court to Determine Its Own Jurisdiction: Competence de la Competence* (Nijhoff 1965) 216; Anne Sheehan, 'Dispute Settlement under UNCLOS: The Exclusion of Maritime Delimitation Disputes' (2005) 24 UQLJ 165, 176.

qualifies as one covered by the consent necessary to establish ICSID's jurisdiction.[170]

4.2.3 Temporality

The critical date doctrine in international law opposes the use of evidence of self-serving conduct intended by the party concerned to improve its position after the dispute has arisen.[171] The *Maffezini v Spain* tribunal identified a 'critical date'[172] had been reached once the dispute in its technical and legal sense had begun to take shape: 'At that point, the conflict of legal views and interests came to be clearly established, leading not long thereafter to the presentation of various claims that eventually came to this Tribunal'.[173]

In two cases before the PCIJ and ICJ, it has been noted that the exact date of the dispute was not decisive but the date of the events leading to the dispute determined whether the respective Court had jurisdiction. In the *Phosphates in Morocco* case and in the *Certain Property* case, the facts for which the dispute arose were found to have predated the critical date. The objections *ratione temporis* were consequently upheld.[174] In the *Electricity Company* and in the *Right of Passage* cases, the disputes were found to have had their source in facts or situations subsequent to the critical date. The objections *ratione temporis* were consequently rejected.[175]

The tribunal in in the *Philip Morris v Australia* found that it had no jurisdiction over the dispute because Philip Morris had restructured its corporate group in February 2011 when was already a 'reasonable prospect' that a specific, foreseeable dispute would arise following the Australian government's announcement in April 2010 of its plain packaging tobacco legislation.[176]

---

170 *Maffezini v Spain*, ICSID Case no ARB/97/7, Decision on Objections to Jurisdiction (25 January 2000) para 96.
171 Robert Pietrowski, 'Evidence in International Arbitration' (2006) 22 Arb Int'l 373, 399. See also *Sanum v Laos* [2016] SGCA 57 (n 2) paras 65 et seq: 'In our judgment, the critical date doctrine remains relevant in this case when considering the various pieces of evidence that the Judge took into account. This does not mean that *any* evidence after the Critical Date is automatically inadmissible but special care would have to be taken in assessing the weight or relevance of such evidence'.
172 *Maffezini v Spain* (n 167) paras 96 et seq.
173 ibid para 98.
174 *Phosphates in Morocco (Italy v France)* [1938] PCIJ Series A/B no 74, 22 et seq; *Certain Property* (n 128) paras 41 et seq.
175 *Electricity Company of Sofia and Bulgaria (Belgium v Bulgaria)* [1939] PCIJ Ser A/B no 77; *Right of Passage over Indian Territory (Portugal v India)* (Preliminary Objections) [1957] ICJ Rep 125. See also Schreuer, 'What is a Legal Dispute?' (n 155).
176 *Philip Morris Asia Ltd (Hong Kong) v Australia*, PCA Case no 2012-12, Award on Jurisdiction and Admissibility (17 December 2015) para 586.

In every case, tribunals and courts refine international procedural rules by testing their veracity against the facts. In the context of investment disputes arising out of uncertain boundaries, the definition of a dispute would have to take on a new nuance in order to prevent parallel proceedings and double recovery.

5   Conclusion: Developing International Procedural Rules

Recent disputes illustrate some of the potential issues which could arise in relation to the extraterritorial effect of investment treaties in the context of uncertain boundaries. Judicial mechanisms to regulate parallel proceedings are being developed, including jurisdiction-regulating mechanisms, agreed coordination mechanisms, hierarchical mechanisms, first-in-time mechanisms, and general coordination mechanisms.[177] Yet, the problems presented by an investment dispute arising from an area of uncertain boundaries presents a peculiar type of parallel proceedings. In these circumstances, what legal rules should govern?

Regardless of the facts of each dispute, international law needs to formulate clear rules to address such potential parallel proceedings. Especially for maritime resources, which is not as susceptible to occupation as land, the operation of law is necessary to create marketable title.[178] Accordingly, continued uncertainty in international law represents risk and raises costs for investment and state development. Normative public international law regimes including state succession and the effect of armed conflict have been proposed. However, substantive legal regimes do not provide a fully satisfactory answer to which investment treaty is applicable.

Existing international procedural rules such as the *Monetary Gold* principle, *res judicata*, and abuse of process pave part of the way towards an organised and coherent international dispute settlement system. In addition, this chapter proposes that the key to formulating a comprehensive rule is not by a normative exploration of policy interests, but by refining international procedural rules through international counsel and tribunals. The definition

---

177   Filip De Ly and Audley Sheppard, 'ILA Interim Report on *Res Judicata* and Arbitration' (2009) 25 Arb Int'l 35, 37; Filip De Ly and Audley Sheppard, 'ILA Final Report on *Res Judicata* and Arbitration' (2009) 25 Arb Int'l 67; Wehland, 'The Regulation of Parallel Proceedings' (n 10) 580 et seq.

178   Lea Brilmayer and Natalie Klein, 'Land and Sea: Two Sovereignty Regimes in Search of a Common Denominator' (2001) 33 NYU J Int'l L & Pol'y 703, 732 et seq.

of a 'dispute'[179] in international law could be developed further when taking into account parallel disputes arising from investments in areas of uncertain boundaries. Identifying general procedural rules that could harmonize the proceedings of tribunals with parallel competing or complementary jurisdiction would promote the international rule of law by circumventing any inconsistencies arising from multiple proceedings.

Note on the Text

Any opinions expressed in this chapter are solely the author's personal views and do not represent the views of any organizations or persons associated with the author. Any description of boundaries as unsettled, contested or uncertain is merely a factual observation of events and should not be taken as a comment on its legal status.

Bibliography

Abi-Saab G, 'Negotiation and Adjudication' in L Boisson de Chazournes, M Kohen, and JE Viñuales (eds), *Diplomatic and Judicial Means of Dispute Settlement* (Nijhoff 2012).

Alvarez JE, 'Beware: Boundary Crossings' (2016) 17 JWIT 171.

Aquarone M-C, 'The 1985 Guinea/Guinea-Bissau Maritime Boundary Case and Its Implications' (1995) 26 Ocean Dev & Int'l L 413.

Ascensio H, 'Abuse of Process in International Investment Arbitration' (2014) 13 Chinese J Int'l L 763.

Aust A, *Modern Treaty Law and Practice* (2nd ed, CUP 2007).

Azarova V, 'Israel's unlawfully prolonged occupation: consequences under an integrated legal framework' (2017) European Council on Foreign Relations Policy Brief <www.ecfr.eu/publications/summary/israels_unlawfully_prolonged_occupation_7294> accessed 13 May 2020.

Berman N, '"But the Alternative Is Despair": European Nationalism and the Modernist Renewal of International Law' (1993) Harv L Rev 1792.

Bethlehem D, 'The End of Geography: The Changing Nature of the International System and the Challenge to International Law' (2014) 25 EJIL 9.

---

179 *Mavrommatis Palestine Concessions* (n 121) 11; Schreuer, 'What is a Legal Dispute?' (n 155) 961 et seq.

Bhatty S and N Lamprou, 'Pitfalls of Investing in Sub-Saharan African Regions with Unsettled Boundaries: How Foreign Investors May Minimize and Manage Investment Risk' (2016) 4 TDM.

Blackaby N and B Juratowitch, 'Hydrocarbons in Disputed Areas' (2015) 44(4) Int'l L News 1.

Blake GH and RE Swarbrick, 'Hydrocarbons and International Boundaries: A Global Overview' in GH Blake and others (eds), *Boundaries and Energy: Problems and Prospects* (Kluwer Law International 1999).

Bohmer L, 'In Now-Public Decisions, Swiss Federal Tribunal Clarifies Reasons for Dismissing Challenges to Two Crimea-Related Investment Treaty Awards against Russia' (*IAReporter*, 16 November 2018) <www.iareporter.com/articles/in-now-public-decisions-swiss-federal-tribunal-clarifies-reasons-for-dismissing-challenges-to-two-crimea-related-investment-treaty-awards-against-russia/> 12 May 2020.

Brand RA, 'Forum Non Conveniens', *Max Planck Encyclopedia of Public International Law* (2019) <https://opil.ouplaw.com/home/MPIL> accessed 14 May 2020.

Brilmayer L and Natalie N, 'Land and Sea: Two Sovereignty Regimes in Search of a Common Denominator' (2001) 33 NYU J Int'l L & Pol'y 703.

Chechi A, *The Settlement of International Cultural Heritage Disputes* (OUP 2014).

Cheng B, *General Principles of Law as Applied by International Courts and Tribunals* (Stevens 1953).

Chinese Foreign Ministry, 'Foreign Ministry Spokesperson Hua Chunying's Regular Press Conference on October 21, 2016' (21 October 2016) <www.fmprc.gov.cn/mfa_eng/xwfw_665399/s2510_665401/t1407743.shtml> accessed 12 May 2020.

Corr A, 'China May Owe the Philippines $177 Billion in South China Sea Rent & Damages' (*Forbes*, 15 July 2016) <www.forbes.com/sites/anderscorr/2016/07/15/the-philippines-should-sue-china-for-177-billion-in-south-china-sea-rent-and-damages/#d405fda60358> accessed 12 May 2020.

Craven M, 'The Problem of State Succession and the Identity of States under International Law' (1998) 9 EJIL 142.

Crawford J, *Brownlie's Principles of Public International Law* (8th ed, OUP 2012).

Cuniberti G, 'Parallel Litigation and Foreign Investment Dispute Settlement' (2006) 21 ICSID Rev 381.

Dancel R, 'Manila Wants South China Sea Outpost to Be Tourism Draw' (*Straits Times*, 17 May 2017) <www.straitstimes.com/asia/se-asia/manila-wants-s-china-sea-outpost-to-be-tourism-draw> accessed 12 May 2020.

Davenport T, 'Submarine Communications Cables and Law of the Sea: Problems in Law and Practice' (2012) 43 Ocean Dev & Int'l L 201.

De Brabandere E, '"Good Faith", "Abuse of Process" and the Initiation of Investment Treaty Claims' (2012) 3 JIDS 609.

De Ly F and A Sheppard, 'ILA Final Report on *Res Judicata* and Arbitration' (2009) 25 Arb Int'l 67.

De Ly F and A Sheppard, 'ILA Interim Report on *Res Judicata* and Arbitration' (2009) 25 Arb Int'l 35.

Dilevka S, 'Arbitration Claims by Ukrainian Investors under the Russia-Ukraine BIT: Between Crimea and a Hard Place?' (*CIS Arbitration Forum*, 17 February 2016) <www.cisarbitration.com/2016/02/17/arbitration-claims-by-ukrainian-investors-under-the-russia-ukraine-bit-between-crimea-and-a-hard-place/> accessed 13 May 2020.

Dumberry P, 'State Succession to Bilateral Treaties: A Few Observations on the Incoherent and Unjustifiable Solution Adopted for Secession and Dissolution of States under the 1978 Vienna Convention' (2014) 28 LJIL 3.

Dumberry P, 'State Succession to BITs in the Context of the Transfer of Territory of Macao to China: Lessons Learned from the *Sanum* Saga' (2018) 35 J Int'l Arb 329.

Dupont P-E, 'Conflicting Maritime Claims in the Gulf of Aden' (15 May 2017) (1) *Int'l L Gazette* 8.

Dupont P-E, 'The Not-So-Curious Case of the Western Sahara Sea' (*The Westphalian*, 13 April 2016) <https://thewestphalian.com/analysis/2016/04/13> accessed on 12 May 2020.

Feldman M, 'Setting Limits on Corporate Nationality Planning in Investment Treaty Arbitration' (2012) 27 ICSID Rev 281.

FI Shihata IFI, 'Towards a Greater Depoliticization of Investment Disputes: The Roles of ICSID and MIGA' (1986) 1 ICSID Rev 1.

Friedman T, *The World is Flat* (Farrar, Straus and Giroux 2005).

Gaffney JP, ' "Abuse of Process" in Investment Treaty Arbitration' (2010) 11 JWIT 515.

Gaillard E, 'Abuse of Process in International Arbitration' (2017) 32 ICSID Rev 17.

Galka M, 'Mapping Every Disputed Territory in the World' (*Metrocosm*, 20 November 2015) <https://metrocosm.com/mapping-every-disputed-territory-in-the-world> accessed 12 May 2020.

Gallagher N and W Shan, *Chinese Investment Treaties: Policies and Practice* (OUP 2009).

Genest A, 'Sudan Bilateral Investment Treaties and South Sudan: Musings on State Succession to Bilateral Treaties in the Wake of Yugoslavia's Breakup' (2014) 3 TDM.

Grant TD, *Aggression against Ukraine: Territory, Responsibility, and International Law* (Palgrave 2015).

Grütters D, 'Catalonia: The Right to Secede and the Right to Self-Determination' (*Oxford Human Rights Hub*, 23 October 2017) <https://ohrh.law.ox.ac.uk/catalonia-the-right-to-secede-and-the-right-to-self-determination/> accessed 12 May 2020.

Hansen R, 'Parallel Proceedings in Investor-State Treaty Arbitration: Responses for Treaty Drafters, Arbitrators and Parties' (2010) 73 MLR 523.

Happ R and S Wuschka, '*Horror Vacui*: Or Why Investment Treaties Should Apply to Illegally Annexed Territories' (2016) 33 J Int'l Arb 245.

Hart N and S Srikumar, 'Investor-State Arbitration before the High Court of Singapore: Territoriality, Nationality and Arbitrability' (2015) 4 Cambridge J Int'l & Comp L 191.

Hepburn J, 'Montenegro to Face Second Known Investment Treaty Claim, This Time over Bankrupt Steelworks' (*IAReporter*, 10 December 2012) <www.iareporter.com/articles/montenegro-to-face-second-known-investment-treaty-claim-this-time-overbankrupt-steelworks> accessed 13 May 2020.

Hernández GI, 'The Interaction between Investment Law and the Law of Armed Conflict in the Interpretation of Full Protection and Security Clause' in F Baetens (ed) *Investment Law within International Law: Integrationist Perspectives* (CUP 2012).

Hofer A, 'Sanctioning Qatar Continued: The United Arab Emirates Is Brought before the ICJ' (EJIL:Talk!, 22 June 2018) <www.ejiltalk.org/sanctioning-qatar-continued-the-united-arab-emirates-is-brought-before-the-icj/> accessed 12 May 2020.

Hofmann R, 'Annexation', *Max Planck Encyclopedia of Public International Law* (2020) <https://opil.ouplaw.com/home/MPIL> accessed 13 May 2020.

Hwang M and A Chang, '*Government of the Lao People's Democratic Republic v Sanum Investments Ltd*: A Tale of Two Letters' (2015) 30 ICSID Rev 506.

Kelsen H, *The Law of the United Nations: A Critical Analysis of Its Fundamental Problems* (first published 1951, The Lawbook Exchange 2000).

Kennedy D, 'International Law and the Nineteenth Century: History of an Illusion' (1997) 17 Quinnipiac L Rev 99.

Klabbers J, 'Cat on a Hot Tin Roof: The World Court, State Succession, and the *Gabčíkovo-Nagymaros* Case' (1998) 11 LJIL 345.

Knop K, *Diversity and Self-Determination in International Law* (CUP 2002).

Kolb R, *The International Court of Justice* (Hart 2014).

Landauer C, 'The Ever-Ending Geography of International Law: The Changing Nature of the International System and the Challenge to International Law: A Reply to Daniel Bethlehem' (2014) 25 EJIL 31.

Lathrop CG, 'Why Litigate a Maritime Boundary? Some Contributing Factors' in N Klein (ed) *Litigation International Law Disputes* (CUP 2014).

Lauterpacht H, 'The Doctrine of Non-Justiciable Disputes in International Law' [1928] (24) Economica 277.

Lowe V, '*Res Judicata* and the Rule of Law in International Arbitration' (1996) 8 Afr J Int'l & Comp L 38.

MacGibbon IC, 'Estoppel in International Law' (1958) 7 ICLQ 468.

Mälksoo L, *Illegal Annexation and State Continuity* (Brill 2003).

Mayorga O, 'Arbitrating War: Military Necessity as a Defense to the Breach of Investment Treaty Obligations' (2013) Harvard Program on Humanitarian Policy and Conflict Research Policy Brief <http://hpcrresearch.org/sites/default/files/publications/081213%20ARBITRATING%20WAR%20%28final%29.pdf> accessed 13 May 2020.

McLachlan C, *Lis Pendens in International Litigation* (Brill 2009).

Milano E and I Papanicolopulu, 'State Responsibility in Disputed Areas on Land and at Sea' (2011) Heidelberg J Int'l L 71.

Milanovic M, 'A Footnote on Secession', (*EJIL:Talk!*, 26 October 2017) <www.ejiltalk.org/a-footnote-on-secession/> accessed 12 May 2020.

Mushkat R, 'Hong Kong and Succession of Treaties' (1997) 46 ICLQ 181.

Oellers-Frahm K, 'Multiplication of International Courts and Tribunals and Conflicting Jurisdiction: Problems and Possible Solutions' (2001) 5 Max Planck UNYB 67.

Ostřanský J, 'The Termination and Suspension of Bilateral Investment Treaties Due to an Armed Conflict' (2015) 6 JIDS 136.

Pereira Coutinho F and Briosa e Gala F, 'David and Goliath Revisited' (2014) 10 Tex J Oil Gas & Energy 429.

Pietrowski R, 'Evidence in International Arbitration' (2006) 22 Arb Int'l 373.

Potestà M, 'Republic of Italy v. Republic of Cuba' (2012) 106 AJIL 341.

Qerimi Q and S Krasniqi, 'Theories and Practice of State Succession to Bilateral Treaties: The Recent Experience of Kosovo' (2013) 14 German LJ 1359.

Reinisch A, 'The Use and Limits of *Res Judicata* and *Lis Pendens* as Procedural Tools to Avoid Conflicting Dispute Settlement Outcomes' (2004) 3 L & Prac Int'l Cts & Tribunals 37.

Reinisch A, 'The Issues Raised by Parallel Proceedings and Possible Solutions' in M Waibel and others (eds), *The Backlash against Investment Arbitration* (Kluwer Law International 2010).

Repousis OG, 'Why Russian Investment Treaties Could Apply to Crimea and What Would This Mean for the Ongoing Russo–Ukrainian Territorial Conflict' (2016) 32 Arb Int'l 459.

Rosenne S, *The Law and Practice of International Court 1920–1996*, vol 3 (Nijhoff 1997).

Ross A, 'Win Declared in West African Offshore Drilling Case' (*Global Arbitration Review*, 18 July 2018) <https://globalarbitrationreview.com/article/1172083/win-declared-in-west-african-offshore-drilling-case> accessed 12 May 2020.

Ryngaert C, *Jurisdiction in International Law* (2nd edn OUP 2015).

Schermers HG and NM Blokker, *International Institutional Law: Unity within Diversity* (5th edn, Brill 2011).

Schill SW, 'W(h)ither Fragmentation? On the Literature and Sociology of International Investment Law' (2011) 22 EJIL 875.

Schreuer C, 'What is a Legal Dispute?' in I Buffard and others (eds), *International Law between Universalism and Fragmentation: Festschrift in Honour of Gerhard Hafner* (Brill 2008).

Schreuer C, 'The Protection of Investments in Armed Conflicts' in F Baetens (ed) *Investment Law within International Law: Integrationist Perspectives* (CUP 2012).

Shaw MN, *International Law* (7th ed., CUP 2014).

Sheehan A, 'Dispute Settlement under UNCLOS: The Exclusion of Maritime Delimitation Disputes' (2005) 24 UQLJ 165.

Sheppard A, 'Res Judicata and Estoppel' in BM Cremades and JDM Lew (eds), *Parallel State and Arbitral Procedures in International Arbitration* (Kluwer Law International 2005).

Shihata I, *The Power of the International Court to Determine Its Own Jurisdiction: Competence de la Competence* (Nijhoff 1965).

Shookman J, 'Too Many Forums for Investment Disputes? ICSID Illustrations of Parallel Proceedings and Analysis' (2010) 27 J Int'l Arb 361.

Sterio M, 'Self-Determination and Secession under International Law: The Cases of Kurdistan and Catalonia' (2018) 22(1) ASIL Insights <www.asil.org/insights/volume/22/issue/1/self-determination-and-secession-under-international-law-cases-kurdistan> accessed 12 May 2020.

Tams CJ, 'The Contentious Jurisdiction of the Permanent Court' in M Fitzmaurice and CJ Tams (eds), *Legacies of the Permanent Court of International Justice* (Nijhoff 2013).

Tams CJ, 'State Succession to Investment Treaties: Mapping the Issues' (2016) 31 ICSID Rev 314.

Thirlway H, 'Territorial Disputes and Their Resolution in the Recent Jurisprudence of the International Court of Justice' (2017) 31 LJIL 1.

Trinidad J, 'The Disputed Waters around Gibraltar' (2016) 86 Brit YB Int'l L 101.

UN Framework Convention on Climate Change, 'COP21 Observer Participation Page' (*United Nations Climate Change*, 2020) <https://unfccc.int/process/conferences/pastconferences/paris-climate-change-conference-november-2015/Observer-participation-in-COP-21-CMP-11> accessed 13 May 2020.

Van Logchem Y, 'Submarine Telecommunication Cables in Disputed Maritime Areas' (2014) 45 Ocean Dev & Int'l L 107.

Voss JO, *The Impact of Investment Treaties on Contracts between Host States and Foreign Investors* (Brill 2011).

Wehland H, *The Coordination of Multiple Proceedings in Investment Treaty Arbitration* (OUP 2013).

Wehland H, 'The Regulation of Parallel Proceedings in Investor-State Disputes' (2016) 31 ICSID Rev 576.

Wellens K, *Negotiations in the Case Law of the International Court of Justice: A Functional Analysis* (Routledge 2016).

Weller M, 'Secession and Self-determination in Western Europe: The Case of Catalonia' (*EJIL:Talk!*, 18 October 2017) <www.ejiltalk.org/secession-and-self-determination-in-western-europe-the-case-of-catalonia/> accessed 12 May 2020.

Williams Z, 'An Update on Disputes under the Russia-Ukraine BIT' (*IAReporter*, 6 July 2017) <www.iareporter.com/articles/an-update-on-disputes-under-the-russia-ukraine-bt/> accessed 13 May 2020.

Xu L, 'China Succeeds in Mining Combustible Ice in South China Sea' (*Xinhua*, 18 May 2017) <www.xinhuanet.com//english/2017-05/18/c_136295598.htm> accessed 12 May 2020.

Zhi Peng BT, 'The International Law Commission's Draft Articles on the Effects of Armed Conflicts on Treaties: Evaluating the Applicability of Impossibility of Performance and Fundamental Change' (2013) 3 Asian J Int'l L 51.

Zimmermann A and JG Devaney, 'Succession to Treaties and the Inherent Limits of International Law', in CJ Tams, A Tzanakopoulos, and A Zimmermann (eds), *Research Handbook on the Law of Treaties* (Edward Elgar 2014).

Živković V, 'Rethinking Interested Parties in ISDS: The Sase of 3rd States' (Kluwer Arbitration Blog, 3 December 2015) <https://arbitrationblog.kluwerarbitration.com/2015/12/03/rethinking-interested-parties-in-isds-the-case-of-3rd-states/> accessed 14 May 2020.

Zou K and Ye Q, 'Interpretation and Application of Article 298 of the Law of the Sea Convention in Recent Annex VII Arbitrations: An Appraisal' (2017) 48 Ocean Dev & Int'l L 331.

CHAPTER 8

Representation of States in Investment Arbitrations Involving Governments Competing for International Recognition

Réka A Papp

1   Introduction

Reports of decisions rendered by investment arbitral tribunals concerning the issue of which government can represent the state party in the proceedings have continually emerged during the course of 2019. The cases involved Venezuela and Yemen, but a number of investment arbitrations are also ongoing against Libya, where the same issue could arise given the continuing civil war raging in the country.[1]

These decisions were rendered in a politically charged atmosphere, where two entities were competing for the acknowledgment of the arbitral tribunals as the sole representative of the state party in the arbitral proceedings. All the entities claimed to be the legitimate representative of the state, and they all enjoyed varying degrees of recognition in the international community. Under these circumstances, it is of particular importance that arbitral tribunals tread with caution. They need to avoid undermining the legitimacy of the decision-making process and in particular accusations of politically motivated or poorly reasoned decisions.

In order to achieve this goal, a coherent legal framework for the arbitral tribunals' analysis has to be elaborated. Such framework must take into account the full legal and factual context of the issue and consider all possible sources to find workable solutions. A brief overview of the rules governing representation

---

1   See, *eg*, Tom Jones and Sebastian Perry, 'Guaidó Calls on ICSID to Take Sides' (*Global Arbitration Review*, 2 May 2019) <https://globalarbitrationreview.com/article/1190944/guaido-calls-on-icsid-to-take-sides> accessed 3 January 2020; Luke E Peterson, 'Award Looms in UNCITRAL Investment Arbitration against Yemen; in Unpublished Ruling, Arbitrators Decided Who Is Rightful Legal Representative of State' (*IAReporter*, 23 December 2019) <www.iareporter.com/articles/award-looms-in-uncitral-investment-arbitration-against-yemen-in-unpublished-ruling-arbitrators-decided-who-is-rightful-legal-representative-of-state/> accessed 12 January 2020.

in international arbitration and international adjudication reveal a complete lack of specific provisions concerning the issue of governments competing for the right to represent a state in judicial proceedings.

The issue of representation in international arbitration is a relatively straightforward one that has not caused many problems or controversies. The central concern is to guarantee the parties' freedom to choose their representatives, be that lawyers or others, as it has a direct influence on the parties' opportunity to present their case and on the way they perceive the fairness and legitimacy of the process.[2] It is true that most international conventions and national arbitration laws do not expressly guarantee the parties' right to select their representatives, but the recognition of this right is generally implied as an inherent aspect of the arbitration process.[3] Most national arbitration laws do not impose any limitations on who may represent a party,[4] and the same is true for institutional rules.[5]

An important aspect of representation is the extent of the powers conferred by the party to its representative. The proof of a representative's authority is not automatically required under all arbitration rules,[6] but the arbitral tribunal can certainly demand proof of authority at any moment during the proceedings.[7] This power, which can be said to be universally recognized, stems from the arbitral tribunal's duty to maintain the integrity of the arbitral proceedings, and in particular to safeguard the other party's rights. In case of doubt,

---

2 Gary Born, *International Commercial Arbitration* (2nd edn, Kluwer Law International 2014) 2833.
3 ibid 2835 et seq.
4 Jason Fry, Simon Greenberg, and Francesca Mazza, *The Secretariat's Guide to ICC Arbitration* (ICC 2012) para 3-668.
5 *Cf*, for instance, United Nations Commission on International Trade Law Rules (UNCITRAL Rules) art 5, International Centre for Settlement of Investment Disputes Rules (ICSID Arbitration Rules) rule 18, London Court of International Arbitration Rules (LCIA Rules) art 18.1, Singapore International Arbitration Centre Rules (SIAC Rules) art 23; Hong Kong International Arbitration Centre Administered Arbitration Rules (HKIAC Rules) art 13.6; Cairo Regional Centre for International Commercial Arbitration Rules (CRCICA Rules) art 5. The arbitration rules of the International Chamber of Commerce (ICC) and Stockholm Chamber of Commerce (SCC) contain no specific provisions concerning the issue of representation. Similarly, certain other arbitration rules, while mentioning party representatives, do not expressly regulate the parties' right to choose theirs.
6 Rule 18 of the ICSID Arbitration Rules constitutes an exception in this regard: party representatives' authority must be notified to the ICSID Secretary General.
7 *Cf*, for instance, ICC Rules art 17, UNCITRAL Rules art 5; LCIA Rules art 18.2; SIAC Rules rule 23; HKIAC Rules art 13.6; CRCICA Rules art 5; Arbitration Rules of the Common Court of Justice of the *Organisation pour l'Harmonisation en Afrique du Droit des Affaires* (OHADA Rules) art 15.

the identity and the extent of powers of a party representative are verified by the arbitral tribunal, or in certain cases by the arbitral institution, based on the proof of authority and under the law applicable to this document.[8]

The vast majority of international arbitration cases involve private parties, and national laws and institutional rules do not contain specific provisions relating to the representation of state parties. On the contrary, the rules of procedure of permanent international courts and tribunals mostly require states to be represented by agents and provide in addition the possibility to appoint other persons to assist them.[9] The International Centre for Settlement of Investment Disputes Convention Arbitration Rules (hereinafter ICSID and ICSID Rules) stand in the middle to the extent that they mention '*agents*' as possible representatives of parties, by which they clearly refer to agents representing states in arbitration proceedings, but without further details.[10] The comprehensive amendment process of the ICSID Rules launched in 2018 does not affect the corresponding provision.[11]

Agents are considered intermediaries between the state and the tribunal before which they appear.[12] The commitments they make during the proceedings bind the state, which is under the obligation to respect and act accordingly to those commitments.[13] Representation by agents in international adjudication is the norm, the appointment of agents being viewed as essential

---

[8] Despite the scarcity of authorities available on the issue, it is safe to say that the law applicable to the formal validity of a power of attorney is the law of the place of execution, and the law applicable to its substance is the law where the services are to be performed; *cf*, in this sense, Margaret R O'Sullivan, 'Conflict of Laws Issues in Drafting and Using Powers of Attorney for the Mobile Client' (2015) 35 Est Tr & Pensions J 94, 107 et seq.

[9] Statute of the International Court of Justice (ICJ) art 42; Rules of Procedure of the European Court of Human Rights (ECtHR) rule 35; Rules of Procedure of the Inter-American Court of Human Rights (IACtHR) art 23; Community Court of Justice of the Economic Community of the West African States (ECOWAS) art 12; Rules of Procedure of the Court of Justice of the European Union (CJEU) art 44(a). The Rules of the International Tribunal for the Law of the Sea refers to agents of Parties, without expressly regulating the issue of representation. Article 4 of the Rules of Procedure of the Iran-US Claims Tribunal (IUSCT) as well as rule 28 of the Rules of the African Court on Human and People's Rights grant the Parties freedom to be represented by any person of their choice.

[10] ICSID Arbitration Rules rule 18.

[11] The Proposals for the Amendment of the ICSID Rules' contains no changes in this regard, see ICSID, 'The Proposals for the Amendment of the ICSID Rules' (2020) 1(4) ICSID Working Paper, 32 et seq (rule 2) <https://icsid.worldbank.org/en/Documents/WP_4_Vol_1_En.pdf> accessed 22 March 2020.

[12] *Georges Pinson (France) v Mexico* (1928) 5 RIAA 327, para 12*bis*.

[13] *Barbados/Trinidad and Tobago* (2006) 45 ILM 800, para 291.

for the proper representation of a state.[14] It is also the default rule before the International Court of Justice (ICJ). Judge Oda, in his Separate Opinion in the *Armed Activities on the Territory of the Congo* case, even considered that when a state is represented by a private lawyer and not an agent, doubts might arise as to whether the case was brought in the interest of the state or for some other reason.[15]

Contrary to proceedings before international courts and tribunals, in investment arbitration states are almost always represented by external counsel, mostly private law firms specialising in arbitration. Agents rarely appear before investment tribunals.[16]

Before 2019, if the issue of state representation emerged at all in investment arbitration proceedings it concerned exclusively the correct identification of the entity in the state apparatus capable of representing the state.[17] For instance, in the *Diag v Czech Republic* case,[18] the investor, a Liechtenstein based business engaged in trading and processing of blood plasma, brought a claim against the Czech Ministry of Health based on a special agreement with the Czech government to arbitrate their dispute under Czech law. Claimant raised concerns about the Czech Republic's representation in the arbitration proceedings leading to the final award.[19] The arbitrators themselves had doubts about whether the Ministry of Health or the Office of the Government Representation in Property Matters was the proper representative of the Czech Republic.[20] The former considered that it had the right to represent the Czech Republic, and that the arbitral tribunal did not have the power to decide the issue based on the arbitration agreement.[21] The latter, however, stated that it was unable to refute or accept the Ministry of Health's position, and that the arbitral tribunal should determine the procedural representation of the state

---

14   Jeremy K Sharpe, 'The Agent's Indispensable Role in International Investment Arbitration' (2018) 33 ICSID Rev 675.
15   *Armed Activities on the Territory of the Congo* (DRC v Uganda) (*Provisional Measures*) (Order of 1 July 2000, Separate Opinion of Judge Oda) [2000] ICJ Rep 131, paras 8 et seq.
16   Sharpe (n 14) 676.
17   *Cf* also *Franz Sedelmayer v Russia*, Arbitration Award (7 July 1998); *cf* also the publicly not available ICSID case mentioned by Sébastian Manciaux, 'The Representation of States before ICSID Tribunals' (2011) 2 JIDS 87, 89.
18   *Diag Human SE v Czech Republic Ministry of Health*, Case no RSP 06/2003, Final Award (4 August 2008).
19   ibid para 27.
20   ibid para 34.
21   ibid para 36.

in accordance with the law.[22] In the end, the issue was finally resolved by the new Minister of Health's statement considering that the Office of the Government Representation in Property Matters was the proper representative of the Czech Republic in the arbitral proceedings.[23]

This scenario is distinct from the cases involving Libya, Yemen and Venezuela insofar as only the identity of the government entity representing the state was contested and not the identity of the government itself. In other words, there were no doubts as to the then Czech government's power to appoint an agent, the issue was which entity could act as an agent in the arbitral proceedings. Nevertheless, the *Diag v Czech Republic* case did raise crucial questions as to the applicable law and the power of the arbitral tribunals to decide on the issue.

While the situation concerning which government can legitimately represent the state in the arbitral proceedings is unprecedented, both public international law and national laws have long been confronted with the related issue of (non)-recognition of governments (section 2). Based on the approaches and solutions elaborated under these two legal systems, and taking into account the specificities of investment arbitration, it is possible to identify several avenues open to arbitral tribunals when they are called upon to decide the question of state representation in case of competing governments (section 3).

2   Recognition of Governments in (Public and Private) International Law

Since acts and commitments made by government agents representing the state in international (arbitration) proceedings bind the state itself, it becomes crucial to know which government can legitimately appoint those agents on the state's behalf. In particular, given the impact such acts and commitments might have on the interests and budget of the State not to mention on the everyday life of its population. The quest for the identity of the government through which the state, itself a nonphysical entity, acts and is represented on the international plane has been undertaken both in public international law and in private international law.

The relevance of the legal notion of recognition stems from the imperfect nature of international law: disputes concerning the existence of a state or

---

22   ibid para 37.
23   ibid para 47.

which government represents a state in international relations cannot be settled through binding judicial processes. Therefore, the position taken by other subjects of international law becomes decisive.[24] Recognition is in principle a unilateral act, although it can also be a collective act by stipulation in a treaty or by declaration by several states.[25] There is no duty to recognise a government, states therefore remain free to grant or withhold recognition from a regime even if it fulfils all necessary criteria.

It is important to specify at the outset that the recognition of governments is a distinct issue from the recognition of states. Once a state is recognized, it continues to be a state, no matter the changes, constitutional or unconstitutional, in government.[26] Consequently, and because international law is not concerned by the constitutionality of the changes in government, the issue of recognition of governments arises only in exceptional situations. Such situations can be when two or more governments compete for control and international recognition following turbulent times of internal conflict or when the previous government lost control over the territory and the apparatus of the state and there is no other entity filling the vacuum.[27]

The exact contours and the conditions of recognition of governments remain uncertain due to the lack of consistency and uniformity of state practice in the field. The situation is further aggravated by the fact that recognition has been withheld, delayed or granted for various reasons not of a legal nature. These include political, ideological, economic, strategic or other interests as well as a desire to intervene in the internal affairs of the other state or to extract promises about the new government's future actions and policy with regard to the recognising state. This has led to abuses of the tool of recognition by many states, which international law has been unable to prevent.[28] It has consequently been argued that collective recognition through an international organization such as the United Nations (hereinafter the UN) could

---

24   Jochen A Frowein, 'Recognition', *Max Planck Encyclopedia of Public International Law* (2010) paras 1, 26 <https://opil.ouplaw.com/home/MPIL> accessed 6 November 2019.
25   ibid paras 1, 4, making reference to the General Treaty for the Re-establishment of Peace (signed 30 March 1856, entered into force 27 April 1856) 114 CTS 409 (Paris Peace Treaty). See also PK Menon, 'The Problem of Recognition in International Law: Some Thoughts on Community Interest' (1990) 59 Nordic J Int'l L 247, 262.
26   *Tinoco Arbitration (Great Britain v Costa Rica)* (1923) 1 RIAA 369, 377; Menon (n 25) 252. See also in this regard Institut de Droit International, 'La reconnaissance des nouveaux Etats et des nouveaux gouvernements' (1936) 39 Annuaire de l'Institut de Droit International 300, preamble.
27   Frowein, 'Recognition' (n 24) para 14.
28   Menon (n 25) 248; Frowein, 'Recognition' (n 24) para 26.

do away with the negative consequences of the unilateral and sometimes abusive (non)-recognition of governments by individual states.[29] While developments within the UN certainly influence the position of many states, the idea of collective recognition has not been further developed or accepted in practice.

Some states, such as the UK,[30] France, Belgium or the Netherlands,[31] decided to abolish the recognition of governments, as it causes more difficulties than it is capable to resolve; essentially due to the fact that governments are often recognised for the new regime's character and policy rather than because they meet the objective criterion of effectiveness.[32] The essential objective of these states was to avoid any embarrassing confusion between recognising a government and approving of it.[33]

It is beyond the scope of this chapter to set out the full history and evolution of the doctrine and state practice relating to the recognition of governments. Nevertheless, it is possible to give a general overview of the most important aspects of the position of public international law, which is in turn essential to determine the approach investment arbitral tribunals should follow when faced with the issue of recognition of governments.

The effectiveness of the entity claiming to be the government is the single most important, and generally undisputed, condition of recognition of governments under public international law.[34] Effectiveness means being in control of at least a larger part of the territory and the administration of the state with no real risk of losing this control in the future.[35] Once established, a government fully in control of the territory should be recognised as the government of the state in question.[36] It is only under exceptional circumstances that an effective government should be denied recognition, in particular when it was set up by foreign intervention.[37] Moreover, the UN Security Council can and

---

29 Menon (n 25) 263–64.
30 *R v Reeves Taylor* [2019] WLR(D) 648, [2019] UKSC 51, [2019] 3 WLR 1073 para 58.
31 Anne Schuit, 'Recognition of Governments in International Law and the Recent Conflict in Libya' (2012) 14 Int'l Comm L Rev 381, 394.
32 Jochen A Frowein, 'De Facto Regime', *Max Planck Encyclopedia of Public International Law* (2013) para 2 <https://opil.ouplaw.com/home/MPIL> accessed 6 November 2019; MJ Peterson, 'Recognition of Governments Should Not Be Abolished' (1983) 77 AJIL 31.
33 Joe Verhoeven, 'La reconnaissance internationale, déclin ou renouveau?' (1993) 39 Annuaire français de droit international 7, 15 et seq.
34 Frowein, 'Recognition' (n 24) para 15.
35 Ibid.
36 ibid para 17; Menon (n 25) 254; Institut de droit international (n 26) art 10.
37 Jochen A Frowein, 'Non-Recognition', *Max Planck Encyclopedia of Public International Law* (2011) para 2 <https://opil.ouplaw.com/home/MPIL> accessed 6 November 2019.

has decided, for instance with respect to Haiti[38] and Sierra Leone,[39] that the overthrow of an established government amounts to a threat to the peace in the sense of article 39 of the UN Charter. In these cases, the Security Council ordered the reinstatement of the previous government, without regard to the effectiveness of the new regimes.

However, states often cite other criteria to justify their decision to grant or to refuse recognition to a foreign government, even when it has established effective control over the territory. These include the consent or acquiescence by the people and the new government's willingness to comply with its international obligations.[40]

Recognition of a new government can be definite and complete (*de jure*) as well as provisional or limited (*de facto*).[41] *De jure* recognition means that the recognising state acknowledges the coming into being of the new government and accepts it as the entity capable of representing fully its state in international relations.[42] States can only recognise one government *de jure* as there can only be one depository of the state's sovereignty.[43]

De facto recognition on the other hand is more difficult to grasp, since its extent can vary depending on the recognising state's interests and can encompass a large number of dealings and contacts between the *de facto* government and the recognising state. In essence, *de facto* recognition expresses the recognising state's willingness to have certain relations with the foreign entity, which can mean a lot or very little.[44] States can recognise several competing regimes or an emerging authority *de facto* while still maintaining *de jure* recognition of the established government.[45]

Reasons for granting *de facto* recognition can be as manifold as its manifestations. In situations where there is uncertainty about whether the newly formed and otherwise effective government would endure or when other more general political interests are at stake, *de facto* recognition is a pragmatic solution enabling the recognising state to carry on its relations with the other state without compromising its interests.

---

38   UNSC Res 841 (16 June 1993) UN Doc S/Res/841, 1 et seq; UNSC Res 940 (31 July 1994) UN Doc S/Res/940, 1 et seq.
39   UNSC Res 1132 (8 October 1997) UN Doc S/Res/ 1132, 1 et seq.
40   Frowein, 'Recognition' (n 24) para 16; Menon (n 25) 253.
41   Institut de Droit International (n 26) art 11.
42   Stefan Talmon, *Recognition of Governments in International Law: With Particular Reference to Governments in Exile* (OUP 2001) 67.
43   ibid 105.
44   ibid 82.
45   ibid 105.

Recognition can be explicit or implied, the latter being more frequent. Recognition can take the form of an express declaration or any other fact that clearly indicates the state's intention to accord recognition to the foreign entity.[46] There are no rules to the modes of recognition, and *de facto* as well as *de jure* recognition have been granted through express declarations or conduct.[47] However, *de jure* recognition is generally granted through direct communication by the recognising state to the foreign government or by way of public announcement.[48] For instance, in the case of the National Transitional Council (NTC) in Libya, the UK that only recognises countries but not governments, expressly stated via the then Foreign Secretary that it no longer recognised Gaddafi regime diplomats as the representatives of the Libyan government, and invited the NTC to appoint a new Libyan diplomatic envoy to take over the Libyan embassy in London.[49] This amounts to a withdrawal of the recognition of the Gadaffi government and the full recognition of the NTC. France and the United Arab Emirates made similarly clear declarations in June 2011 to recognise the NTC as the sole governmental authority in Libya.[50] It is of course an entirely different question whether these recognitions were warranted under international law, as the effectiveness of the NTC in June 2011 was far from being established, Gaddafi's forces still controlling the Western parts of the country and the capital.[51]

There is no exhaustive list of acts that might imply recognition, which should be established based on all the available evidence. In general, it can be said that the forms of conduct that are excluded with a government not recognised *de jure* are the conclusion of a formal bilateral treaty on political matters, final settlements of claims and establishment of formal diplomatic relations.[52] However, given the increased international cooperation in many fields and the great expansion of multilateral relations, non-recognised governments in multilateral organisations and conferences will not be ignored. Diplomats and consuls will pursue a wide variety of negotiations and conclude agreements in particular in technical fields and matters, and even political agreements could be possible with a non-recognised government if expressed informally, such as

---

46 Institut de Droit International (n 26) art 12.
47 Talmon (n 42) 47.
48 Menon (n 25) 259.
49 'UK Expels Gaddafi Diplomats and Recognises Libya Rebels' (*BBC News*, 27 July 2011) <www.bbc.com/news/uk-politics-14306544> accessed 15 January 2020.
50 Schuit (n 31) 396.
51 ibid.
52 Peterson (n 32) 34.

in a press statement or during a state visit.[53] Even the willingness to enter into diplomatic relations or to exchange diplomatic representatives are not necessarily exclusive to situations of *de jure* recognition.[54]

Today, states increasingly avoid proceeding to the recognition of governments and will simply establish a relationship with the entity in question through concrete dealings.[55] As a consequence, it has been argued that the distinction between *de jure* and *de facto* recognition has in fact lost most of its significance.[56]

It follows from the above that the position of public international law concerning the recognition of governments is of limited usefulness given the extreme variations in state practice. In particular, in light of the position of public international law according to which each state is free to choose its political, social and economic system, it is difficult to conceive that the recognition of a state's government could be subject to conditions or anyone's recognition.[57] Notwithstanding the numerous uncertainties surrounding the recognition of governments, effectiveness emerges as a universally accepted, or at least desirable, criterion of a government capable of representing the state in international relations.

2.1 Position of International Judicial Bodies on the (Non)-Recognition of Governments

The question of which government can legitimately represent the state in international relations is not exclusive to state practice. This issue has also been dealt with in international adjudication.

The most relevant decision to the present chapter's subject was rendered in the *Tinoco Arbitration* opposing Great Britain and Costa Rica, dealing with the validity of two contracts entered into by the Tinoco government of Costa Rica and British companies.[58] The sole arbitrator who decided the case, William H Taft, was at the time Chief Justice of the United States and had held the office of President of the United States before. His jurisdiction was based on a treaty of arbitration between Costa Rica and Great Britain concluded in 1922.[59]

---

53 ibid.
54 Talmon (n 42) 72–73, 75–76.
55 Frowein, 'Recognition' (n 24) para 17.
56 ibid.
57 Joe Verhoeven, 'Relations internationales de droit privé en l'absence de reconnaissance d'un État, d'un gouvernement ou d'une situation' (1985) 192 Recueil des Cours 25.
58 *Tinoco Arbitration* (n 26).
59 ibid 375.

The Tinoco government came into power in 1917 by overthrowing the previous one. It assumed undisputed power, called elections and established a new constitution.[60] The Tinoco government fell in 1919; many states, including Great Britain, having never recognized it.[61] In 1922, the newly restored government passed a law invalidating all contracts entered into by the Tinoco government.[62]

In the arbitration, Great Britain maintained that the Tinoco government was, for two years, the *de facto* and *de jure* government of Costa Rica with the acquiescence of its people and with no other government disputing its authority.[63] In response, Costa Rica contended that the Tinoco government and its acts were in violation of the Constitution of Costa Rica of 1871, and therefore the contracts this government concluded were void.[64]

The sole arbitrator first assessed whether the Tinoco government could be considered the *de facto* government of Costa Rica under public international law, capable of assuming binding obligations on behalf of the state of Costa Rica. The sole arbitrator relied on several public international law authorities and concluded that such a *de facto* government exists when it has taken the place of the regularly constituted authorities, and is 'sufficiently established to give reasonable assurance of its permanence, and of the acquiescence of those who constitute the state in its ability to maintain itself, and discharge its internal duties and its external obligations'.[65]

In response to one of Costa Rica's arguments, the sole arbitrator conceded that 'recognition by other Powers is an important evidential factor in establishing proof of the existence of a government in the society of nations'.[66] He added however that when such non-recognition is determined by 'inquiry, not into its de facto sovereignty and complete governmental control, but into its illegitimacy or irregularity of origin, their non-recognition loses something of evidential weight on the issue with which those applying the rules of international law are alone concerned'.[67] The sole arbitrator thus considered that the non-recognition of the Tinoco government by the United States and her then allies Great Britain, France and Italy, independently of the underlying reasons,

---

60 ibid 376.
61 ibid 377.
62 ibid 376.
63 ibid 377.
64 ibid.
65 ibid 378.
66 ibid 380.
67 ibid 381.

could not outweigh the evidence on record demonstrating that the Tinoco government was the *de facto* government of Costa Rica during the relevant period of time.[68]

While the reasoning of the sole arbitrator remains valid as well as convincing and his conclusions well-established under public international law, it must be noted that the situation he faced was more straightforward than the one investment tribunals are confronted with today. The Tinoco government was the *only* effective government of the state, with no other government competing for the control over the territory of the state and international recognition. Nevertheless, the decision points out several fundamental considerations with respect to the recognition of governments, and also draws attention to an important aspect of the problem, to which we will return, namely evidentiary difficulties.

Relevant decisions by other international judicial bodies generally do not directly concern the question of recognition, but rather the effects of non-recognition. In this respect, the ICJ's advisory opinion on the *Legal Consequences for States of the Continued Presence of South Africa in Namibia (South West Africa) Notwithstanding Security Council Resolution 276 (1970)*[69] declares an important principle:

> The non-recognition of South Africa's administration of the Territory should not result in depriving the people of Namibia of any advantages derived from international co-operation. In particular, while official acts performed by the Government of South Africa on behalf of or concerning Namibia after the termination of the Mandate are illegal and invalid, this invalidity cannot be extended to those acts, such as, for instance, the registration of births, deaths and marriages, the effects of which can be ignored only to the detriment of the inhabitants of the Territory.

The ICJ has thus placed emphasis on the protection of the individual inhabitants' rights and interests in order to ensure that their everyday lives remain as undisturbed as possible regardless of the international standing of the authority governing the territory.[70]

---

68   ibid.
69   *Legal Consequences for States of The Continued Presence of South Africa in Namibia (South West Africa) Notwithstanding Security Council Resolution 276 (1970)* (Advisory Opinion) [1971] ICJ Rep 16, 125.
70   On the relevance of the ICJ's *Namibia* Opinion for the application of investment treaties in occupied territories, see Kit De Vriese, chapter 10 in this volume, 329–330 and 343, and Stefan Lorenzmeier, chapter 11 in this volume, 363, 376, and 379.

The European Court of Human Rights (ECtHR) took a similar stance in the *Demopoulos v Turkey* case when it decided that local remedies established by the legislation in Northern Cyprus have to be exhausted before a case can be brought before it. The ECtHR reasoned as follows:

> In the Court's view, the key consideration is to avoid a vacuum which operates to the detriment of those who live under the occupation, or those who, living outside, may claim to have been victims of infringements of their rights. Pending resolution of the international dimensions of the situation, the Court considers it of paramount importance that individuals continue to receive protection of their rights on the ground on a daily basis.
>
> [...] the Court considers that, if there is an effective remedy available for their complaints provided under the auspices of the respondent Government, the rule of exhaustion applies under Article 35 § 1 of the Convention. As has been consistently emphasised, this conclusion does not in any way put in doubt the view adopted by the international community regarding the establishment of the 'TRNC' [Turkish Republic of Northern Cyprus] or the fact that the government of the Republic of Cyprus remains the sole legitimate government of Cyprus. The Court maintains its opinion that allowing the respondent State to correct wrongs imputable to it does not amount to an indirect legitimisation of a regime unlawful under international law.[71]

The ECtHR, while also being mindful of managing its caseload, acknowledged the importance of not ignoring the reality in which people live as well as the need to preserve the efficacy of the protection provided by the European Convention on Human Rights, independently of the international non-recognition of the regime governing the territory. In particular, when the situation will in all likelihood remain unchanged in the future.

As will be shown below, national courts have long been preoccupied by the protection of private interests and the efficacy of their proceedings when deciding what consequences to draw from the non-recognition of governments.

2.2 *Recognition of Governments in Domestic Legal Proceedings: the Approach of National Judges*

Domestic courts have encountered the issue of recognition of governments considerably more frequently than international judicial bodies, but in a different context.

---

71 *Demopoulos v Turkey*, App no 46113/99 (ECtHR, 1 March 2010) para 96.

It is true that the conduct of domestic courts is attributable to the state and can trigger its international responsibility. In the context of recognition of governments, this could be the case if domestic courts explicitly recognised a government established by foreign intervention. Moreover, domestic court decisions could play a role under article 38(1)(d) of the ICJ Statute to confirm a rule, custom or general principle of international law.[72] In this regard, the position of domestic courts concerning the recognition of foreign governments can carry a certain weight under public international law.

However, national judges do not have the power to bind the state in international relations. Whatever their decision concerning the standing of a foreign government, this cannot be conceived as the expression of the official position of their state in international relations.

Decisions of national courts concern the effects of (non)-recognition of a government on the rights and obligations flowing from private relationships. Nonetheless, national courts still have to answer the preliminary question of whether the government in question has been or should be recognised. In this respect, the central issue has rather been the extent of the autonomy national judges enjoy when they have to decide this preliminary question. Put differently: do national courts have to blindly follow the position taken by their respective states concerning the effectiveness of a foreign government? And independently from the answer to this question, what effects can they attach to the (non)-recognition of governments in private relationships?

When it comes to the answer to the first question, at first glance, there seems to be a considerable divide between civil law and common law jurisdictions. Courts in civil law countries enjoy complete autonomy to assess the evidence brought before them as to whether a foreign government has indeed been recognised – and with what effect – by the executive branch of their respective states.[73] On the contrary, courts in common law countries must accept the facts as attested by the executive branch, by way of Foreign Office certificates (UK) and executive certificates or suggestions (US), which in fact means total submission to the political choices of their government in matters of recognition in order to avoid any embarrassment that incongruences between the positions of the executive branch and the judiciary might cause. Despite the limitations on their power to assess certain facts, the independence

---

72   Mads Andenas and Johann R Leiss, 'The Systemic Relevance of "Judicial Decisions" in Article 38 of the ICJ Statute' (2017) 77 Heidelberg J Int'l L 907, 947 et seq, 951.
73   Verhoeven, 'Relations internationales' (n 57) 29.

of the judiciary remains intact in common law countries, too; judges interpret and apply the law in complete autonomy and it is only on the factual plane that their hands are tied.[74] In other words, they have to accept the executive branch's position as to whether a foreign government has been recognised, but they will draw the legal consequences of the (non)-recognition in the case before them as they see fit.

As already explained above, the judiciary does not have the power to recognise or to refuse recognition to a foreign government. Once the executive branch granted or denied recognition, whether it seems justified or not, the judiciary cannot overrule that decision and must abide by it. In this respect, there is no difference between common or civil law jurisdiction. Several recent court decisions illustrate this principle.

In the context of an investment arbitration, the US Court of Appeals for the District of Columbia Circuit held in May 2019 that it was bound by the decision of the executive branch of the United States, which recognised Juan Guaidó as Interim President of Venezuela.[75] Venezuela was opposing the confirmation of an investment arbitration award rendered in favour of a Canadian gold mining company by an arbitral tribunal seated in France under the ICSID Additional Facility Rules. During the proceedings before the Court of Appeals, the administration of Nicolás Maduro requested the court to bar Guaidó and his representatives from arguing the appeal on behalf of Venezuela.[76]

The Court of Appeals considered, based on precedent, that the question of which government is to be regarded as the representative of a foreign state was of a political rather than a judicial nature; and that the executive branch's decision to recognise a foreign government was conclusive on all US courts. The Court of Appeals further remarked that only governments recognised by the United States could have access to the domestic courts, *ie* no other government could bring and maintain a suit in the US courts.[77] As a consequence, and due to the fact that on 23 January 2019, the executive branch recognized Guaidó as the Interim President of Venezuela,[78] the Maduro administration's request was

---

74   ibid 30–31.
75   *Rusoro Mining Ltd v Venezuela*, no 18–7044, Order (DC Cir, 1 May 2019).
76   ibid 1.
77   ibid.
78   Statement from President Donald J Trump Recognizing Venezuelan National Assembly President Juan Guaidó as the Interim President of Venezuela (23 January 2019) <www.whitehouse.gov/briefings-statements/statement-president-donald-j-trump-recognizing-venezuelan-national-assembly-president-juan-guaido-interim-president-venezuela/> accessed 13 December 2019.

rejected.[79] The Court of Appeals' decision was followed by the United States District Court for the District of Columbia in two other cases where it had to address the question of legal representation of Venezuela.[80]

Similarly, when Colonel Gaddafi's government disputed the NTC's right to act on behalf of Libya's Economic Social and Development Fund before the *Tribunal administratif de Paris*,[81] this latter followed and did not question the French government's position to consider the NTC as the only holder of governmental authority in the relations between France and the Libyan state.[82] The *Tribunal administratif de Paris* reasoned that the act of legal and political recognition of the NTC as the sole holder of Libyan governmental authority is inseparable from the conduct of France's international relations and therefore escapes judicial review.

It follows from the above that the freedom civil law judges enjoy compared to common law judges concerns only the assessment of a potential implied recognition of a foreign government and the facts that could attest it. In reality, judges in civil law countries will also often adhere to the executive branch's view.[83] In this respect, the difference in practice between common law and civil law jurisdictions is less pronounced than it would seem at first, except when the executive branch's position goes against an obvious fact, in which case civil law judges can and will diverge from it and proceed to their own appreciation of the facts.[84]

The second set of difficulties national judges encounter concerns the effects to be attached to the non-recognition of governments; the situation being straightforward once a government has been granted recognition by the executive branch of the judge's home state. States enjoy considerable autonomy in the matter, which can lead to divergent outcomes from one country to another.

The issue of participation by a non-recognised government in national proceedings is of particular relevance for the topic of this chapter. Despite some

---

79 *Rusoro Mining Ltd v Venezuela*, Order (n 75) 2.
80 *OI European Group v Venezuela*, no 16-cv-1533, Memorandum Opinion (DDC, 21 May 2019); *OI European Group v Venezuela*, no 16-cv-01533, Memorandum Opinion and Order (DDC, 1 November 2019).
81 TA Paris, Ordonnance du 25 juillet 2011, n°1111788.
82 Statement by the Minister of State, Minister of Foreign and European Affairs, Alain Juppé (7 June 2011) <https://uk.ambafrance.org/LIBYE-Le-Conseil-national-de> accessed 20 December 2019. This Statement specifies that '*Le Conseil national de transition est le seul titulaire de l'autorité gouvernementale, dans les rapports de la France avec l'État libyen et les entités qui relèvent de celui-ci*'.
83 Verhoeven, 'Relations internationales' (n 57) 36.
84 ibid.

shifts in the position of national courts, the general rule widely followed by judges both in civil and in common law jurisdictions, remains that only governments recognised by the executive branch can appear before national courts.[85] It does not matter whether the government is effective or whether diplomatic relations have been broken off with the government is question, as long as recognition has not been withdrawn or granted, the non-recognised government cannot take part in national legal proceedings.

In all other matters, which range from issues of entry into force of treaties to state immunity, validity of death and marriage certificates, conflict of laws and jurisdictions as well as interpretation and application of contractual provisions, positions of national courts vary on a large spectrum. At one end of the spectrum, Swiss judges consider consequently only the effectiveness of the foreign government when it comes to applying its laws or decisions, even if the Swiss government did not grant recognition to the foreign entity.[86] At the other end of the spectrum, US courts adapt their decisions to the interests of the executive branch, which is solely responsible for conducting international relations.[87] It has to be noted that the above conclusions paint a general picture of the different national approaches, which in reality are more nuanced, with possible divergences within the positions of national laws themselves.

Despite the divergences of national case law, two general tendencies can be identified with reasonable certainty. On the one hand, there was a considerable shift towards the application of the criterion of effectiveness, be that of laws, authorities or decisions, and away from considerations of legitimacy or non-recognition.[88] It is indeed understandable, since it is difficult to ignore the reality of the facts that influence private relations in a given country only in order to give effect to a policy of non-recognition adopted by the executive branch on the international plane. The criterion of effectiveness becomes immediately relevant if the executive branch persists in denying recognition to a foreign government that is the effective governing authority in the country. However, in such cases, the judge will have to ascertain the reality of the foreign entity's effectiveness, which can prove to be an extremely difficult task. First, as explained above, determining whether

---

85   ibid 61.
86   *VEB Carl Zeiss Jena v Firma Carl Zeiss Heidenheim*, Swiss Federal Tribunal, Decision (30 March 1965) ATF 91 II 117 para II.4.
87   *Rusoro Mining Ltd v Venezuela*, Order (n 75), *OI European Group v Venezuela*, Memorandum Opinion (n 80), *OI European Group v Venezuela*, Memorandum Opinion and Order (n 80).
88   Verhoeven, 'Relations internationales' (n 57) 108–109, 115, 180–181.

there has been recognition and to what extent by the executive branch under public international law can already be a challenge. And second, in case of non-recognition, national judges do not have at their disposal the necessary tools to collect proof of an entity's effectiveness, which in any event can be almost impossible to demonstrate, in particular without the help of the executive branch.[89]

On the other hand, the majority of national judges take into account first and foremost the need to protect private persons and their interests when determining the consequences of non-recognition, which has proven to be an important corrective mechanism, in particular in the face of overly formalistic approaches.[90] The need to protect private interests can manifest itself in many ways, for instance by giving effect to birth and death certificates issued by a non-recognised entity,[91] applying the law of such an entity because it governs the everyday life of people on the territory or interpreting and applying contractual clauses in accordance with the parties' will and with little or no regard to the position of public international law.[92]

It seems, based on the above observations, that national judges increasingly dissociate themselves from the position of public international law in matters of recognition of governments or even placing private international law over public international law.[93] It is however a natural response to the undefined and unsettled nature of recognition under public international law, and to the fact that public international law does not provide answers to problems that arise in private international law and which national judges have to face.[94] National judges had to elaborate solutions that allow the regulation of private relationships in an international context, with regard to the reality in which these private relationships and interests exist and operate, and which by extension allow private international law to fulfil its function. It is unfortunate that as a consequence the coordination between public international law and private international law has become an illusion in matters of recognition, but as long as the position of public international law remains the same, there cannot be any change without sacrificing essential private international law considerations.

---

89 ibid 191 et seq.
90 ibid 92, 183.
91 ibid 149.
92 A typical example would be clauses that attach certain consequences to times of war, internal turmoil or government measures; ibid 166 et seq.
93 See in this regard ibid 186 et seq.
94 See in this regard ibid 187 et seq.

3   Competing Governments in Investment Arbitration Proceedings

The specific issue of state representation investment arbitral tribunals have been facing with respect to Libya, Venezuela and Yemen presents a real conundrum both from a theoretical and a practical point of view. The issue is narrow and specific: which government can represent the state and appoint agents and counsels in the arbitration proceedings on its behalf? The state which is party to the proceedings does not change, since the legal personality of each state once recognised under international law remains unaffected by changes of government. However, states are abstract entities capable of acting only through an agent. This agent is the government through which a state carries out its international relations, communicates, as well as fulfils obligations and asserts rights in arbitration proceedings.

The solutions public and private international law have to offer in matters of recognition of governments are only partially transposable into the sphere of international investment arbitration, essentially due to its hybrid nature and the specific task with which the arbitral tribunal is entrusted.

Arbitral tribunals that are called upon to decide which government can represent the state in the arbitral proceedings must first embark on answering a number of preliminary questions before elaborating concrete solutions and rendering a decision.

3.1   *Preliminary Issues*

The first preliminary inquiry is a fundamental one: does the arbitral tribunal have the power to even decide on the issue of representation of the state party in the proceedings? In a letter sent to ICSID's Secretary General on 29 April 2019, Venezuelan special attorney general José Ignacio Hernández, appointed by Guaidó, argued that the determination as to which is the legitimate government of Venezuela is not a 'procedural question' and therefore does not fall within the jurisdiction of individual arbitral tribunals and annulment committees to decide as they wish. He considered that only ICSID itself had the authority to resolve the matter and that all pending cases at the Centre that concern Venezuela were to be suspended until it had done so.[95]

Contrary to the special attorney's position, investment arbitral tribunals, whether constituted under the ICSID Convention and Arbitration Rules or otherwise, do have the power and the duty to decide which government represents the state party in the arbitral proceedings.

---

95   Jones and Perry (n 1).

Several ICSID arbitral tribunals have found that they possess inherent powers to deal with any issues necessary for the exercise of their jurisdiction, independently of any statutory reference.[96] In particular, they considered that an investment tribunal 'as a judicial formation governed by public international law [...] has an inherent power to take measures to preserve the integrity of its proceedings'.[97] In other words, arbitral tribunals must be able to prevent the frustration of the proceedings before them and effectively perform their judicial function.

It is not always straightforward to discern a threat to the essential integrity of the arbitral process. It is also true that absent express provisions allowing the arbitral tribunal to determine the representative of a party, the exercise of inherent powers should be rare and carried out only in compelling circumstances.[98] The existence of two or more competing governments all claiming the right to represent the state party in the arbitral proceedings is most certainly a compelling circumstance that threatens the arbitral tribunal's task to render justice and it also violates the other party's right to a fair trial, who cannot be required to answer to several potentially different positions that the competing governments might have in the proceedings. In addition, if the representation of a party in the proceedings remains unclear, it can lead to the annulment of the arbitral award on grounds of violation of the parties' procedural rights. For instance, article 52(1)(a) of the ICSID Convention provides that either party may request annulment of an award on the ground 'that the tribunal was not properly constituted'. If a government not having the power to represent the state appointed a member of the arbitral tribunal, the other party could invoke the improper constitution of the tribunal in the annulment proceedings.[99] All these circumstances taken together justify not only the possibility for the arbitral tribunals to exercise their inherent powers, but it also creates a duty for them to definitely determine the government that has the sole right to represent the state party in the proceedings before them.

---

96 *Hrvatska Elektroprivreda dd v Slovenia*, ICSID Case no ARB/05/24, Tribunal's Ruling Regarding the Participation of David Mildon QC in Further Stages of the Proceedings (6 May 2008) para 33; *Rompetrol Group NV v Romania*, ICSID Case no ARB/06/3, Decision of the Tribunal on the Participation of a Counsel (14 January 2010) para 16; see also in this regard *Interocean Development Company and Interocean Oil Exploration Co v Nigeria*, ICSID Case no ARB/13/20, Procedural Order no 5 on the Claimants' Requests Regarding (i) the Authority of Volterra Fietta Lawyers to Represent the Respondent and (ii) the Source and Terms of the Funding of the Respondent's Defence (15 October 2016) para 67.
97 *Hrvatska Elektroprivreda dd v Slovenia* (n 96) para 33.
98 *Rompetrol Group NV v Romania* (n 96) para 16.
99 Manciaux (n 17) 90.

The existence of inherent powers can equally be deduced from institutional rules,[100] which generally allow arbitral tribunals to decide all questions of procedure that might arise, and which are not governed by the *lex arbitri*, the institutional rules or the parties' agreement. The representation of the parties before the arbitral tribunal is a procedural question, intrinsically linked to the protection of the parties' fundamental procedural rights and thus to the integrity of the arbitral proceedings. This approach has been confirmed by the ICSID Annulment Committee in the *Valores v Venezuela* case.[101] The Annulment Committee held that the question put before them is of limited scope, namely who is empowered to exercise binding procedural acts on behalf of Venezuela in the annulment proceedings.[102] This being a purely procedural issue, the members of the Annulment Committee considered that 'under the provisions of Arts. 44 and 52(4) of the ICSID Convention, and by Rules 19 and 53, the Committee has sufficient powers to resolve the question [sic] Venezuela's procedural representation in this procedure, insofar as the clarification of the point is absolutely necessary for the continuation of the proceedings'.[103]

The Venezuelan special attorney general further argued that the arbitral tribunals' decision on the representation of the Venezuelan state in the arbitral proceedings would mean that these tribunals decide on the international representation of Venezuela and the legitimacy of its government. However, the special attorney general misunderstands the purpose and the scope of the decision an investment arbitral tribunal can take with respect to the recognition of governments. It has been argued in scholarly writings with respect to national courts that a distinction has to be made between recognition of a government as the representative of the state in international relations and the recognition of a government as party to the proceedings; the former being the privilege of the executive branch, but the latter depending solely on the appreciation of the judge based on objective criteria.[104]

While the persuasiveness of this argument might be debated in a purely national context, it is entirely convincing and appropriate when it is transposed to international arbitration. As explained above, recognition of governments is a unilateral act of states whereby they accept to establish international

---

100 As well as from article 44 of the ICSID Convention.
101 *Valores Mundiales SL and Consorcio Andino SL v Venezuela,* ICSID Case no ARB13/11 – Annulment Proceedings Procedural Resolution no 2 (29 August 2019).
102 ibid paras 31–32.
103 ibid 34.
104 Verhoeven, 'Relations internationales' (n 57) 67 making reference to the work of R de Murait.

relations with the government in question. It is undisputed that investment tribunals do not have the authority to decide with which government states will enter into relations. An investment arbitral tribunal's task is to decide the individual dispute submitted to it and to render justice. It is responsible for safeguarding and enforcing both the investor's and the host state's rights by taking into account both of their interests. It is therefore the arbitral tribunal's duty to decide upon all issues necessary to carry out the task entrusted to it by the parties, including deciding which government can represent the state party in the arbitral proceedings.

This decision will only be rendered for the purposes of the arbitral proceedings and will only bind the parties in the context of the proceedings and the award rendered in the proceedings. This is no different from the situation where national courts, despite the executive branch's policy of non-recognition, give effect to laws or acts of a certain regime in order to decide the case before them and to protect the parties' rights.[105] It is true, however, that an arbitral tribunal's decision as to the government that can represent the state party in the proceedings might have a reach beyond the specific arbitral proceedings. For instance, similarly to national court decisions, decisions by arbitral tribunals can be taken into account under article 38(1)(d) of the ICJ Statute.[106]

Another related aspect of the Venezuelan special attorney general's position is his assertion that the question of who can legitimately represent the Venezuelan state in ICSID arbitrations should be decided by the ICSID, an international organisation, and not the individual arbitral tribunals. The special attorney general essentially suggests that there is an entity out there that can decide with binding force on the recognition of governments, and that investment arbitral tribunals should follow the position of such entity. Unfortunately, no such international body exist and there are no binding judicial processes to recognise governments under international law. States would have to specifically empower any international organisation to decide on such matters, which to our knowledge has never been done, and certainly not in relation to the ICSID.

It is equally erroneous to argue that for non-ICSID arbitral tribunals the position of the country of the seat should determine their attitude towards the recognition of governments. This would mean that depending on where

---

[105] In the *Hesperides Hotels v Aegean Holidays Ltd* case, Lord Denning expressly stated that 'the courts of this country can recognise the laws or acts of a body which is in effective control of a territory even though it has not been recognized by Her Majesty's Government de jure or de facto'; *Hesperides Hotels v Aegean Holidays Ltd* [1978] QB 205, 218.
[106] Andenas and Leiss (n 72) 952.

the arbitral tribunal is seated, another government would represent the state in the arbitral proceedings. For instance, if an investment arbitration involving Venezuela were seated in the US or the UK, the special attorney general appointed by Guaidó would represent the state. But were the same arbitration seated in Bolivia or Turkey, no matter how unlikely such a scenario is, Maduro's attorney general would represent the state. In addition, if the same arbitration had a seat in any country of the European Union or Switzerland, in absence of an official position by the executive branch of these countries, the arbitrators would have to decide this question on their own.

The law of the seat determines the general procedural framework of an arbitration and gives nationality to the award for the purposes of the New York Convention of 1958. Courts of the seat will also exercise control over the arbitral award in set aside proceedings. However, the role of the seat does not go beyond these aspects of the arbitration. International arbitral tribunals are not courts of the seat, nor can they be bound by the position of the executive branch in the country of the seat. Considering otherwise would mischaracterise the nature and the purpose of international arbitral tribunals. As a consequence, arbitral tribunals cannot rely on the position adopted by the courts or the government of the country of the seat. There is only one caveat to this conclusion: the international public policy of the seat might set certain boundaries when it comes to the recognition of governments. In principle it is unlikely that international public policy would be triggered by anything less than recognising a government that was set up by foreign intervention or the existence of which was declared a threat to the peace by the UN Security Council, in particular in arbitration-friendly jurisdictions. Similarly, the recognition of the government of the host state by the other state party to the applicable bilateral investment treaty or by state parties to the applicable multilateral treaty is irrelevant to the arbitral tribunal's decision. In any event, given the considerable divergences in state practice when it comes to the recognition of foreign governments, the usefulness of referring to any country's position on this matter is highly doubtful.

Finally, arbitral tribunals are not obliged to abide by decisions rendered by other arbitral tribunals concerning the recognition of governments. In absence of a binding system of precedent in international arbitration, decisions and awards of arbitral tribunals have binding force only between the parties. There is no obligation for arbitral tribunals to follow the positions adopted by other tribunals on any given legal or factual issue; but they are free to do so if they find the previous decision persuasive. Therefore, it is true that different arbitral tribunals might arrive to different conclusions concerning the question which government can represent a given state in the proceedings before them. While this outcome is not desirable, it is inevitable in the system of international arbitration where individual tribunals decide individual disputes and cease to exist once they carry out their mission. Consequently, investment arbitral tribunals are left to their own devices to decide which government to recognise for the purposes of their proceedings.

3.2 Applicable Law and the Criterion of Effectiveness

This brings us to the second main issue arbitral tribunals will have to resolve after having established that they have the power and the duty to decide on their own about the representation of the state in the proceedings: which law should be applied to the question of recognition of governments? There are two possibilities: the law of the country in question or public international law. While municipal law will determine which organ, such as for instance the attorney general, the Minister for Finance or the Ministry of Justice will represent the state as an agent in the arbitration proceedings and with what authority;[107] it cannot answer the question through which government the state can act in the arbitral proceedings or on the international plane.[108]

This can be illustrated by reference to the situation in Venezuela as it developed in 2019. According to article 15(b) of the 'Statute that governs the Transition to Democracy to Re-establish the Full Force and Effect of the Constitution of the Bolivarian Republic of Venezuela', adopted by the National Assembly, Maduro ceased to hold office as President of Venezuela on 10 January 2019 and Guaidó became Interim President of Venezuela. However, according to Maduro, on 8 February 2019, this law was declared null and void under Venezuelan law by the Constitutional Chamber of the *Tribunal Supremo de Justicia* (Republic's Supreme Court of Justice). Guaidó does not deny the truth of this but considers that the *Tribunal Supremo de Justicia* is not a legitimate body of the Republic, its judges having allowed usurpation and violation of human rights. Under these circumstances, municipal law cannot give a satisfactory answer when both parties will question the legitimacy itself of the laws and the institutions applying them.

In addition, civil unrest, civil war, revolution or similar events often overturn regimes through unconstitutional ways and establish new political systems as well as constitutional structures without regard to the previously existing legal rules. In other words, such events can change municipal law so that what was unconstitutional or illegal before, becomes perfectly legal. Therefore, in

---

107   See, in this regard, the *Diag Human SE v Czech Republic Ministry of Health* (n 18).
108   See also in this regard *Valores Mundiales SL and Consorcio Andino SL v Venezuela* (n 101) paras 42–43.

particular in times of internal turmoil and regime transition, it is impossible to determine the government that can represent the state in the arbitral proceedings based on municipal law.

In this respect, it is also worth recalling the related principle set out in article 27 of the Vienna Convention on the Law of Treaties and clearly articulated by the arbitral tribunal in the *Sedelmayer v Russia* case that, 'a country cannot rely on internal rules concerning who has and who has not the authority to represent the country in arbitrations as a defence against liability under international law'.[109]

As a consequence, investment arbitral tribunals should turn to public international law for answers as to the circumstances under which a government be considered able to effectively represent its state in the arbitral proceedings. In other words, which government will be able to respect the commitments made during the proceedings, assert the state's rights effectively and carry out any obligations stemming from the decisions taken by the arbitral tribunal, be that procedural orders or awards. Given the nature of recognition of governments and in particular the extreme variations in state practice, public international law can only offer guidance, but no straightforward answers. According to the overwhelming majority of the doctrine, governments that exercise effective control over larger part of the territory of the state and the state apparatus should be recognised as the representative of the state on the international plane.

Same is true for the arbitral proceedings: an effective government can effectively and fully represent the state in the arbitral proceedings. International law is indifferent to the nature of the change in government and does not deny a government's right to represent its state on the grounds that the change was unconstitutional or seen as illegitimate by other states. The same should hold true for investment arbitral tribunals.[110] While recognition by other states could be an indication of the effectiveness of the government, it is in and of itself not sufficient to conclude that for the purposes of the arbitral proceedings the government in question should be representing the state.

The limits to the principle of effectiveness lie in the answer to the questions whether a government that was set up by foreign intervention or which was deemed by a UN Security Council Resolution a threat to peace under article 39 of the UN Charter should be recognised as the representative of the state in the arbitral proceedings if its effectiveness can be established. After all, from

---

109 *Franz Sedelmayer v Russia* (n 17) 80.
110 This has been confirmed by the Annulment Committee in *Valores Mundiales SL and Consorcio Andino SL v Venezuela* (n 101) paras 42 and 48.

an arbitral tribunal's point of view, such government could very well be the only one that can make commitments and assert rights effectively in the proceedings. However, giving even such limited legitimacy to a government that was set up in denial of the core values shared by the international community would most certainly amount to a violation of international public policy and would lead to the annulment of the final award both in ICSID and non-ICSID arbitrations.

An interesting example is the decision reached by the arbitral tribunal in an UNCITRAL arbitration commenced by Telephony Saba Fon against Yemen. Before the hearings took place in 2018, a controversy had arisen as to which government could represent Yemen in the proceedings.[111] One government claiming to represent Yemen was the Hadi government with only limited presence in the port city of Aden and with its head in exile in Saudi Arabia since 2015, when the Houthi rebels forced him out of the country.[112] The other government was the Houthi government based in the capital city of Saana, controlling key central and Northern provinces of the country.[113] The arbitral tribunal, in an unpublished ruling, decided that the Hadi government, owing to its international recognition by other states and by a UN Security Council Resolution, should be viewed as the one that can represent the state in the proceedings.[114]

At the time the decision was taken, before or in 2018, the Hadi government was in exile and it did not control the largest part of Yemeni territory, the Houthis and the Southern movement also overseeing larger parts of the country. Even the areas under the Hadi government's control were riven with instability.[115] It also did not maintain a functioning state apparatus.[116] It is thus clear that the Hadi government did not fulfil the criterion of effectiveness and possibly could not even have complied with any obligations flowing from a

---

111 Peterson (n 1).
112 European Council on Foreign Relations, 'Mapping the Yemeni Conflict' (2019) <www.ecfr.eu/mena/yemen#cap5> accessed 12 January 2020.
113 ibid.
114 Peterson (n 1).
115 European Council on Foreign Relations (n 112).
116 According to a Saudi Arabian-brokered power sharing agreement signed between the Hadi government and the separatists in the south of the country in November 2019, the Hadi government was to return to Aden to reactivate state institutions. Patrick Wintour, 'Yemen Government Signs Power Sharing Deal with Separatists' (*The Guardian*, 5 November 2019) <www.theguardian.com/world/2019/nov/05/yemen-government-signs-power-sharing-deal-with-separatists> accessed 12 January 2020.

potential adverse final award. The Houthi government being present on the ground certainly exerted a more effective control over its territories.

However, in 2015, the UN Security Council expressed its support for the legitimacy of President Hadi, called to 'all parties and Member States to refrain from taking any actions that undermine the unity, sovereignty, independence and territorial integrity of Yemen, and the legitimacy of the President of Yemen'.[117] Concerning the recognition of the Hadi government by other states, to which the arbitral tribunal referred in its decision, it is unclear which states were considered by the arbitral tribunal. Based on publicly available information, unequivocal recognition of the Hadi government, which would go beyond expressing support for the peaceful resolution of the political crisis or providing military assistance for the Saudi-Arabia led coalition, cannot be established in relation to states other than the members of the Gulf Co-operation Council.

Therefore, the arbitral tribunal's choice was between two governments both lacking full effective control over the territory of the country and the state apparatus, but one of which enjoyed the support of the UN. Under these circumstances, notwithstanding the doubts one can have concerning the capabilities of the Hadi government to effectively assert the state's rights during the proceedings and to comply with commitments and obligations flowing from procedural orders and the arbitral award, the arbitrators took a reasonable stance. It is particularly noteworthy that the arbitral tribunal applied international law to the issue and only made an admittedly superfluous reference to municipal law to confirm its findings.[118]

As is often the case, the real difficulty lies not in the establishment of the criterion of effectiveness itself, but rather in its application based on the available facts.

3.3   *Application of the Criterion of Effectiveness*

The first series of practical difficulties concern the exact degree of effectiveness required, for instance as to the geographical extent of the control necessary to establish effectiveness, and whether there should be a presumption in favour of the established government.[119] The latter proposition seems unfounded from a legal-theoretical point of view, even though in reality it might often be easier to find or accept evidence concerning the effectiveness of a government already in place. The only exception to this conclusion

---

117   UNSC Res 2216 (14 April 2015) UN Doc S/Res/2216, 2.
118   Peterson (n 1).
119   HM Blix, 'Contemporary Aspects of Recognition' (1971) 130 Recueil des Cours 640.

might be situations where there is no effective government emerging after or during a period of civil unrest, and the arbitral tribunal must take a decision.[120]

As to the degree of effectiveness required, there are no hard and fast rules, but control exercised over the bulk of the population or the capital of the country are of particular importance.[121] In addition, it has been argued that the acquiescence of the people should be seen as evidence of the effectiveness of the government, as without some form of acquiescence it is unlikely that the regime in question can exercise control in a sustainable manner.[122]

It has already been pointed out in the context of national court proceedings that obtaining and assessing evidence concerning the effectiveness of a government represents a serious hurdle for domestic courts. It is even more so for arbitral tribunals.

Contrary to national courts, arbitral tribunals cannot require assistance from the executive branch of their state in the matter, nor do they have any means of judicial cooperation with other states at their disposal to collect evidence. Arbitral tribunals rely essentially on the parties to present evidence. However, at times of internal turmoil or transition periods, it is nearly impossible for private investors to obtain meaningful evidence, and evidence presented by the state party's competing governments is unlikely to be more helpful. Moreover, the civil unrests and wars investment tribunals have to assess are increasingly complex, ever-changing and long lasting. Thus, despite of publicly available information provided for instance by UN reports or NGOs present in these countries, it will almost always be extremely difficult to establish with reasonable certainty the facts and whether these amount to effective control.

As an example, the ICSID Annulment Committee established in the *Faviancia v Venezuela* case had to decide upon the legal representation of Venezuela following the events of January 2019. It found, in an unpublished decision rendered on 3 May 2019, that 'the evidence on record does not justify a change in the status quo' and allowed counsel appointed by Maduro's *Procurador General de la Republica* to continue representing the State of Venezuela.[123]

---

120 See in this sense ibid 649.
121 ibid 641.
122 Schuit (n 31) 390.
123 Damien Charlotin and Jarrod Hepburn, 'US Courts Diverge from ICSID Annulment Committee on Venezuela's Representation in International Disputes' (*IAReporter*, 23 May 2019) <www.iareporter.com/articles/us-courts-diverge-from-icsid-annulment-committee-on-venezuelas-representation-in-international-disputes/> accessed 13 January 2020.

The details of the Committee's reasoning remain unknown, but it seems that it is based on the lack of evidence presented by the parties as to the change in government in Venezuela. This might be perceived as a quick and easy way to deal with the sensitive and complicated issue of state representation, in particular since the decision is only two-pages long, but in light of the above it is clear that evidentiary issues remain a serious and very real concern for arbitral tribunals faced with claims of competing governments.

Similarly, the Annulment Committee in the *Valores v Venezuela* case refused to recognise the special attorney general appointed by Guaidó as the rightful representative of Venezuela in the annulment proceedings. The Annulment Committee rightly pointed out that the burden of proof rested with the special attorney general appointed by Guaidó, as he was the one petitioning to change the procedural representation of Venezuela, which even he considered legitimate until 5 February 2019.[124] However, he failed to prove by way of concrete facts that Guaidó's government controlled Venezuelan territory as a valid authority.[125]

Both Committees have thus reached the opposite conclusion than the US Courts, which consider that the special attorney general appointed by Guaidó is the only person capable of representing Venezuela in US court proceedings.

Consequently, the inescapable conclusion is that in reality, due both to evidentiary difficulties and the often complex and volatile situations on the ground, the criterion of effectiveness offers only an illusionary solution to the specific problems of state representation before investment tribunals addressed in this chapter. Nevertheless, and notwithstanding the challenges, arbitral tribunals must render coherent and well-reasoned decisions in order to ensure not only the continuation and integrity of the proceedings, but also to maintain the legitimacy of the decision-making process.

3.4 Roadmap for Arbitral Tribunals Faced with Competing Governments Claiming to Represent the State Party in the Proceedings

As a first step, it is crucial for arbitral tribunals to dissipate the misunderstanding that they would overstep their boundaries and enter into the realm of politics when deciding which government can represent the state in the proceedings. Arbitral tribunals can and must rule upon this question of procedure, as it directly affects the parties' procedural rights and interest and thereby the integrity of the proceedings and the arbitral tribunal's mission to render

---

124 *Valores Mundiales SL and Consorcio Andino SL v Venezuela* (n 101) para 40.
125 ibid para 48.

justice. The arbitral tribunals' ruling will not have effects beyond the arbitral proceedings. In particular, it cannot determine the recognition of the government by states or the international community, nor the extent and nature of the international relations which will be established between the government and other states.

After having carefully set out the basis of its power and duty to render a decision on the issue, the arbitral tribunal should proceed to apply international law and the criterion of effectiveness in order to asses which government can effectively represent the state in the proceedings. The request to determine the representative of the state is most likely to come from one of the competing governments as was the case in the arbitrations involving Venezuela, but it cannot be excluded that the investor should wish to clarify the issue in order to ensure the efficiency of the proceedings. If the request comes at a time when the country is clearly in a period of transition after or during a civil uprising for instance, the arbitral tribunal might consider suspending the proceedings. The suspension must be closely monitored and should not extend over a longer period of time. The suspension should be ordered if there is a reasonable chance that in the foreseeable future the situation might stabilise and one of the competing governments might emerge as the only one claiming to represent the state in the proceedings. A suspension is also necessary during periods of transition in order to avoid premature recognition of a regime.

However, the examples of Venezuela, Yemen or Libya show that arbitral tribunals will most likely be facing situations constantly in flux, where a suspension makes little sense. In these cases, as explained above, arbitral tribunals will be put in an impossible position either because of the insurmountable evidentiary difficulties to establish the level of control exercised by the competing entities or because none of the governments can be said to be the sole effective government of the state.

In addition, arbitral tribunals have little to rely on to guide them in these situations. There might be a UN Security Council resolution expressing support for one of the governments in question, which is of course a strong and persuasive element to consider. However, when such an entity does not have any or only negligible control over the territory, a government in exile for example, caution is to be exercised in order not to go against considerations of fairness to the parties and the efficiency of the proceedings. Even under public international law, such a government should not be granted recognition; and the purpose of the arbitral proceedings also requires an effective government representing the state.

If there is no effective government capable of representing the state in the proceedings due to the internal turmoil in the country and the arbitral tribunal must make a decision, for instance after a time of suspension, it is acceptable to apply a presumption in favour of the already established government as the representative of the state in the proceedings. The legal vacuum must be filled, and this solution has the merit of being foreseeable. As underlined by the Annulment Committee in the *Valores v Venezuela* case, under no circumstances should an arbitral tribunal accept to have the competing governments represent the state party in parallel.[126] Not only is this a solution that defies logic, but it would have catastrophic procedural consequences.

Therefore, it is surprising that in stark contrast to this position, the annulment committee in the *ConocoPhillips v Venezuela* case decided to allow two law firms, one appointed by the Guaidó and one by the Maduro government, to appear on behalf of Venezuela.[127] The arbitral tribunal in the underlying case originally declined to decide the issue during the rectification proceedings considering that submissions by both regimes were substantially identical.[128]

The annulment committee considered that in line with the decisions taken in other ICSID proceedings and following the parties' agreement, it should maintain the *status quo* in Venezuela's representation, which in this case meant allowing two law firms appointed by the two competing governments and already on record to appear before the committee.[129] The annulment committee also found that the possibility of divergences between the positions of the two law firms representing the two governments did not mean that it would not hear and answer the different arguments.[130] Possibly, the fact that annulment proceedings have a narrow scope and both regimes moved to annul the award as well as Claimant's agreement to respond to submissions made by both law firms contributed to the committee's decision. The problem of divergent positions would however be exacerbated in first instance arbitral proceedings, where the reliefs requested and the arguments sustaining them can be manyfold or even contradictory and the burden on claimants consequently heavier.

Finally, when it comes to the question as to who should bear the costs related to the resolution of this particular procedural issue, one cannot but agree

---

126 *Valores Mundiales SL and Consorcio Andino SL v Venezuela* (n 101) para 50.
127 *ConocoPhillips Petrozuata BV, ConocoPhillips Hamaca BV and ConocoPhillips Gulf of Paria BV v Venezuela*, ICSID Case no ARB 07/30, Annulment Proceedings, Order on the Applicant's Representation (3 April 2020).
128 Lisa Bohmer, 'Venezuela Proposes Disqualification of All Three ICSID Ad Hoc Committee Members in Long-Running ConocoPhillips Case' (*IAReporter*, 19 April 2020) <www.iareporter.com/articles/venezuela-proposes-disqualification-of-all-three-icsid-ad-hoc-committee-members-in-long-running-conocophillips-case/> accessed 25 April 2020.
129 ConocoPhillips and others v Venezuela (n 127) paras 31–35.
130 ibid para 36.

with the *Valores* Annulment Committee's position.¹³¹ The request to change Venezuela's representation was made by a third-party: the special attorney appointed by the newly emerged government competing for power. Therefore, it would be unfair to have one of the parties to the proceedings bear all the financial consequences of a procedural incident they have not caused. The parties would thus bear their respective costs, as the ICSID Rules only allow for a party to be the recipient of an order to pay costs.

All in all, there is a heavy burden on the arbitral tribunal, which have to carry out a delicate analysis and not stray out of the realm of legal reasoning in order to avoid any appearance of making a politically motivated decision. But as long as the arbitral tribunal concentrates on the requirements of the arbitral proceedings themselves and in particular on the parties' rights and interests, it will be able to proceed to a coherent legal analysis that might not find universal approval but will withstand scrutiny under the applicable law and logic.

4   Conclusions

In the words of Kelsen '[g]eneral international law is primitive law'.¹³² It is highly decentralised, leaving many aspects of its application to the interested parties, the states themselves.¹³³ As such, it does not provide answers to all legal questions that might arise or the answers provided by state practice are fraught with divergencies, uncertainties and political undertones. The recognition of governments illustrates this problem perfectly.

It is nevertheless part of the mission of investment arbitral tribunals, which apply public international law in sophisticated legal proceedings often involving complex factual matrices and deal with rights and obligations of private persons, to face these uncertainties and rule upon the issue of state representation in order to fulfil their mission of deciding the dispute before them.

Arbitral tribunals have to render a legally coherent decision serving the purposes of the arbitral proceedings while also ensuring coordination and a harmonious relationship with general public international law. It is a difficult and delicate task, but as has been shown before, not an impossible one. As long as arbitral tribunals accept guidance from public international law and tailor the solutions offered to the needs of the arbitral proceedings, they will be able to

---

131   *Valores Mundiales SL and Consorcio Andino SL v Venezuela* (n 101) paras 54–56.
132   Hans Kelsen, 'Recognition in International Law: Theoretical Observations' (1941) 35 AJIL 605, 607.
133   ibid.

efficiently protect the parties' interests as well as the integrity and legitimacy of the decision-making process.

Bibliography

'UK Expels Gaddafi Diplomats and Recognises Libya Rebels' (*BBC News*, 27 July 2011) <www.bbc.com/news/uk-politics-14306544> accessed 15 January 2020.

Andenas M and JR Leiss, 'The Systemic Relevance of "Judicial Decisions" in Article 38 of the ICJ Statute' (2017) 77 Heidelberg J Int'l L 907.

Blix HM, 'Contemporary Aspects of Recognition' (1971) 130 Recueil des Cours 640.

Bohmer L, 'Venezuela Proposes Disqualification of All Three ICSID Ad Hoc Committee Members in Long-Running ConocoPhillips Case' (*IAReporter*, 19 April 2020) <www.iareporter.com/articles/venezuela-proposes-disqualification-of-all-three-icsid-ad-hoc-committee-members-in-long-running-conocophillips-case/> accessed 25 April 2020.

Born G, *International Commercial Arbitration* (2nd edn, Kluwer Law International 2014).

Charlotin D and J Hepburn, 'US Courts Diverge from ICSID Annulment Committee on Venezuela's Representation in International Disputes' (*IAReporter*, 23 May 2019) <www.iareporter.com/articles/us-courts-diverge-from-icsid-annulment-committee-on-venezuelas-representation-in-international-disputes/> accessed 13 January 2020.

European Council on Foreign Relations, 'Mapping the Yemeni Conflict' (2019) <www.ecfr.eu/mena/yemen#cap5> accessed 12 January 2020.

Frowein JA, 'Recognition', *Max Planck Encyclopedia of Public International Law* (2010) <https://opil.ouplaw.com/home/MPIL> accessed 6 November 2019.

Frowein JA, 'Non-Recognition', *Max Planck Encyclopedia of Public International Law* (2011) <https://opil.ouplaw.com/home/MPIL> accessed 6 November 2019.

Frowein JA, 'De Facto Regime', *Max Planck Encyclopedia of Public International Law* (2013) <https://opil.ouplaw.com/home/MPIL> accessed 6 November 2019.

Fry J, S Greenberg, and F Mazza, *The Secretariat's Guide to ICC Arbitration* (ICC 2012).

ICSID, 'The Proposals for the Amendment of the ICSID Rules' (2020) 1(4) ICSID Working Paper <https://icsid.worldbank.org/en/Documents/WP_4_Vol_1_En.pdf> accessed 22 March 2020.

Institut de Droit International, 'La econnaissance des nouveaux Etats et des nouveaux gouvernements' (1936) 39 Annuaire de l'Institut de Droit International 300.

Jones T and S Perry, 'Guaidó Calls on ICSID to Take Sides' (*Global Arbitration Review*, 2 May 2019) <https://globalarbitrationreview.com/article/1190944/guaido-calls-on-icsid-to-take-sides> accessed 3 January 2020.

Kelsen H, 'Recognition in International Law: Theoretical Observations' (1941) 35 AJIL 605.

Manciaux S, 'The Representation of States before ICSID Tribunals' (2011) 2 JIDS 87.

Margaret R O'Sullivan, 'Conflict of Laws Issues in Drafting and Using Powers of Attorney for the Mobile Client' (2015) 35 Est Tr & Pensions J 94.

Menon PK, 'The Problem of Recognition in International Law: Some Thoughts on Community Interest' (1990) 59 Nordic J Int'l L 262.

Peterson LE, 'Award Looms in UNCITRAL Investment Arbitration against Yemen; in Unpublished Ruling, Arbitrators Decided Who Is Rightful Legal Representative of State' (*IAReporter*, 23 December 2019) <www.iareporter.com/articles/award-looms-in-uncitral-investment-arbitration-against-yemen-in-unpublished-ruling-arbitrators-decided-who-is-rightful-legal-representative-of-state/> accessed 12 January 2020.

Peterson MJ, 'Recognition of Governments Should Not Be Abolished' (1983) 77 AJIL 31.

Schuit A, 'Recognition of Governments in International Law and the Recent Conflict in Libya' (2012) 14 Int'l Comm L Rev 381, 394.

Sharpe JK, 'The Agent's Indispensable Role in International Investment Arbitration' (2018) 33 ICSID Rev 675.

Talmon S, *Recognition of Governments in International Law: With Particular Reference to Governments in Exile* (OUP 2001).

Verhoeven J, 'Relations internationales de droit privé en l'absence de reconnaissance d'un État, d'un gouvernement ou d'une situation' (1985) 192 Recueil des Cours 25.

Verhoeven J, 'La reconnaissance internationale, déclin ou renouveau?' (1993) 39 Annuaire français de droit international 7.

Wintour P, 'Yemen Government Signs Power Sharing Deal with Separatists' (*The Guardian*, 5 November 2019) <https://www.theguardian.com/world/2019/nov/05/yemen-government-signs-power-sharing-deal-with-separatists> accessed 12 January 2020.

CHAPTER 9

The Substantive and Procedural Protection of Investments under Article 1 Protocol 1 to the ECHR and Its Value in Cases of Territorial Conflicts

Isabella Risini

1 Introduction

It is safe to say that the drafters of the 1950 Convention for the Protection of Human Rights and Fundamental Freedoms[1] (the Convention, ECHR) and its 1952 Protocol[2] (Protocol 1, the Protocol), which protects property in its first article, did not intend to provide foreign-owned corporate entities with an alternative to the calamities of the customary international law of minimum standards and its deficient enforcement via the law of diplomatic protection for the protection of investments. The European Court of Human Rights (ECtHR, the Court) acknowledged the relevance of the protection of the property of aliens in the framework of the ECHR, which is the subject of this contribution, in its 1986 *Lithgow v UK* judgment. Therein, the Court observed that the entry into force of Protocol 1 had not led to a diminution of the rights of foreign investors.[3] Still, the relationship between the ECHR's human rights protection and the protection of foreign investments poses several questions, some of which this chapter seeks to address.

This contribution is not the first one to shed light on the question of protection of investments and investors under the Convention's framework.[4]

---

1 Convention for the Protection of Human Rights and Fundamental Freedoms (signed 4 November 1950, entered into force 3 September 1953) 213 UNTS 221 (ECHR).
2 Protocol (No 1) to the Convention for the Protection of Human Rights and Fundamental Freedoms (signed 20 March 1952, entered into force 18 May 1954) 213 UNTS 221 (Protocol 1).
3 *Lithgow and others v UK*, App no 9006/80 (ECtHR, 8 July 1986, Merits) para 115.
4 Marius Emberland, *The Human Rights of Companies: Exploring the Structure of ECHR Protection* (OUP 2006); Ursula Kriebaum, *Eigentumsschutz im Völkerrecht: Eine vergleichende Untersuchung zum internationalen Investitionsrecht sowie zum Menschenrechtsschutz* (Duncker & Humblot 2008); Christian Tomuschat, 'The European Court of Human Rights and Investment Protection' in Christina Binder and others (eds), *International in Investment Law for the 21st Century: Essays in Honour of Christoph Schreuer* (OUP 2009); Walid Ben Hamida and Frédérique Coulée (eds), *Convergences and Contradictions between Investment Law and Human Rights Law: A Litigation Approach* (Pedone 2017); Maria Fanou and Vassilis P Tzevelekos,

The considerations offered here are more modest inasmuch they target the specific context of investments in situations of territorial conflict, to which the ECHR system has been exposed for much longer than the law of international investments. The general approach of this chapter, detailed further in section 2, is to highlight the relevant substantive (section 3) and procedural (section 4) characteristics of the ECHR when it comes to investment protection and to compare them with the pertinent aspects of investment protection instruments. Section 5 further explores the possibility that the ECtHR will deal with the large-scale human rights issues that arise from Russia's and Ukraine's actions since 2014 in Eastern Ukraine and Crimea mainly via *non-monetary* measures. The assessment whether foreign investors should consider Strasbourg as an alternative or cumulative forum to arbitration is rounded off with some more detailed background of how specifically Russia and Ukraine have, until now, dealt with their membership in the ECHR and the Council of Europe.

2   The Relevant Framework and Goals of the Analysis

2.1   *Substance, Procedure, Remedies*

The relationship between rights and remedies, between procedure and substance, has been an issue in international investment law.[5] The distinction between the two within the law of the ECHR has equally become more important in the recent past, also as a response to the increasing demands for the subsidiary character of the supervision in Strasbourg.[6] It is further illustrative to note that, in 2019, some 84 percent of cases were in*admissible*.[7] Under article 35(3)(a) ECHR, one of the reasons to dismiss a case is that it is manifestly

---

'The Shared Territory of the ECHR and International Investment Law' in Yannick Radi (ed), *Research Handbook on Human Rights and Investment* (Edward Elgar 2018).

5   *Eg* Relja Radović, 'Between Rights and Remedies: The Access to Investment Treaty Arbitration as a Substantive Right of Foreign Investors' (2019) 10 JIDS 42.

6   Janneke Gerards and Eva Brems (eds), *Procedural Review in European Fundamental Rights Cases* (CUP 2017); Thomas Kleinlein, 'The Procedural Approach of the European Court of Human Rights: Between Subsidiarity and Dynamic Evolution' (2019) 68 ICLQ 91; see also Heribert Golsong, 'Interpreting the European Convention on Human Rights Beyond the Confines of the Vienna Convention on the Law of Treaties' in Ronald St J Macdonald, Franz Matscher, and Herbert Petzold (eds), *The European System for the Protection of Human Rights* (Nijhoff 1993) 150.

7   ECtHR, 'Analysis of Statistics 2019' (January 2020) 11 (chart 9), 15 (chart 11) <www.echr.coe.int/Documents/Stats_analysis_2019_ENG.pdf> accessed 8 June 2020.

ill-*founded*, *ie* a case will not proceed further based on preliminary merits-based considerations.[8]

This contribution is not intended to start a principled discussion on the distinction between and interaction of procedure and substance, and on the place remedies take between them. Rather, it uses the distinction to accentuate certain differences and commonalities between human rights law and the law of investment protection. A further aim is to show that concepts of procedure are closely linked to questions of substance. This is true for *both* human rights law and the law of international investment protection. The rule of the exhaustion of domestic remedies under article 35(1) ECHR will be analyzed in some detail in this regard.

The distinction between procedure and substance is also relevant with regard to available remedies. Remedies can have a dimension of access to justice, which has procedural and substantive aspects. Remedies are also legal consequences of a material breach of human rights. Both concepts are interrelated.[9] This is illustrated by the observation that, in the framework of the protection of property under article 1 Protocol 1, the question whether there has been some kind of compensation in the national proceedings is one of the parameters the Strasbourg court uses to determine whether an interference was proportional.

2.2 *Relevance of Property and Investment Cases in the Framework of the ECHR*

Property cases in the ECHR framework come, in their frequency, third after cases under article 6 ECHR (right to a fair trial) and article 5 ECHR (right to liberty and security). According to statistical information provided by the Court, in all judgments delivered between 1959 and 2017 in which a violation of the Convention or its substantive additional protocols was found, an average of 11.75 percent of the judgments found violations of article 1 Protocol 1.[10]

An effort of looking at the role of the ECtHR as an investment protection forum in more general terms is also worthwhile in view of the ramifications

---

8   See ECtHR, 'Practical Guide on Admissibility Criteria' (31 August 2019), sec III, which is entitled 'Inadmissibility based on the merits' <www.echr.coe.int/Documents/Admissibility_guide_ENG.pdf> accessed 8 June 2020.
9   This emerges already from the table of contents of the standard textbook in this regard by Dinah Shelton, *Remedies in International Human Rights Law* (3rd edn, OUP 2015).
10 ECtHR, 'Overview 1959–2017' (March 2018) 6 <www.echr.coe.int/Documents/Overview_19592017_ENG.pdf> accessed 8 June 2020. In 2017, the share of judgments finding a violation of article 1 Protocol 1 was 8.34 percent, in 2018 8.59 percent, rising to 9.71 percent in 2019. See ECtHR, 'The ECHR in Facts & Figures 2019' (February 2020) <www.echr.coe.int/Documents/Facts_Figures_2019_ENG.pdf> accessed 8 June 2020.

of the March 2018 European Court of Justice judgment in the *Achmea* case,[11] where the Luxembourg court found that investor-state arbitration clauses in intra-European Union (EU) bilateral investment treaties are incompatible with the EU Treaties.[12] In May 2020, 23 EU member states signed an agreement for the termination of their respective bilateral investment treaties.[13] According to that agreement, national courts shall serve as a forum for investment protection instead of investment tribunals. Against this background, it is likely that also the ECtHR will be used more frequently as an investment protection forum.[14]

Between international economic law and human rights, there are many issues worthwhile comparing and exploring. Some broader aspects of the debate have been led in a very principled and theoretical, even ideological, way.[15] It has become a reality that investment protection and human rights law co-exist and are being used cumulatively.[16] With regard to Central and Eastern Europe, Michal Kucera described the cumulative use of the ECHR and investment protection as 're-establishing the commercial rule of law'.[17] There are many different constellations of the interaction between investment law

---

11   ECJ, C-284/16 *Achmea* [2018] ECLI:EU:C:2018:158.
12   For further detail, see Richard Happ and Sebastian Wuschka, 'EU Law and Investment Arbitration: Of Cooperation, Conflict and the EU Legal Order's Autonomy' in Andrea Bjorklund, Franco Ferrari, and Stefan Kröll (eds), *Cambridge Compendium of International Commercial and Investment Arbitration* (CUP 2021, forthcoming).
13   Agreement for the Termination of Bilateral Investment Treaties between the Member States of the European Union (signed 5 May 2020, not in force) [2020] OJ L 169/1.
14   Stephan Balthasar, 'Investment Protection in Europe: International Investment Treaties, the European Convention on Human Rights and the Need for Reform at EU Level' (2018) 16 German Arb J 227, 230.
15   Ernst-Ulrich Petersmann, 'Human Rights and International Economic Law in the 21st Century: The Need to Clarify their Interrelationships' (2001) 4 J Int'l Econ L 3; Philip Alston, 'Resisting the Merger and Acquisition of Human Rights by Trade Law: A Reply to Petersmann' (2002) 13 EJIL 815.
16   As for example in the *Yukos* cases, see Eric De Brabandere, 'Yukos Universal Limited (Isle of Man) v The Russian Federation: Complementarity or Conflict, Contrasting the Yukos Case before the European Court of Human Rights and Investment Tribunals' (2015) 30 ICSID Rev 345. See also Andreas Kulick, *Global Public Interest in International Investment Law* (CUP 2012); Pierre-Marie Dupuy and Jorge E Viñuales, 'Human Rights and Investment Disciplines: Integration in Progress' in Marc Bungenberg and others (eds) *International Investment Law: A Handbook* (CH Beck, Hart, and Nomos 2015).
17   Michal Kucera, 'Convergence and Conflicts between Investment Law and Human Rights Law: A Dispute Settlement Approach – Jurisdiction Ratione Personae' in Walid Ben Hamida and Frédérique Coulée (eds) *Convergences and Contradictions between Investment Law and Human Rights Law: A Litigation Approach* (Pedone 2017) 41. Similarly, Tomuschat (n 4) 655 ('a great service to a culture of stability founded on the rule of law').

and human rights which can only be referred to here.[18] Universal human rights instruments are left outside the present analysis as they do not protect the right to property.[19] Likewise, the other regional human rights systems are left for a more comprehensive study elsewhere, even if specifically Latin America has been in many ways the geographical cradle for the protection of investments.[20]

2.3   Conflict and the ECHR

Despite the end of World War II and the hope for peace in Europe, which the ECHR reflected, *conflict* was still a challenge which, in the eyes of the drafters, needed to be addressed by the Convention. This is evidenced, above all, by the existence of article 15 ECHR, the derogation clause. The provision addresses the way states may act 'in times of war'.[21] From the viewpoint of the Convention, the right to property belongs to the derogable rights, *e contratio* article 15(2) ECHR. This contribution will, however, not deal with the questions arising from the applicability of international humanitarian law in armed conflicts.[22] On a formal level, the Court's material yardstick does not comprise international humanitarian law, although its co-existence is echoed in the Court's jurisprudence.[23]

---

18   Filip Balcerzak, *Investor-State Arbitration and Human Rights* (Brill 2017) 73 et seq, *inter alia* with reference to *Yukos Universal Ltd (Isle of Man) v Russia*, UNCITRAL, PCA Case no 2005-04/AA 227, Final Award (18 July 2014) paras 78 et seq; Ursula Kriebaum, 'Human Rights and International Investment Law' in Yannick Radi (ed), *Research Handbook on Human Rights and Investment* (Edward Elgar 2018) 18 et seq; Silvia Steiniger, 'What's Human Rights Got To Do With It? An Empirical Analysis of Human Rights References in Investment Arbitration' (2018) 31 LJIL 33; Ursula Kriebaum and August Reinisch, 'Property, Right to, International Protection', *Max Planck Encyclopedia of Public International Law* (2019) para 54 <https://opil.ouplaw.com/home/MPIL> accessed 8 June 2020.

19   See International Covenant on Civil and Political Rights (adopted 16 December 1966, entered into force 23 March 1976) 999 UNTS 171 (ICCPR); International Covenant on Economic, Social and Cultural Rights (adopted 16 December 1966, entered into force 3 January 1976) 993 UNTS 3 (ICESCR).

20   See Rodrigo Polanco Lazo and Rodrigo Mella, 'Investment Arbitration and Human Rights Cases in Latin America' in Yannick Radi (ed), *Research Handbook on Human Rights and Investment* (Edward Elgar 2018) 48 et seq, who give examples of cases in which investors relied on the American Convention on Human Rights (adopted 22 November 1969, entered into force 18 July 1978) 1144 UNTS 123.

21   See also ECtHR, 'Guide on Article 15 of the European Convention on Human Rights: Derogation in Time of Emergency' (31 December 2019) <www.echr.coe.int/Documents/Guide_Art_15_ENG.pdf> accessed 8 June 2020.

22   For an overview, see ECtHR, 'Armed Conflicts' (March 2020) <www.echr.coe.int/Documents/FS_Armed_conflicts_ENG.pdf> accessed 8 June 2020.

23   *Eg Hassan v United Kingdom* App no 29750/09 (ECtHR, 16 September 2014).

On 1 January 2020, 15 percent of the individual applications under article 34 ECHR pending before the ECtHR referred to a territorial conflict.[24] Additionally, territorial conflicts underlie most of the inter-state applications pending before the Court under article 33 ECHR, especially those between Ukraine and Russia as well as Georgia and Russia.[25] There is a substantial overlap between the inter-state cases concerning territorial conflicts and individual cases which are potentially well-founded. In the context of the conflict of Ukraine and Russia, the common preliminary question is a question of jurisdiction: which of the two states has jurisdiction under article 1 ECHR in relation to the matters complained of?[26] How these overlapping cases are dealt with by the Court is subject to a reform process.[27] The violent geopolitical conflicts in Eastern Europe have and will have, in turn, an impact on the ECHR and its supervisory system.[28]

The Court's 2020 *Guide on Article 1 of Protocol 1 to the European Convention on Human Rights* identifies groups of cases that concern the situation of the destruction of property in situations of international or internal armed conflict.[29] The non-binding document indicates the relevance of the protection of

---

[24] Council of Europe Steering Committee for Human Rights (CDDH), Committee of Experts on the System of the European Convention on Human Rights, Drafting Group on Effective Processing and Resolution of Cases Relating to Inter-State Disputes, 'Background Paper on the Practice of the European Court of Human Rights with Regard to Inter-State Applications' (23 January 2020) DH-SYSC-IV(2020)02, para 9 <https://rm.coe.int/ 09000016809a4672> accessed 8 June 2020.

[25] ECtHR, 'Inter-State Applications by Date of Introduction of the Applications' (11 September 2019) <www.echr.coe.int/Documents/InterState_applications_ENG.pdf> accessed 8 June 2020. See Geir Ulfstein and Isabella Risini, 'Inter-State Applications under the European Convention on Human Rights: Strengths and Challenges' (*EJIL:Talk!*, 24 January 2020) <www. ejiltalk.org/inter-state-applications-under-the-european-convention-on-human-rights-strengths-and-challenges/> accessed 8 June 2020.

[26] ECtHR Press Unit, 'ECHR to Adjourn Some Individual Applications on Eastern Ukraine Pending Grand Chamber Judgment in Related Inter-State Case' (Press Release ECHR 432 (2018), 17 December 2018).

[27] See CDDH, 'Effective Processing and Resolution of Cases Relating to Inter-State Disputes' (2020) <www.coe.int/en/web/human-rights-intergovernmental-cooperation/effective-processing-and-resolution-of-inter-state-disputes> accessed 8 June 2020.

[28] Mikael Rask Madsen, 'The European Court of Human Rights: From the Cold War to the Brighton Declaration and Backlash' in Karen J Alter, Laurence R Helfer, and Mikael Rask Madsen (eds), *International Court Authority* (OUP 2018).

[29] ECtHR, 'Guide on Article 1 of Protocol No. 1 to the European Convention on Human Rights: Protection of Property' (30 April 2020) <www.echr.coe.int/Documents/Guide_ Art_1_Protocol_1_ENG.pdf> accessed 8 June 2020. It is worthwhile to underline that the materials which stem from various units of the, *eg* the case law guidelines, are not legally binding documents. They are, however, intended to ensure coherence in the Court's extensive case law; see also Mark Villiger, 'The Research Division of the European Court

property in times of conflict. Against this background, the question whether article 1 Protocol 1 and the Strasbourg enforcement machinery have something to offer to investors in the context of territorial conflicts is not one out of place.

Currently, article 1 Protocol 1 is binding upon 45 of the 47 ECHR member states.[30] It is worthwhile to observe that Azerbaijan and Georgia have entered reservations to article 1 Protocol 1 with regard to territories affected by conflicts.[31]

3 Substantive Aspects of the Protection of Property under the ECHR

This section is intended to give an overview of the substantive protection of property in the framework of the ECHR. Further, it is intended to highlight jurisdictional aspects, which are seen here as substantive issues, even though the Court will dismiss a case as inadmissible if it finds itself without jurisdiction *ratione materiae, ratione loci, ratione personae*, or *ratione temporis*.

The contribution does not provide an in-depth comparison concerning standing, *ie* the question of who can claim protection. It suffices to point out that the protection of shareholders under article 1 Protocol 1 falls behind many investment protection instruments in some ways and is broader in others.[32] It is broader inasmuch there is no nationality requirement. Put positively, unlike investment law, human rights law does not exclusively protect foreign property in the context of risky transactions. A further area where the protection is broader relates to creditors of states.[33] The matter of the protection of

---

of Human Rights and Its Relevance for the Court's Case-law' in Koen Lemmens, Stephan Parmentier, and Louise Reyntjens (eds), *Human Rights with a Human Touch: Liber Amicorum Paul Lemmens* (Intersentia 2019) 449.

30 The two states not bound (as of May 2020) by Protocol 1 are Switzerland and Monaco.

31 For the list of reservations currently in force, see Council of Europe Treaty Office, 'Reservations and Declarations for Treaty No. 009 – Protocol to the Convention for the Protection of Human Rights and Fundamental Freedoms' (2020) <www.coe.int/en/web/conventions/full-list/-/conventions/treaty/009/declarations?p_auth=6xJUJLgH> accessed 20 June 2020. The fact that the reservations are listed here does not necessarily mean that the reservations are valid, see, *eg, Assanidze v Georgia*, App no 71503/01 (ECtHR, 8 April 2004) para 140; *Ilaşcu and others v Moldova and Russia*, App no 48787/99 (ECtHR, 4 July 2001, Decision); *Ilaşcu and others v Moldova and Russia*, App no 48787/99 (ECtHR, 8 July 2004, Merits and Just Satisfaction) para 324.

32 For a full overview of the pertinent case law concerning the protection of company shares and other financial instruments, see ECtHR, 'Guide on Article 1 of Protocol No. 1' (n 29), paras 31 et seq; see also *Albert and others v Hungary*, App no 5294/14 (ECtHR, 7 July 2020) paras 120 et seq.

33 Kucera (n 17) 57 et seq.

shareholders, which is in certain ways more limited under the ECHR is closely related with the requirement of the exhaustion of domestic remedies, which is at times difficult for shareholders when the corporate veil is not lifted.[34] However, given that the matter has been subject to many comparisons,[35] and has no specific relevance in the context of territorial conflicts, it is not zoomed into much further. Another aspect worthwhile noting at the outset and which will not be explored in more detail here is that, unlike investment instruments, article 1 Protocol 1 does not guarantee the right to acquire property. Thus, the human right cannot be employed to gain access to foreign markets.[36]

3.1 A Glance at the Drafting History of the Right to Property in the Framework of the ECHR (Including Its Procedural Side)

The drafters of the Convention could not readily agree on a protection of property as a *social* human right.[37] The preamble of the ECHR refers to the (as such and at the time preponderantly) non-binding Universal Declaration of Human Rights (UDHR) of 1948,[38] which formulated the protection of property in its article 17. It has to be recalled that some of the drafters of the UDHR and the ECHR were identical, such as David Maxwell-Fyfe and Fernand Dehousse. The preamble of the ECHR, however, also states that the Convention would only 'take the first steps for the collective enforcement of *certain* of the rights stated in the Universal Declaration.'[39] Those rights were political rights. The social rights in the UDHR were not taken up by the Convention – the right to property is the only exception.

The drafting of article 1 Protocol 1 produced a rather fragmentary text, which left many questions to the interpretation by the now defunct Commission and the Court.[40] *Already in* or *as late as* 1979 (and ever since), the ECtHR clarified in the *Marckx v Belgium* case that article 1 Protocol 1 was 'in substance guaranteeing the right of property'.[41] The provision itself does not contain the term

---

34   *Agrotexim and others v Greece*, App no 14807/89 (ECtHR, 24 October 1995) para 66.
35   See above, n 4.
36   Matthias Ruffert, 'The Protection of Foreign Direct Investment by the European Court of Human Rights' (2000) 43 German YB Int'l L 116, 123.
37   Marco Sassòli, in his foreword to this volume, refers to the tension between collective and individual interests in this regard.
38   Universal Declaration of Human Rights (adopted 10 December 1948) UNGA Res 217 A(III).
39   ECHR preamble (emphasis added).
40   The drafting history has been laid out by William Schabas, *The European Convention on Human Rights: A Commentary* (OUP 2015) 960 et seq.
41   *Marckx v Belgium*, App no 6833/74 (ECtHR, 13 June 1979, Merits and Just Satisfaction) para 63.

property. The heading of the provision 'protection of *property*/protection de la *propriété*' was added only much later, via Protocol 11, which entered into force in 1998.⁴² In terms of substance, the core of article 1 Protocol 1 derives from the notion of property under general international law.⁴³

The provision reads:

1. Every natural or legal person is entitled to the peaceful enjoyment of his possessions. No one shall be deprived of his possessions except in the public interest and subject to the conditions provided for by law and by the general principles of international law.
2. The preceding provisions shall not, however, in any way impair the right of a State to enforce such laws as it deems necessary to control the use of property in accordance with the general interest or to secure the payment of taxes or other contributions or penalties.⁴⁴

Article 1 Protocol 1 does also not speak of *compensation*. This textual situation left the Convention organs with the difficult task to establish a compensation scheme.⁴⁵ It is noteworthy that the Court left, in *Lithgow*, room for a distinction between nationals and non-nationals with regard to compensation. The Court underlined that, for non-nationals, the entry into force of Protocol 1 has not led to a diminution of their rights.⁴⁶ The idea that the ECHR should not be used to lower exisiting standards of protection is also enshrined in article 53 ECHR. Concededly, the provision does not directly apply to the constellation of standards deriving from pre-existing customary international law.

---

42 Protocol No 11 to the Convention for the Protection of Human Rights and Fundamental Freedoms, Restructuring the Control Machinery Established Thereby (adopted 11 May 1994, entered into force 1 November 1998) 2061 UNTS 21.

43 Wolfgang Peukert, 'Artikel 1 Protokoll 1' in Jochen Frowein and Wolfgang Peukert, *Europäische Menschenrechtskonvention: EMRK-Kommentar* (3rd edn, Engel 2009) para 1.

44 The French text is likewise authentic and reads: '(1) Toute personne physique ou morale a droit au respect de ses biens. Nul ne peut être privé de sa propriété que pour cause d'utilité publique et dans les conditions prévues par la loi et les principes généraux du droit international. (2) Les dispositions précédentes ne portent pas atteinte au droit que possèdent les États de mettre en vigueur les lois qu'ils jugent nécessaires pour réglementer l'usage des biens conformément à l'intérêt général ou pour assurer le paiement des impôts ou d'autres contributions ou des amendes.'

45 *James and others v UK*, App no 8793/79 (ECtHR, 21 February 1986) paras 58 et seq; *Lithgow and others v UK* (n 3) paras 111 et seq.

46 *Lithgow and others v UK* (n 3) para 115; see also Georg Ress, 'Reflections on the Protection of Property under the European Convention on Human Rights' in Stephan Breitenmoser and others (eds), *Human Rights, Democracy and the Rule of Law: Liber Amicorum Luzius Wildhaber* (DIKE and Nomos 2007) 625, 632; Matthias Hartwig, 'Der Eigentumsschutz nach Art. 1 des 1. Zusatzprotokolls zur EMRK' (1999) 63 Rabel J Comp & Int'l Priv L 561, 574.

On a procedural level, the original 1950 Convention provided for enforcement *à la carte*, meaning that the individual right to access the now defunct European Commission under ex-article 25 ECHR as well as the later access to the ECtHR under ex-article 46 ECHR depended on the further acceptances (*plural!*) by the respective member states.[47] Today, the individual right to access the ECtHR is enshrined in article 34 ECHR. By now, both the ECHR and international investment instruments provide for the right of private entities to engage the international responsibility of states.[48]

3.2 *Jurisdiction* Ratione Materiae

The property protection offered under article 1 Protocol 1 covers investments.[49] The term investment is used here as a concept to be compared with the kindred concept of possessions as employed by article 1 Protocol 1.[50] They both refer to the *ratione materiae* covered by the respective treaty regime.

The term investment can be defined in many different ways in many different treaty contexts and is usually relative to the respective wording and object and purpose of the underlying investment instrument.[51] It generally requires an engagement of some duration and an assumption of a risk. As a rule, investment treaties limit their application to investments made within the territory of the host state in order to ensure that the host state obtains the benefit of investment.[52]

---

47   For a detailed account, see Ed Bates, *The Evolution of the European Convention on Human Rights* (OUP 2010).

48   Walid Ben Hamida, 'Introductory Overview' in Walid Ben Hamida and Frédérique Coulée (eds), *Convergences and Contradictions between Investment Law and Human Rights Law: A Litigation Approach* (Pedone 2017) 21.

49   For a general overview concerning the right to property as such, see David Harris and others, *Law of the European Convention on Human Rights* (4th edn, OUP 2018) 848 et seq; Maya Beeler-Sigron, 'Protection of Property' in Pieter van Dijk and others (eds), *Theory and Practice of the European Convention on Human Rights* (Intersentia 2018) 851 et seq; Philip Leach, *Taking a Case to the European Court of Human Rights* (4th edn, OUP 2017) 537 et seq.

50   ECtHR, 'Guide on Article 1 of Protocol No. 1' (n 29) paras 4 et seq.

51   Zachary Douglas, 'Property, Investment, and the Scope of Investment Protection Obligations' in Zachary Douglas, Joost Pauwelyn, and Jorge E Viñuales (eds), *The Foundations of International Investment Law* (OUP 2014) 363.

52   See Markus P Beham, chapter 5 in this volume. See also Christina Knahr, 'Investments "In The Territory" of the Host State' in Christina Binder and others (eds), *International in Investment Law for the 21st Century: Essays in Honour of Christoph Schreuer* (OUP 2009) 42 et seq; Richard Happ and Sebastian Wuschka, '*Horror Vacui*: Or Why Investment Treaties Should Apply to Illegally Annexed Territories' (2016) 33 J Int'l Arb 245, 251 et seq; Lucy Reed, Zoe Scanlon, and Dafina Atanasova, 'Protected Investment', *Max Planck Encyclopedia of International Procedural Law* (2018) paras 61 et seq

Comparisons concerning the substantive protection offered by both regimes,[53] ie between the ECHR's key term 'possessions' and investments, show that the ECHR's protection is somewhat broader concerning portfolio investments.[54]

Article 1 Protocol 1 comprises three distinct rules. The first rule, set out in the first sentence of the first paragraph, contains the general principle of the peaceful enjoyment of property. The second rule, contained in the second sentence of the first paragraph, covers deprivation of possessions and subjects it to certain conditions. The third rule, stated in the second paragraph, recognises that the member states are entitled to regulate the use of property in accordance with the general interest. To be deemed compatible with article 1 Protocol 1, interferences must comply with the principle of lawfulness and proportionality.

The first question this translates into is whether there has been an interference with the applicant's right to the peaceful enjoyment of his or her possessions. If the measures which affected the applicant's rights cannot be qualified as either deprivation or control of use of property, it is asked whether the facts of the case can be interpreted in light of the general principle of respect for the peaceful enjoyment of possessions.[55] Many cases stemming from territorial conflicts will fall in the last mentioned, general category.

The case law of the ECHR covers damage and destruction of property[56] and the hindrance of access to property over a long time, as in the Cyprus[57] and Nagorno-Karabakh[58] cases. In the *Loizidou v Turkey* case, Ms Loizidou did

<https://opil.ouplaw.com/home/MPIL> accessed 8 June 2020; Tobias Ackermann, 'Investments under Occupation: The Application of Investment Treaties to Occupied Territory' in Katia Fach Gómez, Anastasios Gourgourinis, and Catharine Titi (eds), *International Investment Law and the Law of Armed Conflict* (Springer 2019) 80.

53 Ursula Kriebaum, 'Is the European Court of Human Rights an Alternative to Investor-State Arbitration?' in Pierre-Marie Dupuy, Ernst-Ulrich Petersmann, and Francesco Francioni (eds), *Human Rights in International Investment Law and Arbitration* (OUP 2009) 219, 231 et seq; Balthasar (n 14) 230 et seq.

54 For a full overview of the pertinent case law concerning the protection of company shares and other financial instruments, see ECtHR, 'Guide on Article 1 of Protocol No. 1' (n 29) paras 31 et seq.

55 ibid para 71.

56 *Eg Selçuk and Asker v Turkey*, App nos 23184/94 and 23185/94 (ECtHR, 24 April 1998, Merits and Just Satisfaction); *Khamidov v Russia*, App no 72118/01 (ECtHR, 15 November 2007, Merits and Just Satisfaction); *Kerimova and others v Russia*, App no 17170/04 (ECtHR, 3 May 2011, Merits and Just Satisfaction); *Damayev v Russia*, App no 36150/04 (ECtHR, 29 May 2012, Merits and Just Satisfaction).

57 *Eg Loizidou v Turkey*, App no 15318/89 (ECtHR, 18 December 1996, Merits).

58 *Chiragov and others v Armenia*, App no 13216/05 (ECtHR, 16 June 2015, Merits); *Sargsyan v Azerbaijan*, App no 40167/06 (ECtHR, 16 June 2015, Merits).

not argue that she had been a victim of expropriation. The Convention organs underlined that she continued to be the formal owner of the plots of land in Northern Cyprus, despite the fact that she had been hindered to peacefully enjoy her possessions since 1974.[59] Thus, where owners are hindered from peacefully enjoying their property rights due to a territorial conflict, they can be entitled to compensation for unjustified interferences with their rights, while they keep their formal title.[60] The arguement that there was an expropriation can be counterproductive in two ways: first, it can be an unnecessary concession. Second, the argument will put the ECtHR in the difficult position to adjudicate on the lawfulness of public acts and, thus, implicit sovereignty issues.

In the law of investment protection, the standards of protection are often described positively as obligations for the host state rather than negatively, as is done with the term interferences under the ECHR. Investment instruments usually oblige host states to refrain from direct and indirect expropriation, require fair and equitable treatment and mandate full protection and security.[61] The latter is in essence a due diligence requirement.[62] It has gained considerable relevance in the context of armed conflicts.[63]

The ECtHR has developed case law regarding positive obligations under article 1 Protocol 1.[64] The actual standard, which can be compared to the full protection and security notion, is a flexible and – for the purposes of this contribution – rather unpredictable one. In the Court's own words:

> In determining the scope of a State's positive obligations, regard must be had to the fair balance that has to be struck between the general interest

---

59 *Loizidou v Turkey*, Merits (n 57) para 64, where the Court notes that Ms Loizidou '*is* the owner' (emphasis added). See also *Loizidou v Turkey*, App no 15318/89 (ECtHR, 28 July 1998, Just Satisfaction) paras 13 and 31.

60 *Loizidou v Turkey*, Merits (n 57) para 63. See also *Chiragov and others v Armenia* (n 58) para 196.

61 See, eg, *Saluka Investments BV v Czech Republic*, Partial Award (17 March 2006) para 484. See also *Amco Asia Corp and others v Indonesia*, ICSID Case no ARB/81/1, Award (20 November 1984); *Eastern Sugar v Czech Republic*, SCC Case no 088/2004, Partial Award (27 March 2007).

62 Christoph Schreuer, 'Full Protection and Security' (2010) 1 JIDS 353.

63 See Emily Sipiorski, chapter 3 n this volume; see also Christina Binder and Philip Janig, chapter 4 in this volume.

64 Eg *Sovtransavto Holding v Ukraine*, App no 48553/99 (ECtHR, 25 July 2002) para 96; *Likvidējamā p/s Selga and Vasiļevska v Latvia*, App no 17126/02 (ECtHR, 1 October 2013, Decision) paras 103 et seq; *Ališić and others v Bosnia and Herzegovina, Croatia, Serbia, Slovenia, and the Former Yugoslav Republic of Macedonia*, App no 60642/08 (ECtHR, 16 July 2014) para 100.

and the interests of the individual, *the diversity of situations obtaining in Contracting States* and the choices which must be made in terms of priorities and resources. Nor must these obligations be interpreted in such a way as to impose an impossible or disproportionate burden.[65]

Outside of the context of territorial conflicts, property-related cases in the framework of the ECHR often involve alleged violations of article 6(1) ECHR (the right to a fair trial), article 13 ECHR (the right to an effective remedy), as well as article 14 ECHR (the prohibition of discrimination). The issues raised thus are not fundamentally different from the usual bouquet of complaints in investor-state contexts where investment agreements typically grant investors the right against expropriation without compensation, to receive fair and equitable treatment, to enjoy minimum standards of due process, and to not to be treated differently from domestic investors. The criteria investment arbitration uses to assess whether there is discrimination are similar.[66] The ancillary protection rights under articles 6, 13, and 14 ECHR and their relationship with the substantive right to property and its built in procedural face under article 1 Protocol 1 will need to undergo more clarification in the jurisprudence. A more explicit argumentation by investors might help clarify the jurisprudence. This presupposes, however, the availability of domestic remedies, which is often not the case in territorial conflicts.[67]

3.3 *Jurisdiction* Ratione Loci *and Jurisdiction* Ratione Personae

In the law of investment protection, jurisdiction *ratione loci* is governed by the notion of investment.[68] In distinction thereto, in the framework of the ECHR, the human rights protection needs to be triggered via article 1 ECHR.[69] Under that provision, jurisdiction *ratione loci* refers to the territorial jurisdiction of member states, thus, the question which state can be held liable. In addition, the two concepts of jurisdiction *ratione personae* and jurisdiction *ratione loci* blend into each other, especially where states are held accountable outside their own territory. Jurisdiction *ratione personae* is somewhat an extension of

---

65 *Ilaşcu and others v Moldova and Russia*, App no 48787/99 (ECtHR, 8 July 2004, Merits and Just Satisfaction) para 332 (emphasis added).
66 Kriebaum, *Eigentumsschutz im Völkerrecht* (n 4) 544.
67 See section 4.1 below.
68 See section 3.2 above and above n 52.
69 The provision reads: 'The High Contracting Parties shall secure to everyone within their jurisdiction the rights and freedoms defined in Section I of this Convention.'

the *ratione loci* jurisdiction – a broader concept, which encompasses the question whether and to what degree a member state is responsible for a certain set of allegations which refer to events outside of its formal borders. The contribution refers both to the Court's guide on article 1 ECHR[70] as well as its 'Practical Guide on Admissibility Criteria', which is concerned mainly with article 35 ECHR.[71] Thus, the issue of jurisdiction *ratione loci* and *ratione personae* has procedural and substantive elements.

The challenge to determine the territorial scope of application of the Convention in the specific context of property protection is not a new one for the Strasbourg organs. The Court has had ample opportunity to develop groups of cases which engage the responsibility of member states outside of their territory.[72] This is in line with the wording of article 33 ECHR, according to which every member state can bring an inter-state application with allegations of human rights violations by – not *in* – another member state. The ECtHR has further held that states retain human rights liability where they have lost control over a certain territory.[73] In order for a case to be admissible *ratione loci*, the alleged violation of the right to property must have taken place within the jurisdiction of the respondent state. The responsibility of a contracting party may also arise out of 'military action – whether lawful or unlawful' and the ensuing effective control over an area outside its national territory.[74] A finding of lack of jurisdiction *ratione loci* will not dispense the Court from examining whether an applicant was under the jurisdiction

---

70   ECtHR, 'Guide on Article 1 of the European Convention on Human Rights: Obligation to Respect Human Rights – Concepts of "Jurisdiction" and Imputability' (31 December 2019) paras 29 et seq <www.echr.coe.int/Documents/Guide_Art_1_ENG.pdf> accessed 8 June 2020.
71   ECtHR, 'Practical Guide on Admissibility Criteria' (n 8).
72   See also the detailed analysis in CDDH, 'Report on the Place of the European Convention on Human Rights in the European and International Legal Order' (2019) CDDH(2019) R92Addendum1, 30 et seq.
73   *Ilaşcu and others v Moldova and Russia*, Merits and Just Satisfaction (n 65). See also ECtHR Research Division, 'Articles 1 and 5: Extra-Territorial Jurisdiction, Jurisdiction of Territorial State Prevented from Exercising Its Authority in Part of Its Territory, and Validity of Detention and Criminal Proceedings in De Facto Entities' (2014) <www.echr.coe.int/Documents/Research_report_articles_1_5_ENG.pdf> accessed 8 June 2020.
74   *Loizidou v Turkey*, App no 15318/89 (ECtHR, 23 March 1995, Preliminary Objections) para 62; *Cyprus v Turkey*, App no 25781/94 (ECtHR, 10 May 2001, Merits) paras 75 et seq; *Ilaşcu and others v Moldova and Russia*, Admissibility, Merits and Just Satisfaction (n 38) para 386; *Issa and others v Turkey*, App no 31821/96 (ECtHR, 16 November 2004, Merits) para 65 et seq (on overall-control at para 70).

ratione personae of one or more contracting states for the purposes of article 1 ECHR.[75]

In turn, the jurisprudence of the Court on jurisdictional matters has led to an extensive amount of scholarship.[76] Specifically, the Court's jurisprudence concerning residual positive obligations of states which lost control over their territory based on sovereign title has been subject to criticism.[77]

This contribution does not provide a new reading of these issues. However, it intends to highlight that, with regard to Crimea, it is for the first time in history that the Strasbourg court has to deal with a formal annexation of territory of one member state by another.[78] It has to be noted that these individual cases under article 34 ECHR as well as the inter-state cases are currently pending before the Court. Many other cases with underlying territorial conflicts are awaiting judgment.[79] It is not clear from the previous case law to what extent Ukraine or Russia are potentially liable for the events in Ukraine. In order to minimize risks, investors should not limit themselves to sue one state in case of a violation of their property rights under the Convention.

4   Procedural Aspects for Investment Litigation under the ECHR

This section gives an overview over procedural requirements which substantially differ from the legal situation in investment protection. At the outset, it

---

75   *Drozd and Janousek v France and Spain*, App no 12747/87 (ECtHR, 26 June 1992) paras 84 et seq; *Ilaşcu and others v Moldova and Russia*, Admissibility, Merits and Just Satisfaction (n 38) para 300.

76   Koen Lemmens, 'General Survey of the Convention' in Pieter van Dijk and others (eds), *Theory and Practice of the European Convention on Human Rights* (Intersentia 2018) 16 et seq; Rick Lawson, 'Really Out of Sight? Issues of Jurisdiction and Control in Situations of Armed Conflict under the ECHR' in Antoine Buyse (ed), *Margins of Conflict: The ECHR and Transitions to and from Armed Conflict* (Intersentia 2011) 57.

77   Marco Milanović, *Extraterritorial Application of Human Rights Treaties: Law, Principles, and Policy* (OUP 2011); Marco Milanović and Tatjana Papić, 'The Applicability of the ECHR in Contested Territories' (2018) 67 ICLQ 779, 799 et seq; Lea Raible, 'Title to Territory and Jurisdiction in International Human Rights Law: Three Models for a Fraught Relationship'(2018) 31 LJIL 315, 316; Conall Mallory, *Human Rights Imperialists: The Extraterritorial Application of the European Convention on Human Rights* (Hart 2020); Lea Raible, *Human Rights Unbound: A Theory of Extraterritoriality* (OUP 2020).

78   In relation to the different situation in the Donbas region, see Stefan Lorenzmeier and Maryna Reznichuk, chapter 13 in this volume.

79   Eg *Georgia v Russia (II)*, App no 38263/08 (ECtHR). See also Stuart Wallace and Conall Mallory, 'Applying the European Convention on Human Rights to the Conflict in Ukraine' (2018) 6 Russian LJ 8.

should not go unobserved that every application needs to be handed to the Court on a form under rule 47 of the Rules of Court.[80] This formal requirement is handled rather strictly. Applicants who complain about property are unlikely to benefit from exceptions provided for in rule 47(5) of the Rules of Court.

The following subsection assesses the requirement of the exhaustion of domestic remedies as contained in article 35(1) ECHR in more detail, especially the exceptions thereto in the context of territorial conflict (section 4.1). The subsequent subsection deals very briefly with the matter of alternative or cumulative litigation, which appears to be handled fairly openly by the ECtHR (section 4.2).

4.1 Exhaustion of Domestic Remedies and Its Exceptions in Situations of Territorial Conflicts

Article 35(1) ECHR has two parts: It comprises the local-remedies rule and the so-called six-month rule.[81] For the purpose of this chapter, it suffices to observe with resepct to the six-month rule that it is applied strictly. For a complaint to interrupt the six-month period, the date of dispatch of the full and complete application (on the rule 47 form) is decisive. It is further important to underline that the mere deprivation of an individual's property is, in principle, an 'instantaneous act' and does not produce a continuing situation in respect of the rights concerned, thus, does not extend the time limit of article 35(1) ECHR.[82] The Cyprus cases have been interpreted as important exceptions, which also relate to the fact that the allegation did not include expropriation.[83] The individual possibility to access the Strasbourg machinery was, during the relevant time frame, very different from today.[84] In view of the special circumstances of the Cyprus cases, especially the procedural circumstances which are not comparable to today's supervisory structure of the Convention, it is advisable to use existing procedural possibilities without undue delay.

---

80 ECtHR, 'Rules of Court' (1 January 2020) <www.echr.coe.int/Documents/Rules_Court_ENG.pdf> accessed 8 June 2020.
81 With the entry into force of Protocol 15, the time frame is cut down to four months. Only two states have not yet ratified the protocol. Protocol No. 15 amending the Convention for the Protection of Human Rights and Fundamental Freedoms (adopted 24 June 2013, not in force) ETS no 213 (Protocol 15).
82 *Blečić v Croatia*, App no 59532/00 (ECtHR, 8 March 2006, Merits) para 86. For the specific case of post-1945 deprivation of possessions under a former regime, see *Preussische Treuhand GmbH & Co KG aA v Poland*, App no 47550/06 (ECtHR 7 October 2008, Decision) paras 55 et seq.
83 *Loizidou v Turkey*, Merits (n 57) paras 39 et seq.
84 See section 3.1 above.

The requirement of the exhaustion of domestic remedies is one which is, on a regular basis, not applicable in the context of investment protection frameworks. On the contrary, one of the purposes of these instruments is to escape many years of vertical exhaustion of domestic remedies.[85] Rather, many bilateral investment treaties mandate cooling-off periods before access to international arbitration is possible.[86] In contrast, the requirement of the exhaustion of domestic remedies under article 35(1) ECHR is an important feature of the Convention and the subsidiary nature of the jurisdiction of the ECtHR. However, in the context of territorial conflicts, the Court has often dispensed with the rule, where it found domestic remedies to be not effective or not available at all.

In the context of the conflict in Chechnya, the Court has reiterated its case law concerning the flexible and not unduly formalistic dispensation from the requirement of the exhaustion of domestic remedies under article 35(1) ECHR.[87] The application of the rule is context-based. The ECtHR underlined that where an arguable claim in respect of killing, torture, or destruction of property involving the responsibility of the state is formulated, 'the notion of an "effective remedy", in the sense of Article 13 of the Convention, entails, in addition to the payment of compensation where appropriate, a thorough and effective investigation capable of leading to the identification and punishment of those responsible and including effective access by the complainant to the investigative procedure.'[88] In cases where property-related violations are alleged outside the ambit of articles 2 and 3 ECHR, the standard may vary.[89]

In the Grand Chamber case of *Chiragov v Armenia*, which centred around the conflict in Nagorno-Karabakh, the Court dispensed from the requirement because the state 'failed to discharge the burden of proving the availability to the applicants of a remedy capable of providing redress in respect of their Convention complaints and offering reasonable prospects of success.'[90]

In the context of prolonged conflicts, such as the one in Northern Cyprus, the Court has held that the domestic remedies available had to be exhausted. It did, however, announce this change in the handling of the rule contained in

---

[85] See only Jeswald W Salacuse, *The Law of Investment Treaties* (2nd edn, OUP 2015) 398.

[86] Aravind Ganesh, 'Cooling off Period', *Max Planck Encyclopedia of International Procedural Law* (2017) <https://opil.ouplaw.com/home/MPIL> accessed 8 June 2020.

[87] *Isayeva v Russia*, App no 57950/00 (ECtHR, 24 February 2005, Merits and Just Satisfaction) para 151 et seq; *Kerimova and others v Russia* (n 56) paras 212 et seq.

[88] *Kerimova and others v Russia* (n 56) para 215.

[89] *Damayev v Russia* (n 56) paras 108 et seq.

[90] *Chiragov and others v Armenia* (n 58) para 120; similarly, *Sargsyan v Azerbayan* (n 58) para 119.

article 35 (1) ECHR. In the *Xenides-Arestis v Turkey* pilot judgment of December 2005, the Court considered that the respondent state must introduce a remedy in the Turkish Republic of Northern Cyprus (TRNC) which secures genuinely effective redress for the Convention violations identified in the judgment.[91] In response to the *Xenides* judgment, the TRNC set up the so-called Immovable Property Commission (IPC). The IPC started its work in March 2006. In its 2010 admissibility decision in the case of *Demopoulos and others v Turkey*, the Grand Chamber found that the IPC provides for an effective remedy and dismissed property-related complaints emanating from Cyprus for the non-exhaustion of domestic remedies.[92] The Court argued that it had a subsidiary role in the protection of human rights as enshrined in the Convention.[93] It thus required the exhaustion of domestic remedies in the TRNC.

In sum, conflict situations may lead to a successful argument by an applicant in favour of dispensing with the requirement to exhaust domestic remedies under article 35(1) ECHR. If a conflict persists over a long time (which it already does in Ukraine), the rule might be applied differently over time as the example of Northern Cyprus shows.

A dispensation from the rule allows, at first sight, faster access to the ECtHR. However, the other side of this medal is that the Strasbourg court is then in a situation akin to a court of first instance. This means that the facts of each case need to be ascertained, which is potentially time consuming. In cases of territorial conflict, facts will often be disputed, thus, to establish facts is a considerable challenge, all the more for a Court which is already very busy. In the specific context of conflicts, the Court has developed standards regarding the required level of proof for the claim of ownership.[94]

4.2 *Alternative or Cumulative Litigation before the ECHR*

This subsection deals with the question whether the ECtHR can be used as an additional forum to litigate investment claims in view of article 35(2)(b) ECHR, which states that the Court shall not deal with an application which, among others, 'has already been submitted to another procedure of international

---

91 *Xenides-Arestis v Turkey*, App no 46347/99 (ECtHR, 22 December 2005, Merits) para 40 and para 5 of the dispositive. Some authors refer to the case also as quasi-pilot judgment because the Court has not identified the case as a pilot case, Philip Leach and others, *Responding to Systemic Human Rights Violations* (2010) 156.
92 *Demopoulos and others v Turkey*, App nos 46113/99 and others (ECtHR, 1 March 2010, Decision). The Court's approach was confirmed in *Meleagrou and others v Turkey*, App no 14434/09 (ECtHR, 2 April 2013, Decision).
93 *Demopoulos and others v Turkey* (n 92) para 69.
94 ECtHR, 'Guide on Article 1 of Protocol No. 1' (n 29) paras 63 et seq.

investigation or settlement and contains no relevant new information.' The ECtHR has been rather liberal in allowing seemingly similar cases.[95] With regard to the *Yukos* case, the Court was not very strict at the merits stage.[96] It rendered a just satisfaction (article 41 ECHR) judgment[97] only weeks after an arbitral tribunal had rendered awards in the context of PCA proceedings.[98] The ECtHR declined to look into the merits of a case where a prior decision on the merits existed at the date on which the Court examined the case.[99] In another case, the Court has also considered whether the applicant had abused the right of application by concealing the intention to use another international forum, the International Labour Organization's Committee on Freedom of Association.[100]

The problems (potentially) caused by forum shopping between several available human rights instruments has been assessed by the Steering Committee for Human Rights (CDDH) in late 2019.[101] The analysis, however, did not take into account mechanisms under investment protection law.[102] Overall, the potential problems with cumulative proceedings under the ECHR and investment treaties should not be overestimated. Where the substantive provisions differ, especially in their wording, different interpretations of different norms do not pose a problem for the coherence of international judicial decisions. The wording of article 1 Protocol 1 is fragmentary. Compared to the usually more explicit and precise provisions which were drafted for a specific, usually bilateral context, a conflict based on different norms does not arise. Further, it is important to distinguish who is the litigant or applicant: is it a shareholder, is it a legal person? Where there is no identity of the

---

95   *Folgerø and others v Norway*, App no 15472/02 (ECtHR, 14 February 2006, Decision); *Hilal Mammadov v Azerbaijan*, App no 81553/12 (ECtHR, 4 February 2016) para 103 et seq.
96   *Oao Neftyanaya Kompaniya Yukos v Russia*, App no 14902/04 (ECtHR, 20 September 2011, Merits) paras 520 et seq.
97   *Oao Neftyanaya Kompaniya Yukos v Russia*, App no 14902/04 (ECtHR, 31 July 2014, Just Satisfaction).
98   *Hulley Enterprises Ltd (Cyprus) v Russia*, UNCITRAL, PCA Case no 226, Final Award (18 July 2014); *Veteran Petroleum Ltd (Cyprus) v Russia*, UNCITRAL, PCA Case no AA228, Final Award (18 July 2014); *Yukos Universal Ltd (Isle of Man) v Russia* (n 18).
99   *Peraldi v France*, App no 2096/05 (ECtHR, 7 April 2009, Decision).
100 *National Union of Rail, Maritime and Transport Workers v UK*, App no 31045/10 (ECtHR, 8 April 2014, Merits and Just Satisfaction) para 48.
101 CDDH, 'Report on the Place of the European Convention on Human Rights in the European and International Legal Order' (n 72) 81 et seq. See also Hans-Jörg Behrens, 'Forum Shopping – Eine Herausforderung für den internationalen Menschenrechtsschutz' (2020) 47 EuGRZ 171.
102 In this respect, see Christine Sim, chapter 7 in this volume.

parties and the substantive provisions, there is no danger of formally divergent decisions.

5 The Prospects of Investment Protection Regarding Current Territorial Conflicts under the ECHR

This section assesses the prospects of investment protection cases in the framework of the ECHR in the context of territorial conflicts. It discusses the implications the ECHR's caseload has on the discharge of its functions (5.1), addresses potential remedies (5.2) and familiarizes the reader with the instrument of pilot judgment proceedings (5.3), which represents in essence a *non-monetary* approach of the Court to deal with systemic or large-scale human rights violations which typically arise during and in the aftermath of territorial conflicts. Then, Ukraine (5.4) and Russia (5.5) are put in an – admittedly selective – spotlight. Overall, the prospects of success for investment claims in terms of *financial* compensation seem to be very limited.

5.1 *The ECtHR's Caseload*

The ECtHR is a *very* busy court. Some 60,000 applications were pending in Strasbourg at the turn of the year 2019/2020.[103] The Court does not provide statistical information as to how long a case usually takes to be decided. As a rule of thumb, the Court endeavors to deal with cases within three years after they have been brought[104] – a duration that is somewhat comparable to the average duration of investor-state arbitration, that is, about four years.[105] The length of the proceedings before the Court varies depending on the complexity of the case, the formation to which it is assigned, the diligence of the parties in providing the Court with information, the conduct of the relevant authorities, and many other factors, such as the holding of a hearing or referral to the Grand Chamber.

The *Yukos v Russia* case,[106] an investment protection case outside of the context of a territorial conflict, took roughly ten years from the date of its

---

103 ECtHR, 'Pending Applications Allocated to a Judicial Formation' (31 December 2019) <www.echr.coe.int/Documents/Stats_pending_2020_BIL.pdf> accessed 8 June 2020.
104 ECtHR, 'The ECHR in 50 Questions' (2014) 9 <www.echr.coe.int/Documents/50Questions_ENG.pdf> accessed 8 June 2020.
105 José M Álvarez Zárate and others, 'Duration of Investor-State Dispute Settlement Proceedings' (2020) 21 JWIT 300, 311.
106 *Oao Neftyanaya Kompaniya Yukos v Russia*, Just Satisfaction (n 97).

introduction in Strasbourg in April 2004 to a judgment on the merits in 2011 and the just satisfaction judgment in July 2014. Similarly, the case of *Industrial Financial Consortium Investment Metallurgical Union v Ukraine* took more than 13 years.[107] The famous *Loizidou v Turkey* case began in 1974 with the Turkish intervention in Cyprus, when Ms Loizidou was deprived of her property in the North of the island. The case was brought to Strasbourg and before the now defunct Commission in 1989. Turkey had accepted the right to individual petition under ex-article 25 ECHR only in 1987. Turkey accepted the jurisdiction of the Court under ex-article 46 ECHR in 1990. The Court rendered the just satisfaction award in 1998 and ultimately paid it in 2003.[108] It is, at this point, worthwhile to underline that the *Loizidou* case as an individual case was so important because of the unsuccessful inter-state litigation up to that point. It is unlikely that such an individual case would be decided by way of example in today's conflict between Ukraine and Russia.

One of the responses to the heavy workload of the Court is a priority policy, established in 2009 'with a view to speeding up the processing and adjudication of the most important, serious and urgent cases.'[109] The legal basis for this policy is contained in rule 41 of the Rules of Court. The Court may derogate from these criteria so as to give priority to a particular application.

In essence, there are eight categories of cases, comprising inter-state applications and seven categories of individual applications under article 34 ECHR. The first three categories of individual cases are dedicated to (I.) urgent applications, in particular risk to life or health of the applicant, the applicant deprived of liberty as a direct consequence of the alleged violation of his or her Convention rights, (II.) applications raising questions capable of having an impact on the effectiveness of the Convention system (in particular a structural or endemic situation that the Court has not yet examined, pilot-judgment procedure) or applications raising an important question of general interest (in particular a serious question capable of having major implications for domestic legal systems or for the European system) and (III.) to the core rights (articles 2, 3, 4, and 5(1) of the Convention).

---

107 *Industrial Financial Consortium Investment Metallurgical Union v Ukraine*, App no 10640/05 (ECtHR, 26 June 2018, Merits and Just Satisfaction).
108 See Council of Europe Committee of Ministers, 'Resolution Concerning the Judgment of the European Court of Human Rights of 28 July 1998 in the Loizidou Case against Turkey' (2003) ResDH(2003)190. See also below, n 123.
109 ECtHR, 'The Court's Priority Policy' (not dated) <www.echr.coe.int/Documents/Priority_policy_ENG.pdf> accessed 8 June 2020.

Property cases regularly do not fall within the 'important, serious and urgent'-category.[110] According to a press release of December 2018, the Court procedurally connected the approximately 5.000 individual applications relating to Eastern Ukraine to the inter-state proceedings *Ukraine v Russia (re Eastern Ukraine)*.[111]

5.2 Financial Compensation, Just Satisfaction and Litigation Costs, Enforcement

In the framework of human rights law, restitution arguably still plays a larger role than in the context of international investment arbitration. Cases regarding restitution in the aftermath of the (democratic) changes in Central and Eastern Europe are an important example.[112] In terms of financial consequences for human rights breaches, the Court has been careful not to provide financial incentives for even more human rights litigation by a cautious approach of awarding just satisfaction under article 41 ECHR. Even the *Yukos* award mentioned above is dwarfed by the sums the PCA tribunal awarded. A financial consequence of a violation is no automatism under the law of the Convention. The Court will only award just satisfaction where a specific claim has been submitted in line with the requirements set out in rule 60 of the Rules of Court. The Court's practice direction for just satisfaction is a valuable reference.[113] Just satisfaction may be afforded under article 41 ECHR in respect of (a) pecuniary damage, (b) non-pecuniary damage, and (c) costs and expenses. There are no court fees for the applicants in proceedings before the ECtHR. Thus, litigation before the Court might be less costly than arbitration.

---

110   ECtHR, 'Analysis of Statistics 2019' (n 7).
111   ECtHR Press Unit, Press Release ECHR 432 (2018) (n 26). Meanwhile, investment tribunals have already adjudicated some of the cases arising out of the territorial conflict between Ukraine and Russia, for further details on the mostly confidential awards see Sebastian Wuschka, 'Investment Tribunals Adjudicating Claims Relating to Occupied Territories – Curse or Blessing?' in Antoine Duval and Eva Kassoti (eds), *The Legality of Economic Activities in Occupied Territories* (Routlege 2020) 235.
112   ECtHR, 'Guide on Article 1 of Protocol No. 1' (n 29) paras 346 et seq; Antoine Buyse, 'Lost and Regained? Restitution as a Remedy for Human Rights Violations in the Context of International Law' (2008) 68 Heidelberg J Int'l L 129, 132. See also Fionnuala Ní Aoláin, 'Transitional Justice and the European Convention on Human Rights' (2017) Geneva Academy of International Humanitarian Law and Human Rights, Academy Briefing no 10, 33 et seq <https://repository.graduateinstitute.ch/record/295768?ln=en> accessed 8 June 2020.
113   ECtHR, 'Practice Direction Just Satisfaction Claims' (2007) <www.echr.coe.int/Documents/PD_satisfaction_claims_ENG.pdf> accessed 8 June 2020.

In terms of compensation for property-related violations, the Court stated in the 1986 *Lithgow v UK* case that the introduction of Protocol 1 did not mean that existing standards in customary international law, *ie* that of prompt, adequate, and effective compensation for foreign-owned property, would be lowered.[114] In practice, the Court does not seem to distinguish, in the application of article 41 ECHR, between foreign owned and other property.[115] The Court further underlines that article 41 ECHR requires an equitable application of the provision.[116] In sum, it is important to provide for a convincing and detailed calculation for pecuniary damages, including the use of expert calculations.[117] In addition, the Court can award non-pecuniary damages where frustration and suffering has had a negative impact on individuals.[118] This possibility goes beyond the reach of investment protection.

The Court can order the reimbursement of costs and expenses for both national proceedings and the proceedings before the Strasbourg court. Overall, the reimbursement is only possible in so far as it has been shown that costs and expenses have been actually and necessarily incurred and are reasonable as to quantum.[119]

The judgments of the Court are final and binding under article 46 ECHR. However, it has to be recalled that, unlike, for example, articles 53 and 54 of the ICSID Convention[120] or the possibilities offered under the New York Convention,[121] Strasbourg's judgments are not enforceable titles. This is a disadvantage which is especially relevant where respondent states are recalcitrant. As will be shown below, both Ukraine and Russia might resist the execution of judgments not in their favour. In order to provide a full picture, it must be added here that annulment proceedings in the framework of the law of

---

114   *Lithgow and others v UK* (n 3) para 115.
115   *Bimer SA v Moldova*, App no 15084/03 (ECtHR, 10 July 2007) paras 62 et seq.
116   *Marini v Albania*, App no 3738/02 (ECtHR, 18 December 2007) para 191; *Zslinsat, Spol SRO v Bulgaria*, App no 57785/00 (ECtHR, 10 January 2008, Just Satisfaction) para 41.
117   *Rosenzweig and Bonded Warehouses Ltd v Poland*, App no 51728/99 (ECtHR, 5 June 2012, Just Satisfaction) paras 39 et seq.
118   ibid.
119   *Iatridis v Greece*, App no 31107/96 (ECtHR, 25 March 1999, Just Satisfaction) para 54.
120   Convention on the Settlement of Investment Disputes between States and Nationals of Other States (adopted 18 March 1965, entered into force 14 October 1966) 575 UNTS 159 (ICSID Convention).
121   United Nations Convention on the Recognition and Enforcement of Foreign Arbitral Awards (adopted 10 June 1958, entered into force 7 June 1959) 330 UNTS 3 (New York Convention).

investment protection can be an obstacle in the enforcement of awards as well.[122]

5.3 Pilot Judgments – General Non-Monetary Measures

An ECtHR judgment is binding and final under article 46 ECHR. The Committee of Ministers supervises the execution of judgments in a peer review-proceeding in which sovereign states are the peers.[123] This type of proceeding is overall fairly efficient, probably the best human rights oversight mechanism today. However, it has its limitations, especially if respondent states remain recalcitrant.

The role of the supervision of judgments has been, in part, acquired by the Court itself. One of the measures the Court has come up with to tackle structural, systemic human rights issues are so-called pilot judgments. A pilot judgment addresses a systemic issue in a leading case. Other parallel or clone cases will be resolved by adjudicating one specific case. Its aim is ultimately to prompt the respondent state to create an effective domestic remedy. The Strasbourg court started using this type of measure because it was overwhelmed by cases. Repetitive well-founded cases were and are a burden to the Strasbourg supervisory system.[124] This type of proceeding has no formal grounding in the Convention.[125] Since February 2011, rule 61 of the Rules of Court, which do not have the status of international law, provide for a legal basis.

Pilot judgments have been identified to provide a way to ease the transition of states in the *aftermath* of conflict.[126] The *Broniowski v Poland*

---

122 See, for the context of the *Yukos* case, Felix Boor, 'Die Aufhebung der Yukos-Schiedssprüche des Court of Arbitration vor dem Bezirksgericht in Den Haag – nur der Anfang einer langen Vollstreckungsodysee?' (2016) 54 Archiv des Völkerrechts 297.
123 The department of the execution of judgments at the ECtHR provides, analogously to the 'HUDOC-ECHR' system, the 'HUDOC-EXEC' database. In the database, the status of execution of judgments are rendered transparent. See ECtHR Department for the Execution of Judgments, 'HUDOC-EXEC' (2020) <https://hudoc.exec.coe.int/> accessed 8 June 2020.
124 Luzius Wildhaber, 'Pilot Judgments in Cases of Structural or Systemic Problems on the National Level' in Rüdiger Wolfrum and Ulrike Deutsch (eds), *The European Court of Human Rights Overwhelmed by Applications: Problems and Possible Solutions* (Springer 2009).
125 ECtHR Press Unit, 'Factsheet – Pilot Judgments' (May 2020) <www.echr.coe.int/Documents/FS_Pilot_judgments_ENG.pdf> accessed 8 June 2020. See, for the background on the reform discussions, Marten Breuer, 'Urteilsfolgen bei strukturellen Problemen – Das erste "Piloturteil" des EGMR, Anmerkung zum Fall Broniowski gegen Polen' (2004) 31 EuGRZ 445, 447. See also Marten Breuer, 'Zur Fortentwicklung der Piloturteilstechnik durch den EGMR' (2012) 39 EuGRZ 1.
126 Antoine Buyse, 'Airborne or Bound to Crash? The Rise of Pilot Judgments and Their Appeal as a Tool to Deal with the Aftermath of Conflict' in Antoine Buyse (ed), *Margins of Conflict: The ECHR and Transitions to and from Armed Conflict* (Intersentia 2011) 175.

case[127] was the first pilot judgment. It stems from the context of the Second World War, when the borders of the Polish state were rearranged both in the West and in the East. Poland had undertaken to compensate displaced persons. However, some 100,000 inhabitants of the Bug River region never received compensation. Mr Broniowski was one of the many affected persons. The pilot proceedings induced changes in the national legislation providing for a 20 percent compensation of the original value, which the Strasbourg court held to be within the margin of appreciation of Poland.[128] The remaining cases were struck from the list.[129]

The type of proceeding was also employed in the context of the Turkish occupation of Northern Cyprus in *Xenides-Arestis v Turkey*[130] and was applied to the situation in Eastern Turkey.[131] The case of *Suljagić v Bosnia and Herzegovina*[132] concerned systemic problems due to deficiencies in repayment scheme for foreign currency deposited before the dissolution of the Socialist Federal Republic of Yugoslavia (SFRY). The applicant, a Bosnian national, complained about the failure to issue state bonds which, as provided for by Bosnian law, would enable savings deposited by individuals in Bosnian banks before the dissolution of the SFRY to be reimbursed. The Court observed that more than 1,350 similar cases were pending before it. In November 2010, having concluded that the matter had been resolved, the Court closed the pilot-judgment procedure in question.[133]

Without zooming in too deeply into the type of proceeding,[134] one aspect has to be underlined: the Court actively seeks to ensure that structural issues, including property issues in the aftermath of conflicts, are solved on the national level. This might be also the approach of the Court in the current conflicts between Ukraine and Russia – all the more so in light of the fact that member states have, via Protocol 15 (which is not yet in force), expressly enshrined the principle of subsidiarity in the preamble of the Convention. Certainly, the pilot judgment proceedings do not bar the Court from issuing just satisfaction judgments in case the respective respondent state does not

---

127 *Broniowski v Poland*, App no 31443/96 (ECtHR, 28 September 2005, Friendly Settlement).
128 *Wolkenberg v Poland*, App no 50003/99 (ECtHR, 4 December 2007, Decision).
129 *EG and 175 other Bug River Applications v Poland*, App no 50425/99 (ECtHR, 23 September 2008, Decision).
130 *Xenides-Arestis v Turkey* (n 91).
131 *Icyer v Turkey*, App no 18888/02 (ECtHR, 12 January 2006, Decision).
132 *Suljagić v Bosnia and Herzegovina*, App no 27912/02 (ECtHR, 3 November 2009).
133 *Zadrić v Bosnia and Herzegovina*, App no 18804/04 (ECtHR, 16 November 2010, Decision).
134 Leach, *Taking a Case* (n 49) 86 et seq.

solve the underlying issue, as it has done in *Xenides-Arestis v Turkey*. However, the Court prefers to address large scale cases by non-pecuniary measures.

5.4 *A Spotlight on Ukraine*

Ukraine's human rights record, showing very serious systemic problems when it comes to the enforcement of human rights, is illustrated here in some more detail in order to help assess whether it would be worthwhile for investors to pursue claims against Ukraine in the framework of the ECHR.[135] Ukraine alone accounts for some 12 percent of the Court's overall caseload. Specifically, the non-enforcement of domestic final judgments, especially judgments delivered against entities owned or controlled by the state, and to the lack of an effective remedy in this respect, is sobering.

In October 2017, the Grand Chamber of the Court delivered its judgment in *Burmych and others v Ukraine*.[136] The case represents a total of about 29,000 repetitive and well-founded applications concerning the non-enforcement of domestic judgments which have been submitted to the Court since 1999. Since the beginning of 2016, the Court has continued to receive a large number of such applications, over 200 per month.[137]

In October 2010, the Court delivered a pilot judgment in the *Yuriy Nikolayevich Ivanov v Urkaine* case.[138] It stressed that specific reforms in Ukraine's legislation and administrative practice should be implemented without delay to resolve this problem, and set a deadline for mid-2011 for the creation of an effective domestic remedy in this respect. The Court invited the respondent state to settle on an *ad hoc* basis all similar applications, at the time, some 1,600 cases, lodged with it before the delivery of the pilot judgment. It decided to adjourn the examination of similar cases. Given that the measures called for by the Court in its pilot judgment were not adopted within

---

135   ECtHR Press Unit, 'Press Country Profile – Ukraine' (January 2020) <www.echr.coe.int/Documents/CP_Ukraine_ENG.pdf> accessed 8 June 2020.
136   *Burmych and others v Ukraine*, App no 46852/13 (ECtHR, 12 October 2017, Striking Out). See Lize Glas, 'Burmych v Ukraine Two Years Later: What About Restoral?' (*Strasbourg Observers*, 17 September 2019) <https://strasbourgobservers.com/2019/09/17/burmych-v-ukraine-two-years-later-what-about-restoral/> accessed 8 June 2020; Geir Ulfstein and Andreas Zimmermann, '*Certiorari* through the Backdoor? The Judgment by the European Court of Human Rights in *Burmych and Others v. Ukraine* in Perspective' (2018) 17 L & Prac Int'l Cts & Tribunals 289.
137   *Burmych and others v Ukraine* (n 136) para 44.
138   *Yuriy Nikolayevich Ivanov v Ukraine*, App no 40450/04 (ECtHR, 15 October 2009, Merits and Just Satisfaction).

the deadline set, in February 2012, the Court decided to resume examination of the frozen applications raising similar issues. In the 2017 *Burmych* judgment, the Grand Chamber noted that despite the significant lapse of time since the *Ivanov* pilot judgment, Ukraine had still not implemented the requisite general measures capable of addressing the root causes of the systemic problem identified by the Court nor provided an effective remedy securing redress to all victims at the national level. After some 18 years of dealing with *Ivanov*-type cases, the Grand Chamber, by a 10:7 majority, concluded that 'nothing is to be gained, nor would justice be best served, by the repetition of its findings in a lengthy series of comparable cases, which would place a significant burden on its own resources, with a consequent impact on its considerable caseload.'[139] Citing article 37(1)(c) ECHR, the Grand Chamber decided to strike 12,148 repetitive follow-up applications from its list of cases. In perspective, in the beginning of 2017, some 80,000 cases were pending before the Court. The Committee of Ministers, which is entrusted with the supervision of the judgments of the Court, has the cases on its agenda.[140] What the *Burmych* judgment shows is that the Strasbourg machinery meets its limits where a state does not cooperate and implements neither national nor international judgments.

5.5   The Council of Europe, the ECHR, and Russia

Russia is the largest state party of the Council of Europe.[141] It signed the Convention and Protocol 1 in 1996, and ratified both in 1998. The protection of private property in the Russian legal order does not look back on a long tradition. Russia's ratification of the Convention and of Protocol 1 was therefore not just *usual business*.[142] The hope that Russia would, as a member of the Council of Europe, benefit from the 'School of Democracy' was a desire that was hard to reconcile with the realities from the beginning.[143]

---

139   *Burmych and others v Ukraine* (n 136) para 174.
140   For the status of the cases, see Department for the Execution of Judgments, 'HUDOC-EXEC' (n 123).
141   ECtHR Press Unit, 'Press Country Profile – Russia' (February 2020) <www.echr.coe.int/Documents/CP_Russia_ENG.pdf> accessed 8 June 2020.
142   Vladislav Starzhenetskiy, 'Property Rights in Russia: Reconsidering the Socialist Legal Tradition' in Lauri Mälksoo and Wolfgang Benedek (eds), *Russia and the European Court of Human Rights: The Strasbourg Effect* (CUP 2017) 297 et seq.
143   Lauri Mälksoo, 'Russia, Strasbourg and the Paradox of a Human Rights Backlash' in Lauri Mälksoo and Wolfgang Benedek (eds), *Russia and the European Court of Human Rights: The Strasbourg Effect* (CUP 2017) 4.

Describing the current relationship between the Council of Europe, the parent organization of the ECtHR, and Russia as *difficult* is an understatement.[144] The July 2014 just satisfaction award in the case of *Yukos v Russia*,[145] an award of Euro 1,866,104,634 (1.86 billion) accelerated the development of sophisticated methods of Russian 'resistance'[146] to the Court's judgments.[147] The award remains the largest in the history of the Convention. The unprecedented amount 'presented an unsolvable dilemma for the Russian authorities from the financial, reputational and political points of view.'[148]

The execution of judgments by the Court is overseen by the Committee of Ministers of the Council of Europe, a political organ. The inherent limits in this supervisory function are illustrated here by reference with the way the Council of Europe as such dealt with the conflict between Russia and Ukraine since 2014.[149]

The Parliamentary Assembly of the Council is the deliberative organ of the Council of Europe. It is made up of members of national parliaments of the 47 Council of Europe member states.[150] The Assembly has been a vocal actor in Europe over the decades when it came to reactions to a state's failure to comply with the Statute of the Council of Europe.[151] The Assembly's reaction often can

---

144 Caroline von Gall, 'Gemeinsam für den Frieden und die Einheit Europas? Der Europarat und Russland' (*Verfassungsblog*, 5 May 2019) <https://verfassungsblog.de/gemeinsam-fuer-den-frieden-und-die-einheit-europas-der-europarat-und-russland/> accessed 8 June 2020.
145 *Oao Neftyanaya Kompaniya Yukos v Russia*, Just Satisfaction (n 97).
146 Matthias Hartwig, 'Vom Dialog zum Disput? Verfassungsrecht vs. Europäische Menschenrechtskonvention – Der Fall der Russländischen Föderation' (2017) 44 EuGRZ 1, 14 et seq; Vladislav Starzhenetskiy, 'The Execution of ECHR Judgments and the "Right to Object" of the Russian Constitutional Court' in Marten Breuer (ed), *Principled Resistance to ECHR Judgments – A New Paradigm?* (Springer 2019) 267.
147 Russia's share in the category of enhanced supervision cases is almost 20 percent of cases overall, followed by Ukraine with a similar sizeable chunk. See ECtHR Department for the Execution of Judgments, 'Main States with Cases under Enhanced Supervision' (not dated) <https://rm.coe.int/5-main-states-with-cases-under-enhanced-supervision-eng/16807b8a62> accessed 8 June 2020; Council of Europe Committee of Ministers, 'Supervision of the Execution of Judgments and Decisions of the European Court of Human Rights 2019' (2020) <https://rm.coe.int/annual-report-2019-1/16809e1c59> accessed 8 June 2020.
148 Starzhenetskiy, 'Execution of ECHR Judgments' (n 146) 268.
149 Council of Europe Parliamentary Assembly, Committee on Legal Affairs and Human Rights, 'Implementation of the Judgments of the European Court of Human Rights, 10th Report: Russian Federation' (4 February 2020) AS/Jur (2020) 05.
150 Philip Leach, 'The Parliamentary Assembly of the Council of Europe' in Stefanie Schmahl and Marten Breuer (eds), *The Council of Europe* (OUP 2016).
151 Eckart Klein, 'Membership and Observer Status' in Stefanie Schmahl and Marten Breuer (eds), *The Council of Europe* (OUP 2016) 65 et seq. See also Andrew Drzemczewski,

be seen in contrast to the ones of the Committee of Ministers of the Council of Europe. The Committee of Ministers is composed of one representative of each member state, according to Article 14 of the Statute of the Council of Europe. It brings together the ministers of foreign affairs or their deputies.

Russia discontinued payments to the Council of Europe after its voting rights in the Parliamentary Assembly had been suspended following the its annexation of Crimea and its actions in Eastern Ukraine.[152] The Parliamentary Assembly regarded the violation of the territorial integrity of Ukraine as a grave violation of the Statute of the Council of Europe.[153] In fact, a large part of Ukraine's territory is affected, is 'in limbo'. In the summer of 2019, the Parliamentary Assembly of the Council of Europe restored the voting rights of the Russian delegation in a controversial vote.[154] The Committee of Ministers had, in May 2019, appealed to the 'shared responsibility for democratic security in Europe.'[155] It noted, without referring expressly to Russia, that, 'having regard to the importance of the elections of the Secretary General and of judges to the European Court of Human Rights, [it] would welcome that delegations of all member states take part in the next June part-Session of the Parliamentary Assembly'.[156] The Committee of Ministers further observed the

> urgent need to develop synergies and provide for co-ordinated action by the two statutory organs, in recognition of their respective mandates, in order to strengthen the Organization's ability to react more effectively in situations where a member State violates its statutory obligations or does not respect the standards, fundamental principles and values upheld by the Council of Europe.[157]

'The Prevention of Human Rights Violations: Monitoring Mechanism of the Council of Europe' in Linos-Alexander Sicilianos (ed), *The Prevention of Human Rights Violations* (Brill Nijhoff 2001).

152   Council of Europe Parliamentary Assembly, 'Reconsideration on Substantive Grounds of the Previously Ratified Credentials of the Russian Delegation' (2014) Resolution 1990.

153   See also Lauri Mälksoo, 'The Annexation of Crimea and Balance of Power in International Law' (2019) 30 EJIL 303, who describes the annexation of Crimea as 'probably the most challenging event for the foundations of international law in the last decade.'

154   Council of Europe Parliamentary Assembly, 'Challenge, on Substantive Grounds, of the Still Unratified Credentials of the Parliamentary Delegation of the Russian Federation' (2019) Resolution 2292.

155   Council of Europe Committee of Ministers, 'A Shared Responsibility for Democratic Security in Europe' (17 May 2019) Decision CM/Del/Dec(2019)129/2.

156   ibid para 4.

157   ibid para 6. See also Council of Europea Parliamentary Assembly, 'Strengthening the Decision-making Process of the Parliamentary Assembly Concerning Credentials and Voting' (25 June 2019) Resolution 2287, para 4.

One of the main arguments to keep Russia within the Council of Europe was the preservation of the right of individual application under article 34 ECHR. In the end, however, Russia's membership in the Council of Europe has the potential to threaten the credibility of the whole organization.

6 Conclusion

The claim the title of this contribution makes is that there is value in the way article 1 Protocol 1 to the ECHR protects investments in cases of territorial conflicts.

Substantively, there is indeed merit in this statement. Investments and investors enjoy considerable protection via article 1 Protocol 1. The possibilities for just satisfaction under article 41 ECHR regarding the compensation for interferences with foreign owned property are not necessarily limited by the way the Court deals with national cases. The *prompt, adequate and effective* standard has neither been confirmed nor ruled out for foreign-owned property.[158]

Often, the Court resorts to equity. This approach avoids direct comparisons of compensation standards. In turn, much depends on the level of diligence in which the claims are substantiated. While judgments of the ECtHR are binding under article 46 ECHR, they are not enforceable titles.

Procedurally, there are considerable hurdles to access the ECtHR. Where the disruptive shock of violence renders domestic remedies unavailable or ineffective, the requirement to exhaust domestic remedies under article 35 (1) ECHR can be dispensed with. However, the fact-finding necessary to provide the basis for a judgment poses another challenge for a Court which is very busy and usually functions as a review instance. The heavy workload of the Court, which does not prioritize property cases, adds another grain of salt from the perspective of investors considering Strasbourg as a forum.

The Strasbourg system has been exposed to situations of territorial conflict and the ensuing cases where title to territory and actual control over it are not congruent. The case law indicates that the Court prefers to deal with these situations via non-monetary measures which aim to improve the situation beyond individual cases. While this does not exclude that individual cases are going to be adjudicated, the calls for a more subsidiary role of the Court, which have been enshrined in Protocol 15, might affect individual cases, including

---

158 *Gasus Dosier- und Fördertechnik GmbH v The Netherlands*, App no 15375/89 (ECtHR, 23 February 1995) para 59.

individual cases related to investments of aliens, stemming from territorial conflicts.

Overall, the place of investment protection under the framework of the ECHR is one to be considered. Even if the Strasbourg court is not looking for more business than it already has, it can be seen as an additional forum which offers substantive protection with considerable procedural hurdles. The enforcement of possible judgments depends on the goodwill of the respective respondent states. The expectations for investment protection in the conflict between Ukraine and Russia should be managed carefully. Systemic issues, including those regarding property-related issues, are likely to remain on the agenda of the Court, and the Council of Europe at large, for a long time.

Bibliography

Ackermann T, 'Investments under Occupation: The Application of Investment Treaties to Occupied Territory', in K Fach Gómez, A Gourgourinis, and C Titi (eds), *International Investment Law and the Law of Armed Conflict* (Springer 2019).

Alston P, 'Resisting the Merger and Acquisition of Human Rights by Trade Law: A Reply to Petersmann' (2002) 13 EJIL 815.

Álvarez Zárate JM and others, 'Duration of Investor-State Dispute Settlement Proceedings' (2020) 21 JWIT 300.

Balcerzak F, *Investor – State Arbitration and Human Rights* (Brill 2017).

Balthasar S, 'Investment Protection in Europe: International Investment Treaties, the European Convention on Human Rights and the Need for Reform at EU Level' (2018) 16 German Arb J 227.

Bates E, *The Evolution of the European Convention on Human Rights* (OUP 2010).

Beeler-Sigron M, 'Protection of Property', in P van Dijk and others (eds), *Theory and Practice of the European Convention on Human Rights* (Intersentia 2018).

Behrens H-J, 'Forum Shopping – Eine Herausforderung für den internationalen Menschenrechtsschutz.' (2020) 47 EuGRZ 171.

Ben Hamida W and F Coulée (eds), *Convergences and Contradictions between Investment Law and Human Rights Law: A Litigation Approach* (Pedone 2017).

Ben Hamida W, 'Introductory Overview', in W Ben Hamida and F Coulée (eds), *Convergences and Contradictions between Investment Law and Human Rights Law: A Litigation Approach* (Pedone 2017).

Boor F, 'Die Aufhebung der Yukos-Schiedssprüche des Court of Arbitration vor dem Bezirksgericht in Den Haag – nur der Anfang einer langen Vollstreckungsodysee?' (2016) 54 Archiv des Völkerrechts 297.

Breuer M, 'Urteilsfolgen bei strukturellen Problemen – Das erste "Piloturteil" des EGMR, Anmerkung zum Fall Broniowski gegen Polen' (2004) 31 EuGRZ 445.

Breuer M, 'Zur Fortentwicklung der Piloturteilstechnik durch den EGMR' (2012) 39 EuGRZ 1.

Buyse A, 'Lost and Regained? Restitution as a Remedy for Human Rights Violations in the Context of International Law' (2008) 68 Heidelberg J Int'l L 129.

Buyse A, 'Airborne or Bound to Crash? The Rise of Pilot Judgments and Their Appeal as a Tool to Deal with the Aftermath of Conflict', in A Buyse (ed), *Margins of Conflict: The ECHR and Transitions to and from Armed Conflict* (Intersentia 2011).

Council of Europe Committee of Ministers, 'Supervision of the Execution of Judgments and Decisions of the European Court of Human Rights 2019' (2020) <https://rm.coe.int/annual-report-2019-1/16809e1c59> accessed 8 June 2020.

Council of Europe Steering Committee for Human Rights (CDDH), Committee of Experts on the System of the European Convention on Human Rights, Drafting Group on Effective Processing and Resolution of Cases Relating to Inter-State Disputes, 'Background Paper on the Practice of the European Court of Human Rights with Regard to Inter-State Applications' (23 January 2020) DH-SYSC-IV(2020)02, para 9 <https://rm.coe.int/090000168o9a4672> accessed 8 June 2020.

Council of Europe Steering Committee for Human Rights (CDDH), 'Effective Processing and Resolution of Cases Relating to Inter-State Disputes' (2020) <www.coe.int/en/web/human-rights-intergovernmental-cooperation/effective-processing-and-resolution-of-inter-state-disputes> accessed 8 June 2020.

Council of Europe Treaty Office, 'Reservations and Declarations for Treaty No. 009 – Protocol to the Convention for the Protection of Human Rights and Fundamental Freedoms' (2020) <www.coe.int/en/web/conventions/full-list/-/conventions/treaty/009/declarations?p_auth=6xJUJLgH> accessed 20 June 2020.

De Brabandere E, 'Yukos Universal Limited (Isle of Man) v The Russian Federation: Complementarity or Conflict, Contrasting the Yukos Case before the European Court of Human Rights and Investment Tribunals' (2015) 30 ICSID Rev 345.

Douglas Z, 'Property, Investment, and the Scope of Investment Protection Obligations', in Z Douglas, J Pauwelyn, and JE Viñuales (eds), *The Foundations of International Investment Law* (OUP 2014).

Drzemczewski A, 'The Prevention of Human Rights Violations: Monitoring Mechanism of the Council of Europe', in L-A Sicilianos (ed), *The Prevention of Human Rights Violations* (Brill Nijhoff 2001).

Dupuy P-M and JE Viñuales, 'Human Rights and Investment Disciplines: Integration in Progress' in M Bungenberg and others (eds) *International Investment Law: A Handbook* (CH Beck, Hart, and Nomos 2015).

ECtHR, 'The Court's Priority Policy' (not dated) <www.echr.coe.int/Documents/Priority_policy_ENG.pdf> accessed 8 June 2020.

ECtHR, 'Practice Direction Just Satisfaction Claims' (2007) <www.echr.coe.int/Documents/PD_satisfaction_claims_ENG.pdf> accessed 8 June 2020.

ECtHR, 'The ECHR in 50 Questions' (2014) <www.echr.coe.int/Documents/50Questions_ENG.pdf> accessed 8 June 2020.

ECtHR, 'Overview 1959–2017' (March 2018) 6 <www.echr.coe.int/Documents/Overview_19592017 ENG.pdf> accessed 8 June 2020.

ECtHR, 'Practical Guide on Admissibility Criteria' (31 August 2019) <www.echr.coe.int/Documents/Admissibility_guide_ENG.pdf> accessed 8 June 2020.

ECtHR, 'Inter-State Applications by Date of Introduction of the Applications' (11 September 2019) <www.echr.coe.int/Documents/InterState_applications_ENG.pdf> accessed 8 June 2020.

ECtHR, 'Guide on Article 1 of the European Convention on Human Rights: Obligation to Respect Human Rights – Concepts of "Jurisdiction" and Imputability' (31 December 2019) <www.echr.coe.int/Documents/Guide_Art_1_ENG.pdf> accessed 8 June 2020.

ECtHR, 'Guide on Article 15 of the European Convention on Human Rights: Derogation in Time of Emergency' (31 December 2019) <www.echr.coe.int/Documents/Guide_Art_15_ENG.pdf> accessed 8 June 2020.

ECtHR, 'Pending Applications Allocated to a Judicial Formation' (31 December 2019) <www.echr.coe.int/Documents/Stats_pending_2020_BIL.pdf> accessed 8 June 2020.

ECtHR, 'Analysis of Statistics 2019' (January 2020) <www.echr.coe.int/Documents/Stats_analysis_2019_ENG.pdf> accessed 8 June 2020.

ECtHR, 'Rules of Court' (1 January 2020) <www.echr.coe.int/Documents/Rules_Court_ENG.pdf> accessed 8 June 2020.

ECtHR, 'The ECHR in Facts & Figures 2019' (February 2020) <www.echr.coe.int/Documents/Facts_Figures_2019_ENG.pdf> accessed 8 June 2020.

ECtHR, 'Armed Conflicts' (March 2020) <www.echr.coe.int/Documents/FS_Armed_conflicts_ENG.pdf> accessed 8 June 2020.

ECtHR, 'Guide on Article 1 of Protocol No. 1 to the European Convention on Human Rights: Protection of Property' (30 April 2020) <www.echr.coe.int/Documents/Guide_Art_1_Protocol_1_ENG.pdf> accessed 8 June 2020.

ECtHR Department for the Execution of Judgments, 'Main States with Cases under Enhanced Supervision' (not dated) <https://rm.coe.int/5-main-states-with cases-under-enhanced-supervision-eng/16807b8a62> accessed 8 June 2020.

ECtHR Department for the Execution of Judgments, 'HUDOC-EXEC' (2020) <https://hudoc.exec.coe.int/> accessed 8 June 2020.

ECtHR Press Unit, 'Press Country Profile – Ukraine' (January 2020) <www.echr.coe.int/Documents/CP_Ukraine_ENG.pdf> accessed 8 June 2020.

ECtHR Press Unit, 'Press Country Profile – Russia' (February 2020) <www.echr.coe.int/Documents/CP_Russia_ENG.pdf> accessed 8 June 2020.

ECtHR Press Unit, 'Factsheet – Pilot Judgments' (May 2020) <www.echr.coe.int/Documents/FS_Pilot_judgments_ENG.pdf> accessed 8 June 2020.

ECtHR Research Division, 'Articles 1 and 5: Extra-Territorial Jurisdiction, Jurisdiction of Territorial State Prevented from Exercising Its Authority in Part of Its Territory, and Validity of Detention and Criminal Proceedings in De Facto Entities' (2014) <www.echr.coe.int/Documents/Research_report_articles_1_5_ENG.pdf> accessed 8 June 2020.

Emberland M, *The Human Rights of Companies: Exploring the Structure of ECHR Protection* (OUP 2006).

Fanou M and VP Tzevelekos, 'The Shared Territory of the ECHR and International Investment Law' in Y Radi (ed), *Research Handbook on Human Rights and Investment* (Edward Elgar 2018).

Ganesh A, 'Cooling off Period', *Max Planck Encyclopedia of International Procedural Law* (2017) <https://opil.ouplaw.com/home/MPIL> accessed 8 June 2020.

Gerards J and E Brems (eds), *Procedural Review in European Fundamental Rights Cases* (CUP 2017).

Glas L, 'Burmych v Ukraine Two Years Later: What About Restoral?' (*Strasbourg Observers*, 17 September 2019) <https://strasbourgobservers.com/2019/09/17/burmych-v-ukraine-two-years-later-what-about-restoral/> accessed 8 June 2020.

Golsong H, 'Interpreting the European Convention on Human Rights Beyond the Confines of the Vienna Convention on the Law of Treaties' in RSJ Macdonald, F Matscher, and H Petzold (eds), *The European System for the Protection of Human Rights* (Nijhoff 1993).

Happ R and S Wuschka, '*Horror Vacui*: Or Why Investment Treaties Should Apply to Illegally Annexed Territories' (2016) 33 J Int'l Arb 245.

Happ R and S Wuschka, 'EU Law and Investment Arbitration: Of Cooperation, Conflict and the EU Legal Order's Autonomy' in A Bjorklund, F Ferrari, and S Kröll (eds), *Cambridge Compendium of International Commercial and Investment Arbitration* (CUP 2021, forthcoming).

Harris D and others, *Law of the European Convention on Human Rights* (4th edn, OUP 2018).

Hartwig M, 'Der Eigentumsschutz nach Art. 1 des 1. Zusatzprotokolls zur EMRK' (1999) 63 Rabel J Comp & Int'l Priv L 561.

Hartwig M, 'Vom Dialog zum Disput? Verfassungsrecht vs. Europäische Menschenrechtskonvention – Der Fall der Russländischen Föderation' (2017) 44 EuGRZ 1.

Hodgson M and A Campbell, 'Damages and Costs in Investment Treaty Arbitration Revisited' (*Global Arbitration Review*, 14 December 2017) <https://globalarbitrationreview.com/article/1151755/damages-and-costs-in-investment-treaty-arbitration-revisited> accessed 8 June 2020.

Klein E, 'Membership and Observer Status' in Stefanie Schmahl and Marten Breuer (eds), *The Council of Europe* (OUP 2016).

Kleinlein T, 'The Procedural Approach of the European Court of Human Rights: Between Subsidiarity and Dynamic Evolution' (2019) 68 ICLQ 91.

Knahr C, 'Investments "In The Territory" of the Host State' in C Binder and others (eds), *International in Investment Law for the 21st Century: Essays in Honour of Christoph Schreuer* (OUP 2009).

Kriebaum U, *Eigentumsschutz im Völkerrecht: Eine vergleichende Untersuchung zum internationalen Investitionsrecht sowie zum Menschenrechtsschutz* (Duncker & Humblot 2008).

Kriebaum U, 'Is the European Court of Human Rights an Alternative to Investor-State Arbitration?' in P-M Dupuy, E-U Petersmann, and F Francioni (eds), *Human Rights in International Investment Law and Arbitration* (OUP 2009).

Kriebaum U, 'Human Rights and International Investment Law' in Y Radi (ed), *Research Handbook on Human Rights and Investment* (Edward Elgar 2018).

Kriebaum U and A Reinisch, 'Property, Right to, International Protection', *Max Planck Encyclopedia of Public International Law* (2019) <https://opil.ouplaw.com/home/MPIL> accessed 8 June 2020.

Kucera M, 'Convergence and Conflicts between Investment Law and Human Rights Law: A Dispute Settlement Approach – Jurisdiction Ratione Personae' in W Ben Hamida and F Coulée (eds) *Convergences and Contradictions between Investment Law and Human Rights Law: A Litigation Approach* (Pedone 2017).

Kulick A, *Global Public Interest in International Investment Law* (CUP 2012).

Lawson R, 'Really Out of Sight? Issues of Jurisdiction and Control in Situations of Armed Conflict under the ECHR' in A Buyse (ed), *Margins of Conflict: The ECHR and Transitions to and from Armed Conflict* (Intersentia 2011).

Leach P and others, *Responding to Systemic Human Rights Violations* (2010).

Leach P, 'The Parliamentary Assembly of the Council of Europe' in S Schmahl and M Breuer (eds), *The Council of Europe* (OUP 2016).

Leach P, *Taking a Case to the European Court of Human Rights* (4th edn, OUP 2017).

Lemmens K, 'General Survery of the Convention' in P van Dijk and others (eds), *Theory and Practice of the European Convention on Human Rights* (Intersentia 2018).

Madsen MR, 'The European Court of Human Rights: From the Cold War to the Brighton Declaration and Backlash' in KJ Alter, LR Helfer, and MR Madsen (eds), *International Court Authority* (OUP 2018).

Mälksoo L, 'Russia, Strasbourg and the Paradox of a Human Rights Backlash' in L Mälksoo and W Benedek (eds), *Russia and the European Court of Human Rights: The Strasbourg Effect* (CUP 2017).

Mälksoo L, 'The Annexation of Crimea and Balance of Power in International Law' (2019) 30 EJIL 303.

Mallory C, *Human Rights Imperialists: The Extraterritorial Application of the European Convention on Human Rights* (Hart 2020).

Milanović M, *Extraterritorial Application of Human Rights Treaties: Law, Principles, and Policy* (OUP 2011).

Milanović M and T Papić, 'The Applicability of the ECHR in Contested Territories' (2018) 67 ICLQ 779.

Ní Aoláin F, 'Transitional Justice and the European Convention on Human Rights' (2017) Geneva Academy of International Humanitarian Law and Human Rights, Academy Briefing no 10 <https://repository.graduateinstitute.ch/record/295768?ln=en> accessed 8 June 2020.

Petersmann E-U, 'Human Rights and International Economic Law in the 21st Century: The Need to Clarify their Interrelationships' (2001) 4 J Int'l Econ L 3.

Peukert W, 'Artikel 1 Protokoll 1' in J Frowein and W Peukert, *Europäische Menschenrechtskonvention: EMRK-Kommentar* (3rd edn, Engel 2009).

Polanco Lazo R and R Mella, 'Investment Arbitration and Human Rights Cases in Latin America' in Y Radi (ed), *Research Handbook on Human Rights and Investment* (Edward Elgar 2018).

Radović R, 'Between Rights and Remedies: The Access to Investment Treaty Arbitration as a Substantive Right of Foreign Investors' (2019) 10 JIDS 42.

Raible L, 'Title to Territory and Jurisdiction in International Human Rights Law: Three Models for a Fraught Relationship' (2018) 31 LJIL 315.

Raible L, *Human Rights Unbound: A Theory of Extraterritoriality* (OUP 2020).

Reed L, Z Scanlon, and D Atanasova, 'Protected Investment', *Max Planck Encyclopedia of International Procedural Law* (2018) <https://opil.ouplaw.com/home/MPIL> accessed 8 June 2020.

Ress G, 'Reflections on the Protection of Property under the European Convention on Human Rights' in Stephan Breitenmoser and others (eds), *Human Rights, Democracy and the Rule of Law: Liber Amicorum Luzius Wildhaber* (DIKE and Nomos 2007)

Ruffert M, 'The Protection of Foreign Direct Investment by the European Court of Human Rights' (2000) 43 German YB Int'l L 116.

Salacuse JW, *The Law of Investment Treaties* (2nd edn, OUP 2015).

Schabas W, *The European Convention on Human Rights: A Commentary* (OUP 2015).

Schreuer C, 'Full Protection and Security' (2010) 1 JIDS 353.

Shelton D, *Remedies in International Human Rights Law* (3rd edn, OUP 2015).

Starzhenetskiy V, 'Property Rights in Russia: Reconsidering the Socialist Legal Tradition' in L Mälksoo and W Benedek (eds), *Russia and the European Court of Human Rights: The Strasbourg Effect* (CUP 2017).

Starzhenetskiy V, 'The Execution of ECHR Judgments and the "Right to Object" of the Russian Constitutional Court' in M Breuer (ed), *Principled Resistance to ECHR Judgments – A New Paradigm?* (Springer 2019).

Steiniger S, 'What's Human Rights Got To Do With It? An Empirical Analysis of Human Rights References in Investment Arbitration' (2018) 31 LJIL 33.

Tomuschat C, 'The European Court of Human Rights and Investment Protection' in C Binder and others (eds), *International in Investment Law for the 21st Century: Essays in Honour of Christoph Schreuer* (OUP 2009).

Ulfstein G and A Zimmermann, '*Certiorari* through the Backdoor? The Judgment by the European Court of Human Rights in *Burmych and Others v. Ukraine* in Perspective' (2018) 17 L & Prac Int'l Cts & Tribunals 289.

Ulfstein G and I Risini, 'Inter-State Applications under the European Convention on Human Rights: Strengths and Challenges' (*EJIL:Talk!*, 24 January 2020) <www.ejiltalk.org/inter-state-applications-under-the-european-convention-on-human-rights-strengths-and-challenges/> accessed 8 June 2020.

Villiger M, 'The Research Division of the European Court of Human Rights and Its Relevance for the Court's Case-law' in K Lemmens, S Parmentier, and L Reyntjens (eds), *Human Rights with a Human Touch: Liber Amicorum Paul Lemmens* (Intersentia 2019).

von Gall C, 'Gemeinsam für den Frieden und die Einheit Europas? Der Europarat und Russland' (*Verfassungsblog*, 5 May 2019) <https://verfassungsblog.de/gemeinsam-fuer-den-frieden-und-die-einheit-europas-der-europarat-und-russland/> accessed 8 June 2020.

Wallace S and C Mallory, 'Applying the European Convention on Human Rights to the Conflict in Ukraine' (2018) 6 Russian LJ 8.

Wildhaber L, 'Pilot Judgments in Cases of Structural or Systemic Problems on the National Level' in R Wolfrum and U Deutsch (eds), *The European Court of Human Rights Overwhelmed by Applications: Problems and Possible Solutions* (Springer 2009).

Wuschka S, 'Investment Tribunals Adjudicating Claims Relating to Occupied Territories – Curse or Blessing?' in A Duval and E Kassoti (eds), *The Legality of Economic Activities in Occupied Territories: International, EU Law and Business and Human Rights Perspectives* (Routlege 2020).

PART 3

Investment Law and Its Application to Annexed Territories and in 'Frozen' Conflicts

∴

CHAPTER 10

The Application of Investment Treaties in Occupied or Annexed Territories and 'Frozen' Conflicts: *Tabula Rasa* or *Occupata*?

Kit De Vriese

1   Introduction

Annexation, 'the domestic legal act of a State purporting to extend sovereignty over a piece of territory over which it has gained effective control through non-consensual forcible means',[1] is an unlawful mode of acquisition of territory in international law.[2] It often follows from (belligerent) occupation.[3] Yet, occupation does not always involve a state claiming the occupied territory as part of its territory.[4] 'Lawful occupation' includes forms of territorial administration and peacekeeping and will be treated separately.

More recently, and especially since the rise of international investment law (IIL), several additional questions have emerged. This includes the potential failure of respecting international investment agreements (IIAs) and the rights of individual foreign investors while prioritising military/political objectives. This nexus between investment treaties, armed conflict and territorial changes is finally coming of age. The '*terra nullius*'[5] of this nexus is slowly but steadily being explored by international tribunals. These have primarily been established following Russia's occupation and subsequent annexation of

---

1   Daniel Costelloe, 'Treaty Succession in Annexed Territory' (2016) 65 ICLQ 343, 353.
2   But this has not always been the case, see Rainer Hofmann, 'Annexation', *Max Planck Encyclopedia of Public International Law* (2020) para 1 <https://opil.ouplaw.com/home/MPIL> accessed 4 March 2020.
3   Convention (IV) respecting the Laws and Customs of War on Land and its Annex: Regulations concerning the Laws and Customs of War on Land (adopted 18 October 1907, entered into force 26 January 1910) 36 Stat. 2277 (Hague Regulations) art 42: 'Territory is considered to be occupied when it is actually placed under the authority of the hostile army'; *Armed Activities on the Territory of the Congo (DRC v Uganda)* [2005] ICJ Rep 168, para 172.
4   Costelloe (n 1) 354.
5   Sebastian Wuschka, 'Investment Claims and Annexation: Where General International Law and Investment Law Collide?' in Mesut Akbaba and Giancarlo Capurro (eds), *International Challenges in Investment Arbitration* (Routledge 2019) 21.

the Autonomous Republic of Crimea and the City of Sevastopol (hereinafter 'Crimea') in 2014.

While investment obligations in 'mere' armed conflict have been examined recently,[6] to the author's knowledge this has never been applied to occupation/annexation before. Against this background, this chapter will examine how international investment law holds the occupying/annexing state and perhaps the *de jure* sovereign accountable for (their) negative acts and omissions regarding foreign investments/property. It will argue that this depends on the type of aggression. The bilateral investment treaty (BIT) with the aggressor-state will *usually* apply. However, there are some exceptions to this proposed dichotomy.

Next to answer the controversial question which IIA applies during occupation/annexation, an arbitral tribunal has to steer clear of dangerous waters such as international politics, the (il)legality of occupation and its judicial validation, and jurisdiction.

The examined international legal rules primarily include, but are not limited to, BITs, as there is a vast legal framework of pre-BIT treaties, IIAs and state practice.[7] The recent case of the Crimea will be used for IIL issues during annexation. The (in)applicability of the 1998 Russia-Ukraine BIT and other BITs will be addressed in this chapter, to the extent that it concerns jurisdiction, admissibility and applicable law. Issues like the qualification of the Crimean crisis and the (il)legality of the use of force by Russia will only be briefly touched upon in this chapter for two reasons.[8] Russia repeatedly decided not to participate in cases instituted by Ukrainian claimants, until it changed strategy.[9] Furthermore, the outcome of the cases and the awards rendered have not been published. Reference to these cases depends largely on secondary literature and reports.

---

6   Jure Zrilič, *The Protection of Foreign Investment in Times of Armed Conflict* (OUP 2019) 14. He notes that the application of investment treaties in occupied and annexed territories merits its own research.
7   Ofilio J Mayorga, 'Occupants, Beware of BITs: Applicability of Investment Treaties to Occupied Territories' (2016) 19 Pal YB Int'l L 136, 145 et seq.
8   For an outline of the events leading up to annexation by Russia and its consequences for international law, see Patrick Dumberry, 'Requiem for Crimea: Why Tribunals Should Have Declined Jurisdiction over the Claims of Ukrainian Investors against Russian [*sic*] under the Ukraine–Russia BIT' (2018) 9 JIDS 506, 508 et seq.
9   Compare respectively *Everest Estate LLC and others v Russia*, PCA Case no 2015-36, Press Release (9 August 2016), and *Limited Liability Co Lugzor and others v Russia*, PCA Case no 2015-29, Press Release (28 November 2019).

In general, following the order of proceedings before international investment tribunals,[10] the relevant BIT – if there is one applicable to the case[11] – and its jurisdictional conditions and applicable law are examined (section 3). Investment tribunals will then address the BIT's correlation with the general IHL framework, including the content of the latter and a possible application of the *lex specialis* principle. However, as the latter discussion is more general it will be discussed in section 2.

Although outside this chapter's scope, it is still worth mentioning that states will usually be able to invoke 'pure' IHL defences (to validly exempt them from the law and courts of the occupied state among others), *eg* by proving that they separated potential targets from densely populated areas, and/or the essential security and emergency (or: non-precluded measures) clauses.[12] For example, Ukraine could invoke this in the Crimea cases: Russia's annexation and Ukraine's loss of control over the territory amounted to an irresistible force which could not be foreseen or controlled.[13] Next, the investment tribunal will assess whether the measures in question were *bona fide* measures and not disguised protectionist measures (good faith review). An assessment of the obligations under IIL will then usually be conducted.[14] Finally, the tribunal will proceed to (the effect of hostilities on) the damages stage and states can, again,

---

10 Based on Ira Ryk-Lakhman, 'IHL-Based Defenses in Investment Arbitration' (2018) Workshop Series on Investment Law and Policy.

11 If not, diplomatic protection offers a way out, but this will not be examined in this chapter. For an analysis applied to the Crimea crisis, see Natalia Tuzheliak, 'Investors at Conflict's Crossroads: An Overview of Available International Courts and Tribunals in the Crimean Context' (2017) 6 UCLJLJ 14, 39 et seq. The question then still is what substantive obligations could be relied upon. For Ukraine, this will obviously not be an efficient alternative for its relations towards Russia.

12 Mayorga (n 7) 162 et seq. For *force majeure*, see Christina Binder and Philipp Janig, chapter 4 in this volume.

13 ILC, 'Articles on Responsibility of States for Internationally Wrongful Acts' (2001) annexed to UNGA Resolution 56/83 UN Doc A/56/83 [2001] (Articles on State Responsibility); *Autopista Concesionada de Venezuela CA v Venezuela*, ICSID Case no ARB/00/5, Award (23 September 2003) para 108 required proof of the impossibility of performance, unforeseeability of the intervening event, and non-attributability of the intervening event; Yarik Kryvoi, 'Protecting Foreign Investors in Crimea: Is Investment Arbitration an Option?' (*CIS Arbitration Forum*, 29 July 2014) <www.cisarbitration.com/2014/07/29/protecting-foreign-investors-in-crimea-is-investment-arbitration-an-option/> accessed 29 November 2018.

14 See Ira Ryk-Lakhman, chapter 2 in this volume, and Emily Sipiorski, chapter 3 in this volume. See also Kit De Vriese, 'That Other Crisis: Extraterritorial Application of Investment Standards During Occupation and Annexation' (*Kluwer Arbitration Blog*, 30 June 2020) <http://arbitrationblog.kluwerarbitration.com/2020/06/30/that-other-crisis-extraterritorial-application-of-investment-standards-during-occupation-and-annexation/?doing_wp_cron=1598004139.7670049667358398437500> accessed 30 June 2020.

rely on IHL considerations to escape the award.[15] Yet, the latter issue and issues of state responsibility (*eg* the overall and effective control tests) will only be discussed to the extent that they are relevant to IIL.[16]

2   Investments during Occupation

2.1   *The Intersection of International Investment and Humanitarian Law*

Traditionally, treaties between belligerent states ceased to have effects with the outbreak of hostilities,[17] but this rule was never absolute. Some treaties provided for their applicability during armed conflict,[18] while territorial treaties created (persisting) rights *in rem*.[19] Moreover, occupants had to justify their measures through military necessity.[20] In any case, the traditional rule lost its meaning after the Second World War and the adoption of the Geneva Conventions.[21] These reintroduced the principle that international agreements of the occupied state bind the occupant,[22] usually with the condition that these agreements have to be relevant to the maintenance of public order and civil life.[23] While this chapter will mainly address unlawful occupation and annexation,[24] article 43 of the Hague Regulations 1907[25] stipulates the following for *lawful* occupation:

---

15 Based on the 1969 Declaration on Social Progress and Development, any damages caused to foreign investors in the Crimea should be compensated if the causal link can be proven; Kryvoi (n 13).

16 The criterion is usually one of effective control: Eyal Benvenisti, 'Occupation, Belligerent', *Max Planck Encyclopedia of Public International Law* (2009) para 1 <https://opil.ouplaw.com/home/MPIL> accessed 4 March 2020.

17 Arnold N Pronto, 'The Effect of War on Law – What Happens to Their Treaties When States Go to War?' (2013) 2 Cambridge J Int'l & Comp L 227, 230.

18 Tobias Ackermann, 'The ILC Draft Articles on the Effects of Armed Conflicts on Treaties: Room for Termination or Suspension of Bilateral Investment Treaties?' (2016) Minerva Center for the Rule of Law under Extreme Conditions Working Paper, 2 et seq <http://minervaextremelaw.haifa.ac.il/images/Ackermann_Armed_Conflicts_and_BITs_Minerva_Working_Paper.pdf> accessed 15 May 2020.

19 Lester H Woolsey, 'Peaceful War in China' (1938) 32 AJIL 314, 320 as cited in Mayorga (n 7) 146.

20 *Deserters of Casablanca (France v Germany)* (1909) 3 AJIL 755.

21 Mayorga (n 7) 150, 157. Together with the concept of subjugation (*debellatio*) – which gave the occupant the right to create legislation.

22 ibid 152.

23 Eyal Benvenisti, *The International Law of Occupation* (OUP 2012) 83.

24 *Cf* sections 2.2 and 3 below.

25 Other provisions relevant to occupation are arts 52, 53, as well as several provisions of the Fourth Geneva Convention and its additional protocols.

The authority of the legitimate power having in fact passed into the hands of the occupant, the latter shall take all the measures in his power to restore, and ensure, as far as possible, public order and safety, while respecting, unless absolutely prevented, the laws in force in the country.[26]

This provision of IHL and the general IIL regime seem to contrast, respectively prioritising the war effort and protecting investments. When two fields of law coexist, intersect, and formulate different conclusions, one usually identifies the specific norm which supersedes the general norm (*lex specialis derogat generalis*).[27] The more specific norm should contain the general norm in its scope of application.[28] Ultimately, the definition and solution of a conflict between treaties or a treaty and general international law must be primarily derived from the common intention of the parties,[29] but this is unlikely in cases of armed conflict.

The effects of IHL on general international law and IIL are substantial. The *Nuclear Weapons* and *Palestinian Wall* advisory opinions of the International Court of Justice (ICJ) could be seen as representing the orthodox approach: (only) those principles of IIL which must yield to IHL are disapplied.[30]

---

26 Note that 'authority' is not the same as 'sovereignty'. In general, the rationale of this provision is to avoid a legal vacuum after the ousted government loses control. Yet, this will prove difficult regarding BITs. The inclusion of 'public order and safety' was a mere consequence of merging earlier instruments: Benvenisti, *The International Law of Occupation* (n 23) 43, 69; Tobias Ackermann, 'Investments Under Occupation: The Application of Investment Treaties to Occupied Territory' in Katia Fach Gómez, Anastasios Gourgourinis, and Catharine Titi (eds), *International Investment Law and the Law of Armed Conflict* (Springer 2019) 75.

27 This 'normative conflict' is mainly due to the fragmentation of international law: Zrilič (n 6) 162.

28 Articles on State Responsibility art 55(4); Gleider I Hernández, 'The Interaction between Investment Law and the Law of Armed Conflict in the Interpretation of Full Protection and Security Clauses' in Freya Baetens (ed), *Investment Law within International Law: Integrationist Perspectives* (CUP 2013) 26; Ryk-Lakhman (n 10) 24; Suzanne Spears and Maria Fogdestam-Agius, 'Protection of Investments in War-Torn States: A Practitioner's Perspective on War Clauses in Bilateral Investment Treaties' in Katia Fach Gómez, Anastasios Gourgourinis, and Catharine Titi (eds), *International Investment Law and the Law of Armed Conflict* (Springer 2019) 306. See also Tillmann Rudolf Braun, chapter 1 in this volume.

29 Joost Pauwelyn, 'The Role of Public International Law in the WTO: How Far Can We Go' (2001) 95 AJIL 535, 552.

30 *Legality of the Threat or Use of Nuclear Weapons* (Advisory Opinion) [1996] ICJ Rep 226, para 25; *Legal Consequences of the Construction of a Wall in the Occupied Palestinian Territory* (Advisory Opinion) [2004] ICJ Rep 136, para 106; Freya Baetens, 'When International Rules

Hernández adds that if IHL is departed from by using military necessity, treaties continue to apply, as necessity is a *defence* and not an *exception* to derogate from the applicable law.³¹ The orthodox approach thus prioritises IHL. Despite IIL's specific regime between one state and foreign investors, IHL obligations are specific *vis-à-vis* the specific circumstances of the situation in which the investment is made.³² Another argument in support of the more specific status of IHL norms could be that many customary IHL obligations have attained *jus cogens* status, from which no derogation is permitted and as such constitute *lex specialis*.³³

Others have argued that IIL, rather than IHL provides greater protection to investors' lives and property, as the latter excludes economic considerations and means for redress from its scope.³⁴ It also *enforces* the substantive law provided by IHL, for example by scrutinising the occupant's obligations under article 43 Hague Regulations through a BIT,³⁵ as investments can easily lose their protection under occupation or military use.³⁶

Nevertheless, *lex specialis* could avoid an 'apparent' conflict (compatibility/complementarity),³⁷ or integrate two norms.³⁸ An example of complementarity is that an investor could succeed under the BIT's (extended) armed conflict clause instead of the full protection and security (FPS) provision, as due diligence is easy to meet for the state, and it is suggested that FPS

Interact: International Investment Law and the Law of Armed Conflict' (*Investment Treaty News*, 7 April 2011) <www.iisd.org/itn/2011/04/07/when-international-rules-interact-international-investment-law-and-the-law-of-armed-conflict/> accessed 10 March 2020. *Cf* Pauwelyn (n 29) 539. noting that having *lex specialis* character does not mean that it is *lex specialis* vis-à-vis all rules of international law.

31 Hernández (n 28) 30.
32 Ryk-Lakhman (n 10) 24.
33 ibid; *cf* section 3 below.
34 Zrilič (n 6) 161 et seq; Spears and Fogdestam-Agius (n 28) 289.
35 Mayorga (n 7) 174. For the same argument regarding human rights treaties, see Marko Milanović, *Extraterritorial Application of Human Rights Treaties: Law, Principles, and Policy* (OUP 2011) 96.
36 As was the case in *Asian Agricultural Products Ltd (AAPL) v Sri Lanka*, ICSID Case no ARB/87/3, Award (27 June 1990) para 82.
37 As opposed to a genuine conflict described above. Milanović (n 35) 102. When the conflict is neither avoidable nor resolvable, a political solution is warranted.
38 Zrilič (n 6) 186; Mayorga (n 7) 174. This is 'consistent', as opposed to 'creative' and 'forced' avoidance: Milanović (n 35) 106 et seq. Neither treaty practice nor compliance by states suggests that *lex specialis* is merely a sub-species of harmonious interpretation, rather than a norm of conflict resolution. States do often not comply with IHL too: ibid 115 et seq. He even says '*lex specialis*' should be avoided altogether. This fits into the presumption against conflict (or for continuity) in international law: Pauwelyn (n 29) 541 et seq.

could modify the interpretation of an armed conflict clause.³⁹ This chapter will exactly try to mitigate such a conflict and reconcile the two approaches, upholding IHL in some situations (*eg* lawful occupation) and IIL in others (*eg* when investors have no other recourse during annexation). Mayorga argues that complementarity is more likely in cases of short-lived occupations indeed, as these are motivated exclusively by the occupant's military objectives.⁴⁰

Article 31(3)(c) of the Vienna Convention on the Law of Treaties (VCLT) sets out the second method: systemic integration.⁴¹ Several investment tribunals have indeed accepted that a BIT is not a 'self-contained legal system' and has to be interpreted through systemic integration,⁴² despite the lack of precedent. While the *Asian Agricultural Products Ltd (AAPL)* tribunal was not clear on which obligations outside the BIT can be adjudicated by an investment tribunal, the door is open to apply IHL in cases of occupation (and *a fortiori* annexation).⁴³ However, this comes with a caveat: tribunals should be careful not to second-guess IHL norms and military objectives.⁴⁴

2.2 To the Occupier Belong the Spoils ... in Principle

Ackermann argues that dynamic treaty interpretation, supported by the object and purpose of the treaty, leads to the conclusion that 'the laws in force in the country' (article 43 Hague Regulations) also include IIAs, especially when they are almost always accompanied by a domestic statute (in dualist

---

39 Spears and Fogdestam-Agius (n 28) 308.
40 Mayorga (n 7) 175.
41 Vienna Convention on the Law of Treaties (adopted 23 May 1969, entered into force 27 January 1980) 1155 UNTS 331 (VCLT). There has to exist a relevant a rule of international law which is applicable between parties and their relations: *Oil Platforms (Iran v USA)* (Merits) [2003] ICJ Rep 161, paras 41 et seq, which held that *jus ad bellum* principles were 'relevant' to the interpretation of FCN treaties. Integration has two benefits: i) it ensures that investor-state arbitration remains possible during armed conflict, and ii) it allows assessment of state conduct in occupied territory under IHL: Mayorga (n 7) 169.
42 *AAPL v Sri Lanka* (n 36) para 21; *LG&E Energy Corp, LG&E Capital Corp and LG&E International Inc v Argentina*, ICSID Case no ARB/02/1, Decision on Liability (3 October 2006) para 97.
43 Christoph Schreuer, 'War and Peace in International Investment Law' in Katia Fach Gómez, Anastasios Gourgourinis, and Catharine Titi (eds), *International Investment Law and the Law of Armed Conflict* (Springer 2019) 3. This is strengthened by referring to international law in applicable law provisions like Convention on the Settlement of Investment Disputes Between States and Nationals of Other States (adopted 8 March 1965, entered into force 14 October 1966) 575 UNTS 159 (ICSID Convention) art 42(1).
44 Spears and Fogdestam-Agius (n 28) 296. Other problems include the misinterpretation of foreign norms and concepts: Zrilič (n 6) 193.

systems).⁴⁵ Including IIAs also seems to be in line with the general principle in the International Law Commission's (ILC) Draft Articles on the Effects of Armed Conflict on Treaties ('Draft Articles'),⁴⁶ which presumes the continuity of treaties (see article 3).⁴⁷ Moreover, they set out an indicative list of treaties whose subject-matter implies continued operation during armed conflict. These include Treaties of Friendship, Commerce and Navigation (FCN) treaties and treaties concerning private rights, human rights treaties, and treaties concerning dispute settlement.⁴⁸ The ILC Commentary, noting that human rights treaties are an extension of the first two categories, also includes BITs.⁴⁹ The presumption of continuity of treaties in armed conflict seems to apply *a fortiori* to lawful occupation.⁵⁰ The Commentary explicitly refers to 'treaties creating a territorial regime' which protect human rights of the local population.⁵¹

The principle of continuity for war-torn states' treaties is still good law and a sound policy principle when it comes to treaty relations between the occupied and a *third state*. For investment cases, the BIT between them can be applied, at least for the unoccupied part of the country. The same conclusion holds under the *lawful* and *extended* territorial administration of the entire country, which is truly subrogated in the rights of the original government. This does not prevent occupied states from invoking IHL defences and circumstances precluding wrongfulness.⁵²

Another question relates to the IIA applicable to the occupied part of the state: Mayorga argues that foreign investors could file a claim under the BIT between the occupying and third state by way of 'indirect' or 'derivative' consent, parallel to establishing the *ad hoc* tribunals through Security Council resolutions.⁵³ Article 43 Hague Regulations could indeed be interpreted that

---

45 Ackermann, 'Investments Under Occupation' (n 26) 73, referring to *Navigational and Related Rights (Costa Rica v Nicaragua)* [2009] ICJ Rep 213, paras 66 et seq. See also Wuschka, 'Investment Claims and Annexation' (n 5) 28, arguing that IIAs are part of the state's legal order, which is protected by the laws of occupation.
46 ILC, 'Draft Articles on the Effects of Armed Conflict on Treaties, with Commentaries' (2011) UN Doc A/66/10, 179.
47 In general, there is a presumption against conflict and for continuity in international law; Pauwelyn (n 29) 541 et seq.
48 Draft Articles on the Effects of Armed Conflict on Treaties, art 7 and Annex lit (e), (f) and (k). However, one should be aware of the risk of overgeneralisation: not all armed conflicts are the same and not all treaty provisions are affected by hostilities; Zrilič (n 6) 65.
49 ILC, 'Draft Articles on the Effects of Armed Conflict on Treaties' (n 46) para 48.
50 Ackermann, 'Investments Under Occupation' (n 26) 70 et seq.
51 ILC, 'Draft Articles on the Effects of Armed Conflict on Treaties' (n 46) para 48.
52 ILC, 'Draft Articles on the Effects of Armed Conflict on Treaties' (n 46) art 18.
53 Mayorga (n 7) 142, 161.

way,⁵⁴ but article 43 is not the only factor to be taken into account. Furthermore, Wuschka believes that this would make *all* dispute settlement clauses that have been signed by the *de jure* sovereign applicable.⁵⁵ Ackermann fears the far-reaching consequences for the occupant, including the impossibility to withdraw from the treaty, and distinguishes investment from criminal tribunals: states, not individuals, are the subjects of BITS.⁵⁶ One could add that it is difficult to see the analogy between indirect consent through *binding* Security Council resolutions and *voluntary* BITS.

The indirect character of article 43 indeed justifies the insignificance of the occupied state in this regard. This seems to be accepted in practice. Claims have only been filed under the *Russia*-Ukraine BIT; no cases under a third state-*Ukraine* or third state-*Russia* BIT have been registered for investment claims after the occupation and subsequent annexation of Crimea.⁵⁷ In sum, the BIT with the occupying state, which controls the territory effectively, must be applied from a legal perspective. This solution does not only find support in the object and purpose of the treaty. The customary international law theory of acquired rights protects factual situations created by the respective BIT, such as state succession.⁵⁸ This should be no different for occupation/annexation. Although *foreign* investors are merely third parties to the treaty under the VCLT,⁵⁹ they have acquired certain rights under it.⁶⁰

This solution thus follows the alternative approach to *lex specialis*, prioritising investors and economic considerations whilst providing a means to enforce substantive IHL. From a policy perspective, another advantage of this approach – also backed up by practice – is that investors from the unoccupied part of the state are now within the scope of the treaty. Ukrainian investors can file a claim for the treatment of their investments in Crimea – and these have indeed been the only claims.

However, between the occupied and occupying state, the situation is a bit more complex. The Draft Articles marginalised this transfer of international legal obligations during occupation.⁶¹ While article 43 of the Hague Regulations

---

54 '[...] while respecting, unless absolutely prevented, the laws in force in the country'.
55 Wuschka, 'Investment Claims and Annexation' (n 5) 26 et seq.
56 Mayorga (n 7) 161; Ackermann, 'Investments Under Occupation' (n 26) 79.
57 Although claims under the latter seem possible under the moving treaty-frontiers rule; Sebastian Wuschka, 'Das Investitionsschutzrecht: Rechtssicherheit für deutsche Investoren auf der Krim?' (2017) 26 Wirtschaft und Recht in Osteuropa 193. *Cf* section 3 below.
58 Daniel P O'Connell, 'The Doctrine of Acquired Rights and State Succession', (1950) 27 Brit YB Int'l L 92.
59 VCLT art 70(1)(b); ILC, 'Fifth Report on the Law of Treaties' (1966) II YBILC 265, art 66(3).
60 Michael Waibel, 'Brexit and Acquired Rights' (2018) 111 AJIL 440, 442 et seq.
61 Mayorga (n 7) 158.

emphasises continuity, it also mentions that the occupant 'shall take all the measures in his power to restore, and ensure, as far as possible, public order and safety'. This phrase justifies the application of the occupier's BITs to the occupied territory. Indeed, a similar reasoning has been used for human and labour rights treaties, because of these (customary) international, quasi-universal legal obligations.[62] The ICJ in *Armed Activities on the Territory of the Congo* merely relied upon article 43 and its continuity requirement because of *inter-state* violations.[63] As a matter of analogy, there is room for the extra-territorial application of (bilateral investment) treaties during occupation.[64] Admitted, the international legal obligations of the occupying state may not be the same in terms of specific BIT provisions, but it usually provides for some sort of investment protection. Thus, apart from some exceptions, one may therefore put forward the following qualified principle:

> *Principle 1* – Although the occupant cannot alter the legal system of the occupied territory considerably (article 43 Hague Regulations), investment treaties of the *occupying* state apply to occupied territory.

The occupant is even entitled to conclude *new* treaties if three additional conditions are fulfilled: (i) they are necessary for the benefit of the population; (ii) the occupant acts in its own name; and (iii) the created obligations elapse with the end of the occupation.[65] The last two requirements are usually not difficult to meet. Lorenzmeier argues that investment treaties do not benefit the population as a whole and must thus be categorically excluded from such an extraterritorial application.[66]

One should be careful with such categorical exclusions. In contrast to humanitarian treaties,[67] investment treaties could indeed be more beneficial

---

62   Milanović (n 35) 123; Mayorga (n 7) 155–156.
63   *Armed Activities on the Territory of the Congo* (n 3) paras 242 et seq; Mayorga (n 7) 156.
64   Ackermann, 'Investments Under Occupation' (n 26) 72 et seq.
65   Benvenisti, *The International Law of Occupation* (n 23) 86; Ackermann, 'Investments Under Occupation' (n 26) 72. *Contra*: Robert Tadlock, 'Occupation Law and Foreign Investment in Iraq: How an Outdated Doctrine Has Become an Obstacle to Occupied Populations' (2004) 39 USF L Rev 227, 249, proposing a 'lowest common denominator' approach, only making it possible to make changes in accordance with foreign investment rules of neighbouring countries.
66   Stefan Lorenzmeier, chapter 11 in this volume.
67   As being the scope of the exception in *Legal Consequences for States of The Continued Presence of South Africa in Namibia (South West Africa) Notwithstanding Security Council Resolution 276 (1970)* (Advisory Opinion) [1971] ICJ Rep 16, para 122.

to a privileged group of investors rather than the local population, especially considering 'negative spill overs' on the human rights regime.[68] However, apart from some studies carefully concluding a positive impact on foreign direct investment, more economic-empirical research needs to be done,[69] especially on investments in territory under the factual/legal control of another state.[70] A recent report by the Organisation for Economic Cooperation and Development was equally prudent.[71] No societal advantages will be cherry-picked from that report and displayed here as a general authority for societal advantages of IIAs. A case-by-case assessment by an international court or tribunal should determine whether a particular IIA is beneficial for the population, if it finds that conclusive in the first place. As a side bonus, they usually benefit foreign investors who can fall between the two stools of having the occupying or the occupant's BIT with their (third) country of nationality applied (*cf* section 3 below).

Second, Lorenzmeier rightly sees the importance of the *Front Polisario* case of the Court of Justice of the European Union (CJEU). On the other hand, he concludes too quickly that it is authority for the fact that free trade agreements and investment treaties are not beneficial for the population as a whole. The CJEU indeed held that it is sufficient that the implementation of the Association Agreement with Morocco receives the consent of the occupied Western Saharans (albeit as a third party). However, in the same paragraph, it notes that this applies 'without it being necessary to determine whether such implementation is likely to harm it or, on the contrary, to benefit it'.[72]

The exception in the *Namibia* advisory opinion, *ie* the extraterritorial application of multilateral (humanitarian) treaties that positively affect the local population, could indeed be read as extending to the occupant's investment treaties, as they could benefit the population as argued above. Moreover, while

---

68 Jonathan Bonnitcha, Lauge N Skovgaard Poulsen, and Michael Waibel, *The Political Economy of the Investment Treaty Regime* (OUP 2017) 251 et seq.

69 ibid 155 et seq, 179 et seq, referring to 24 studies with a positive correlation.

70 This is difficult, as BITs with these territories are very recent or non-existent. Palestine, for example, only signed five BITs, of which two have not entered into force: <https://investmentpolicy.unctad.org/international-investment-agreements/countries/158/state-of-palestine> accessed 10 March 2020. However, it is not difficult to see that without these BITs certain capital inflow would miss its mark.

71 Joachim Pohl, 'Societal Benefits and Costs of International Investment Agreements: A Critical Review of Aspects and Available Empirical Evidence' (2018) OECD Working Paper on International Investment 2018/01 <www.oecd-ilibrary.org/finance-and-investment/societal-benefits-and-costs-of-international-investment-agreements_e5f85c3d-en> accessed 15 May 2020.

72 ECJ, C–104/16, *Council v Front Polisario* [2016] ECLI:EU:C:2016:973, para 106.

the advisory opinion mainly concerned multilateral treaties (and thus not *bilateral* investment treaties), the responsibility of the occupant (whether or not under a treaty) is triggered in any case: '[p]hysical control of a territory, and not sovereignty or legitimacy or title, is the basis of State liability for acts affecting other States'.[73] This is an obligation of due diligence: the occupant only has to do what is reasonably possible.[74]

Several Crimea tribunals have reportedly held that 'an occupying power may be held responsible *under a BIT* for its conduct in the occupied territory'.[75] Without stating this explicitly, the *PJSC Ukrnafta* and *Stabil* tribunals seem to use this as a *fait accompli* for determining whether *de facto* territory constitutes territory under the BIT (see section 3.2).[76]

As stated above, there are three notable exceptions to the principle of continuity. These can be used to escape Lorenzmeier's concerns regarding a rigid application of the *Namibia* exception. First, Ackermann was quick to note that mere temporary occupations – whether or not lawful – like the United States in Iraq would not fall under this extraterritorial application of IIAs.[77] Subrogating the US in all of Iraq's rights and obligations and applying the US-third state BIT (*eg* providing full protection and security treatment) would be excessive, especially regarding the fact that the Coalition Provisional Authority included other states as well. Thus, only stabilised long-term occupations should be covered by the principle above. This might explain the ICJ's reliance on article 43 of the Hague Regulations in *Armed Activities*. A possible criterion for long-term occupations is economic integration in the occupant's economic and political system.[78] This exception is justified by the 'object and purpose' of the laws of occupation, *ie* preserving the *status quo* and the dispossessed state's sovereignty.

A second exception should exist when the dispossessed state expresses its will to continue the protection of investments and does not consent to such extraterritorial application. After all, extending article 43 Hague Regulations to

---

73 *Legal Consequences for States of The Continued Presence of South Africa in Namibia* (n 67) para 118 *in fine*.
74 Milanović (n 35).
75 Marat Davletbaev, 'The Applicability of Russia-Ukraine BIT Treaty to Investments in Crimea: Current Status and Future Developments' (*Lexology*, 31 May 2017) <www.lexology.com/library/detail.aspx?g=ea62373e-8e20-4fb8-b2ec-f5ac295dfc3f> accessed 10 March 2020. Emphasis added.
76 See, on jurisdiction, Swiss Federal Tribunal, Judgment no 4A_396/2017 and no 398/2017 (16 October 2018).
77 Ackermann, 'Investments Under Occupation' (n 26) 84. *Contra*: Tadlock (n 65).
78 Ackermann, 'Investments Under Occupation' (n 26) 84.

IIAs is relative ('unless absolutely prevented') and indirect (lacking consent by the occupying state).[79] This exception finds support in the *Front Polisario* case too.[80] Even though Ackermann does not distinguish occupation from annexation, unlike the present chapter, he distinguishes the case through the object and purpose of IIAs (protecting individual interests).[81] Yet, it seems logical that an automatic application of the occupant's BITs, and possibly other laws and treaties, to occupied territory would result in a loss of *de jure* sovereignty and inability to legislate by the dispossessed state. Therefore, international courts and (investment) tribunals could temper the automatic extraterritorial application of BITs for situations of occupation by examining situations case-by-case – which is their task in the first place. Without ruling on the legality of those situations, the occupation of Western Sahara (without a government in place) – and Crimea – seem completely different to that of Iraq or Palestine which could guarantee protection under their own investment laws.[82] Regarding the legal aspects of the BIT in question, other criteria include, but are not limited to: (i) the definition of investment; (ii) whether this must be an active investment (rather than passively holding assets)[83]; and (iii) whether they are protected prior to the IIA's entry into force.[84]

A third exception should exist when the occupied state has *not* concluded a BIT with the occupying state at all. The logic of *Armed Activities*, ie applying international human rights standards to which both states are parties, does not hold then. When neither occupied nor occupying state has a BIT in place, investors are simply not covered by the treaty. The international minimum standard still applies to all states, whether or not they are party to a BIT. However, there may be no tribunal with jurisdiction to apply it.

3   Jurisdiction and Applicable Law for Investment Disputes in Annexed Territory

Investment treaties belong to the category of treaties that refer to territory for treaty obligations to apply: only investments made in a specific territory are

---

79   ibid 11.
80   *Front Polisario* (n 72).
81   Ackermann, 'Investments Under Occupation' (n 26) 86.
82   For the latter, see Law on the Encouragement of Investment in Palestine (1998).
83   *Eg* Energy Charter Treaty art 1(6).
84   See, in the context of the Russia-Ukraine BIT, Sebastian Wuschka, 'Zuständigkeit von Investitionsschiedsgerichten für Klagen mit Bezug zur Annexion der Krim' (2019) German Arb J 93, 100.

covered.[85] Thus, as the *PJSC Ukrnafta* Tribunal rightly noted,[86] a preliminary issue concerns whether the issue under consideration falls within the scope of the treaty, *ie* whether the tribunal has material, spatial, temporal, and personal jurisdiction.[87] More generally, the jurisdiction of any investment tribunal is based on the consent of states and investors.[88] Nevertheless, as introduced for occupation in section 2, also during annexation the main issue is whether that consent extends to the annexed territory. Such consent is logically denied by the aggressor-state.[89]

3.1 *Jurisdiction* Ratione Materiae

Material jurisdiction usually refers to the (disputed) definition of investment and whether that includes the particular investment.[90] This was not a point of discussion in the Crimea cases, however. In *PJSC Ukrnafta* and *Stabil*, for example, the tribunal quickly accepted that petrol stations are investments under the BIT's definition (article 1(1)).[91] Other heads of jurisdiction, and whether material jurisdiction is a standalone head of jurisdiction, are more disputed.

However, even if an investment tribunal confirms its jurisdiction, as all the Crimea tribunals have done, the (il)legality of the occupation/annexation and its judicial validation can remain a huge elephant in the room for material jurisdiction.[92] Following annexation, formerly protected foreign investors

---

85   Costelloe (n 1) 348.
86   While this decision has not been published, the subsequent judgment by the Swiss Federal Tribunal on the respective set-aside application offers a look into the reasoning of the former: Swiss Federal Tribunal (n 76) para 4.2.
87   This in contrast to Repousis who focuses on jurisdiction *ratione personae*; Odysseas G Repousis, 'Why Russian Investment Treaties Could Apply to Crimea and What Would This Mean for the Ongoing Russo–Ukrainian Territorial Conflict' (2016) 32 Arb Int'l 459, 462. Wuschka treats jurisdiction *ratione materiae* and *personae* as manifestations of *ratione temporis* jurisdiction, as this is often the case in investment treaties: Wuschka, 'Investment Claims and Annexation' (n 5) 22 et seq.
88   Yuval Shany, 'Jurisdiction and Admissibility' in Cesare Romano, Karen Alter, and Yuval Shany (eds), *The Oxford Handbook of International Adjudication* (OUP 2013) 782.
89   *Everest Estate*, Press Release (n 9). For Mayorga's argument of 'indirect' consent, *cf* section 2.2 above.
90   Eg Campbell McLachlan, Laurence Shore, and Matthew Weiniger, *International Investment Arbitration* (2nd edn, OUP 2017) 10, 217 et seq.
91   Swiss Federal Tribunal (n 76) para 4.2.
92   Mayorga (n 7) 141; G Matteo Vaccaro-Incisa, 'Crimea Investment Disputes: Are Jurisdictional Hurdles Being Overcome Too Easily?' (9 May 2018) <www.ejiltalk.org/crimea-investment-disputes-are-jurisdictional-hurdles-being-overcome-too-easily/comment-page-1/> accessed 10 March 2020.

do not have legal recourse anymore and find themselves in a – relative[93] – legal vacuum: neither the BIT with the aggressor-state (given the illegality of its authority) nor that with the dispossessed state (given the lack of effective protection) seems to apply.[94] Regarding the latter, it is generally accepted that this is *a fortiori* the case when the state is completely annexed and thus extinct.[95] Furthermore, a change in sovereignty could constitute a supervening impossibility to perform (article 61 VCLT) or a fundamental change of circumstances (*rebus sic stantibus*, article 62 VCLT) which suspend the treaty.[96] It will however be difficult to prove their requirements, respectively a material impossibility or essential to the consent of the parties and radically transforms the parties' obligations.[97] Furthermore, the VCLT does not provide for a partial suspension/termination in the sense of excluding the occupied/annexed territory. However, for supervening impossibility to perform, a broader view could be adopted, including the disappearance of the treaty's objectives (investments in the entire territory of the *occupied* state) and means for performance.[98]

---

93 Dumberry, 'Requiem for Crimea' (n 8) 518. The international minimum standards and its implications still apply, see section 2.2 above. Furthermore, Ukrainian investors do have recourse to the European Court of Human Rights, which Happ & Wuschka omit to state in their article: Richard Happ and Sebastian Wuschka, *'Horror Vacui*: Or Why Investment Treaties Should Apply to Illegally Annexed Territories' (2016) 33 J Int'l Arb 245.

94 Dumberry, 'Requiem for Crimea' (n 8) 517; Happ and Wuschka (n 93) 247. This is only reinforced when it specifically refers to that territory (*cf* section 3.2 below), or when it is concluded *intuitu personae* (*cf* section 3.4 below): Costelloe (n 1) 373 et seq.

95 Arnold Duncan McNair, *The Law of Treaties* (Clarendon Press 1961) 592 et seq, referring to the cases of Algeria, San Domingo, Upper Burma, Hawaii, Transvaal Republic and Orange Free State, Congo Free State, Korea and Austria.

96 ECJ, C-162/96 *A Racke GmbH & Co v Hauptzollamt Mainz* [1998] 3 CMLR 219 paras 55 et seq; Costelloe (n 1) 373 et seq. Article 73 VCLT stating that its provisions 'shall not prejudice any question that may arise in regard to a treaty from the outbreak of hostilities between States', read together with article 18 Draft Articles, probably implies that it may create legal consequences not covered by the VCLT rather than not applying to armed conflict at all. A state should be able to choose between the two regimes, as none of them is *lex specialis* but *inter alia* have different consequences, including the notification procedure under the VCLT: Zrilič (n 6) 84 et seq.

97 *Fisheries Jurisdiction (Germany v Iceland)* (Jurisdiction) [1973] ICJ Rep 49 para 43; *Gabčíkovo-Nagymaros Project (Hungary v Slovakia)* [1997] ICJ Rep 7 para 104; Josef Ostránsky, 'The Termination and Suspension of Bilateral Investment Treaties Due to an Armed Conflict' (2015) 6 JIDS 136, 139 et seq; Schreuer (n 43) 8. The claim in the *Racke* case (n 96) seems to be successful only because the armed conflict was accompanied by the dissolution of Yugoslavia: Zrilič (n 6) 81 et seq.

98 Schreuer (n 43) 7.

Sovereignty disputes are usually not part of the material jurisdiction of arbitration tribunals,[99] but could fall within their incidental jurisdiction, *ie* jurisdiction over a(n) (substantive) issue that is incidental to the issue outside of the jurisdiction *ratione materiae*.[100] Some Crimea tribunals have side-stepped this issue on the basis of the effectiveness of the *de facto* situation.[101] Yet, just as has been argued for IHL norms (section 2), there seems to be no reason why investment tribunals could not follow the reasoning of other international courts and tribunals. As such, they could declare to have incidental jurisdiction to determine whether the other state committed an unlawful use of force ex article 2(4) UN Charter (through article 31(3)(c) VCLT).[102] Furthermore, the principles of *Kompetenz-Kompetenz* and *jura novit curia* require that, in default proceedings (*ie* when the parties do not appear), the question whether the dispute or any ancillary claim is within its jurisdiction must be answered *ex officio* (*eg* ICSID arbitration rule 42(4)).[103] For *forum prorogatum*, however, *ie* an implicit agreement regarding jurisdiction, the objective jurisdictional requirements of article 25 of the ICSID Convention (the existence of a legal dispute

---

99 Peter Tzeng, 'Investments on Disputed Territory: Indispensable Parties and Indispensable Issues' (2017) 14 Braz J Int'l L 121, 123.

100 Peter Tzeng, 'The Implicated Issue Problem: Indispensable Issues and Incidental Jurisdiction' (2018) 50 New York U J Int'l L & Pol 447, fn 31.

101 *Aeroport Belbek LLC and Mr. Igor Valerievich Kolomoisky v Russia*, PCA Case no 2015-07, Interim Award (24 February 2017) (not public); *PJSC CB PrivatBank and Finance Co Finilon LLC v Russia*, PCA Case no 2015-21, Interim Award (24 February 2017) (not public); *Everest Estate LLC and others v Russia*, PCA Case no 2015-36, Decision on Jurisdiction (20 March 2017) (not public); *PJSC Ukrnafta v Russia*, PCA Case no 2015-34, Award on Jurisdiction (26 June 2017) (not public); *Stabil LLC and others v Russia*, PCA Case no 2015-35, Award on Jurisdiction (26 June 2017) (not public); *Lugzor LLC and others v Russia*, PCA Case no 2015-29, Tribunal's Letter (29 August 2017); Dumberry (n 8) 525. It could be argued that the lack of opposition to the application of the Russia–Ukraine BIT could circumvent the need for a determination on jurisdiction, see Repousis (n 87) 469 et seq.

102 *Questions of Interpretation and Application of the 1971 Montreal Convention Arising from the Aerial Incident at Lockerbie (Libya v USA)* (Preliminary Objections) [1998] ICJ Rep 115, para 10; *M/V "Saiga" (No 2) Case (Saint Vincent and the Grenadines v Guinea)* [1999] ITLOS Rep 10, para 155.

103 Christoph Schreuer and others, *The ICSID Convention: A Commentary* (2nd edn, CUP 2009) 530; Dumberry (n 8) 517. Contrary to contested proceedings, where the tribunal has a discretionary power (*proprio motu*) to determine this (ICSID Arbitration Rule 41(2)). Wuschka notes that this distinction should be maintained despite the confusion in the case law which argues for *ex officio* proceedings in both cases. In default non-ICSID proceedings an *ex officio* review is, just as for ICSID cases, warranted: Sebastian Wuschka, 'Procedural Aspects of the Obligation of Non-Recognition Before International Investment Tribunals' in Katia Fach Gómez, Anastasios Gourgourinis, and Catharine Titi (eds), *International Investment Law and the Law of Armed Conflict* (Springer 2019) 6 et seq.

arising directly out of an investment; nationality; and consent in writing) still apply.[104]

However, the danger of scrutinising the territorial dispute is reinforced by the duty to render an enforceable award (against the aggressor-state) and the controversial political nature of occupation/annexation.[105] Applying the annexing state's investment treaties could result in the judicial validation of the annexation or unlawful occupation.[106] For example, current investment claims under BITs between third states and Russia may contradict the UN Resolution on the Territorial Integrity of Ukraine.[107] Furthermore, adjudicating whilst ignoring the parties' consent, carries another intrinsic risk: transforming the investment tribunal into an all-inclusive forum prioritising the conduct of hostilities (which the tribunal is not qualified to do in the first place).[108] Investment tribunals usually have more competences than jurisdiction on the 'interpretation and application' of the treaty.[109] While they usually have jurisdiction over 'any dispute between either [c]ontracting party and the investor of the other [c]ontracting party',[110] they can only assess IHL's *effects* on the applicability of the BIT, not 'pure' IHL issues.[111] There must thus always be a link with the investment. Investment tribunals would otherwise become *pseudo-* international criminal tribunals, which primarily deal with IHL violations. However, it is indeed difficult to draw such a line, as the Crimea tribunals – and before that the *AAPL* tribunal – have shown.

Perhaps investment tribunals' legitimacy would thus benefit from avoiding a lack of jurisdiction and solving general international law issues first, preferably in a bifurcated procedure on jurisdiction. The jurisdictional issues discussed below are indeed classic examples of what could lead to such bifurcation,[112] as occupation/annexation leads to (i) substantive and not frivolous jurisdictional challenges; (ii) which, if successful, would materially reduce the proceedings

---

104   Wuschka, 'Procedural Aspects of the Obligation of Non-Recognition Before International Investment Tribunals' (n 103) 142. It must be noted that these requirements only apply to the ICSID framework.
105   Dumberry, 'Requiem for Crimea' (n 8) 521.
106   Mayorga (n 7) 141.
107   UNGA Res 68/262 (2014) UN Doc A/RES/68/262.
108   Ryk-Lakhman (n 10) 14 et seq.
109   Russia–Ukraine BIT art 10(1).
110   Russia–Ukraine BIT art 9(1).
111   Ryk-Lakhman (n 10) 16 et seq.
112   *Eg* UNCITRAL Rules art 21(4). This was exactly the case in several Crimea cases, *eg Aeroport Belbek* (n 101) Press Release (6 December 2017).

at the next phase; and (iii) which are not as intertwined with the merits that an early determination would save time and costs.[113]

Still, several tribunals refuse(d) to render a determination on a legal issue outside their jurisdiction *ratione materiae*.[114] Tzeng refutes using investment tribunals altogether as they only rarely examine their jurisdiction if no objection is raised by the parties, they often reject *amicus curiae* briefs, and tend to be very proactive in answering legal questions (instead of making a formal determination on the status of the annexed territory).[115] Furthermore, BIT preambles usually refer to protecting investments, which would make the settlement of territorial/maritime disputes under BITs rather exotic, unless closely connected to the investment issue.[116] Even if they tackle issues of territorial acquisition, investment tribunals will (for reasons of legitimacy) be reluctant to recognise them as (un)lawful and will consequently attach challenge, annulment, or unenforceability to their award.[117] One could thus object to investment tribunals as being *the* place to solve public international law issues. Such concerns have value, but so do investment tribunals. Legal questions (such as title to territory) should be distinguished from political ones (such as transfer).[118] Investment tribunals should not address the latter.[119]

An alternative could be the European Court of Human Rights (ECtHR) and its case law on extraterritorial application of human rights treaties,[120] but it seems again not well placed to solve international legal issues like territorial

---

113 *Glamis Gold Ltd v USA*, Procedural Order no 2 (Revised) (31 May 2005) para 12(c).
114 Tzeng, 'Indispensable Parties and Indispensable Issues' (n 99) 131 et seq, referring to *ADM v Mexico* and *CPI v Mexico* which both refused to make a finding on Mexico's defence as those required a determination on the lawfulness of US measures. Yet, his argument that the Crimea tribunals can hold that there is no territorial dispute, is unconvincing, as then a position on the territorial dispute is taken. For the argument that the non-recognition obligation could be extended to corporations regarding state contracts in Ukraine, see Patrick Dumberry, *A Guide to State Succession in International Investment Law* (Edward Elgar Publishing 2018) 202 et seq.
115 Peter Tzeng, 'Sovereignty over Crimea: A Case for State-to-State Investment Arbitration' (2014) 41 Yale J Int'l L 459, 462 et seq.
116 Thomas D Grant, 'International Dispute Settlement in Response to an Unlawful Seizure of Territory: Three Mechanisms' (2015) 16 Chicago J Int'l L 1, 33.
117 Happ and Wuschka (n 93) 255.
118 Robert Jennings, *The Acquisition of Territory in International Law* (first published 1963, MUP 2017) 88.
119 Vladimir Gladyshev, 'Russian Domestic Law in Crimea-Related Investment Arbitrations: Issues and Pitfalls' (2017) Colloquium International Investment Law & the Law of Armed Conflict, Athens, 10 (not published).
120 *Ukraine v Russia (re Crimea)* App no 20958/14 (ECtHR, 11 September 2019). For an analysis, see Isabella Risini, chapter 9 in this volume; Tuzheliak (n 11) 28 et seq.

disputes. The ICJ or a tribunal under Annex VII of the UN Convention on the Law of the Sea (UNCLOS) seem preferable: they respectively settle territorial and maritime disputes, as its judges have experience in territorial disputes, are state-appointed and thus have more legitimacy.[121] Otherwise, this could lead to inequitable results and adjudicate certain territorial issues while ignoring others.[122] Indeed, regarding the Crimea crisis, it seems that Ukraine has taken both avenues to sue Russia, as well as proceedings before the International Criminal Court.[123] While proceedings based on general international law (*ie* non-treaty law) before investment tribunals are extremely rare,[124] another alternative would be an inter-state dispute resolution mechanism (*eg* article 10 Russia-Ukraine BIT) for interpretation[125] and application issues (including which state should protect investments in that territory). This could give Ukraine a seat at the table and give subsequent tribunals more legitimacy when dealing with those issues.[126]

3.2 *Jurisdiction* Ratione Loci

3.2.1 Legal or Factual Territory?

To answer the question whether spatial jurisdiction (*ratione loci*) covers *de facto* territory (*eg* the Crimea as Russian territory), interpretation of the terms 'territory' and 'jurisdiction' through article 31(1) VCLT and the effectiveness principle is key.[127] Costelloe gives the example of article 11(1) of the Austria-Ukraine BIT which (merely) extends the application of the treaty to parties' sovereign (*de jure*) territory: only when investments are made in that territory, application of the treaty is triggered.[128] However, going beyond mere systemic

---

121 Tzeng, 'Indispensable Parties and Indispensable Issues' (n 99) 131 et seq.
122 ibid 132.
123 Tzeng, 'Sovereignty over Crimea' (n 115) 460; Laura Rees-Evans, 'Litigating the Use of Force: Reflections on the Interaction between Investor-State Dispute Settlement and Other Forms of International Dispute Settlement in the Context of the Conflict in Ukraine' in Katia Fach Gómez, Anastasios Gourgourinis, and Catharine Titi (eds), *International Investment Law and the Law of Armed Conflict* (Springer 2019) 183 et seq.
124 This is also due to the fact that they are a remnant of pre-BIT diplomatic protection: ibid 5. A reason for not filing such a claim could be that such a tribunal could have interpreted the Russia–Ukraine BIT to the detriment of investors.
125 Including the word 'territory', *cf* section 3.2 below.
126 Tzeng, 'Sovereignty over Crimea' (n 115) 466 et seq; Zrilič (n 6) 228; Davletbaev (n 75); Vaccaro-Incisa (n 92); Dumberry, *State Succession in International Investment Law* (n 114) 245 et seq.
127 Costelloe (n 1) 364, 366.
128 ibid 364 et seq. This is strengthened by the other qualifier, 'in accordance with international law', regarding maritime disputes.

integration, a normative judgment by a tribunal seems to equate a judgment on the lawfulness of the occupation/annexation.[129]

State succession usually provides for straightforward answers when territory is lawfully transferred (*eg* cession and succession). This happens also in investment arbitration.[130] The often-cited case in this respect is *Sanum Investments*, in which it was held that treaties automatically apply to successor states, unless this is inconsistent with the object and purpose of the treaty or radically change the conditions of their operation.[131]

Different problems occur when territory is transferred illegally, as is the case for annexation. In light of the *jus cogens* prohibition of aggression and the impossibility to acquire territory by force, it is not straightforward to apply the moving treaty-frontiers rule. The latter is found in article 15 Vienna Convention on the Succession of States in Respect of Treaties (VCST),[132] and implicitly in article 29 VCLT,[133] stipulating that a treaty automatically applies to all (new) territory of the contracting state. The term 'territory' in those provisions refers to territories over which the state has sovereignty 'in accordance with international law' (article 6 VCST).[134] Yet, both articles 29 VCLT and 15 VCST are not absolute, they only *presume* the application to a party's entire legal territory, but do not *limit* it to that territory.[135] The Swiss Federal Tribunal in *Ukrnafta* and *Stabil* noted that the VCLT argues for a *dynamic* understanding of territory.[136]

---

129 *Cf* section 3.1 above.

130 See in general: Christian J Tams, 'State Succession to Investment Treaties: Mapping the Issues' (2016) 31 ICSID Rev 314; Dumberry, *A Guide to State Succession in International Investment Law* (n 114).

131 *Sanum Investments Ltd v Laos*, PCA Case no 2013-13, Award on Jurisdiction (13 December 2013) para 230. For an overview and critique of the episode, see Dumberry, *A Guide to State Succession in International Investment Law* (n 114) 162 et seq.

132 Vienna Convention on the Succession of States in Respect of Treaties (concluded 23 August 1978, entered into force 6 November 1996) 1946 UNTS 3 (VCST).

133 Repousis (n 87) 464 calls article 15 VCST *lex specialis* to article 29 VCLT.

134 Costelloe (n 1) 347, 350; Asaf Niemoj, 'The Protection of Investments in Disputed Territories: A Panel Hosted by BIICL's Investment Treaty Forum' (*Kluwer Arbitration Blog*, 17 May 2017) <http://arbitrationblog.kluwerarbitration.com/2017/05/17/the-protection-of-investments-in-disputed-territories-a-panel-hosted-by-biicls-investment-treaty-forum/> accessed 29 November 2018; Dumberry, *State Succession in International Investment Law* (n 114) 215. Costelloe argues that also the Commentary on article 29 VCLT suggests such a limitation.

135 Costelloe (n 1) 359. This is supported by the ILC's discussion of article 29 VCLT: Karl Doehring, 'The Scope of the Territorial Application of Treaties – Comments on Art. 25 of the ILC's 1966 Draft Articles on the Law of Treaties' (1967) Heidelberg J Int'l L 483, 488; Happ and Wuschka (n 93) 258.

136 Swiss Federal Tribunal (n 76) para 4.3.2, referring to Mark E Villiger, *Commentary on the 1969 Vienna Convention on the Law of Treaties* (Martinus Nijhoff 2009) 7.

Furthermore, the limited application of the VCST during occupation (articles 39, 40 VCST) and the carve-out of situations not in conformity with international law in article 6 only mean that situations are assumed to be in accordance with international law if not covered by the VCLT/VCST.[137] Such a reference to legality is true for most treaties concluded since the UN Charter.[138] It was also the premise of the CJEU's *Front Polisario* judgment, in which it limited the territorial scope of the Association Agreement, the 'territory of the Kingdom of Morocco', to the *internationally recognised* territory of Morocco, excluding the Western Sahara.[139] Those provisions do not *per se* mean that the moving treaty-frontiers rule cannot be applied to annexations. What makes those provisions on moving treaty-frontiers inapplicable is that no *legal* transfer of territory occurs during illegal occupation/annexation.[140] The application of the moving treaty-frontiers rule to those cases could have the adverse and undesirable effect of legitimising aggression.

One could argue that the customary international law rule on the moving treaty-frontiers still applies, which includes article 29 VCLT, *a fortiori* when no definition of territory can be found in the (investment) treaty.[141] It therefore applies to all territories under a state's effective jurisdiction/control.[142] This has indeed been Ukraine's approach as non-disputing party in the Crimea cases and the tribunals have relied heavily upon this.[143] It is unclear why that would extend treaties to *de facto* territory, however, as this depends on practice of states which can invoke a violation of *jus cogens* and make or break the application of the moving treaty-frontiers rule.[144] These arguments regarding customary international law are therefore not persuasive.

This leaves only the third option. A particular treaty *can* refer back to general international law – and it often does – and as such extend the scope of a treaty to *de facto* territory.[145] This is in line with the case-by-case approach of this

---

137 ILC, 'Draft Articles on Succession of States in respect of Treaties, with Commentaries' (1974) II(1) YB Int'l L 181, art 6(1). *Contra*: Dumberry, *A Guide to State Succession in International Investment Law* (n 114) 198 et seq.
138 Vaccaro-Incisa (n 92).
139 *Front Polisario* (n 72).
140 Costelloe (n 1) 358 et seq; Dumberry, 'Requiem for Crimea' (n 8) 514 et seq.
141 McNair (n 95) 116 et seq; Happ and Wuschka (n 93) 260. *Contra*: Dumberry, 'Requiem for Crimea' (n 8) 515.
142 ibid.
143 Rees-Evans (n 123) 179.
144 Costelloe (n 1) 358; Dumberry, 'Requiem for Crimea' (n 8) 515.
145 Eugene Kontorovich, 'Economic Dealings with Occupied Territory' (2015) 53 Colum J Transnat'l L 584, 636. as cited in Ackermann, 'Investments Under Occupation' (n 26) 83. It is thus roughly equated to the private international law concept of *renvoi*.

chapter. For example, article 1(4) Russia-Ukraine BIT defines territory as 'the territory of the Russian Federation or the territory of Ukraine, as well as their respective exclusive economic zone [(EEZ)] and continental shelf, defined in accordance with international law'.

In contrast to other Russian BITs (with *eg* Norway or Turkey), there is an extra comma after 'shelf', which means that the referral to international law could be applied to the EEZ and the continental shelf only, or to both of them *and* territory, or only to territory.[146] By applying a textual approach, one could thus argue that the material scope is 'territory [...] defined in accordance with international law', ie *de jure* territory (the default criterion).[147]

Several means of interpretation, which are also part of general international law, argue against such a conclusion. One should not be able to justify its claims through its own illegal acts (*ex injuria jus non oritur*).[148] This is supported by the Draft Articles.[149] Furthermore, the door to *de facto* territory is opened by applying the principle of effectiveness (*ut magis valeat quam pereat*, found in article 31(1) VCLT) and consequently ignoring the comma. That way only the EEZ and continental shelf are qualified by the comma, and the BIT is interpreted in line of the Russia-Norway and Russia-Turkey BITs. This seems to have been the approach of the *Ukrnafta* and *Stabil* tribunals,[150] referring to (i) article 29 VCLT; (ii) dictionaries that do not require sovereignty criteria for their definition of territory; (iii) Russia's ability to legislate; (iv) Russia's inability to blow hot (annexing the Crimea) and cold (not applying its own BITs) simultaneously; and (v) the object and purpose of the BIT (providing recourse

---

146 Mykhaylo Soldatenko, 'Ongoing Territorial Challenges in Crimea Cases: Putting Everest v. Russia in Context' (*Kluwer Arbitration Blog*, 5 November 2018) <http://arbitrationblog.kluwerarbitration.com/2018/11/05/territorial-challenges-expected-in-crimea-cases-putting-everest-v-russia-in-context/> accessed 29 November 2018.
147 Vaccaro-Incisa (n 92).
148 *Eg Legal Consequences for States of The Continued Presence of South Africa in Namibia* (n 67) (Dissenting Opinion Judge Dillard) 167. Equivalent maxims are *nemo auditor turpitudinem suam allegans* and *nullus commodum capere de sua injuria propria*.
149 ILC, 'Draft Articles on the Effects of Armed Conflict on Treaties' (n 46) art 15: 'A State committing aggression within the meaning of the Charter of the United Nations and resolution 3314 (XXIX) of the General Assembly of the United Nations shall not terminate or withdraw from a treaty or suspend its operation as a consequence of an armed conflict that results from the act of aggression if the effect would be to the benefit of that State.'
150 Swiss Federal Tribunal (n 76) para. 4.3. Germany–Russia BIT art 1(2), the wording of which does not preclude the application of the treaty to Russia's annexed territory; see Wuschka, 'Rechtssicherheit für deutsche Investoren auf der Krim?' (n 57) 196. *Contra*: Dumberry, 'Requiem for Crimea' (n 8) 524. He argues that therefore tribunals should *not* conclude that Crimea is part of Russia to avoid legitimisation of the situation.

for investors).¹⁵¹ Through the latter, the tribunals clearly upheld the *Sanum Investments* exception, which only has to be applauded in light of consistency and systemic integration (*cf* section 2.1).

One could add that article 29 itself provides room for derogation in the BIT: '[u]nless a different intention appears from the treaty or is otherwise established'.¹⁵² In *Everest Estate*, reportedly¹⁵³ the tribunal avoided this textual issue and merely held that the Russia-Ukraine BIT applies to Crimea because that was the case at the time of its adoption in 1998 (irrespective of whether investors qualified as foreign).¹⁵⁴ No matter the approach, concluding that the BIT applies to *de facto* territory under effective control of Russia should be favoured to avoid the legal vacuum described above. Sometimes an illegal act must be upheld and effective to the extent that it provides for a remedy, but it can never be on an innocent party to prove an *ab initio* nullity, especially not when jurisdiction is non-compulsory.¹⁵⁵ In this scenario, Crimea is considered to be part of Russia, disregarding the illegality of the annexation.¹⁵⁶

3.2.2 Strategy of Aggressor-States

The issue of (extra)territorial application will only emerge when the occupying/annexing state denies the applicability of its BITs to the *de facto* territory (like in the Crimea dispute), or when it does *not* consider the occupied/annexed territory as part of its territory. The latter is improbable as the aggressor-state will want to benefit from the occupation/annexation.¹⁵⁷ Investment treaties will thus almost always automatically apply due to the preclusive character of the sovereignty claim. In the long term, however, a decrease in foreign direct investment in the annexed territories is rather logical.¹⁵⁸

Respondent states could follow several strategies to avoid extraterritorial application of their investment treaties. First and foremost, they could argue on the facts that the territory is neither occupied nor annexed at all – which will be very difficult to maintain – nor part of the state's territory.¹⁵⁹ Russia

---

151 Soldatenko (n 146); Rees-Evans (n 123) 187 et seq.
152 Ackermann, 'Investments Under Occupation' (n 26) 81 et seq.
153 Soldatenko (n 146); Rees-Evans (n 123) 186.
154 *Cf* section 3.4 below.
155 Robert Jennings, 'Nullity and Effectiveness in International Law' in Robert Jennings (ed), *Cambridge Essays in International Law: Essays in Honour of Lord McNair* (Stevens & Sons 1965) 72, 76 et seq.
156 Dumberry, 'Requiem for Crimea' (n 8) 507, 511 et seq.
157 Costelloe (n 1) 372; Happ and Wuschka (n 93) 261 et seq.
158 Dumberry, 'Requiem for Crimea' (n 8) 532. He therefore argues for consistent non-recognition of annexations by tribunals.
159 Kryvoi (n 13).

did indeed not deny that Crimea was not covered by the BIT, merely that the tribunal(s) wrongly upheld a dynamic interpretation of territory.[160] Second, aggressor-states could claim that the BIT does not apply to the annexed territory and object to the tribunal's jurisdiction, because it was not understood as territory at the time of the adoption of the BIT.[161] Russia has done so in the *PJSC Ukrnafta* and *Stabil* cases.[162] These objections are extremely illogical, as they are inconsistent with the territorial claim. Non-appearance would therefore be a better solution.[163] Indeed, this seemed to be Russia's strategy in all cases.[164] A third avenue could be to argue that the tribunal only has jurisdiction over investment disputes, not over the legal determination of territorial disputes and thus one should insist on investments made in the sovereign territory of the state.[165] Russia has started to participate in the pending cases 'in order to express its position comprehensively and ensure better protection of its rights' and has challenged jurisdictional decisions and awards of the tribunals.[166] Indeed, as argued above, adopting a position on the legality of the occupation/annexation and interpreting and applying provisions referring to 'territory' will lead to the tribunal taking a position on the underlying territorial dispute (*eg* through incidental jurisdiction) and could thus cause legitimacy issues.[167]

A solution to the latter for tribunals could be to frame the sovereignty issue over Crimea as a factual matter, which would make the breach of investment protections the only relevant legal issue.[168] The investor's claim could thus be made directly upon the fact of occupation/annexation, thus severing title from respondent's treaty obligation.[169] Alternatively, an implicit *ad hoc* agreement could be the way to apply BITs extraterritorially based on the respondent state's non-objection to jurisdiction on that ground

---

160 Swiss Federal Tribunal (n 76) para. 4.3.2.
161 *Cf* section 3.3 below on jurisdiction *ratione temporis*.
162 Swiss Federal Tribunal (n 76) para. 4.3.1. See also: Tzeng, 'Indispensable Parties and Indispensable Issues' (n 99) 133; Repousis (n 87) 470; Niemoj (n 134).
163 Costelloe as cited in Niemoj (n 134).
164 See, *eg*, *Lugzor LLC* (n 101).
165 Niemoj (n 134); Soldatenko (n 146).
166 *Lugzor LLC* (n 101). While it has 'not participated hitherto because the jurisdictional position appeared clear – the Tribunal lacks jurisdiction', now '[p]articipation has simply become a practical necessity because some recent tribunal decisions have gone awry on basic principles of Public International Law'.
167 Niemoj (n 134); Vaccaro-Incisa (n 92).
168 For this solution regarding the UNCLOS dispute, see Peter Tzeng, 'Ukraine v. Russia and Philippines v. China: Jurisdiction and Legitimacy' (2017) 46 Denv J Int'l L & Pol'y 1, 7.
169 Jennings (n 155) 77 et seq.

when the state participates in the proceedings.[170] Moreover, the occupying/annexing state cannot avoid its responsibilities due to the estoppel principle (*venire contra factum proprium non valet*),[171] otherwise it would create fewer obligations than under the lawful acquisition of territory (*ex injuria jus non oritur*), for example by submitting a case to the local courts of the annexed territory.[172]

3.2.3 Towards a *Namibia*-Like Exception for Investment Treaties

Treaties have to be interpreted in accordance with their object and purpose (article 31 VCLT), especially when they are silent on their application to certain 'territory', but this is unlikely as they usually refer to the state's territory, its coastal sea and the areas where the state is entitled to exercise sovereignty (in accordance with international law).[173] Leaving matters of state succession aside, like for occupation, a solution could lie in the application of IIAS to the annexed territory, analogous to the extraterritorial application of human rights treaties on the basis of the treaty's object and purpose (protecting people's or peoples' rights).[174] Human rights treaties often refer to 'jurisdiction' as a basis for extraterritorial application, in occupied territory.[175] Yet, territory and jurisdiction have different objectives: jurisdiction refers to the threshold requirement for a state to be bound by a treaty in a specific territory, triggering their human rights obligations towards individuals, while its territorial application and articles 29 VCLT and 15 VCST concern pure geographical and internal matters within the state to uphold minimal stability.[176]

---

170 Happ and Wuschka (n 93) 265; Wuschka, 'Procedural Aspects of the Obligation of Non-Recognition Before International Investment Tribunals' (n 103) 148.
171 Happ and Wuschka (n 93) 261 et seq.
172 ibid 263 et seq; Wuschka, 'Investment Claims and Annexation' (n 5) 31 et seq; Wuschka, 'Procedural Aspects of the Obligation of Non-Recognition Before International Investment Tribunals' (n 103) 148 et seq. *Contra*: Dumberry, 'Requiem for Crimea' (n 8) 527.
173 *Cf* Russia–Ukraine BIT art 1(4) above; Happ and Wuschka (n 93) 260.
174 *Legal Consequences of the Construction of a Wall in the Occupied Palestinian Territory* (n 30) para. 112; Mayorga (n 7) 17; Costelloe (n 1) 350, 359 et seq, 372; Niemoj (n 134). See in general Milanović (n 35).
175 Convention for the Protection of Human Rights and Fundamental Freedoms (adopted 4 November 1950, entered into force 3 September 1953) 213 UNTS 221 (ECHR) art 1; *Loizidou v Turkey*, App no 15318/89 (ECtHR, 23 March 1995, Preliminary Objections) para 62; *Ilaşcu and others v Moldova and Russia* ECHR 2004–VII 1, paras 310 et seq; Costelloe (n 1) 367.
176 ibid 371 et seq; Lea Raible, 'Title to Territory and Jurisdiction in International Human Rights Law: Three Models for a Fraught Relationship' (2018) 31 LJIL 315, 323. Costelloe (n 1) refers to respectively ECHR arts 1 (jurisdiction) and 56 (territorial application).

In *Ilaşcu*, the ECtHR held that the relevant test to apply treaties extraterritorially in occupied territories is twofold: all the facts limiting the effective exercise over a state's territory should be considered, as well the state's own conduct.[177] As has been argued above, this includes *unlawful* occupation or, *a fortiori*, annexation. Applying the annexing state's treaties in a limited way whilst suspending the dispossessed state's treaties in *de facto* territory could find support in the *lex specialis* character of IHL,[178] article 40 VCST and article 73 VCLT.[179] It is thus an example of how IHL and IIL can cooperate rather than conflict.

However, two caveats should be made. IIAs are by their nature narrower than eg article 1 ECHR and must be interpreted and applied individually: there is a difference between 'treaties purporting to govern State conduct generally, [...] and those purporting to govern State conduct with respect to a particular territory'.[180] The purpose of the rules on international armed conflict, on the other hand, is exactly to apply extraterritorially.[181]

The main impediment to an extraterritorial application of investment treaties to annexed or illegally occupied territory – different to occupation – is that this seems to be in conflict with the customary and *jus cogens* obligation of non-recognition.[182] It is a decentralised enforcement mechanism of the prohibition of territorial acquisition by force.[183] Investment tribunals also have to follow this principle of general international law.[184] Yet, as argued above, following the approach by the ICJ in the *Namibia* advisory opinion and the ECtHR in *Loizidou* and *Cyprus v Turkey*, (investment) treaties that seem to

---

177   *Ilaşcu* (n 175) para 313; Costelloe (n 1) 368.
178   *Cf* section 2 above.
179   Costelloe (n 1) 355; *cf* section 3.1 above.
180   ibid 359, 371. *Eg* the treaty's purpose under consideration in *Legal Consequences of the Construction of a Wall in the Occupied Palestinian Territory* (n 30) is to regulate parties' conduct in general, rather than with regards to specific territory.
181   ibid 361.
182   'Friendly Relations Declaration' UNGA Res 2625 (XXV) (1970) art 1; *Military and Paramilitary Activities in and against Nicaragua (Nicaragua v USA)* (Merits) [1986] ICJ Rep 14 para 188; *Legal Consequences of the Construction of a Wall in the Occupied Palestinian Territory* (n 30) para 159; Articles on State Responsibility art 41(2). Note that also acts implying such recognition are excluded: ILC, 'Report of the Commission to the General Assembly on the Work of its 53rd Session' (2001) UN Doc A/56/10, 287, para 5.
183   Costelloe (n 1) 356.
184   *Methanex Corp v USA*, Award (3 August 2005), para. 24; Dumberry, 'Requiem for Crimea' (n 8) 527 et seq. Even if this obligation only applies to states, tribunals should be sensitive about exercising such disputed jurisdiction; Wuschka, 'Investment Claims and Annexation' (n 5) 26.

recognise an illegal regime could survive when they are beneficial for the local population.¹⁸⁵ Therefore, the second principle will be formulated as follows:

> *Principle 2* – Investment treaties of the annexing State do *not* generally apply to annexed territory, as they would recognise an illegal situation. Investment treaties of the dispossessed State thus logically apply. The former only apply when the wording of the BIT permits it and investors have no other effective remedies.

Furthermore, individual interests rather than title and sovereignty are another decisive factor for the (extra)territorial application of an investment treaty.¹⁸⁶ Claimants will, in line with the object and purpose of the IIA (the protection of the investor and the development of economic cooperation)¹⁸⁷ argue for their extraterritorial application based on effective control to establish jurisdiction and substantive protections, as they want to avoid the legal vacuum.¹⁸⁸ The *Namibia* advisory opinion suggests that one should not apply the obligation of non-recognition of illegal situations too rigidly on individuals, in line with the very notion of sovereignty, the laws of occupation and the object and purpose of the IIA.¹⁸⁹ Using *jus cogens* to resolve the normative conflict between non-recognition and extraterritorial application is difficult in the first place, because it does not allow balancing conflicting interests.¹⁹⁰ Hierarchy is also difficult in a system based on consensual law-making between states – and consent extends to this extraterritorial application.¹⁹¹ Moreover, international

---

185 *Legal Consequences for States of The Continued Presence of South Africa in Namibia* (n 67) para 125; See also: *Loizidou v Turkey*, App no 15318/89 (ECtHR, 18 December 1996, Merits) para 45; *Cyprus v Turkey*, App no 25781/94 (ECtHR, 10 May 2001) para 96; Costelloe (n 1) 376 et seq; Davletbaev (n 75).
186 Costelloe (n 1) 363; Ackermann, 'Investments Under Occupation' (n 26) 86.
187 *Sanum* (n 131) para 240. This was also the reasoning of the Swiss Supreme Court in *Russia v A* [2018] Case no 4A_396/2017, BGE 144 III 559 (Swiss Federal Tribunal); Simon Bianchi, 'The Applicability of the Ukraine-Russia BIT to Investment Claims in Crimea: A Swiss Perspective' (*Kluwer Arbitration Blog*, 16 March 2019) <http://arbitrationblog.kluwer-arbitration.com/2019/03/16/the-applicability-of-the-ukraine-russia-bit-to-investment-claims-in-crimea-a-swiss-perspective/> accessed 16 March 2019.
188 Tzeng, 'Indispensable Parties and Indispensable Issues' (n 99) 133; Happ and Wuschka (n 93) 253. *Contra*: Dumberry, *State Succession in International Investment Law* (n 103) 216, arguing that only basic human rights protection can be applied extraterritorially.
189 Benvenisti, *The International Law of Occupation* (n 23) 85 et seq; Ackermann, 'Investments Under Occupation' (n 26) 88.
190 Milanović (n 35) 103.
191 ibid.

courts and tribunals are not states and are thus not bound by article 41(2) of the Articles on State Responsibility and the obligation of non-recognition of illegal situations.[192] Still, for reasons set out above, investment tribunals will be reluctant to follow this argument.[193]

BITs that are beneficial for the local population are thus an exception to Principle 2 and can be applied extraterritorially. While this exception can thus become quite broad, it is important to see it as a deviation from the principle of non-recognition of illegal situations.

The argument for the extraterritorial application of the annexing state's BITs in this section is not always desirable. The dispossessed state's and investors' acknowledgement of *de facto* aggressor-state's sovereignty may be interpreted as accepting the new *status quo*.[194] Even when territory is claimed through mere *de facto* sovereignty, other states may regard it as a *fait accompli* after a significant period of time.[195] Furthermore, regarding the example of Crimea, it is generally accepted – at least by states – that Russia succeeded the Soviet Union,[196] but this means that the latter's practice on leaving questions of state responsibility outside the jurisdiction of tribunals is still applicable in Russia's IIAs.[197]

3.3 *Jurisdiction* Ratione Temporis

Also for temporal jurisdiction, one must examine the applicable IIA. The Russia-Ukraine BIT (27 November 1998) requires that the investments should have been made after 1 January 1992 (article 12), *ie* the dissolution of the Soviet Union. This was the decisive question in the eyes of the *Ukrnafta* and *Stabil* tribunals, as well as the Swiss Federal Tribunal, and was thus answered in favour

---

192 Wuschka, 'Procedural Aspects of the Obligation of Non-Recognition Before International Investment Tribunals' (n 103) 186.
193 ibid 5.
194 Davletbaev (n 75). This can be seen in the claims filed by *Naftogaz* and *Oschadbank* (both state-owned companies): Dumberry, 'Requiem for Crimea' (n 8) 522 et seq. See also De Vriese (n 14), noting that the extraterritorial application of substantive investment protections, rather than treaties, could provide an alternative.
195 Costelloe (n 1) 347, 352 et seq. He notes that an agreement on the moving treaty-frontiers rule can always be concluded between the occupying and occupied state, but this will be unlikely for the unlawful acquisition of territory.
196 Patrick Dumberry, *State Succession to International Responsibility* (Martinus Nijhoff 2007) 150 et seq; Patrick Dumberry, 'An Uncharted Question of State Succession: Are New States Automatically Bound by the BITs Concluded by Predecessor States Before Independence?' (2015) 6 JIDS 74, 90 et seq.
197 Costelloe (n 1) 373.

of the investors.[198] However, examining the different heads of jurisdiction one-by-one, as the tribunals did – and this chapter does – was criticised by Russia for being too compartmentalised ('*Schubladisierung*'): the definition of investment itself (*ratione materiae*) contains a temporal and territorial element.[199] Indeed, 'the dividing line between persons and things is not exact',[200] and in practice they are often intertwined, but a more compartmentalised academic discussion has its merits for clarity.

One could argue that investments were made within the original BIT and the domestic legal framework before the occupation. The Crimea was not part of Russia at the time of the conclusion of the BIT in 1998 and non-recognition means that it still is not.[201] Yet, Ukrainian investments in the Crimea are then not covered by the Russia-Ukraine BIT (from a policy perspective), and the occupied state could invoke circumstances precluding wrongfulness, thus risking a complete legal vacuum. On the other hand, even if one could follow the changing borders, or better, the extraterritorial approach,[202] the principle of non-retroactivity of treaties (article 28 VCLT) applies, absent provisions to the contrary.[203] Ukrainian investments pre-2014 (the year of annexation) are then not covered, as they were not 'foreign' yet nor made *intuitu personae* in Russia.[204]

Both approaches thus prove to be unsatisfactory for foreign and Ukrainian investors. The only way out – again – seems to be the effective interpretation of the specific BIT (article 1(1) and (4)). This would not require an *ab initio* investment in the *other* state, or better, an *ab initio* investment in the other state *but for* the event of a border shift.[205] As long as *ratione personae* jurisdiction (nationality or legal seat) is satisfied at the time of the *infringement*,[206] the non-retroactivity can thus be neutralised. This is particularly true if one follows a modern liberal approach of investments *ratione personae*, including protection of certain rights and values, rather than Russia's old conservative definition of a monetary injection.[207]

---

198   Swiss Federal Tribunal (n 76) para 4.2; Soldatenko (n 146).
199   ibid para 4.4.1.
200   McLachlan, Shore, and Weiniger (n 90) 10.
201   Kryvoi (n 13).
202   *Cf* section 3.2 above.
203   Costelloe (n 1) 362 et seq.
204   Vaccaro-Incisa (n 92).
205   This was exactly the approach of the *Ukrnafta* and *Stabil* tribunal: Swiss Federal Tribunal (n 76) para 4.2.
206   Zachary Douglas, *The International Law of Investment Claims* (CUP 2009) 290 et seq. See also: Swiss Federal Tribunal (n 76) para 4.4.3.
207   Wuschka, 'Zuständigkeit von Investitionsschiedsgerichten Für Klagen Mit Bezug Zur Annexion Der Krim' (n 84) 99.

Requiring an *ab initio* investment would clearly be against the object and purpose of the BIT and exclude many investments.[208] The *Everest Estate* tribunal held that an investment on the territory of the other contracting state *at the time of the alleged breach* suffices.[209] Extraterritorial application of Russia's IIAs thus seems to be reinforced by its temporal application.[210] Indeed, the *Aeroport Belbek* and *Privatbank* tribunals allegedly held that Russia owed obligations *vis-à-vis* Ukrainian investors from the moment the Accession Agreement was signed, rejecting the claimants' argument that this was the case since the Russian occupation.[211] This is confirmed by principle 1 and reinforced by Ukraine's and its (state-owned) investors' compliance with Russian law.

Temporal jurisdiction is also linked to the requirement that the investment be made in accordance with the domestic law of the host state, found in many BITs.[212] As investment tribunals must refer to domestic law for a range of issues,[213] this will probably also be the case in the Crimea disputes.[214] Regarding jurisdiction *ratione temporis*, one could argue that under article 1(5) Russia-Ukraine BIT, Ukrainian law would be applied for legal relations before 18 March 2014 'if it is consistent with the rules of Russian laws' and that the Russian transitional law would become applicable after that.[215] That states that Ukrainian investments in Crimea are only covered once they are re-registered as Russian businesses.[216] This seems to be an attempt by Russia to avoid liability under any third state-Russia BIT. Article 1(2)(b) defines investors as 'any legal entity, set up or instituted in conformity with the legislation prevailing on the territory of the given Contracting Party'. Thus, Ukrainian law rather than

---

208   Soldatenko (n 146) referring to *Ukrnafta* (n 101), *Stabil* (n 101), and *Everest Estate* (n 101) (citing *PacRim v El Salvador*, ICSID Case no ARB/09/12, Decision on Jurisdiction (1 June 2012), where the Tribunal found that the investor was not required to have proper nationality *ab initio* as long as it possessed it prior to the state breach).

209   Belén Olmos Giupponi, 'Exploring the Links Between Nationality Changes and Investment Claims Arising Out of Armed Conflicts: The Case of Russian Passportization in Crimea' in Katia Fach Gómez, Anastasios Gourgourinis, and Catharine Titi (eds), *International Investment Law and the Law of Armed Conflict* (Springer 2019) 166.

210   However, the use of 'carried out' in that provision could be a basis for Russia to argue that investments shall be initially made into Russian territory, which is not the case when the control over the territory changes later; Soldatenko (n 146).

211   Rees-Evans (n 123) 16.

212   Vaccaro-Incisa (n 92).

213   From attribution of conduct over nationality to property rights, see in general: Jarrod Hepburn, *Domestic Law in International Investment Arbitration* (OUP 2017) 2.

214   Gladyshev (n 119).

215   Russian Federal Constitutional Law N6-FKZ [2014] on the acceptance of Crimea and Sevastopol into the Russian Federation, as cited in ibid 11.

216   Vaccaro-Incisa (n 92).

Russian domestic law should be applied.[217] Furthermore, applying Russian law legitimises the Russian annexation.[218] Like fruits of the poisonous tree, all products of the annexation should be void.[219] The only exception to the principle of non-recognition carved out here is the extraterritorial application of BITs during annexation. In practice, however, applying a Russian BIT while referring to Ukrainian law will be difficult to maintain: referring to Russian law seems to be the lesser of two evils (not applying any BIT).

3.4 *Jurisdiction* Ratione Personae

Notwithstanding the express provision that investments need to be made in the other state, a restrictive interpretation would lead to the conclusion that only *foreign* investments are covered.[220] As argued above, this nationality or legal seat requirement raises the question whether originally domestic investments should benefit from protection under international investment law.[221] This was exactly the argument made by Russia in the *PJSC* proceedings before the Swiss Supreme Court, but this was dismissed on (i) a textual *and* (ii) teleological approach of article 1(1) Russia-Ukraine BIT; (iii) the 'asset-based' (contrary to a cross-border 'transaction-based') non-exhaustive list of investments;[222] (iv) the well-established principle that conditions for jurisdiction *ratione personae* must be fulfilled at the time of the breach; and (v) the principle of good faith.[223] Furthermore, not including investors of the occupied country within the BIT protection would treat them unfairly compared to other foreign investors.[224] Denying domestic investors BIT protection while giving benefits to the aggressor-state would go against the 'synallagmatic relationship' envisaged

---

217 ibid.
218 Gladyshev (n 119) 1 et seq.
219 Thomas D Grant, *Aggression against Ukraine: Territory, Responsibility, and International Law* (Palgrave Macmillan 2015).
220 *Bayview Irrigation District and others v Mexico*, ICSID Case no ARB(AF)/05/1, Award (19 June 2007) para 105; *Canadian Cattlemen for Fair Trade v USA*, Award on Jurisdiction (28 January 2008) para 147 (limiting foreign investment to the commitment of financial resources and excluding mere cross-border trade activities); Christina Knahr, 'Investments "in the Territory" of the Host State' in Christina Binder and others (eds), *International Investment Law for the 21st Century: Essays in Honour of Christoph Schreuer* (OUP 2009) 51 et seq.
221 Wuschka, 'Investment Claims and Annexation' (n 5) 33.
222 The Swiss Federal Tribunal followed a similar qualitative assessment of the investment, see Swiss Federal Tribunal (n 76) para 4.4.1.
223 *Russia v A* (n 187); Bianchi (n 187). See also Vaccaro-Incisa (n 92).
224 *Ukrnafta* (n 100); Vaccaro-Incisa (n 91). However, in the Crimea, the percentage of other foreign investors was very modest, and generally not made *intuitu personae* in Russia.

by BITS, *ie* protection and encouragement.[225] According to the *Ukrnafta* tribunal, companies incorporated under Ukrainian law qualified as investor under article 1(2).[226] In short, investment claims by Ukrainian investors were internationalised through Russia's annexation of Crimea.[227]

There is one caveat: a tribunal cannot apply a BIT with more than one respondent state (*eg* applying the Germany-Russia BIT against Russia *and* Ukraine), otherwise it would violate its jurisdiction *ratione personae*.[228] This is based on the *admissibility* doctrine of indispensable parties. A claim is inadmissible if the legal interests of a state outside its jurisdiction *ratione personae* would be affected by and form the 'very subject-matter' of the decision,[229] which requires a 'prerequisite determination' on its legal responsibility.[230] Admissibility is different from jurisdiction: it concerns situations in which a tribunal should refrain from exercising its jurisdiction and thus gives the tribunal some policy options as to which cases to accept (contrary to jurisdiction).[231] This doctrine will render a claim under a 'disputed-territory-BIT' inadmissible, as the latter requires a prerequisite determination on title to territory.[232] According to Tzeng, however, this statement suffers from four problems, which one could divide into two categories. On the one hand, the doctrine incentivises the state not to participate in the proceedings and ignore its responsibility while upholding its sovereignty claim.[233] On the other hand, he relativizes the scope of investment cases: the very subject-matter of an investment claim is the breach of protection standards rather than the sovereignty issue (which is part of the *ratio decidendi*) and the award is merely a *res inter alios acta* between the investor and the respondent (*eg* Russia).[234] Ukraine's legal interests

---

225   *Ukrnafta* (n 100) and *Everest* (n 101) as cited in ibid.
226   Bianchi (n 187). The reasoning of the Swiss Supreme Court (n 187) also applies here.
227   Wuschka, 'Zuständigkeit von Investitionsschiedsgerichten für Klagen mit Bezug zur Annexion der Krim' (n 84) 99.
228   Tzeng, 'Indispensable Parties and Indispensable Issues' (n 99) 123.
229   *Monetary Gold Removed from Rome in 1943 (Italy v France, UK, USA)* (Preliminary Question) [1954] ICJ Rep 19, para 32.
230   *Certain Phosphate Lands in Nauru (Nauru v Australia)* (Preliminary Objections) [1992] ICJ Rep 240, para 55. For the argument that the principle applies to international arbitration, see Noam Zamir, 'The Applicability of the Monetary Gold Principle in International Arbitration' (2017) 33 Arb Int'l 523.
231   *Accordance with International Law of the Unilateral Declaration of Independence in Respect of Kosovo* (Advisory Opinion) [2010] ICJ Rep 403, 415 et seq; Shany (n 88) 780, 786, 796.
232   Tzeng, 'Indispensable Parties and Indispensable Issues' (n 99) 125 et seq, arguing, however, that this is not the case for non-state actors, as those need not to consent.
233   ibid 126. This is indeed what Russia has done in the Crimea cases.
234   Tzeng, 'Indispensable Parties and Indispensable Issues' (n 99) 126.

(the territorial dispute) do not necessarily form the very subject-matter of the investor-state dispute (article 9 Russia-Ukraine BIT), as the BIT also provides for a state-state track (article 10).[235]

Wuschka's view is more convincing: even if the question on the disputed territory is a preliminary determination for the investor-state dispute, this has to be done by using the specific definition of territory in the investment treaty.[236] This seemed to be the reasoning of the *Ukrnafta* tribunal.[237] The subsequent Swiss Supreme Court decision confirmed that article 29 VCLT makes the BIT applicable to *de facto* territory, and as Russia did not contest that fact and the irrelevance of the illegality of the annexation, it confirmed the award.[238] Indeed, merely using dispute settlement tools, based on *de facto* control by one of the contracting states, is not equivalent to implicitly/explicitly recognising (illegal) annexation.[239] This goes for both investor-state as inter-states disputes.

4 Conclusion

This chapter addressed the question how both the occupying and annexing state can be held accountable for their acts and omissions regarding foreign investments and property. It examined several situations and discovered two main principles, which are each other's antipode. Annexation is perhaps the simplest: *jus cogens* forbids extraterritorial application, but an effective interpretation of specific IIAs can lead to protection in favour of the investor. Conversely, extraterritorial application of the IIA between the occupying and occupied state seems warranted, despite the plea for continuity in article 43 Hague Regulations. Logically, this is not the case when there is no IIA in the first place, although the international minimum standard can still apply. There are further exceptions in the form of temporary occupations and willing occupied states to continue protection by agreement. Furthermore, this chapter

---

235 *Cf Ecuador v USA*, PCA Case no 2012-5, Prof Michael Reisman, Expert Opinion with Respect to Jurisdiction (24 April 2012) paras. 4, 20–21 as cited in Repousis (n 86) 480.
236 Wuschka, 'Investment Claims and Annexation' (n 5) 33–34. *Cf* Ukraine as non-disputing party and Russia both accepting the Crimea as part of Russia in *Everest Estate*.
237 Bianchi (n 187).
238 ibid.
239 Nikos Lavranos, 'The New Frontier: Investment Treaty Disputes in Times of War and Annexations' (*Practical Law Arbitration Blog*, 13 December 2017) <http://arbitrationblog.practicallaw.com/the-new-frontier-investment-treaty-disputes-in-times-of-war-and-annexations/> accessed 25 March 2019.

has argued that the IIA between the occupying state and a third state regarding the occupied territory apply on the basis of teleological interpretation and/or the acquired rights of foreign investors. It certainly does not apply because of indirect/derivative consent. The IIA between a third state and the unoccupied part of the state logically remains in force.

Although this chapter focused on the situation in the Crimea, it has tried to provide a general framework for future situations and can thus be a beacon of light for tribunals to navigate through the waters of *jus cogens* and the dense network of IIAs. Investment claims can then be assessed through several substantive standards, *eg* advanced armed conflict clauses.[240] Those add something to the customary IHL standard of article 43 Hague Regulations, as they extend the possibility of compensation to non-international armed conflicts and give investors a *procedural* right to claim compensation directly from the host state, next to their substantive protection.[241] In the case of Crimea, one could argue that investors do not have the possibility to claim damages from the Russian Government (as it does not accept jurisdiction), nor have any achievable claim against Ukraine (which can rely on the *force majeure* exception). Still, claims against the latter are not impossible. Assuming that the procedural hurdle can be tackled, and jurisdiction can actually be established – as this chapter argues – the awards still have to be enforced.[242] This has been the case for several of the Crimea awards, for example the *Everest Estate* award, for which the Hague Court of Appeal has rejected Russia's application to suspend its enforcement.[243]

Investor-state dispute settlement is yet another example of the rising importance of the individual in international law.[244] However, a readjustment of established international law principles (like the obligation not to recognise illegal situations) would cause adverse effects. In the case of the Crimea, those rules seem to frustrate the transnational movement of investments as protected by BITs. This chapter has circumvented that *jus cogens* rule and indeed accommodated that tension inherent to (international) law, *ie* between effectiveness and flexibility.[245] Other possibilities are regional human rights

---

240 These are not discussed in this chapter but in several chapters in Part 1 of this volume. See also De Vriese (n 14).
241 Heather L Bray, 'SOI – Save Our Investments: International Investment Law and International Humanitarian Law' (2013) 14 JWIT 578, 581 et seq; Spears and Fogdestam-Agius (n 28) 295. They found some exceptions in the Libya–Korea and Syria–Slovakia BITs, re-introducing national and MFN treatment in the advanced armed conflict clause.
242 Kryvoi (n 13).
243 Hague Court of Appeal, Judgment no 200.250.714-01 (11 June 2019).
244 Wuschka, 'Investment Claims and Annexation' (n 5) 21, 32; Happ and Wuschka (n 93) 264.
245 Jennings (n 155) 72 et seq.

bodies or mere IHL protection, but they are likely to circumvent the issue as well.[246] Perhaps the only exception is the ICJ, which could address the *jus cogens* question when adjudicating diplomatic protection claims. Furthermore, in cases of loss of territory or protracted armed conflict (both cause a large number of claims), a single post-conflict tribunal, reminiscent of the Iran-US Claims Tribunal, would be a better option in transition to peace.[247]

Nevertheless, the power of investment law and tribunals to break open frozen conflicts such as the one in Crimea, but potentially many more, cannot be underestimated. After all, next to enforcing IHL, investment arbitration captures situations which would otherwise not be scrutinised (such as the situation in the Crimea), and thus brings them to the attention of the international community. It may generate several positive effects on international law and politics: it enhances public scrutiny over armed conflicts,[248] and it might even depoliticise international disputes.[249]

Note on the Text

This chapter is an edited version of the dissertation submitted for the LLM (Cantab) degree. I am hugely indebted to Dr Michael Waibel, Tobias Ackermann, Sebastian Wuschka and my dear friend and colleague Dhruv Sharma for their constructive feedback on previous drafts.

Bibliography

Ackermann T, 'The ILC Draft Articles on the Effects of Armed Conflicts on Treaties: Room for Termination or Suspension of Bilateral Investment Treaties?' (2016) Minerva Center for the Rule of Law under Extreme Conditions Working Paper <http://minervaextremelaw.haifa.ac.il/images/Ackermann_Armed_Conflicts_and_BITs_Minerva_Working_Paper.pdf> accessed 15 May 2020.

Ackermann T, 'Investments Under Occupation: The Application of Investment Treaties to Occupied Territory' in K Fach Gómez, A Gourgourinis, and C Titi (eds), *International Investment Law and the Law of Armed Conflict* (Springer 2019).

---

246 Happ and Wuschka (n 93) 250.
247 Gladyshev (n 121); Zrilič (n 6) 204 et seq; Lavranos (n 239).
248 Ryk-Lakhman (n 10) 51.
249 In general, see Ursula Kriebaum, 'Evaluating Social Benefits and Costs of Investment Treaties: Depoliticization of Investment Disputes' (2018) 33 ICSID Rev 14.

Baetens F, 'When International Rules Interact: International Investment Law and the Law of Armed Conflict' (*Investment Treaty News*, 7 April 2011) <www.iisd.org/itn/2011/04/07/when-international-rules-interact-international-investment-law-and-the-law-of-armed-conflict/> accessed 10 March 2020.

Benvenisti E, 'Occupation, Belligerent', *Max Planck Encyclopedia of Public International Law* (2009) <https://opil.ouplaw.com/home/MPIL> accessed 4 March 2020.

Benvenisti E, *The International Law of Occupation* (OUP 2012).

Bianchi S, 'The Applicability of the Ukraine-Russia BIT to Investment Claims in Crimea: A Swiss Perspective' (*Kluwer Arbitration Blog*, 16 March 2019) <http://arbitrationblog.kluwerarbitration.com/2019/03/16/the-applicability-of-the-ukraine-russia-bit-to-investment-claims-in-crimea-a-swiss-perspective/> accessed 16 March 2019.

Bonnitcha J, LN Skovgaard Poulsen, and M Waibel, *The Political Economy of the Investment Treaty Regime* (OUP 2017).

Bray HL, 'SOI – Save Our Investments: International Investment Law and International Humanitarian Law' (2013) 14 JWIT 578.

Costelloe D, 'Treaty Succession in Annexed Territory' (2016) 65 ICLQ 343.

Davletbaev M, 'The Applicability of Russia-Ukraine BIT Treaty to Investments in Crimea: Current Status and Future Developments' (*Lexology*, 31 May 2017) <www.lexology.com/library/detail.aspx?g=ea62373e-8e20-4fb8-b2ec-f5ac295dfc3f> accessed 10 March 2020.

De Vriese K, 'That Other Crisis: Extraterritorial Application of Investment Standards During Occupation and Annexation' (*Kluwer Arbitration Blog*, 30 June 2020) <http://arbitrationblog.kluwerarbitration.com/2020/06/30/that-other-crisis-extraterritorial-application-of-investment-standards-during-occupation-and-annexation/?doing_wp_cron=1598004139.7670049667358398437500> accessed 30 June 2020.

Doehring K, 'The Scope of the Territorial Application of Treaties – Comments on Art. 25 of the ILC's 1966 Draft Articles on the Law of Treaties' (1967) Heidelberg J Int'l L 483.

Douglas Z, *The International Law of Investment Claims* (CUP 2009).

Dumberry P, *State Succession to International Responsibility* (Martinus Nijhoff 2007).

Dumberry P, 'An Uncharted Question of State Succession: Are New States Automatically Bound by the BITs Concluded by Predecessor States Before Independence?' (2015) 6 JIDS 74.

Dumberry P, *A Guide to State Succession in International Investment Law* (Edward Elgar Publishing 2018).

Dumberry P, 'Requiem for Crimea: Why Tribunals Should Have Declined Jurisdiction over the Claims of Ukrainian Investors against Russian [sic] under the Ukraine–Russia BIT' (2018) 9 JIDS 506.

Gladyshev V, 'Russian Domestic Law in Crimea-Related Investment Arbitrations: Issues and Pitfalls' (2017) Colloquium International Investment Law & the Law of Armed Conflict, Athens (not published).

Grant TD, *Aggression against Ukraine: Territory, Responsibility, and International Law* (Palgrave Macmillan 2015).

Grant TD, 'International Dispute Settlement in Response to an Unlawful Seizure of Territory: Three Mechanisms' (2015) 16 Chicago J Int'l L 1, 33.

Happ R and S Wuschka, '*Horror Vacui*: Or Why Investment Treaties Should Apply to Illegally Annexed Territories' (2016) 33 J Int'l Arb 245.

Hepburn J, *Domestic Law in International Investment Arbitration* (OUP 2017).

Hernández GI, 'The Interaction between Investment Law and the Law of Armed Conflict in the Interpretation of Full Protection and Security Clauses' in F Baetens (ed), *Investment Law within International Law: Integrationist Perspectives* (CUP 2013).

Hofmann R, 'Annexation', *Max Planck Encyclopedia of Public International Law* (2020) <https://opil.ouplaw.com/home/MPIL> accessed 4 March 2020.

Jennings R, *The Acquisition of Territory in International Law* (first published 1963, MUP 2017).

Jennings R, 'Nullity and Effectiveness in International Law' in R Jennings (ed), *Cambridge Essays in International Law: Essays in Honour of Lord McNair* (Stevens & Sons 1965).

Knahr C, 'Investments "in the Territory" of the Host State' in C Binder and others (eds), *International Investment Law for the 21st Century: Essays in Honour of Christoph Schreuer* (OUP 2009).

Kontorovich E, 'Economic Dealings with Occupied Territory' (2015) 53 Colum J Transnat'l L 584.

Kriebaum U, 'Evaluating Social Benefits and Costs of Investment Treaties: Depoliticization of Investment Disputes' (2018) 33 ICSID Rev 14.

Kryvoi Y, 'Protecting Foreign Investors in Crimea: Is Investment Arbitration an Option?' (*CIS Arbitration Forum*, 29 July 2014) <www.cisarbitration.com/2014/07/29/protecting-foreign-investors-in-crimea-is-investment-arbitration-an-option/> accessed 15 May 2020.

Lavranos N, 'The New Frontier: Investment Treaty Disputes in Times of War and Annexations' (*Practical Law Arbitration Blog*, 13 December 2017) <http://arbitrationblog.practicallaw.com/the-new-frontier-investment-treaty-disputes-in-times-of-war-and-annexations/> accessed 25 March 2019.

Mayorga OJ, 'Occupants, Beware of BITs: Applicability of Investment Treaties to Occupied Territories' (2016) 19 Pal YB Int'l L 136.

McLachlan C, L Shore, and M Weiniger, *International Investment Arbitration* (2nd edn, OUP 2017).

McNair AD, *The Law of Treaties* (Clarendon Press 1961).

Milanović M, *Extraterritorial Application of Human Rights Treaties: Law, Principles, and Policy* (OUP 2011).

Niemoj A, 'The Protection of Investments in Disputed Territories: A Panel Hosted by BIICL's Investment Treaty Forum' (*Kluwer Arbitration Blog*, 17 May 2017) <http://arbitrationblog.kluwerarbitration.com/2017/05/17/the-protection-of-investments-in-disputed-territories-a-panel-hosted-by-biicls-investment-treaty-forum/> accessed 10 March 2020.

O'Connell DP, 'The Doctrine of Acquired Rights and State Succession', (1950) 27 Brit YB Int'l L 92.

Olmos Giupponi B, 'Exploring the Links Between Nationality Changes and Investment Claims Arising Out of Armed Conflicts: The Case of Russian Passportization in Crimea' in K Fach Gómez, A Gourgourinis, and C Titi (eds), *International Investment Law and the Law of Armed Conflict* (Springer 2019).

Ostránsky J, 'The Termination and Suspension of Bilateral Investment Treaties Due to an Armed Conflict' (2015) 6 JIDS 136.

Pauwelyn J, 'The Role of Public International Law in the WTO: How Far Can We Go' (2001) 95 AJIL 535.

Pohl J, 'Societal Benefits and Costs of International Investment Agreements: A Critical Review of Aspects and Available Empirical Evidence' (2018) OECD Working Paper on International Investment 2018/01 <www.oecd-ilibrary.org/finance-and-investment/societal-benefits-and-costs-of-international-investment-agreements_e5f85c3d-en> accessed 15 May 2020.

Pronto AN, 'The Effect of War on Law – What Happens to Their Treaties When States Go to War?' (2013) 2 Cambridge J Int'l & Comp L 227.

Raible L, 'Title to Territory and Jurisdiction in International Human Rights Law: Three Models for a Fraught Relationship' (2018) 31 LJIL 315.

Rees-Evans L, 'Litigating the Use of Force: Reflections on the Interaction between Investor-State Dispute Settlement and Other Forms of International Dispute Settlement in the Context of the Conflict in Ukraine' in K Fach Gómez, A Gourgourinis, and C Titi (eds), *International Investment Law and the Law of Armed Conflict* (Springer 2019).

Repousis OG, 'Why Russian Investment Treaties Could Apply to Crimea and What Would This Mean for the Ongoing Russo–Ukrainian Territorial Conflict' (2016) 32 Arb Int'l 459.

Ryk-Lakhman I, 'IHL-Based Defenses in Investment Arbitration' (2018) Workshop Series on Investment Law and Policy.

Schreuer C and others, *The ICSID Convention: A Commentary* (2nd edn, CUP 2009).

Schreuer C, 'War and Peace in International Investment Law' in K Fach Gómez, C Titi, and A Gourgourinis (eds), *International Investment Law and the Law of Armed Conflict* (Springer 2019).

Shany >, 'Jurisdiction and Admissibility' in C Romano, K Alter, and Y Shany (eds), *The Oxford Handbook of International Adjudication* (OUP 2013).

Soldatenko M, 'Ongoing Territorial Challenges in Crimea Cases: Putting Everest v. Russia in Context' (*Kluwer Arbitration Blog*, 5 November 2018) <http://arbitrationblog.kluwerarbitration.com/2018/11/05/territorial-challenges-expected-in-crimea-cases-putting-everest-v-russia-in-context/> accessed 29 November 2018.

Spears S and M Fogdestam-Agius, 'Protection of Investments in War-Torn States: A Practitioner's Perspective on War Clauses in Bilateral Investment Treaties' in K Fach Gómez, A Gourgourinis, and C Titi (eds), *International Investment Law and the Law of Armed Conflict* (Springer 2019).

Tadlock R, 'Occupation Law and Foreign Investment in Iraq: How an Outdated Doctrine Has Become an Obstacle to Occupied Populations' (2004) 39 USF L Rev 227.

Tams CJ, 'State Succession to Investment Treaties: Mapping the Issues' (2016) 31 ICSID Rev 314.

Tuzheliak N, 'Investors at Conflict's Crossroads: An Overview of Available International Courts and Tribunals in the Crimean Context' (2017) 6 UCLJLJ 14.

Tzeng P, 'Sovereignty over Crimea: A Case for State-to-State Investment Arbitration' (2014) 41 Yale J Int'l L 459.

Tzeng P, 'Investments on Disputed Territory: Indispensable Parties and Indispensable Issues' (2017) 14 Braz J Int'l L 121.

Tzeng P, 'Ukraine v. Russia and Philippines v. China: Jurisdiction and Legitimacy' (2017) 46 Denv J Int'l L & Pol'y 1.

Tzeng P, 'The Implicated Issue Problem: Indispensable Issues and Incidental Jurisdiction' (2018) 50 New York U J Int'l L & Pol 447, fn 31.

Vaccaro-Incisa GM, 'Crimea Investment Disputes: Are Jurisdictional Hurdles Being Overcome Too Easily?' (9 May 2018) <www.ejiltalk.org/crimea-investment-disputes-are-jurisdictional-hurdles-being-overcome-too-easily/comment-page-1/> accessed 24 November 2018.

Villiger ME, *Commentary on the 1969 Vienna Convention on the Law of Treaties* (Martinus Nijhoff 2009).

Waibel M, 'Brexit and Acquired Rights' (2018) 111 AJIL 440.

Woolsey LH, 'Peaceful War in China' (1938) 32 AJIL 314.

Wuschka S, 'Das Investitionsschutzrecht: Rechtssicherheit für deutsche Investoren auf der Krim?' (2017) 26 Wirtschaft und Recht in Osteuropa 193.

Wuschka S, 'Investment Claims and Annexation: Where General International Law and Investment Law Collide?' in M Akbaba and G Capurro (eds), *International Challenges in Investment Arbitration* (Routledge 2019).

Wuschka S, 'Procedural Aspects of the Obligation of Non-Recognition Before International Investment Tribunals' in K Fach Gómez, A Gourgourinis, and C Titi (eds), *International Investment Law and the Law of Armed Conflict* (Springer 2019).

Wuschka S, 'Zuständigkeit von Investitionsschiedsgerichten für Klagen mit Bezug zur Annexion der Krim' (2019) German Arb J 93.

Zamir N, 'The Applicability of the Monetary Gold Principle in International Arbitration' (2017) 33 Arb Int'l 523.

Zrilič J, *The Protection of Foreign Investment in Times of Armed Conflict* (OUP 2019).

CHAPTER 11

The Duty of Non-Recognition and EU Free Trade Agreements: Lessons for Investment Law from the Case of *Front Polisario*

Stefan Lorenzmeier

1 Introduction

The European Union (EU), as a subject of public international law under article 47 of the Treaty on European Union (TEU), is very active in the conclusion of genuine free trade agreements as well as association agreements,[1] which usually contain, among others, a part on free trade with third states[2] or other subjects of international law.[3] An association in accordance with article 217 of the Treaty on the Functioning of the European Union (TFEU) is the closest form of cooperation between the EU and a third (non-member) state.[4]

Some of the agreements concluded by the EU potentially also apply on disputed territories, when parts of the territory of the other party to the agreement are under occupation or that other party is indeed itself an occupying power. The latter was the case in the *Front Polisario* set of judgments of the

---

1 See section 4.1.1 below for an elaboration of the types of agreements.
2 *Eg* the agreements concluded with Morocco. The association agreement referred to is the Euro-Mediterranean Agreement establishing an association between the European Communities and their Member States, of the one part, and the Kingdom of Morocco, of the other part [2000] OJ L 70/1; the free trade agreement is an Agreement in the form of an Exchange of Letters between the European Union and the Kingdom of Morocco concerning reciprocal liberalization measures on agricultural products, processed agricultural products, fish and fishery products, the replacement of Protocols No 1, 2 and 3 and their Annexes and amendments to the Euro-Mediterranean Agreement [2012] OJ L 241/2.
3 See, *eg*, the Euro-Mediterranean Interim Association Agreement on trade and cooperation between the European Community and the Palestine Liberation Organization (PLO) for the benefit of the Palestinian Authority of the West Bank and the Gaza Strip [1997] OJ L 187/3, and the Stabilisation and Association Agreement between the European Union and the European Atomic Energy Community with Kosovo [2016] OJ L 71/1.
4 Concerning association agreements, see Piet Eeckhout, *EU External Relations Law* (2nd edn, OUP 2011) 124 et seq; Christoph Vedder, 'The EEA in the Union's Legal Order' in Finn Arnesen and others (eds), *Agreement on the European Economic Area: A Commentary* (Nomos, CH Beck, and Hart 2018) 101 et seq.

Court of Justice of the European Union (CJEU).⁵ In these cases, the scope of application of several agreements concluded between the EU and the Kingdom of Morocco had been silent on the fact that Morocco considers the territory of the Western Sahara as its own state territory and, thereby, neglects the right of self-determination of the Western Sahrawis as recognized by the International Court of Justice (ICJ) in its *Western Sahara* advisory opinion.⁶

This chapter examines the legal consequences this situation entails for free trade agreements and investment treaties concluded by the EU with other subjects of international law. Firstly, it explores the duty of non-recognition as accepted under customary international law (section 2) and under the law of the EU (section 3). The subsequent part shows the effects of the duty of non-recognition as part of the corpus of international law on the EU and its existing agreements (section 4), before turning to the specific case of investment law and illustrating the duty of non-recognition's effect on existing and potential future investment treaties (section 5). The results are tied up in a concluding part (section 6).

2   The Duty of Non-Recognition under Public International Law

The duty of non-recognition of illegal acts under public international law has been advocated for since the 1930s.⁷ The doctrine prescribes that a factual situation must not be recognized under public international law because of strong reservations as to the legality of actions that have been adopted by a subject of international law. It is dogmatically founded in the principle that legal rights cannot derive from an illegal situation⁸ and has first been acknowledged by the ICJ in its *Namibia* advisory opinion of 1971.⁹ There, the Court stated that a duty of non-recognition existed as to the territorial administration of the territory of Namibia by South Africa, which essentially obliged the member states of the United Nations to acknowledge the illegality and invalidity of South Africa's continued presence in Namibia.¹⁰ The Court's statement is an expression of

---

5   General Court, T–512/12 *Front Polisario I* [2015] ECLI:EU:T:2015:953; ECJ, C–104/16 P *Front Polisario II* [2016] ECLI:EU:C:2016:973; ECJ, C–266/16 *Western Sahara Campaign* [2018] ECLI:EU:C:2018:118.
6   *Western Sahara* (Advisory Opinion) [1975] ICJ Rep 12.
7   Malcolm Shaw, *International Law* (8th edn, CUP 2017) 347.
8   *Ex injuria jus non oritur*, see ibid 347.
9   *Legal Consequences for States of the Continued Presence of South Africa in Namibia (South West Africa) notwithstanding Security Council Resolution 276 (1970)* (Advisory Opinion) [1971] ICJ Rep 16.
10 ibid 54.

the general rule that territorial acquisitions by states are not to be recognized by other states when achieved through means inconsistent with international law, *eg* the threat or use of force.[11]

Said rule was embedded in more general terms in the International Law Commission's (ILC) Articles on State Responsibility.[12] Their article 41(2) affirms that 'no state shall recognize as lawful a situation created by a serious breach within the meaning of Art. 40 [...]'. Article 40, in turn, describes a serious breach as a gross violation or systematic failure to fulfil an obligation arising under a peremptory norm of public international law.[13] This was further clarified in the ICJ's *Palestinian Wall* advisory opinion.[14] In it, the ICJ held that the right of self-determination, which it found violated, constituted an *erga omnes* right[15] and that, therefore, all states were under an obligation not to recognize the illegal situation arising from the construction of a wall in the occupied Palestinian territory.[16] This legal principle is also embodied in the

---

11 See Draft Declaration on the Rights and Duties of States, annexed to UNGA Res 375 (IV) (1949); Shaw (n 7) 347 et seq; several UNGA Resolutions, especially the 'Friendly Relations Declaration' UNGA Res 2625 (XXV) (1970), the 'Definition of Aggression' UNGA Res. 3314 (XXIX) (1974) and UNGA Res 68/262 (2014) on the territorial integrity of Ukraine.

12 ILC, 'Articles on Responsibility of States for Internationally Wrongful Acts' (2001), annexed to UNGA Res 56/83 (12 December 2001) UN Doc A/56/83 (ILC Articles on State Responsibility). For the EU, the similarly worded articles 41 and 42 of the Draft Articles on the Responsibility of International Organization (2011) would be applicable, should they evolve into treaty law. At the moment, for states as well as international organizations, only the customary rules of the said principles are applicable. See *eg* Philipp Stegmann, *Responsibility of the EU and its Member States under International Investment Protection Agreements* (Springer 2019) 79 et seq.

13 On *jus cogens* norms, see Alexander Orakhelashvili, *Peremptory Norms in International Law* (OUP 2006). According to his assessment, *jus cogens* and *erga omnes* obligations are two sides of the same coin and are virtually coextensive, ibid 286 et seq. The ICJ refrains from coining a norm as *jus cogens* and tends to state its *erga omnes* character.

14 *Legal Consequences of the Construction of a Wall in the Occupied Palestinian Territory* (Advisory Opinion) [2004] ICJ Rep 136.

15 ibid para 156. Also: *East Timor (Portugal v Australia)* [1995] ICJ Rep 90, para 29; 'Friendly Relations Declaration' UNGA Res 2625 (XXV) (1970). The ILC accepted it even as a peremptory norm of international law, see ILC, 'Fragmentation of International Law: Difficulties arising from the Diversification and Expansion of International Law' UN Doc A/CN.4/L.702 [2006] para 33; James Crawford, *Brownlie's Principles of Public International Law* (8th edn, OUP 2012) 596. On the right to self-determination in general: Elena Konnova, 'The Right to Self-Determination and Time' in Sebastian Wuschka and others (eds), *Zeit und Internationales Recht* (Mohr Siebeck 2019).

16 *Legal Consequences of the Construction of a Wall in the Occupied Palestinian Territory* (n 14) para 159. See recently *Legal Consequences of the Separation of the Chagos Archipelago from Mauritius in 1965* (Advisory Opinion) [2019] para 180 <www.icj-cij.org/en/case/169/advisory-opinions> accessed 21 January 2020.

Friendly Relations Declaration,[17] which states that 'every state has the duty to promote, through joint or separate action, realization of the principle of [...] self-determination of peoples [...].'[18] Essentially, the recognition as lawful of a situation created by a serious breach of international law is not just the recognition of a fact. It also lends legitimacy to the acts and tends to consolidate an illegal legal regime.[19] By contrast, the widespread recognition of a legal act as unlawful has the opposite effect. This is the *raison d'être* of the duty of non-recognition.

It can be deduced from the above-mentioned ICJ advisory opinions as well as scholarly opinions[20] that the duty of non-recognition of illegal acts is limited in two respects. First, it applies only to violations of international norms with an *erga omnes* or *jus cogens* character. This can also be derived, for instance, from article 42(2) of the ILC Articles on State Responsibility.[21] The violation of norms that do not possess this nature can only be addressed by the usual rules governing international wrongful acts. In reliance on these, the victim state of the unlawful act may not recognize the resulting situation as lawful, but no international obligations of other subjects of international law exist to do the same.

In this respect, it may be questioned whether international law should develop in the direction of a full application of the duty of non-recognition to all acts not in compliance with law. This would significantly broaden its scope of application and would strengthen the effective enforcement of the international legal system. Moreover, any redress to state responsibility implicitly

---

17   UNGA Res 2625 (XXV) (1970). The principle of self-determination as laid down in the Friendly Relations Declaration has evolved to the status of customary international law, see eg Daniel Thürer and Thomas Burri, 'Self-Determination', *Max Planck Encyclopedia of Public International Law* (2008) para 12 <https://opil.ouplaw.com/home/MPIL> accessed 21 January 2020.

18   UNGA Res 2625 (XXV); *Legal Consequences of the Separation of the Chagos Archipelago from Mauritius* (n 16) para 180.

19   Crawford (n 15) 600.

20   Crawford (n 15) 598 et seq; Jochen A Frowein, 'Non-Recognition', *Max Planck Encyclopedia of Public International Law* (2011) para 6 <https://opil.ouplaw.com/home/MPIL> accessed 21 January 2020. Critical to some of the legal effects of the duty of non-recognition: Stefan Talmon, 'The Duty Not to "Recognize as Lawful" a Situation Created by the Illegal Use of Force or Other Serious Breaches of a Jus Cogens Obligation: An Obligation without Real Substance?' in Jean-Marc Thouvenin and Christian Tomuschat (eds), *The Fundamental Rules of the International Legal Order: Jus Cogens and Obligations Erga Omnes* (Brill 2005) 9 et seq.

21   ILC Articles on State Responsibility art 41(2). See ILC, 'Fragmentation of International Law' (n 15) para 33; *Crawford* (n 15) 596.

leads to the non-recognition of the illegal act in question by the violated subject of international law. This suggestion, however, faces several difficulties. The rules on state responsibility know a wide variety of applicable remedies,[22] which are not limited to the non-acceptance of an illegal act, and its application is in the discretion of the subject of international law the rights of which have been violated. Limiting this discretion would not necessarily foster international peace and be helpful to solve a critical situation, because international relations should remain flexible in order to avoid and solve tensions and violations of the international legal order. This flexibility would be set aside. As a result, a development of international law in the direction of non-recognition of all illegal acts of subjects of international law faces serious obstacles and does not seem to be a recommendable option at the moment.

A second limitation of the duty of non-recognition arises from its exceptions. The duty of non-recognition is relative even in the case of a violation of a *jus cogens* or *erga omnes* norm. In its *Namibia* advisory opinion, the ICJ recognized an exception to the rule. While it found that in cases of illegal territorial acquisition, treaties with the rule-breaker must generally not be applied to the territory in question, this was not true in case of (multilateral) treaties if their non-application adversely affects the people inhabiting the territory ('*Namibia* exception').[23] The telos of this exception is that a violation of an *erga omnes* rule shall not operate to the detriment of the rights of the people of the territory as protected by human rights or humanitarian law treaties. Whether the exception should not be extended to bilateral treaties of the same effect remains unsettled in international law and will be explored below.[24] Given the rather limited scope of application of the duty of non-recognition, it probably would support the enforcement of and respect for international law if it was applied to all international wrongful acts, not only norms with a special status. However, such an approach is not backed by sufficient state practice at the moment and therefore cannot be considered part of customary international law.

3   The Duty of Non-Recognition under EU Law

This part of the chapter addresses the application of the international duty of non-recognition under the law of the European Union (EU law). In this context,

---

22   See ILC Articles on State Responsibility art 30 et seq.
23   *Legal Consequences for States of the Continued Presence of South Africa in Namibia* (n 9) para 122.
24   See section 5.1 below.

it scrutinizes whether the EU is bound by the duty in its external actions also by its foundational instruments. For this, the primary law of the Union – the EU treaties, especially articles 3(5)(2) and 21(2) and (3) TEU – are analysed.

Article 3(5)(2) TEU states in general terms and in the relevant part for our analysis that the EU shall, 'in its relations with the outside world, contribute to the strict observance and development of international law.' 'Strict observance' in the sense of the provision is only given if the EU complies with the rules of public international law.[25]

Article 21 TEU, which defines the principles and objectives of the Union's external action, further elaborates on the rule of strict observance of international law. Paragraph 1 of the provision reaffirms that the EU's 'actions shall be guided by [...] respect for [...] international law.' Article 21(2)(b) prescribes that the Union shall consolidate and support the principles of international law. Finally, paragraph 3 determines that '[t]he Union shall respect the principles and pursue the objectives set out in paragraphs 1 and 2 in the development and implementation of the different areas of the Union's external action covered by [...] Part Five of the Treaty on the Functioning of the European Union [...].' The term 'respect' in article 21(2) and (3) TEU means that the acts of the EU dealing with its external affairs have to comply with the existing body of public international law because otherwise the legal requirement of 'strict observance' in article 3(5)(2) TEU could not be effectively upheld. Thus, the EU is in a position to develop international law, yet it is bound by the already existing corpus of public international law and is legally barred from conducting unlawful acts in its external actions.

The strict observance of international law principle is reflected in the TFEU as well. Article 205 TFEU prescribes that '[t]he Union's action on the international scene [...] shall be guided by the principles, pursue the objectives and be conducted in accordance with the general provisions laid down in chapter 1 of title V of the Treaty on European Union', which is a reference to, among others, article 21 TEU. The EU's competence to conclude free trade agreements, either in accordance with article 207(3) or article 217 TFEU is laid down in Part Five of the TFEU and has to be exercised in accordance with the principles of international law. Moreover, the case-law of the European Court of Justice (ECJ) illustrates that existing customary rules of public international law become an integral part of the Union's legal order[26] with a special hierarchical

---

25   See recently: ECJ, C-363/18 *Organisation juive européenne* [2019] ECLI:EU:C:2019:954 para 48.
26   ECJ, C-181/73 *Haegeman* [1974] ECR 449; ECJ C-162/96 *Racke* [1998] ECR I-3655.

position situated between the Union's primary law, *ie* the TEU and TFEU, and its secondary law.[27]

As such, the duty of non-recognition as prescribed under customary international law has to be 'respected', *ie* applied, by the EU in its internal and external actions. International agreements of the EU become an integral part of the Union's internal legal order[28] as well by the use of secondary Union law, namely decisions in accordance with article 218 (6) TFEU.[29] Thus, the secondary law, namely the stated decisions on association agreements and free trade agreements taken in accordance with article 218 (6) TFEU, have to comply with the applicable rules of international law. Secondary acts, which are not in accordance with international law, are or can be declared void due to their violation of the Union's primary law. As a result, the EU must also comply with the right of self-determination of peoples, as a right of customary international law, in its external actions and is legally barred from concluding treaties that violate this right or any other rule of international law.

4   Effects of the Duty of Non-Recognition on EU Association and Free Trade Agreements

The legal effects of the application of the duty of non-recognition in case of a violation of an *erga omnes* or *jus cogens* right by an EU Association or Free Trade Agreement are scrutinized next. The *Front Polisario* judgments of the CJEU serve as an example for the application of the duty of non-recognition in Union law. This section, first, sets out the legal effects of the duty of non-recognition. Secondly, it analyses the territorial application of an already concluded treaty which is violating the right of self-determination. Finally, it will be scrutinized whether the *Namibia* exception applies to free trade provisions of an international agreement concluded by the EU.

---

27   Article 216(2) TFEU, which applies not only to international treaties but to all sources of international law. See ECJ, C–162/96 *Racke* (n 26).

28   *Haegeman* (n 26); generally: Mario Mendez, *The Legal Effects of EU Agreements* (OUP 2013).

29   Stefan Lorenzmeier, 'The Procedural and Substantial Requirements of the European Union's Accession to the ECHR' in Stefan Lorenzmeier and Vasilka Sancin (eds), *Contemporary Issues of Human Rights Protection in International and National Settings* (Nomos 2018) 198 et seq.

4.1 Effects on the Union's Treaty Relations

4.1.1 EU Free Trade and Association Agreements

Before delving into the in-depth analysis of the effects of the duty of non-recognition, it is helpful to explain, as a preliminary step, the relevant legal content of free trade and association agreements of the Union. Free trade agreements, on the one hand, are usually concluded in accordance with article 207(3) TFEU and are part of the Union's Common Commercial Policy formulated under article 207(1) TFEU, an exclusive competence of the Union in relation to its member states. Unlike traditional free trade agreements, which usually only address conventional trade barriers such as tariffs, modern EU trade agreements are far more ambitious and competitiveness-driven. They include, *inter alia*, provisions on intellectual property rights, competition and environmental standards.[30] Association agreements, on the other, are governed by article 217 TFEU and constitute the closest form of cooperation between the EU and a third country. They are used to establish privileged links across a broad spectrum of EU policies.[31] A number of association agreements have been concluded between the EU and certain Mediterranean countries, including Morocco.[32] These agreements cover a wide range of areas and can also create a competitive-driven free trade area[33] covering a wide range of areas.[34]

4.1.2 Legal Effects of the Duty of Non-Recognition in General

The legal effects of the duty of non-recognition on treaties are disputed in practice and academia.[35] In advisory opinions on *Namibia*, which concerned the continued presence of South Africa in Namibia (South West Africa),[36] on the *Palestine Wall* issue, which was about the construction of a permanent physical barrier by Israel on Palestinian territory[37] and *Chagos*, which addressed the decolonization of Mauritius and the separation of the Chagos archipelago

---

30 So-called 'Deep and Comprehensive Free Trade Agreements' (DCFTAs); see Panos Koutrakos, *EU International Relations Law* (2nd edn, Hart 2015) 380.
31 Eeckhout (n 4) 127.
32 Koutrakos (n 30) 397.
33 ibid 398.
34 See *eg* the deep and comprehensive free trade area established by the EU–Ukraine Association Agreement [2014] OJ L 161/3.
35 *Eg* Daniel Costelloe, 'Treaty Succession in Annexed Territory' (2016) 65 ICLQ 343, 358 et seq with further references.
36 An overview is given by Christof Heyns and Magnus Killander, 'South West Africa/Namibia (Advisory Opinion and Judgements)', *Max Planck Encyclopedia of Public International Law* (2007) <https://opil.ouplaw.com/home/MPIL> accessed 21 January 2020.
37 See Arthur Watts, 'Israeli Wall Advisory Opinion', *Max Planck Encyclopedia of Public International Law* (2007) <https://opil.ouplaw.com/home/MPIL> accessed 21 January 2020.

from it,[38] the ICJ pronounced on recognized principles for the duty of non-recognition. In its ground-breaking *Namibia* advisory opinion, the ICJ stated that any action which implies a recognition of an illegal act as legal constitutes a violation of public international law.[39] This was further developed by the ICJ in the *Palestinian Wall* and the *Chagos Archipelago* advisory opinions, where the Court found that the respective illegal act entailed the international responsibility of the perpetrating state.[40] Otherwise, the illegal situation could not be brought to an end.[41] Moreover and for the context in question, it has to be borne in mind that the right of self-determination of the peoples is defined by the entirety of a non-self-governing territory, the peoples entitled to self-determination are covered by the ambit of the right to territorial integrity.[42] Thus, the right of self-determination applies to the whole territory of the people in question, whose integrity forms an integral part of self-determination.

In its *Namibia* advisory opinion, the ICJ established that, in the case of illegally annexed or illegally acquired territory, new treaties that recognize the illegal situation shall not be concluded and existing treaties shall not be invoked or applied in a manner contrary to international law.[43] Thus, in general, the duty of non-recognition of territorial claims requires states not to accept the applicability of treaties to the territory in question.[44] As already hinted at above, the Court recognized an exception to this general prohibition when it comes to (multilateral) treaties whose non-application may adversely affect

---

38 An overview can be found at ICJ, 'Legal Consequences of the Separation of the Chagos Archipelago from Mauritius in 1965: Overview of the Case' (2020) <www.icj-cij.org/en/case/169> accessed 21 January 2020.

39 *Legal Consequences for States of the Continued Presence of South Africa in Namibia* (n 9) para 121.

40 *Legal Consequences of the Separation of the Chagos Archipelago from Mauritius in 1965* (n 16) para 177.

41 *Haya de la Torre (Colombia v Peru)* [1951] ICJ Rep 71, 82. For instance, the United Kingdom has to terminate its administration of the Chagos Archipelago as rapidly as possible, see *Legal Consequences of the Separation of the Chagos Archipelago from Mauritius* (n 16) paras 178, 182.

42 ibid para 160.

43 *Legal Consequences for States of the Continued Presence of South Africa in Namibia* (n 9) para 122 ('States are under obligation to abstain from entering into treaty relations with South Africa in all cases in which the Government of South Africa purports to act on behalf of or concerning Namibia. With respect to existing bilateral treaties, member States must abstain from invoking or applying those treaties or provisions of treaties concluded by South Africa on behalf of or concerning Namibia which involve active intergovernmental co-operation.').

44 Frowein (n 20) para 4.

the people of a given region, in that case Namibia.[45] The implications of this so-called 'Namibia exception' for the present analysis is explored further below. However, in general, the duty of non-recognition of territorial claims will have the consequence that states must not accept the applicability of treaties to the territory in question.

In essence, the ICJ's jurisprudence on the duty of non-recognition and the right of self-determination, as expressed in the three advisory opinions, and as accepted under public international law more generally, will, at first, lead to a duty to interpret territorial clauses in a way that is in accordance with public international law, since this appears as the smoothest way of avoiding a violation of international law by a treaty provision. If this is not possible, the treaty must not be invoked or applied and will have to be terminated or amended in order to comply with the duty of non-recognition. Since EU law, as has been shown, requires from the EU strict adherence to international law, the same rules apply to treaties concluded by the EU and have to be respected by the organs of the Union.

4.2 The Term 'Territory' in Treaty Law

The application of treaties to disputed territories could conflict with the duty on non-recognition, begging the question how the territorial scope of the treaty in question is to be understood. Usually, EU agreements are applicable on the territories of the EU (or, rather, its member states) and the relevant other state party.[46] If the scope of territorial application extends beyond the land territory, as, for instance, in the CETA Agreement between the EU and Canada,[47] it must be borne in mind that the duty of non-recognition also applies with regard to the exclusive economic zone or the continental shelf, which are

---

45 *Legal Consequences for States of the Continued Presence of South Africa in Namibia* (n 9) para 122.

46 See *eg* Euro-Mediterranean Agreement establishing an association between the European Communities and their Member States, of the one part, and the Kingdom of Morocco, of the other part [2000] OJ EU L 70/1, art 94: 'territory of the Kingdom of Morocco'. The scope of application is, for instance, further elaborated in the CETA agreement with Canada, Comprehensive Economic and Trade Agreement between Canada and the European Union [2017] OJ L 11/23: CETA article 1.3 prescribes the geographical application concerning Canada to: (i) the land territory, air space, internal waters, and territorial sea of Canada; (ii) the exclusive economic zone of Canada, as determined by its domestic law, consistent with Part V of the United Nations Convention on the Law of the Sea, done at Montego Bay on 10 December 1982 (UNCLOS); and, (iii) the continental shelf of Canada, as determined by its domestic law, consistent with Part VI of UNCLOS.

47 Comprehensive Economic and Trade Agreement between Canada and the European Union (CETA) [2017] OJ L 11/23.

under a state's jurisdiction. This extension of sovereign rights to these areas must also be lawful; otherwise the exercise of such rights must not be recognized as lawful.

In lack of precise treaty definitions, the meaning of the term 'territory' as used in international treaties has to be defined further. Under general international law, the notion of territory 'embraces all the land, internal waters and territorial sea, and the airspace above them over which a party has sovereignty.'[48] For bilateral treaties, such as the Association Agreement of the EU with the Kingdom of Morocco,[49] this means that it will extend to the entire territory of the parties[50] unless its subject-matter or nature dictates otherwise.[51] Additionally, under public international law, the title to the territory must be lawful and, in general, the term 'territory' constitutes a judgment with respect to the lawfulness of the territorial acquisition.[52]

4.2.1   The General Court of the European Union

These principles were arguably not fully respected by the EU's General Court in its *Front Polisario* ruling.[53] The background of the dispute before the European

---

48   Anthony Aust, 'Treaties, Territorial Application', *Max Planck Encyclopedia of Public International Law* (2006) para 2 <https://opil.ouplaw.com/home/MPIL> accessed 21 January 2020; Anthony Aust, *Modern Treaty Law and Practice* (2nd edn, CUP 2013) 178.

49   Euro-Mediterranean Agreement (n 46). The further applicable agreement was an Agreement in the form of an Exchange of Letters between the European Union and the Kingdom of Morocco (n 2).

50   Article 29 of the Vienna Convention on the Law of Treaties (adopted 23 May 1969, entered into force 27 January 1980) 1155 UNTS 331 (VCLT) states that 'a treaty is binding upon each party in respect of its entire territory'. The provision does not cover the entire issue regarding the application of a treaty to a territory, it is limited to the binding force of a treaty, see Kerstin von der Decken, 'Art. 29' in Oliver Dörr and Kirsten Schmalenbach (eds), *Vienna Convention on the Law of Treaties: A Commentary* (2nd edn, Spinger 2018) para. 1.

51   Aust, 'Treaties, Territorial Application' (n 48), para 5. Territorial extension clauses can for instance be found in some investment treaties, whose territorial scope extends to the exclusive economic zone and or the continental shelf of a state; see in this regard also Marco Benatar and Valentin Schatz, chapter 6 in this volume. Colonial extension clauses, whereby the colonial power could decide upon the territorial scope of a treaty for its colonies, are not used anymore, see von der Decken (n 50) para 10.

52   Costelloe (n 35) 366. The ICJ did not have to rule on this issue in its *East Timor* decision, although it had been argued by the parties; see *East Timor* (n 15) para 35.

53   According to article 19(1)(1) TEU, the Court of Justice of the European Union shall include the Court of Justice, the General Court and specialized courts. As such, the General Court is the court of first instance for all matters with a natural or legal person as claimant and the Court of Justice has the role of an appeals court. On the decision, see Guillaume van der Loo, 'EU Trade Agreements with 'Disputed' Territories' in Inge Govaere and Sacha Garben (eds), *The Interface between EU and International Law* (Hart 2019) 250 et seq.

courts was an application lodged by Front Polisario, the national liberation movement of the people of the Western Sahara, against the EU in front of the General Court, which challenged the validity of the latter's decision to conclude an association agreement with Morocco[54] and claimed that the General Court should annul the contested decision of the European Union.[55] According to Morocco, this agreement was also legally applicable to the territory of the Western Sahara.[56] The territory of Western Sahara is in its large part *de facto* controlled by Morocco, whereas the Front Polisario only controls a small bit of it.[57]

The General Court found no rule of customary international law prohibiting the conclusion of an international treaty which may be applied on a disputed territory.[58] In its view, a statement of the UN Under-Secretary-General for Legal Affairs and Legal Counsel did not lead to a different conclusion. In response to a request from the members of the Security Council, the Under-Secretary-General expressed his opinion on the lawfulness of the decisions taken by the Moroccan authorities concerning the offer and signature of contracts for the prospection of mineral resources in Western Sahara made with foreign companies. In his letter, he states that

> the recent State practice, though limited, is illustrative of an opinio juris on the part of both administering Powers and third States: where resource exploitation activities are conducted in Non-Self-Governing Territories for the benefit of the peoples of those Territories, on their behalf or in consultation with their representatives, they are considered compatible with the [United Nations] Charter obligations of the administering Power and in conformity with the General Assembly resolutions and the principle of 'permanent sovereignty over natural resources' enshrined therein.[59]

---

54   See above n 46.
55   *Front Polisario I* (n 5) para 29 et seq.
56   On the 'lawfare' and the different cases relating to Western Sahara initiated by the Front Polisario see Thomas D Ruys, 'The Role of State Immunity and Act of State in the NM Cherry Blossom Case and the Western Sahara Dispute' (2019) 68 ICLQ 67.
57   *Front Polisario I* (n 5) para 16. See also Sven Simon, 'Western Sahara' in Christian Walter, Antje von Ungern-Sternberg, and Kavus Abushov (eds), *Self-Determination and Secession in International Law* (OUP 2014) 255 et seq.
58   *Front Polisario I* (n 5) para 205.
59   Letter dated 29 January 2002 from the Under-Secretary for Legal Affairs, the Legal Counsel, addressed to the President of the Security Council (12 February 2002) UN Doc S/2002/161, para 24.

In the Under-Secretary-General's opinion, therefore, it is of the utmost relevance for the legality of the claim whether the people of the respective territory have accepted the exploitation of their natural resources. If this is not the case, the territorial claim would not be in compliance with the principle of self-determination of people. This is supported by the following further explanations of the Under-Secretary:

> while the specific contracts which are the subject of the Security Council's request are not in themselves illegal, if further exploration and exploitation activities were to proceed in disregard of the interests and wishes of the people of Western Sahara, they would be in violation of the principles of international law applicable to mineral resource activities in Non-Self-Governing Territories.[60]

As a general rule, the principle of self-determination requires the approval of the Western Sahrawis for the application of agreements concluded by Morocco on the territory of the Western Sahara. This principle, as stated by the Under-Secretary, is not limited to exploration and exploitation treaties. The General Court, however, had not correctly applied it in its *Front Polisario* ruling.

4.2.2 The European Court of Justice

The decision of the General Court was appealed by the Council of the European Union to the ECJ. In its appeal decision, the ECJ dismissed the reasoning of the General Court and came to the opposite conclusion. It interpreted the clause 'territory of the Kingdom of Morocco', embodied in article 94 of the EU-Morocco Association Agreement, as meaning the 'international recognized territory of Morocco' excluding the territory of the Western Sahara[61] and, as a result, limited the territorial scope of the agreement.[62] The ECJ based its ruling upon the principle of self-determination as a legally enforceable right erga omnes and its status as one of the essential principles of international law, which applies to all non-self-governed territories.[63] An extension of the territorial scope of the association agreement with Morocco would only be lawful

---

60   ibid para 25.
61   *Front Polisario II* (n 5) para 126.
62   On the international status of the Western Sahara, see *Front Polisario I* (n 5) paras 1 et seq; Rainer Hofmann, 'Annexation', *Max Planc Encyclopedia of Public International Law* (2020) para 37 <https://opil.ouplaw.com/home/MPIL> accessed 15 May 2020.
63   *Front Polisario II* (n 5) para 88; see also *East Timor* (n 15) para 29.

if the people of the Western Sahara would have agreed to it, which was not the case.[64]

The ECJ's limitation of the scope of the association agreement is in line with the ICJ's advisory opinion on the Western Sahara.[65] There, the ICJ held that the territory of the Western Sahara could not be considered *terra nullius* and that neither Mauretania nor Morocco exercised territorial sovereignty over Western Sahara. In addition, the ICJ confirmed the right of self-determination for the Sahrawi people.[66] In essence, the ECJ applied articles 3(5), 21(2) and (3) TEU and article 205 TFEU in respect of the existing corpus of international law, in the case at bar the right to self-determination, to the EU-Morocco Association Agreement without stating the provisions of the TEU explicitly.

If the territorial scope of a treaty cannot be limited by interpretation, because the disputed territory is explicitly mentioned in the respective treaty, the parties to the agreement have to abstain from invoking or applying the relevant treaty, as long as the non-performance does not adversely affect the population in the disputed territories, which is the case for human rights treaties and which will be explored next. The EU would be under an obligation stemming from the stated provisions of EU primary law to act accordingly.

The General Court therefore erred by stating that the EU institutions enjoy a wide discretion as to whether it is appropriate to conclude an agreement with a non-member state, which will be applied on a disputed territory.[67] This discretion is reduced by the applicable rules of international law due to articles 3(5), 21(2) and (3) TEU,[68] even if they are complex and imprecise. Under the rules established by the Treaty of Lisbon, the EU courts are not any more limited in their judicial review to assess whether the competent EU institution made manifest errors of assessment.[69] Quite to the contrary, they have to respect the applicable international law and to make sure that EU acts do not lead to a violation of international law. As a consequence, the ECJ ruled in *Front Polisario* that an extension of the association agreement with Morocco on the territory of the Western Sahara would also constitute a breach of article 34 VCLT, the principle of relative effect of treaties, according to which treaties must not harm or profit third parties – that is, in the present

---

64 *Front Polisario II* (n 5) paras 105 et seq.
65 *Western Sahara* (n 6).
66 ibid para 162.
67 *Front Polisario I* (n 5) para 223.
68 Similarly Van der Loo (n 53) 245.
69 In this respect ECJ C–162/96 *Racke* (n 26) para 52.

case, the people of Western Sahara as a subject of international law – without their consent.[70]

The approach of the ECJ has been criticised in academia for, *inter alia*, applying incorrectly several rules of the VCLT,[71] especially the rules on treaty interpretation and the territorial application of treaties.[72] This critique does not seem to pay appropriate regard to the special status of the right of self-determination in combination with the duty of non-recognition as expressed by the ICJ in its *Namibia* advisory opinion and its more recent case-law.[73] If the duty of non-recognition is applicable, the EU is under a duty not to recognize an illegal situation. The application of the concluded treaties to the territory of Western Sahara would entail such an unlawful recognition, namely the recognition that the internationally recognized territory of Morocco includes the unlawfully occupied territory. To bring the treaty in line with the duty of non-recognition by means of interpretation of the territorial clause seems to be far more practical. It further less significantly intrudes with the intention of the parties to conclude a legally valid agreement with the Kingdom of Morocco. Otherwise, the EU would have been obligated to terminate the agreement and to conclude a new one, which does not seem to be adequate in the given situation. Additionally, an application of the *pacta tertiis* rule only in state-to-state relations would run counter to the special status of a non-self-governed territory under the principle of self-determination and an application of the subsequent practice-provision as entailed in article 31(3)(b) VCLT, as proposed in academic writings[74] due to the application of the EU-Morocco treaties on the territory of the Western Sahara prior to the judgment of the ECJ would also run counter to the principle of self-determination and as such constitute a violation of international law, to which the EU is legally barred.

---

70 *Front Polisario II* (n 5) para 107. On the ruling, see also Eva Kassoti, 'The Legality under International Law of the EU's Trade Agreements covering Occupied Territories: A Comparative Study of Palestine and Western Sahara' (2017) CLEER Working Papers 2017/3 <www.asser.nl/media/3934/cleer17-3_web.pdf> accessed 15 May 2020.

71 In the present context, the VCLT is only applicable insofar as it codified customary rules of international law; see VCLT art 3.

72 See Jed Odermatt, 'Council of the European Union v. Front Populaire pour la liberation de la Sagueia-El-Hamra et du Rio de Oro (Front Polisario)' (2017) 111 AJIL 731, 736; Eva Kassoti, 'The EU's Duty of Non-Recognition and the Territorial Scope of Trade Agreements Covering Unlawfully Acquired Territories' (2019) 3 Europe and the World: A Law Review 1 et seq (with further references).

73 See section 2 above.

74 Odermatt (n 72) 736; Kassoti (n 72); Peter Hilpold, '"Self-Determination at the European Courts: The *Front Polisario* Case" or "The Unintended Awakening of a Giant"' (2017) 2 European Papers 907.

4.3 Non-Territorial Zones as Territory?

Additionally, it has to be examined whether terrestrial non-territorial zones, *eg* (certain) maritime zones, do also belong to the 'territory' of a state or other subject of public international law. In a different context, but also in respect with a treaty of the EU with Morocco, the ECJ had to decide upon this issue as well. In the *Western Sahara Campaign* decision on the application of the Fisheries Partnership Agreement between the EU and Morocco[75] and its 2013 Protocol,[76] the ECJ upheld its *Front Polisario* ruling even for fishery resources on the territory of the Western Sahara and its adjacent waters.[77] In this litigation, the treaty-term 'waters falling within the sovereignty or jurisdiction' had to be interpreted by the ECJ. According to article 2 UNCLOS, the territorial sea is part of the sovereignty of a coastal state, whereas it enjoys only jurisdiction in the adjacent waters to the territorial sea, article 55 f UNCLOS.[78] The latter does not belong to a coastal state's territory.[79] This reasoning had been followed by the ECJ as well. Having recourse to articles 55 et seq UNCLOS, the ECJ held that only the coastal state was able to regulate the waters adjacent to its territorial sea and that the territory of the Western Sahara did not belong to the territory of Morocco, which, thus, could not exercise jurisdiction over it and the adjacent waters.[80] Moreover, Morocco does not have sovereignty over the territorial waters of the Western Sahara in line with the above-mentioned *Front Polisario*-ruling. The 2013 Protocol goes even further and does not entail a territorial clause but uses the term 'Moroccan fishing zone', which can also be found in article 2(a) Fisheries Agreement and should have the identical meaning as defined there, namely the waters falling within the jurisdiction of the

---

75 Fisheries Partnership Agreement between the EU and the Kingdom of Morocco [2007] OJ L 78/31.
76 Protocol between the European Union and the Kingdom of Morocco setting out the fisheries opportunities and financial contribution provided for in the Fisheries Partnership agreement between the European Union and the Kingdom of Morocco [2013] OJ L 328/2.
77 *Western Sahara Campaign* (n 5) paras 65 et seq. Advocate-General Melchior Wathelet analysed the situation in depth in paras 145 et seq of his opinion; ECJ, C–266/16 *Western Sahara Campaign*, Opinion by AG Melchior Wathelet.
78 For further references see the commentaries by Richard Barnes, 'Art. 2' in Alexander Proelß (ed), *United Nations Convention on the Law of the Sea: A Commentary* (Beck and Hart 2017); Alexander Proelß, 'Art. 55' in Alexander Proelß (ed), *United Nations Convention on the Law of the Sea: A Commentary* (Beck and Hart 2017); Alexander Proelß, 'Art. 56' in Alexander Proelß (ed), *United Nations Convention on the Law of the Sea: A Commentary* (Beck and Hart 2017).
79 Proelß, 'Art. 56' (n 78) para 9.
80 *Western Sahara Campaign* (n 5) paras 68 et seq.

Kingdom of Morocco.[81] These waters are limited to the internationally recognized territory and jurisdictional zones of Morocco and thereby the territorial scope of the 2013 Protocol did also not extend to the waters of the Western Sahara.[82]

Advocate-General *Wathelet*, whose task is to assist the Court by giving his legal opinion on relevant cases,[83] even considered it a violation of the duty of non-recognition by the EU if Morocco autonomously applied it to the waters of the Western Sahara in disregard of the Western Sahrawis' right of self-determination.[84] This view is supported by the ICJ's notion that maritime rights derive from the coastal state's sovereignty over land and, as such, the terrestrial territorial situation must be taken as starting point for the determination of the maritime rights of a coastal state.[85] Moreover, the ICJ also found that '[t]he title of a State to the continental shelf and to the exclusive economic zone is based on the principle that the land dominates the sea through the projection of the coasts or the coastal fronts.'[86] The land is, in the words of the ICJ, 'the legal source of the power which a State may exercise over territorial extensions to seaward.'[87]

To conclude, under the EU's primary law, the treaty term 'territory' does only entail the international recognized part of the land of a treaty partner. It neither covers unfounded territorial claims if they violate the rights of other states or other subjects of international law, nor does it extend to terrestrial non-territorial zones in which another power lawfully exercises its rights. This is especially so for the exercise of jurisdiction at sea due to the well-accepted principle that the land dominates the sea.

---

81 ibid para 78.
82 ibid para 82.
83 Article 252(2) TFEU states in this respect that '[i]t shall be the duty of the Advocate-General, acting with complete impartiality and independence, to make, in open court, reasoned submissions on cases which [...] require his involvement.'
84 *Western Sahara Campaign*, AG Wathelet (n 77) paras 187 et seq.
85 *Maritime Delimitations and Territorial Questions between Qatar and Bahrain (Qatar v Bahrain)* [2001] ICJ Rep 40, para 185; *Maritime Delimitation in the Black Sea (Romania v Ukraine)* [2009] ICJ Rep 61, para 77; *Territorial and Maritime Dispute (Nicaragua v Colombia)* [2012] ICJ Rep 624, para 140; *Western Sahara Campaign*, AG Wathelet (n 77) para 190.
86 *Maritime Delimitation in the Black Sea* (n 85) para 77; *Territorial and Maritime Dispute* (n 85) para 140. See also *Maritime Delimitations and Territorial Questions between Qatar and Bahrain* (n 85) para 185.
87 *North Sea Continental Shelf* (Germany/Denmark; Germany/Netherlands) [1969] ICJ Rep 3, para 96; *Territorial and Maritime Dispute* (n 85) 140.

4.4 Application of the 'Namibia Exception' to EU Trade Agreements?

The ICJ's *Namibia* advisory opinion continues to be an influential source for the duty of non-recognition and its contents, also in the context of the EU *Front Polisario* cases. The ECJ's decisions are in line with the general prohibition of applying treaties to unlawfully occupied territory, as established in *Namibia*. However, this prohibition is not absolute. The ICJ recognized an exception for certain categories of treaties. While states must not apply bilateral treaties to the territory in question, the ICJ continued that 'the same rule cannot be applied to certain general conventions such as those of a humanitarian character, the non-performance of which may adversely affect the people of Namibia.'[88] Whether this '*Namibia* exception' is also applicable to free trade agreements has not been clarified yet. In the *Front Polisario* case, the ECJ did not have recourse to the category of treaties whose non-application would have an adverse effect on the people (in the following referred to as 'benevolent treaties'). This silence could be read as implicitly rejecting the idea that the Association Agreement with Morocco was part of this category of treaties. Yet, it could be argued that association agreements and free trade agreements create – in general – a positive effect on trade, which is, *inter alia*, reflected by article XXIV GATT. These instruments thereby contribute to the well-being of the population, which is why their non-application could have adverse effects for the people living on the territory. They could accordingly be qualified as benevolent under the *Namibia* exception.

The General Court dealt with this issue only briefly in its *Front Polisario* decision. It held that for an association or free trade agreement to be considered as a benevolent treaty, it is in light of the special status of the right of self-determination absolutely necessary that the agreement in question guarantees that the exploitation of natural resources is carried out for the benefit of the inhabitants of the territory enjoying the right to self-determination.[89] A 'neutral' agreement merely facilitating the export of products from an occupied territory to the EU, whether or not they originate from exploitation beneficial to its inhabitants, does not fulfil these criteria.[90] A clear indicator for a benevolent effect of an agreement is an affirmative act of the people of the territory in question. The General Court did not accept the status of a 'benevolent treaty' for the association agreement and the 2012 Protocol thereto due to a lack of an affirmative act by the people of the Western Sahara concerning the

---

88 *Legal Consequences for States of the Continued Presence of South Africa in Namibia* (n 9) para 122.
89 *Front Polisario I* (n 5) para 239.
90 ibid.

exploitation of their national resources.[91] This is persuasive given the special status of the right violated in the case, the right of self-determination of the Western Sahrawis, and due to the general prohibition of acts violating the principle of self-determination of people if the act in question has not been accepted by the affected people.

The purported view of the General Court seems also to be also generally in accordance with the content of the right of self-determination as accepted under international law. The economic well-being is expressly mentioned in article 1 ICCPR and article 1 ICESCR as a part of the right of self-determination. The application of a free trade agreement or association agreement concluded by a third party applicable on the territory under self-determination would automatically constitute a violation of the right to self-determination due to a breach of the customary third-party rule as laid down in article 34 VCLT.

As regards the counter-argument that the Kingdom of Morocco is not prevented by the terms of the agreement from guaranteeing that the exploitation of the natural resources of Western Sahara is to be carried out for the benefit of its inhabitants, it suffices to note that the free trade agreement between the EU and Morocco does not guarantee an exploitation of the natural resources of Western Sahara that is beneficial to its inhabitants either. It is entirely neutral in that regard and, stemming from the foregoing, the opposite view could only be accepted if the people of the Western Sahara accepted the exploitation of their territory.[92]

---

91   ibid paras 235 et seq.
92   The recently adopted Council Decision on the conclusion of the agreement in the form of an Exchange of Letters between the European Union and the Kingdom of Morocco on the amendment of Protocols 1 and 4 to the Euro-Mediterranean Agreement establishing an association between the European Communities and their Member States, of the one part, and the Kingdom of Morocco, of the other part 2019/217 [2019] OJ L 34/1, will extend the territorial scope of the agreement on the territory of the Western Sahara because, according to the Joint report by the Commission and the European External Action Service on Benefits for the People of Western Sahara and Public Consultation on Extending Tariff Preferences to Products from Western Sahara (SWD(2018) 346 final), 'there are signs that economic activity generated by exports to the EU creates local jobs and thus helps all parts of the population, regardless of background, to a greater or lesser extent. These benefits would be compromised if exports to the EU did not enjoy the same tariff preferences as those granted to Morocco.'. This agreement would, in line with the foregoing, constitute a violation of the principle of self-determination of the people of the Western Sahara as well. See in a similar vein Eva Kassoti, 'The Empire Strikes Back: The Council Decision Amending Protocols 1 and 4 to the EU-Moroccan Association Agreement' (2019) 4 European Papers 307, 307 et seq.

However, association and free trade agreements of the EU or other subjects of international law do not only benefit the capital-exporting party, as it is usually the case in investment treaties or clauses but grant a right to free trade to both parties of the respective agreement. Thus, both sides do directly benefit from the trade arrangements. Whether free trade is good for the peoples of the two parties to the agreement remains at least unclear and is sometimes rather doubtful. In addition, the correlation of the aim of the agreement, fostering free trade, and its benevolent effect remains unresolved. Moreover, the non-application of a free trade agreement does not necessarily adversely affect the people in a certain territory due to the far looser correlation of free trade and its effects on the people as compared to, for instance, the application of a human rights treaty. A lose correlation could be proven by almost every possible subject matter of a treaty and their regard as a 'benevolent treaty' would water down the *Namibia* exception and, as a result, constitute a far too wide-reaching exception for the duty of non-recognition.[93] As a result, the *Namibia* exception cannot be applied for free trade agreements or clauses in other treaties.

5 Effects of the Duty of Non-Recognition on Investment Treaties

While the *Front Polisario* cases concerned only trade and association treaties, the question arises whether the conclusion reached by the ECJ can be transferred to the context of investment law as well. Such a cross-regime consideration can help clarifying the legal effects of the duty of non-recognition in the context of investment treaties (as well as investment chapters within broader agreements). Accordingly, the purpose of this section is to identify lessons learned from the *Front Polisario* case and draw parallels to existing and future investment treaties that potentially concern disputed territories. To this end, this part of the chapter proceeds as follows: it, first, discusses in how far the results found in case of the EU's association and free trade agreements also apply to investment treaties. To this end, the section critically reflects on the 'investment law specialism' sometimes invoked in this regard and ultimately reject the application of the *Namibia* exception to investment treaties. In a second step, the section assesses the effects of the duty of non-recognition on existing investment treaties, that is, their non-application to disputed territories.

---

93 See also the arguments given below against the application of the *Namibia* exception to investment treaties and clauses.

The final section presents some considerations as to the prospects for future treaty drafting.

5.1 'Investment Law Specialism'?

As elaborated above, the General Court found that the trade and association agreements in question were not to be qualified as 'benevolent' but rather 'neutral' instruments. The *Namibia* exception, therefore, could not apply. How is the issue to be decided in case of investment treaties? A literal reading of the *Namibia* advisory opinion would speak against an application of the exception due to the bilateral nature of most investment treaties. In *Namibia*, the ICJ accepted only multilateral treaties as falling within this category. In light of the development of international law since the early 1970s, however, the restriction of the exception's application to multilateral treaties is far from convincing and should be overcome. Decisive for the classification of treaties as falling under the category of 'benevolent treaties' should rather exclusively be the subject-matter of the respective treaty and not its character as a bi- or multilateral treaty.

Moreover, it could be argued that investment agreements fall within the category of a benevolent treaty. As opposed to free trade agreements, investment treaties grant individuals a legal right to 'defend' their investment against any treatment by the host state not in compliance with the underlying investment treaty.[94] At their heart, the provisions on investment protection belong to the set of provisions against illegal expropriation of foreigners in a host country.[95] As such, they could be considered as embodying a human right and their non-application may adversely affect the people in a given region.[96] Historically, they are rooted in the law of aliens and the international protection of foreigners,[97] which, in turn, also influenced the development of international human rights law.

---

94 Matthias Herdegen, *Principles of International Economic Law* (2nd edn, OUP 2016) 439.
95 On the legal nature of international investment law, see Rudolf Dolzer and Christoph Schreuer, *Principles of International Investment Law* (2nd edn, OUP 2012) 19 et seq.
96 For a discussion of investment protection under article 1 of Protocol no 1 to the ECHR, see Isabella Risini, chapter 9 in this volume. For the 'investment as property' theory: Zachary Douglas, 'Property, Investment and the Scope of Investment Protection Obligations' in Zachary Douglas, Joost Pauwelyn, and Jorge E Viñuales (eds), *The Foundations of International Investment Law: Bringing Theory into Practice* (OUP 2014) 372 et seq.
97 On the law of aliens see Stephan Hobe, 'The Development of the Law of Aliens and the Emergence of General Principles of Protection under Public International Law' in Marc Bungenberg and others (eds), *International Investment Law: A Handbook* (CH Beck, Hart, and Nomos 2015) 7 et seq.

Yet, the human rights analogy is not fully convincing.[98] Unlike human rights, investment treaties are aimed at protecting only a specific group of individuals, namely foreign investors, and only at best indirectly at benefitting the people in the territory through the promise of economic development. The people or their human rights would not be compromised by the non-application of an investment treaty, also because they are not in a position to invoke the investment treaty's protection standards. The lack of individual enforcement mechanisms may exist in the case of other types of agreements as well, including agreements on the rules of armed conflict.[99] However, these agreements directly address the affected people during armed conflicts and grant them certain rights and protection. Human rights treaties applicable on a territory under the jurisdiction of a state[100] are part of this category, too. These agreements grant rights to all people living on the territory under the jurisdiction of a state. Investment treaties that do not benefit the population in a comparable way therefore have to be distinguished from human rights treaties for the purpose of the *Namibia* exception: They fall within different legal categories. The non-application of the duty of non-recognition in the recent practice of arbitral tribunals, which apply the Ukrainian-Russian BIT to Ukrainian investors that invested in now Russian-controlled Crimea,[101] does not seem to pay the required regard to these differences between investment treaties and human rights treaties.[102]

Moreover, the exception to the rule of non-recognition has to be applied in a strict manner due to the serious nature of the violation. The duty of non-recognition itself only applies in exceptional circumstances, if an *erga omnes* and/or *jus cogens* norm is violated. The duty of non-recognition, as a means of enforcing these fundamental norms, should only be limited on the basis of strong justification. Bilateral investment treaties do not fulfil this standard.[103]

---

98 On the difference between investment and human rights law see also, *eg*, Anne Peters, *Beyond Human Rights* (CUP 2016) 318 et seq.

99 Geneva Conventions I–IV (adopted 12 August 1949, entered into force 21 October 1950) 75 UNTS 31, 85, 135, 287, and Additional Protocols I–II (adopted 8 June 1977, entered into force 7 December 1978) 1125 UNTS 3, 609.

100 *Eg* International Covenant on Civil and Political Rights (adopted 16 December 1966, entered into force 23 March 1976) 999 UNTS 171, European Convention for the Protection of Human Rights and Fundamental Freedoms (adopted 04 November 1950, entered into force 3 September 1953) 213 UNTS 221.

101 See *eg Case 4A_396/2017* (2019) 17(2) German Arb J 93 (Swiss Federal Tribunal).

102 In this context, it has to be noted that the issue has not been raised in the proceedings due to the claimants' interest in the application of the Ukraine–Russia BIT.

103 See also the analysis by Patrick Dumberry, *A Guide to State Succession in International Investment Law* (Edward Elgar 2018) para 6.168.

They are ordinary international agreements covering a certain subject matter, which is important but not as important as the human rights of the people living in a territory in question despite their importance for international economic development.

Otherwise, the principle of self-determination could be compromised and the people could ultimately be deprived of the full enjoyment of their self-determination due to the application of an investment treaty on their territory without their consent.[104] The reasoning is applicable *mutatis mutandis* for a duty to settle conflicts in accordance with international law, *eg* before an arbitral tribunal. These tribunals do not enjoy a special status under international law either.

Thus, an 'investment law specialism' cannot be accepted in this regard and also no legal lacunae, in which an international investment treaty or clause could be applied, is given in the situation at hand.

5.2 The Duty of Non-Recognition and Existing Treaties

As should be recalled, existing investment treaties or investment clauses in treaties, the conclusion of which falls within the competence of the EU,[105] have to be in compliance not only with the Union's primary law but also with international law more generally. Investment treaties or free trade agreements that include an investment clause thus have to respect, in particular, international *erga omnes* and *jus cogens* norms. Any violation of such rules would lead to the non-application or non-invocation of the treaty as such or parts of it under the duty of non-recognition, if they are not void *ipso facto* in accordance with article 53 VCLT.[106]

Moreover, it has to be recognized that territorial claims usually fall into the category of a *jus cogens* or *erga omnes* norm and that illegal claims shall

---

104 Differently Costelloe (n 35) 375 et seq.
105 See the already famous 2018 *Achmea* decision of the ECJ, C–284/16 *Achmea* [2018].
106 The same would apply before arbitral tribunals, investment courts or a multilateral investment court (to be) created by current and future international agreements of the EU, *eg* the investment court system created by the Comprehensive Economic and Trade Agreement between Canada and the European Union (CETA) [2017] OJ L 11/23. For instance, article 8.31 (1) of the CETA prescribes that the 'Tribunal established [...] shall apply this agreement as interpreted in accordance with [...] other rules and principles of international law applicable between the parties.' The duty of non-recognition as being part of the general corpus of international customary law is one of the referenced 'rules of international law applicable between the parties', the EU and Canada. On the compatibility of the investment court system with the EU legal order, see recently also ECJ, *Opinion 1/17* [2019] ECLI:EU:C:2019:341.

not be recognized under the duty of non-recognition applicable for the EU. In accordance with the duty of non-recognition, all Union acts violating an international norm of *erga omnes* or *jus cogens* character are invalid under EU law and the provisions of a concluded agreement cannot be invoked or applied externally or internally. Regarding territorial claims or disputes, in which usually either the *erga omnes* and *jus cogens* rights of the right of self-determination or the prohibition of the use of force are applicable, this would lead to the need to reduce the territorial scope of a treaty (as illustrated above),[107] if this is possible or, otherwise, in the non-application of the agreement in question.

For free trade or investment treaties concluded by other subjects of international law within their respective competence, the rule applies as well, since other subjects of public international law are bound by the customary rule of the duty of non-recognition of illegal *erga omnes* and *jus cogens* rights in the same manner as the EU, at least seen from the perspective of general international law.

5.3 *Prospects for Future Treaty Drafting*

Based on the foregoing, the EU should be strongly encouraged to include more detailed territorial clauses in any new investment treaties or investment clauses in agreements concluded not only with third states that are involved in territorial disputes but with any other country. Such clauses would clarify the territorial scope of the treaty and clarify the applicable law in situations of illegal changes of territory. After all, these are a violation of one of the foundations of the international system, which aims at establishing peaceful relations by delineating territorial claims of states and other subjects of public international law. In the EU's treaty practice, territorial clauses can for instance be found in the association agreements with Georgia[108] and Moldova,[109] but not in the association agreement with Ukraine, which is due to the fact that the agreement had already been finalized at the time of the beginning of the Ukrainian-Russian conflict. Essentially, it was even one of the reasons for the conflict.[110]

In any event, clearly defined territorial clauses should become part of any investment treaty, not only limited to those concluded by the EU. After all, the arguments developed throughout this chapter do not only apply to the

---

107 See section 4.2.2 above.
108 Association Agreement with Georgia [2014] OJ L 261/1, art 429.
109 Association Agreement with Moldova [2014] OJ L 260/4, art 462.
110 See Guillaume Van der Loo, *The EU-Ukraine Association Agreement and Deep and Comprehensive Free Trade Area* (Brill 2016).

agreements concluded by the EU. They are valid for all agreements in case of disputed territories. A territorial clause would help to clarify the legal situation.

6 Conclusions

The chapter has shown that the duty of non-recognition of illegal acts, as a rule of customary international law, applies only to violations of norms having an *erga omnes* or *jus cogens*-character. As a consequence of this duty, treaties must generally not be applied to unlawfully occupied territory. Yet, the duty is inapplicable if the non-recognition of a treaty to a given territory would adversely affect the people living in the territory under the ICJ's *Namibia* exception.

The EU, as a subject of public international law, is bound by the general rules of international law, which includes this duty of non-recognition. Accordingly, their external free trade or association agreements, if in violation of the duty, would breach international law and thereby run counter also to the Union's internal law. Decisions concluding such agreements would be void. However, instead of declaring entire treaties void, the ECJ, in its *Front Polisario* line of judgments, interpreted the territorial clause and the term 'territory' as restricting the territorial scope of application to internationally recognized territory of a state. That way, the ECJ upheld the validity of the decision of the EU Council under article 218(6) TFEU to conclude an association agreement with Morocco.

Otherwise, the application of free trade and association agreements would have violated the duty of non-recognition as well as the right to self-determination of the people of Western Sahara. Although the duty of non-recognition does not apply in case the non-application of a treaty would adversely affect the people living in the relevant territory, free trade and association agreements of the EU do not constitute benevolent treaties in the meaning of the '*Namibia* exception'. Unlike human rights or humanitarian law treaties, they do not directly benefit the people living on a given territory. Despite their different structure, the same result applies to investment treaties. These agreements directly benefit foreign investors, but not the people in the affected territory. The indirect benevolent effect is too remote to be legally relevant.

As a result, existing treaties must be interpreted in accordance with international law. Their territorial application thus must be restricted to the sovereign territory and lawfully controlled maritime zones of their parties. If such an interpretation is not possible due to a special territorial clause in the agreement, the agreement cannot be applied. It therefore seems advisable for future treaty drafting to insert clearly defined territorial clauses in any future agreements, although this might be complicated in a given situation, since – as the case of the EU–Ukraine Association Agreement illustrates – not all territorial conflicts are foreseeable.

Bibliography

Aust A, 'Treaties, Territorial Application', *Max Planck Encyclopedia of Public International Law* (2006) <https://opil.ouplaw.com/home/MPIL> accessed 21 January 2020.

Aust A, *Modern Treaty Law and Practice* (2nd edn, CUP 2013).

Barnes R, 'Art. 2' in A Proelß (ed), *United Nations Convention on the Law of the Sea: A Commentary* (Beck and Hart 2017).

Costelloe D, 'Treaty Succession in Annexed Territory' (2016) 65 ICLQ 343.

Crawford J, *Brownlie's Principles of Public International Law* (8th edn, OUP 2012).

Dolzer R and C Schreuer, *Principles of International Investment Law* (2nd edn, OUP 2012).

Douglas Z, 'Property, Investment and the Scope of Investment Protection Obligations' in Z Douglas, J Pauwelyn and JE Viñuales (eds), *The Foundations of International Investment Law: Bringing Theory into Practice* (OUP 2014).

Dumberry P, *A Guide to State Succession in International Investment Law* (Elgar 2018).

Eeckhout P, *EU External Relations Law* (2nd edn, OUP 2011).

Frowein JA, 'Non-Recognition', *Max Planck Encyclopedia of Public International Law* (2011) <https://opil.ouplaw.com/home/MPIL> accessed 21 January 2020.

Herdegen M, *Principles of International Economic Law* (2nd edn, OUP 2016).

Heyns C and M Killander, 'South West Africa/Namibia (Advisory Opinion and Judgements)', *Max Planck Encyclopedia of Public International Law* (2007) <https://opil.ouplaw.com/home/MPIL> accessed 21 January 2020.

Hobe S, 'The Development of the Law of Aliens and the Emergence of General Principles of Protection under Public International Law' in M Bungenberg and others (eds), *International Investment Law: A Handbook* (CH Beck, Hart, and Nomos 2015).

Hofmann R, 'Annexation', *Max Planc Encyclopedia of Public International Law* (2020) <https://opil.ouplaw.com/home/MPIL> accessed 15 May 2020.

ICJ, 'Legal Consequences of the Separation of the Chagos Archipelago from Mauritius in 1965: Overview of the Case' (2020) <www.icj-cij.org/en/case/169> accessed 21 January 2020.

Kassoti E, 'The Legality under International Law of the EU's Trade Agreements covering Occupied Territories: A Comparative Study of Palestine and Western Sahara' (2017) CLEER Working Papers 2017/3 <www.asser.nl/media/3934/cleer17-3_web.pdf> accessed 15 May 2020.

Kassoti E, 'The Empire Strikes Back: The Council Decision Amending Protocols 1 and 4 to the EU-Moroccan Association Agreement' (2019) 4 European Papers 307.

Kassoti E, 'The EU's Duty of Non-Recognition and the Territorial Scope of Trade Agreements Covering Unlawfully Acquired Territories' (2019) 3 Europe and the World: A Law Review 1.

Konnova E, 'The Right to Self-Determination and Time' in Sebastian Wuschka and others (eds), *Zeit und Internationales Recht* (Mohr Siebeck 2019).

Koutrakos P, *EU International Relations Law* (2nd edn, Hart 2015).

Lorenzmeier S, 'The Procedural and Substantial Requirements of the European Union's Accession to the ECHR' in S Lorenzmeier and V Sancin (eds), *Contemporary Issues of Human Rights Protection in International and National Settings* (Nomos 2018).

Mendez M, *The Legal Effects of EU Agreements* (OUP 2013).

Odermatt J, 'Council of the European Union v. Front Populaire pour la liberation de la Sagueia-El-Hamra et du Rio de Oro (Front Polisario)' (2017) 111 AJIL 731.

Orakhelashvili A, *Peremptory Norms in International Law* (OUP 2006).

Peter Hilpold, ' "Self-Determination at the European Courts: The *Front Polisario* Case" or "The Unintended Awakening of a Giant" ' (2017) 2 European Papers 907.

Peters A, *Beyond Human Rights* (CUP 2016).

Proelß A, 'Art. 55' in A Proelß (ed), *United Nations Convention on the Law of the Sea: A Commentary* (Beck and Hart 2017).

Proelß A, 'Art. 56' in A Proelß (ed), *United Nations Convention on the Law of the Sea: A Commentary* (Beck and Hart 2017).

Ruys TD, 'The Role of State Immunity and Act of State in the NM Cherry Blossom Case and the Western Sahara Dispute' (2019) 68 ICLQ 67.

Shaw MN, *International Law* (8th edn, CUP 2017).

Simon S, 'Western Sahara' in C Walter, A von Ungern-Sternberg, and K Abushov (eds), *Self-Determination and Secession in International Law* (OUP 2014).

Stegmann P, *Responsibility of the EU and its Member States under International Investment Protection Agreements* (Springer 2019).

Talmon S, 'The Duty Not to "Recognize as Lawful" a Situation Created by the Illegal Use of Force or Other Serious Breaches of a Jus Cogens Obligation: An Obligation without Real Substance?' in J-M Thouvenin and C Tomuschat (eds), *The Fundamental Rules of the International Legal Order: Jus Cogens and Obligations Erga Omnes* (Brill 2005).

Thürer D and T Burri, 'Self-Determination', *Max Planck Encyclopedia of Public International Law* (2008) <https://opil.ouplaw.com/home/MPIL> accessed 21 January 2020.

Van der Loo G, *The EU-Ukraine Association Agreement and Deep and Comprehensive Free Trade Area* (Brill 2016).

Van der Loo G, 'EU Trade Agreements with 'Disputed' Territories' in I Govaere and S Garben (eds), *The Interface between EU and International Law* (Hart 2019).

Vedder C, 'The EEA in the Union's Legal Order' in Finn Arnesen and others (eds), *Agreement on the European Economic Area: A Commentary* (Nomos, CH Beck, and Hart 2018).

von der Decken K, 'Art. 29' in Oliver Dörr and Kirsten Schmalenbach (eds), *Vienna Convention on the Law of Treaties: A Commentary* (2nd edn, Spinger 2018).

Watts A, 'Israeli Wall Advisory Opinion', *Max Planck Encyclopedia of Public International Law* (2007) <https://opil.ouplaw.com/home/MPIL> accessed 21 January 2020.

CHAPTER 12

Assessing the Role and Effects of Domestic Investment Statutes in Frozen Conflict Situations: The Example of Transnistria/Pridnestrovie

Vladlena Lisenco and Karsten Nowrot

1   By Way of a Start: On the (Political) Abnormality and (Economic) Normality of Frozen Conflict Situations

Although until now no generally recognized definition of 'frozen conflicts' and their core criteria exists, such situations are frequently characterized by the emergence and continued presence of non-recognized or only partially recognized autonomous territorial entities.[1] These actors are also referred to as, among others, non-recognized states, state-like entities, quasi-states, entities short of statehood or stabilized *de facto* regimes.[2] Their origins often lie in a former (and currently inactive) internal or international armed conflict and/or only semi-successful secessionist movements. Respective examples are provided by the Republic of Abkhazia, the Republic of Artsakh (more commonly known as Nagorno-Karabakh), the Donetsk People's Republic, the Luhansk People's Republic as well as the Republic of South Ossetia, but also – outside of the post-Soviet realm – by the Republic of China (frequently referred to as Taiwan), the Republic of Somaliland and the Turkish Republic of Northern Cyprus.

There are certainly different answers to the question as to the necessary elements and prerequisites of statehood under public international law in general[3] – and whether they are fulfilled in a given case. Moreover, there are surely various possibilities to position oneself on the side of, or in fact potentially also

---

1   Generally, on the concept of frozen conflicts and its core characteristics, see Thomas D Grant, 'Frozen Conflicts and International Law' (2017) 50 Cornell Int'l LJ 361.
2   Specifically, on the concept of stabilized *de facto* regimes and their status under public international law, see Jochen A Frowein, 'De Facto Regime', *Max Planck Encyclopedia of Public International Law* (2013) paras 1 et seq <https://opil.ouplaw.com/home/MPIL> accessed 6 November 2019.
3   Generally, on the elements of statehood from the perspective of international law see, James Crawford, *The Creation of States in International Law* (2nd edn, OUP 2006) 37 et seq.

somewhere between, the so-called 'constitutive theory' and/or the 'declaratory theory' in the in principle age-old and still ongoing discussion about the legal relevance and effects of the recognition of states in particular.[4] Irrespective of these issues, however, the incontrovertible fact remains that for the time being, and probably for quite some time to come, these non-recognized autonomous territorial entities as being a common feature of frozen conflict situations are, from a political perspective, clearly more of an abnormality in an international system comprising mostly of recognized states.[5] Moreover, and again seen from a political standpoint, they are not only an anomaly, but often even perceived as something like 'irritants' in the global community. The potential threat to international stability and security thereby results from their very existence as well as in particular from the possibility that the underlying frozen conflict with the territorially affected recognized country might again turn into an active armed conflict, theoretically at any moment.[6]

Nevertheless, in many other ways, and in particular also when viewed from an economic perspective, these non-recognized territorial entities usually present themselves as rather normal political communities: meaning, they are typically not more abnormal than the quite diverse members of the global community of recognized states. In order to support this perception, attention might for example be drawn to the reasons that speak in favour of also integrating these territorial regimes into the global economy and its legal order. In order to illustrate the arguments for a preferably close, because in principle mutual beneficial, relationship between non-recognized territorial entities on

---

4   For a more in-depth treatment of the issue of recognition of states including the relevance of the declaratory and constitutive theory of recognition see James Crawford, *Brownlie's Principles of Public International Law* (9th edn, OUP 2019) 134 et seq; Stefan Talmon, 'The Constitutive Versus the Declaratory Theory of Recognition: *Tertium Non Datur?*' (2004) 75 Brit YB Int'l L 101. Concerning the inconsistency of state practice relating to the legal effects attributed to the recognition of states see also Robert Jennings and Arthur Watts, *Oppenheim's International Law*, vol 1 (9th edn, Longman 1992) 129 ('state practice is inconclusive and may be rationalised either way').

5   Nina Caspersen, 'States without Sovereignty: Imitating Democratic Statehood' in Nina Caspersen and Gareth Stansfield (eds), *Unrecognized States in the International System* (Routledge 2011) 78 ('More widespread recognition is needed for these entities to function as normal entities in the international system of sovereign states; […].'); and specifically with regard to Taiwan Steve Charnovitz, 'Taiwan's WTO Membership and its International Implications' (2006) 1 Asian J WTO & Int'l Health L & Pol'y 401, 423 ('Taiwan is an anomaly in international relations. It is a self-governing, stable, prosperous nation whose identity is sharply contested.').

6   On this perception see Kristin M Bakke, 'After the War Ends: Violence and Viability of Post-Soviet Unrecognized States' in Nina Caspersen and Gareth Stansfield (eds), *Unrecognized States in the International System* (Routledge 2011) 90.

the one hand as well as the international economic system and its transboundary normative framework on the other hand, it seems useful to briefly highlight two main aspects or dimensions of this relationship.

First, viewed from the external economic perspective of other territorial players in the international system, among them in particular recognized states and their private business actors, the respective territorial entities, including their populations and natural, human as well as other resources, not infrequently provide for valuable business opportunities. These opportunities exist, for example, in the form of additional consumers and thus market demands for imported products and services as well as in the form of places to profitably undertake foreign investments. Moreover, and particularly highlighting the in principle given desirability to integrate also the respective regimes into the transnational economic legal order, these transboundary business prospects by other countries and their economic actors should, from their perspective, preferably also be secured and stabilized on the basis of legal rules applying to transnational trade and investment transactions in order to, among others, facilitate a reduction of transaction costs.[7]

These expectations not only refer to, among others, the legal order of the World Trade Organization (WTO), well-known to be fundamentally aimed at ensuring legal certainty in international trade as a necessary prerequisite 'to create the predictability needed to plan future trade'[8] and for the optimal allocation of economic resources by its at present already 164 members, but also by private business actors to achieve the welfare-creating effects of international economic relations.[9] They also first and foremost include the transnational normative framework dealing with foreign investments, since among the primary purposes pursued by this legal regime is the promotion as well as protection of foreign investments and thus the intention to create favourable conditions for investments and to stimulate private initiative on the basis of a stable, predictable and secure normative environment.[10]

---

7   Generally thereto John H Jackson, 'Global Economics and International Economic Law' (1998) 1 J Int'l Econ L 1, 5.
8   GATT Panel, *United States – Taxes on Petroleum and Certain Imported Substances*, Report of the Panel adopted on 17 June 1987, L/6175 - 34S/136, para 5.2.2; see also WTO, *Russia: Measures Concerning Traffic in Transit – Panel Report* (5 April 2019) WT/DS512/R, para 7.79.
9   Specifically on the interests of private economic actors as mirrored in the purposes pursued by the WTO legal order see WTO, *United States: Sections 301–310 of the Trade Act of 1974 – Panel Report* (11 December 1999) WT/DS152/R, para 7.73.
10 See thereto as well as on other purposes pursued by international investment law *Daimler Financial Services AG v Argentina*, ICSID Case no ARB/05/1, Award (22 August 2012) paras 161 et seq; Rudolf Dolzer and Christoph Schreuer, *Principles of International Investment Law* (2nd edn, OUP 2012) 22.

Second, looking at the present issue from the internal economic and, equally important, also political perspective of the public authorities and the population of the non-recognized territorial entities in question, it seems appropriate to recall that a functioning, preferably prosperous, economy is of paramount importance in order to achieve and provide public services and other welfare gains for the population as well as to foster the social stability of the political community as a whole.[11] While this finding certainly applies in principle equally to both recognized countries and stabilized *de facto* regimes, striving for economic stability and prosperity appears to be of particular importance for territorial entities that are still in the phase of seeking recognition by the international community of states. In the course of this endeavor as well as to enhance their chances of success, they often engage in imitating effective statehood, thereby conveying the message to the world that they have created viable and sustainable territorial entities with state-like and stable organizational structures worthy of international recognition.[12]

In addition, establishing and maintaining political and legal conditions for a prosperous economy might also have the desirable effect of reducing the economic dependence of the territorial regime in question on its respective patron state(s), the existence of which is a quite common feature of frozen conflict situations.[13] Furthermore considering that economic activities and relations are today first and foremost, if not even by now almost inherently, also international and thus transboundary in character, with a stable and prosperous business environment in political communities therefore also being dependent upon a closer integration into the international economic system, it becomes obvious that the category of territorial actors here at issue, including their private commercial players, normally also have a strong interest in establishing and intensifying trade and investment relations with other countries; again preferably on the more stable and secure basis of transnational normative regulations in the realm of global trade and investment law.

Against this background, this contribution intends to describe and evaluate more specifically the particular investment law context of, and especially the respective regulatory approaches adopted by, another central territorial actor

---

11   On this issue specifically in the context of non-recognized territorial entities see Pal Kolstø and Helge Blakkisrud, 'Living with Non-Recognition: State- and Nation-Building in South Caucasian Quasi-States' (2008) 60 Eur-Asia Stud 483, 493 et seq; Caspersen (n 5) 79; Daria Isachenko, 'On the Political Economy of Unrecognised State-Building Projects' (2009) 44(4) Int'l Spectator 61.
12   On this phenomenon or strategy see already Caspersen (n 5) 73 et seq.
13   See thereto Caspersen (n 5) 82 et seq; Kolstø and Blakkisrud (n 11) 507.

in one of the current 'core examples of frozen conflicts',[14] namely the Pridnestrovian Moldavian Republic (more commonly known as Pridnestrovie or Transnistria) situated – depending on the perspective – east of, or in the east of, the Republic of Moldova. Thereby, particular attention will be devoted to the regulatory features and normative relevance of the Law of the Pridnestrovian Moldavian Republic on State Support for Investment Activities that more recently entered into force on 1 June 2018.[15] For this purpose, the following assessment is divided into four main parts.

In a first step, we will provide some useful background information on the case of Pridnestrovie with a particular focus, already suggested by the primary research interest of this contribution, on the current economic situation and the investment climate in this autonomous territorial entity (section 2). The second part, primarily in order to illustrate the importance of the recently adopted Pridnestrovian investment statute, will be devoted to a brief evaluation of the current (ir)relevance of international investment treaties for foreign investors doing business in Pridnestrovie (section 3). Against this background, the third and central section is intended to give a systematic overview and assessment of the notable regulatory features characterizing the 2018 Pridnestrovian investment law (section 4). Based on the findings made in the third part, the contribution concludes, in a fourth step, with an attempt to evaluate the Pridnestrovian investment regime in light of the overall normative relevance of domestic investment statutes, thereby in particular also addressing the question whether frozen conflict situations are actually also exercising an influence on the content and regulatory approaches of investment codes adopted by concerned territorial actors (section 5).

2   Where Are We Now? The Case and Context of Pridnestrovie and Its Investment Climate

The origins of, and subsequent developments related to, the frozen conflict between Moldova and Pridnestrovie that also involves a number of other international actors, among them the Russian Federation, the Organization for Security and Co-operation in Europe (OSCE), the European Union (EU) and Ukraine, have been already quite extensively described, analyzed and narrated

---

14   Grant (n 1) 377.
15   Law of the Pridnestrovian Moldavian Republic no 123-3-VI on State Support for Investment Activities (8 May 2018), CA3 18–19.

in scholarly publications as well as other sources.[16] Despite this by now more than considerable amount of academic literature and other documents, it is incontrovertible that the existence of, and evidence for, many alleged facts, details and causal links are still uncertain, disputed and controversially perceived; ultimately, as it is not infrequently the case, giving rise to a number of different narratives and counter-narratives. Furthermore, it seems appropriate to recall also in the context of this frozen conflict that '[t]here is always a perspective from which a story is told, which is never neutral'.[17] In other words, there is hardly, if ever, an entirely objective 'view from nowhere' in narration.[18]

Bearing in mind these limits as also inherent in all descriptions of, and narrations on, the frozen conflict over Pridnestrovie, we consider it for the purposes of the present analysis sufficient to provide our readers with a very brief – and most certainly also, like all others, not necessarily entirely objective – overview of the complex historical and political background, and then focus primarily on some recent facts and figures related to the Pridnestrovian economy.

Whereas it has occasionally been argued that the roots and real origins of the current frozen conflict can in fact be traced back a few centuries ago and while it is undoubtedly always important not to neglect the effects of distant historical developments, the more proximate and direct causes for the present situation actually relate to comparatively recent events and policies taking place in the transition period from the final stages of the Soviet 'Perestroika' in the late 1980s over the collapse of the USSR to the dawn of the post-Soviet era in the beginning of the 1990s. It could be said that the unfolding developments were particularly triggered by certain clear signs, increasingly visible towards the end of the 1980s, that the then Moldavian Soviet Socialist Republic (MSSR) aspired sovereign statehood. More specifically, the Supreme Soviet of the MSSR enacted legal regulations in the second half of 1989 making the

---

16   From the numerous literature on this topic see, *eg*, Francois Finck, 'Border Check Point, the Moldovan Republic of Transnistria' in Jessie Hohmann and Daniel Joyce (eds), *International Law's Objects* (OUP 2018) 162; Christopher J Borgen, 'Moldova: Law and Complex Crises in a Systemic Borderland' (2016) 59 German YB Int'l L 115; Bill Bowring, 'Transnistria' in Christian Walter, Antje von Ungern-Sternberg, and Kavus Abushov (eds), *Self-Determination and Secession in International Law* (OUP 2014) 157.

17   Andrea Bianchi, 'International Adjudication, Rhetoric and Storytelling' (2018) 9 JIDS 28, 34 ('There is always a perspective from which a story is told, which is never neutral. The standpoint from which one looks at things determines what one sees. In other words, one's perspective shapes the reality one experiences.').

18   Generally thereto Thomas Nagel, *The View from Nowhere* (OUP 1986) 3 ('This book is about a single problem: how to combine the perspective of a particular person inside the world with an objective view of that same world, the person and his viewpoint included.').

Romanian language with its Latin script the official state language, thus effectively replacing the Russian language with its Cyrillic letters. In addition, the same body decided in April 1990 to adopt a new tricolour flag as well as a new national anthem that happened to be the same as that of Romania. Moreover, the MSSR proclaimed its sovereignty on 23 June 1990, thus effectively changing its status within the USSR.

These developments gave rise to increased concerns in parts of the population that the now apparently newly sovereign MSSR would in the foreseeable future attempt a (re-)unification with Romania, among them in particular the strong Russian minority in the territories east of the river Dnestr/Dniester or Nistru (Trans-Dniestria) as well as the Gagauz in the south of Moldova.[19] As a result, resistance movements emerged in Pridnestrovie as well as Gagauzia from 1989 onwards. Upon further escalation of the political tensions, Pridnestrovie, claiming the legitimate exercise of a right of external self-determination, declared on 2 September 1990 its independence from the MSSR and its new status as a republic within the USSR. Although this proclamation was never accepted by the political bodies of the latter, it ultimately contributed to the first armed clashes between Moldovan armed forces and police forces on the one hand, and separatist paramilitaries on the other hand near the city of Dubosari in November 1990.

However, large-scale fighting only began at the end of 1991 and lasted until the middle of 1992. It was stopped as a result of a direct intervention of the Russian armed forces being stationed in Pridnestrovie at that time under the command of General *Lebed*. The fighting resulted in approximately one thousand persons killed and probably more than 100,000 refugees, mostly in the form of internally displaced persons. The fighting ended on 21 July 1992 with the conclusion of a ceasefire agreement between Moldova and Russia on the basis of what was then – and in principle still remains as of today – the *status quo* and foreseeing, among others, the establishment of a peacekeeping force including members of the Russian, Moldovan and Pridnestrovian armed forces. Furthermore, the agreement provided for an immediate ceasefire and the creation of a demilitarized security zone extending 10 kilometers from the Nistru on each side of the river, including the town of Bendery on the right bank. A set of principles for the peaceful settlement of the dispute was also announced, namely, respect for the sovereignty and territorial integrity

---

19   The Gagauz, a people of Turkish origin but Orthodox believers, constitute 3.5% of Moldova's population. In 1995, the Gagauz Territorial Administrative Unit was established, granting this ethnic group considerable administrative and cultural autonomy and thus settling peacefully the respective separatist conflict that erupted in 1991.

of Moldova, the need for a special status for Pridnestrovie, and the right of its inhabitants to determine their future in case Moldova were to unite with Romania. Some control mechanisms were also proposed, including the setting up of a Joint Control Commission.

As a consequence of this ceasefire agreement, Pridnestrovie was at least *de facto* effectively separated from the rest of Moldova. In addition, the fighting largely stopped, leading to the emergence of a frozen conflict situation. Ever since that time, there have been in the by now already twenty-seven years following these events numerous proposals and initiatives aimed at reaching a solution to the conflict that is acceptable to all actors involved. Thereby, a quite prominent role is played by the 'Permanent Conference for Political Questions in the Framework of the Negotiating Process for the Transdniestrian Settlement', also referred to as the '5+2 settlement process' (Moldova and Pridnestrovie as the direct parties to the conflict; the OSCE, the Russian Federation and Ukraine as mediators of the settlement; and the EU and the USA as observers).[20]

More recently, towards the end of 2013, the Party of Socialists of the Republic of Moldova presented a new plan envisioning a quite far-reaching federal restructuring of this country with the aim to accommodate concerns and reservations on the side of Pridnestrovie. A similar project is at present promoted by the current Moldovan President, *Igor Dodon*, who suggests the creation of a federation comprising of three autonomous regions: Moldova, Pridnestrovie as well as Gagauzia. The project includes a bicameral parliament consisting of a senate and a house of representatives, a common government as well as a president directly elected jointly by the peoples from all three regions. Although the chances of successfully implementing these conceptual ideas are extremely difficult to predict, it is noteworthy that there appears to be more recently a general trend pointing towards an improvement in the bilateral relations between Moldova and Russia. More specifically, the appointment of the Russian Deputy Prime Minister *Dmitry Kozak* by the Russian President *Putin* as his 'Representative for the Development of Commercial-Economic Relations with the Republic of Moldova' in July 2018 might, in light of respective developments in present-day Moldova and nevertheless with all due caution, be interpreted as a sign that the efforts and negotiations aimed at identifying and implementing a sustainable and mutually beneficial solution for this decades-long frozen conflict are currently gaining new momentum. *Kozak* is

---

20 See thereto also more recently for example Antal Berkes, 'Frozen Conflicts, Consolidation of *De Facto* Regimes and the Obligation of Timely Cooperation' in Sebastian Wuschka and others (eds), *Zeit und Internationales Recht* (Mohr Siebeck 2019) 173, 178 et seq.

known for having promoted in 2003 the so-called 'Kozak plan' for resolving the Pridnestrovian conflict on the basis of a federalization of Moldova, an idea that was at that time rejected by the Moldovan side.

Irrespective of what the future has in store for this autonomous territorial entity, Pridnestrovie with its territory of 4,163 square kilometers and a current population of approximately 470,000 people has in the course of its already twenty-nine years of existence as an independent actor established, at a quite early stage, a functioning governmental system based on the model of a presidential republic with its own constitution approved by a national referendum on 24 December 1995 and entering into force in January 1996, a developed financial and tax systems, a modern communication infrastructure, an army (which is actually larger than the Moldovan army), a police, a security service, a national flag, a coat of arms and an anthem. The head of Pridnestrovie is the President, elected for a term of five years, as the head of the country and the guarantor of the Constitution and laws of the country, who directs and coordinates the activities of all structures of state power, represents the country in international relations, and is the Commander-in-Chief of the armed forces. The supreme legislative and representative body of Pridnestrovie is the Supreme Council, elected for a term of five years by majority rule. The Supreme Council is headed by the Chairman of the Supreme Council, elected from among the deputies (a total of 43 deputies are elected).

Moreover, this autonomous territorial entity has developed, originally on the basis of the respective resources existing in the former MSSR, an economic system that is currently first and foremost also characterized by international trade and investment relations. Thereby, in the beginning of the previous decade, the transition from a planned Soviet-style economy to an economic system also characterized by market elements was progressively implemented. Overall, Pridnestrovie can be considered as a developed industrial-agrarian region. Its economy is dominated by electric power, ferrous metallurgy engineering and metalworking, electrical, chemical, light industry, food industry, forestry and woodworking, printing as well as a building materials industry. The core of the industrial sectors of Pridnestrovie includes approximately 150 larger enterprises of various forms of ownership, with the largest production centres being the cities of Tiraspol, Bender and Rybnitsa. For 2018, the gross domestic product (GDP) amounted to more than 807 million Euro, an increase of 2.52% compared to 2017. The GDP structure was characterized by a clear dominance of the production sector (31%) and non-market services (27%), followed by trade (14%) and the agricultural sector (9%).

The foreign trade turnover of Pridnestrovie in 2018 amounted to a total of 1.913,2 million US-Dollars, of which the imports were worth 1.216 million

US-Dollars and the exports amounted to 697 million US-Dollars. According to the current customs statistics methodology, this figure is more than the figure for 2017 by 394.2 million US-Dollars: exports increased by 30.3%, imports by 26.6%.

Among the main imported goods are primary energy, mineral fertilizers, agricultural machinery, paper, road and rail transport, household appliances and computers, cotton raw materials, industrial wood as well as consumer goods. The export structure is currently dominated by metals and metal products (36%), fuel and energy products (17%), foodstuffs and raw materials (16%), textile materials and products (9%) as well as footwear (6%). The main export destinations of Pridnestrovie are at present Moldova (30.4%), Ukraine (19%), Romania (15.9%), the Russian Federation (10.2%), Italy (6%), Germany (5.6%), Poland (3.7%) and Slovakia (1.9%).[21]

Finally, and of particular relevance for the research focus of this contribution, Pridnestrovie has attracted foreign investments by investors from, among others, Russia, Italy, Germany, Romania, Austria, Bulgaria, Ukraine and Moldova with their production facilities involving, for example, agriculture, metalworking, pharmaceutical industry, women's footwear, as well as work shoes.

3 No Treaties, Nowhere: On the Current (Ir)Relevance of International Investment Agreements for Foreign Investors in Pridnestrovie

In order to illustrate the importance of the recently adopted domestic investment statute for foreign investors doing business in Pridnestrovie, it seems useful to briefly describe and evaluate the existing international legal framework of investment treaties – or lack thereof – applicable to this autonomous territorial entity. First of all, Pridnestrovie itself has not (yet) concluded any bilateral, regional or multilateral investment agreements with other countries. However, this finding should not give rise to the perception that this actor is lacking the necessary treaty-making power under public international law to enter into respective treaty relations.

Regardless of whether one considers it as an unrecognized state or merely as a stabilized *de facto* regime, there is a general consensus that territorial

---

21 All these and the above-mentioned statistics and other information are based on data provided by the Ministry of Economic Development as well as the State Customs Committee of Pridnestrovie.

entities like Pridnestrovie – as at least partial subjects of international law – also enjoy in principle the capacity to conclude international (investment) agreements with states and certain other actors in the international system. This is *inter alia* illustrated by the example of Taiwan being a party to quite a number of bilateral investment treaties (BITs) and free trade agreements as well as, among others, being a member of the WTO. The fact that Pridnestrovie has yet to activate its treaty-making powers in practice thus first and foremost merely indicates that this actor and/or other countries have for political reasons abstained from entering into respective treaty relations. Moreover, if viewed from an international legal perspective, the possibility cannot entirely be ruled out that the motive of an alleged relevance, also in the present context, of the obligation of non-recognition[22] might contribute for the time being to the reluctance on the side of at least some third countries to conclude respective international economic agreements with Pridnestrovie.

Nevertheless, in light of this current absence of investment treaties concluded by Pridnestrovie itself, the question arises – and is indeed worth at least briefly addressing – as to the potential applicability of investment agreements concluded by other countries to certain foreign investors and investments in this territorial entity. In this regard, it seems helpful for the purposes of systemisation to distinguish between two scenarios. The first of them assumes, based on the declaratory theory of the recognition of states,[23] that Pridnestrovie has – as a result of its declaration of independence on 2 September 1990 or subsequent developments such as the first independence referendum of 1 December 1991, the ceasefire agreement signed on 21 July 1992 or the second independence referendum of 17 September 2006 – acquired statehood and thus the status of a country under public international law. Adopting this perspective opens up the possibility to consider the legal relevance of in particular BITs ratified by Moldova and the former Soviet Union, applicable to those foreign investors whose home states have concluded respective agreements, by way of state succession.

Such a continuation of (investment) treaty obligations on the occasion of a succession of states, understood as the replacement of one country by another

---

22 Generally on the obligation of non-recognition under public international law see *Legal Consequences of the Construction of a Wall in the Occupied Palestinian Territory* (Advisory Opinion) [2004] ICJ Rep 136, 200; *Accordance with International Law of the Unilateral Declaration of Independence in Respect of Kosovo* (Advisory Opinion) [2010] ICJ Rep 403, 437 et seq.

23 See thereto already briefly section 1 above.

in the responsibility for the international relations of territory,[24] is in principle surely not only conceivable, but in fact even considered to be the general rule in accordance with article 34(1)(a) of the 1978 Vienna Convention on Succession of States in respect of Treaties in situations of secessions. Nevertheless, there seem to be at least two reasons to assume that caution is warranted in this regard in the case of Pridnestrovie, in particular in the relevant context of BITs. First, specifically concerning the possible succession of this territorial entity to prior BITs concluded by Moldova, it should be recalled that the first Moldovan BIT, namely the one concluded with the United States, actually only entered into force in November 1994. Consequently, it is only under the assumption that Pridnestrovie acquired statehood at a comparatively late stage of its emergence and existence as an autonomous territorial entity, such as on the occasion of the second independence referendum of September 2006, that the issue of state succession with regard to Moldovan BITs could at all be of potential practical relevance.

Second, and even more notable since applying equally to Moldovan BITs as well as those entered into by the former Soviet Union, a broad consensus exists among international legal scholars in light of relevant state practice that the general rule of automatic state succession with regard to multilateral and bilateral agreements as enshrined in article 34 of the 1978 Vienna Convention on Succession of States in respect of Treaties currently does not reflect customary international law[25] and is even occasionally considered to be one of the reasons for the comparatively low number of ratifications of this normative ordering treaty.[26] To the contrary, it appears increasingly – and rightly – recognized in the admittedly only more recently intensified discussion[27] on the

---

24 See Vienna Convention on Succession of States in respect of Treaties (adopted 23 August 1978, entered into force 6 November 1996) 1946 UNTS 3 (VCST) art 2(1)(b). See also Crawford, *Brownlie's Principles* (n 4) 409.

25 On this perception see Crawford, *Brownlie's Principles* (n 4) 423 et seq; Anthony Aust, *Modern Treaty Law and Practice* (3rd edn, CUP 2013) 321 et seq; Jan Klabbers, 'Cat on a Hot Tin Roof: The World Court, State Succession, and the *Gabčikovo-Nagymaros* Case' (1998) 11 LJIL 345, 348 et seq; Alexander Orakhelashvili, *Akehurst's Modern Introduction to International Law* (8th edn, Routledge 2019) 310–311; Christian J Tams, 'State Succession to Investment Treaties: Mapping the Issues' (2016) 31 ICSID Review 314, 326 and 334; Patrick Dumberry, 'State Succession to Bilateral Treaties: A Few Observations on the Incoherent and Unjustifiable Solution Adopted for Secession and Dissolution of States under the 1978 Vienna Convention' (2015) 28 LJIL 13.

26 On this perception see Detlef F Vagts, 'State Succession: The Codifiers' View' (1993) 33 Va J Int'l L 275, 287 et seq; Tams (n 25) 326.

27 Concerning the finding that this issue has only more recently started to attract scholarly attention, see Patrick Dumberry, 'State Succession to BITs: Analysis of Case Law in the Context of Dissolution and Secession' (2018) 34 Arb Int'l 445; Tams (n 25) 315.

relationship between the general rules of public international law governing state succession and the international legal regime on the protection of foreign investments, that – in the absence of an at least tacit agreement to the contrary of all contracting parties concerned – new states are not automatically bound by BITs entered into by the predecessor state.[28] Consequently, under this first scenario a possible state succession with regard to treaties would also in the case of Pridnestrovie apply neither to Moldovan BITs nor to those investment treaties concluded by the former Soviet Union.

The second scenario, obviously reflecting the currently still dominant perception of Pridnestrovie and its legal status in the international system,[29] presupposes that this territorial entity also as of today continues to form a part of Moldova. Already in light of the presumption stipulated in article 29 of the 1969 Vienna Convention on the Law of Treaties as well as corresponding customary international law[30] stating that a treaty is binding upon each contracting party in respect of its entire territory, it is under this second scenario in principle beyond any reasonable doubt that Moldovan BITs also apply to the territory of Pridnestrovie. This finding seems particularly true since Moldova – in notable contrast to its approach towards other treaties like the Convention on Cybercrime,[31] the Convention on Information and Legal Co-operation concerning

---

[28] See thereto *European American Investment Bank AG (Austria) v Slovak Republic*, Award on Jurisdiction (22 October 2012) paras 79 et seq; Patrick Dumberry, 'An Unchartered Question of State Succession: Are New States Automatically Bound by the BITs Concluded by Predecessor States before Independence?' (2015) 6 JIDS 74; Patrick Dumberry, *A Guide to State Succession in International Investment Law* (Edward Elgar 2018) 33 et seq; see, however, for a more cautious assessment in this regard also Tams (n 25) 334 et seq.

[29] See UNGA Res 72/282 (26 June 2018) UN Doc A/RES/72/282; *Sandu and others v Moldova and Russia* App nos 21034/05 and seven others (ECtHR, 17 July 2018) para 34; see thereto also Borgen (n 16) 115; Bowring (n 16) 157.

[30] Vienna Convention on the Law of Treaties of 23 May 1969, 1155 UNTS 331. On the status of article 29 as also reflecting customary international law see *Sanum Investments Ltd v Laos*, PCA Case no 2013-13, Award on Jurisdiction (13 December 2013) para 220; Kerstin von der Decken, 'Article 29 VCLT' in Oliver Dörr and Kirsten Schmalenbach (eds), *Vienna Convention on the Law of Treaties* (2nd edn, Springer 2018) para 3; Richard Happ and Sebastian Wuschka, '*Horror Vacui*: Or Why Investment Treaties Should Apply to Illegally Annexed Territories' (2016) 33 J Int'l Arb 245, 256; Matthew Kennedy, 'Overseas Territories in the WTO' (2016) 65 ICLQ 741, 747.

[31] See Declaration contained in a letter from the Ministry of Foreign Affairs and European Integration of Moldova and in the instrument of ratification deposited on 12 May 2009 <www.coe.int/en/web/conventions/full-list/-/conventions/treaty/185/declarations?p_auth=qAYdMSkb&_coeconventions_WAR_coeconventionsportlet_enVigueur=false&_coeconventions_WAR_coeconventionsportlet_searchBy=state&_coeconventions_WAR_coeconventionsportlet_codePays=MOL&_coeconventions_WAR_coeconventionsportlet_codeNature=4> accessed 6 November 2019 ('In accordance with

'Information Society Services',³² the International Convention for the Suppression of Acts of Nuclear Terrorism,³³ the Convention on the Settlement of Investment Disputes Between States and Nationals of Other States (ICSID Convention),³⁴ and the European Convention for the Protection of Human Rights and Fundamental Freedoms (ECHR)³⁵ – has in the present context of its BITs apparently not made any declarations intending to limit the territorial scope of application of the respective agreements.

Despite this conclusion, however, there appear to exist again at least two arguments in favour of assuming that this general applicability of Moldovan BITs is only of very limited practical relevance for foreign investors doing business in Pridnestrovie. First, a valid and convincing argument can be made that any acts adopted by Pridnestrovian public authorities that allegedly violate protection standards benefiting foreign investors under Moldovan BITs are not attributable to Moldova and thus cannot give rise to a successful claim

---

Article 38, paragraph 1 of the Convention, the Republic of Moldova specifies that the provisions of the Convention will be applied only on the territory controlled effectively by the authorities of the Republic of Moldova.').

32 See Declaration contained in the instrument of ratification deposited on 19 March 2010 <www.coe.int/en/web/conventions/full-list/-/conventions/treaty/180/declarations?p_auth=qAYdMSkb> accessed 6 November 2019 ('According to Article 11 of the Convention, the Republic of Moldova declares that, until the full re-establishment of its territorial integrity, the provisions of the Convention will be applied only on the territory controlled effectively by the authorities of the Republic of Moldova.').

33 See the Declaration made on the Occasion of the Ratification on 18 April 2008 <https://treaties.un.org/pages/ViewDetailsIII.aspx?src=TREATY&mtdsg_no=XVIII-15&chapter=18&Temp=mtdsg3&clang=_en> accessed 6 November 2019 ('Until the full re-establishment of the territorial integrity of the Republic of Moldova, the provisions of the Convention will be applied only on the territory controlled effectively by the authorities of the Republic of Moldova.').

34 See the Notification on Exclusion of Territories in accordance with article 70 ICSID Convention made by Moldova on the occasion of depositing its instrument of ratification on 5 May 2011 <https://icsid.worldbank.org/en/Pages/about/MembershipStateDetails.aspx?state=ST92> accessed 6 November 2019 ('Following Article 70 of the Convention, the Republic of Moldova specifies that the provisions of the Convention shall be applied only on the territory effectively controlled by the authorities of the Republic of Moldova.').

35 See the relevant part of the Declaration contained in the instrument of ratification deposited on 12 September 1997: 'The Republic of Moldova declares that it will be unable to guarantee compliance with the provisions of the Convention in respect of omissions and acts committed by the organs of the self-proclaimed Trans-Dniester republic within the territory actually controlled by such organs, until the conflict in the region is finally definitively resolved.' Thereto as well as on the (very limited) legal relevance of this declaration see in particular *Ilașcu and others v Moldova and Russia* ECHR 2004–VII 1, 11, 19 et seq; William A Schabas, *The European Convention on Human Rights* (OUP 2015) 938 (art 57).

for compensation in investment arbitration proceedings initiated by foreign investors against this country under one of its BITs. This finding is based on the international legal regime on state responsibility as in principle also applicable to investment treaty relations,[36] in particular the rules concerning the (non-) attribution of conduct of insurrectional and secessionist movements to the state at issue as for example at least implicitly enshrined in article 10 of the 2001 Articles on State Responsibility developed by the International Law Commission (ILC) and also reflecting customary international law.[37]

Second, attention might be drawn and recourse taken to the concept of estoppel in the present context. It is submitted that a sound argument can be made that a foreign investor who has previously, knowingly and intentionally, established close (contractual) contacts with Pridnestrovian public authorities against the presumed or even explicit will of the Moldovan government is prevented from subsequently invoking the protection granted under Moldovan BITs and from initiating dispute settlement proceedings against Moldova. Estoppel constitutes a well-recognized general principle of law in the sense of article 38(1)(c) Statute of the International Court of Justice.[38] Against this background, the applicability of this concept in the modern context of treaty-based investor-state arbitration is in principle beyond reasonable doubt,[39] already when taking into account that also this legal regime 'cannot be read and interpreted in isolation from public international law and its general principles'.[40]

---

36 On this finding, in particular concerning the rules on attribution at issue in the present context, see James Crawford, 'Investment Arbitration and the ILC Articles on State Responsibility' (2010) 25 ICSID Rev 127, 132 et seq; Martins Paparinskis, 'Investment Treaty Arbitration and the (New) Law of State Responsibility' (2013) 24 EJIL 617, 627 et seq; Jarrod Hepburn, 'Domestic Investment Statutes in International Law' (2018) 112 AJIL 658, 679.

37 See ILC, Draft Articles on Responsibility of States for International Wrongful Acts, with Commentaries, ILC Yearbook 2001, vol II, pt two, 50 et seq, with additional references.

38 Generally on the concept of estoppel in public international law see *Case Concerning the Temple of Preah Vihear (Cambodia v Thailand)* [1962] ICJ Rep 6, 32 et seq; Bin Cheng, *General Principles of Law as Applied by International Courts and Tribunals* (Stevens 1953) 143 et seq; Crawford, *Brownlie's Principles* (n 4) 406 et seq.

39 See also, eg, Andreas Kulick, 'About the Order of Cart and Horse, Among other Things: Estoppel in the Jurisprudence of International Investment Arbitration Tribunals' (2016) 27 EJIL 107, 112 et seq; Emily Sipiorski, *Good Faith in International Investment Arbitration* (OUP 2019) 197; Karsten Nowrot and Emily Sipiorski, 'Approaches to Arbitrator Intimidation in Investor-State Dispute Settlement: Impartiality, Independence, and the Challenge of Regulating Behaviour' (2018) 17 L & Prac Int'l Cts & Tribunals 178, 191 et seq.

40 *Phoenix Action Ltd v Czech Republic*, ICSID Case no ARB/06/5, Award (15 April 2009) para 78; see also *Urbaser SA and others v Argentina*, ICSID Case no ARB/07/26, Award (8 December 2016) para 1200.

Finally, also under this second scenario, the question again arises as to the potential relevance of BITs concluded by third countries to foreign investors in Pridnestrovie. This applies in particular to Russian BITs. Since its 2004 judgment in the case of *Ilascu and others v Moldova and Russia*, it is well-known that the European Court of Human Rights has consistently held that, first and factually, Pridnestrovie's 'high level of dependency on Russian support provided a strong indication that the Russian Federation continued to exercise effective control and a decisive influence over the Transdniestrian authorities'[41] as well as that, second and normatively, in light of these findings, and since the ECHR can also apply extraterritorially in cases where a contracting party exercises effective control over an area outside its national territory,[42] applicants alleging a violation of one of their rights and freedoms under this human rights treaty taking place in Pridnestrovie are within the jurisdiction of Russia in the sense of article 1 ECHR.[43] However, this jurisprudence initially only allows for the conclusion that foreign investors in Pridnestrovie benefit from international legal protection under the ECHR, including the right to property under article 1 of Protocol No 1 to the ECHR,[44] and are in this regard with certain chances of success entitled to initiate proceedings in Strasbourg against Moldova and in particular also Russia.

Despite cautious pleas to the contrary,[45] it seems – already in light of a literal interpretation of the relevant provisions – at least doubtful whether this line of reasoning could also be had recourse to in order to establish an extraterritorial scope of application of investment treaties. Whereas the respective jurisprudence of the European Court of Human Rights is based on a broad reading of the phrase 'within their jurisdiction' under article 1 ECHR, at least most, if not all, BITs – including investment treaties signed by Russia[46] – as

---

41   *Sandu and others v Moldova and Russia* (n 29) para 36; see also already in particular *Ilaşcu and others v Moldova and Russia* (n 35) paras 28 et seq, 311 et seq, 376 et seq.
42   Generally thereto Schabas (n 35) Art. 1 ECHR, 100 et seq, with further references.
43   *Ilascu and others v Moldova and Russia* (n 41) paras 311 et seq, 376 et seq; *Sandu and others v Moldova and Russia* (n 29) paras 36 et seq.
44   See thereto more recently *Sandu and others v Moldova and Russia* (n 29) paras 63 et seq.
45   See, especially in the context of Crimea, the argumentation by Happ and Wuschka (n 30) 245.
46   See Russia–Sweden BIT (1995), in particular the definition of 'territory' provided for in its art 1(4): 'The term 'territory' shall mean the territory of the Kingdom of Sweden or the territory of the Russian Federation, as well as those maritime areas, such as an exclusive economic zone and a continental shelf, adjacent to the outer limit of that territorial sea of the respective State, over which it exercises, in accordance with international law, sovereign rights and jurisdiction for the purposes of exploration, exploitation and conservation of natural resources.' For a quite similar approach see also Russia–Singapore BIT (2010) art 1(5).

well as the already above-mentioned article 29 of the 1969 Vienna Convention on the Law of Treaties employ the different and arguably considerably narrower term 'territory',[47] thus requiring a territorial nexus between the investment and the territory of the respondent host state[48] and consequently excluding the possibility of an extraterritorial applicability of respective BITs based on considerations of an alleged effective control over an area outside of the contracting party's national territory. In the context here at issue – and in particular unlike the circumstances underlying the current discussions on the situation in Crimea and its implications for the realm of international investment treaties[49] – the authors are not aware of anybody claiming that Pridnestrovie is at present a part of the Russian Federation, thus excluding the applicability of Russian BITs. In sum, there appear to be at present no investment treaties that could be of practical relevance for, and in particular grant effective international protection to, foreign investors and their respective activities in Pridnestrovie.

4 The 2018 Pridnestrovian Law on State Support of Investment Activities: Identifying and Assessing Some Notable Regulatory Features

The lack of pertinent BITs or other investment treaties[50] as well as the rather meager normative layer of relevant customary international law in particular in the form of the vague and disputed international minimum standard[51] that arguably applies to and obliges also territorial entities beyond the state, both

---

47 On this perception, specifically with regard to article 29 of the 1969 Vienna Convention on the Law of Treaties, see also already Daniel Costelloe, 'Treaty Succession in Annexed Territory' (2016) 65 ICLQ 343, 347, 358; Patrick Dumberry, 'Requiem for Crimea: Why Tribunals Should Have Declined Jurisdiction over the Claims of Ukrainian Investors against Russian [sic] under the Ukraine-Russia BIT' (2018) 9 JIDS 506, 515; Syméon Karagiannis, 'The Territorial Application of Treaties' in Duncan B Hollis (ed), *The Oxford Guide to Treaties* (OUP 2012) 305, 318 et seq; von der Decken (n 30) paras 34 et seq.

48 Generally on this issue see Christina Knahr, 'The Territorial Nexus between an Investment and the Host State' in Marc Bungenberg and others (eds), *International Investment Law: A Handbook* (CH Beck, Hart, and Nomos 2015).

49 On this discussion see Happ and Wuschka (n 30) 245; Dumberry, 'Requiem for Crimea' (n 47) 506.

50 See thereto section 3 above.

51 Generally on this standard and its possible normative elements see Patrick Dumberry, *The Formation and Identification of Rules of Customary International Law in International Investment Law* (CUP 2016) 61 et seq, 96 et seq, with numerous further references.

serve as clear indications for the practical relevance of other sources of law for foreign investors in Pridnestrovie. Among them are contractual arrangements concluded between respective public authorities and investors as well as the domestic legal system of the host state or, for that matter perhaps more accurately, the host entity. While specific aspects of foreign investment projects are most certainly subject to various national laws and regulations, Pridnestrovie has – in the same way as the majority of countries and other economies in the world[52] – more recently adopted a domestic investment statute that now provides a central legal regime for undertaking and operating investments in this territorial entity and, already in light of this qualification, thus deserves taking a closer look at.

In order to provide a systematic overview and evaluation of the notable regulatory features characterizing the Law of the Pridnestrovian Moldavian Republic on State Support for Investment Activities, which entered into force on 1 June 2018, it is useful to recall that these host country's legislative acts are often said to pursue two overarching purposes: to encourage and to control foreign investments.[53] While this perception is most certainly not entirely incorrect, we submit that one can also, more specifically and thus more accurately, distinguish between six main functions exercised by domestic investments statutes like the respective Pridnestrovian legal regime of 2018, namely to define the relevant economic actors and business transactions (section 4.1), to provide a public law-based normative steering framework for investments (section 4.2), to establish the institutions and procedures for administering investments (section 4.3), to provide for means aimed at promoting and facilitating investments (section 4.4), to ensure legal protection for investors and their investments (section 4.5), as well as to foresee venues and procedures for the settlement of investment disputes (section 4.6).

---

52 See UNCTAD, 'Investment Laws – A Widespread Tool for the Promotion and Regulation of Foreign Investment' (2016) Investment Policy Monitor: Special Issue, 2 <https://unctad.org/en/pages/newsdetails.aspx?OriginalVersionID=1388> accessed 15 May 2020 ('UNCTAD research finds that at least 108 countries have an investment law.'). See in this connection also the regularly updated UNCTAD database on domestic investment laws, UNCTAD, 'Investment Laws Navigator' (*Investment Policy Hub*, 2020) <https://investmentpolicy.unctad.org/investment-laws> accessed 15 May 2020.

53 See Jeswald W Salacuse, *The Three Laws of International Investment* (OUP 2013) 90; UNCTAD, 'Investment Laws – A Widespread Tool' (n 52) 2; Campbell McLachlan, Laurence Shore, and Matthew Weiniger, *International Investment Arbitration – Substantive Principles* (2nd edn, OUP 2017) 44; Markus Burgstaller and Michael Waibel, 'Investment Codes', *Max Planck Encyclopedia of Public International Law* (2011) para 2 <https://opil.ouplaw.com/home/MPIL> accessed 6 November 2019.

4.1 Definition of Covered Investments and Investors

Supporting the view that national investment laws and international investment treaties not infrequently contain quite similar provisions,[54] the overwhelming majority of the respective domestic statutes – in the same way as, among others, BITs – include stipulations defining or at least further specifying the relevant types of business transactions as well as the economic actors concerned.[55] This also applies to the 2018 Pridnestrovian investment statute. Thereby, the definition of 'investment' stipulated in article 2(1)(a) and (b) of this statute, focusing on the establishment of a new business entity under Pridnestrovian law or the acquisition of long-term interests in an existing enterprise, follows the – compared to a broad asset-based approach – more limited enterprise-based approach. This approach characterizes roughly one-third of all currently existing domestic investment laws[56] as well as in the realm of international investment treaties or models thereof, among others, article 1611 of the former 1988 Canada–United States Free Trade Agreement[57] and article 1(4) of the 2015 Indian Model BIT.[58] Article 1(2)(a) and (b) further limit the material scope of application by excluding certain types of investments, among them those in non-profit organizations as well as respective business transactions for educational, charitable, scientific or religious purposes.[59] To the contrary, article 2(1) states in its last sentence that investments can be domestic and foreign; thus indicating that the 2018 Pridnestrovian investment statute belongs to the majority of related domestic legal regimes[60] that do not address foreign investors only, but apply to both foreign and domestic investors. The notion of 'investor' itself is further specified for the purposes of the 2018 Pridnestrovian

---

54 On this perception see UNCTAD, 'Investment Laws – A Widespread Tool' (n 52) 2.
55 See thereto Hepburn (n 36) 658; Michele Potestà, 'The Interpretation of Consent to ICSID Arbitration Contained in Domestic Investment Laws' (2011) 27 Arb Int'l 149, 150; UNCTAD, 'Investment Laws – A Widespread Tool' (n 52) 4.
56 UNCTAD, 'Investment Laws – A Widespread Tool' (n 52) 4; generally on the approach of an enterprise-based definition of investments see also UNCTAD, *Key Terms and Concepts in IIAs: A Glossary* (2004) 96 et seq; UNCTAD, *International Investment Agreements: Key Issues*, vol 1 (2004) 195.
57 Canada–USA FTA (1988).
58 See India's Model Bilateral Investment Treaty (2015) <http://investmentpolicyhub.unctad.org/Download/TreatyFile/3560> accessed 6 November 2019; see thereto also Grant Hanessian and Kabir Duggal, 'The Final 2015 Indian Model BIT: Is This the Change the World Wishes to See?' (2017) 32 ICSID Rev 216, 217 et seq.
59 Generally on the underlying issue see Sabine Konrad, 'Protection for Non-Profit Organizations' in Marc Bungenberg and others (eds), *International Investment Law: A Handbook* (CH Beck, Hart, and Nomos 2015).
60 See thereto UNCTAD, 'Investment Laws – A Widespread Tool' (n 52) 2.

investment statute in its article 2(2), adopting the quite common broad regulatory approach of including both natural persons as well as juridical persons.

4.2 Public Law-Based Normative Steering Framework for Investments

Unlike at least most traditional BITs and other international investment agreements, national investment laws do not focus exclusively or even primarily on investment protection. Rather, adopting a much broader regulatory approach,[61] one of their central functions is the establishment of what might appropriately be referred to as an overarching public law-based normative steering framework for undertaking and operating this type of business transactions that is also aimed at controlling and channeling investment projects in, as well as for the benefit of, the country or other territorial entity at issue.[62] In this regard, there seem to be at least four regulatory aspects worth highlighting in the present context of the 2018 Law of the Pridnestrovian Moldavian Republic on State Support for Investment Activities.

First, similar to most domestic investment statutes,[63] article 3(2) and (3) stipulate certain sector-specific entry restrictions for organizations with foreign investments, a term that is defined in article 2(3) as a commercial entity in which a foreign investor owns at least 30 percent of the capital. Adopting a kind of 'negative list' approach, article 3(2) prohibits respective organizations with foreign investments from carrying out certain activities explicitly deemed to be of strategic importance for the national defence and security. This includes the development, manufacturing, sales, storage and transportation of weapons and ammunition (lit a), the production and sale of narcotic drugs and other substances that are hazardous to health (lit b), the importation, manufacturing, planting and sale of substances and crops containing narcotic, toxic and psychotropic substances (lit c) as well as the treatment of patients and animals suffering from dangerous diseases (lit d).[64] Viewed from a global comparative perspective, this list is especially remarkable for its brevity. In other words, the number of prohibited sectors and business activities seems to be quite limited

---

61   On this finding see also already Jonathan Bonnitcha, 'Investment Laws of ASEAN Countries: A Comparative Review' (2017) International Institute for Sustainable Development Report, 4 <www.iisd.org/library/investment-laws-asean-countries-comparative-review> accessed 15 May 2020>.

62   Generally on this finding see also Salacuse, *The Three Laws of International Investment* (n 53) 89 et seq; Hepburn (n 36) 662 et seq.

63   UNCTAD, 'Investment Laws – A Widespread Tool' (n 52) 5; Salacuse, *The Three Laws of International Investment* (n 53) 92 et seq.

64   Article 3(2) lit d furthermore specifies that the diseases at issue are determined according to a list established and issued by the government of Pridnestrovie.

and furthermore does not apply to foreign investments below the threshold of 30 percent of the capital, thus indicating a quite liberal approach with regard to the entry and establishment of foreign investments in Pridnestrovie.

Nevertheless, the following article 3(3) foresees, again in the interest of national defence and security, a second layer of restrictions applying to those organizations with foreign investments in which foreign nationals or foreign legal persons own 50 percent or more of the shares. These economic entities are, in addition to restrictions provided for in article 3(2), also prevented from business activities such as the operation of gas and oil pipelines, power lines (except for telecommunication lines), heat supply networks and water supply (lit b), the organization and conducting of gambling and betting (lit c), the preparation of radio and television programs as well as publishing activities (lit d), and the operation of public transportation networks (lit e). However, the final sentence of article 3(3) stipulates two notable exceptions to this rule, stating that these restrictions do not apply to, first, business entities whose shares have been acquired by foreign investors in the course of a privatization of state-owned property or, second, to corporations whose shares are owned by individuals that are residents of, and legal persons that are duly incorporated in, the Russian Federation.

It is in particular this last-mentioned stipulation granting preferential treatment to residents and juridical persons of a single country on a unilateral basis outside the context of regional economic integration regimes that seems to be, at a minimum, a very rare if not unique provision in the global context of domestic investment statutes and appears to be, already against this background and at least at first sight, quite remarkable. Thereby, it should be recalled that, viewed from a legal perspective, such a regulatory approach is not objectionable since most-favoured-nation (MFN) treatment is neither included as a protection standard for foreign investors in the 2018 Pridnestrovian investment statute, nor a rule of general customary international law[65] that would arguably also bind Pridnestrovie. Nevertheless, and seen from a political perspective, this stipulation surely serves as a clear reminder that we are dealing here in the case of Pridnestrovie with a frozen conflict situation generally characterized by not infrequently involving the existence of a so-called patron state[66] and that this context also needs to be taken into account when assessing the

---

65 On the last-mentioned finding see also Christian Tietje, 'Begriff, Geschichte und Grundlagen des Internationalen Wirtschaftssystems und Wirtschaftsrechts' in Christian Tietje (ed), *Internationales Wirtschaftsrecht* (2nd edn, De Gruyter 2015) § 1 para 93.
66 See thereto already section 1 above.

regulatory content of individual legislative acts adopted by actors involved in this frozen conflict.

Second, exercising governmental control over investment activities that credibly takes into account also important aspects like the interests on the side of investors in legal certainty as well as foreseeability and proportionality of governmental conduct and thus ultimately observance of central elements of the rule of law requires, among others, a transparent stipulation of the supervisory competences bestowed upon public agencies in this regard as well as of the applicable sanctions regime in cases of non-compliance with statutory or contractual obligations on the side of investors. As far as the 2018 Pridnestrovian investment statute is concerned, respective legislative determinations are for example enshrined in article 21, providing for a quite detailed account of the Authorized Investment Agency's powers to monitor the compliance of investors with the terms and conditions of the respective investment agreements concluded between the investor and respective public authorities in the sense of article 2(10) of the statute. Furthermore, to mention but two additional examples, article 22 stipulates the prerequisites for a mutually agreed, and in particular also for a unilateral, early termination of these investment agreements prior to the expiration date, whereas article 23, complementing this provision, includes a listing of the legal consequences arising from a respective termination of an investment agreement.

The third aspect of the present public law-based normative steering framework briefly worth drawing attention to concerns the stipulation of investors' obligations; a regulatory approach that has *de lege lata* until now not gained widespread recognition in the realm of investment treaty practice. Yet, it is increasingly recognized at the level of domestic investment statutes.[67] This trend is further confirmed by the 2018 Pridnestrovian investment law that explicitly enshrines in its article 4(2) respective obligations of investors. That said, this provision confines itself to stipulating the most commonly stated obligation of these economic actors to comply with the existing legislation of Pridnestrovie (lit a) as well as to fulfil the obligations of the respective contractual agreement with the Pridnestrovian government (lit b). It is thus abstaining from legislating more specific, and potentially more far-reaching, (corporate social responsibility) obligations of these business actors to contribute in the course of their business activities to the promotion and realization of broader public interest

---

67   See UNCTAD, 'Investment Laws – A Widespread Tool' (n 52) 8; Karsten Nowrot, 'Obligations of Investors' in Marc Bungenberg and others (eds), *International Investment Law: A Handbook* (CH Beck, Hart, and Nomos 2015) 1170 et seq.

concerns like the protection of human rights, core labour and social standards, consumer interests as well as the environment.[68]

Fourth and finally, the channeling function of national investment legislation often finds its manifestation in affirmative specifications of those economic sectors and activities in which the undertaking of investments is particularly welcomed by the country or other territorial entity at issue.[69] And indeed, respective normative guidance for potential investors is also provided in the present context by the distinction between so-called 'priority investment projects' and other investment activities that forms one of the central steering elements of the 2018 Pridnestrovian investment statute. Article 2(2) defines a priority investment project for the purposes of this legislation in rather abstract terms as measures involving an investment in the creation of a new production facility in Pridnestrovie. More specifically and with regard to the type of priority activities covered by this category, article 14(2) states from an export-oriented perspective that all activities of Pridnestrovian legal entities whose share of exports in the course of a priority investment project accounts for a minimum of 90 percent of the total sales revenue qualify as priority activities. In addition, article 14(3) stipulates that – regardless of the share of exports – all activities in the industrial sectors and the agroindustry shall, with certain exceptions as laid down in this provision as well as in the subsequent paragraph 4, qualify as a priority activity for the purposes of a priority investment project. As we shall see in subsequent sections, this distinction between priority investment projects and other (non-prioritized) investment undertakings can very well be considered as one of the defining elements, if not even *the* defining element, of the 2018 Pridnestrovian investment statute's overall regulatory structure.

4.3   Institutions and Procedures for the Administration of Investments

Already in light of the fact that the effective implementation of a normative steering regime aimed at promoting and regulating investment activities usually necessitates some form of institutional and procedural administrative framework, it is hardly surprising that the 2018 Pridnestrovian investment law – like many other domestic investment statutes[70] – also includes provisions establishing public agencies and other bodies as well as specific procedures

---

68 For a critical view on this reluctant regulatory attitude see generally UNCTAD, 'Investment Laws – A Widespread Tool' (n 52) 11.
69 See thereto Salacuse, *The Three Laws of International Investment* (n 53) 95 et seq.
70 On this finding see also UNCTAD, 'Investment Laws – A Widespread Tool' (n 52) 6; Salacuse, *The Three Laws of International Investment* (n 53) 106 et seq.

for the administration of investments. From an institutional perspective, the two main governmental agencies created in order to fulfil these administrative tasks are the Investment Board and the Authorized Investment Agency.

In accordance with article 2(11), the Investment Board presents itself as a collective body established by the Pridnestrovian government in order to coordinate the activities related to the undertaking and operation of investments in this territorial entity. Subsequently, article 20(2) provides further details on the composition of this committee. Chaired by the Deputy Chairman of the Pridnestrovian government, it comprises of six additional members, among them two other representatives of the Government, three representatives of the Supreme Council (the parliamentary assembly) as well as one representative of the Central Bank. The specific functions and competences of the Investment Board in the processes of public investment administration are not codified in a single provision. Rather, they can be derived from various different stipulations in the 2018 investment statute. Its responsibilities include, for example, involvement in the examination of and decisions regarding applications for investment incentives under article 12(4), article 18(2) and (3), the decision on whether to apply the guarantee of legislation stability as foreseen in article 16(5), a participation in the processes prior to the signing of contractual agreements with investors in accordance with article 20 as well as a central role in decisions on the early termination of respective investment agreements under article 22(5) and (6).

The second governmental agency referred to in the 2018 Pridnestrovian investment law is the Authorized Investment Agency as designated by the government under article 2(12) and being entitled to involve specialists from other governmental bodies as well as external advisors and experts in accordance with article 2(12) as well as article 10(1). As indicated by article 20(2), the Investment Agency is envisioned to assist the Investment Board in its work by, among others, gathering and preparing the information and documents for the meetings of the later body. In addition, albeit to a certain extent related to these support functions, the tasks entrusted to the Investment Agency concern in particular the direct interactions with, and assistance for, prospective and established investors in Pridnestrovie. In this regard, this agency serves as the addressee of investors' applications for investment incentives under article 12(1) and (4) as well as of applications for the guarantee of legislation stability in the sense of article 16(4), is involved in the preparation of contractual investment agreements in accordance with article 20(4) and provides a considerable number of advice and support services for investors as further specified in form and content in article 10(2) to (5). Furthermore, other competences and responsibilities of the Authorized Investment Agency include the monitoring of compliance by investors with the terms and conditions agreed upon in investment contracts under article 21 as well as an involvement in the processes potentially leading to an early termination of these investment agreements in accordance with article 22(4) and (5).

Viewed from a procedural perspective, it seems noteworthy – albeit far from unknown in the global realm of domestic investment statutes[71] – that the 2018 Pridnestrovian investment law does not contain a general procedure for the registration or other types of governmental involvement in the undertaking of investments. Moreover, in particular the stipulation enshrined in article 3(1), whereby investors have the right to invest in any object and type of entrepreneurial activities except as otherwise provided by this investment statute, seems to allow the conclusion that this legal regime in principle does not foresee a specific requirement for especially also foreign investors to register or seek approval from governmental authorities prior to undertaking a respective investment. Rather, the specific procedures for the administration of investments that are included in the 2018 Pridnestrovian investment law are predominantly concerned with priority investment projects,[72] namely, aside from applications for the guarantee of legislation stability in the sense of article 16(4), in particular the application process for investment incentives in accordance with article 12, the respective process leading to the signing of an investment contract between the investor and the Pridnestrovian government under article 20 as well as the administrative procedure concerning an early termination of such an agreement in accordance with article 22.

4.4   Promotion and Facilitation of Investment

As already indicated by the full name, 'Law of the Pridnestrovian Moldavian Republic on State Support for Investment Activities', of the statute at issue and further confirmed by article 1(1), stating that this law establishes procedures for providing special state guarantees and incentives for investment activities, the promotion and facilitation of investments undoubtedly presents itself, contrary to the common regulatory approach of BITs and other investment treaties, as the central objective of this legal regime. It thereby primarily serves the purpose, emphasized in article 9(1), of increasing production capabilities in Pridnestrovie by creating new manufacturing enterprises and jobs as well as by advancing the skills of the workforce. In light of this finding, it seems hardly

---

71   See UNCTAD, 'Investment Laws – A Widespread Tool' (n 52) 6.
72   See thereto already section 4.2 above.

surprising that also a clear majority of the provisions of the 2018 Pridnestrovian investment law address the issues of promoting and facilitating investments.[73]

In line with the stipulation included in article 9(2), the individual measures foreseen in this regard can be broadly systemized by distinguishing between three different categories of regulatory approaches. The first type of provisions is intended to facilitate the undertaking and operationalization of investments by establishing procedures and arrangements conducive to enable special and simplified interactions between prospective and established investors on the one hand and state authorities on the other hand. Aside from, *inter alia*, the option, granted to certain types of investors under article 19, to maintain accounting records and submit financial statements solely in accordance with common international financial reporting standards such as the United States Generally Accepted Accounting Principles (US-GAAP) or the International Financial Reporting Standards (IFRS standards) issued by the International Accounting Standards Board (IASB) of the IFRS Foundation, the most obvious manifestation of this regulatory approach is the reference to a so-called 'one-stop shop' in article 10(2) to (5) as a single point of contact for investors who implement priority investment projects[74] to receive assistance from the Authorized Investment Agency.

The institutional and procedural concept of a 'one-stop shop' is until now only rarely foreseen in domestic investment statutes,[75] but for example well-known in the context of the EU Services Directive.[76] The incorporation of this institutional feature in the Pridnestrovian investment law, whose practical importance can hardly be over-emphasized, serves as a clear indication that this legal regime is guided by the idea of investment facilitation in a comprehensive sense to the obvious benefit of particularly foreign investors. This perception is further supported by the guarantee of government transparency in accordance with article 7(1) and (2), stipulating that the Pridnestrovian state authorities will make publicly available all laws and regulations affecting the interests of investors and shall provide in principle open access to additional information to these business actors upon their request. Such a legal assurance

---

73   On a possible distinction between regulatory measures aimed at promoting investments on the one hand and those facilitating investments on the other hand see UNCTAD, 'Investment Laws – A Widespread Tool' (n 52) 9. Generally on these purposes pursued by domestic investment statutes see also Salacuse, *The Three Laws of International Investment* (n 53) 99 et seq.

74   See thereto already section 4.2 above.

75   See the respective finding in UNCTAD, 'Investment Laws – A Widespread Tool' (n 52) 9.

76   See Directive 2006/123/EC of the European Parliament and of the Council of 12 December 2006 on Services in the Internal Market [2006] OJ EU L 376/36, art 6.

and procedure are surely quite common at least in countries governed by the rule of law. Nevertheless, they are until now only seldom to be found in domestic investment statutes.[77]

The underlying aim of the second category of provisions being of relevance in the present context is the promotion and encouragement of investments on the basis of offering of fiscal, financial and other incentives to investors who implement priority investment projects. article 11 foresees three types of investment incentives that prospective investors are entitled to apply for under the 2018 Pridnestrovian investment law. Among them is the possibility of grants-in-kind from the government to the investor under article 15, a measure that might refer to, among others, the free use of land plots, buildings, machinery and vehicles in the sense of article 15(3). Furthermore, another investment incentive available for priority investment projects that include the establishment of new production facilities concerns fiscal benefits in the form of temporary exemptions from taxes and other charges like corporate income tax, land tax, and social tax, the details of which are laid down in article 17. Finally, the investment statute also foresees the right of investors to apply for financial incentives in the form of direct investment subsidies granted on a free-of-charge and non-repayable basis in accordance with article 18.

The third type of provisions envisioned under article 9(2) to serve the purpose of contributing to the promotion and facilitation of investments are characterized by the stipulation of legal guarantees for investment activities (lit a). While the regulations that fall into this third category are undoubtedly first and foremost also legislated with the intention to encourage new investments, and whereas this underlying motive surely applies to both investment treaties and domestic investment statutes, the respective substantive and procedural investment protection standards are commonly – and in principle rightly – dealt with separately from the issues of investment promotion and facilitation. Following this general conceptual and analytical trend, the respective stipulations are also in the present context the subjects of the two subsequent sections.[78]

4.5   Legal Protection for Investors and Their Investments

As for example already indicated by the fact that most of the currently more than 2,930 BITs[79] are titled 'Treaty Concerning the Promotion and Protection of Investments' or in line with some variations thereof, international investment treaty law is traditionally – and also today – primarily concerned with

---

77   See thereto UNCTAD, 'Investment Laws – A Widespread Tool' (n 52) 10.
78   See sections 4.5 and 4.6 below.
79   UNCTAD, *World Investment Report 2019: Special Economic Zones* (UN 2019) 99.

the protection of foreign investors and their investments.[80] To the contrary, investment protection has never been the sole or at least dominant function of domestic investment statutes whose content overall tend to be inspired by considerably broader regulatory approaches.[81] That said, many national investment laws also contain – already in the interest of investment promotion[82] – certain provisions that are quite similar to the substantive protection standards enshrined in BITs and other investment treaties.[83]

This finding also applies to the 2018 Pridnestrovian investment law. Admittedly, this legal regime – in the same way as most of the other currently existing investment statutes[84] – does not openly include guarantees of fair and equitable treatment, of MFN treatment[85] as well as of full protection and security to foreign investors as commonly found in international investment treaties. However, it explicitly foresees in particular the protection of investments in case of expropriation (article 8) and legal guarantees in connection with the transfer of funds (article 6). It thus adopts an approach that finds itself in principle again in conformity with the majority of domestic investment laws.[86]

With regard to the guarantee of investors' property rights, article 8 distinguishes between expropriations as the result of a conversion of property owned by individuals and private legal persons into state property (nationalizations) on the one hand and requisition of private property on the other hand.[87] While both types, in order to be lawful, have to be provided for by law in accordance with article 8(1), the regulation on lawful nationalizations in article 8(2) is at least equally noteworthy for the requirements it does not mention in this regard as for those conditions that it explicitly stipulates. Contrary to what is

---

80 On this perception see also Jeswald W Salacuse, *The Law of Investment Treaties* (2nd edn, OUP 2015) 124 et seq.
81 See thereto already section 4.2 above.
82 See section 4.4 above.
83 On this finding see also already McLachlan, Shore and Weiniger (n 53) 44; Hepburn (n 36) 658.
84 UNCTAD, 'Investment Laws – A Widespread Tool' (n 52) 6 et seq; Bonnitcha (n 61) 4; Antonio R Parra, 'Principles Governing Foreign Investment, as Reflected in National Investment Codes' (1992) 7 ICSID Rev 428, 435.
85 See thereto also already section 4.2 above.
86 See UNCTAD, 'Investment Laws – A Widespread Tool' (n 52) 6 et seq; Parra (n 84) 437 et seq; Hepburn (n 36) 658; Burgstaller and Waibel (n 53) para 29.
87 It seems worth emphasizing that expropriation of land ownership, often an important issue also in the realm of international investment law, is of merely marginal relevance in the context of Pridnestrovie since, in accordance with article 5 of the 1996 Pridnestrovian Constitution, all land is in the exclusive ownership of the state with citizens and foreign investors being entitled to land use only on a short-term or long-term lease basis.

probably now part of customary international law,[88] article 8(2) does explicitly require neither that – unlike the stipulation in article 8(3) concerning requisitions – the state measure at issue serves a public purpose nor that it must not be discriminatory. Furthermore, although this provision foresees that investors shall be compensated for the losses incurred as a consequence of the expropriatory act and that the compensation shall be paid within a period of eighteen months, it is somewhat conspicuously silent on the other two elements of the (in-)famous 'Hull formula', namely the issues of adequate and effective compensation. In this regard, the 2018 Pridnestrovian investment law appears to belong to the – in fact quite populous – class of domestic investment statutes that foresee some 'flexibility' in the calculation of compensation.[89] In particular, a comparative reading of article 8(2) and the provision on requisition in article 8(3) might allow the conclusion that adequate compensation in cases of nationalizations under article 8(2) is not always envisioned to be equivalent to the market value of the expropriated investment.[90] This requirement is explicitly stipulated only with regard to the scenario of requisitions under article 8(3). Aside from this condition applicable to the valuation and calculation of compensation, article 8(3) furthermore requires that requisition of investors' property shall only be permissible, first, in the event of natural disasters, accidents, epidemics, epizootics and other extreme circumstances, as well as, second, in the public interest, and, third, on the basis of a lawful decision taken by state authorities. Finally, it seems worth drawing attention to the fact that article 8 of the 2018 Pridnestrovian investment law, in line with roughly 80 percent of the currently existing domestic investment statutes,[91] confines its scope of application to direct expropriations. The legislative act thus excludes indirect expropriations and thereby avoids, among others, the quite 'thorny' issue well-known from the realm of investment treaties of articulating and specifying the difference between indirect expropriation and legitimate regulatory measures in furtherance of general welfare purposes.[92]

---

[88] On this perception see Dolzer and Schreuer (n 10) 99 et seq; Ursula Kriebaum, 'Expropriation' in Marc Bungenberg and others (eds), *International Investment Law: A Handbook* (CH Beck, Hart, and Nomos 2015) 1018.

[89] See thereto UNCTAD, 'Investment Laws – A Widespread Tool' (n 52) 7.

[90] Generally on this issue see Irmgard Marboe, *Calculation of Compensation and Damages in International Investment Law* (OUP 2017) 43 et seq.

[91] UNCTAD, 'Investment Laws – A Widespread Tool' (n 52) 7.

[92] See thereto Gebhard Bücheler, *Proportionality in Investor-State Arbitration* (OUP 2015) 125 et seq; Kriebaum (n 88) 971 et seq; Karsten Nowrot, 'How to Include Environmental Protection, Human Rights and Sustainability in International Investment Law?' (2014) 15 JWIT 612, 628 et seq.

The legal guarantees in connection with the transfer of funds under article 6 address and take into account a fundament concern for foreign investors when making an investment abroad.[93] In the same way as respective stipulations in most other domestic investment statutes, the provision starts out in article 8(1)(a) with a general right of investors to transfer abroad proceeds resulting from their investments, followed by a non-exhaustive list of examples of legitimate, and thus covered, transactions and purposes. Nevertheless, the provision also reflects the recognized need to balance the at times diverging interests of host territories and investors by foreseeing certain limitations to the right to transfer of funds.[94] Thereby, article 6(1)(a) initially clarifies that respective transactions are only permitted once the investors have honored their tax obligations and other compulsory payments; an approach that finds itself in conformity with many other domestic investment statutes.[95] However, contrary to many other investment treaties and national investment laws stipulating specific other limitations like cases where creditors' rights are at risk or cases of serious balance-of payments difficulties, article 6(1)(a) furthermore subjects the right to transfer in a rather comprehensive way to the existing legislation of Pridnestrovie. Such a regulatory approach used to be particularly prominent for example in a number of BITs concluded by China in the 1980s and in principle allows a change in the host territory's laws at any time.[96] Consequently, it grants to investors in essence only the comparatively modest protection against transfer restrictions that violate the host territory's laws and regulations.[97]

Unlike a considerable number of other domestic investment statutes as well as most international investment treaties, the 2018 Pridnestrovian investment law does not explicitly include a guarantee of national treatment for foreign investors. Nevertheless, such a general right of foreign investors, most certainly

---

93 On this perception see *Continental Casualty Co v Argentina*, ICSID Case no ARB/03/9, Award (5 September 2008) para 239; as well as for a more detailed assessment Carsten Kern, 'Transfer of Funds' in Marc Bungenberg and others (eds), *International Investment Law: A Handbook* (CH Beck, Hart, and Nomos 2015) 871 et seq.

94 Generally thereto Kern (n 93) 872 and 878; Dolzer and Schreuer (n 10) 212 et seq.

95 UNCTAD, 'Investment Laws – A Widespread Tool' (n 52) 8.

96 However, at least investors implementing priority investment projects are potentially protected against subsequent legislative changes on the basis of the guarantee of legislation stability under article 16, at least as long as one does not consider article 6 to be *lex specialis* as far as limitations on the transfer of funds are concerned.

97 See generally on this regulatory approach and its consequences UNCTAD, *International Investment Arrangements: Trends and Emerging Issues* (UN 2006) 39; Kern (n 93) 878 et seq; Dolzer and Schreuer (n 10) 214.

subject to exceptions and qualifications as stipulated in the statute itself, to be accorded a treatment no less favourable than that which is accorded by Pridnestrovian public authorities to investments of domestic investors might arguably be inferred from the stipulation enshrined in article 4(1), stating that (foreign and domestic) investors have equal rights. Even if one is not willing to follow this argumentation, it seems appropriate to recall that the mere fact that a certain right or legal guarantee is not included in an investment statute does not mean that a territorial entity does not offer it to foreign investors on the basis of its constitution or other legislative acts.[98] This finding also applies to Pridnestrovie. In fact, article 5(1) states that all investors, domestic and foreign, are enjoying full and unconditional protection of their rights and interests as ensured by the Pridnestrovian Constitution, by other laws and regulation as well as – with a view to a possible future – by international treaties concluded and ratified by this territorial entity. This provision is also noteworthy for the fact that it stipulates in its paragraph 2 an entitlement for investors to compensation for damages caused by illegal actions or omissions of Pridnestrovian public authorities. It thus establishes – or hints at the existence of – a kind of Pridnestrovian 'state liability law' to the benefit of domestic and foreign investors.

A final provision that also deserves attention in the present context of investment protection under the 2018 Pridnestrovian investment statute is the 'stabilization clause' included in article 16. Whereas article 5(3) merely guarantees to all investors the – at least in theory largely self-evident – stability of the content of investment agreements concluded between the investor and respective public authorities except for amendments by mutual consent, article 16 provides those investors who implement priority investment projects[99] with the option to rely on a considerably more far-reaching stabilization clause. In general, this type of provisions is aimed at providing stability and predictability for investors, with the consequences of, among others, reducing their transaction costs, by largely exempting them for a certain and often quite long period of time from those subsequent legislative amendments in the host state that might negatively affect their business environment and their profit expectations.[100] Stabilization clauses were for many decades a quite common

---

98   See thereto already UNCTAD, 'Investment Laws – A Widespread Tool' (n 52) 6.
99   See thereto already section 4.2 above.
100 Generally on stabilization clauses and their context see Rudolf Dolzer, *Petroleum Contracts and International Law* (OUP 2018) 191 et seq; Morris Besch, 'Typical Questions Arising within Negotiations' in Marc Bungenberg and others (eds), *International Investment Law: A Handbook* (CH Beck, Hart, and Nomos 2015) 106 et seq.

element of state contracts as well as of many domestic investment statutes. More recently, however, these provisions are increasingly critically perceived due to the constraints imposed by them on the regulatory autonomy of host states in furtherance of other public interest concerns.[101]

Viewed against this background, the regulatory approach enshrined in article 16 provides for a quite balanced and politically as well as legally sound solution to the complex issue of stabilization clauses. On the one hand, it guarantees in its paragraph 1 the stability of the business environment for investors in the event of legislative changes in Pridnestrovie with the procedure for requests aimed at applying this guarantee in cases of a deterioration of the business environment being established and detailed in its paragraphs 4 and 5. Overall, these stipulations grant investors quite far-reaching legal protection. On the other hand, article 16(2) exempts certain legislative changes from the substantive scope of application of this stabilization clause, in particular as far as labour legislation, the regulation of minimum wages and salaries as well as laws on pricing are concerned. Based on this differentiated steering approach, the provision thus enables the host territory, in the present case Pridnestrovie, to exercise, without additional legal constraints, its regulatory competences in order to effectively promote and protect also other public interest concerns of its population.

4.6 Settlement of Investment Disputes

No assessment of a normative steering instrument in the realm of investment law would be complete without at least a word – and usually much more than that – on its dispute settlement mechanisms or lack thereof. On the one hand, the increased effectiveness of, and recourse to, the legal regime on the settlement of investment disputes, in particular in the form of international investment arbitration between foreign investors and host states in recent decades, is a central factor that has undoubtedly strongly contributed to the current importance and global visibility of international investment law and illustrates the significance of this issue in the eyes of many foreign investors as well as other actors. On the other hand, it is equally well-known that it is first and foremost this concept of international investor-state arbitration and its implementation in practice that has more recently been quite critically perceived and thereby continues to be a key element in a development that resulted in the legal regime on the protection of foreign investments as a whole being

---

[101] For a quite comprehensive discussion of these issues see more recently Jola Gjuzi, *Stabilization Clauses in International Investment Law* (Springer 2018).

now – again – increasingly controversially debated. And indeed, as well as further supporting the central importance of this issue, one of the few features of domestic investment statutes that has attracted already for quite some time a certain scholarly attention is the design of their respective dispute settlement provisions, in particular the interpretation of the arbitration clauses not infrequently enshrined therein.[102]

The central provision in the 2018 Pridnestrovian investment law addressing the issue of dispute settlement appears to be, at least at first sight, article 24 bearing the title 'Resolution of Investment Disputes'. However, a closer look at this regulation from a systematic perspective reveals that its scope of application is limited by the definition of 'investment dispute' under article 2(5), stipulating that this term only covers a dispute arising in connection with the contractual obligations of the investor and respective public authorities on the basis of an investment agreement in the sense of article 2(10). In other words, article 24 seems to be confined to investment contracts and thus does not cover, among others, disputes between investors and Pridnestrovian public authorities that concern the interpretation and application of other domestic laws and regulations, including the 2018 Pridnestrovian investment statute itself.

Within its scope of application, article 24(1) foresees that investment disputes shall preferably be resolved through negotiations or in accordance with the (alternative) dispute resolution procedure that has been agreed by the parties in their investment contract. This provision is thus essentially referring to the dispute settlement venues and mechanisms consensually determined by the investor and the Pridnestrovian government in the specific state contract. And indeed, also the current 'Standard Bilateral Investment Agreement on Investing and the Provision of Investment Preferences within the Implementation of the Investment Priority Project' adopted by the Pridnestrovian government in May 2018 envisions in its paragraph 9(2) that '[i]n the event that disagreements and disputes cannot be resolved by the Parties within one month by negotiation, these disputes shall be resolved by the Parties in …'.[103] It

---

102   See Parra (n 84) 444 et seq; Potestà (n 55) 149 et seq; Christoph Schreuer and others, *The ICSID Convention – A Commentary* (2nd edn, CUP 2009) art 25 paras 392 et seq; Dolzer and Schreuer (n 10) 256 et seq; Michael Waibel, 'Investment Arbitration: Jurisdiction and Admissibility' in Marc Bungenberg and others (eds), *International Investment Law: A Handbook* (CH Beck, Hart, and Nomos 2015) 1225 et seq; as well as Burgstaller and Waibel (n 53) para 31.

103   Standard Bilateral Investment Agreement on Investing and the Provision of Investment Preferences within the Implementation of the Investment Priority Project, Annex 1 to the Decree of the Government of the Pridnestrovian Moldavian Republic no 159 of 18 May 2018.

thus allows and expects the parties to determine respective venues and procedures that can be domestic or international in character.

In case the investment dispute at issue cannot be resolved in accordance with the means foreseen in article 24(1), the following article 24(2) stipulates that it shall be settled either in the domestic Pridnestrovian courts or before those courts and tribunals that are determined by the parties in their investment contract. This provision thus again primarily refers to the consensual decision on appropriate domestic or international dispute settlement venues and procedures as included in the state contract. Whether this regulatory approach grants foreign investors direct access to effective international legal remedies on the basis of an unconditional prior consent to transboundary arbitration on the side of Pridnestrovie depends, first, on the individual dispute settlement venues and mechanisms chosen by the parties to the agreement as well as, second, most certainly on the specific wording of the respective arbitration clause.

In addition, the 2018 Pridnestrovian investment statute itself explicitly foresees the option of a recourse to domestic as well as international courts and tribunals in two scenarios. First, as already indicated in the previous section,[104] article 16 provides investors implementing priority investment projects[105] with the option to rely on a quite far-reaching stabilization clause and to apply, in situations of an alleged deterioration of the business environment, for a guarantee of legislation stability in the sense of article 16(4). In case this application is rejected by the competent Investment Board, article 16(5) stipulates that this executive decision can be contested by the investor in the courts, including courts with international jurisdiction. Thereby, the last-mentioned option of recourse to international courts and tribunals is not further specified in article 16(5). Nevertheless, a systematic reading of this provision suggests, also in the interest of practicability, that this option again depends on the respective determination of dispute settlement venues agreed upon in the specific investment contract.

Second, article 8(3) grants investors the right to initiate a judicial or quasi-judicial review of the determination of the market value of their requisitioned property, used as a basis to specify the amount of compensation to which the owner is entitled. Concerning suitable dispute settlement venues, this provision foresees access to domestic Pridnestrovian courts, national courts of other countries as well as international courts and tribunals. However, the last

---

104   See already section 4.5 above.
105   See thereto already section 4.2 above.

two options are again – and this time explicitly – dependent upon a respective determination made in the individual investment contract. In article 8 we find once more one of those provisions that are at least as remarkable for what they not stipulate than for the regulations they include. It is noteworthy, that article 8 confines the explicit access to legal remedies to the comparatively narrow issue of the determination of the market value of requisitioned property. It thus excludes not only a judicial review of the legality of the requisition itself but in particular also of the lawfulness of, including the appropriate amount of compensation to be paid in connection with, nationalizations in the sense of article 8(2).[106]

Nevertheless, with regard to the last-mentioned issues as well as regarding other disputes between investors and Pridnestrovian public authorities that concern the interpretation and application of domestic laws and regulations, including the 2018 Pridnestrovian investment statute itself, access to judicial remedies – at least before the domestic courts of Pridnestrovie – might arguably be indirectly inferred from the general guarantees of legal protection for investors under article 5(1) and (2). Furthermore, and specifically referring to expropriations in the form of nationalizations in accordance with article 8(2), a valid argument can be made, that respective legislative measures potentially affect the guarantee of legislation stability under article 16. Therefore, they would enable those investors that implement priority investment projects to seek protection, ultimately including access to dispute settlement mechanisms, under article 16(4) and (5). This implies that one does not consider article 8(2) to be *lex specialis* as far as nationalizations are concerned.[107]

In sum, the provisions on the settlement of investment disputes as enshrined in the 2018 Pridnestrovian investment statute, in the same way as those included in the majority of the other domestic investment laws currently in force,[108] do not offer a unilateral advance consent by Pridnestrovie to international arbitration for foreign investors. However, as implied in particular by its article 8(3) and article 24, the statute at least acknowledges the possibility of recourse to international dispute settlement venues and procedures in

---

106 See thereto already section 4.5 above.
107 Generally on this issue, albeit referring to stabilization clauses included in state contracts, see Dolzer and Schreuer (n 10) 98 ('Even clauses in agreements between the host state and the investor that freeze the applicable law for the period of the agreement ("stabilization clauses") will not necessarily stand in the way of a lawful expropriation.').
108 See UNCTAD, 'Investment Laws – A Widespread Tool' (n 52) 10; see also specifically with regard to the situation in ASEAN countries Bonnitcha (n 61) 4 ('no ASEAN country grants advance consent to investor-state arbitration in its investment law').

cases in which the investor and the Pridnestrovian government have agreed to respective mechanisms in their investment contract. Furthermore, the investment law, at least in certain scenarios, also recognizes the right of investors to have access to judicial remedies in domestic courts.

5   By Way of a Conclusion: Measuring the 2018 Pridnestrovian Investment Law in Light of the Normative Importance of Domestic Investment Statutes – 'Same Same But Different' due to a Frozen Conflict Situation?

It has been more recently not infrequently emphasized that domestic investment statutes have until now – with the possible exceptions of the content and legal effects of their arbitration clauses[109] as well as questions related to their overall normative character as 'ordinary' domestic laws or rather as unilateral acts under public international law[110] – attracted comparatively little attention in the legal literature,[111] especially in light of the considerable and by now almost unmeasurable number of publications devoted to BITs, investment chapters in regional economic integration agreements as well as other international investment treaties. This scholarly focus is to a certain extent understandable and hardly surprising; it is well-known that the international legal framework on the protection of foreign investments comprises primarily of treaty law. The currently more than 2930 BITs together with some 385 other international agreements that include investment-related provisions[112] constitute already for a number of decades the central normative 'backbone' of this legal regime.

Nevertheless, the times appear to be changing also in this regard. International investment law has more recently entered a phase of reformation and reconceptualization that is primarily characterized by various efforts of states to regain some their 'policy space' vis-à-vis foreign investors and to stress the importance of regulatory autonomy of host states in order to allow them to pursue the promotion and protection of other public interest concerns such

---

109   See thereto already section 4.6 above.
110   On this debate see David D Caron, 'The Interpretation of National Foreign Investment Laws as Unilateral Acts under International Law' in Mahnoush H Arsanjani and others (eds), *Looking to the Future – Essays on International Law in Honor of W. Michael Reisman* (Brill 2011) 649 et seq; Hepburn (n 36) 667 et seq.
111   On this perception see UNCTAD, 'Investment Laws – A Widespread Tool' (n 52) 11; Bonnitcha (n 61) 4; Hepburn (n 36) 659.
112   UNCTAD, *World Investment Report 2019* (n 79) 99.

as sustainable development. The specific policy responses so far suggested or already implemented in this regard most certainly vary considerably from country to country. Nevertheless, there is currently a clear and global tendency by states to either renegotiate and replace existing agreements with new treaties that 'down-grade' the legal position previously enjoyed by foreign investors by, among others, stipulating new constraints to the substantive protection standards and by limiting the access to international dispute settlement mechanisms or even to unilaterally terminate their BITs altogether[113] and to substitute the previous investment treaty protection by adopting new domestic investment statutes. South Africa is a well-known example for the last-mentioned investment policy approach.[114]

As a result of these developments, the importance of BITs and other investment treaties as normative steering instruments for investors and host states is to a certain extent declining, while at the same time the significance of other sources of law in the international investment regime is – again – on the rise. This applies for example to so-called 'state contracts' concluded between foreign investors and host state authorities, but in particular also to national investment laws that provide for domestic legal frameworks specifically addressed also to the undertakings of foreign investors.

Aside from these global tendencies, their underlying motives and their normative consequences, we can identify in the context of this contribution another type of scenarios as well as alternative set of reasons – so far much less noted and appreciated in scholarly writings – that also indicate the continued and potentially even growing importance of state contracts and especially also domestic investment statutes in the international economic system. It concerns the situation of autonomous territorial entities that have emerged – and are likely here to stay – as the result of frozen conflicts and that, primarily for

---

113 Generally on this current trend in international investment treaty-making and -unmaking see UNCTAD, *World Investment Report 2018: Investment and New Industrial Policies* (UN 2018) 88; UNCTAD, *World Investment Report 2019* (n 79) 100; Karsten Nowrot, 'Termination and Renegotiation of International Investment Agreements' in Steffen Hindelang and Markus Krajewski (eds), *Shifting Paradigms in International Investment Law* (OUP 2016) 230 et seq.

114 See UNCTAD, unctad, Investment Policy Monitor no 20 (2018) 4 <https://unctad.org/en/PublicationsLibrary/diaepcb2018d5_en.pdf> accessed 15 May 2020. For a more in-depth assessment of the new South African Protection of Investment Act that came into effect on 13 July 2018 and its investment policy context see Malebakeng Agnes Forere, 'The New South African Protection of Investment Act – Striking a Balance between Attraction of FDI and Redressing the Apartheid Legacies' in Fabio Morosini and Michelle Ratton Sanchez Badin (eds), *Reconceptualizing International Investment Law from the Global South* (CUP 2018).

political reasons unrelated to economic aspects in the narrow sense, have abstained from signing, or have due to a lack of potential treaty partners been until now unable to conclude, BITs or other investment treaties.[115] It is first and foremost also in the context of these territorial actors, and the present case of Pridnestrovie serves as a vivid example in this regard, that we see an investment policy approach that, voluntarily or involuntarily, substitutes international investment treaty regimes by relying on state contracts and domestic investment statutes, thereby contributing to the persistent or even rising relevance of these alternative sources of transnational investment law.

A final question that potentially arises in this regard – and seems worth addressing in particular bearing in mind the primary research focus of this contribution – concerns the influence possibly exercised by the existence of frozen conflict situations on the regulatory approaches and content of domestic investment statutes. In other words and more specifically, are the investment laws adopted by unrecognized territorial entities in frozen conflicts notably different from respective legal steering instruments of recognized countries? One might for example presume that the, compared to 'ordinary' state actors, frequently more peculiar political and security context of these territorial entities somehow also finds its manifestation in certain regulatory approaches enshrined in their local normative frameworks dealing with domestic and transboundary economic relations. In addition, to mention but one further example, one could image that stabilized *de facto* regimes more often decide to introduce particularly foreign investment-friendly legislation in order to compensate for the possible 'economic costs of non-recognition'[116] and, in this connection, especially to overcome potential reservations on the side of foreign investors.[117]

In the course of this contribution, this complex issue cannot be addressed in something even close to a comprehensive way; in particular, as far as the identification of findings is concerned that might legitimately be considered representative and thus in principle applicable to all, or at least the majority, of the unrecognized territorial entities currently existing in the international system. In the end, all of these different territorial regimes in frozen conflict

---

115   On the in principle undisputed (investment) treaty-making capacity of these autonomous territorial actors under public international law see already section 3 above.

116   Scott Pegg, *International Society and the De Facto State* (Ashgate 1998) 43.

117   On the possibility of such reservations see the perception expressed by Caspersen (n 5) 82 ('Their lack of recognition and precarious position makes them [unrecognized states] highly unattractive to foreign investors […].'); as well as by Kolstø and Blakkisrud (n 11) 505 ('foreign investors will be wary of dealing with the separatists').

situations are in many ways quite unique actors, each being influenced by its own specific political and economic context, and, after all, we have confined ourselves to taking a closer look 'merely' at the case of Pridnestrovie. Nevertheless, with regard to the specific investment law context of Pridnestrovie, the analysis undertaken in this contribution allows for at least two notable findings that might also potentially be helpful for possible future research dealing with this question on a much broader empirical scale.

First, there seems to be only one stipulation in the 2018 Pridnestrovian investment statute that has very few, if any, pendants in the global realm of domestic investment codes and can, moreover, legitimately be interpreted as mirroring, and being considerably influenced by, the frozen conflict situation of Pridnestrovie. The provision at issue is article 3(3) granting preferential treatment to residents and legal persons of a single country, namely the Russian Federation, on a unilateral basis;[118] thereby indicating the important role played by Russia as the patron state of Pridnestrovie.[119] Aside from this rather unique stipulation, however, there are no regulatory features enshrined in this domestic investment statute whose existence can be attributed to the specific political and security context of a frozen conflict situation. In particular, also the sector-specific entry restrictions for foreign investments stipulated in the interest of national defence and security in article 3 are, if viewed from a global perspective, rather reflecting a comparatively liberal investment policy approach[120] and are thus far from indicative of being motivated by a more peculiar security environment.

Second, and despite this last-mentioned finding, the 2018 Pridnestrovian investment statute overall does not distinguish itself by being an extraordinary or even excessively foreign investment-friendly piece of legislation. Admittedly, and in addition to its quite liberal approach towards the admission of foreign investments, this legal regime is undoubtedly characterized by a strong focus on investment promotion and facilitation as for example evidenced by the concept of a 'one-stop shop' as a single point of contact for investors as well as the quite remarkable and far-reaching investment incentives foreseen in articles 15 et seq.[121] However, the substantive and procedural protection standards stipulated in the statute[122] are, at best, in line with the respective

---

118　See thereto already section 4.2 above.
119　Generally on the phenomenon of patron states in the context of frozen conflict situations, see already section 1 above.
120　See thereto also already section 4.2 above.
121　See already section 4.4 above.
122　For a more detailed evaluation, see section 4.5 above.

regulatory approaches that can be found in many other domestic investment laws, and surely cannot legitimately give rise to an accusation of the 2018 Pridnestrovian investment statute being unduly one-sided and partial in favour of investors' interests. The same applies most certainly to the provisions on the settlement of investment disputes.[123]

Thereby, it seems important to emphasize that these findings are not meant to be understood as indicating regulatory deficits of this legal regime. Rather, they initially merely reveal that the features of the 2018 Pridnestrovian investment law are not primarily motivated by an attempt to compensate for possible 'economic costs of non-recognition'. Moreover, and quite to the contrary, they also serve as an illustration that the design of this domestic investment law seems to be guided by overall progressive, quite well-adjusted and thus modern regulatory approaches that find themselves in conformity with current global trends in investment policy- and law-making. After all, it is by now increasingly recognized among governments of industrialized and developing countries, practitioners and scholars alike, that at the level of designing international and domestic investment laws as well as in the realm of investor-state dispute settlement mechanisms, the central challenge lawmakers and other relevant actors are as of today ever more faced with is to provide for an appropriate and thus acceptable balance between the legally-protected economic interests of foreign investors and the domestic steering capacity or policy space of host states to allow the later to pursue the promotion and protection of other public interest concerns to the benefit of their populations and global public goods.

These findings bring us at last, at the end of this contribution, again to the perception introduced already at the very beginning of it. The fact that the 2018 Pridnestrovian investment statute, if evaluated from a global comparative perspective, ultimately presents itself – with very few exceptions – as a rather normal domestic investment law, further supports the view that non-recognized autonomous territorial entities like Taiwan or Pridnestrovie, despite being something of an anomaly in the international inter-state system, are usually rather normal political communities, in particular also as far as economic aspects are concerned. And, in the same way as most other political communities, they want to attract foreign investments without, however, unduly compromising their policy space and regulatory autonomy in order to also pursue the promotion and protection of other public interest concerns.

---

123 See thereto also already section 4.6 above.

Bibliography

Aust A, *Modern Treaty Law and Practice* (3rd edn, CUP 2013).

Bakke KM, 'After the War Ends: Violence and Viability of Post-Soviet Unrecognized States' in N Caspersen and G Stansfield (eds), *Unrecognized States in the International System* (Routledge 2011).

Berkes A, 'Frozen Conflicts, Consolidation of *De Facto* Regimes and the Obligation of Timely Cooperation' in S Wuschka and others (eds), *Zeit und Internationales Recht* (Mohr Siebeck 2019).

Besch M, 'Typical Questions Arising within Negotiations' in M Bungenberg and others (eds), *International Investment Law: A Handbook* (CH Beck, Hart, and Nomos 2015).

Bianchi A, 'International Adjudication, Rhetoric and Storytelling' (2018) 9 JIDS 28.

Bonnitcha J, 'Investment Laws of ASEAN Countries: A Comparative Review' (2017) International Institute for Sustainable Development Report <www.iisd.org/library/investment-laws-asean-countries-comparative-review> accessed 15 May 2020>.

Borgen CJ, 'Moldova: Law and Complex Crises in a Systemic Borderland' (2016) 59 German YB Int'l L 115.

Bowring B, 'Transnistria' in C Walter, A von Ungern-Sternberg, and K Abushov (eds), *Self-Determination and Secession in International Law* (OUP 2014).

Bücheler G, *Proportionality in Investor-State Arbitration* (OUP 2015).

Burgstaller M and M Waibel, 'Investment Codes', *Max Planck Encyclopedia of Public International Law* (2011) <https://opil.ouplaw.com/home/MPIL> accessed 6 November 2019.

Caron DD, 'The Interpretation of National Foreign Investment Laws as Unilateral Acts under International Law' in MH Arsanjani and others (eds), *Looking to the Future – Essays on International Law in Honor of W. Michael Reisman* (Brill 2011).

Caspersen N, 'States without Sovereignty: Imitating Democratic Statehood' in N Caspersen and G Stansfield (eds), *Unrecognized States in the International System* (Routledge 2011).

Charnovitz S, 'Taiwan's WTO Membership and its International Implications' (2006) 1 Asian J WTO & Int'l Health L & Pol'y 401.

Cheng B, *General Principles of Law as Applied by International Courts and Tribunals* (Stevens 1953).

Costelloe D, 'Treaty Succession in Annexed Territory' (2016) 65 ICLQ 343.

Crawford J, *The Creation of States in International Law* (2nd edn, OUP 2006).

Crawford J, 'Investment Arbitration and the ILC Articles on State Responsibility' (2010) 25 ICSID Rev 127.

Crawford J, *Brownlie's Principles of Public International Law* (9th edn, OUP 2019).

Dolzer R and C Schreuer, *Principles of International Investment Law* (2nd edn, OUP 2012).

Dolzer R, *Petroleum Contracts and International Law* (OUP 2018).

Dumberry P, 'An Unchartered Question of State Succession: Are New States Automatically Bound by the BITs Concluded by Predecessor States before Independence?' (2015) 6 JIDS 74.

Dumberry P, 'State Succession to Bilateral Treaties: A Few Observations on the Incoherent and Unjustifiable Solution Adopted for Secession and Dissolution of States under the 1978 Vienna Convention' (2015) 28 LJIL 13.

Dumberry P, *The Formation and Identification of Rules of Customary International Law in International Investment Law* (CUP 2016).

Dumberry P, *A Guide to State Succession in International Investment Law* (Edward Elgar 2018).

Dumberry P, 'Requiem for Crimea: Why Tribunals Should Have Declined Jurisdiction over the Claims of Ukrainian Investors against Russian [sic] under the Ukraine-Russia BIT' (2018) 9 JIDS 506.

Dumberry P, 'State Succession to BITs: Analysis of Case Law in the Context of Dissolution and Secession' (2018) 34 Arb Int'l 445.

Finck F, 'Border Check Point, the Moldovan Republic of Transnistria' in J Hohmann and D Joyce (eds), *International Law's Objects* (OUP 2018).

Forere MA, 'The New South African Protection of Investment Act – Striking a Balance between Attraction of FDI and Redressing the Apartheid Legacies' in F Morosini and MR Sanchez Badin (eds), *Reconceptualizing International Investment Law from the Global South* (CUP 2018).

Frowein JA, 'De Facto Regime', *Max Planck Encyclopedia of Public International Law* (2013) <https://opil.ouplaw.com/home/MPIL> accessed 6 November 2019.

Gjuzi J, *Stabilization Clauses in International Investment Law* (Springer 2018).

Grant TD, 'Frozen Conflicts and International Law' (2017) 50 Cornell Int'l LJ 361.

Hanessian G and K Duggal, 'The Final 2015 Indian Model BIT: Is This the Change the World Wishes to See?' (2017) 32 ICSID Rev 216.

Happ R and S Wuschka, '*Horror Vacui*: Or Why Investment Treaties Should Apply to Illegally Annexed Territories' (2016) 33 J Int'l Arb 245.

Hepburn J, 'Domestic Investment Statutes in International Law' (2018) 112 AJIL 658.

Isachenko D, 'On the Political Economy of Unrecognised State-Building Projects' (2009) 44(4) Int'l Spectator 61.

Jackson JH, 'Global Economics and International Economic Law' (1998) 1 J Int'l Econ L 1.

Jennings R and A Watts, *Oppenheim's International Law*, vol I (9th edn, Longman 1992).

Karagiannis S, 'The Territorial Application of Treaties' in DB Hollis (ed), *The Oxford Guide to Treaties* (OUP 2012).

Kennedy M, 'Overseas Territories in the WTO' (2016) 65 ICLQ 741.

Kern C, 'Transfer of Funds' in M Bungenberg and others (eds), *International Investment Law: A Handbook* (CH Beck, Hart, and Nomos 2015).

Klabbers J, 'Cat on a Hot Tin Roof: The World Court, State Succession, and the *Gabčikovo-Nagymaros* Case' (1998) 11 LJIL 345.

Knahr C, 'The Territorial Nexus between an Investment and the Host State' in Marc Bungenberg and others (eds), *International Investment Law: A Handbook* (CH Beck, Hart, and Nomos 2015).

Kolstø P and H Blakkisrud, 'Living with Non-Recognition: State- and Nation-Building in South Caucasian Quasi-States' (2008) 60 Eur-Asia Stud 483.

Konrad S, 'Protection for Non-Profit Organizations' in M Bungenberg and others (eds), *International Investment Law: A Handbook* (CH Beck, Hart, and Nomos 2015).

Kriebaum U, 'Expropriation' in M Bungenberg and others (eds), *International Investment Law: A Handbook* (CH Beck, Hart, and Nomos 2015).

Kulick A, 'About the Order of Cart and Horse, Among other Things: Estoppel in the Jurisprudence of International Investment Arbitration Tribunals' (2016) 27 EJIL 107.

Marboe I, *Calculation of Compensation and Damages in International Investment Law* (OUP 2017).

McLachlan C, L Shore, and M Weiniger, *International Investment Arbitration – Substantive Principles* (2nd edn, OUP 2017).

Nagel T, *The View from Nowhere* (OUP 1986).

Nowrot K, 'How to Include Environmental Protection, Human Rights and Sustainability in International Investment Law?' (2014) 15 JWIT 612.

Nowrot K, 'Obligations of Investors' in M Bungenberg and others (eds), *International Investment Law: A Handbook* (CH Beck, Hart, and Nomos 2015).

Nowrot K, 'Termination and Renegotiation of International Investment Agreements' in S Hindelang and M Krajewski (eds), *Shifting Paradigms in International Investment Law* (OUP 2016).

Nowrot K and E Sipiorski, 'Approaches to Arbitrator Intimidation in Investor-State Dispute Settlement: Impartiality, Independence, and the Challenge of Regulating Behaviour' (2018) 17 L & Prac Int'l Cts & Tribunals 178.

Orakhelashvili A, *Akehurst's Modern Introduction to International Law* (8th edn, Routledge 2019).

Paparinskis M, 'Investment Treaty Arbitration and the (New) Law of State Responsibility' (2013) 24 EJIL 617.

Parra AR, 'Principles Governing Foreign Investment, as Reflected in National Investment Codes' (1992) 7 ICSID Rev 428.

Pegg S, *International Society and the De Facto State* (Ashgate 1998).

Potestà M, 'The Interpretation of Consent to ICSID Arbitration Contained in Domestic Investment Laws' (2011) 27 Arb Int'l 149.

Salacuse JW, *The Three Laws of International Investment* (OUP 2013).

Salacuse JW, *The Law of Investment Treaties* (2nd edn, OUP 2015).

Schabas WA, *The European Convention on Human Rights* (OUP 2015).

Schreuer C and others, *The ICSID Convention – A Commentary* (2nd edn, CUP 2009).

Sipiorski E, *Good Faith in International Investment Arbitration* (OUP 2019).

Talmon S, 'The Constitutive Versus the Declaratory Theory of Recognition: *Tertium Non Datur?*' (2004) 75 Brit YB Int'l L 101.

Tams CJ, 'State Succession to Investment Treaties: Mapping the Issues' (2016) 31 ICSID Review 314.

Tietje C, 'Begriff, Geschichte und Grundlagen des Internationalen Wirtschaftssystems und Wirtschaftsrechts' in C Tietje (ed), *Internationales Wirtschaftsrecht* (2nd edn, De Gruyter 2015).

UNCTAD, *International Investment Agreements: Key Issues*, vol I (2004).

UNCTAD, *Key Terms and Concepts in IIAs: A Glossary* (2004).

UNCTAD, *International Investment Arrangements: Trends and Emerging Issues* (UN 2006) 39.

UNCTAD, 'Investment Laws – A Widespread Tool for the Promotion and Regulation of Foreign Investment' (2016) Investment Policy Monitor: Special Issue <https://unctad.org/en/pages/newsdetails.aspx?OriginalVersionID=1388> accessed 15 May 2020.

UNCTAD, Investment Policy Monitor no 20 (2018) <https://unctad.org/en/PublicationsLibrary/diaepcb2018d5_en.pdf> accessed 15 May 2020.

UNCTAD, *World Investment Report 2018: Investment and New Industrial Policies* (UN 2018).

UNCTAD, *World Investment Report 2019: Special Economic Zones* (UN 2019).

UNCTAD, 'Investment Laws Navigator' (*Investment Policy Hub*, 2020) <https://investmentpolicy.unctad.org/investment-laws> accessed 15 May 2020.

Vagts DF, 'State Succession: The Codifiers' View' (1993) 33 Va J Int'l L 275.

von der Decken K, 'Article 29 VCLT' in Oliver Dörr and Kirsten Schmalenbach (eds), *Vienna Convention on the Law of Treaties* (2nd edn, Springer 2018).

Waibel M, 'Investment Arbitration: Jurisdiction and Admissibility' in M Bungenberg and others (eds), *International Investment Law: A Handbook* (CH Beck, Hart, and Nomos 2015).

CHAPTER 13

Investment Law and the Conflict in the Donbas Region: Legal Challenges in a Special Case

Stefan Lorenzmeier and Maryna Reznichuk

1 Introduction

The current state of bilateral relations between Ukraine and the Russian Federation is extremely complex, both factually and legally. The events of the Euromaidan in Ukraine between November 2013 and February 2014 did not only oust the former Ukrainian government but led to territorial disputes in the country as well. Besides the *de facto* territorial change of Crimea from Ukraine to Russia, which took place on 21 March 2014 when Russia annexed the peninsula,[1] military hostilities in the Donbas / Luhansk region took place. These led to the establishment of two new entities on Ukrainian territory, namely the Peoples' Republics of Donetsk (DNR) and Luhansk (LNR).[2]

The two new entities declared their independence from Ukraine in April 2014 and a referendum fostering the situation was held in May 2014. Neither of these acts was recognized internationally. As of April 2014, Ukraine used military means to regain control of the occupied territory, but was not successful in its endeavor due to strong support for the new entities by Russia, whose military forces intervened actively in the fighting.[3] International mediation resulted in the conclusion of the first Minsk Agreement, which aimed at the establishment of a cease-fire between the warring parties. Yet, this plan was

---

1 President of Russia, 'Laws on admitting Crimea and Sevastopol to the Russian Federation' (Press Release, 21 March 2014) <http://en.kremlin.ru/acts/news/20625> accessed 10 May 2020.
2 On their legal systems see Roman Petrov, 'Legal Systems of Donetsk/Luhansk Peoples' Republics and Their Status under International and European Law' in Benedikt Harzl and Roman Petrov (eds), *Non-Recognised Entities in International and EU Law* (Brill 2021, forthcoming).
3 Sabine Fischer, 'The Donbas Conflict, Opposing Interests and Narratives, Difficult Peace Process', SWP Research Paper 5 (April 2019) 9. Regarding Crimea, see *eg* Kit De Vriese, chapter 10 in this volume; Stefan Lorenzmeier 'Investment Disputes in the Annexed Crimea from the Perspective of International Law', in Benedikt Harzl and Roman Petrov (eds), *Non-Recognised Entities in International and EU Law* (Brill 2021, forthcoming).

not as successful as originally hoped. Even after a second agreement (Minsk II), the situation in the region remains unstable. According to UN estimates, about 13000 persons have been killed in the conflict so far and cease-fire violations are taking place regularly.[4]

Under customary international law, following the principle of territorial integrity of states, settled borders are privileged. A territorial change is only legal under very strict conditions.[5] Additionally, the territorial integrity of a state belongs to the corpus of fundamental principles of international law. The declaration of independence by the DNR and LNR does not comply with the international legal order. The new entities have not been recognized by the international community,[6] which is a political indicator for not fulfilling the established criteria for statehood, and are not regarded as states by the international community.[7] Especially, the requirements for the exercise of a remedial secession[8] under the rule of self-determination of peoples as expressed in treaty and customary law[9] were not fulfilled in the Donbas territory.[10] Furthermore, the referendi for independence held in the DNR and LNR do not bear significance under public international law.[11]

Unlike Crimea, the separatist Donbas territory has not been annexed by the Russian Federation. Whether or not it is unofficially and effectively controlled by Russia is a question of fact, which however strongly point in this direction. Official acts of the Russian state are rare. Yet, strong indicators for Russian influence exists with respect to the DNR and LNR separatist entities. These include the introduction of the Russian ruble in the region, Russia's

---

4 See, *eg*, OHCHR, Report on the Human Rights Situation in Ukraine, 16 August to 15 November 2015, <www.ohchr.org/Documents/Countries/UA/28thReportUkraine_EN.pdf> accessed 10 May 2020, 6 et seq.

5 Gleider I Hernández, 'Territorial Change, Effects Of', *Max Planck Encyclopedia of Public International Law* (2010) para 2 <https://opil.ouplaw.com/home/MPIL> accessed 6 November 2019.

6 Only South Ossetia, another internationally non-recognized entity, recognized the DNR and LNR.

7 See *eg* Malcolm Shaw, *International Law* (8th ed CUP 2017) 331.

8 Daniel Thürer and Thomas Burri, 'Self-Determination', *Max Planck Encyclopedia of Public International Law* (2008) para 17 <https://opil.ouplaw.com/home/MPIL> accessed 10 May 2020.

9 Yves Beigbeder, 'Referendum', *Max Planck Encyclopedia of Public International Law* (2011) paras 4 et seq <https://opil.ouplaw.com/home/MPIL> accessed 10 May 2020.

10 Jure Vidmar, 'The Annexation of Crimea and the Boundaries of the Will of the People' (2015) 16 German LJ 365 et seq.

11 See the *Kosovo* advisory opinion, *Accordance with International Law of the Unilateral Declaration of Independence in Respect of Kosovo* (Advisory Opinion) [2010] ICJ Rep 403, paras 102 et seq. On the opinion, see Ralph Wilde, 'Kosovo (Advisory Opinion)', *Max Planck Encyclopedia of Public International Law* (2011) <https://opil.ouplaw.com/home/MPIL> accessed 10 May 2020.

policy of 'passportization',[12] its 'humanitarian assistance' to the people in the separatist areas and the way in which the investigations regarding the shooting of the passenger flight MH 17 are conducted.[13] Moreover, observations from the Organization for Security and Co-operation in Europe (OSCE) foster the thesis of Russian influence on the DNR and LNR entities.[14] It seems as if neither the DNR nor the LNR are viable as regimes without strong Russian support on all state levels and the supply of weapons and military personnel, although Russian soldiers are officially only in the territory on their own account and not deployed.[15] Additionally, there is a determining influence of Russia on the politics of the insurgents. They are heavily dependent on the already mentioned Russian military supply in terms of weapons and personnel as well as other means of support, for instance finances and resources.

Despite the foregoing, Ukraine does still exercise *de jure* sovereignty over the relevant territory but lacks *de facto* control. Since the new holders of the effective power in the region expropriated foreign but especially also Ukrainian assets in the Donbas region, the aim of this chapter is to analyze the impact of this situation on investments in the separatist territories of the Donbas and to identify the applicable legal norms for affected international and Ukrainian investors. It first clarifies the status of the Donbas under international and Ukrainian law, whether the situation could be considered a Russian occupation, as also in the case of Crimea, and what this means for international investments (section 2). The chapter then looks at the rules of the internal laws on investment protection of Ukraine, on the one hand, and of the separatist entities on the other hand (section 3.1 and 3.2), before it addresses questions of international humanitarian law (IHL, section 3.3), of the bilateral investment treaties (BITs) and the Russian-Ukrainian bilateral investment treaty (the 1998 BIT)[16] in particular (section 3.4), and of human rights law, specifically the European Convention on Human Rights and Fundamental Freedoms (ECHR,

---

12   Benedikt Harzl, 'Passportizatsiya revisited: Extraterritorial naturalization in the case of Abkhazia and South Ossetia' in Benedikt Harzl and Roman Petrov (ed), *Non-Recognised Entities in International and EU Law* (Brill 2021, forthcoming).
13   Georg Scherpf and Nikita Kondrashov, 'Investment Protection and Arbitration in the CIS Region' (2020) 18 German Arb J 8, 14.
14   See the various reports of the OSCE Special Monitoring Mission to Ukraine, <www.osce.org/ukraine-smm/reports> accessed 10 May 2020.
15   Fischer (n 3) 14. Russia claims that the Russian soldiers are 'on vacation' and 'on their own account' in the Donbas region.
16   Agreement between the Government of the Russian Federation and the Cabinet of Ministers of Ukraine on the Encouragement and Mutual Protection of Investments dated 27 November 1998.

section 3.5). As a final step, it addresses obligations the DNR and LNR might be under as a matter of international law, before concluding (section 4).

2   Russian Occupation?

2.1   *The Status of the Donbas Region under International Law*

As just outlined, in a first step, the international legal status of the separatist territories needs to be clarified, and especially whether Russia can be regarded as an occupying power in these separatist territories. Article 42 of the 1907 Hague Regulations provides that a 'territory is considered occupied when it is actually placed under the authority of the hostile army' and that the 'occupation extents only to the territory where such authority has been established and can be exercised'. According to official Russian statements, there is no Russian involvement in the region, because neither the military personnel nor the military means have been deployed. The Russian soldiers active in the Donbas area are acting on their own behalf. The Ukrainian side contests this assumption. Thus, the interpretation of the term 'authority' in article 42 becomes of crucial importance. The definition of 'authority' is based on factual criteria.[17] For a situation to qualify as a belligerent occupation, the forces of at least one state would need to exercise (effective) control over the territory of another state without the latter's state volition.[18] Effective control does not require that occupation forces are present at all places at all times.[19] The ability of the occupying force to send detachments of troops is sufficient to make its authority felt within a reasonable time.[20]

However it is disputed, whether actual or potential control would suffice for the exercise of effective control. The International Court of Justice (ICJ) in its *Armed Activities on the Territory of the Congo* case opted for actual control of the occupying forces.[21] A different opinion was endorsed *inter alia* by the International Criminal Tribunal for the Former Yugoslavia (ICTY)[22] and Judge

---

17 *Armed Activities on the Territory of the Congo (DRC v Uganda)* (Separate Opinion of Judge Kooijmans) [2005] ICJ Rep 306, para 38.
18 Eyal Benvenisti, 'Occupation, Belligerent', *Max Planck Encyclopedia of Public International Law* (2009) para 1 <https://opil.ouplaw.com/home/MPIL> accessed 10 May 2020.
19 ibid para 8.
20 ibid.
21 *Armed Activities on the Territory of the Congo (DRC v Uganda)* [2005] ICJ Rep 168, paras 173, 177.
22 ICTY, *Prosecutor v Naletilic and Martinovic*, IT-98-34-T, 31 March 2003.

Kooijmans[23] in his separate opinion in the *Armed Activities* case. *Kooijmans* noted explicitly that an occupying army cannot avoid its obligations by simply refusing to set up any system of government on its own.[24] He went even further and accepted the exercise of authority in cases where an armed invasion enabled a rebel movement to gain control over parts of the territory.[25] On the basis of the foregoing, it is legally irrelevant whether an occupying power exercises its control directly or indirectly through local forces and authorities.[26] Yet, also for the exercise of potential control, a military presence on the territory of another state seems to be required.

Factually, unlike in the case of Uganda's presence in the Democratic Republic of the Congo or of Russia's presence on Crimea and as described in the introduction, Russia does not exercise direct control over the occupied Donbas territory. It further did not, at least not officially, exercise military or security actions in the Donbas area. Thus, strong indications of Russian influence exist with respect to the DNR and LNR entities, but no open involvement of organs of the Russian state.

Further, it might be doubtful whether the introduction of a new currency and the issuance of passports can be used as criteria to establish actual or potential control over territory.[27] In this context, the telos of the rules of occupation should be taken into account. Like other norms of international humanitarian law,[28] the law of occupation is intended to provide reliable rules for the population in the occupied territory and aims at avoiding unnecessary hardships by establishing a reliable legal regime. In this regard, it has to be borne in mind that 'occupation' has also acquired a very pejorative connotation and occupants tend to use euphemistic terms for their position.[29] This is especially true for Russia's involvement in the events in Eastern Ukraine in light of the international condemnation of the annexation of Crimea and the sanctions imposed by the international community.[30] Against this background, Russia has very convincing reasons to shy away from terming its influence an 'occupation'. It only admits to support the insurrectional movements in the DNR and LNR.[31]

---

23 *Armed Activities on the Territory of the Congo* (Separate Opinion of Judge Kooijmans) (n 17) para 49.
24 ibid paras 36–64.
25 ibid para 48.
26 ibid para 49.
27 Scherpf and Kondrashov (n 13) 14.
28 See *eg* the preambular paragraphs of the 1907 Hague Convention.
29 Eyal Benvenisti, *The International Law of Occupation* (OUP 1993) 212.
30 See Lorenzmeier (n 3).
31 Fischer (n 3) 24 et seq.

Additionally, the main feature of the law of occupation is that a foreign power substitutes its authority for the authority of the former power. Yet, the situation in the DNR and LNR differs from other instances in which independent national liberation movements received support from other powers, *eg* the Contras in the Nicaragua conflict, due to the absolute dependency of the DNR and LNR on Russian supplies of all kinds. This support led to Ukraine's incapability to exercise actual control in the separatist territories and to a replacement of its state structures by Russian-influenced structures. In essence, although there is no actual official involvement of a hostile army, the situation in the separatist territories of the Donbas shows all features of an occupation. Thus, only the armed support for the insurgents led to their ability to control parts of Ukraine's Luhansk and Donetsk regions. Additionally, Russia's ongoing support on all levels, as described above, was and still is crucial for the sheer existence of the DNR and LNR.

In sum, the situation in the Donbas differs factually from the well-established types of occupation. The Russian army is not officially involved and acts of organs of the Russian state are complicated to detect. This could lead to the assumption that there was no Russian 'authority' in the Donbas area. On the contrary, the two created entities DNR and LNR are fully dependent on Russia for their existence, which is the classic case of an occupation, *eg* in Northern Cyprus. Therefore, unofficially Russia seems to exercise actual control over the separatist territories, but officially it does not even exercise potential control. In such a factual and legal vacuum, recourse should be had to the telos of the law of occupation, the protection of the people living on the territory. This aim can only be fulfilled by a power that is in a position to exercise control over the Donbas, which, in the given situation, is Russia.

As a result, the interpretation of 'authority' in article 42 Hague Regulations should also encompass situations in which a power is exercising effective control without claiming to do so. In this case, the problem seems to be more of a practical nature, namely difficulties in collecting convincing evidence. However, there is admittedly no case law supporting the proposed interpretation of article 42 of the Hague Regulations, yet.

2.2 *The Legal Status of Ukraine's Occupied Territories under Ukrainian Law*

This analysis under international law is complemented by Ukraine's own approach to the matter under domestic law. Ukrainian law defines the legal status of the occupied territories in the Donbas region in the Law on Certain Aspects of State Policy on Securing State Sovereignty over the Temporarily

Occupied Territories of the Donetsk and Luhansk Oblasts[32] as well as the Law on Ensuring the Rights and Freedoms of Citizens and the Legal Regime in the Temporarily Occupied Territory of Ukraine.[33] These laws in particular set out Ukraine's position that there is a temporary occupation by the Russian Federation of these territories of Ukraine, which is illegal and does not create any territorial rights for the Russian Federation.

The Ukrainian Helsinki Human Rights Union Report[34] states that there are two separate legal regimes of armed conflict in the Donbas region: a non-international armed conflict between the Armed Forces of Ukraine and other military formations of Ukraine on one side and organized anti-government armed groups of the DNR and LNR on the other side; and an international armed conflict between the Armed Forces of Ukraine and other military formations of Ukraine on one side and separate divisions of Armed Forces of the Russian Federation on the other side.

In light of these statements and also Ukraine's legislation on the matter, Ukraine appears to consider the conflict in the Donbas region as an international armed conflict. Also the Ukrainian legislator still focused on the application of the Additional Protocol 1 to the Geneva Conventions[35] in the preamble to the Law on Certain Aspects of State Policy on Securing State Sovereignty over the Temporarily Occupied Territories of the Donetsk and Luhansk Oblasts. The law further clarified, summarized and systematically described the main elements of the legal position of Ukraine by stating that the armed forces of the Russian Federation and the occupation administration of the Russian Federation have established and exercise overall control over the temporarily occupied territories in Donetsk and Luhansk regions.

2.3 The Legal Status of Ukraine's Donbas Region and Its Implications for the Protection of Foreign Investors

The assumption that the Donbas region is occupied by Russia from the perspective of public international law as well as the political and legal position of

---

32 Law of Ukraine on Certain Aspects of State Policy on Securing State Sovereignty over the Temporarily Occupied Territories of the Donetsk and Luhansk Oblasts, no 2268-VIII.
33 Law of Ukraine on Ensuring the Rights and Freedoms of Citizens and the Legal Regime in the Temporarily Occupied Territory of Ukraine, no 1207-VII.
34 Ukrainian Helsinki Human Rights Union, Report 'War and Human Rights'(2015), <https://helsinki.org.ua/files/docs/1439184931.pdf> accessed 10 May 2020, p 11–12.
35 Protocol Additional to the Geneva Conventions of 12 August 1949, and relating to the Protection of Victims of International Armed Conflicts (Protocol I) (adopted 8 June 1977, entered into force 7 December 1978) 1125 UNTS 3 (AP 1).

Ukraine brings about many legal challenges, not the least of which is the need to develop an effective legal mechanism to protect the rights of investors in the temporarily occupied territories. This issue is exacerbated by the fact that Russia does not recognize *de facto* control over certain territories of Donetsk and Luhansk. The legislative consolidation of liability for material damage to the Russian Federation under Ukrainian law does not mean automatic return of lost funds and reliable protection of rights of foreign investors before domestic courts. Despite the national investment legislation, it must therefore be assumed that, in the temporarily occupied territories of Ukraine, there is no effective mechanism to protect the rights of foreign investors during the occupation regime.

On the international plane, it is also noteworthy how Ukraine has chosen to address the situation when ratifying the Additional Protocol between the Government of Ukraine and the Government of the Republic of Croatia that amended the Croatia-Ukraine BIT:

> Since the Autonomous Republic of Crimea and the City of Sevastopol, which form an integral part of the territory of Ukraine, are temporarily occupied territories, the provisions of this Agreement do not apply to these territories until the Ukrainian jurisdiction over them is fully restored. As a result of the armed aggression, the territories of certain regions of Donetsk and Luhansk regions are actually occupied territories and controlled by the Russian Federation. The Government of Ukraine does not guarantee full and effective control and protection of investments in these territories.[36]

Ukraine thereby demonstrates a clear position, namely that it seeks the full assignment of responsibility for actions taking place in the Donbas region to the Russian Federation. At least in relation to Croatian investors, the statement will allow Ukraine to avoid possible investment claims related to these parts of the territory of Ukraine before the restoration of the jurisdiction of Ukraine over them.

---

36 President of Ukraine, Statement During the Ratification of the Additional Protocol on Amendments to the Agreement between the Government of Ukraine and the Government of the Republic of Croatia, 4 October 2017 (English translation by the authors), <https://zakon.rada.gov.ua/laws/show/2151-19/sp:max100?sp=:max100&lang=uk> accessed 10 May 2020.

3   Investment Protection

Ukrainian and international companies economically active in the separatist territories have been harmed and, for instance, expropriated by the DNR and LNR entities.[37] This section will scrutinize the legality of these acts under domestic and international law and highlight potential avenues for investors to seek legal redress in this extraordinary situation.

First, we will illustrate the relevant rules of Ukrainian domestic law (section 3.1). Second, IHL will be addressed (section 3.2). Third, investment treaties and in particular the application of the 1998 BIT between Ukraine and Russia (section 3.3) will be looked at. Finally, the ECHR (section 3.4) will become the last instrument our inquiry focuses on, before we briefly turn to international obligations the DNR and LNR themselves might be considered to be under (section 3.5).

3.1   *Ukrainian Domestic Law*

3.1.1   Ukraine's General Investment Legislation

As part of a short overview of the national legislation of Ukraine in the field of protection of foreign investment, it should be stated that today's framework consists of the certain norms of the Commercial Code of Ukraine as well as the especially enacted Law of Ukraine on the Regime of Foreign Investments,[38] which is the successor to the previous Law on Investment Activity and the Law on the Protection of Foreign Investments in Ukraine.[39]

Article 397 of the Commercial Code of Ukraine entails several guarantees for foreign investors, including the application of state guarantees for the protection of foreign investment in the case of changes in the legislation on foreign investment, guarantees against forced removal, as well as guarantees against illegal actions of authorities and their officials, compensation of losses to foreign investors, guarantees in case of termination of investment activity and guarantees for the transfer of profits and the use of income from foreign investments.[40]

---

37   See *eg* German Advisory Group Ukraine, 'The Effect of Company Seizures and Trade Suspension in Donbas', Newsletter no 106 (August 2017), www.beratergruppe-ukraine.de/wordpress/wp-content/uploads/2017/08/Newsletter_106_2017_German-Advisory-Group.pdf.

38   Law of Ukraine on the Regime of Foreign Investments (last amended on 31 May 2016), <https://investmentpolicy.unctad.org/investment-laws/laws/253/ukraine-law-on-the-regime-of-foreign-investments> accessed 10 May 2020.

39   ibid art 27.

40   This is a parallel legal regime to the enforcement of Ukrainian BITs, see Ukrainian Constitution art 9.

According to article 10 of the Law on The Regime of Foreign Investment, foreign investors have the right to compensation of losses, including lost profits and moral damage caused to them as a result of actions, inactivity or improper performance by the state bodies of Ukraine or their officials of the obligations under the legislation with respect to a foreign investor or enterprise with foreign investments.

Article 26 of the Ukrainian law on the Regime of Foreign Investments provides that

> disputes between foreign investors and the state on issues of state regulation of foreign investments and activities of enterprises with foreign investments are subject to consideration in the courts of Ukraine, unless otherwise stipulated by international treaties of Ukraine. All other disputes are subject to consideration in the courts of Ukraine or by agreement of the parties-in arbitration courts, including abroad.

Recourse to Ukrainian domestic law with respect to the Donbas region will likely be fruitless for both domestic and international investors for various reasons. First, Ukraine has clearly reaffirmed its national position concerning its responsibility of the Russian Federation for compensation of all investors' losses and it is likely that Ukrainian courts would concur with respect to claims against the Ukrainian government. Second, since the domestic legislation provides mainly for protection against acts by the Ukrainian state, it is not easily conceivably how Ukrainian courts might hold Russia accountable under the above-mentioned provisions. Finally, even if Ukrainian courts exercised jurisdiction over the matter, the Ukrainian authorities are not in a position to change the factual situation due to the Russian *de facto* control. Any such judgment could not be enforced. Bringing together these points, investment activities during the occupation regime do not enjoy effective legal protection under any of the Ukrainian domestic guarantees.

3.1.2 Investment Legislation of Ukraine Regarding the Protection of Investors' Rights in the Temporarily Occupied Territories

In light of these circumstances, Ukraine established additional regulatory acts that could also form the basis for the protection of investors' rights in the Donbas region: The Law of Ukraine on Certain Aspects of State Policy on Securing State Sovereignty over the Temporarily Occupied Territories of the Donetsk and Luhansk Oblasts,[41] which was long-awaited, designates the DNR and LNR

---

41 See n 32, also known as the 'Law on the Reintegration of Donbas'.

as the 'representatives of the occupation administrations of Russia'. However, there is a legal gap in the law on the procedure for bringing material damage. While a separate regime exists for Crimea in relation to economic activity in the temporarily occupied territory in order to implement the provisions of article 13 of the Law of Ukraine on Ensuring the Rights and Freedoms of Citizens and the Legal Regime in the Temporarily Occupied Territory of Ukraine,[42] there is no separate law regarding Donbas which would regulate economic activity in the temporarily occupied territories of Donetsk and Luhansk. Overall, the above-mentioned legal acts therefore do not provide a legal mechanism for the enforcement of their norms. Thus, there still remains an objective need for the development and implementation at the legislative level of more effective, efficient and constructive law models for the settlement of economic disputes in the Donbas region during the temporary occupation.

3.2   Regulatory Instruments of the DNR and LNR

The two administering entities in the Donbas region have themselves established their own institutional mechanism, including a 'Ministry of Justice' and a 'Ministry of Economic Development'. The latter organisation deals with the formation of investment platforms, in which relevant proposals for interested investors are placed. In 2017, the launch of an investment portal was one of the priorities of the DNR and LNR. As of today, the investment portal has received basic content and is regularly updated with new reference and analytical information.

At the moment, large and strategically important enterprises in the republics are under external management. The authorities consider the attraction of private investment as an opportunity for cooperation between the DNR and private business in areas in which the 'Republic' has traditionally been a monopolist (*eg* energy and transport infrastructure). To implement this mechanism, the DNR's Council Committee on Budget, Finance and Economic Policy, together with representatives of the Ministry of Economic Development and other authorized specialists, adopted the Law on Public-Private and Municipal-Private Partnership.[43] This instrument has been developed as a basis for other laws on foreign investments, *eg* on investment activities in

---

42   See n 33. On 12 August 2014, Ukraine adopted a separate Law of Ukraine On the Formation of a Free Economic Zone 'Crimea' and the Peculiarities of Economic Activity in the Temporarily Occupied Territory of Ukraine, no 1636–VII.

43   Law of the Donetsk People's Republic on Public-Private and Municipal-Private Partnership, no 188-INNS (11 August 2017). This and further regulatory acts of the DNR are available at <https://dnrsovet.su/en/> accessed 10 May 2020.

the DNR, on concessions and on the development of small and medium-sized enterprises.

The issue of recognition of these acts as legal acts, which could be part of Ukrainian law,[44] is clearly defined in the Ukrainian legislation. According to article 2 of the Law of Ukraine on Certain Aspects of State Policy on Securing State Sovereignty over the Temporarily Occupied Territories of the Donetsk and Luhansk Oblasts, the activities of the armed forces of the Russian Federation and the occupation administration of the Russian Federation in the Donetsk and Luhansk regions are illegal. Any act issued in connection with such activities is invalid and does not create any legal consequences, except for documents confirming the birth or death of a person in the temporarily occupied territories in the Donetsk and Luhansk regions.

3.3 *International Humanitarian Law*

In these circumstances, IHL could grant protection to investors in the case of, for instance, an illegal expropriation, since the Donbas is, as illustrated above, to be considered occupied territory of Ukraine. The relevant corpus of international humanitarian law consists of the 1899 and 1907 Hague Regulations[45] and the four Geneva Conventions[46] and the Additional Protocols thereto.[47] For present purposes, the 1907 Hague Regulations, especially their article 46, could be brought forward in the context of control over the separatist areas of the Donbas and the occupation regime since it exempts private property from

---

44   See, in this respect, Vladlena Lisenco and Karsten Nowrot, chapter 12 in this volume, illustrating the situation with respect to laws enacted in Transnistria.

45   Convention (IV) respecting the Laws and Customs of War on Land and its Annex: Regulations concerning the Laws and Customs of War on Land (adopted 18 October 1907, entered into force 26 January 1910) 36 Stat 2277 (Hague Regulations).

46   Geneva Convention for the Amelioration of the Condition of the Wounded and Sick in Armed Forces in the Field (adopted 12 August 1949, entered into force 21 October 1950) 75 UNTS 31 (First Geneva Convention); Geneva Convention for the Amelioration of the Condition of Wounded, Sick and Shipwrecked Members of Armed Forces at Sea (adopted 12 August 1949, entered into force 21 October 1950) 75 UNTS 85 (Second Geneva Convention); Geneva Convention Relative to the Treatment of Prisoners of War (adopted 12 August 1949, entered into force 21 October 1950) 75 UNTS 135 (Third Geneva Convention); Geneva Convention Relative to the Protection of Civilian Persons in Time of War (adopted 12 August 1949, entered into force 21 October 1950) 75 UNTS 287 (Fourth Geneva Convention).

47   Additional Protocol 1 (n 35); Protocol Additional to the Geneva Conventions of 12 August 1949, and relating to the Protection of Victims of Non-International Armed Conflicts (Protocol II) (adopted 8 June 1977, entered into force 7 December 1978) 1125 UNTS 609 (Additional Protocol 2).

confiscation.[48] According to the ICJ in its *Wall* advisory opinion, the provision is applicable in cases of occupation, even in long-term ones.

However, it is questionable which entity is legally responsible for any acts contrary to article 46 in the Donbas region. Since the events in 2014, Ukraine does not exercise effective control over the territory, but the *de jure* control. DNR and LNR respectively do not exercise the *de facto* control due to their absolute dependence on Russia.[49] As explained above, Russia has to be regarded as the occupying power in accordance with article 42 Hague Regulations.

Russia's denial of influence is legally irrelevant. Rather, it is important whether an influence by Russia on the politics of the DNR and LNR can be proven and whether the conduct of the two entities can be attributed to the Russian Federation under international law. Generally, all subjects of international law, *ie* mostly states, can only carry out their activities through individuals whose conduct has to be imputed to the respective state.[50]

3.3.1 Rules of Attribution

For lack of a treaty, to establish attribution of conduct to a state, recourse has to be had to customary rules of international law.[51] These rules are codified in articles 4 – 11 of the International Law Commission's Articles on State Responsibility (ASR).[52] Article 4 ASR establishes that the acts of state organs are attributable to a state. In the *Bosnia Genocide* case, the ICJ clarified that this does not only apply to *de jure* organs of a state, but also to person or entities not having the status of a *de jure* organ, if these entities act in complete dependence on the state of which they are merely the instruments.[53] Thus, not the formal legal status is decisive but the reality of the relationship.[54] The ICJ applied the complete dependency test in a very strict manner. It did not attribute the actions

---

48   Article 46 provides: 'Family honour and rights, the lives of persons, and private property, as well as religious convictions and practice, must be respected. Private property cannot be confiscated.'
49   Council of Europe, Parliamentary Assembly, Resolution 2133 of 12 October 2016, no 5.
50   Luigi Condorelli and Claus Kress, 'The Rules of Attribution: General Considerations' in James Crawford, Alain Pellet and Simon Olleson (eds), *The Law of International State Responsibility* (OUP 2010) 221.
51   For article 8 ASR explicitly: *Application of the Convention on the Prevention and Punishment of the Crime of Genocide (Bosnia and Herzegovina v Serbia and Montenegro)* [2007] ICJ Rep 43 para 407.
52   ILC, 'Articles on Responsibility of States for Internationally Wrongful Acts' (2001) annexed to UNGA Resolution 56/83 UN Doc A/56/83 [2001].
53   *Application of the Convention on the Prevention and Punishment of the Crime of Genocide* (n 51) para 392; Condorelli and Kress (n 50) 221, 230.
54   Condorelli and Kress (n 50) 221, 230.

on Bosnian territory to Yugoslavia because the insurgents did not always act in a way consistent with Yugoslav orders.[55] Powerful ties were not enough.[56] Whether this is different and the very high threshold of the complete dependency test can considered fulfilled in the case of the DNR and LNR in eastern Ukraine is doubtful. It remains a matter of fact.

Additionally, article 11 ASR is not applicable due to Russia's non-adoption of the DNR and LNR acts as its own. Article 10(2) ASR, which addresses the conduct of an insurrectional movement succeeding in establishing a new state, is also not of relevance in the given context, since neither the DNR nor the LNR fulfil the requirements of a state. Article 9 ASR cannot be used either because the insurrectional movements do not act on behalf of Ukraine.

Thus, it is article 8 ASR that remains. According to that provision, 'the conduct of a person or group of persons shall be considered an act of state under international law if the person or group of persons is in fact acting on the instructions of, or under the direction or control of, that state in carrying out the conduct'. This covers cases where state organs recruit or instigate private persons or groups who acts as 'auxiliaries' while remaining outside of the official structure of a state.[57] Included are, for instance, private individuals who are not specifically commissioned by the state but are sent as 'volunteers' to neighboring countries or who are instructed to carry out missions abroad.[58]

Potentially, the Russian soldiers as well as other personnel active in the Donbas entities and for their organs fall under this provision. The decisive question is whether these persons were acting 'under the direction or control' of Russia. Two different tests are known in international law in this respect: the effective control test and the overall control test. The effective control test has first been relied upon by the ICJ in its *Nicaragua* decision. It attributes the conduct of individuals to a state if this state directs or enforces the acts of the individuals.[59] The overall control test has first been used by the ICTY in its *Tadic* decision. In the *Tadic* case, the Appeals Chamber of the ICTY stressed that the degree of control may vary in light of the factual circumstances of each case and that a strict standard cannot be applied in all circumstances.[60] Under that approach,

---

55 *Application of the Convention on the Prevention and Punishment of the Crime of Genocide* (n 51) paras 394 et seq.
56 ibid.
57 ILC, Draft Articles on Responsibility of States for International Wrongful Acts, with Commentaries, ILCYB 2001, vol II, pt 2, 47, article 8 para 2.
58 ibid.
59 *Military and Paramilitary Activities in and against Nicaragua (Nicaragua v USA)* (Merits) [1986] ICJ Rep 14, paras 109 and 115.
60 ICTY, *Prosecutor v Dusko Tadic*, IT-94-1-A, ILM [1999] p 1518, para 117.

in order to attribute the acts of individuals to a state, 'it must be proved that the State wields overall control over a group not only by equipping and financing the group but also by coordinating or helping in the planning of its military activity'.[61]

However, the less strict overall control test has only been applied in cases of individual criminal responsibility, not in cases of attribution of conduct to a state. It has further been rejected by the ICJ in the subsequent *Bosnia Genocide* case. According to the ICJ, the wider overall control test is not in conformity with the stricter effective control test and does not comply with article 8 ASR[62] because the overall control test stretches too far the connection between the conduct of a state's organs and its international responsibility.[63] Additionally, in its *Armed Activities on the Territory of the Congo* ruling, the ICJ did not accept the responsibility of Uganda for the acts of a private group trained and militarily supported by Uganda. Instead, it adhered to the effective control test as expressed in *Nicaragua*[64] and only accepted attribution of acts of the Ugandan army on Congolese territory.[65]

3.3.2   Attribution and Interpretation

Regarding private conduct and its attribution to a state, the ICJ's interpretation of article 8 ASR would lead to a different result than the interpretation of article 42 Hague regulations concerning the determination of the occupying power. This seems to be contradictory, yet not to the ICJ. According to the court, the attribution of state conduct under the rules of state responsibility does not have to be equated with the interpretation of other international norms such as the interpretation of the term 'authority' in article 42 Hague Regulations. The ICJ explicitly stated in the *Bosnia Genocide* case that it is not necessary to adopt the same test for the resolution of two different issues.[66] The degree and nature of a state's involvement in acts on another territory can very well differ from the nature and degree of involvement required to give rise to that state's responsibility for a specific act committed in the course of a conflict.[67]

---

61   ibid para 131.
62   *Application of the Convention on the Prevention and Punishment of the Crime of Genocide* (n 51) paras 402 et seq.
63   ibid para 406.
64   *Armed Activities on the Territory of the Congo* (n 21), paras 160 et seq.
65   ibid para 175.
66   *Application of the Convention on the Prevention and Punishment of the Crime of Genocide* (n 51) para 405.
67   ibid.

Further, the court relied upon the underlying rationale of the rules of state responsibility. It noted:

> a State is responsible only for its own conduct, that is to say the conduct of persons acting, on whatever basis, on its behalf. That is true of acts carried out by its official organs, and also by persons or entities which are not formally recognized as official organs under internal law but which must nevertheless be equated with State organs because they are in a relationship of complete dependence on the State. Apart from these cases, a State's responsibility can be incurred for acts committed by persons or groups of persons – neither State organs nor to be equated with such organs – only if, assuming those acts to be internationally wrongful, they are attributable to it under the rule of customary international law reflected in Article 8 [...]. This is so where an organ of the State gave the instructions or provided the direction pursuant to which the perpetrators of the wrongful act acted or where it exercised effective control over the action during which the wrong was committed.[68]

The ICJ's approach has been heavily criticized in scholarly writings,[69] in particular for not paying due regard to the difference of international criminal law and the rules of attribution of conduct to states, especially in the context of IHL.[70] IHL is not concerned with individual criminal responsibility but the interpretation of a notion like 'occupation' in article 42 Hague Regulations, which inherently requires the attribution of conduct of individuals to a state. A different reasoning and decision in these two cases is anything but convincing because it would lead to contradicting results with respect to the same subject-manner.[71] In these circumstances, as a simple matter of logic, the application of different tests for attribution of individual acts to a state seems unwarranted, although this might be so in a different context.[72]

---

68 ibid para 406.
69 Antonio Cassese, 'The *Nicaragua* and *Tadić* Tests Revisited in Light of the ICJ Judgment on Genocide in Bosnia' (2007) 18 EJIL 651; Condorelli and Kress (n 49) 221, 234.
70 ibid.
71 A similar reasoning has been used by the ICJ in *Military and Paramilitary Activities in and against Nicaragua* (n 59) paras 216, 219.
72 So the reasoning of the ICJ in *Application of the Convention on the Prevention and Punishment of the Crime of Genocide* (n 51) para 405.

3.3.3 Interim Result

Whether Russian effective control can be proven for potential acts in violation of investors' rights in the Donbas region depends again on the relevant facts. However, it does not seem as if the acts known to the public and relied upon in this contribution would fulfil the ICJ's effective control test. Thus, if the *Bosnia Genocide* reasoning is followed, any acts harming investors in the Donbas area cannot be attributed to Russia under article 8 ASR and Russia cannot be held responsible for them. The *de facto* control of the DNR and LNR does not suffice.

However, as set out above, the ICJ's reasoning is not absolutely conclusive. In light of the arguments in favour of a parallel interpretation of the rules of occupation and the rules of state responsibility, the approach of the ICJ seems to be less convincing and should be adjusted. As a result, if this approach is followed, acts harming foreign companies in the DNR and LNR could be attributable to Russia.

3.4 *Bilateral Investment Treaties*

Investment treaties are not automatically dissolved in times of war.[73] For Ukrainian investments in the Donbas, the 1998 BIT between Ukraine and Russia could cover the situation if its territorial application can be established. The same would be the case for investments by third-state nationals (that is nationals of other states than Russia and Ukraine) under investment treaties between Russia and their home states. In both cases, the relevant question is the same, namely whether Russia can be considered bound by its investment treaty obligations towards Ukrainian or other foreign investors in relation to the Donbas region.

Article 1 of the Russian-Ukrainian BIT (as also treaties with third states would) defines the territorial scope of the agreement as 'the territory of the Russian Federation or the territory of Ukraine and also their respective exclusive economic zone and the continental shelf as defined in conformity with international law'. As stated above, the territory of the DNR and LNR separatist entities have only been occupied, but – unlike Crimea[74] – not annexed and therefore are not even from Russia's perspective part of the Russian territory. It is still part of the Ukrainian territory.

---

[73] Christoph Schreuer, 'War and Peace in International Investment Law', in Katia Fach Gómez, Anastasios Gourgourinis and Catharine Titi (eds), *International Investment Law and the Law of Armed Conflict* (Springer 2019) 8.

[74] With respect to Crimea in this regard, see Kit De Vriese (n 3) and Stefan Lorenzmeier (n 3).

3.4.1 Moving Treaty-Frontiers Rule

Yet, the treaty could be applicable in line with the moving treaty-frontiers rule. Under this concept, which belongs to the corpus of customary law,[75] the territorial scope of a treaty is automatically extended to newly acquired territory from the acquisition onwards.[76] However, unlike the situation in Crimea, the Russian Federation did not acquire – legally or illegally – the territory of the Donbas. Further, this principle is only applicable in cases of a legal transfer of territory. Otherwise, the effects of the prohibition of the use of force as laid down in article 2(4) UN Charter would be compromised. As a result, the internationally accepted moving treaty-frontiers rule is not applicable for occupied territories such as the separatist areas in the Donbas.

3.4.2 *De Facto* Control

However, the treaty might be applied if the *de facto* control of Russia over the DNR and LNR suffices. For instance, with respect to the annexation of Crimea several arbitral tribunals and the Swiss Federal Tribunal held during set-aside proceedings that the 1998 BIT applied on the peninsula – without the necessity to decide on the legality of the annexation of Crimea into the territory of the Russian Federation – because of Russia's exercise of *de facto* control.[77] In essence, the Swiss Federal Tribunal ruled that Crimea was covered by the territorial scope of the Russian-Ukrainian BIT.[78] It reached this conclusion by relying on article 29 VCLT and, unconvincingly, the moving treaty-frontiers rule.[79]

Although the judgment of the Swiss Federal tribunal seems to be conclusive in light of its procedural rules, it is not paying enough regard to the international legal order. Its reasoning on the moving treaty-frontiers rule in particular neglects other international legal principles to the required extent and constitutes itself a breach of public international law. An application of the principle of *de facto* control over the Donbas territory would violate the territorial integrity of Ukraine, one of the cornerstones of the international legal order. The application of the doctrine of *de facto* control over a territory would

---

75 Kerstin von der Decken, 'Art. 29' in Kerstin Schmalenbach and Oliver Dörr (eds), *Vienna Convention on the Law of Treaties, A Commentary* (Springer, 2nd edn 2018) para 27.
76 Richard Happ and Sebastian Wuschka, '*Horror Vacui*: Or Why Investment Treaties Should Apply to Illegally Annexed Territories' (2016) 33 J Int'l Arb 245, 257.
77 See only Swiss Federal Tribunal, Judgment of 16 October 2018, 4A_396/2017 (2019) 17(2) German Arb J 93. An almost identical decision was rendered by the Swiss Federal Tribunal on the same day concerning a parallel decision of the same tribunal in the related case of *Stabil and other v Russia*.
78 ibid para 4.2.
79 ibid para 4.3.

disregard the international legal system and therefore cannot be upheld in the circumstances at hand. Otherwise, a different conclusion would constitute an indirect recognition of the illegal occupation. This can also be inferred from article 43 Hague Regulations, analysed below, which grants only temporary rights to the occupying power. Foremost, the occupying power has to respect the laws in force in the (occupied) country. Whether the term 'laws in force in the country' relates only to the existing legislation of the occupied territory at the time of occupation or also later enacted law is an additional unsettled aspect. International temporal law would speak in favour of the first strain as long as a different intention could be found by interpretation of the respective treaty norm, in our case article 43 Hague Regulations. Such an interpretation does not seem to be convincing given that otherwise the only partly occupied state would be in a position to change its national laws subsequently and the occupying state would be in a position to respect these laws.

3.4.3 Article 43 Hague Regulations

The application of article 43 Hague Regulations might lead to a different conclusion. Under this provision, in case

> the authority of the legitimate power having in fact passed into the hands of the occupant, the latter shall take all the measures in his power to restore and ensure, as far as possible, public order and safety, while respecting, unless absolutely prevented, the laws in force in the country.

The norm prescribes the occupant's obligations in the occupied territory[80] and shall fill in the temporary legal vacuum created by an occupation.[81] If the acts of occupation can be attributed to Russia, as argued here, the burden to fulfil the provision is upon Russia as well.

Interestingly, it can be argued that the 'the laws in force in the country' do encompass ratified bilateral investment treaties as well.[82] Following this argument, the 1998 Russian-Ukrainian BIT as part of Ukrainian law could be applied in the separatist areas of the Donbas. Additionally, the occupant only has to 'respect, unless absolutely prevented' the Ukrainian laws. First, this wording

---

80 Tobias Ackermann, 'Investments under Occupation' in Katia Fach Gómez, Anastasios Gourgourinis and Catherine Titi (eds), *International Investment Law and the Law of Armed Conflict* (Springer 2019) 71.
81 Benvenisti (n 29) 67.
82 In this respect especially Ofilio J Mayorga, 'Occupants, Beware of BITs: Applicability of Investment Treaties to Occupied Territories' (2016) 19 Pal YB Int'l L 136, 142.

establishes only an obligation of conduct, not one of result.[83] The occupant must only act in conformity with the standard of due diligence,[84] which is again qualified by military necessity. Secondly, and this is probably even more important, the dispute-settlement mechanism in the BIT, does not bind the occupying power which has only to respect the local laws. This term does in neither case establish the jurisdiction of an international arbitral tribunal. To that effect, the consent of Russia as the occupying power would be needed.[85]

From a legal point of view, subsuming BITs under the term 'laws in force in the country' does not come without problems. First, it would only be possible under a dynamic interpretation of the provision since, historically, the term does only encompass domestic laws.[86] A dynamic interpretation, in turn, is only possible if one can consider that the parties to a treaty have given their consent to such an interpretative approach. Whether a dynamic interpretation can be considered part of the object and purpose of article 43 Hague Regulations[87] has to be determined in line with the consent of the parties. However, this is more and more unlikely the older the respective treaty is, since the concept of dynamic interpretation is a rather novel one in international law and, as such, rather doubtful in the case of the 1907 Hague Regulations. It seems far more apt to conclude more recent treaties on the issue, as done with the Geneva Conventions and the Additional Protocols thereto. Thus, we would argue that BITs are not covered by the term 'laws in force in the country', while keeping in mind that both opinions lead to very similar practical consequences for aggrieved investors.

As a result, the situation in the separatist areas does neither fall within the territorial ambit of bilateral investment treaties, nor is article 43 Hague Regulations applicable for BITs. Even the concurring view does not lead to an enforceable right for foreign investors.

3.5 *The European Convention on Human Rights and Fundamental Freedoms*

Next, the ECHR could offer another avenue in the case of, *eg*, expropriations in the separatist territories of the Donbas.[88] The Russian Federation joined

---

83   *Armed Activities on the Territory of the Congo* (n 21) paras 178 et seq.
84   Ackermann (n 80) 77.
85   Conclusive: ibid, 77 et seq with further arguments. Opposite: Mayorga (n 81) 166 et seq.
86   Ackermann (n 80) 73.
87   In this vein Ackermann (n 80) 73.
88   To date, there are over 6500 pending applications before the ECtHR in connection with the events in Crimea and Eastern Ukraine. See ECtHR, Country Profile Russia, last

the Council of Europe on 28 February 1996, and ratified the Convention on 30 March 1998. Ukraine is also a member of the Council of Europe.

The relevant provision for present purposes is article 1 of the ECHR's Protocol no 1: 'Every natural or legal person is entitled to the peaceful enjoyment of his possessions'. Furthermore, also an invocation of articles 13 (right to an effective remedy) and 14 (prohibition of discrimination) of the ECHR seems possible. Thus, a case against Russia and / or Ukraine in front of the European Court of Human Rights (ECtHR) seems promising.

The ECHR's territorial scope is determined by its article 1. According to this provision, the Convention is applicable within the 'jurisdiction' of the contracting parties. The occupied territories of the Donbas area are still part of the territory of Ukraine and do fall within its jurisdiction in the meaning of article 1 ECHR.[89] However, in cases in which a state is prevented from exercising its authority in part of its territory, like Ukraine is in the Donbas region, its responsibility under the ECHR is limited to discharging positive obligations.[90] These include measures needed to re-establish control over the territory in question, as an expression of its jurisdiction, and measures to ensure respect for individual rights.[91] Under the first head, the state has a duty to assert or reassert its sovereignty over the territory and to refrain from any acts supporting the separatist regime.[92] Under the second head, the state must take judicial, political, or administrative measures to secure the applicant's individual rights.[93] Both obligations have not been violated by Ukraine and the acts of expropriation under the Convention do not fall within their jurisdiction.

Yet, one could also consider the separatist regions of the Donbas to fall within the jurisdiction of the Russian Federation. Like in the ECtHR's *Catan* case concerning Moldova and Transnistria,[94] Russia denies any responsibility for the acts of the DNR and LNR entities. In that case, the ECtHR held, first, that

---

updated February 2020, <https://echr.coe.int/Documents/CP_Russia_ENG.pdf> accessed 10 May 2020, 29.

89 *Sargsyan v Azerbaijan*, App no 40167/06 (ECtHR, 16 June 2015 [GC]) para 130; *Catan and Others v Moldova and Russia*, App no 43370/04 (ECtHR, 19 October 2012 [GC]) para 109.

90 *Sargsyan v Azerbaijan* (n 89) para 131; *Ilaşcu and others v Moldova and Russia*, App no 48787/99 (ECtHR, 8 July 2004, Merits and Just Satisfaction) para 335.

91 *Ilaşcu and others v Moldova and Russia* (n 90) para 339; *Sargsyan v Azerbaijan* (n 89) para 131.

92 *Ilaşcu and others v Moldova and Russia* (n 90) para 340; *Sargsyan v Azerbaijan* (n 89) para 131.

93 *Ilaşcu and others v Moldova and Russia* (n 90) para 346; *Sargsyan v Azerbaijan* (n 89) para 131.

94 *Catan and Others v Moldova and Russia* (n 89).

'jurisdiction' differs from the rules of state responsibility expressed by the ICJ in *Bosnia Genocide*.[95] It considered this requirement to be fulfilled by the Russian Federation's exercise of 'effective control' over the territory.[96] Unlike the rules on state responsibility, effective control for the establishment of jurisdiction means 'decisive influence', which can be deducted from the military, political and economic influence of a state over the separatist government.[97] Therefore, in the present case, the military support must be pivotal in preventing the Ukrainian army from regaining control over the separatist regions and the economic and political support has to be absolutely necessary for the survival of the DNR and LNR entities.[98] Neither the DNR nor the LNR are viable without the strong Russian support on all state levels. Additionally, Russia did not invoke article 15 ECHR so far, which limits the application of the Convention in times of an armed conflict. Thus, the Russian Federation is exercising 'decisive influence' and 'effective control' in the Donbas region and the committed expropriations are within its jurisdiction in the meaning of article 1 ECHR.[99]

Article 1(1)(2) of Protocol no 1 is the ECHR's protection of property and prescribes that 'no one shall be deprived of his possessions except in the public interest and subject to the conditions for by law and the general principles of international law'. Since any takings of property by the DNR and LNR regimes likely takes place without compensation of the expropriated natural or legal persons, the requirements of this provisions should be easily established. In such case, the ECtHR grants the private party just satisfaction under article 41 ECHR, which can lead to the full sum of the expropriation. However, the ECtHR's jurisprudence demonstrates a reluctance to award the full amount of damages as just satisfaction due to the court's approach to compensation.

Moreover, it has to be borne in mind that article 41 ECHR does not grant a legally enforceable title to the winning party of a case. It is only a statement of the ECtHR which sum would constitute a 'just satisfaction' in the circumstances of a case before it. Thus, even if Ukrainian companies would be entitled to receive just satisfaction, the enforcement of this could and likely would result in difficulties. According to article 46(1) ECHR, only the state party to a conflict

---

95 ibid para 115.
96 ibid para 116.
97 ibid para 122.
98 ibid paras 118 et seq.
99 Along the same line, the government of Ukraine has repeatedly stated in its proceedings against Russia before the ECtHR that Russia has exercised and continues to exercise overall control over Donetsk and Luhansk territories by controlling separatists and armed groups. See, *eg*, the statement of 17 February 2017, <www.kmu.gov.ua/ua/news/249734247> accessed 10 May 2020.

has to abide by the final judgment of the ECtHR, it is not enforceable in national courts of member states of the ECHR against Russia.[100] In sum, article 1 AP I to the ECHR could be an avenue for aggrieved investors to have recourse against expropriations in the separatist areas of the DNR and LNR, but it will likely be difficult for these investors to actually obtain 'just satisfaction' in the meaning of article 41 ECHR.

3.6   DNR / LNR – De Facto *Control?*

Insurgents and belligerents may also be considered as subjects of international law holding the effect that they are bound by the rules of international law with respect to the conduct of hostilities. This would mean the DNR and LNR respectively would be bound by the rules of the Hague Regulations themselves. Required is, however, that they are *de facto* administering a certain territory.[101] As pointed out above, it is in light of the Russian determining influence[102] rather doubtful – and not the view of the authors – whether the governments of the two republics are indeed in charge of the administration of the separatist territories and whether they are responsible for the expropriations of Ukrainian and foreign investors.

A different conclusion has to be drawn if two propositions are not given. First, if the facts point to the effective administration of the territory by the DNR and LNR respectively, which is not the view of the authors, and, secondly, if the concept of *de facto* control is accepted under customary international law, the two separatist republics would be legally responsible for the expropriations of non-DNR and non-LNR investors. In such a situation, the legal enforcement of a claim for foreign investors is even more burdensome than in the case of the attribution of the acts to the Russian Federation. Neither of the entities is a member of the Council of Europe and, therefore, a case cannot be brought to the ECtHR. The only international possibility would be an agreement between the investors and the respective separatist entity establishing an international arbitral tribunal. The applicable law could be, *eg*, the Hague Regulations. Yet, this seems to be an extremely hypothetical case, to say the least, given the lack of *de facto* control of the DNR and LNR.

---

100   Article 46(2) ECHR provides that the supervision of judgments is done by the Committee of Ministers of the Council of Europe, a mostly political body.
101   Shaw (n 7) 195 with further references.
102   See Council of Europe, Parliamentary Assembly, Resolution 2133 of 12 October 2016, no 5. Also, the decision of the ECtHR in *Khlebik v Ukraine*, App no 2945/16 (ECtHR, 25 July 2017), is pointing in this direction.

3.7 Interim Result

The part on international investment protection has clearly shown the legal issues associated with the illegal expropriations in the separatist areas of the Donbas region. The BIT between Ukraine and Russia or Russian BITs with other states are not applicable because the areas in question still fall within the sovereignty of Ukraine and do belong to its territory. Article 43 Hague Regulations, even if it is applicable in the situation of Ukraine, does also not grant a legally enforceable right to investors.

The second option, to invoke article 46 Hague Regulations due to the occupied status of the region, remains at least doubtful in light of the jurisprudence of the ICJ in the *Bosnia Genocide* case. According to this judgment, the acts of the DNR and LNR republics are not attributable to Russia. This chapter proposed a different reading of the rules on attribution, which is, however, not yet affirmed by an international tribunal.

Most promising for expropriated investors seems to be the third option, to bring a case in front of the ECtHR. In its jurisprudence, the ECtHR interpreted the applicability of the ECHR more extensively than the ICJ, also encompassing states enjoying 'decisive control' over a different territory. Yet, the just satisfaction granted by the ECtHR is complicated to enforce and does not always equate with the expropriated sum.

4 Conclusion

Effective investment protection in the occupied territories of the Donbas region is legally an extremely complicated task. Unlike the annexation of Crimea, Russia does not recognize overall control or even influence over the temporarily occupied territories of the Donetsk and Luhansk oblasts, so in the case of lost assets of foreign investors in the Donbas region a different approach has to be applied. Taking into account the publicly known information, we came to the conclusion that Russia exercises overall control over the occupied Donbas territory and the actions of the DNR and LNR, which are not attributable to Russia under the ASR, are attributable to Russia under article 42 of the Hague Regulations, since that provision's requirements of attribution differ from the norms of the ASR. Russia therefore must be regarded as an occupying power in the Donbas region.

This has a notable effect for the protection of foreign investments. Although the Ukrainian-Russian BIT is not applicable for the expropriations in the Donbas area and Ukrainian national law cannot effectively protect expropriated investors, two venues seems to be promising: Cases claiming a violation of international humanitarian law in front of an international court or tribunal or of article 1 of the ECHR's Protocol no 1 in front of the ECtHR could be brought forward. Yet, both fora show weaknesses. Russia would have to consent to the jurisdiction of an international court or tribunal, which seems rather unlikely. More promising seems to be to bring cases in front of the ECtHR, which unfortunately only grants 'just satisfaction' and not full compensation of an expropriated sum. Additionally, cases before the ECtHR also take some time, which may not speak in favour of the ECtHR as the proper forum.

On the national level, Ukraine has enacted several norms to protect investors. Yet, due to the lack of effective enforcement in the occupied territory, these legal provisions cannot tackle the issue at its roots. Moreover, Ukraine has already stated that it does not guarantee full and effective control and protection of investments in these territories.[103] The statement reaffirms Ukraine's position to equally exempt itself from BIT obligations.

In conclusion, the legal protection for foreign investors in the Donbas is far weaker than in annexed Crimea. The risks for achieving a full compensation of the expropriated sums are greater and the process as such is far more burdensome and lengthy.

Note on the Text

This research has been sponsored by the Alexander von Humboldt Foundation in the framework of the Research Group Linkage Programme funded by the German Federal Ministry of Education and Research and the German Academic Exchange Program respectively.

Bibliography

Ackermann T, 'Investments under Occupation' in K Fach Gómez, A Gourgourinis and C Titi (eds), *International Investment Law and the Law of Armed Conflict* (Springer 2019).

Beigbeder Y, 'Referendum', *Max Planck Encyclopedia of Public International Law* (2011) <https://opil.ouplaw.com/home/MPIL> accessed 10 May 2020.

Benvenisti E, *The International Law of Occupation* (OUP 1993).

---

103 President of Ukraine, Statement during the ratification of the Additional Protocol on Amendments to the Agreement between the Government of Ukraine and the Government of the Republic of Croatia (n 36).

Cassese A, 'The *Nicaragua* and *Tadić* Tests Revisited in Light of the ICJ Judgment on Genocide in Bosnia' (2007) 18 EJIL 651.

Condorelli L and C Kress, 'The Rules of Attribution: General Considerations' in J Crawford, A Pellet, and S Olleson (eds), *The Law of International State Responsibility* (OUP 2010).

ECtHR, Country Profile Russia, (last updated February 2020) <https://echr.coe.int/Documents/CP_Russia_ENG.pdf> accessed 10 May 2020.

Eyal Benvenisti, 'Occupation, Belligerent' *Max Planck Encyclopedia of Public International Law* (2009) <https://opil.ouplaw.com/home/MPIL> accessed 10 May 2020.

Fischer S, 'The Donbas Conflict, Opposing Interests and Narratives, Difficult Peace Process', SWP Research Paper 5 (April 2019).

German Advisory Group Ukraine, 'The Effect of Company Seizures and The effect of company seizures and trade suspension in Donbas Trade Suspension in Donbas', Newsletter no 106 (August 2017), <www.beratergruppe-ukraine.de/wordpress/wp-content/uploads/2017/08/Newsletter_106_2017_German-Advisory-Group.pdf> accessed 10 May 2020.

Happ R and S Wuschka, '*Horror Vacui*: Or Why Investment Treaties Should Apply to Illegally Annexed Territories' (2016) 33 J Int'l Arb 245.

Harzl B, 'Passportizatsiya revisited: Extraterritorial naturalization in the case of Abkhazia and South Ossetia' in B Harzl and R Petrov (ed), *Non-Recognised Entities in International and EU Law* (Brill 2021, forthcoming).

Hernández GI, 'Territorial Change, Effects Of', *Max Planck Encyclopedia of Public International Law* (2010) <https://opil.ouplaw.com/home/MPIL> accessed 10 May 2020.

Lorenzmeier S, 'Investment Disputes in the Annexed Crimea from the Perspective of International Law' in B Harzl and R Petrov (ed), *Non-Recognised Entities in International and EU Law* (Brill 2021, forthcoming).

Mayorga OJ, 'Occupants, Beware of BITs: Applicability of Investment Treaties to Occupied Territories' (2016) 19 Pal YB Int'l L 136.

OSCE Special Monitoring Mission to Ukraine, <www.osce.org/ukraine-smm/reports> accessed 10 May 2020.

Petrov R, 'Legal systems of Donetsk/Luhansk People's Republics and their status under international and European Law' in B Harzl and R Petrov (eds), *Non-Recognised Entities in International and EU Law* (Brill 2021, forthcoming).

President of Russia, 'Laws on admitting Crimea and Sevastopol to the Russian Federation' (Press Release, 21 March 2014) <http://en.kremlin.ru/acts/news/20625> accessed 10 May 2020.

President of Ukraine, Statement during the ratification of the Additional Protocol on Amendments to the Agreement between the Government of Ukraine and the Government of the Republic of Croatia, 4 October 2017 <https://zakon.rada.gov.ua/laws/show/2151-19/sp:max100?sp=:max100&lang=uk> accessed 10 May 2020.

Scherpf G and N Kondrashov, 'Investment Protection and Arbitration in the CIS Region' (2020) 18 German Arb J 8.

Schreuer C, 'War and Peace in International Investment Law', in K Fach Gómez, A Gourgourinis, and C Titi (eds), *International Investment Law and the Law of Armed Conflict* (Springer 2019).

Shaw M, *International Law* (8th ed CUP 2017).

Thürer D and T Burri, 'Self-Determination', *Max Planck Encyclopedia of Public International Law* (2008) <https://opil.ouplaw.com/home/MPIL> accessed 10 May 2020.

Ukrainian Helsinki Human Rights Union, Report 'War and Human Rights' (2015), <https://helsinki.org.ua/files/docs/1439184931.pdf> accessed 10 May 2020.

Vidmar J, 'The Annexation of Crimea and the Boundaries of the Will of the People' (2015) 16 German LJ 365.

von der Decken K, 'Art. 29' in Kerstin Schmalenbach and Oliver Dörr (eds), *Vienna Convention on the Law of Treaties, A Commentary* (Springer, 2nd edn 2018).

Wilde R, 'Kosovo (Advisory Opinion)', *Max Planck Encyclopedia of Public International Law* (2011) <https://opil.ouplaw.com/home/MPIL> accessed 10 May 2020.

CHAPTER 14

International Investment Law in the Context of State Fragility: Full Protection and Security and Fair and Equitable Treatment

Johanna Baumann

1   Introduction

International investment law assumes functioning statehood. An effective government, administration, and court system as well as a stable economy are vital to allow foreign investments to prosper. At the same time, they are indispensable conditions for the implementation of guarantees given by states through their conclusion of investment treaties. A functioning police apparatus, for example, is needed to accord foreign investors, just as any other citizen or company in the country, with protection. And an effective administration, as another example, is required to ensure foreign investors to conduct their businesses without arbitrary interferences by the state. Yet, what happens if this basic assumption of a functioning host state is disturbed? The issue of what is called state fragility is not a problem that international investment law addresses directly. Even general international law has its focus primarily on the question of emergence and dissolution of states. Development, changes or even temporary lack of statehood, in contrast, have not as often been subjects of intense discussion.[1]

Although the expression 'fragile state' has first been introduced in the early 1990s, the term has ever since been mainly discussed in a political science context. International law, including international investment law, has not dealt with state fragility in a comparable way. Overall, international investment law deals only to a limited extent with certain aspects that may become relevant in connection with and during an investment relationship. There are many matters that are not regulated in investment treaties, such as remedies, treaty interpretation, contract succession or defences. The same

---

1   Zaryab Iqbal and Harvey Starr, *State Failure in the Modern World* (Stanford University Press 2015) 14; Mohammed Nuruzzaman, 'Revisiting the Category of Fragile and Failed States in International Relations' (2009) 46 Int'l Stud 271, 272.

applies to the subject of state fragility and its accompanying problem areas. Even though the scope of investment agreements of the new generation has increased significantly,[2] not all aspects of the investment relationship are touched upon despite its long-term character. During the time period of an investment relationship, significant changes in relation to both the foreign investor and the host state can occur. Regarding the host state, limitations on its statehood could emerge, eventually resulting in its fragility. State fragility, on the one hand, and armed conflicts, on the other, often accompany each other. Ineffective government and, thus, a state being incapable to perform its functions present an ideal basis for violence and aggression. At the same time, existing armed conflicts are reasons of internal instability that can ultimately promote state fragility.

Despite the numerous unregulated issues in international investment law, international investment law and state fragility have a correlation: While international investment law attempts to protect an investment against possibly emerging political risks,[3] political risks are realised in a fragile state in a particularly pronounced manner.

This chapter deals with the impact of state fragility on protection standards of international investment law. In its first part, the chapter examines the main characteristic of fragile states – ineffective power of the state. It also analyses the relevant manifestations of state fragility – namely failing states and failed states (section 2). In its second part, the chapter focuses on the effects of state fragility on the protection standards fair and equitable treatment (FET) and full protection and security (FPS) (section 3). As to the impact on these protection standards, a distinction is made between failing states and failed states. In relation to FET, the chapter examines whether, in view of the fragility of a host state, legitimate expectations of a foreign investor are to be relativized. In this regard, the fact that state fragility is a sliding scale is relevant so that the development from failed state to failing state and from stable state to failing state must be given attention. With respect to FPS, the chapter, at first, examines how the due diligence required from a host state is to be understood and, based thereon, whether and how due diligence is met in a fragile state.

---

2 *Eg* the USA Model BIT: while the USA Model BIT of 1984 roughly had a volume of eight pages, the USA Model BIT of 2012 already has a volume of 42 pages. Nevertheless, many relevant aspects remain unaddressed.
3 In the context of this paper, the term 'political risks' not only includes political risks as such but also economic and security risks, see section 2.2 below.

2 Characteristics and Manifestations of State Fragility Relevant in the Context of International Investment Law

State fragility is the generic term for states with structures and institutions that are marked by massive shortcomings regarding their core responsibilities and functions. The term represents a sliding scale of states that show characteristics of fragility. The problem of state fragility manifests itself in various ways. It affects all aspects of a state so that it has impacts at the level of economy and governance on the one hand, and at the level of the nation state on the other.[4] Within these levels, several characteristics associated with fragile states can be identified. Each of them exists in different forms and to different extents in states affected by state fragility.[5] However, it is the characteristic of ineffective government that is relevant in the context of international law. Although the respective manifestation of this characteristic is strongly dependent on the individual case, making it a variable scenario,[6] this does not alter the fact that ineffective government is inherent to all scenarios of state fragility.[7] The variations of state fragility with different degrees of ineffective government are *failed* states and *failing* states. States that are currently classified as fragile state are, on the one hand, Somalia as an example for a failed state and, on the other hand, Libya as an example for a failing state:

For more than two decades, Somalia has been known as the failed state *par excellence*. Since the Somali civil war in 1991, there has been no state authority in the territory of the former Democratic Republic of Somalia exercising control over the entire territory. Instead, various groups exercise and claim control over certain parts of Somalia (*eg* Somaliland and Puntland). The fragmentation of territorial sovereignty results in state power not being effectively

---

4 Lothar Brock and others, *Fragile States* (Polity Press 2012) 159; *cf* Gerard Kreijen, *State Failure, Sovereignty and Effectiveness: Legal Lessons from the Decolonization of Sub-Saharan Africa* (Brill Nijhoff 2004) 86 et seq.

5 Yasmine Shamsie and Andrew Thompson, *Haiti: Hope for a Fragile State* (Wilfrid Laurier UP 2006) 3; *cf* David Carment, Stewart Prest, and Yiagadeesen Samy, *Security, Development and the Fragile State* (Routledge 2010) 7; these characteristics include, *inter alia*, low economic performance, the existence of pronounced militarism and the exercise of state power primarily by the elite.

6 Neyire Akpinarli, *The Fragility of the Failed State Paradigm: A Different International Law Perception of the Absence of Effective Government* (Brill Nijhoff 2010) 97; *cf* Carment, Prest and Samy (n 5) 4 et seq.

7 For example, especially Turkey respectively Turkish investors have been investing in Somalia for several years, but a BIT signed between the two states on 1 June 2016 has still not entered into force – due to the lack of ratification caused by Somalia's ineffective government and thus, leaving investors without any investment treaty protection.

exercised by the internationally recognised government of the Federal Republic of Somalia. Consequently, it is obvious in the case of Somalia that overall ineffective government exists which is the main characteristic of a failed state. This is intensified by the fact that public order within Somalia is not maintained throughout the state but is in part characterised by considerable violence and disorganisation. Furthermore, the international exercise of state power is primarily characterised by ineffectiveness so that international rights and obligations are not met.[8]

Since the Arab Spring in 2011, Libya is scarred by national conflicts and the existence of two rival governments in the east and west of its territory. Nevertheless, Libya still shows a sufficient level of effectively exercised state power – despite the use of violence in connection with the revolutionary aspirations of the Arab Spring and the shift in its domestic political situation following the events of 2011.[9] The internationally recognised government in Tripoli does not exercise effective control over the entire territory and the state is struggling with civil war in some of its regions. However, economic performance – especially within the public oil sector – still takes place and basic state functions are exercised.[10] Libya is therefore still to be classified as a failing state – at least for the time being as its domestic situation seems to be worsening.

2.1 *Ineffective Government*

State power in a fragile state is characterised by the fact that it is no longer exercised effectively.[11] The main features of ineffective government are the lack

---

8   For a closer look at the situation in Somalia, see Deutsche Gesellschaft für Internationale Zusammenarbeit, 'Somalia' (2020) <www.giz.de/en/worldwide/33495.html> accessed 20 March 2020.

9   As a consequence of the events in Libya following the Arab Spring in 2011, a large number of investment arbitration proceedings have been initiated against Libya most of which are still pending, *eg, Etrak İnşaat Taahut ve Ticaret Anonim Sirketi v Libya* (ICC Arbitration); *Güriş İnşaat ve Mühendislik AŞ v Libya* (ICC Arbitration); *DS Construction FZCO v Libya*, PCA Case no 2017–21. See, in relation to the associated question of the representation of states in investment arbitrations involving competing claims to govern the country, see Réka A Papp, chapter 8 in this volume, 264–269.

10   For a closer look at Libya's situation, see Deutsche Gesellschaft für Internationale Zusammenarbeit, 'Libya' (2020) <www.giz.de/en/worldwide/69197.html> accessed 20 March 2020.

11   This does not correspond to the requirement of effectively exercised state power according to the definition of a state under international law, according to which it is necessary that a state has a state population, state territory and effective state power exercised by a government.

of exercise of state functions and, consequently, the exercise of power by private individuals instead of state institutions.

2.1.1 Lack of Exercise of State Functions

A characteristic feature of the ineffectiveness of state power is that state institutions, such as the administrative apparatus, are no longer intact. Basic state functions also include the establishment and maintenance of an education and health system as well as an economic and structural infrastructure within the national territory.[12] The applicable law can no longer be enforced[13] which is the defining criterion for the effectiveness of a government. Another consequence of the erosion of state power is that, due to the absence of effective state institutions, the basic functions of the state, such as the sustained provision of security, order and legal protection, can no longer be guaranteed.[14] Furthermore, political goods to be provided by a state, including the existence of political structures and a banking system, are no longer fully ensured.[15]

2.1.2 Exercise of Power by Private Individuals

The deficiency in a fragile state caused by the ineffectiveness of state power is partly overcome by the fact that private actors increasingly step to the fore and act instead of state institutions,[16] leading to a 'privatization of the state'.[17] As a result, the use of violence by both state and private actors as well as the intensity of violence may increase steadily as the two sides act against each other.[18] This also results in considerable conflict and chaos within the fragile state which can ultimately lead to a worsening of the situation. If no *de facto* government is given in such an exercise of power by private individuals, such

---

12 Chiara Giorgetti, *A Principled Approach to State Failure – International Community Actions in Emergency Situations* (Brill Nijhoff 2010) 43; *cf* Akpinarli (n 6) 11 et seq.
13 Giorgetti (n 12) 43.
14 Akpinarli (n 6) 11; Giorgetti (n 12) 43; *cf* Daniel Thürer, 'Der Wegfall effektiver Staatsgewalt: "The Failed State"' in Daniel Thürer, Matthias Herdegen, and Gerhard Hohloch (eds), *Der Wegfall effektiver Staatsgewalt: The Failed State* (CF Müller 1995) 12.
15 Giorgetti (n 12) 43; *cf* Robert Rotberg, 'The Failure and Collapse of Nation-States' in Robert Rotberg (ed), *When States Fail* (Princeton University Press 2003) 11.
16 Robin Geiß, *Failed State* (Duncker & Humblot 2005) 45; Pietro Pustorino, 'Failed States and International Law: The Impact of UN Practice on Somalia in Respect of Fundamental Rules of International Law' (2010) 53 German YB Int'l L 727.
17 Thürer (n 14) 12.
18 Chiara Giorgetti, 'Why Should International Law be Concerned About State Failure' (2010) 16 ILSA J Int'l L 469; Thürer (n 14) 12.

private acts are attributed to the host state. It incurs legal responsibility for such acts pursuant to article 9 of the ILC Articles on State Responsibility.[19]

2.2 Political Risks

State fragility is closely linked to the realisation of political risks in a host state. Although it lacks a generally accecpted definition, the conceptual notion of the term 'political risks' includes the occurrence of unwanted repercussions of political activities.[20] They are unwanted since they constitute interferences with a foreign investment by the respective host state that adversely affect such investments.[21] Such interferences can consist of instability or violence in a host country, or barriers imposed by the government of a host country, such as discriminatory taxation.[22] They encompass not only political risks as such, *eg* the change of political directions, but also economic and security aspects such as the existence of riots.[23]

According to the Multilateral Investment Guarantee Agency (MIGA), political risks rank second place among possible constraints to foreign investments, especially in developing countries.[24] As mostly developing countries belong to states being affected by state fragility,[25] political risks and their realisation are particularly relevant in this regard.

2.3 Manifestations of State Fragility

It has already been mentioned above that there are two manifestations of state fragility: *failed* states and *failing* states. Both manifestations reflect different degrees of state fragility. In particular regarding the characteristic of ineffective

---

19 If private acts constitute a general *de facto* government, it replaces the relevant (former) state organs. Acts of a *de facto* government are not encompassed by article 9, but by article 4 of the ILC Articles on State Responsibility; *cf* ILC, 'Report of the International Law Commission on the Work of its 53rd Session' UN Doc A/56/10 (2001) 110.

20 Kaj Hobér and Joshua Fellenbaum, 'Political Risk Insurance and Investment Treaty Protection' in Marc Bungenberg and others (eds), *International Investment Law: A Handbook* (CH Beck, Hart, and Nomos 2015) 1519; Stephen Kobrin, 'Political Risk; A Review and Reconsideration' (1979) 10 J Int'l Business Stud 67.

21 Molly Zohn, 'Filling the Void; International Legal Structures and Political Risk in Investment' (2007) 31 Fordham Int'l L J 230.

22 *Cf* Kobrin (n 20) 67.

23 *Cf* Hobér and Fellenbaum (n20) 1519; Kobrin (n 20) 67.

24 Multilateral Investment Guarantee Agency, *World Investment and Political Risk 2013* (2013) 18.

25 See oecd, *States of Fragility 2018* (oecd 2018) <www.oecd.org/dac/states-of-fragility-2018-9789264302075-en.htm> accessed 20 March 2020.

government, there are considerable differences between these two manifestations that have to be described in more detail.

2.3.1 Failed State

For a failed state, the decisive characteristic is that there has been a complete loss of effective state power.[26] In such a case, none of the three powers of the state – the executive, the judiciary and the legislative branch – are fully functioning which results in a power vacuum.[27] This power vacuum can be replaced by an order created by non-state actors which, however, may be based primarily on violence and oppression.[28] When the orderly organisational structure of the state and the associated state monopoly on the use of power have almost completely disappeared, there is no longer an effective exercise of state power and the relevant state can be classified as a failed state.[29] This means that none of the above-mentioned essential functions of a state are still present in any meaningful way. It exists a complete downfall of statehood.[30] Yet, since international law assumes the continuity of states, the consequence for a state affected by such extensive fragility is not the loss of its quality as a state.[31] The rationale of the continuity principle is that, firstly, the obligations of a state under international law should be maintained for as long as possible as otherwise they would cease to exist. Secondly, the development of a vacuum should be avoided as it provides potential for annexation.

State failure not only involves a lack of exercise of governmental functions. It affects the state structures in their entirety, including the government itself.[32] Due to its lack of effective state power, a failed state is incapable of fulfilling even the basic functions of a state.[33] As a result, not only the population of the affected state suffers from the consequences, but also its international partners, since its ability to fulfil international and national obligations is highly disrupted.[34] Nevertheless it cannot be assumed that a failed state is unwilling to fulfil these functions.[35] Rather, due to the inoperative and (in

---

26 Robin Geiß, 'Failed States: Legal Aspects and Security Implications' (2004) 47 German YB Int'l L 457; Iqbal and Starr (n 1) 20.
27 Geiß, *Failed State* (n 16) 45.
28 *Cf* Geiß, 'Failed States: Legal Aspects and Security Implications' (n 26) 457.
29 Geiß, *Failed State* (n 16) 55 et seq; Thürer (n 14) 12.
30 Geiß, 'Failed States: Legal Aspects and Security Implications' (n 26) 467.
31 James Crawford, *The Creation of States in International Law* (2nd edn, OUP 2007) 678 et seq.
32 Giorgetti (n 12) 44.
33 Geiß, 'Failed States: Legal Aspects and Security Implications' (n 26) 467; Kreijen (n 2) 97.
34 Giorgetti (n 12) 44; Thürer (n 14) 12 et seq.
35 Giorgetti (n 12) 44; *cf* Akpinarli (n 6) 14.

most parts) missing state organs, there is hardly any possibility for the failed state to effectively meet its actual functions and obligations.[36] This leaves the question open whether a failed state can actually breach its international legal obligations since a failed state is unable to act. However, under certain circumstances, attribution of private acts to the failed state according to the rules of attribution as stipulated in Chapter II of the ILC Articles on State Resonsibility may be possible as the failed state continues to exist as a legal entity.

2.3.2 Failing State

In contrast to the failed state, the state power of a failing state is merely partially ineffective.[37] This partial ineffectiveness lies either in the partly collapse of a state's (*de jure*) sovereign power or in the loss of a state's (*de facto*) sovereignty in a part of its state territory.[38] The state power in a failing state is affected by a crisis in such a way that it is not always in a position to easily perform all of its tasks and obligations. State power is not fully effective and – with respect to the territory affected, *eg* by armed conflict – failing states are states in which the state's monopoly on the use of force and the guarantee of security may be restricted. Depending on the degree to which the organs are affected by the state's ineffectiveness, there may also be corresponding restrictions leading to non-fulfilment of state functions and obligations.

3 Full Protection and Security and Fair and Equitable Treatment in the Context of State Fragility

In a state marked by fragility, the effective power does not exist either wholly or to a partial extent and political risks are realised. Consequently, not only the executive and judicial powers but also the legislature is severely affected. This in turn has various effects not only on the national but also on the international level: Treaties are not adhered to and obligations are not fulfilled. With respect to international investment law, the protection standards of FET and FPS are the most relevant ones in the context of state fragility. This is not only because almost every investment treaty contains these protection standards and also

---

36 Geiß, 'Failed States: Legal Aspects and Security Implications' (n 26) 467; Pustorino (n 16) 727.
37 Pustorino (n 16) 728; *cf* Riikka Koskenmäki, 'Legal Implications Resulting from State Failure in Light of the Case of Somalia' (2004) 73 Nordic J Int'l L 1, 5.
38 Pustorino (n 16) 728.

foreign investors invoke these standards the most.[39] As will be outlined below, they also create obligations to act or to conduct themselves in a particular way, the performance of which might be impacted in a state of fragility. These possible effects fragility can have on the compliance with international investment law are outlined in the following by reference to both FET and FPS.

3.1 The Standards' Content

Prior to discussing the effects of state fragility on the protection standards of FET and FPS, the content of these protection standards will be briefly summarised.

3.1.1 Fair and Equitable Treatment

The classic understanding of the scope of the standard of fair and equitable treatment is to protect a foreign investor from any action by the host state that is arbitrary, grossly unfair, unjustified, discriminatory or lacks due process.[40] However, this understanding no longer prevails today; rather, a broad interpretation of the clause is applied.[41] The provision is understood to mean that treatment according to fair and equitable standards cannot be separated from stable and predictable business conditions in the host state.[42] What ultimately matters are the foreign investor's legitimate expectations; if these are frustrated, this is a violation of the standard of fair and equitable treatment.[43] For the expectations of a foreign investor to be given and, above all, to be legitimate, the host state must have created an act of trust as their basis.[44] The

---

39   Dolzer and Schreuer (n 42) 130, 160 et seq; Christoph Schreuer, 'Fair and Equitable Treatment' (2005) 6 JWIT 357. According to UNCTAD statistics, FPS has been invoked by foreign investors in 230 different investment treaty arbitrations since 2000. FET has even been invoked in more than 460 investment treaty arbitrations since 2000. For more data, see UNCTAD, 'Investment Dispute Settlement Navigator' (*Investment Policy Hub*, 2020) <http://investmentpolicyhub.unctad.org/ISDS/AdvancedSearch> accessed 20 March 2020.

40   *Waste Management, Inc v Mexico*, ICSID Case no ARB(AF)/00/3, Award (30 April 2004) para 98; Surya Subedi, *International Investment Law: Reconciling Policy and Principle* (3rd edn, Hart 2016) 214.

41   Andrea Schernbeck, *Der Fair and Equitable Treatment Standard in internationalen Investitionsschutzabkommen* (Nomos 2013) 20; Subedi (n 40) 213.

42   *CMS Gas Transmission Co v Argentina*, ICSID Case no ARB/01/8, Award (12 May 2005) para 276; *Técnicas Medioambientales Tecmed, SA v Mexico*, ICSID Case no ARB(AF)/00/2, Award (29 May 2003) para 154; Rudolf Dolzer and Christoph Schreuer, *Principles of International Investment Law* (2nd edn, OUP 2012) 145.

43   *Tecmed v Mexico* (n 42) para 154.

44   Dolzer and Schreuer (n 42) 145; Schernbeck (n 41) et seq.

expectations are based on the legal framework in force in the host state and on all explicit or implicit representations by the host state.[45] Host states have the duty to ensure a certain stability as well as a calculable business environment for foreign investors by, among other things, creating a transparent and stable legal framework.[46]

3.1.2 Full Protection and Security

In contrast to other protection standards under international investment agreements that primarily relate to the state's duties to omit certain conduct, FPS provides that a host state shall actively take measures to safeguard a foreign investment.[47] FPS clauses require a host state to actively protect a foreign investment from negative impacts by third parties but also by itself.[48] This refers to such impairments which can either be attributed to the host state directly, for example an active intervention by the armed forces of the host state,[49] or are attributed to it indirectly, being the result of omissions on the host state's part to prevent damage to foreign investments by third parties.[50] The protection to be provided under this clause concerns physical protection of a foreign investment.[51] It does not require a host state to actually succeed in taking the measure and does not provide an absolute guarantee from the host state that it will protect the foreign investor from any harm.[52] In fact, a host state is merely obliged to exercise due diligence in this regard.[53] Furthermore, FPS does not protect a foreign investor against a state's exercise of its right to legislate or regulate in a manner which may negatively affect an investment, as

---

45 Dolzer and Schreuer (n 42) 145.
46 *Olin Holdings Ltd v Libya*, ICC Case no 20355/MCP, Final Award (25 May 2018) para 311.
47 Heather L Bray, 'SOI – Save Our Investments: International Investment Law and International Humanitarian Law' (2013) 14 JWIT 578, 583; Dolzer and Schreuer (n 42) 162.
48 Eric De Brabandere, 'Host States' Due Diligence Obligations in International Investment Law' (2015) 42 Syracuse J Int'l L & Com 319, 332; Christoph Schreuer, 'Full Protection and Security' (2010) 1 JIDS 353.
49 *Asian Agricultural Products Ltd (AAPL) v Sri Lanka*, ICSID Case no ARB/87/3, Final Award (27 June 1990) para 67; Jeswald W Salacuse and Nicholas Sullivan, 'Do BITs Really Work? An Evaluation of Bilateral Investment Treaties and Their Grand Bargain' (2005) 46 Harv Int'l L J 67, 83.
50 *American Manufacturing & Trading Inc v Zaire*, ICSID Case no ARB/93/1, Award (21 February 1997) para 6.08; Dolzer and Schreuer (n 42) 162.
51 *Saluka Investments BV v Czech Republic*, Partial Award (17 March 2006) para 483; De Brabandere (n 48) 332; cf *Tecmed v Mexico* (n 42) paras 175 et seq. See, however, Emily Sipiorski, chapter 3 in this volume, 102–103.
52 However, this is the legal opinion in *AAPL v Sri Lanka* (n 49) para 26.
53 How due diligence in the context of FPS is to be understood, especially in relation to state fragility, will be shown in section 3.2.2.1 below.

long as the host state acts reasonably and with the intent to serve an objectively rational public interest.[54]

3.2 Effects of State Fragility on Compliance with FET and FPS Standards

As will have become clear by these brief descriptions of the standards' contents, both the FET and the FPS standard impose a set of obligations on host states and are, thus, closely related to the host state's ability act. As fragile states are restricted or unable to act and to abide by their legal obligations, the effects of state fragility are particularly evident under the protection standards of FET and FPS. In the case of FPS, this is because the standard requires the host state to take active measures to protect a foreign investor from adverse effects. A fragile state, especially a failed state, lacks the capacity to act and thus, may not be able to take any action to protect foreign investors. Regarding FET, its particular relevance in connection with fragile states is first of all based on the fact that the clause has a broad scope of application.[55] In addition, by also protecting a foreign investor's legitimate expectations, FET refers to a due exercise of state power by a host state – something which might be lacking in a fragile state.

3.2.1 Fair and Equitable Treatment

The determination of a violation of the standard of FET in the scenario of state fragility requires an examination of the specific circumstances of the individual case. In particular with respect to the protection of legitimate expectations of a foreign investor, it is necessary for a violation of FET that the foreign investors' expectations regarding the circumstances of their investment in the host state, which are ultimately frustrated, are based on an established act of trust by the host state. In this regard, also the conditions in the host state are crucial, since they form an integral part of the basis of the investor's expectations.[56] It is therefore essential to examine whether – under the conditions of state fragility with its two main manifestations, failing state and failed state – foreign

---

54 The question whether FPS also includes legal protection is highly disputed; tribunals denying legal protection under FPS: *AES Summit Generation Ltd and AES-Tisza Erömü Kft v Hungary*, ICSID Case no ARB/07/22, Award (23 September 2010) para 13.3.2.; *Suez, Sociedad General de Aguas de Barcelona, SA and Vivendi Universal SA v Argentina*, ICSID Case no ARB/03/19, Decision on Liability (30 July 2010) paras 158 et seq; tribunals having the view that legal protection is included in FPS: *Siemens AG v Argentina*, ICSID Case no ARB/02/8, Award (17 January 2007) para 303; *Sempra Energy International v Argentina*, ICSID Case no ARB/02/16, Award (28 September 2007) para 323.
55 Dolzer and Schreuer (n 42) 130, 132.
56 Cf *Bayindir Insaat Turizm Ticaret Ve Sanayi AS v Pakistan*, ICSID Case no ARB/03/29, Award (27 August 2009) para 197.

investors' expectations can be legitimate at all. As 'the dominant element'[57] of FET, legitimate expectations are the sole focus of the following discussion.

When speaking of an investor's legitmate expectations, these expectations refer to a legal and administrative environment that is both predictable and stable and which is characterised by transparency and consistency.[58] This element of the FET standard protects an investor's expectations, among others, concerning the state's adherence to due process and fair principles during its decision making processes.[59] It also encompasses the protection of expectations regarding the benefits of existing economic rights that form an essential component of an investment.[60] Expectations are legitimate and protected, if the host state has created an element of trust on which the expectations of the foreign investor are ultimately based upon.

In the context of fragility, it has to be assessed whether expectations of a foreign investor can be legitimate and if so, whether their frustration can constitute a violation the standard of FET.

3.2.1.1 Relativisation of Legitimate Expectations

The exact content of the standard of FET depends on the circumstances of the particular case.[61] The prevailing political, socio-economic, cultural and historical conditions in the host states are important elements to consider.[62] Whether a possible crisis-prone status quo of the host state also should be taken into account and could then lead to a relativisation of the legitimacy of the expectations is a different matter.[63] This is especially true since the standard of FET is an absolute standard of protection.[64]

---

57 *Saluka v Czech Republic* (n 51) para 302.
58 *Tecmed v Mexico* (n 42) para 154; *EnCana Corp v Ecuador*, LCIA Case no UN3481, Award (3 February 2006) para 158; Andrew Newcombe and Lluis Paradell, *Law and Practice of Investment Treaties: Standards of Treatment* (Wolters Kluwer 2009) 280.
59 Newcombe and Paradell (n 58) 280.
60 ibid 280.
61 *Noble Ventures, Inc v Romania*, ICSID Case no ARB/01/11, Award (12 October 2005) para 181; *Waste Management, Inc v Mexico* (n 40) para 99.
62 *Duke Energy Electroquil Partners & Electroquil SA v Ecuador*, ICSID Case no ARB/04/19, Award (16 August 2008) para 340; *cf Generation Ukraine, Inc v Ukraine*, ICSID Case no ARB/00/9, Award (16 September 2003) para 20.37.
63 Nick Gallus, 'The Influence of the Host State's Level of Development on International Investment Treaty Standards of Protection' (2005) 6 JWIT 711, 715 et seq; Ursula Kriebaum, 'Are Investment Treaty Standards Flexible Enough to Meet the Needs of Developing Countries?' in Freya Baetens (ed), *Investment Law Within International Law* (CUP 2016) 334 et seq.
64 Gallus (n 63) 712.

There is a notable tension: On the one hand, the expectations a foreign investor has at the time of making an investment must be protected from unforeseen changes.[65] On the other hand, it must be possible for the host state to respond to changed conditions and to take any necessary measures in this regard. A foreign investor cannot expect a host state to refrain from any regulatory acts. In this respect, FET and in particular the protection of the investor's legitimate expectations serve to balance these two aspects and to solve the aforementioned tension.[66] It can therefore be assumed that the legitimacy of the expectations of a foreign investor depends on the given circumstances of the individual case and thus, is relative.[67] This is particularly true in the case of political instability and unrest within a host state. Due to the foreign investor's own duty to exercise due diligence,[68] a foreign investor must be aware of the economic, political and social situation of the host state.[69] The expectations of a foreign investor of an unrestricted functioning of the organs of the host state and a full granting of legal security cannot be regarded as legitimate in a host state situation marked by instability.[70]

State fragility is not a phenomenon that occurs suddenly, but which becomes apparent in advance through certain characteristics. In this context, the time

---

65 André von Walter, 'The Investor's Expectations in International Investment Arbitration' in August Reinisch and Christina Knahr (eds), *International Investment Law in Context* (Eleven International Publishing 2008) 173, 175.

66 *Saluka v Czech Republic* (n 51) para 305; Kriebaum (n 63) 339.

67 Gallus (n 63) 714; see also arbitration practice which shows that the legitimate expectations of a foreign investor vary in every country; *MTD Equity Sdn. Bhd. and MTD Chile SA v Chile*, ICSID Case no ARB/01/7, Award (25 May 2004) paras 114 et seq; *Generation Ukraine, Inc v Ukraine* (n 62) para 20.37; *Metalclad Corp v Mexico*, ICSID Case no ARB(AF)/97/1, Award (30 August 2000) para 99. Furthermore, a recognition of the level of development as well as the system differences of the contracting states involved have been explicitly included within the framework of FET of COMESA's investment protection agreement, so that article 14(3) of the agreement states: '[...] Member States understand that different Member States have different forms of administrative, legislative and judicial systems and that Member States at different levels of development may not achieve the same standards at the same time [...]'.

68 As in each investment project, a potential investor must conduct – in their own interest – a comprehensive due diligence investigation in relation to the potential risks concerning the planned investment project.

69 Matthäus Fink, 'Grenzen des arabischen Wandels aufgrund von Investitionsschutzrecht? Betrachtungen anhand der Situation in Ägypten und Libyen' (2012) 72 Heidelberg J Int'l L 483, 511; cf *Bayindir v Pakistan* (n 56) para 197.

70 Cf *Bayindir v Pakistan* (n 56) para 193 et seq in case political instability exists; regarding the times after a civil war: *Toto Costruzioni Generali SpA v Lebanon*, ICSID Case no ARB/07/12, Award (7 June 2012) para 245.

at which the legitimacy of expectations is to be assessed is disputed: Most tribunals are of the opinion that merely the moment of the initial investment is decisive.[71] However, since investments are not always made in a single stage but sometimes in several stages, each stage constitutes a new relevant timing for the determination of the legitimacy of an investor's expectations.[72] Thus, a foreign investor bears the obligation to identify the risks of the foreign investment – before starting the investment but also during the entire duration of the investment.

The foreign investor is obliged to observe and exercise due diligence regarding the development and implementation of foreseeable political changes that may adversely affect the investment. If the foreign investor disregards these obligations or misjudges the circumstances, the foreign investor will not be able to successfully invoke a violation of legitimate expectations and, thus, a violation of the standard of FET. The expectations of the foreign investor must be adapted to the given circumstances in the fragile host state. This gives rise to different scenarios relating to both the failed state and the failing state, since failed states and failing states show different degrees of state fragility.

3.2.1.2 Effects of the Relativisation of Legitimate Expectations in the Context of State Fragility

To recall, there is a qualitative difference between a failed state and a failing state: The ineffective government in a failed state is much more pronounced than in a failing state. It can be assumed that the manifestation of a failing state forms a preliminary stage to a failed state. This means that even before state failure occurs, there has already been a certain and not insignificant degree of state fragility. Therefore, state failure is not an abrupt and completely unexpected occurrence. Even before its characterisation as a failed state, certain political risks have already been realised in the respective state and led to its instability. Consequently, it must be examined whether and to what degree a foreign investor's expectations are legitimate and if a breach of FET is given in the scenario of a failed state.

---

71 *Duke Energy v Ecuador* (n 62) para 340; *Saluka v Czech Republic* (n 51) para 329; *LG&E Energy Corp, LG&E Capital Corp, and LG&E International Inc v Argentina*, ICSID Case no ARB/02/1, Decision on Liability (3 October 2006) para 130.

72 Christoph Schreuer and Ursula Kriebaum, 'At What Time Must Legitimate Expectations Exist?' in Jacques Werner and Arif Hyder Ali (eds), *A Liber Amicorum: Thomas Wälde: Law Beyond Conventional Thought* (CMP 2009) 265, 276; cf *Frontier Petroleum Services Ltd v Czech Republic*, Final Award (12 November 2010) para 287.

A foreign investor that has made an investment at a time when characteristics of a fragile state have already existed cannot reasonably expect that there will be no deterioration in the host state's relevant situation. There can be no legitimate expectations of a foreign investor that the prevailing circumstances will remain largely unchanged in a fragile state and will not affect an investment. The reason for this is simply that an already fragile host state is in a transitional situation.[73] It is doubtful whether, on such a basis, a host state could even make sufficient representations to justify any expectations of the foreign investor and, hence, lend them legitimacy.

A development from a failing state to a failed state does not necessarily have to take place. Yet, it cannot be ruled out and is not completely unlikely due to the danger of a what has been described as a vicious cycle[74] concerning state fragility. Accordingly, the expectation of a foreign investor who, although the host state is a failing state, assumes that the conditions relevant to an investment in the host state will not change significantly, cannot be regarded as legitimate. For instance, a foreign investor cannot expect the existence of a predictable and stable executive and a functioning judicial system that provide a positive investment environment if state fragility exists.[75] State fragility by definition includes instable political conditions which imply a deficit and hardly uniform exercise of government. Investment protection agreements are, however, not 'insurance policies against bad business judgments',[76] meaning that the foreign investor's failure to recognise the relevant circumstances in the host country precludes a claim that supposedly legitimate expectations have been violated.[77] Given that a foreign investor has to be aware that the host state of the investment is in a situation of economic, political and social

---

73 *Cf,* concerning situations of states after (armed) conflicts, Rahim Moloo and Alex Khachaturian, 'Foreign Investment in a Post-Conflict Environment' (2009) 10 JWIT 341.

74 Wim Naudé, Amelia Santos-Paulino, and Mark McGillivray, 'Fragile States: An Overview' in Wim Naudé, Amelia Santos-Paulino, and Mark McGillivray (eds), *Fragile States: Causes, Costs and Responses* (OUP 2011) 7; 'vicious cycle' insofar as a higher risk of conflicts exists in fragile states – due to their generally rather low development status – which can possibly lead to further conflicts and thus, increasing fragility.

75 In *Bayindir v Pakistan* (n 56) para 193 the Tribunal rejected the plausibility of the legitimate expectations of a foreign investor in the event of political instability within the host state.

76 *Emilio Agustín Maffezini v Spain*, ICSID Case no ARB/97/7, Award (13 November 2000) para 64.

77 *Cf* Kendra Leite, 'The Fair and Equitable Treatment Standard: A Search for a Better Balance in International Investment Agreements' (2016) 32 Am U Int'l L Rev 363, 389; Markus Wagner, 'Regulatory Space in International Trade Law and International Investment Law' (2014) 36 U Pa J Int'l L 1, 52.

uncertainty due to its already existing fragility, expectations can only be regarded as legitimate if they properly factor in the context of the fragility of the host state. With regard to the failing state and the question of whether the protection standard of FET is violated in such a case, a distinction must be made between two additional scenarios: On the one hand, the development of an originally stable host state towards a failing state and, on the other hand, the development from a failed state towards a failing state.[78] The two scenarios mentioned must be distinguished from each other since the basis of trust created by the host state and, thus, the associated legitimacy of the expectations of a foreign investor differ. This distinction naturally also affects the question of a potential violation of FET in the case of a failing state.

In contrast to the failed state, the failing state has no significant preliminary stage regarding state fragility. Consequently, there is no obvious indication of a potential imminent restriction of effective state power and, thus, of the possible emergence of state fragility in its manifestation as a failing state. It can therefore be assumed that the occurrence of a failing state is usually unexpected. A proper example is the so-called Arab Spring. Within a few weeks or months, a wave of protests, uprisings and unrest spread across the Arab-speaking world in North Africa and the Middle East during the spring of 2011. These events took place unexpectedly and have had an impact not only on political and social levels, but also on foreign investments. Numerous cases against states involved in the Arab Spring have been brought before investment tribunals. This primarily relates to Egypt and Libya.[79]

A foreign investor – due to such unforeseen changes – cannot recognise the impending characteristic of a failing state to the same extent as is the case with the impending characterisation as a failed state. The expectations of a foreign investor with regard to the circumstances in the host state relevant to

---

78   Strictly speaking, the latter does not qualify as a failing state since the ordinary meaning of the term 'failing state' rather refers to a deteriorating than an improving development, however, it shows similar issues to that of a failing state so that it is nevertheless referred to in this chapter.

79   As a result of the Arab Spring, several investment disputes have been brought against Libya and Egypt, some of which have been settled and some of which have not yet been decided, eg *Trasta Energy v Libya* (UNCITRAL), *Cengiz İnşaat Sanayi ve Ticaret AS v Libya* (ICC Arbitration), *Yosef Maiman, Merhav (Mnf) Ltd, Merhav Ampal Group Ltd, and Merhav Ampal Energy Holdings Ltd Partnership v Egypt*, PCA Case no 2012/26. Investors have primarily invoked a breach of FET or FPS or indirect expropriation. Irrespective of their political systems, both Libya and Egypt have been relatively stable states before the events in the spring of 2011. In contrast to the condition of Libya already outlined before (see section 2 above), the political situation in Egypt has settled and stabilised to a large extent shortly after the Arab Spring.

the investment cannot include the possible state fragilility and need not be adjusted accordingly. Furthermore, the existence of a trust basis established by the host state which is necessary for the legitimate expectations of a foreign investor cannot be ruled out either. Rather, a foreign investor can legitimately expect stability, as the host state, which to date has been stable, has created a sufficient basis of trust. There is no relativisation of the legitimate expectations of a foreign investor in the event a stable state evolves into a failing state, as the decisive moment for estimating the legitimacy of expectations is the first stage of an investment, *ie* its start. Therefore, a violation of the investor's legitimate expectations and, at the same time, a disregard for the protection standard of FET in the development of a formerly stable host state towards a failing state can be assumed, if domestic changes of various kinds occur in the host state which prove to be detrimental for the foreign investor's investment.

On the other hand, attention also needs to be paid to the possibility that a failed state develops into a failing state by regaining its effective state power. In view of the problems associated with state failure described above, it is unlikely that a failed state will immediately become a stable state. Rather, a gradual development takes place so that, as if in a transitional stage, the characteristics associated with the failing state are first erstablished. A host state that carries out such a development is on the verge of recovery in terms of its state power and thus, also in terms of its overall stability. However, the host state is in a phase of transformation which continues to involve considerable uncertainties although it also poses many business opportunities for potential foreign investors.[80] On such a basis, it cannot be assumed that legal stability and consistent conditions can be guaranteed within the fragile host state. In this respect, the presumption of a trust basis created by the host state must be denied. Many tribunals, especially in relation to post-soviet countries, *eg* the tribunals in *Parkerings-Compagniet AS v Lithuania* and *William Nagel v Czech Republic*, ruled that expectations of a foreign investor made in a transitional situation and requiring fundamentally stable circumstances must be regarded as illegitimate.[81] Instead, these expectations must be adapted to and relativised in accordance with the corresponding situation in view of the fragility of the host state and the uncertainties associated with the transformation. A violation of the supposedly legitimate expectations of a foreign investor and

---

80   With respect to post-conflict situations of states: Moloo and Khachaturian (n 73) 341.
81   *Parkerings-Compagniet AS v Lithuania*, ICSID Case no ARB/05/8, Award (11 September 2007) paras 335 et seq; *William Nagel v Czech Republic*, SCC Case no 049/2002, Award (9 September 2003) para 293; similar in regard to circumstances after a civil war: *Toto Costruzioni v Lebanon* (n 70) para 246.

a breach of the protection standard of FET have to be excluded if a failed state develops into a failing state.

3.2.2 Full Protection and Security

As already outlined above, unlike other provisions in international investment agreements, the FPS standard requires the host state of a foreign investment to perform certain actions in particular situations in order to protect foreign investments from impairments.[82]

3.2.2.1 *The Notion of Due Diligence: Purely Objective or Modified in Accordance with the Host State's Status Quo*

As part of the FPS standard, the host state of an investment shall exercise the required protection and security with due diligence. This is a generic legal term which is not uniformly understood in terms of its substance. In particular, it is controversial whether instability and a lower level of development of a host state should inform the level of due diligence required within the framework of FPS.

The tribunal in *AAPL v Sri Lanka*, for instance, applied a purely objective understanding of due diligence. The tribunal stated that '[…] nothing more nor less than the reasonable measures of prevention, which a well-administered government could be expected to exercise under similar circumstances'[83] constitutes the content of the due diligence obligation. From this perspective, the FPS standard does not permit any modification of what can be regarded as duly diligent in light of the concrete circumstances of the individual case in fragile host states. Pursuant to this purely objective notion, it should always depend on what measures a well-administered government would have taken. The level of the required due diligence is high and its starting point are the appropriate preventive measures that could be expected from a well-administered, *ie* stable, host state.[84] Such an approach does not leave any room for the consideration of possible instabilities and limited resources of any kind of the host state.[85] The same requirements for due diligence relating to the protection of foreign investments that apply to entirely stable host states would apply to fragile host states. Whether it is in fact possible for the relevant

---

82 De Brabandere (n 48) 332; Schreuer, 'Full Protection and Security' (n 48) 353.
83 Alwyn Freeman, 'Responsibility of States for Unlawful Acts of Their Armed Forces' (1955) 88 Recueil des Cours 263, 277 et seq, quoted after *AAPL v Sri Lanka* (n 49) para 77.
84 *Cf* ibid paras 77 et seq.
85 *Cf* ibid paras 77 et seq; *AMT v Zaire* (n 50) paras 6.05 et seq; *Wena Hotels Ltd v Egypt*, ICSID Case no ARB/98/4, Award (8 December 2000) para 84.

fragile host state to take the same measures as a stable host state, especially considering the fragile state's lack of resources, must be completely disregarded in this purely objective view.

In contrast, others argue that a purely objective understanding of due diligence cannot be taken as a basis. Rather, the status quo of a host state of a foreign investment needs to play a role.[86] Therefore, it has been explicitly argued that the extent of care required by a host state has to be based on the conditions currently prevailing in that state.[87] The criterion to be used in this regard should be the resources available to the host state and thereby indirectly its level of development as well as the degree of its stability.[88] It cannot be assumed that stable host states, on the one hand, and unstable host states, on the other, are capable in an identical way of providing protection and security for foreign investors.[89] Otherwise, the same standard would be required from unstable and from stable host states, which could eventually lead to different measures being taken by the host state in favour of nationals and foreigners respectively. To prevent a violation of FPS and the accompanying violation of an international protection standard, there would then be unequal treatment by host states between foreigners and nationals, with foreigners being treated better than nationals. To eliminate this circumstance, the legal principle of *diligentia quam in suis* could be applied.[90] It would then be required to exercise

---

86 Newcombe and Paradell (n 58) 310; cf *Pantechniki SA Contractors & Engineers (Greece) v Albania*, ICSID Case no ARB/07/21, Award (30 July 2009) paras 77 et seq.

87 *Pantechniki v Albania* (n 86) para 77; *El Paso Energy International Co v Argentina*, ICSID Case no ARB/03/15, Award (31 October 2011) para 523; Gleider I Hernández, 'The Interaction Between Investment Law and the Law of Armed Conflict in the Interpretation of Full Protection and Security Clauses' in Freya Baetens (ed), *Investment Law Within International Law* (CUP 2016) 42; Newcombe and Paradell (n 58) 310.

88 *Pantechniki v Albania* (n 86) para 81 explicitly refers to the view of Newcombe and Paradell (n 58) 310 and cites as follows '[...] state's level of development and stability as relevant circumstances in determining whether there has been due diligence. An investor investing in an area with endemic civil strife and poor governance cannot have the same expectation of physical security as one investing in London, New York or Tokyo'.

89 *Pantechniki v Albania* (n 86) paras 77 et seq; Newcombe and Paradell (n 58) 310.

90 Ian Brownlie, *Principles of Public International Law* (7th edn, OUP 2008) 526; *diligentia quam in suis* is a legal principle of the Roman law; it has been referred to by Max Huber in *Spanish Zone of Morocco* with relation to the extent of diligence owed by a state towards foreigners and there it is set forth that a state is 'obliged to exercise only that degree of vigilance which corresponds to the means at its disposal [...] the vigilance which from the point of view of international law a state is required to exercise, may be characterised as diligentia quam in suis'. *Spanish Zone of Morocco (Great Britain v Spain)* (1925) 2 RIAA 615, 644.

such a care as in one's own affairs.[91] Ultimately, this would also lead to a modified notion of what constitutes diligently exercised protection and security since the prevailing circumstances in the host state are at least indirectly relevant when the principle *diligentia quam in suis* is applied. What a host state would exercise towards its own nationals is closely related to the state's available resources and capabilities.

3.2.2.2 Modification of Due Diligence in View of State Fragility?

Having discussed the views regarding the general possibility of modifying the understanding of due diligence required within the protection standard of FPS, it is now to be examined whether the modified understanding of due diligence can be applied in the case of state fragility. With regard to state fragility, reference can be made to the case of *Pantechniki v Albania*, in which it was argued that

> [a] failure of protection and security is to the contrary likely to arise in an unpredictable instance of civic disorder which could have been readily controlled by a powerful state but which overwhelms the limited capacities of one which is poor and fragile. There is no issue of incentives or disincentives with regard to unforeseen breakdowns of public order; it seems difficult to maintain that a government incurs international responsibility for failure to plan for unprecedented trouble of unprecedented magnitude in unprecedented places. The case for an element of proportionality in applying the international standard is stronger than with respect to claims of denial of justice.[92]

This shows the partially held view that a host state which already shows indications of state fragility could easily be held responsible for violations of the standard of FPS.[93] However, it is rather the understanding of due diligence

---

91 The modified notion described at the beginning of this section is a reflection of the legal principle of *diligentia quam in suis*. The Tribunal in *LESI SpA and ASTALDI SpA v Algeria*, ICSID Case no ARB/05/3, Award (12 November 2008) determined the notion of the due diligence standard in the context of FPS by comparing the level of protection given by a host state to its own nationals to the level of protection granted to foreigners – thus, by applying the legal principle of *diligentia quam in suis* although it does not explicitly refer to this principle.
92 *Pantechniki v Albania* (n 86) para 77.
93 This view is, *inter alia*, held by Dolzer and Schreuer (n 42) 162; Freeman (n 84) 277 et seq, cited in *AAPL v Sri Lanka* (n 49) para 77.

owed by the host state that should be modified according to the prevailing circumstances within the respective host state.

With regard to the possible application of a modified notion of due diligence to a fragile state, an important distinction must be made between two different scenarios: Firstly, the inability of the host state to take measures to protect a foreign investor and, secondly, the unwillingness of the host state to take appropriate protective measures in favour of a foreign investor.[94] If a host state refuses to grant a foreign investor protection and security measures, even though possible for the host state, this constitutes a violation of FPS.[95] By contrast, the situation in which it is not even possible for a host state to provide protection and security in favour of a foreign investor due to a lack of resources is fundamentally different.[96] In the case of a fragile state, it cannot be assumed that there is an unwillingness *per se* on the part of the state to carry out its state duties and functions. In fact, because of the significant limitation of the effective state power of the fragile state, it can be assumed that it is merely incapable of fulfilling its state tasks and functions.

With regard to the differentiation between the inability and unwillingness of a host state, it can be argued that it does not seem acceptable to disadvantage a host state if, due to its structural weaknesses, it does not have sufficient resources to protect foreign investors and therefore cannot meet the requirements of FPS. Yet, by releasing structurally weaker host states from obligations under FPS, no incentive is created for such host states to improve their own overall status.[97] For these host states, such an improvement would bring with it the threat of a possible violation of FPS if protection and security are still not provided with the required due diligence. Furthermore, a host state may, by malice, deliberately refrain from creating and establishing the resources necessary for the exercise of the requirement to sufficiently provide protection and security in order to maintain its inability to meet the standard of protection

---

94   *Cf Pantechniki v Albania* (n 86) para 82.

95   *Cf Ampal-American and others v Egypt*, ICSID Case no ARB/12/11, Decision on Liability and Heads of Loss (21 February 2017) paras 288 et seq.

96   *Cf Ampal* (n 95) paras 283 et seq; *Pantechniki v Albania* (n 86) para 77; *LESI SpA and ASTALDI SpA v Algeria* (n 91) para 181.

97   The tribunal in *Pantechniki v Albania* (n 86) para 77 also differentiates between denial of justice on the one hand and protection and security on the other hand; merely with regard to denial of justice it can be assumed that a state is not given any incentive to improve its situation if its structural weakness and limited resources are taken into consideration – not with relation to protection and security – since the legal system is based on a deliberate choice by the state whereas a state's failure to protect and secure is likely to arise in unpredictable instances and thus, is not a deliberate choice by the state.

and thus, to prevent a violation FPS in the long term. Although such an approach by the host state which contradicts good faith could in theory lead to the assumption that FPS has been infringed, it is difficult for the investor claiming the infringement to prove causality of the host state's behaviour for the violation of FPS.[98]

Therefore, and in view of the opportunities for abuse on the part of host states opened up by a differentiated approach with regard to FPS, it structural weaknesses and a lack of resources within a host state should not lead to the assumption that the standard of protection is not violated.[99] Due to the possibility of exploiting in a targeted manner the adaptation of the standard of due diligence to the stability of a host state in order to circumvent a potentially liability for violation of international law, the level of development of a host state cannot play any role in the context of the due due diligence required by FPS. The constant adjustment of the understanding of what constitutes due diligence to the specific conditions prevailing within the relevant host state would lead to a considerable reduction in legal certainty and stability. If an adjustment were done in each case, the actual objectives of international investment agreements – legal certainty and stabilisation – would be counteracted. Foreign investors, but also host states, would have difficulties in estimating what would constitute a measure conducted with sufficient due diligence, ultimately leading to tribunals having to answer this question.

Above all, it seems dogmatically preferable that the considerations advocated for a modification of due diligence in the event of state crises and instabilities should be considered at the level of the justification of an interference in foreign investors' rights.[100] In this way, sufficient account can be taken of the

---

98 See below.
99 According to Dolzer and Schreuer (n 42) 162, the lack of resources crucial for the exercise of the necessary measures should not result in the host state being exempted from the requirement to provide protection and security with the required diligence.
100 Possible justifications for a host state for negatively interfering in foreign investor's rights are necessity and *force majeure* (generally on *force majeure* in conflict scenarios see Christina Binder and Philipp Janig, chapter 4 in this volume, 119–127). Necessity can possibly be invoked by a host state if the measures affecting a foreign investment were taken to safeguard an essential interest against a grave and imminent peril and do not seriously impair an essential interest of the state(s) towards which the obligation exists or the international community as a whole (see article 25 of the ILC Articles on State Responsibility). However, the requirements for successfully invoking necessity are high so that it seems doubtful these are met in every concrete scenario of state fragility. As the cases concerning the economic crisis of Argentina in 2001 as well as the cases following the effects of the Arab Spring in 2011 have shown, investment tribunals oftentimes deny the recognition of necessity, even if state fragility has occurred – as is especially the case

adverse circumstances in which a host state in crisis finds itself while, at the same time, there is neither the possibility of abuse nor the risk of legal uncertainty or a reduced stabilisation effect due to the inconsistent understanding of the content of due diligence.

All aspects considered, a merely objective notion of due diligence regarding FPS should be applied. This results in the same understanding of 'due diligence' in every host state: It depends on what measures a well-administered government would have taken in the relevant situation – and not on the stability or status quo of the respective host state.

3.2.2.3   Failed State

Having pointed out that an objective standard should be applied concerning due diligence, the effects of this view on the scenario of a failed state are set out in the following. Due to a failed state's ineffective government and the related lack of state resources, there is no prospect that a level of due diligence can be applied by a failed state in favour of the protection and security of a foreign investor that corresponds to that of a well-administered government. It can be even assumed that, due to the paralysis within a failed state, the latter is certainly not able to observe any discernible degree of diligence regarding the protection and security of foreign investors or investments. The comprehensive paralysis in a failed state precludes the possibility that organs of a failed state intervene in support of foreign investors, even though FPS requires a foreign investor's protection from adverse intervention by third parties through the host state. A breach of FPS is evident: due to the clearly discernible ineffectiveness of the state authority and the associated paralysis in the failed state, the proof of the causality of the host state's failure to exercise due diligence leading to the infringement can be provided without any problems by the affected foreign investor.

In the context of state failure, it could also be argued that a foreign investor must be aware that different circumstances prevail in an unstable state as in industrialised countries and that, accordingly, the same standard of protection cannot be applied globally.[101] This is particularly true in the scenario of the failed state which already had a successively deteriorating status before the actual state failure occurred. Subsequently, what has been said about the standard of FET in fragile states would be applicable *mutatis mutandis* and the host state's obligations would be correspondingly modified. In contrast to

---

with relation to the Arab Spring. The same applies to *force majeure* and its strict and high requirements.

101   *Pantechniki v Albania* (n 86) paras 77 et seq; Newcombe and Paradell (n 58) 310.

the standard of FET, however, FPS does not provide that the expectations of the foreign investor regarding the condition of the investment are of importance within the understanding of the content of FPS. The reason is that – as already shown above[102] – FET, at least as far as the protection of legitimate expexations is concerned, is a protection standard in which a relationship of trust builds the investment protection standard's core. Therefore, the (justified) subjective perspective of a foreign investor is of central importance and ultimately legitimises the subjective approach to FET. In comparison to this, FPS does not refer to a reasonably established basis of trust of a foreign investor. This therefore leaves no room for any subjective expectations in relation to FPS and a purely objective approach to this investment protection standard. Whatever the foreign investor's expectations of the prosperity of the investment project are and however legitimate they may be, they are irrelevant to the standard of care required by the host state to protect and secure foreign investments. A merely objective standard must therefore be used, without the expectations of the foreign investor being of significance to FPS.

With regard to the failed state, it is to be noted that, due to its profound state crisis, it is not in a position to meet the requirements imposed by FPS. It is not capable of successfully performing what is expected of a well-administered government in a comparable situation to protect a foreign investor. Accordingly, in the case of the failed state, there is a violation of FPS as the failed state cannot protect an investment from adverse interferences by third parties.[103]

3.2.2.4 Failing State

In the following, it shall be discussed how and whether the status as a failing state affects the investment protection standard of FPS. As mentioned above, a purely objective notion of due diligence based on a well-administered government is used as a comparison parameter and no importance is attached to the expectations of the foreign investor.

In contrast to a failed state, the failing state does not have a comprehensive paralysis, but is only partially impaired in its effective state power. Most of the state's power is functioning. As a result, the failing state is in principle able to protect and secure foreign investors and thus, is able to comply with the requirement to provide protection and security. However, there are individual cases in which the partly limited effectiveness of the failing state's state power is reflected in the fact that foreign investors are not protected from

---

102 See section 3.1.1 above.
103 This leaves aside aspects of a possible justification, especially under *force majeure*.

adverse interventions as due diligence requires.[104] In such cases, the failing state is not able to observe the due diligence required by a well-administered government for the protection of foreign investors due to its partially ineffective government. Therefore, whenever a failing state reflects the limited effectiveness of state power, the requirement of protection and security in favour of foreign investors is disregarded. Since there is no comprehensive paralysis of the state structure in the failing state, it is possible for the failing state (as opposed to a failed state) to actively commit acts of infringement through its own state organs. In a failing state, the possibility of causing an impairment of the foreign investment is thus not limited to private actors but encompasses state actors. The objective approach to due diligence does not lead to failing host states always violating FPS. It depends on the circumstances of the individual case if a well-administered government would have acted comparably.

4   Conclusions

Foreign investments are of great importance for fragile states since they can have stabilising influence. Investments are an essential element in rebuilding a state and promoting progress and are, thus, especially crucial in situations of state fragility. Political risks and the pronounced ineffectiveness of state power in fragile states can, however, discourage foreign investment in fragile states while at the same time such investments provide significant support to fragile states in regaining stability and are therefore urgently needed.

A fragile state exhibits several characteristics that are relevant to the investment law context – above all, the ineffective power of the state and the general realisation of political risks. State fragility, with its manifestations of failed state and failing state, has different effects on the investment protection standards of FET and FPS:

As regards the protection standard of FET, the expectations that can be considered as legitimate on a foreign investor's part are relative in relation to the context of state fragility. Depending on whether a failing state transforms into

---

104   For example, during the so-called Arab Spring in Egypt in 2011, during which private militant groups exploited the situation in a systematic manner to launch attacks against foreign investors, among others. Despite the fact that at that time Egypt had a failing state status (part of the state power was ineffective and law enforcement was deficient), a violation of the requirement to grant protection and security was assumed, *Ampal v Egypt* (n 95) paras 284 et seq.

a failed state or a failed state transforms into a failing state respectively, expectations of a foreign investor concerning a stable and secure investment environment are to be considered illegitimate. This ultimately results in denying a violation of the FET standard where aspects of state fragility affect a foreign investment. However, if a stable state turns into a failing state, a breach of FET could be given as a foreign investor's expectations of a positive investment environment are still to be considered legitimate.

With respect to FPS, the protection to be granted by the host state cannot be adapted to the circumstances prevailing in the host state. Otherwise, legal uncertainty, possibilities of abuse and dogmatic inaccuracy could arise. This may lead to a violation of FPS in the case a fragile host state fails to accord protection to foreign investors. Thereby, the proof of causality required from the foreign investor in case of a failing state will not as easily be furnished as in the case of a failed state.[105] The only partial ineffectiveness of state power in the failing state does not lead to an entire standstill of state structures and a paralysis of the activities of the failing state. This prohibits an assumption that a failing state has automatically failed to exercise due diligence as soon as foreign investments are harmed. Rather, providing proof that a lack of due diligence on the part of a failing state ultimately led to the foreign investment being harmed will not be easy for the investor in a failing state and requires an examination of the specific individual case.[106]

However, even if an FPS violation is found, invoking *force majeure* may, in the individual case, provide a justification. In both scenarios of state fragility, the question of applicability of possible justifications of the fragile host state – especially the aspect of *force majeure* – is of relevance.[107] In view of the legal uncertainties and dogmatic imprecision that this would entail, the fragility of a host state should not be taken into account at the level of a possible violation of the protection standard FPS. Rather, the circumstances associated with state fragility should only be considered at the level of a possible justification for a violation of an investment protection standard.

---

105   *Cf Noble Ventures, Inc v Romania* (n 61) para 166.
106   See, in this respect, also Tillmann Rudolf Braun, chapter 1 in this volume, 46–48, who argues for a shifting of the burden of proof in conflict scenarios. His arguments are, however, not simply transferable to the situation of failed or failing states, since also the state party to the arbitration will be limited in its endeavours to comply with a potentially shifted burden.
107   For a closer look on *force majeure* and contrary conclusion in the context of international investment law and conflict scenarios, see Christina Binder and Philipp Janig, chapter 4 in this volume, 119–127.

Bibliography

Akpinarli N, *The Fragility of the Failed State Paradigm: A different International Law Perception of the Absence of Effective Government* (Brill Nijhoff 2010).

Bray H, 'Save Our Investments, International Investment Law and International Humanitarian Law' (2013) 14 JWIT 578.

Brock L and others, *Fragile States* (Polity Press 2012).

Brownlie I, *Principles of Public International Law* (7th edn, OUP 2008).

Carment D, S Prest, and Y Samy, *Security, Development and the Fragile State* (Routledge 2010).

Crawford J, *The Creation of States in International Law* (2nd edn, OUP 2007).

De Brabandere E, 'Host States' Due Diligence Obligations in International Investment Law' (2015) 42 Syracuse J Int'l L & Com 319.

Dolzer R and C Schreuer, *Principles of International Investment Law* (2nd edn, OUP 2012).

Fink M, 'Grenzen des arabischen Wandels aufgrund von Investitionsschutzrecht? Betrachtungen anhand der Situation in Ägypten und Libyen' (2012) 72 Heidelberg J Int'l L 483.

Gallus N, 'The Influence of the Host State's Level of Development on International Investment Treaty Standards of Protection' (2005) 6 JWIT 711.

Geiß R, 'Failed States: Legal Aspects and Security Implications' (2004) 47 German YB Int'l L 457.

Geiß R, *Failed States* (Duncker & Humblot 2005).

Giorgetti C, *A Principled Approach to State Failure – International Community Actions in Emergency Situations* (Brill Nijhoff 2010).

Giorgetti C, 'Why Should International Law be Concerned About State Failure' (2010) 16 ILSA J Int'l L 469.

Hernández G, 'The Interaction Between Investment Law and the Law of Armed Conflict in the Interpretati-on of Full Protection and Security Clauses' in F Baetens (ed), Investment Law Within International Law (CUP 2016).

Hobér K and J Fellenbaum, 'Political Risk Insurance and Investment Treaty Protection' in M Bungenberg and others (eds), *International Investment Law:* A Handbook (CH Beck, Hart, and Nomos 2015).

Iqbal Z and H Starr, *State Failure in the Modern World* (Stanford UP 2015).

Kobrin K, 'Political Risk; A Review and Reconsideration' (1979) 10 J Int'l Business Stud 67.

Koskenmäki R, 'Legal Implications Resulting from State Failure in Light of the Case of Somalia' (2004) 73 Nordic J Int'l L 1.

Kreijen G, *State Failure, Sovereignty and Effectiveness: Legal Lessons from the Decolonization of Sub-Saharan Africa* (Brill Nijhoff 2004).

Kriebaum U, 'Are Investment Treaty Standards Flexible Enough to Meet the Needs of Developing Countries?' in F Baetens (ed), *Investment Law Within International Law* (CUP 2016).

Leite K, 'The Fair and Equitable Treatment Standard: A Search for a Better Balance in International Investment Agreements' (2016) 32 Am U Int'l L Rev 363.

Moloo R and A Khachaturian, 'Foreign Investment in a Post-Conflict Environment' (2009) 10 JWIT 341.

Naudé W, A Santos-Paulino, and M McGillivray, 'Fragile States: An Overview' in W Naudé, A Santos-Paulino and M McGillivray (eds), *Fragile States: Causes, Costs and Responses* (OUP 2011) 1.

Newcombe AP and L Paradell, *Law and Practice of Investment Treaties: Standards of Treatment* (Wolters Kluwer 2009).

Nuruzzaman M, 'Revisiting the Category of Fragile and Failed States in International Relations' (2009) 46 Int'l Stud 271.

Pustorino P, 'Failed States and International Law: The Impact of UN Practice on Somalia in Respect of Fundamental Rules of International Law' (2010) 53 German YB Int'l L 727.

Rotberg R, 'The Failure and Collapse of Nation-States' in R Rotberg (ed), *When States Fail* (Princeton UP 2003).

Salacuse J and N Sullivan, 'Do BITs Really Work: An Evaluation of Bilateral Investment Treaties and Their Grand Bargain' (2005) 46 Harv Int'l LJ 67.

Schernbeck A, *Der Fair and Equitable Treatment Standard in internationalen Investitionsschutzabkommen* (Nomos 2013).

Schreuer C and U Kriebaum, 'At What Time Must Legitimate Expectations Exist?' in J Werner and AA Hyder (eds), *A Liber Amicorum: Thomas Wälde: Law Beyond Conventional Thought* (CMP 2009).

Schreuer C, 'Full Protection and Security' (2010) 1 JIDS 353.

Shamsie Y and A Thompson, *Haiti: Hope for a Fragile State* (Wilfrid Laurier UP 2006) 3.

Subedi S, *International Investment Law* (3rd edn, Hart 2016).

Thürer D, 'Der Wegfall effektiver Staatsgewalt: "The Failed State"' in D Thürer, M Herdegen, and G Hohloch (eds), *Der Wegfall effektiver Staatsgewalt: The Failed State* (CF Müller 1995).

von Walter A, 'The Investor's Expectations in International Investment Arbitration' in A Reinisch and C Knahr (eds), *International Investment Law in Context* (Eleven International Publishing 2008) 173.

Wagner M, 'Regulatory Space in International Trade Law and International Investment Law' (2014) 36 U Pa J Int'l L 1.

Zohn M, 'Filling the Void; International Legal Structures and Political Risk in Investment' (2007) 31 Fordham Int'l LJ 230.

Index

agents *see* representatives
arbitral tribunals
    duties of   230, 265
    jurisdiction *see* jurisdiction of arbitral tribunals
    mandate of   3, 192, 194, 230, 320, 335
    powers of   90, 101, 194, 228, 264–266
annexation   10, 319
    Crimea and Russia   1, 196–199, 217–218, 294, 308, 319–320, 327, 330–332, 339–343, 346–353, 402
    effective control and   185, 196–198, 200, 319–320, 341, 345
    investor-state dispute settlement and   210, 227, 326, 351–353
    jurisdiction of arbitral tribunals and   11, 192–200, 224, 448
    jurisdiction of states and   285
    non-recognition of *see* non-recognition
    prohibition of the use of force and   223, 338, 344
    sovereign rights and   183–186, 198, 201
    sovereignty and   209, 224–225, 235, 338, 344, 433
    treaties and *see* treaties, moving-treaty frontiers rule; treaties, extraterritorial application
armed conflict
    effects on treaties *see* treaties, continuity during armed conflict
    international   56, 67, 344, 387
    non-international   19–21, 26–27, 32–33, 38–39, 41–42, 44–45, 49, 67–68, 97–98, 387

border conflicts *see* territorial disputes

China   150–155, 191, 232–233, 235–236, 387, 416
compensation
    in case of *force majeure*   127–133
    under 'extended' war clauses   38–40, 73–76, 116–118
    under 'simple' war clauses   115–116
    under 'strict' war clauses   118
    under the 2018 Priednestrovian investment law   414–415, 420–421
    under Ukrainian domestic law   439–440
    see also European Convention on Human Rights, compensation for violation
counsel *see* representation
Court of Justice of the European Union   282–283
    Front Polisario   170, 329–330, 359–360, 369–375
customary international law   4, 56, 188, 280, 403, 414–415
    see also war clauses, customary international law and
Crimea *see* annexation, Crimea and Russia

de facto regime   x, 10, 12, 197–198, 387–426
    Abkhazia   161, 164, 191, 387
    Donetsk People's Republic   387, 434–436, 453
    frozen conflict and   10, 353, 387–391, 407–408, 423–425
    investment protection and   332, 387–426
    Luhansk People's Republic   434–436, 453
    'legislation' of   403–409, 441–442
    Nagorno-Karabakh   387
    Northern Cyprus   160, 296–297, 344, 387
    Somaliland   387
    South Ossetia   161, 164, 191, 387
    Transnistria / Priednistrovie   344, 387–426
    moving treaty-frontiers
    see also effective control, non-state actors by
diplomatic protection   40–41, 280, 353
disputed maritime zones   179–182
    implicated investment disputes   188–192, 194–200
    investment treaties and   190–192
    limits on jurisdiction of arbitral tribunals and   188–194, 337, 374–375
    overlapping entitlements in case of   180–182, 374–375
domestic investment laws / statutes   403–426, 439–442

Donbas 431–455
  Russian influence 432–433
  see also effective control, non-state actors by

effective control
  governments by 252–253 *see also* recognition of governments
  jurisdiction and 196–198, 341, 345, 443, 461–463
  non-state actors by 434, 462–463
  sovereignty and 196–198, 319, 461–463
  see also annexation, effective control and
enforcement
  arbitral awards 260, 352
  judgments *see* European Court of Human Rights, enforcement of judgments
epistemic communities xv, 7
European Convention on Human Rights 280–310, 450–453
  compensation for violation 288, 302, 309, 452
  investment law compared to 289, 336–337, 344, 452
  jurisdiction 10, 285, 292–294, 343, 402, 451–452
  possession 289–290
  property, right to 280, 287–292, 402, 452
  remedies 281–282, 301–302, 452
  see also European Court of Human Rights
European Court of Human Rights 280–310, 336–337, 402, 452–453
  cost of litigation 301–302
  domestic remedies, exhaustion of 295–297
  enforcement of judgments 280, 301–303, 305, 452–453
  forum shopping 298
  investor-state dispute settlement compared 44–45, 291, 336–337
European Union 12, 141, 268, 283, 359–384
expropriation 75–76, 291–292, 379, 414–415, 421, 452–455

failed state *see* state fragility
failing state *see* state fragility
fair and equitable treatment 72n90, 90–91, 291, 349, 466–467
  legitimate expectations 468–475

relevance of circumstances 468–475
state fragility and 468–475
force majeure 112–133
  consequences 129–133
  duty to compensate and *see* compensation, in situations of *force majeure*
  full protection and security and 114, 125–127, 479n100, 483
  invocation 127–129, 352
  state fragility and 479n100, 483
  war clauses and 125, 352
fragmentation of international law x–xi, 2, 20, 35, 84, 214, 226 see also *normative conflict*
frozen conflict *see de facto* regime
full protection and security 28–29, 33, 35, 84–107, 114, 291, 324, 467–468
  content 88–98, 467–468
  due diligence 92–96, 324, 467, 475–482
  environmental impact and 88, 94–95, 101–106
  force majeure and *see force majeure*, full protection and security and
  investor contribution / complicity and 98–101
  relevance of circumstances 89, 114–115, 475–480
  state fragility and 475–482

general principles
  effectiveness 340
  estoppel 119, 343, 401
  force majeure 119
  good faith 128–129, 349
Georgia 161–165, 191, 285–286

hostilities *see* armed conflict
human rights law *see* European Convention on Human Rights

international humanitarian law ix, xiv, 26–28, 61, 68, 70–71, 225, 284
  customary rules 31, 58–60
  international investment law and xiv, 7, 20–21, 28, 31–35, 40–45, 48–49, 73–79, 95, 322–325
  military necessity 19, 28–31, 60–61, 77–78, 323–324
  appropriation and destruction of property ix, 61–65

INDEX 489

investment
    under the 2018 Priednestrovian
        investment law   405–406
    see also jurisdiction of arbitral
        tribunals, definition of investment
        and investor
investor
    under the 2018 Priednestrovian
        investment law   405–406
    see also jurisdiction of arbitral tribunals,
        definition of investment and investor
investor-state dispute settlement
    annexation and *see* annexation, investor-
        state dispute settlement and
    competing governments and   246–278
    parallel proceedings and *see* parallel
        proceedings
    proceedings before the European Court of
        Human Rights compared *see* European
        Court of Human Rights, investor-state
        dispute settlement compared
Iraq   330
Israel   68, 165–167, 190

jurisdiction of states
    non-territorial zones   374–375
jurisdiction of arbitral tribunals
    definition of investment and
        investor   332, 347–349
    domestic law and   348–349
    forum prorogatum   334–335
    incidental   334, 342
    indispensable parties / *Monetary Gold*
        doctrine   192–194, 228, 238, 350
    investment dispute   188
    material (*ratione materiae*)   188–192,
        194–195, 332–337
    personal (*ratione
        personae*)   192–194, 349–351
    spatial (*ratione loci*)   179n16, 182–187,
        189, 337–346
    temporal (*ratione temporis*)   346–349
jus ad bellum   ix, xi–xii, 70
jus cogens   324, 339, 344–345,
    351–353, 361–363
jus in bello see international humanitarian
    law

Korea
    North Korea   156, 158

South Korea   156–159
Kosovo   168–169

lex specialis see normative conflict
Libya   1, 22, 246, 254, 261, 275, 460–461, 473

maritime zones *see* disputed maritime
    zones
Moldova   390–403

national investment laws *see* domestic
    investment laws / statutes
non-recognition, duty of
    content   224, 360–363, 397
    Front Polisario and   329–330, 339, 376
    investor-state arbitral tribunals
        and   320, 378–383
    law of the European Union and   363–365,
        376–378
    '*Namibia* exception'   257, 329–330,
        343–346, 376–378
    status   323, 338, 344, 352
    Western Sahara and   190, 196, 331,
        339, 376–377
normative conflict
    international investment law and
        international humanitarian
        law between see international
        humanitarian law, international
        investment law and
    lex specialis   xii, 24, 31–35, 323–324, 327,
        344, 416n96, 421
    treaty interpretation and   xiii, 39, 44, 49,
        69–71, 334

occupation   58–59, 67–68, 72, 160, 165, 176,
    225, 319, 322–331, 434–437
    conclusion of treaties and   328–329
    see also annexation
Organization for Security and Co-operation
    in Europe   391, 394, 433

Palestine   165–167, 190, 331
parallel proceedings   209–239, 297–298
    abuse of process   229–230, 238
    legal dispute   230–238
    lis pendens   228–229
    res judicata   228–229, 238
Priednestrovie *see de facto* regime,
    Transnistria / Priednestrovie

property
- appropriation and destruction of 58–79, 116–117
- investment and 28, 39, 44, 48–49, 65–79, 320, 324, 351
- protection under human rights law *see* European Convention on Human Rights, right to property

recognition of governments 250–263
- *de facto* governments 253
- *de facto* regimes 387
- *de jure* governments 253
- effectiveness of government 252, 262, 263, 273–274
- effects of 250, 261–263
- in private international law 263
- modes of 254–255
- recognition of states distinguished 251
- *Tinoco* arbitration 255–257

representatives
- agent 248–249
- counsel 249
- parties in international arbitration of 247–249
- state in legal proceedings of 248–249, 261–262

Russia
- Crimea and *see* annexation, Crimea and Russia
- Donbas region and 432–433
- European Court of Human Rights and 306–309
- Transnistria and 391–396, 402, 407, 425

sovereignty *see* annexation, sovereignty and
Soviet Union 161, 221, 346, 392, 397–399
state fragility
- failed state 464–465
- failing state 465
- investment protection and 458–483
- political risk and 463
- state responsibility and 467
- *see also* fair and equitable treatment, state fragility and; full protection and security, state fragility and

state practice
- moving treaty-frontiers rule and 339

recognition of governments and 250–255
state responsibility and 346
treatment of foreign property and 61–62, 67
state responsibility 43, 61–62, 64, 67, 74, 77, 85, 112–113, 226, 346, 451–452, 463
- attribution 443–447
- circumstances precluding wrongfulness 321 *see also* force majeure
- insurgencies and 4, 400
- state fragility and 467
state-state dispute settlement 212, 227, 285, 350–351
state succession 140, 218, 327, 338, 343, 346, 397–399
systemic integration *see* fragmentation of international law; normative conflict

Taiwan 150–151, 155–156, 387, 396, 426
territorial disputes 1, 280, 285–286, 337
territory
- European Court of Justice 371–373
- notion in international law 141–142, 182–183, 337–341, 343–344, 371, 399
- notion in investment treaties 139–171, 182–187, 337–346, 351, 402–403
Transnistria/Priednestrovie *see de facto* regime, Transnistria/Priednestrovie
treaties
- continuity during armed conflict 226, 325–326
- customary international law and 69
- extraterritorial application 198, 238, 328–331, 336, 341–349, 351, 402–403
- interpretation 55, 57, 325
- moving treaty-frontiers rule 221, 238, 338–339, 448 *see also* state practice, moving treaty-frontiers rule and
- spatial scope *see* territory
- supervening impossibility to perform 112–113, 333

Ukraine 200, 217–218, 81, 305–306, 321, 335, 337, 339, 348–351, 391, 394, 396, 431, 433, 437–441, 451; *see also* annexation, Crimea and Russia

Venezuela 260–261, 264, 266, 269, 273–277

war clauses   54–79, 115–118
   burden of proof   46–47, 76, 118
   compensation under *see* compensation
   customary international law and   40, 58–79
   destruction of investments   54–79, 117
   extended war clauses   33, 38, 54–79, 116–118, 352
   force majeure and *see force majeure*, war clauses and
   interpretation   35–45, 49, 54–79
   'necessity of the situation'   38, 41–45, 57, 65–79, 117–118
   requisitioning of investments   54–79, 117–118
World Trade Organization   212–213, 389, 397

Yemen   9, 246, 264, 271–272

Printed in the United States
By Bookmasters